MODESTY Blaise
THE KILLING GAME

Modesty Blaise: The Killing Game
ISBN: 9781785653001

Published by Titan Books,
A division of Titan Publishing Group Ltd.
144 Southwark St.
London SE1 0UP

A CIP catalogue record for this title is available from the British Library.

First edition: 2017

10 9 8 7 6 5 4 3 2

Printed in Lithuania

Grateful thanks to William Gardiner and Geoff Malyon from Solo Syndication for their help in the production of this book, and to Alun and Paul Michael for all their support and for Paul's fantastic introduction. And many thanks, of course, to Daphne Alexander and Kate McAll, for their fabulous introductions.

What did you think of this book? We love to hear from our readers. Please email us at: **readerfeedback@titanemail.com**, or write to us at the above address.

To receive advance information, news, competitions, and exclusive offers online, please sign up for the Titan newsletter on our website: **www.titanbooks.com**

MODESTY Blaise

THE KILLING GAME

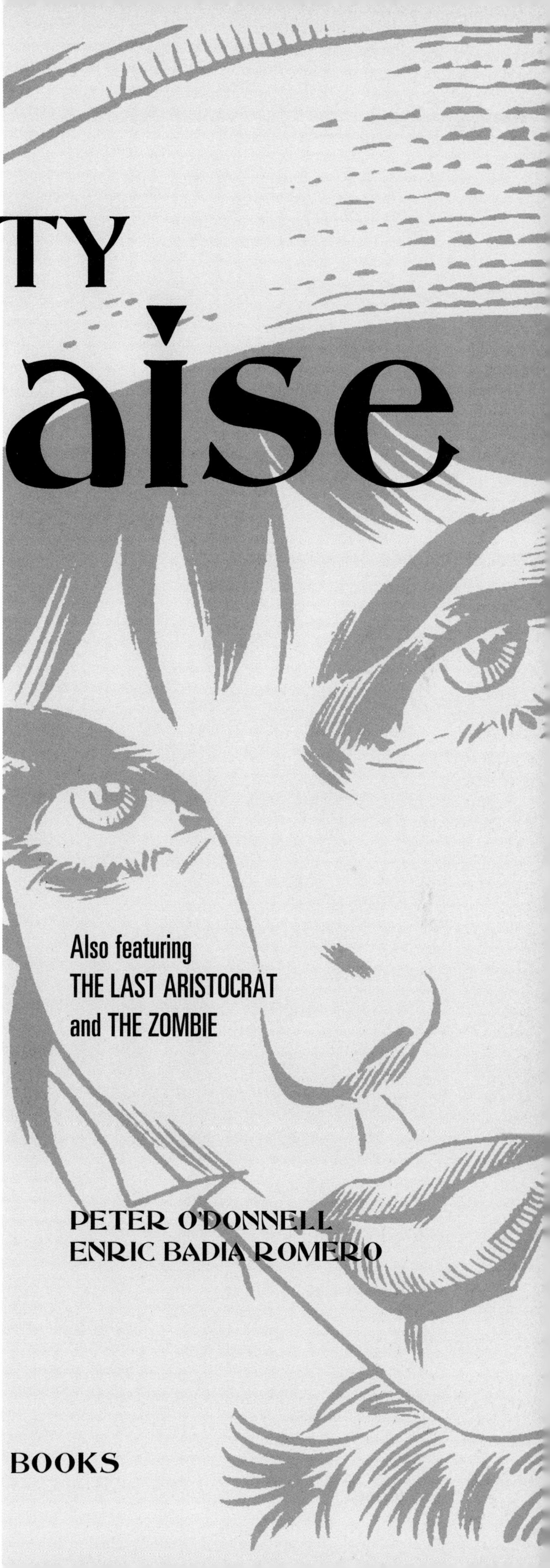

Also featuring
THE LAST ARISTOCRAT
and THE ZOMBIE

PETER O'DONNELL
ENRIC BADIA ROMERO

TITAN BOOKS

MODESTY AND ME

HE'S DANGEROUS... IF I HAD HACKLES THEY'D BE BRISTLING NOW...

NOT JUST A TEENSY BIT OVER THE TOP?

NO, NO... YOU MUST **EXPRESS** YOURSELF, OR YOU MIGHT HAVE A NERVOUS BREAKDOWN

She was always there: in the hardbacks on the bookshelf at home, next to the Madeleine Brent ones, signed 'With love Daddy'; in the three comic strip frames on the kitchen wall; in the copy of the *Evening Standard* on the hall table which Dad brought home every evening, the comic strips page always read. I didn't know who she was or what she was like to start with, that came later, but she was always there.

Growing up with Modesty was fascinating for me as a child, a teenager, an adult and has been even as a parent. So too were the realisations and surprises about grandpa, grandpa the writer. I'll call him Peter here. A few of those stand out in my mind.

Laughing out loud at Willie Garvin. If you've read Modesty Blaise before you'll have been there.

You can imagine how funny it was for a little boy who had never heard the word pseudonym to find out that his grandpa was also a woman (writer) or years later to finally

Top: The Killing Game - 9969
Above: The Last Aristocrat - 9955
Right: The Killing Game - 10019

realise the subtle connection between Madeleine Brent and Modesty Blaise, their common initials.

As a teenager I remember being slouched on the settee reading the Modesty Blaise strips, rarely able to stop until reading the last frame. I remember turning off the light too late because I had to see what happened next in the novels. I was lucky with the strips to have the luxury of reading them in a book like this. I am not sure how I would have coped reading them in the *Evening Standard* and having to wait until the next day for the next frame, or worse, having to wait over the weekend after the Friday cliffhanger.

The frustration of finishing the Modesty strips was healed by being able to plough into the Garth, Romeo Brown and Tug Transom strips which Peter wrote. All of them different, all enjoyable and, although I confess to having not read them for a long time, I do remember one thing, they all made me feel as if I was afflicted with the same curse that Modesty gave: can't stop reading.

This was when I started to realise the incredible volume and rate of output that Peter produced, on an old typewriter, month after month, year after year. In one month alone, not an atypical one, he would write 15 to 20 short stories and 50 to 100 comic strip frames. Also, since to me Modesty had always been there, I was surprised to learn that Peter had a twenty year writing career before he even created Modesty.

Another surprise was going to the theatre with Peter as a young boy and seeing his name on the programme. We were watching his play, *Mr Fothergill's Murder*.

For someone who produced so many comic strip stories, it still amuses me that Peter's drawing ability was at the other end of the spectrum from his writing ability. Here the credit must go to Jim Holdaway, the original artist who brought Modesty to life visually, to Enric Romero who drew her for so many years, and also to the other three artists, Neville Colvin, John Burns and Pat Wright. All had the difficult task of interpreting the doodles that Peter sent and turning them into the thousands of fabulous graphics we have had the pleasure to read.

For all his creativity, Peter simply put it all down to effort. I once heard a school pupil ask him how to go about writing a story. Without a hint of flippancy he simply said, "sit down with a piece of paper and write" because that is how he did it.

Then there's what Modesty means to me and what she meant to Peter. For him, he cared for her like a loved one. After all, they had a forty-year relationship. As well as Modesty herself, what meant most to Peter about his work was what the readers and fans thought, in particular his fellow writers.

For me, I love to hear of the way that those readers and writers talk about Modesty with genuine excitement and passion. Stef Penney, who has written the scripts for the recent BBC radio dramatizations of several of the Modesty Blaise novels, epitomises this enthusiasm. Also, it is mind-boggling how many times some of those fans confess to having read the books. It is a credit to the stories' depth and ability to entertain that readers keep going back to them.

I feel pride hearing what Modesty means to people and the effect she has on them: to hear how she can give inspiration, provide solace and perspective, feel like a friend, be a role model and even a pick-me-up. As a parent, I can see what an inspiration she can be, especially for girls. She is fairly wholesome as ex-criminals go. I can't think of any other former felons I'd be happy for my girls to be inspired by.

Finally, I don't know what it is like for other readers but at times I still find it easy to forget, especially when reading the novels, that Modesty and Willie are fictional. They were made to be so alive. How did that come out of one writer's head? I'll leave the last word to Peter to explain how he did it.

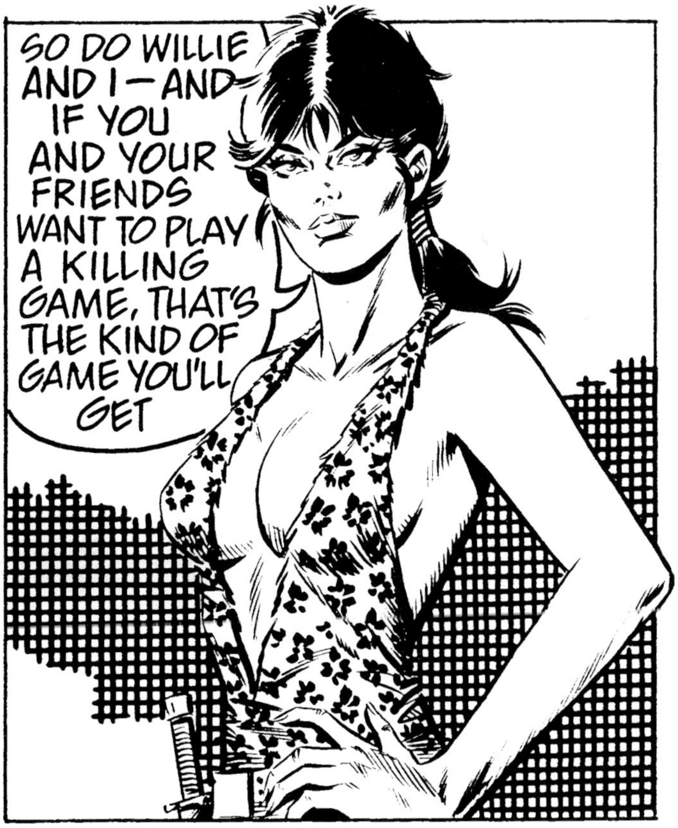
SO DO WILLIE AND I — AND IF YOU AND YOUR FRIENDS WANT TO PLAY A KILLING GAME, THAT'S THE KIND OF GAME YOU'LL GET

PAUL MICHAEL

Paul Michael is the grandson of Peter O'Donnell.

ALL IN THE MIND

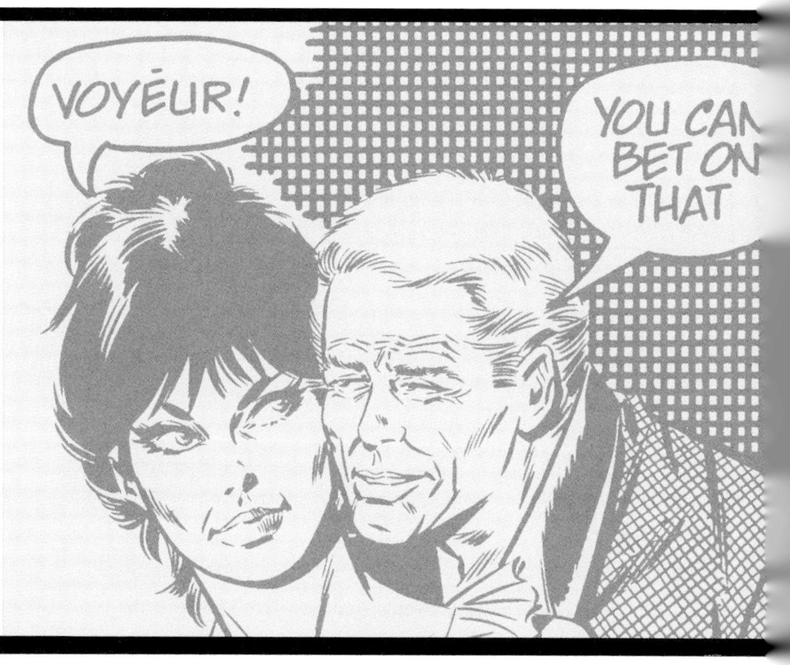
VOYEUR!
YOU CAN BET ON THAT

Long ago, when I was six years old, I made a discovery. It happened when I began to write my First Story, which I proposed to inscribe in a small red notebook I'd found. Full of enthusiasm, I laboriously spelled out the words, *Wonce upon a tim ther was a man...*

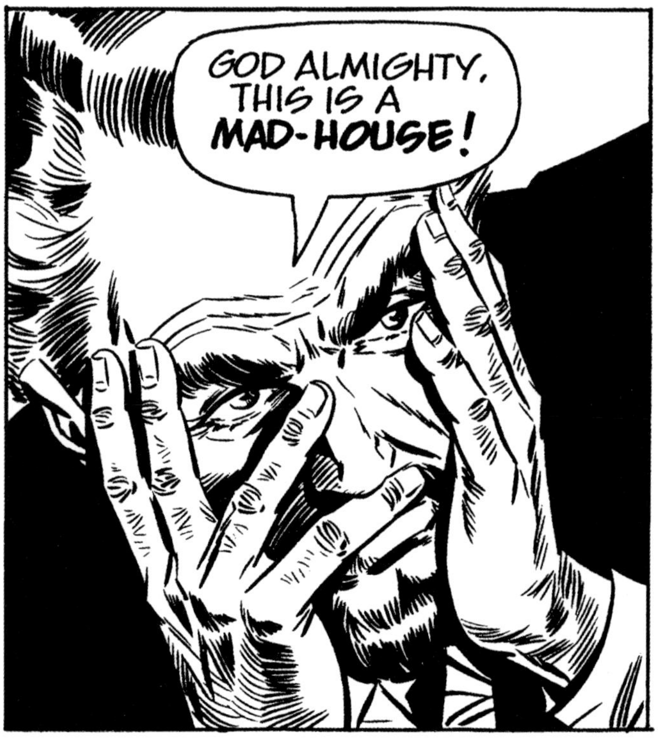
GOD ALMIGHTY, THIS IS A MAD-HOUSE!

And there the whole project ground to a dead stop, not to be resumed for ten years, and then with a somewhat different opening. I had been granted, at that tender age, the traumatic revelation that if you want to write a story you must first have an Idea. It was, in a way, like a very retarded Newton discovering that apples always fall *down*. Just as everybody had always known this thing about apples, I later found that everybody had always known this thing about Ideas. In fact, a favourite question put to writers of fiction, in whatever medium, is - where do you get your ideas?

I always tell lies about this, because the truth is so humiliating. I give the answer I've heard other writers give, and say modestly that any little thing can stimulate an idea - a three-line paragraph in a newspaper, a photograph, a scrap of overheard conversation, a sound, a sight, anything at all can be seized upon instantly by the Sensitive and Receptive Mind of the Writer.

I only wish this did happen with me, but unfortunately my response to stimuli is so delayed you'd never believe it. The sad truth is that I have hundreds, perhaps thousands, of little holes in the top of my brain, caused by I know not what, and through these holes slip everything I see, hear, read, or experience. Down, down they go into a kind of musty cellar just above the stalk, or *pons varolii*, thereby leaving the working surface clear for such titanic and recurring problems as remembering what day it is, not putting on odd socks, and recalling what it was I came upstairs for just now.

You can get an image of what I mean if you think of those street gratings where you can look down and see the detritus of years lying below. An age-bleached cigarette packet, a pre-war toffee-apple stick or matchbox, dead beetles, yellowing scraps of newspaper (with three-line paragraphs), and indeterminate lumps, all being slowly buried under a carpet of dust. Now, when I have to write anything, which is all the time, the preliminary process is to shake up this jumble in the cellars of the mind and try to get it into some sort of pattern, rather like shaking a kaleidoscope.

The actual technique of shaking is the real problem. I have tried yoga, standing on my head in the hope that a lot of stuff will fall out of the holes and onto the working surface, to provide raw material for an Idea. But Newtonian physics doesn't seem to work in the mysterious labyrinth of the brain, and the only result is bloodshot eyes.

I have also tried the method of having a pad and pencil beside the bed in case I'm woken from sleep by some brilliant inspiration trickling out from the cellars while I'm horizontal. This did happen once, and in the early hours I woke with a Great Idea almost coming out of one ear. Bedside light on... grope for pencil... scribble scribble... then back to happy sleep. In the morning I found I'd written *Poached egg defies cynicism.*

No. The only technique that works for me is Effort. Like Uri Geller bending forks, I find that if I try really hard I can overcome the laws of physics and, as it were, draw a kind of whirlpool of mixed debris up through the holes and onto the working surface, there to be picked over and shuffled around until an Idea is born.

After that there's nothing to it but blood and tears, toil and sweat - but not for everybody, to my constant chagrin. I have known writers, seemingly normal chaps with only one head, who can turn out 10,000 words of good stuff in a *day*, and enjoy it. Now I'm not one to complain, but this is grossly unfair to holes-in-the-brain cases like me, and I can only say I hope it rains on them. They've never had to bend a fork in their lives.

PETER O'DONNELL

Left top: The Zombie - 10087
left: The Zombie - 10166
Right: The Killing Game - 9969

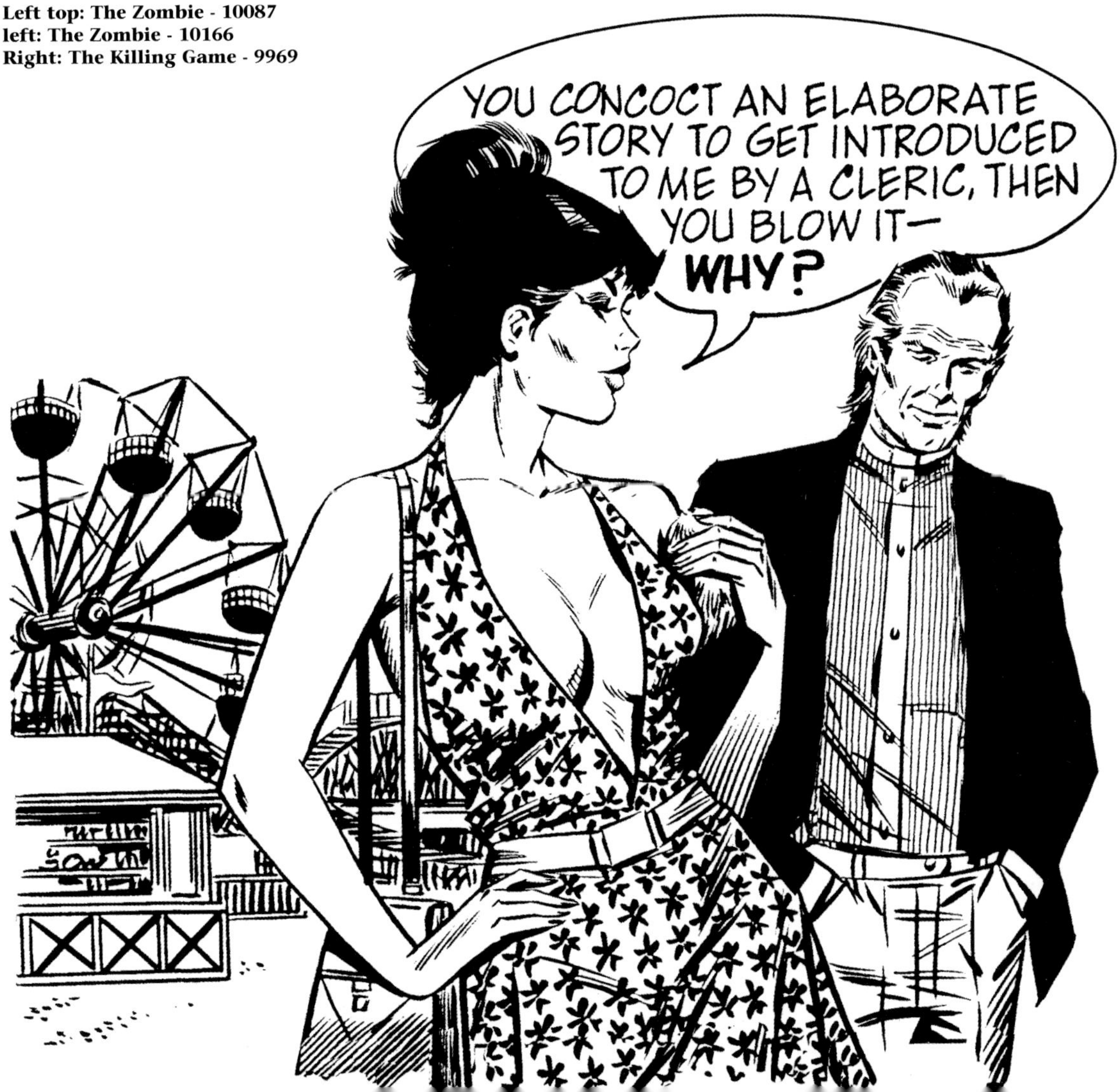
YOU CONCOCT AN ELABORATE STORY TO GET INTRODUCED TO ME BY A CLERIC, THEN YOU BLOW IT— WHY?

THE LAST ARISTOCRAT

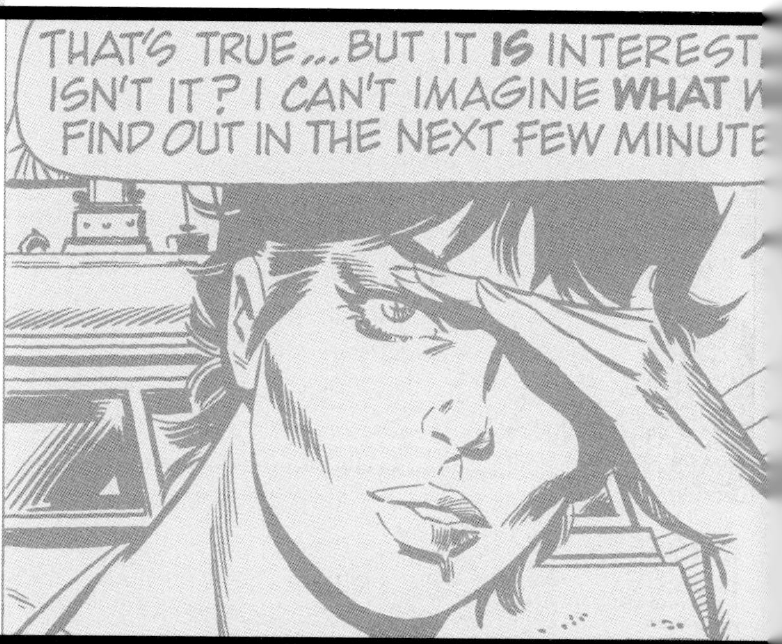
THAT'S TRUE... BUT IT IS INTEREST
ISN'T IT? I CAN'T IMAGINE WHAT
FIND OUT IN THE NEXT FEW MINUTE

One of the special pleasures of Modesty Blaise is the beautiful choice of locations: this time the island of Corfu. Here we find one of Modesty's old criminal contacts has a base. Peter O'Donnell once again weaves a tightly plotted adventure featuring yet another strong female villain: this time the ludicrously aristocratic Granny Smythe; the keeper of bacterial bombs, butlers and stately homes.

We also find the recurring character of journalist Guido the Jinx (a delicious tongue teaser of a name) who is ultimately the catalyst of this charming tale. Guido, as Lawrence Blackmore informs us in his terrific 'Modesty Blaise Companion', appears in no less than four stories in all: Guido The Jinx, Story 65, Milord and this one. Here he enters the story in the most astonishing fashion, descending via a parachute that ends unceremoniously in the ocean. A bemused Modesty and Willie look on from a glamorous yacht and eventually have to jump in to help.

'Is there a girl with him?' Willie asks. 'How can he possibly tell from such a distance?' Sir Gerald replies in astonishment. Willie, as we well know by now, can sniff out the scent of the girls over a very great distance.

In fact Aniela, Guido's outrageously flirtatious fiancée, would rather canoodle with Willie (and who can really blame her!). They have come to invite Modesty to their wedding (and Aniela insists Willie must "give her away", a wonderful euphemism suggesting another sort of invitation perhaps?) But Guido would rather leave his lady at the altar than miss an opportunity for mischief. In another surprising master stroke of plot by Peter O'Donnell Guido the Jinx uses his own wedding as subterfuge to go to Granny Smythe's estate and get the low down on her meeting with a terrorist who's hell bent on buying bacterial bombs. And thus another whirligig ensues...

A most delightful and ingenious tale by the ever inventive and playful Peter O'Donnell.

DAPHNE ALEXANDER

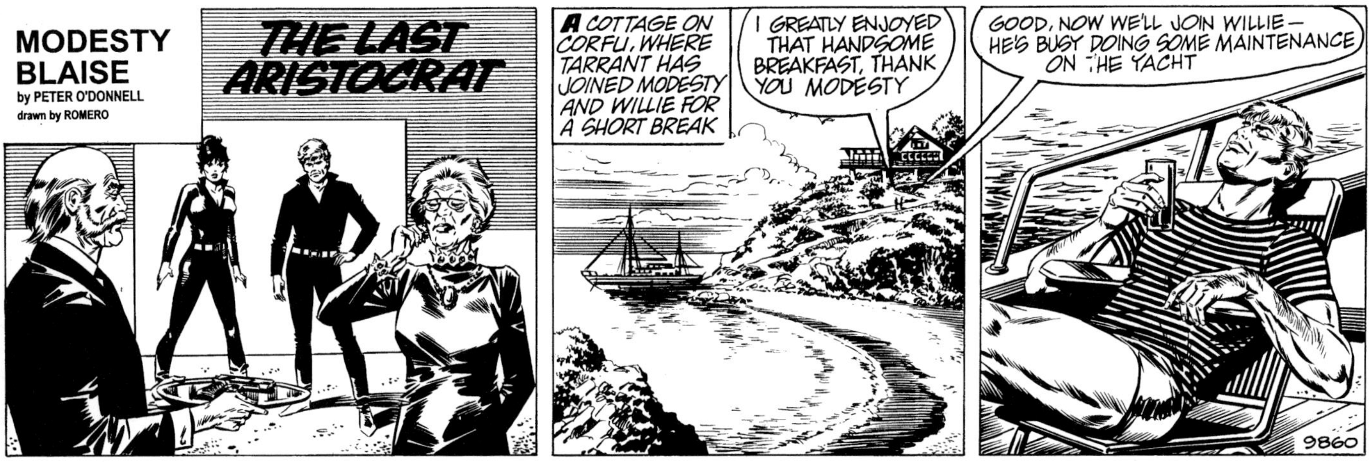

MODESTY BLAISE
by PETER O'DONNELL
drawn by ROMERO
THE LAST ARISTOCRAT
A COTTAGE ON CORFU, WHERE TARRANT HAS JOINED MODESTY AND WILLIE FOR A SHORT BREAK
I GREATLY ENJOYED THAT HANDSOME BREAKFAST, THANK YOU MODESTY
GOOD, NOW WE'LL JOIN WILLIE — HE'S BUSY DOING SOME MAINTENANCE ON THE YACHT
9860

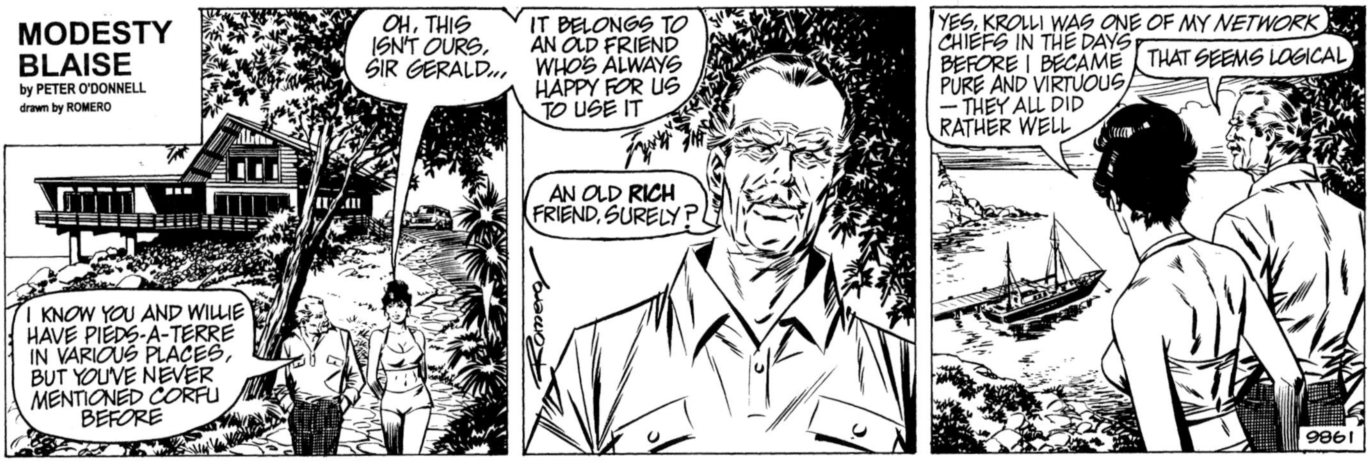

MODESTY BLAISE
by PETER O'DONNELL
drawn by ROMERO
I KNOW YOU AND WILLIE HAVE PIEDS-A-TERRE IN VARIOUS PLACES, BUT YOU'VE NEVER MENTIONED CORFU BEFORE
OH, THIS ISN'T OURS, SIR GERALD...
IT BELONGS TO AN OLD FRIEND WHO'S ALWAYS HAPPY FOR US TO USE IT
AN OLD RICH FRIEND, SURELY?
YES, KROLLI WAS ONE OF MY NETWORK CHIEFS IN THE DAYS BEFORE I BECAME PURE AND VIRTUOUS — THEY ALL DID RATHER WELL
THAT SEEMS LOGICAL
9861

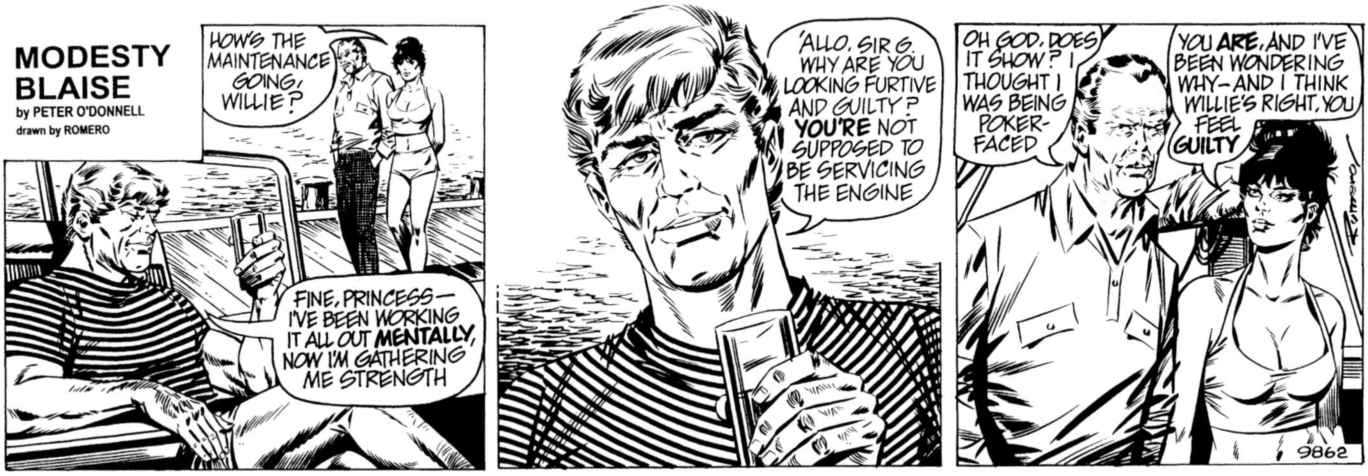

MODESTY BLAISE
by PETER O'DONNELL
drawn by ROMERO
HOW'S THE MAINTENANCE GOING, WILLIE?
FINE, PRINCESS — I'VE BEEN WORKING IT ALL OUT MENTALLY, NOW I'M GATHERING ME STRENGTH
'ALLO, SIR G. WHY ARE YOU LOOKING FURTIVE AND GUILTY? YOU'RE NOT SUPPOSED TO BE SERVICING THE ENGINE
OH GOD, DOES IT SHOW? I THOUGHT I WAS BEING POKER-FACED
YOU ARE, AND I'VE BEEN WONDERING WHY — AND I THINK WILLIE'S RIGHT, YOU FEEL GUILTY
9862

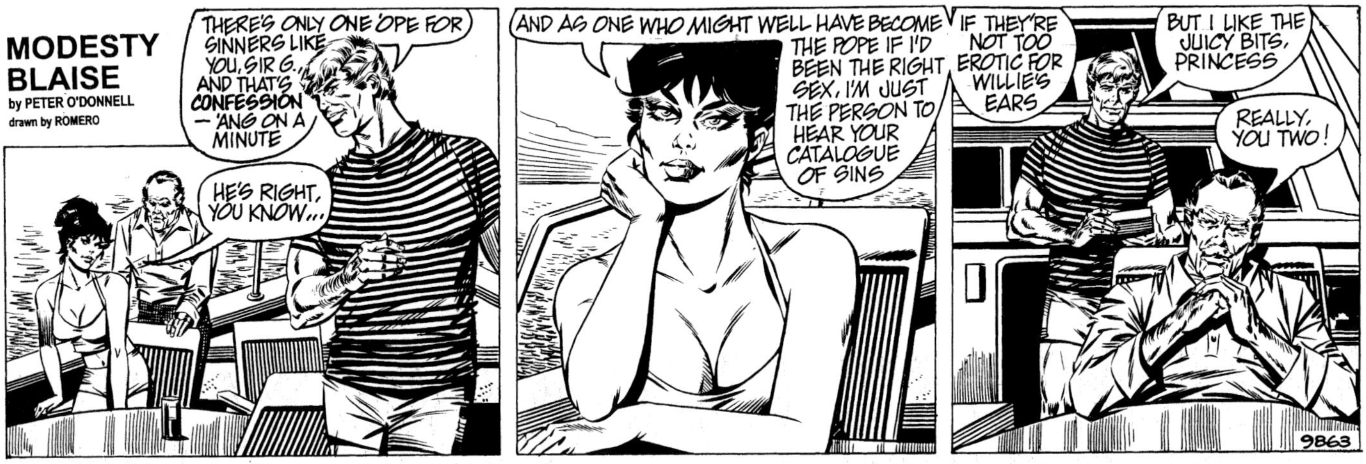

MODESTY BLAISE
by PETER O'DONNELL
drawn by ROMERO
THERE'S ONLY ONE 'OPE FOR SINNERS LIKE YOU, SIR G., AND THAT'S CONFESSION — 'ANG ON A MINUTE
HE'S RIGHT, YOU KNOW...
AND AS ONE WHO MIGHT WELL HAVE BECOME THE POPE IF I'D BEEN THE RIGHT SEX, I'M JUST THE PERSON TO HEAR YOUR CATALOGUE OF SINS
IF THEY'RE NOT TOO EROTIC FOR WILLIE'S EARS
BUT I LIKE THE JUICY BITS, PRINCESS
REALLY, YOU TWO!
9863

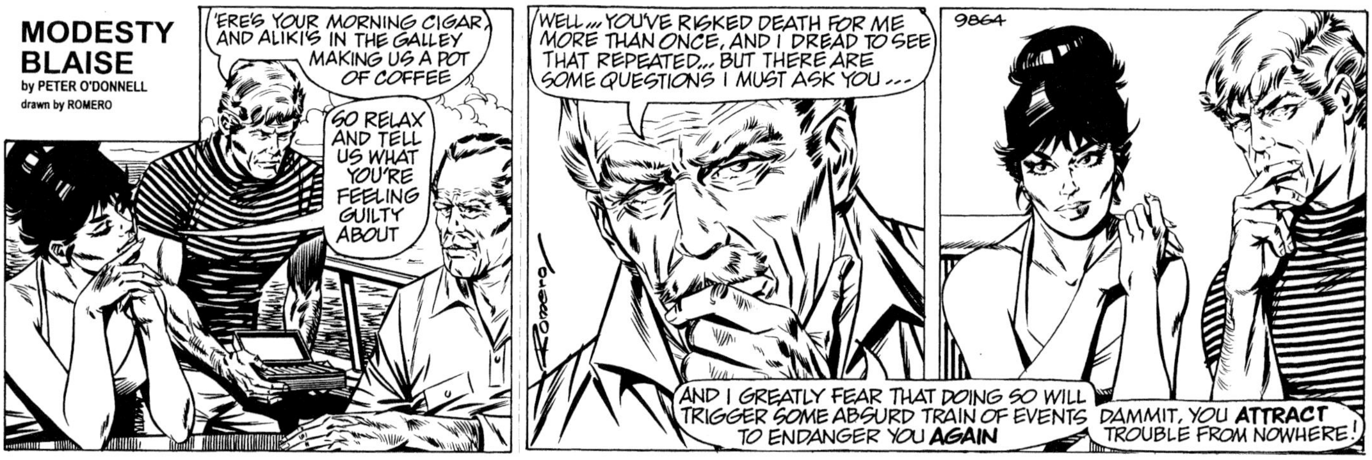
MODESTY BLAISE
by PETER O'DONNELL
drawn by ROMERO
'ERE'S YOUR MORNING CIGAR AND ALIKI'S IN THE GALLEY MAKING US A POT OF COFFEE
SO RELAX AND TELL US WHAT YOU'RE FEELING GUILTY ABOUT
WELL... YOU'VE RISKED DEATH FOR ME MORE THAN ONCE, AND I DREAD TO SEE THAT REPEATED... BUT THERE ARE SOME QUESTIONS I MUST ASK YOU...
AND I GREATLY FEAR THAT DOING SO WILL TRIGGER SOME ABSURD TRAIN OF EVENTS TO ENDANGER YOU **AGAIN**
ROMERO
9864
DAMMIT, YOU **ATTRACT** TROUBLE FROM NOWHERE!

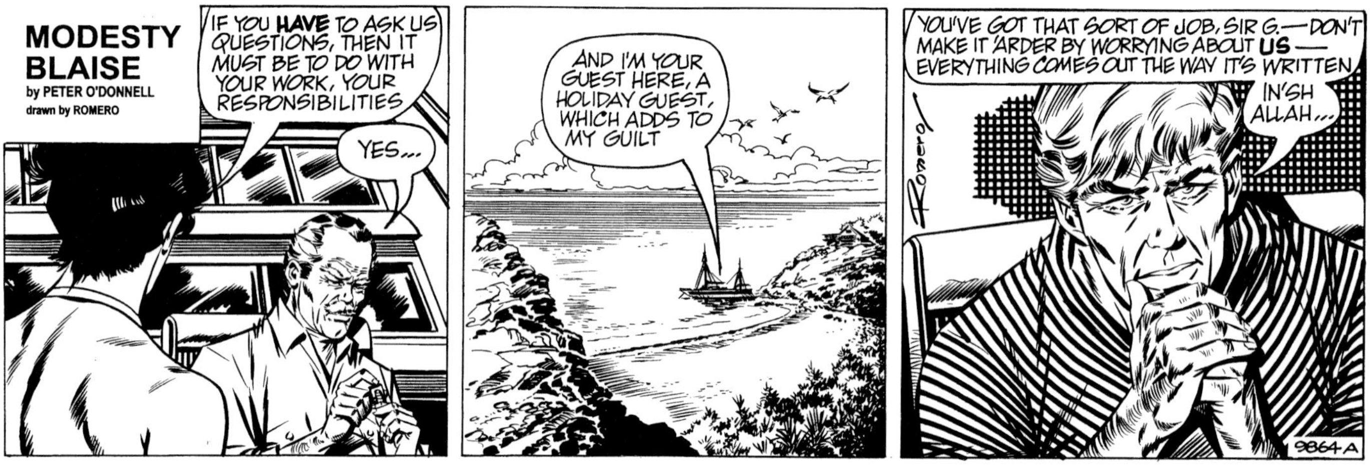
MODESTY BLAISE
by PETER O'DONNELL
drawn by ROMERO
IF YOU **HAVE** TO ASK US QUESTIONS, THEN IT MUST BE TO DO WITH YOUR WORK, YOUR RESPONSIBILITIES
YES...
AND I'M YOUR GUEST HERE, A HOLIDAY GUEST, WHICH ADDS TO MY GUILT
YOU'VE GOT THAT SORT OF JOB, SIR G.—DON'T MAKE IT 'ARDER BY WORRYING ABOUT **US**—EVERYTHING COMES OUT THE WAY IT'S WRITTEN
IN'SH ALLAH...
ROMERO
9864 A

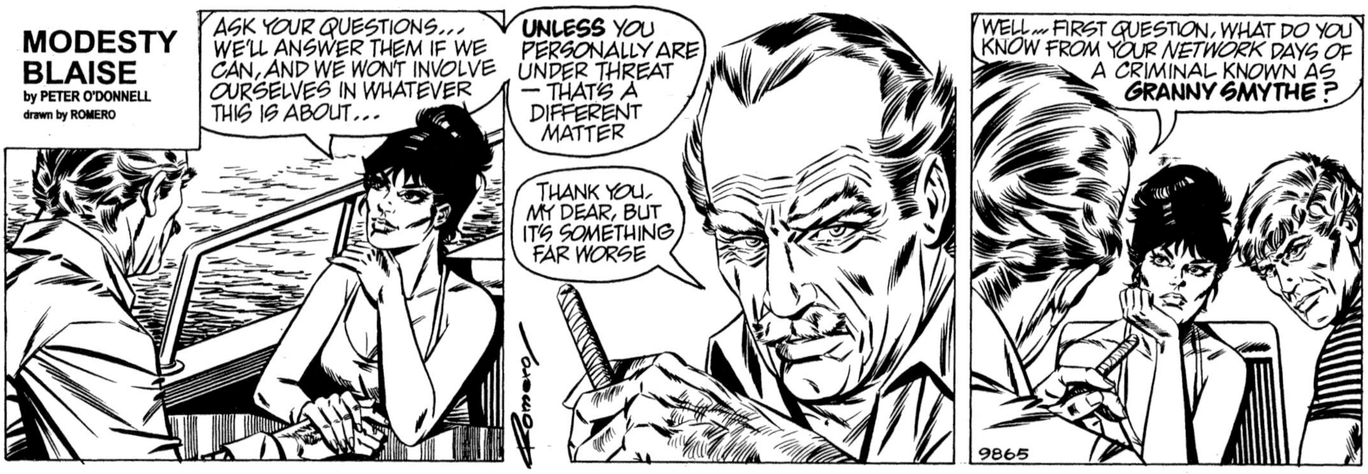
MODESTY BLAISE
by PETER O'DONNELL
drawn by ROMERO
ASK YOUR QUESTIONS... WE'LL ANSWER THEM IF WE CAN, AND WE WON'T INVOLVE OURSELVES IN WHATEVER THIS IS ABOUT...
UNLESS YOU PERSONALLY ARE UNDER THREAT—THAT'S A DIFFERENT MATTER
THANK YOU, MY DEAR, BUT IT'S SOMETHING FAR WORSE
ROMERO
WELL... FIRST QUESTION. WHAT DO YOU KNOW FROM YOUR *NETWORK* DAYS OF A CRIMINAL KNOWN AS **GRANNY SMYTHE**?
9865

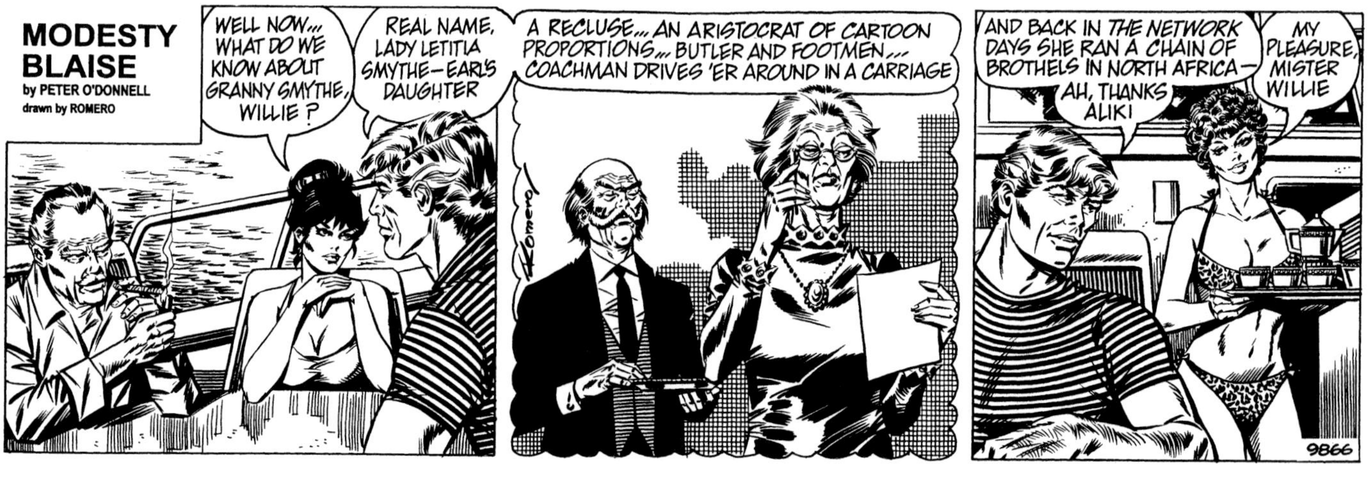
MODESTY BLAISE
by PETER O'DONNELL
drawn by ROMERO
WELL NOW... WHAT DO WE KNOW ABOUT GRANNY SMYTHE, WILLIE?
REAL NAME, LADY LETITIA SMYTHE—EARL'S DAUGHTER
A RECLUSE... AN ARISTOCRAT OF CARTOON PROPORTIONS... BUTLER AND FOOTMEN... COACHMAN DRIVES 'ER AROUND IN A CARRIAGE
ROMERO
AND BACK IN *THE NETWORK* DAYS SHE RAN A CHAIN OF BROTHELS IN NORTH AFRICA—
AH, THANKS ALIKI
MY PLEASURE, MISTER WILLIE
9866

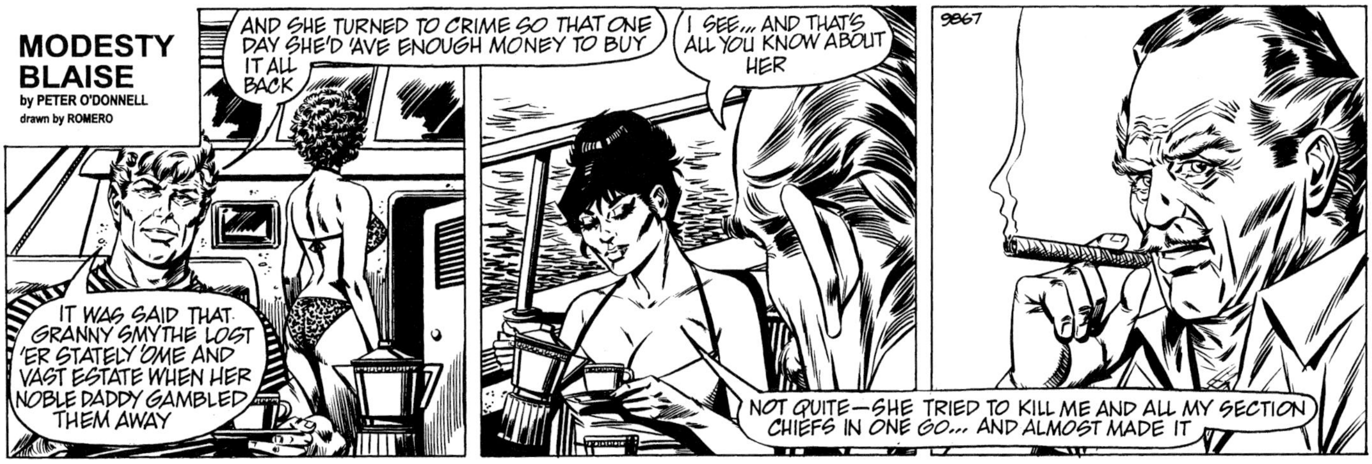
MODESTY BLAISE
by PETER O'DONNELL
drawn by ROMERO
AND SHE TURNED TO CRIME SO THAT ONE DAY SHE'D 'AVE ENOUGH MONEY TO BUY IT ALL BACK
IT WAS SAID THAT GRANNY SMYTHE LOST 'ER STATELY 'OME AND VAST ESTATE WHEN HER NOBLE DADDY GAMBLED THEM AWAY
I SEE... AND THAT'S ALL YOU KNOW ABOUT HER
9867
NOT QUITE—SHE TRIED TO KILL ME AND ALL MY SECTION CHIEFS IN ONE GO... AND ALMOST MADE IT

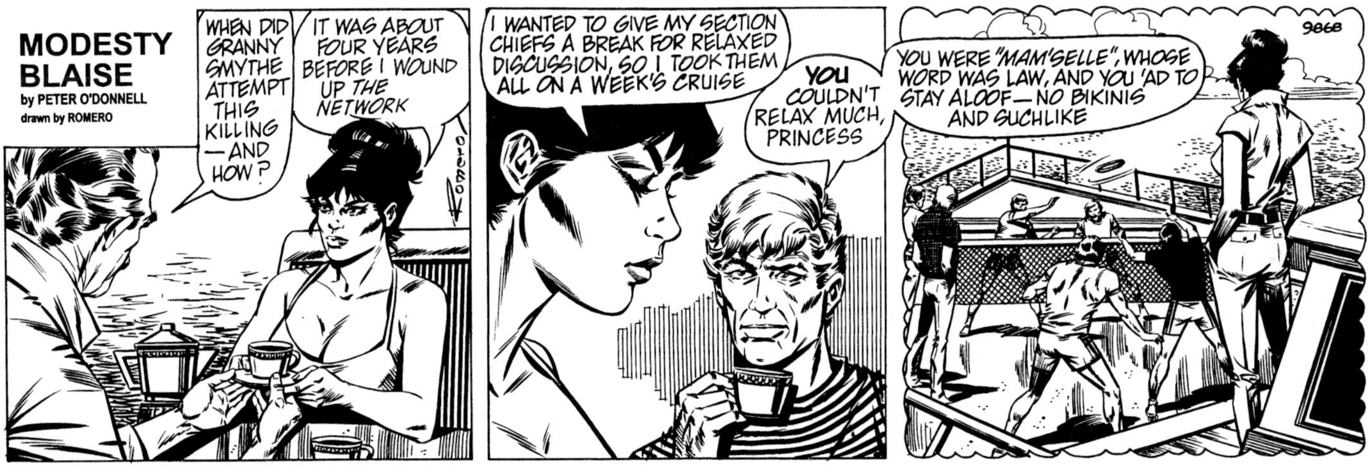
MODESTY BLAISE
by PETER O'DONNELL
drawn by ROMERO
WHEN DID GRANNY SMYTHE ATTEMPT THIS KILLING —AND HOW?
IT WAS ABOUT FOUR YEARS BEFORE I WOUND UP THE NETWORK
I WANTED TO GIVE MY SECTION CHIEFS A BREAK FOR RELAXED DISCUSSION, SO I TOOK THEM ALL ON A WEEK'S CRUISE
YOU COULDN'T RELAX MUCH, PRINCESS
9868
YOU WERE "MAM'SELLE", WHOSE WORD WAS LAW, AND YOU 'AD TO STAY ALOOF— NO BIKINIS AND SUCHLIKE

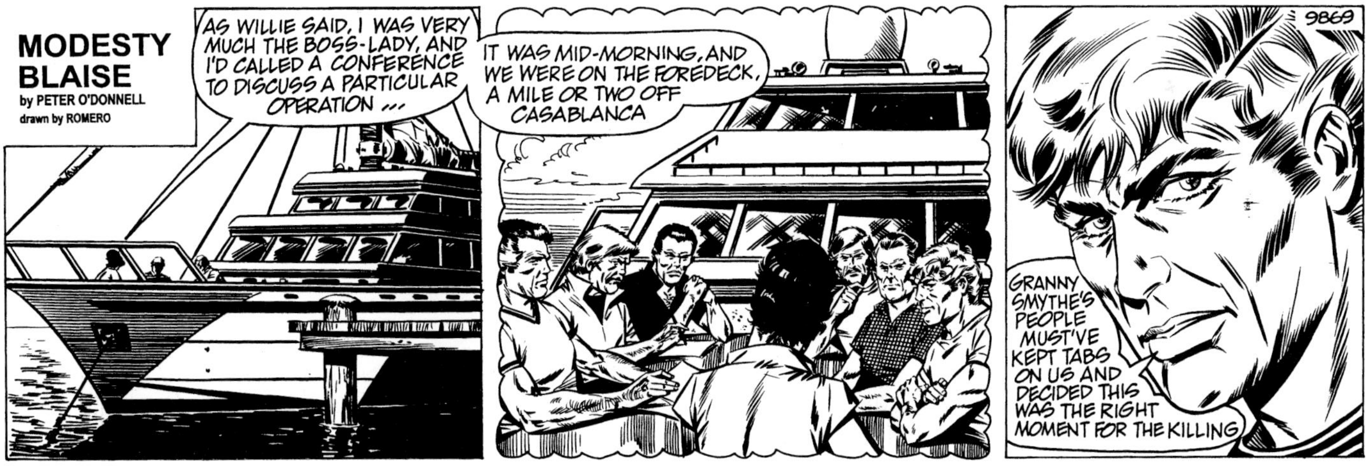
MODESTY BLAISE
by PETER O'DONNELL
drawn by ROMERO
AS WILLIE SAID, I WAS VERY MUCH THE BOSS-LADY, AND I'D CALLED A CONFERENCE TO DISCUSS A PARTICULAR OPERATION...
IT WAS MID-MORNING, AND WE WERE ON THE FOREDECK, A MILE OR TWO OFF CASABLANCA
9869
GRANNY SMYTHE'S PEOPLE MUST'VE KEPT TABS ON US AND DECIDED THIS WAS THE RIGHT MOMENT FOR THE KILLING

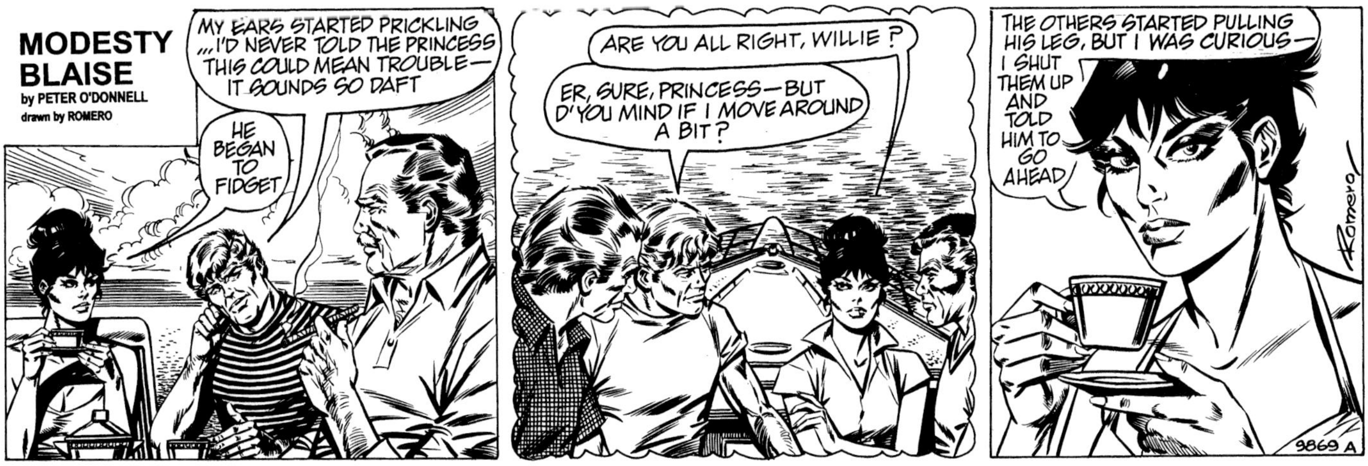
MODESTY BLAISE
by PETER O'DONNELL
drawn by ROMERO
MY EARS STARTED PRICKLING ...I'D NEVER TOLD THE PRINCESS THIS COULD MEAN TROUBLE— IT SOUNDS SO DAFT
HE BEGAN TO FIDGET
ARE YOU ALL RIGHT, WILLIE?
ER, SURE, PRINCESS—BUT D'YOU MIND IF I MOVE AROUND A BIT?
THE OTHERS STARTED PULLING HIS LEG, BUT I WAS CURIOUS— I SHUT THEM UP AND TOLD HIM TO GO AHEAD
Romero
9869 A

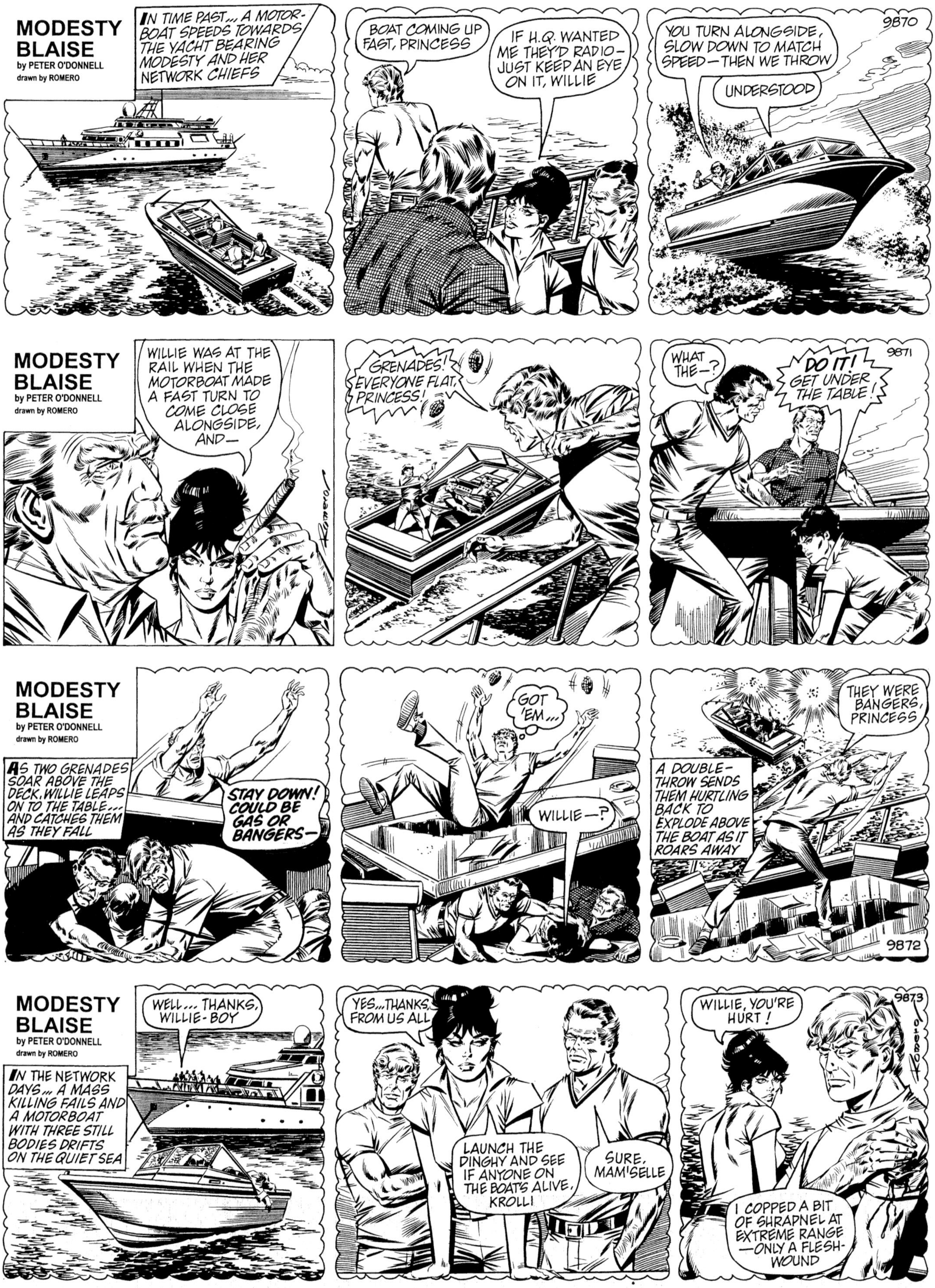
MODESTY BLAISE
by PETER O'DONNELL
drawn by ROMERO
IN TIME PAST... A MOTOR-BOAT SPEEDS TOWARDS THE YACHT BEARING MODESTY AND HER NETWORK CHIEFS
BOAT COMING UP FAST, PRINCESS
IF H.Q. WANTED ME THEY'D RADIO—JUST KEEP AN EYE ON IT, WILLIE
9870
YOU TURN ALONGSIDE, SLOW DOWN TO MATCH SPEED—THEN WE THROW
UNDERSTOOD
MODESTY BLAISE
by PETER O'DONNELL
drawn by ROMERO
WILLIE WAS AT THE RAIL WHEN THE MOTORBOAT MADE A FAST TURN TO COME CLOSE ALONGSIDE, AND—
ROMERO
GRENADES! EVERYONE FLAT, PRINCESS!
9871
WHAT THE—?
DO IT! GET UNDER THE TABLE!
MODESTY BLAISE
by PETER O'DONNELL
drawn by ROMERO
AS TWO GRENADES SOAR ABOVE THE DECK, WILLIE LEAPS ON TO THE TABLE... AND CATCHES THEM AS THEY FALL
STAY DOWN! COULD BE GAS OR BANGERS—
GOT 'EM...
WILLIE—?
THEY WERE BANGERS, PRINCESS
A DOUBLE-THROW SENDS THEM HURTLING BACK TO EXPLODE ABOVE THE BOAT AS IT ROARS AWAY
9872
MODESTY BLAISE
by PETER O'DONNELL
drawn by ROMERO
WELL... THANKS, WILLIE-BOY
IN THE NETWORK DAYS... A MASS KILLING FAILS AND A MOTORBOAT WITH THREE STILL BODIES DRIFTS ON THE QUIET SEA
YES... THANKS, FROM US ALL
LAUNCH THE DINGHY AND SEE IF ANYONE ON THE BOAT'S ALIVE, KROLL!
SURE, MAM'SELLE
9873
WILLIE, YOU'RE HURT!
I COPPED A BIT OF SHRAPNEL AT EXTREME RANGE—ONLY A FLESH-WOUND

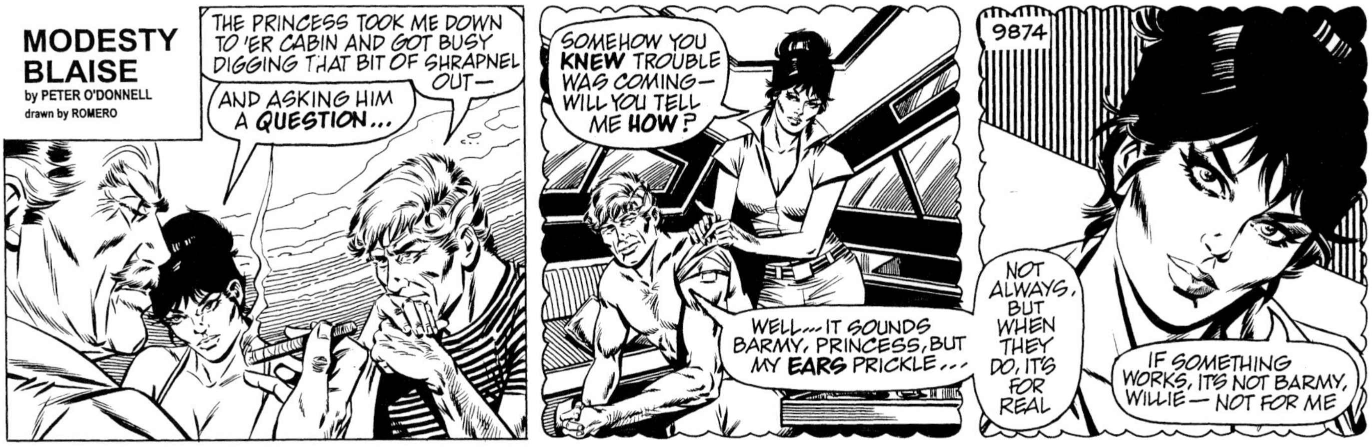
MODESTY BLAISE
by PETER O'DONNELL
drawn by ROMERO
THE PRINCESS TOOK ME DOWN TO 'ER CABIN AND GOT BUSY DIGGING THAT BIT OF SHRAPNEL OUT—
AND ASKING HIM A QUESTION...
SOMEHOW YOU KNEW TROUBLE WAS COMING— WILL YOU TELL ME HOW?
WELL... IT SOUNDS BARMY, PRINCESS, BUT MY EARS PRICKLE...
9874
NOT ALWAYS, BUT WHEN THEY DO, IT'S FOR REAL
IF SOMETHING WORKS, IT'S NOT BARMY, WILLIE — NOT FOR ME

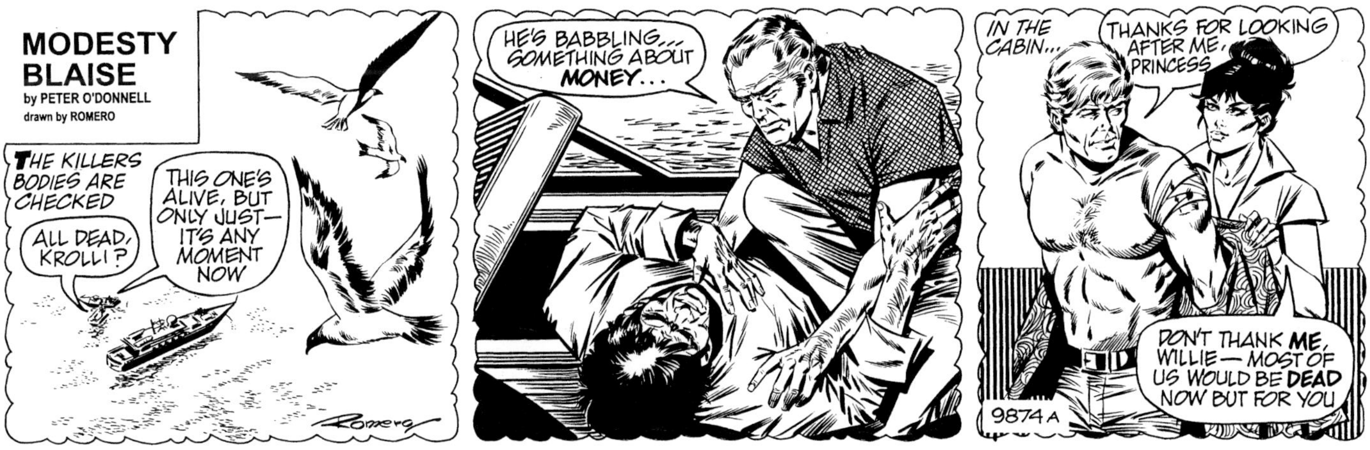
MODESTY BLAISE
by PETER O'DONNELL
drawn by ROMERO
THE KILLERS BODIES ARE CHECKED
ALL DEAD, KROLLI?
THIS ONE'S ALIVE, BUT ONLY JUST— IT'S ANY MOMENT NOW
ROMERO
HE'S BABBLING... SOMETHING ABOUT MONEY...
IN THE CABIN...
THANKS FOR LOOKING AFTER ME, PRINCESS
DON'T THANK ME, WILLIE — MOST OF US WOULD BE DEAD NOW BUT FOR YOU
9874 A

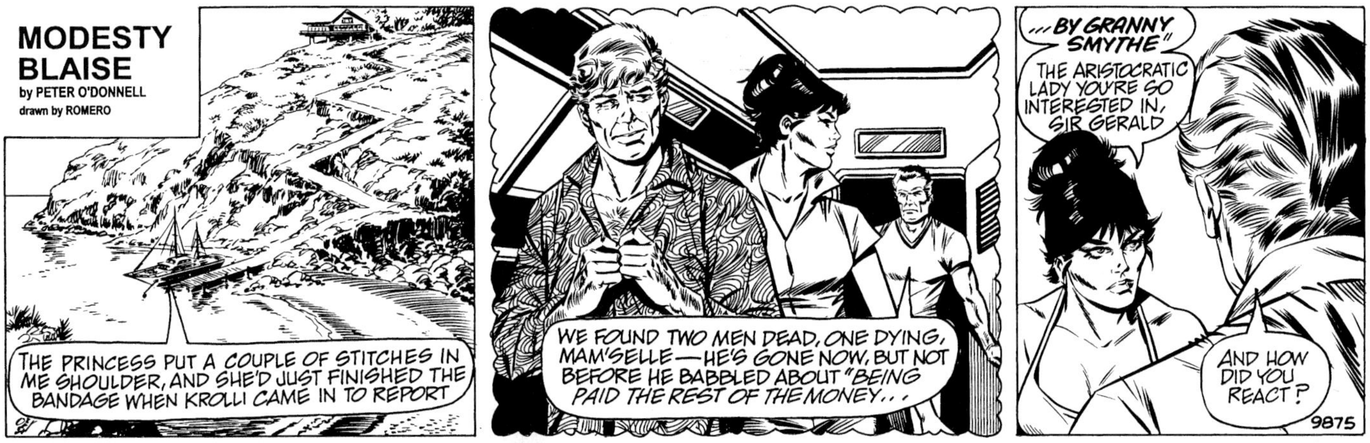
MODESTY BLAISE
by PETER O'DONNELL
drawn by ROMERO
THE PRINCESS PUT A COUPLE OF STITCHES IN ME SHOULDER, AND SHE'D JUST FINISHED THE BANDAGE WHEN KROLLI CAME IN TO REPORT
WE FOUND TWO MEN DEAD, ONE DYING, MAM'SELLE — HE'S GONE NOW, BUT NOT BEFORE HE BABBLED ABOUT "BEING PAID THE REST OF THE MONEY...
..."BY GRANNY SMYTHE"
THE ARISTOCRATIC LADY YOU'RE SO INTERESTED IN, SIR GERALD
AND HOW DID YOU REACT?
9875

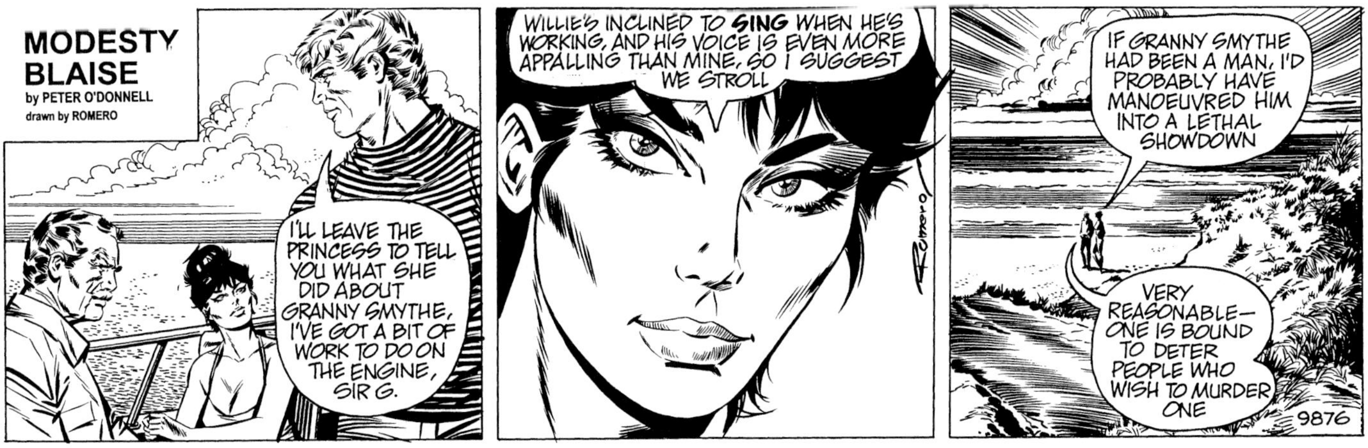
MODESTY BLAISE
by PETER O'DONNELL
drawn by ROMERO
I'LL LEAVE THE PRINCESS TO TELL YOU WHAT SHE DID ABOUT GRANNY SMYTHE, I'VE GOT A BIT OF WORK TO DO ON THE ENGINE, SIR G.
WILLIE'S INCLINED TO SING WHEN HE'S WORKING, AND HIS VOICE IS EVEN MORE APPALLING THAN MINE, SO I SUGGEST WE STROLL
ROMERO
IF GRANNY SMYTHE HAD BEEN A MAN, I'D PROBABLY HAVE MANOEUVRED HIM INTO A LETHAL SHOWDOWN
VERY REASONABLE— ONE IS BOUND TO DETER PEOPLE WHO WISH TO MURDER ONE
9876

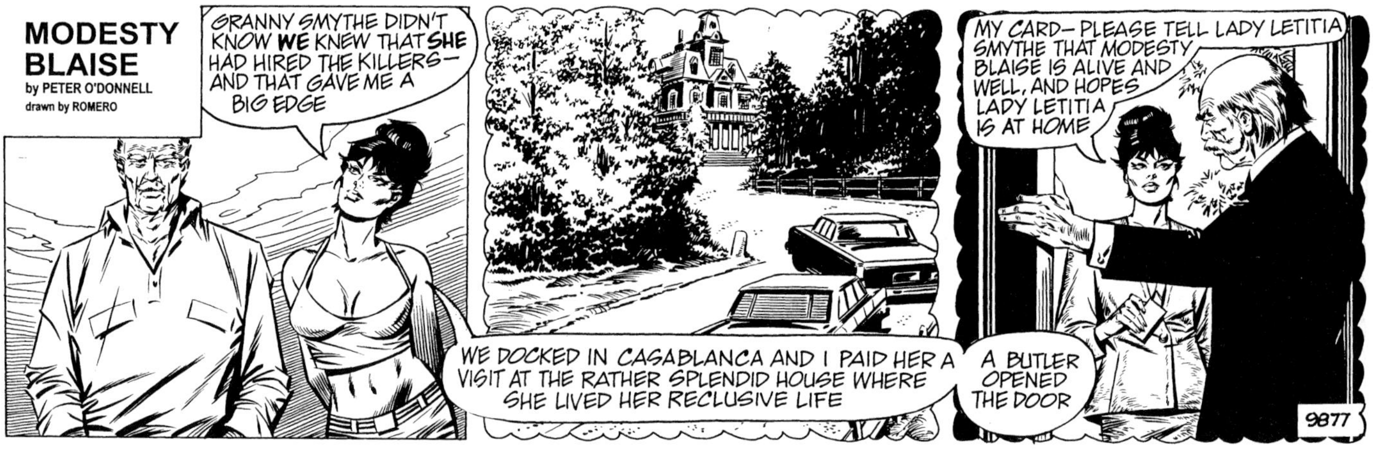
MODESTY BLAISE
by PETER O'DONNELL
drawn by ROMERO
GRANNY SMYTHE DIDN'T KNOW **WE** KNEW THAT **SHE** HAD HIRED THE KILLERS— AND THAT GAVE ME A BIG EDGE
WE DOCKED IN CASABLANCA AND I PAID HER A VISIT AT THE RATHER SPLENDID HOUSE WHERE SHE LIVED HER RECLUSIVE LIFE
A BUTLER OPENED THE DOOR
MY CARD— PLEASE TELL LADY LETITIA SMYTHE THAT MODESTY BLAISE IS ALIVE AND WELL, AND HOPES LADY LETITIA IS AT HOME
9877

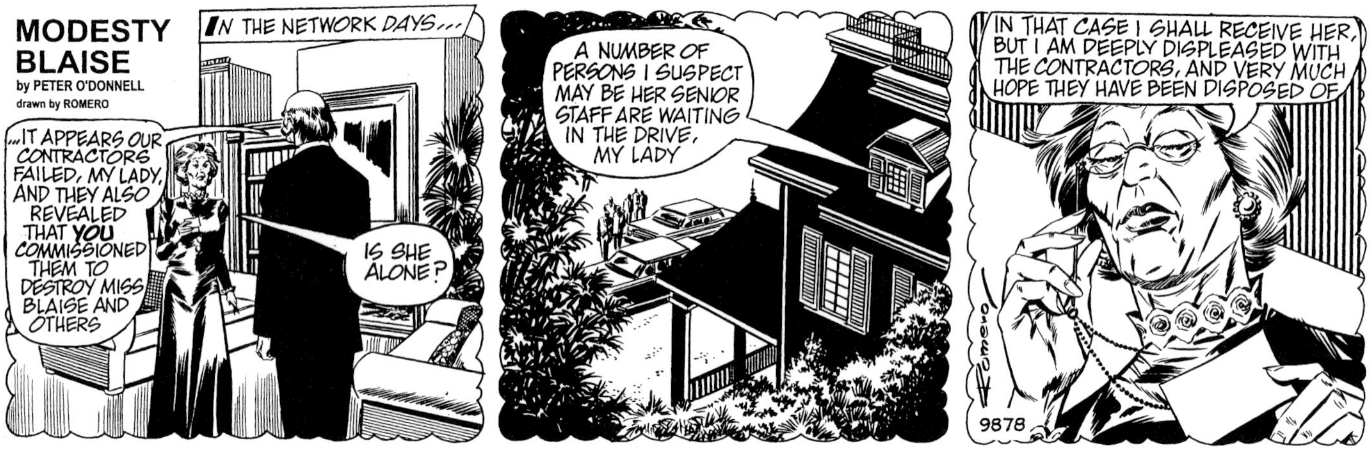
MODESTY BLAISE
by PETER O'DONNELL
drawn by ROMERO
IN THE NETWORK DAYS...
...IT APPEARS OUR CONTRACTORS FAILED, MY LADY, AND THEY ALSO REVEALED THAT **YOU** COMMISSIONED THEM TO DESTROY MISS BLAISE AND OTHERS
IS SHE ALONE?
A NUMBER OF PERSONS I SUSPECT MAY BE HER SENIOR STAFF ARE WAITING IN THE DRIVE, MY LADY
IN THAT CASE I SHALL RECEIVE HER, BUT I AM DEEPLY DISPLEASED WITH THE CONTRACTORS, AND VERY MUCH HOPE THEY HAVE BEEN DISPOSED OF
9878

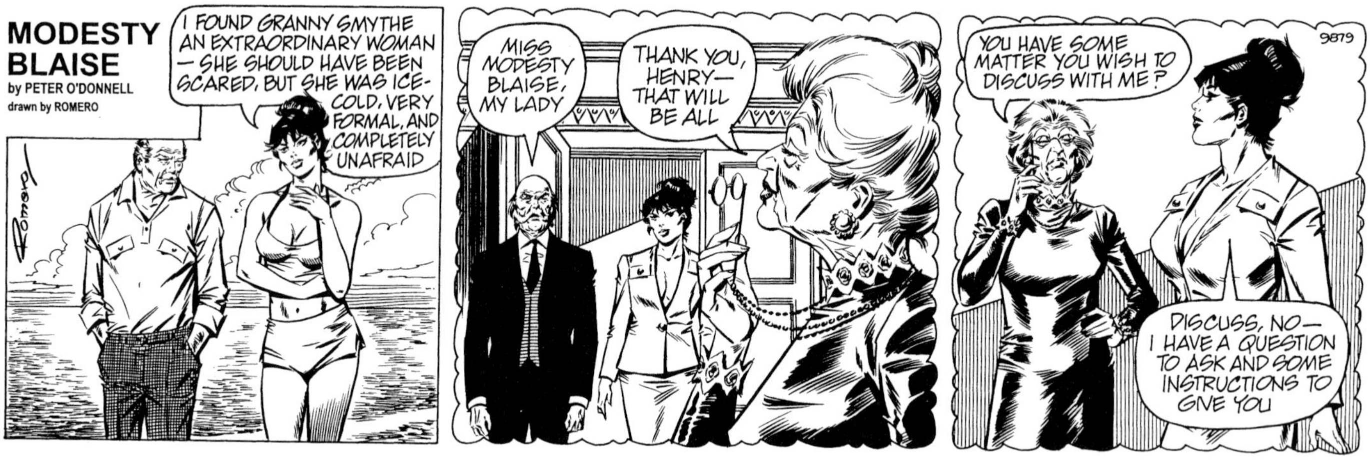
MODESTY BLAISE
by PETER O'DONNELL
drawn by ROMERO
I FOUND GRANNY SMYTHE AN EXTRAORDINARY WOMAN —SHE SHOULD HAVE BEEN SCARED, BUT SHE WAS ICE-COLD, VERY FORMAL, AND COMPLETELY UNAFRAID
MISS MODESTY BLAISE, MY LADY
THANK YOU, HENRY— THAT WILL BE ALL
9879
YOU HAVE SOME MATTER YOU WISH TO DISCUSS WITH ME?
DISCUSS, NO— I HAVE A QUESTION TO ASK AND SOME INSTRUCTIONS TO GIVE YOU

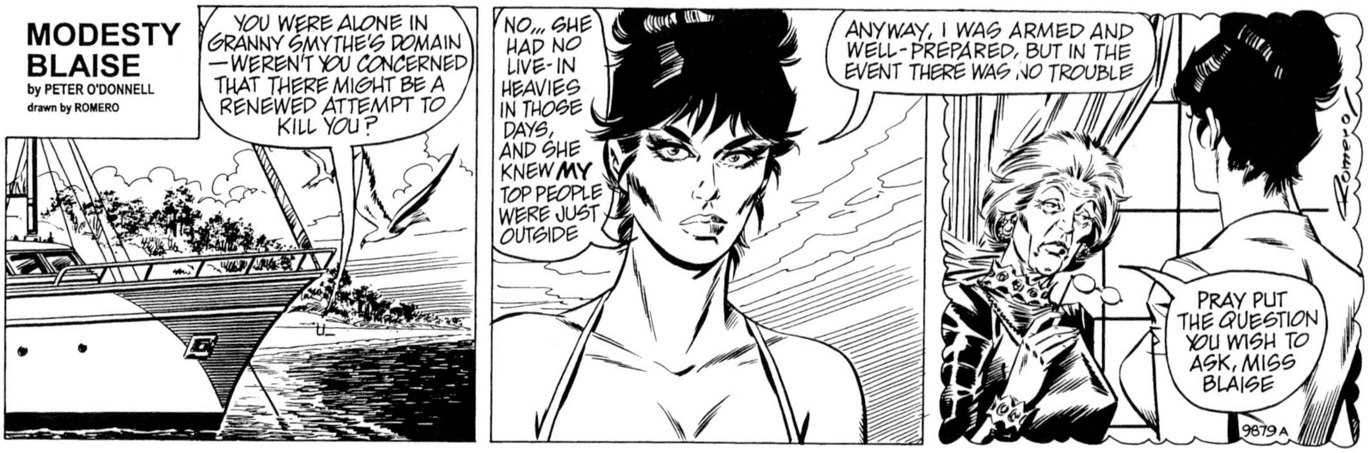
MODESTY BLAISE
by PETER O'DONNELL
drawn by ROMERO
YOU WERE ALONE IN GRANNY SMYTHE'S DOMAIN —WEREN'T YOU CONCERNED THAT THERE MIGHT BE A RENEWED ATTEMPT TO KILL YOU?
NO... SHE HAD NO LIVE-IN HEAVIES IN THOSE DAYS, AND SHE KNEW **MY** TOP PEOPLE WERE JUST OUTSIDE
ANYWAY, I WAS ARMED AND WELL-PREPARED, BUT IN THE EVENT THERE WAS NO TROUBLE
PRAY PUT THE QUESTION YOU WISH TO ASK, MISS BLAISE
9879 A

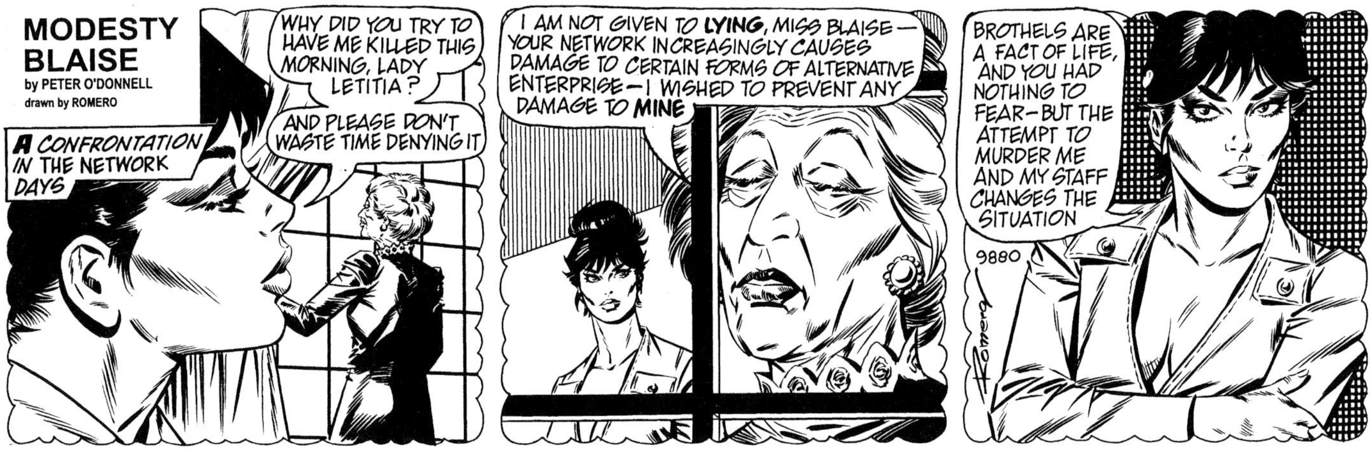
MODESTY BLAISE
by PETER O'DONNELL
drawn by ROMERO
A CONFRONTATION IN THE NETWORK DAYS
WHY DID YOU TRY TO HAVE ME KILLED THIS MORNING, LADY LETITIA?
AND PLEASE DON'T WASTE TIME DENYING IT
I AM NOT GIVEN TO LYING, MISS BLAISE — YOUR NETWORK INCREASINGLY CAUSES DAMAGE TO CERTAIN FORMS OF ALTERNATIVE ENTERPRISE — I WISHED TO PREVENT ANY DAMAGE TO MINE
BROTHELS ARE A FACT OF LIFE, AND YOU HAD NOTHING TO FEAR — BUT THE ATTEMPT TO MURDER ME AND MY STAFF CHANGES THE SITUATION
9880
Romero

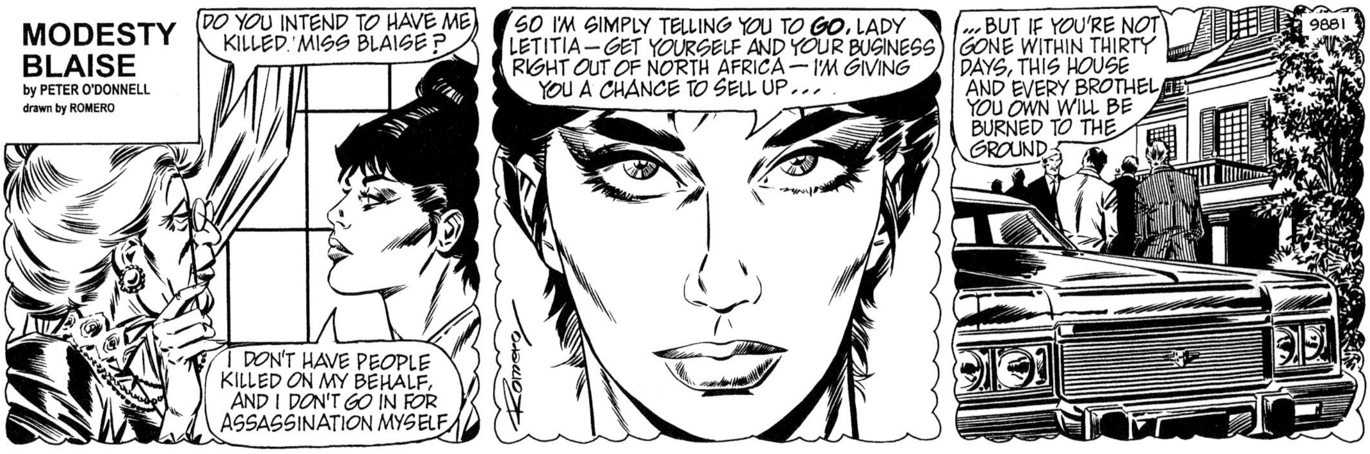
MODESTY BLAISE
by PETER O'DONNELL
drawn by ROMERO
DO YOU INTEND TO HAVE ME KILLED, MISS BLAISE?
I DON'T HAVE PEOPLE KILLED ON MY BEHALF, AND I DON'T GO IN FOR ASSASSINATION MYSELF
SO I'M SIMPLY TELLING YOU TO GO, LADY LETITIA — GET YOURSELF AND YOUR BUSINESS RIGHT OUT OF NORTH AFRICA — I'M GIVING YOU A CHANCE TO SELL UP...
Romero
...BUT IF YOU'RE NOT GONE WITHIN THIRTY DAYS, THIS HOUSE AND EVERY BROTHEL YOU OWN WILL BE BURNED TO THE GROUND
9881

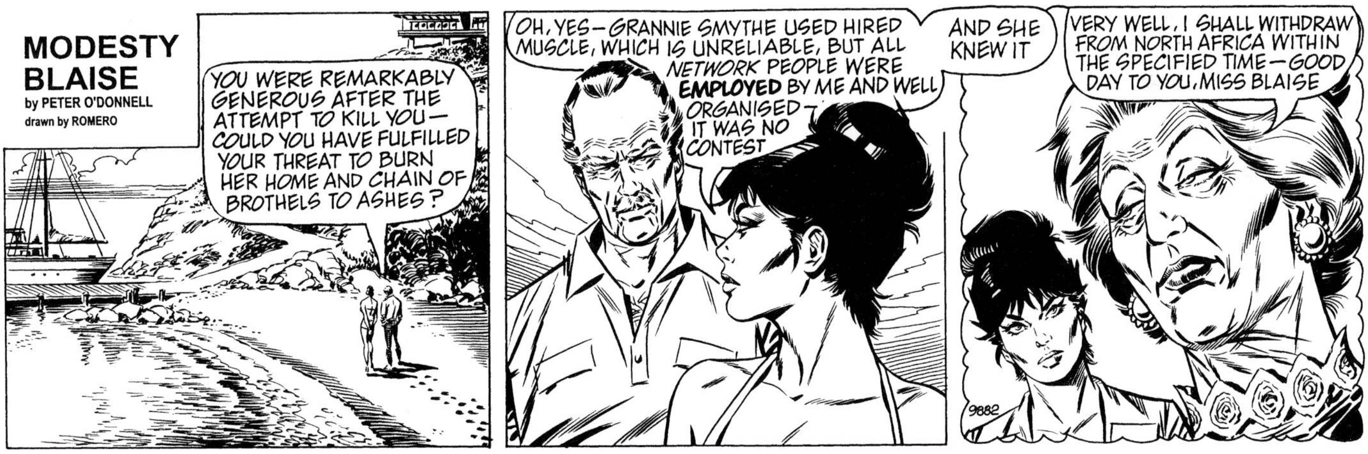
MODESTY BLAISE
by PETER O'DONNELL
drawn by ROMERO
YOU WERE REMARKABLY GENEROUS AFTER THE ATTEMPT TO KILL YOU — COULD YOU HAVE FULFILLED YOUR THREAT TO BURN HER HOME AND CHAIN OF BROTHELS TO ASHES?
OH, YES — GRANNIE SMYTHE USED HIRED MUSCLE, WHICH IS UNRELIABLE, BUT ALL NETWORK PEOPLE WERE EMPLOYED BY ME AND WELL ORGANISED — IT WAS NO CONTEST
AND SHE KNEW IT
VERY WELL, I SHALL WITHDRAW FROM NORTH AFRICA WITHIN THE SPECIFIED TIME — GOOD DAY TO YOU, MISS BLAISE
9882

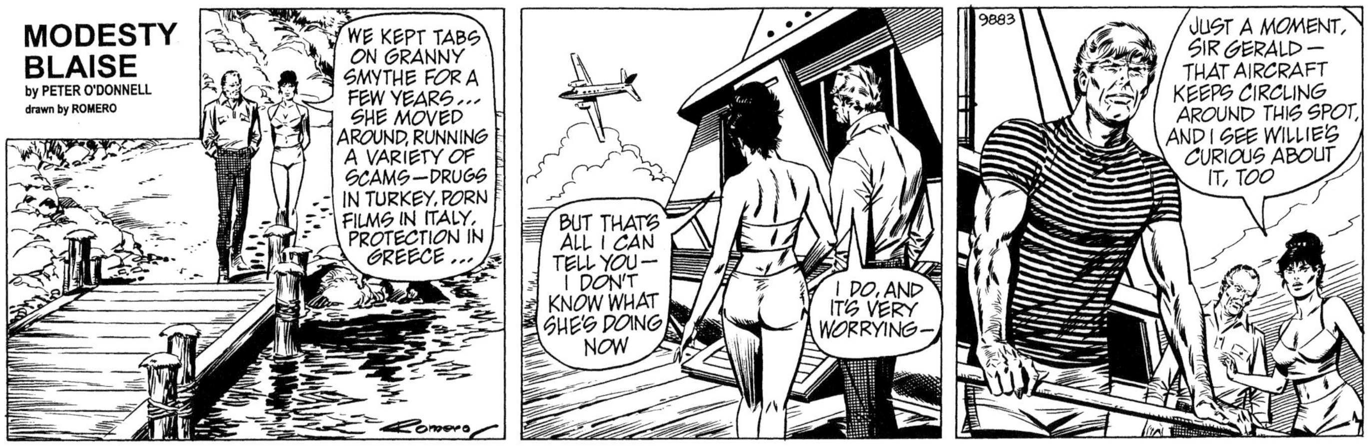
MODESTY BLAISE
by PETER O'DONNELL
drawn by ROMERO
WE KEPT TABS ON GRANNY SMYTHE FOR A FEW YEARS... SHE MOVED AROUND, RUNNING A VARIETY OF SCAMS — DRUGS IN TURKEY, PORN FILMS IN ITALY, PROTECTION IN GREECE...
Romero
BUT THAT'S ALL I CAN TELL YOU — I DON'T KNOW WHAT SHE'S DOING NOW
I DO, AND IT'S VERY WORRYING —
9883
JUST A MOMENT, SIR GERALD — THAT AIRCRAFT KEEPS CIRCLING AROUND THIS SPOT, AND I SEE WILLIE'S CURIOUS ABOUT IT, TOO

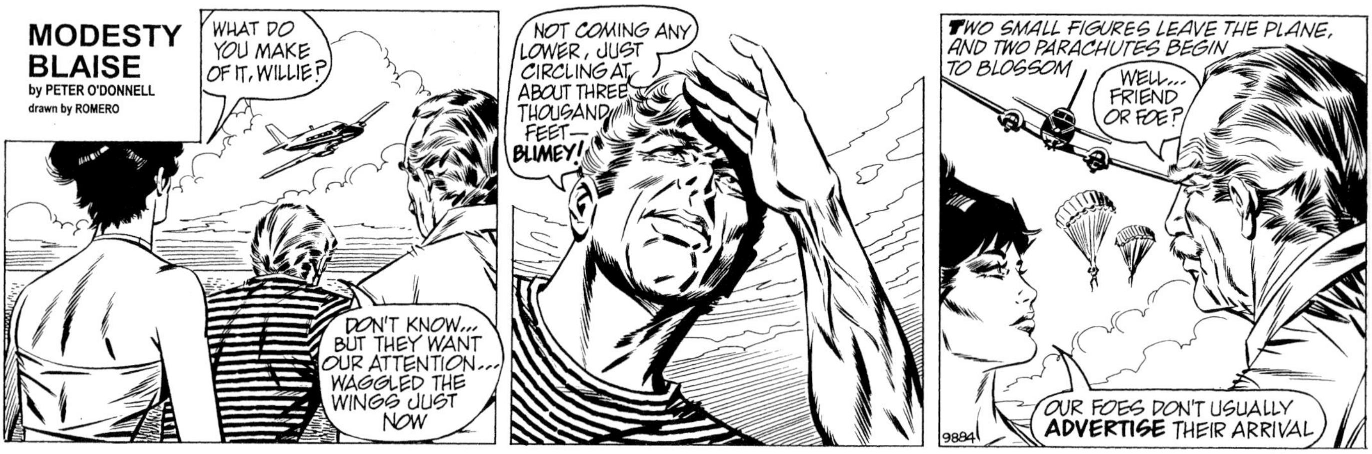
MODESTY BLAISE
by PETER O'DONNELL
drawn by ROMERO
WHAT DO YOU MAKE OF IT, WILLIE?
DON'T KNOW... BUT THEY WANT OUR ATTENTION... WAGGLED THE WINGS JUST NOW
NOT COMING ANY LOWER, JUST CIRCLING AT ABOUT THREE THOUSAND FEET— BLIMEY!
TWO SMALL FIGURES LEAVE THE PLANE, AND TWO PARACHUTES BEGIN TO BLOSSOM
WELL... FRIEND OR FOE?
OUR FOES DON'T USUALLY ADVERTISE THEIR ARRIVAL
9884

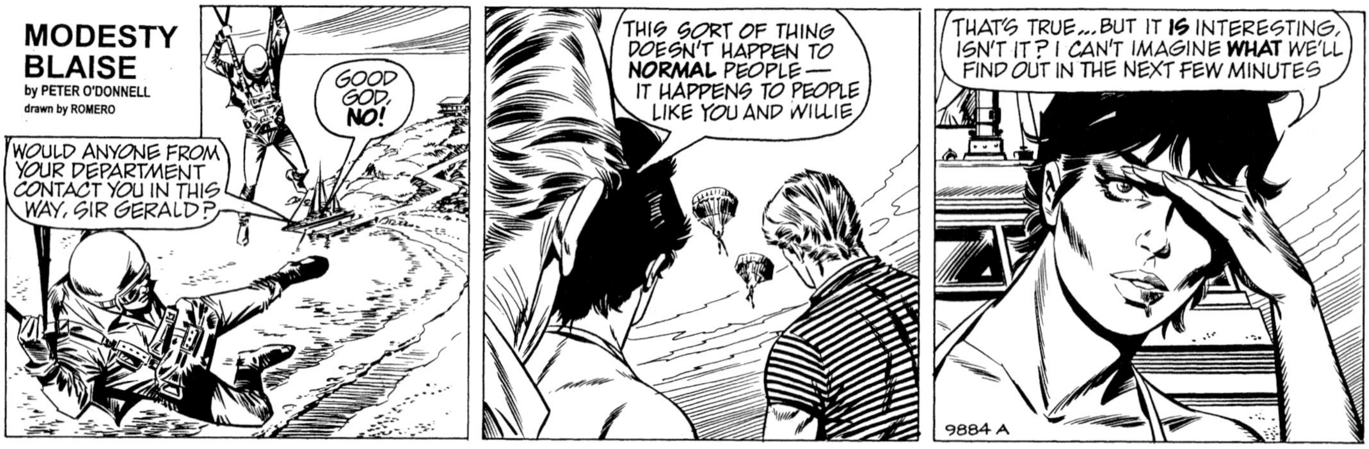
MODESTY BLAISE
by PETER O'DONNELL
drawn by ROMERO
WOULD ANYONE FROM YOUR DEPARTMENT CONTACT YOU IN THIS WAY, SIR GERALD?
GOOD GOD, NO!
THIS SORT OF THING DOESN'T HAPPEN TO NORMAL PEOPLE — IT HAPPENS TO PEOPLE LIKE YOU AND WILLIE
THAT'S TRUE... BUT IT IS INTERESTING, ISN'T IT? I CAN'T IMAGINE WHAT WE'LL FIND OUT IN THE NEXT FEW MINUTES
9884 A

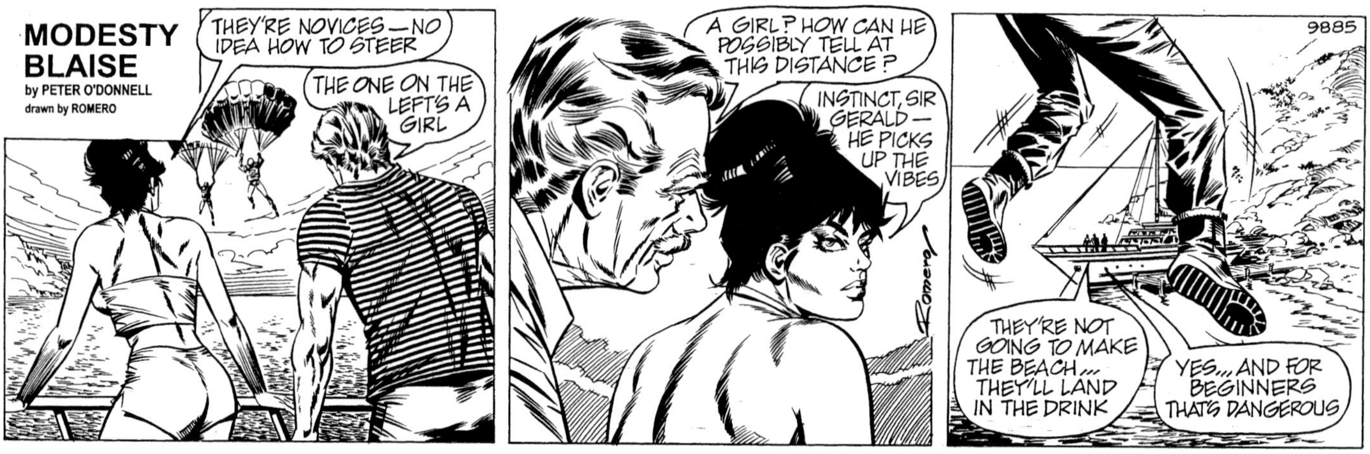
MODESTY BLAISE
by PETER O'DONNELL
drawn by ROMERO
THEY'RE NOVICES — NO IDEA HOW TO STEER
THE ONE ON THE LEFT'S A GIRL
A GIRL? HOW CAN HE POSSIBLY TELL AT THIS DISTANCE?
INSTINCT, SIR GERALD — HE PICKS UP THE VIBES
9885
THEY'RE NOT GOING TO MAKE THE BEACH... THEY'LL LAND IN THE DRINK
YES... AND FOR BEGINNERS THAT'S DANGEROUS

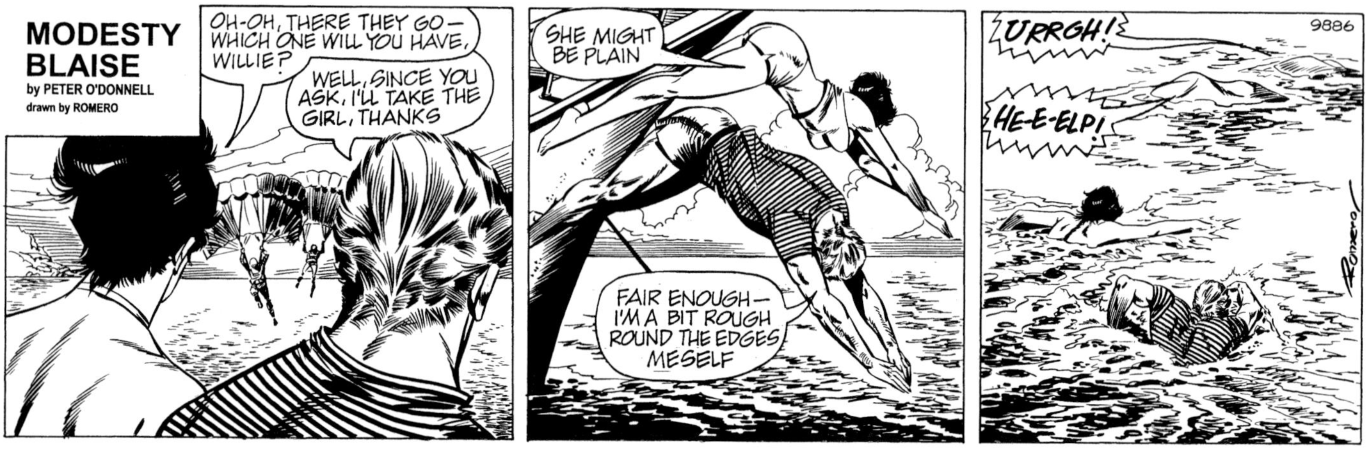
MODESTY BLAISE
by PETER O'DONNELL
drawn by ROMERO
OH-OH, THERE THEY GO — WHICH ONE WILL YOU HAVE, WILLIE?
WELL, SINCE YOU ASK, I'LL TAKE THE GIRL, THANKS
SHE MIGHT BE PLAIN
FAIR ENOUGH — I'M A BIT ROUGH ROUND THE EDGES MESELF
URRGH!
HE-E-ELP!
9886

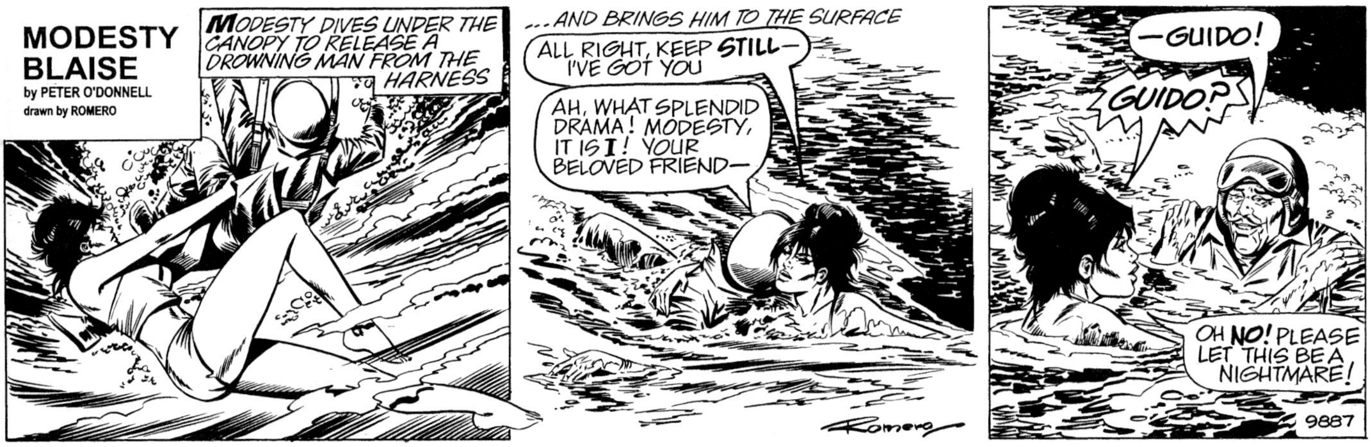
MODESTY BLAISE
by PETER O'DONNELL
drawn by ROMERO
MODESTY DIVES UNDER THE CANOPY TO RELEASE A DROWNING MAN FROM THE HARNESS
...AND BRINGS HIM TO THE SURFACE
ALL RIGHT, KEEP STILL— I'VE GOT YOU
AH, WHAT SPLENDID DRAMA! MODESTY, IT IS I! YOUR BELOVED FRIEND—
—GUIDO!
GUIDO?
OH NO! PLEASE LET THIS BE A NIGHTMARE!
Romero
9887

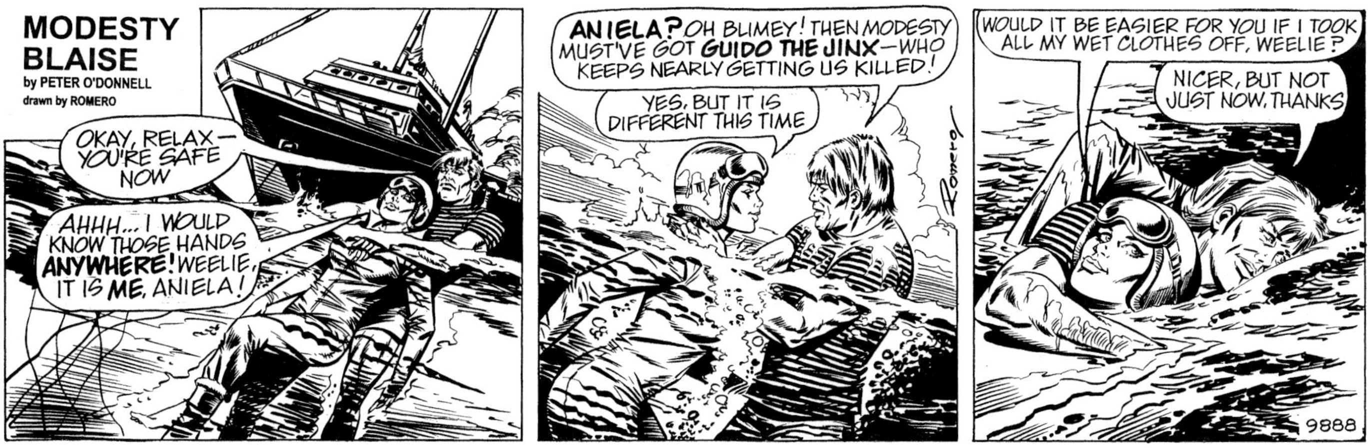
MODESTY BLAISE
by PETER O'DONNELL
drawn by ROMERO
OKAY, RELAX— YOU'RE SAFE NOW
AHHH... I WOULD KNOW THOSE HANDS ANYWHERE! WEELIE, IT IS ME, ANIELA!
ANIELA? OH BLIMEY! THEN MODESTY MUST'VE GOT GUIDO THE JINX—WHO KEEPS NEARLY GETTING US KILLED!
YES, BUT IT IS DIFFERENT THIS TIME
Romero
WOULD IT BE EASIER FOR YOU IF I TOOK ALL MY WET CLOTHES OFF, WEELIE?
NICER, BUT NOT JUST NOW, THANKS
9888

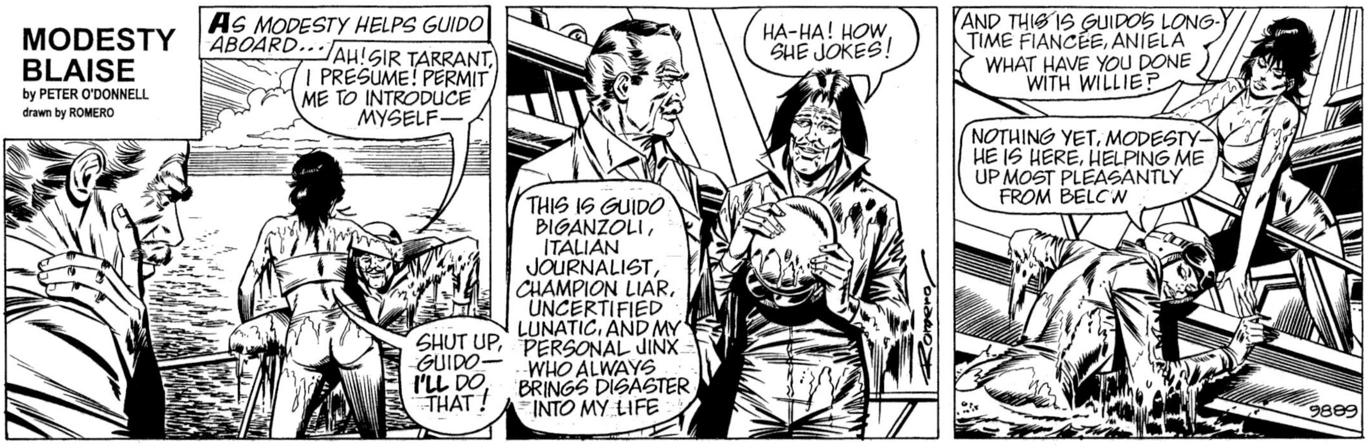
MODESTY BLAISE
by PETER O'DONNELL
drawn by ROMERO
AS MODESTY HELPS GUIDO ABOARD...
AH! SIR TARRANT, I PRESUME! PERMIT ME TO INTRODUCE MYSELF—
SHUT UP, GUIDO— I'LL DO THAT!
THIS IS GUIDO BIGANZOLI, ITALIAN JOURNALIST, CHAMPION LIAR, UNCERTIFIED LUNATIC, AND MY PERSONAL JINX WHO ALWAYS BRINGS DISASTER INTO MY LIFE
HA-HA! HOW SHE JOKES!
Romero
AND THIS IS GUIDO'S LONG-TIME FIANCÉE, ANIELA WHAT HAVE YOU DONE WITH WILLIE?
NOTHING YET, MODESTY— HE IS HERE, HELPING ME UP MOST PLEASANTLY FROM BELOW
9889

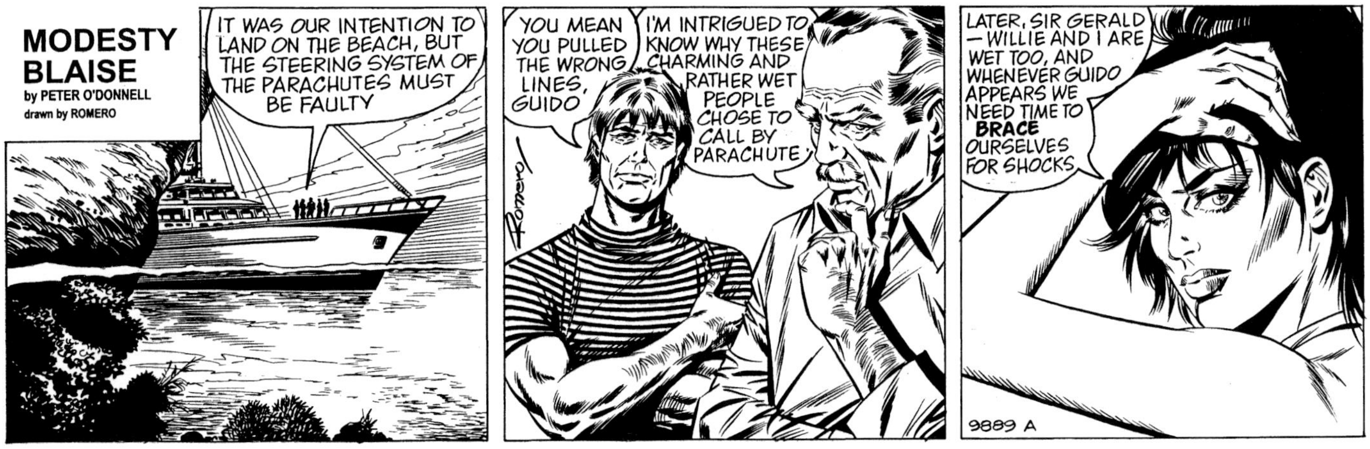
MODESTY BLAISE
by PETER O'DONNELL
drawn by ROMERO
IT WAS OUR INTENTION TO LAND ON THE BEACH, BUT THE STEERING SYSTEM OF THE PARACHUTES MUST BE FAULTY
YOU MEAN YOU PULLED THE WRONG LINES, GUIDO
I'M INTRIGUED TO KNOW WHY THESE CHARMING AND RATHER WET PEOPLE CHOSE TO CALL BY PARACHUTE
Romero
LATER, SIR GERALD —WILLIE AND I ARE WET TOO, AND WHENEVER GUIDO APPEARS WE NEED TIME TO BRACE OURSELVES FOR SHOCKS
9889 A

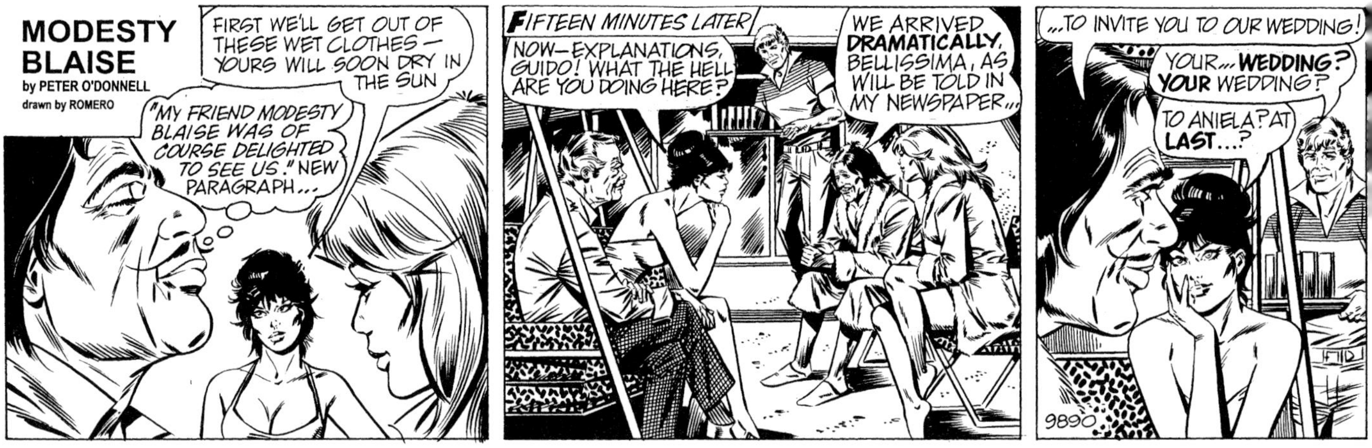
MODESTY BLAISE
by PETER O'DONNELL
drawn by ROMERO
FIRST WE'LL GET OUT OF THESE WET CLOTHES — YOURS WILL SOON DRY IN THE SUN
"MY FRIEND MODESTY BLAISE WAS OF COURSE DELIGHTED TO SEE US." NEW PARAGRAPH...
FIFTEEN MINUTES LATER
NOW—EXPLANATIONS, GUIDO! WHAT THE HELL ARE YOU DOING HERE?
WE ARRIVED DRAMATICALLY, BELLISSIMA, AS WILL BE TOLD IN MY NEWSPAPER...
...TO INVITE YOU TO OUR WEDDING!
YOUR... WEDDING? YOUR WEDDING?
TO ANIELA? AT LAST...?
9890

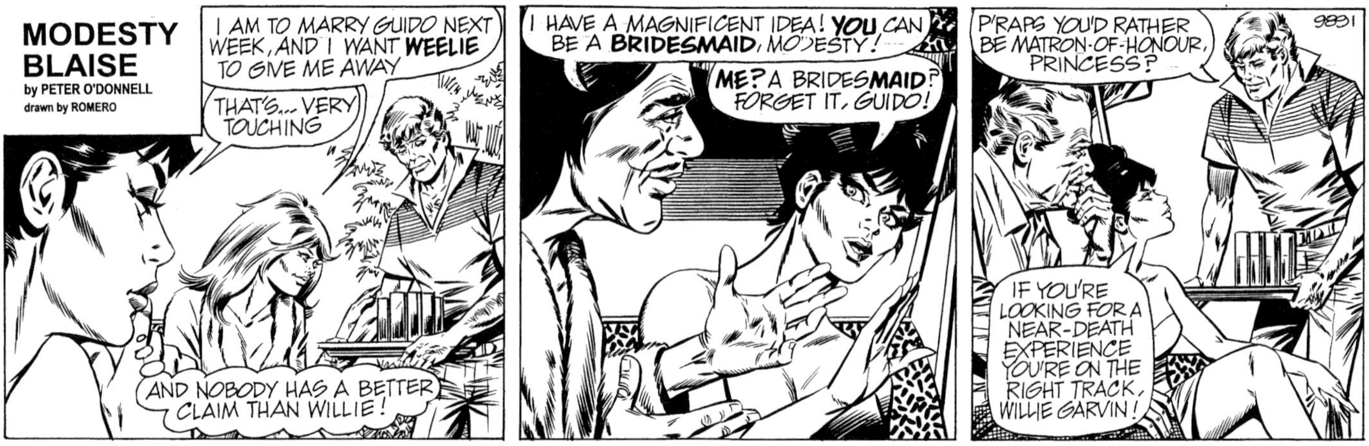
MODESTY BLAISE
by PETER O'DONNELL
drawn by ROMERO
I AM TO MARRY GUIDO NEXT WEEK, AND I WANT WEELIE TO GIVE ME AWAY
THAT'S... VERY TOUCHING
AND NOBODY HAS A BETTER CLAIM THAN WILLIE!
I HAVE A MAGNIFICENT IDEA! YOU CAN BE A BRIDESMAID, MODESTY!
ME? A BRIDESMAID? FORGET IT, GUIDO!
9891
P'RAPS YOU'D RATHER BE MATRON-OF-HONOUR, PRINCESS?
IF YOU'RE LOOKING FOR A NEAR-DEATH EXPERIENCE YOU'RE ON THE RIGHT TRACK, WILLIE GARVIN!

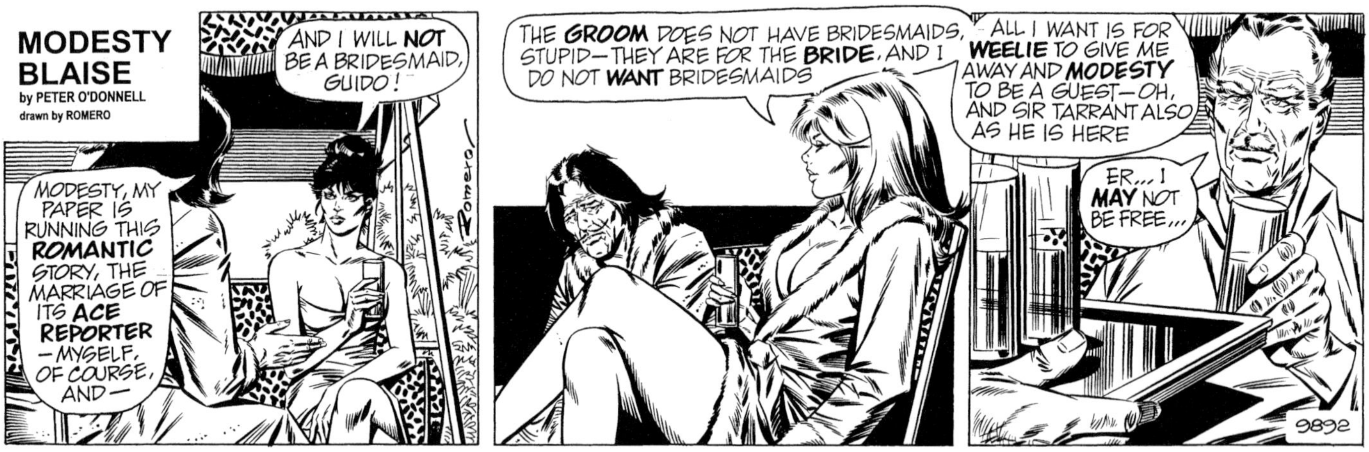
MODESTY BLAISE
by PETER O'DONNELL
drawn by ROMERO
AND I WILL NOT BE A BRIDESMAID, GUIDO!
MODESTY, MY PAPER IS RUNNING THIS ROMANTIC STORY, THE MARRIAGE OF ITS ACE REPORTER — MYSELF, OF COURSE, AND—
Romero
THE GROOM DOES NOT HAVE BRIDESMAIDS, STUPID—THEY ARE FOR THE BRIDE, AND I DO NOT WANT BRIDESMAIDS
ALL I WANT IS FOR WEELIE TO GIVE ME AWAY AND MODESTY TO BE A GUEST—OH, AND SIR TARRANT ALSO AS HE IS HERE
ER... I MAY NOT BE FREE...
9892

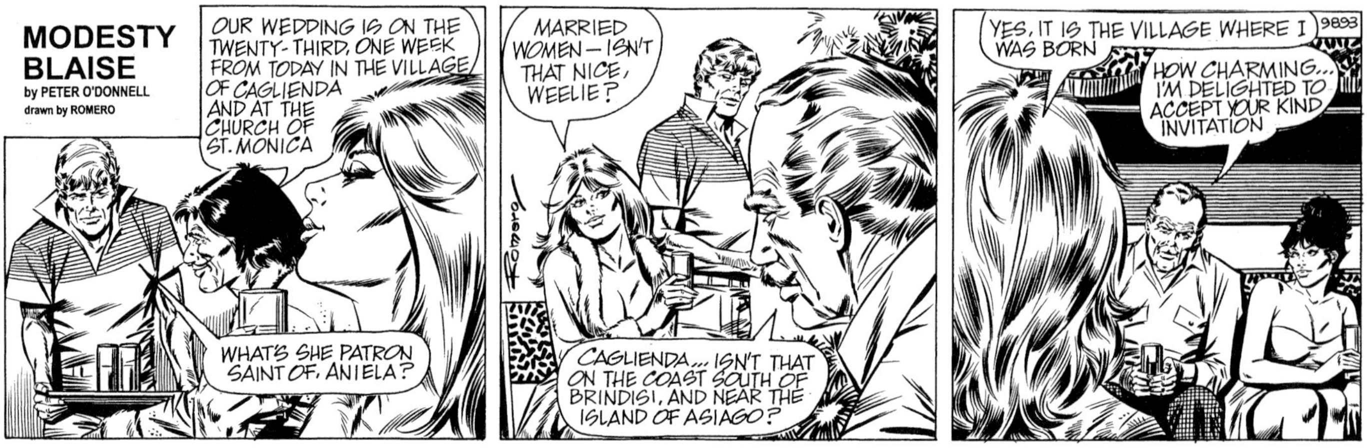
MODESTY BLAISE
by PETER O'DONNELL
drawn by ROMERO
OUR WEDDING IS ON THE TWENTY-THIRD, ONE WEEK FROM TODAY IN THE VILLAGE OF CAGLIENDA AND AT THE CHURCH OF ST. MONICA
WHAT'S SHE PATRON SAINT OF, ANIELA?
MARRIED WOMEN — ISN'T THAT NICE, WEELIE?
Romero
CAGLIENDA... ISN'T THAT ON THE COAST SOUTH OF BRINDISI, AND NEAR THE ISLAND OF ASIAGO?
9893
YES, IT IS THE VILLAGE WHERE I WAS BORN
HOW CHARMING... I'M DELIGHTED TO ACCEPT YOUR KIND INVITATION

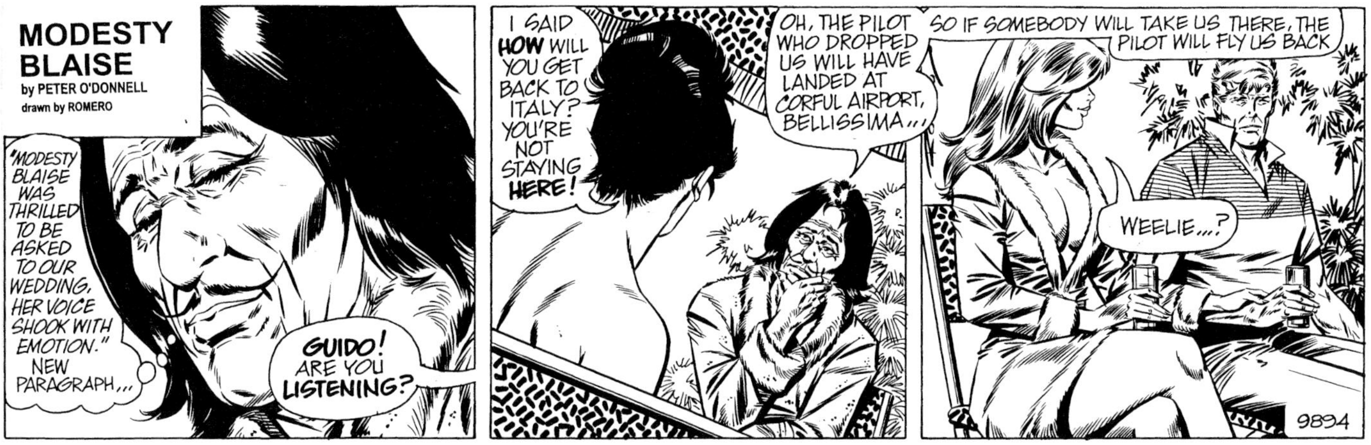
MODESTY BLAISE
by PETER O'DONNELL
drawn by ROMERO
"MODESTY BLAISE WAS THRILLED TO BE ASKED TO OUR WEDDING, HER VOICE SHOOK WITH EMOTION." NEW PARAGRAPH...
GUIDO! ARE YOU LISTENING?
I SAID HOW WILL YOU GET BACK TO ITALY? YOU'RE NOT STAYING HERE!
OH, THE PILOT WHO DROPPED US WILL HAVE LANDED AT CORFUL AIRPORT, BELLISSIMA...
SO IF SOMEBODY WILL TAKE US THERE, THE PILOT WILL FLY US BACK
WEELIE...?
9894

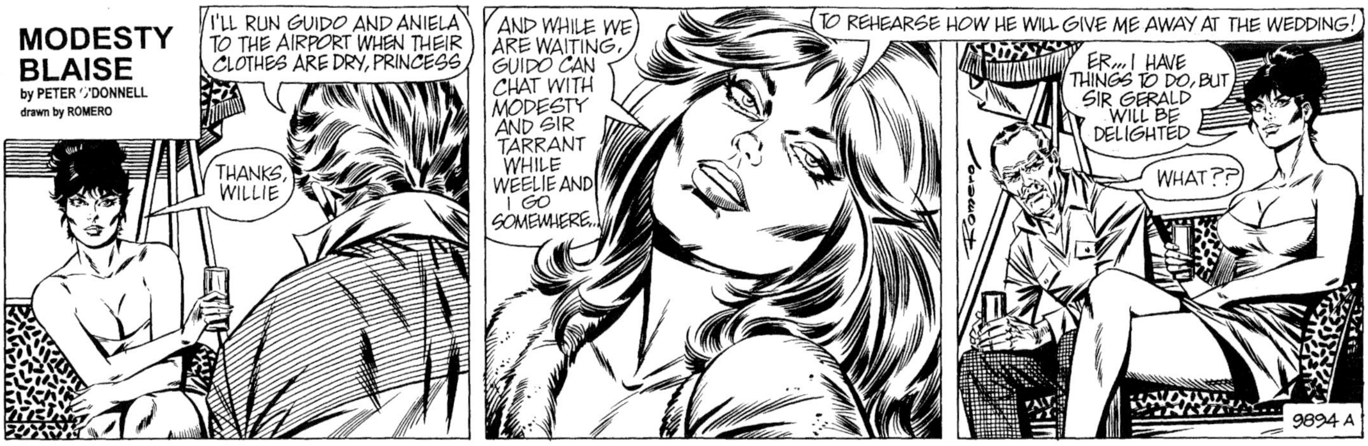
MODESTY BLAISE
by PETER O'DONNELL
drawn by ROMERO
I'LL RUN GUIDO AND ANIELA TO THE AIRPORT WHEN THEIR CLOTHES ARE DRY, PRINCESS
THANKS, WILLIE
AND WHILE WE ARE WAITING, GUIDO CAN CHAT WITH MODESTY AND SIR TARRANT WHILE WEELIE AND I GO SOMEWHERE...
TO REHEARSE HOW HE WILL GIVE ME AWAY AT THE WEDDING!
ER... I HAVE THINGS TO DO, BUT SIR GERALD WILL BE DELIGHTED
WHAT??
9894 A

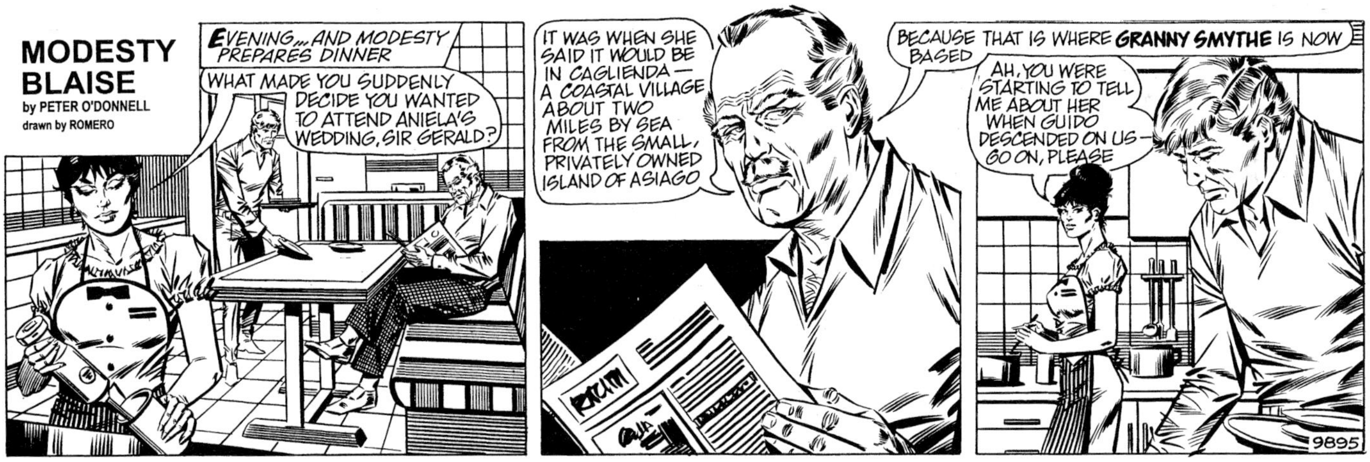
MODESTY BLAISE
by PETER O'DONNELL
drawn by ROMERO
EVENING... AND MODESTY PREPARES DINNER
WHAT MADE YOU SUDDENLY DECIDE YOU WANTED TO ATTEND ANIELA'S WEDDING, SIR GERALD?
IT WAS WHEN SHE SAID IT WOULD BE IN CAGLIENDA — A COASTAL VILLAGE ABOUT TWO MILES BY SEA FROM THE SMALL, PRIVATELY OWNED ISLAND OF ASIAGO
BECAUSE THAT IS WHERE GRANNY SMYTHE IS NOW BASED
AH, YOU WERE STARTING TO TELL ME ABOUT HER WHEN GUIDO DESCENDED ON US — GO ON, PLEASE
9895

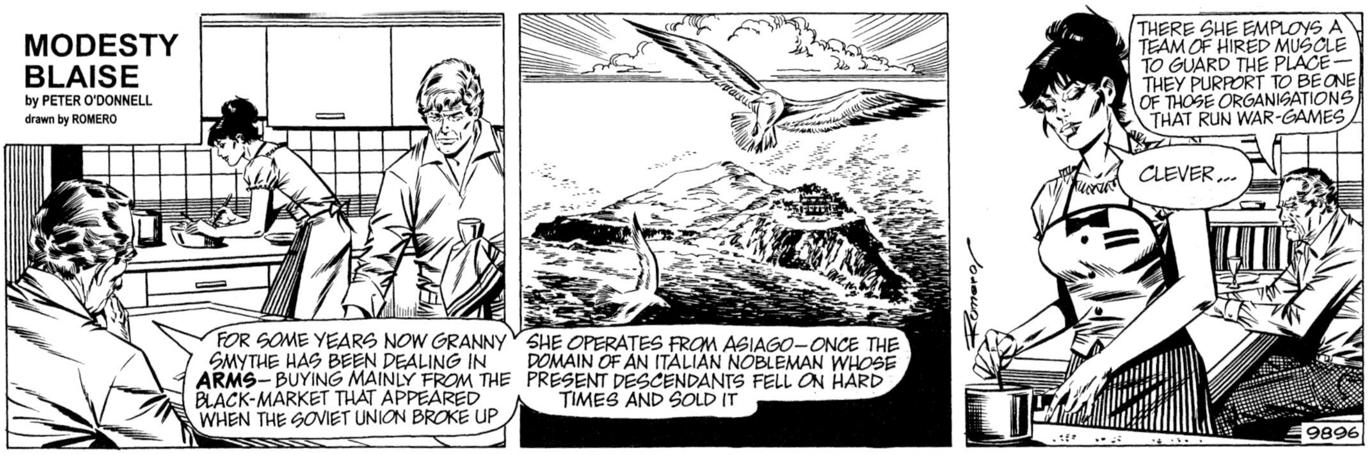
MODESTY BLAISE
by PETER O'DONNELL
drawn by ROMERO
FOR SOME YEARS NOW GRANNY SMYTHE HAS BEEN DEALING IN ARMS — BUYING MAINLY FROM THE BLACK-MARKET THAT APPEARED WHEN THE SOVIET UNION BROKE UP
SHE OPERATES FROM ASIAGO — ONCE THE DOMAIN OF AN ITALIAN NOBLEMAN WHOSE PRESENT DESCENDANTS FELL ON HARD TIMES AND SOLD IT
THERE SHE EMPLOYS A TEAM OF HIRED MUSCLE TO GUARD THE PLACE — THEY PURPORT TO BE ONE OF THOSE ORGANISATIONS THAT RUN WAR-GAMES
CLEVER...
9896

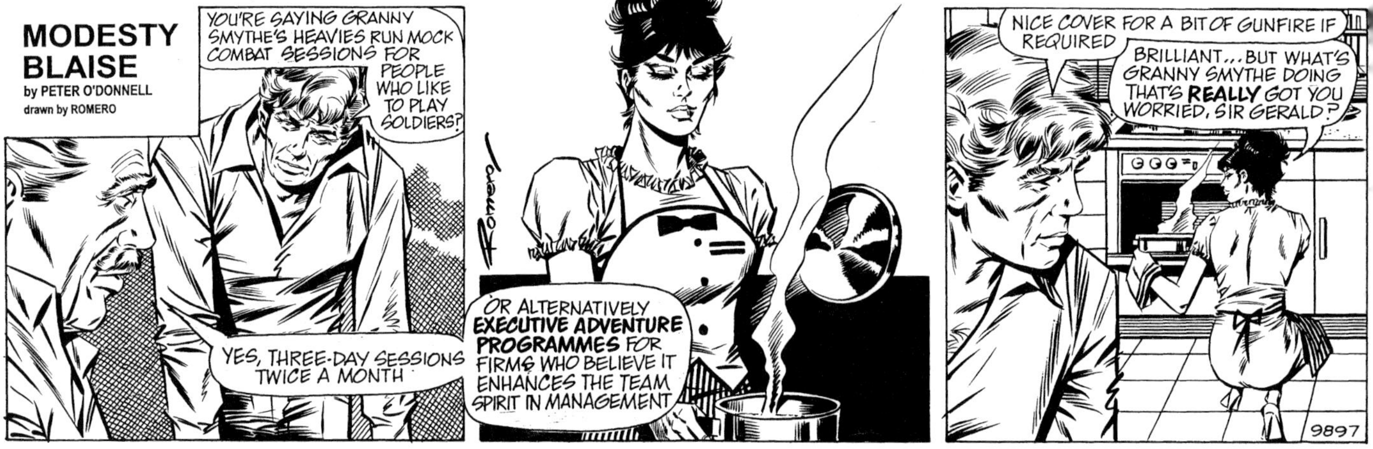
MODESTY BLAISE
by PETER O'DONNELL
drawn by ROMERO
YOU'RE SAYING GRANNY SMYTHE'S HEAVIES RUN MOCK COMBAT SESSIONS FOR PEOPLE WHO LIKE TO PLAY SOLDIERS?
YES, THREE-DAY SESSIONS TWICE A MONTH
OR ALTERNATIVELY **EXECUTIVE ADVENTURE PROGRAMMES** FOR FIRMS WHO BELIEVE IT ENHANCES THE TEAM SPIRIT IN MANAGEMENT
NICE COVER FOR A BIT OF GUNFIRE IF REQUIRED
BRILLIANT... BUT WHAT'S GRANNY SMYTHE DOING THAT'S **REALLY** GOT YOU WORRIED, SIR GERALD?
9897

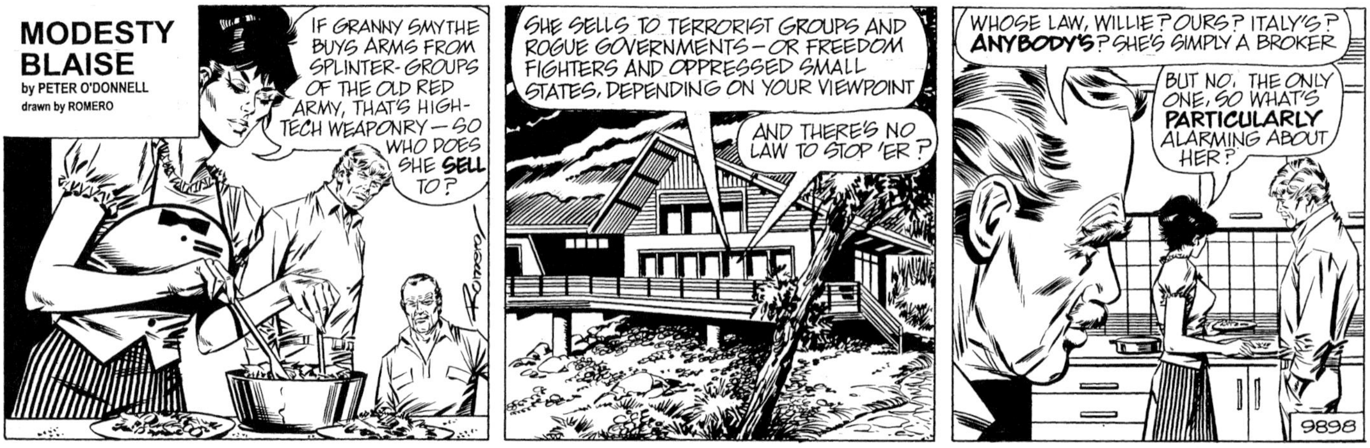
MODESTY BLAISE
by PETER O'DONNELL
drawn by ROMERO
IF GRANNY SMYTHE BUYS ARMS FROM SPLINTER-GROUPS OF THE OLD RED ARMY, THAT'S HIGH-TECH WEAPONRY — SO WHO DOES SHE **SELL** TO?
SHE SELLS TO TERRORIST GROUPS AND ROGUE GOVERNMENTS — OR FREEDOM FIGHTERS AND OPPRESSED SMALL STATES, DEPENDING ON YOUR VIEWPOINT
AND THERE'S NO LAW TO STOP 'ER?
WHOSE LAW, WILLIE? OURS? ITALY'S? **ANYBODY'S**? SHE'S SIMPLY A BROKER
BUT NO, THE ONLY ONE, SO WHAT'S **PARTICULARLY** ALARMING ABOUT HER?
9898

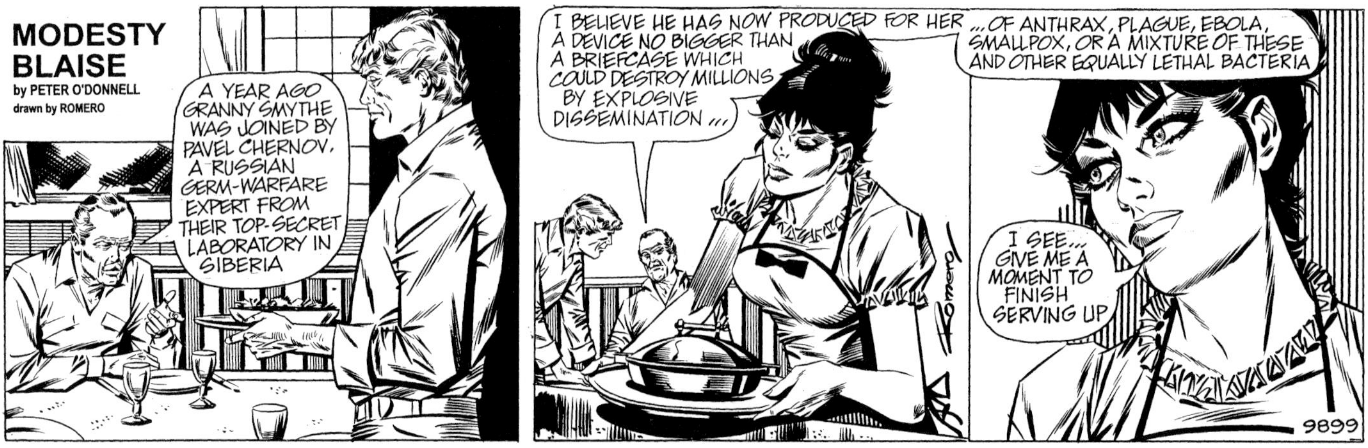
MODESTY BLAISE
by PETER O'DONNELL
drawn by ROMERO
A YEAR AGO GRANNY SMYTHE WAS JOINED BY PAVEL CHERNOV, A RUSSIAN GERM-WARFARE EXPERT FROM THEIR TOP-SECRET LABORATORY IN SIBERIA
I BELIEVE HE HAS NOW PRODUCED FOR HER A DEVICE NO BIGGER THAN A BRIEFCASE WHICH COULD DESTROY MILLIONS BY EXPLOSIVE DISSEMINATION...
...OF ANTHRAX, PLAGUE, EBOLA, SMALLPOX, OR A MIXTURE OF THESE AND OTHER EQUALLY LETHAL BACTERIA
I SEE... GIVE ME A MOMENT TO FINISH SERVING UP
9899

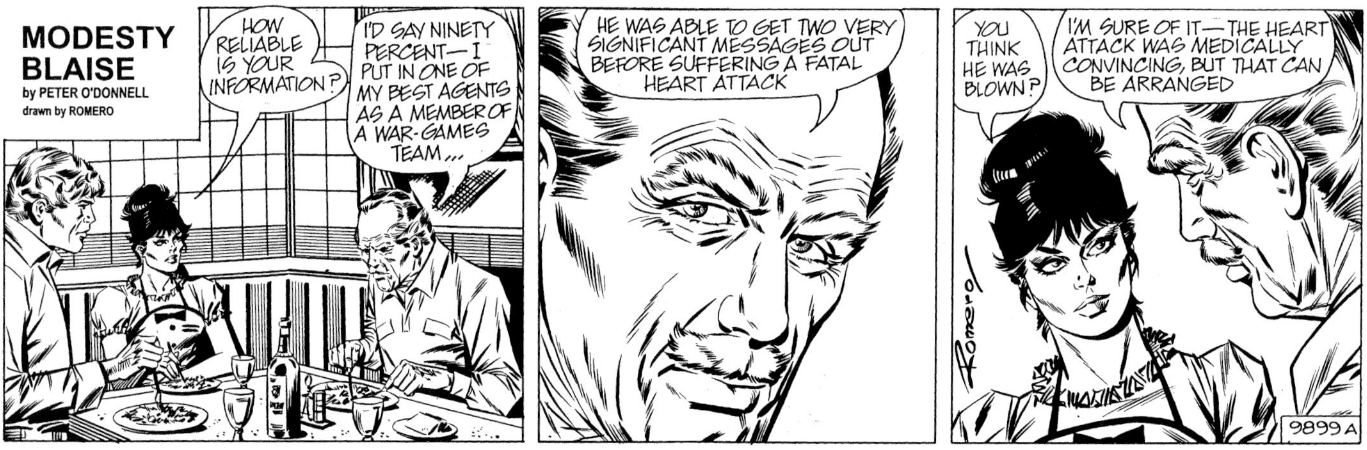
MODESTY BLAISE
by PETER O'DONNELL
drawn by ROMERO
HOW RELIABLE IS YOUR INFORMATION?
I'D SAY NINETY PERCENT — I PUT IN ONE OF MY BEST AGENTS AS A MEMBER OF A WAR-GAMES TEAM...
HE WAS ABLE TO GET TWO VERY SIGNIFICANT MESSAGES OUT BEFORE SUFFERING A FATAL HEART ATTACK
YOU THINK HE WAS BLOWN?
I'M SURE OF IT — THE HEART ATTACK WAS MEDICALLY CONVINCING, BUT THAT CAN BE ARRANGED
9899 A

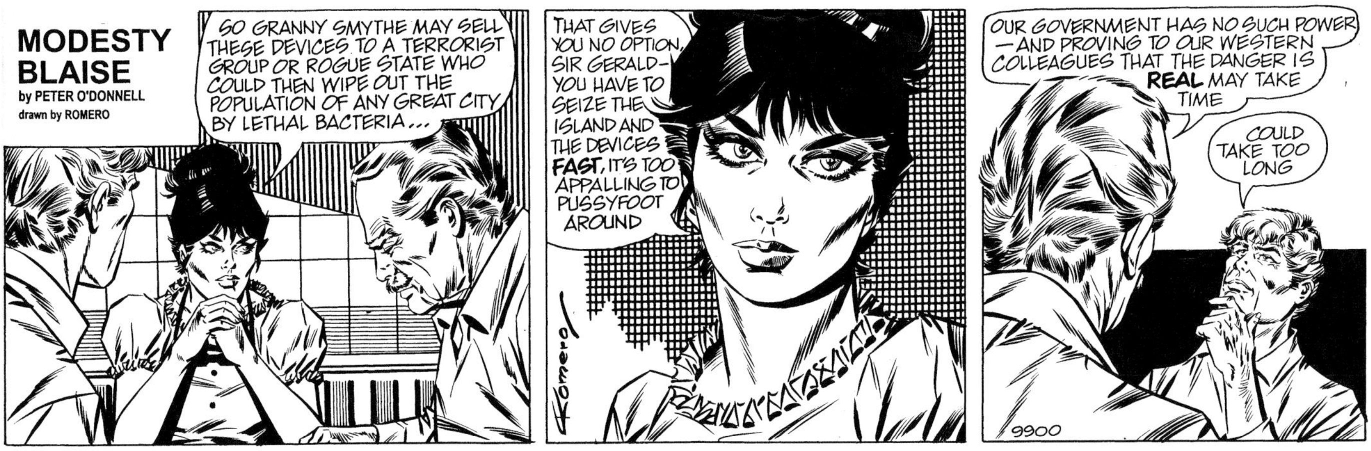
MODESTY BLAISE
by PETER O'DONNELL
drawn by ROMERO
SO GRANNY SMYTHE MAY SELL THESE DEVICES TO A TERRORIST GROUP OR ROGUE STATE WHO COULD THEN WIPE OUT THE POPULATION OF ANY GREAT CITY BY LETHAL BACTERIA...
THAT GIVES YOU NO OPTION, SIR GERALD— YOU HAVE TO SEIZE THE ISLAND AND THE DEVICES FAST, IT'S TOO APPALLING TO PUSSYFOOT AROUND
ROMERO
OUR GOVERNMENT HAS NO SUCH POWER —AND PROVING TO OUR WESTERN COLLEAGUES THAT THE DANGER IS REAL MAY TAKE TIME
COULD TAKE TOO LONG
9900

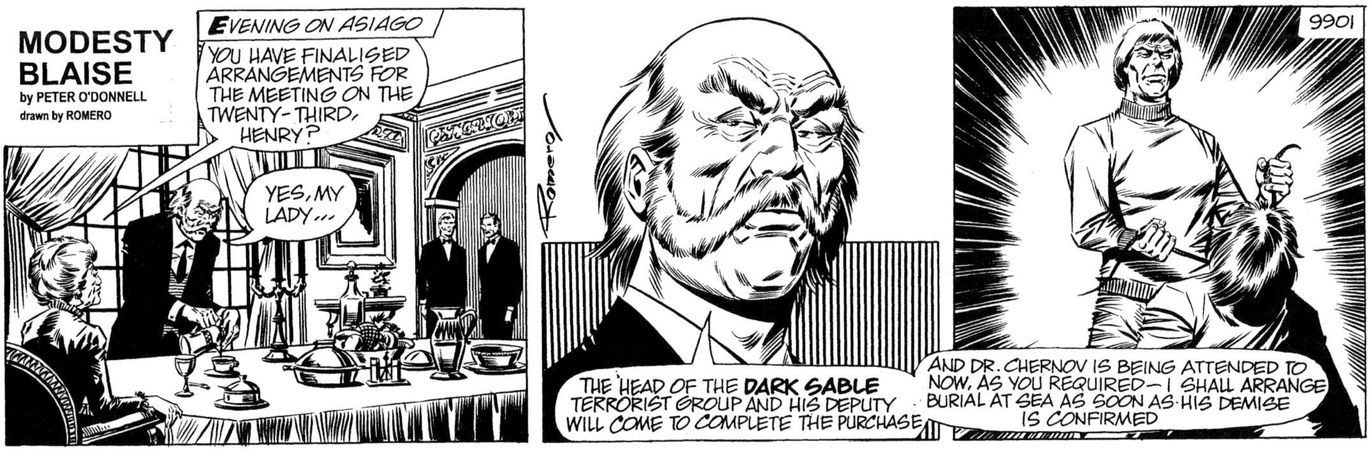
MODESTY BLAISE
by PETER O'DONNELL
drawn by ROMERO
EVENING ON ASIAGO
YOU HAVE FINALISED ARRANGEMENTS FOR THE MEETING ON THE TWENTY-THIRD, HENRY?
YES, MY LADY...
ROMERO
THE HEAD OF THE DARK SABLE TERRORIST GROUP AND HIS DEPUTY WILL COME TO COMPLETE THE PURCHASE
9901
AND DR. CHERNOV IS BEING ATTENDED TO NOW, AS YOU REQUIRED— I SHALL ARRANGE BURIAL AT SEA AS SOON AS HIS DEMISE IS CONFIRMED

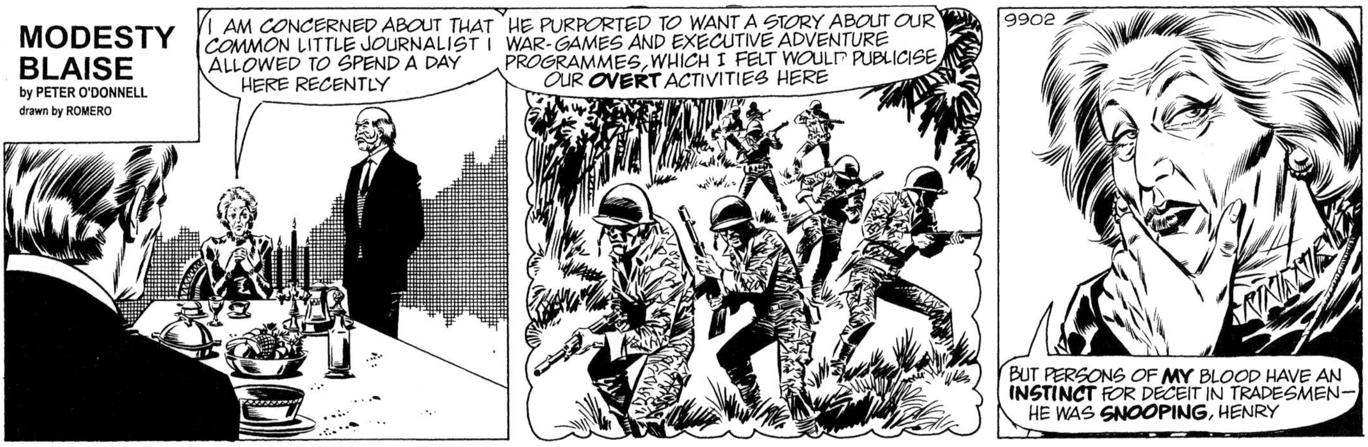
MODESTY BLAISE
by PETER O'DONNELL
drawn by ROMERO
I AM CONCERNED ABOUT THAT COMMON LITTLE JOURNALIST I ALLOWED TO SPEND A DAY HERE RECENTLY
HE PURPORTED TO WANT A STORY ABOUT OUR WAR-GAMES AND EXECUTIVE ADVENTURE PROGRAMMES, WHICH I FELT WOULD PUBLICISE OUR OVERT ACTIVITIES HERE
9902
BUT PERSONS OF MY BLOOD HAVE AN INSTINCT FOR DECEIT IN TRADESMEN— HE WAS SNOOPING, HENRY

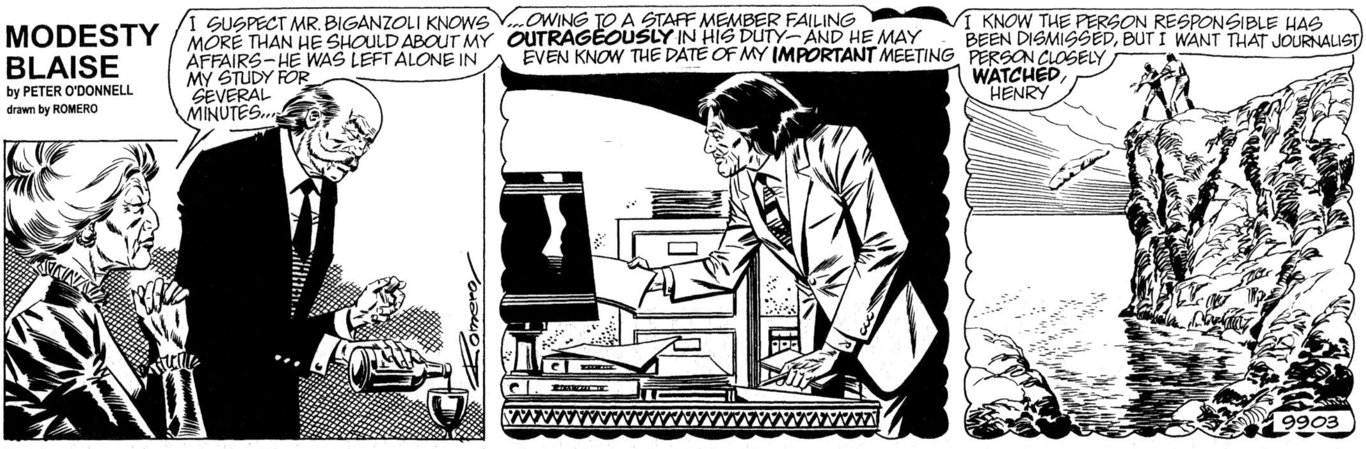
MODESTY BLAISE
by PETER O'DONNELL
drawn by ROMERO
I SUSPECT MR. BIGANZOLI KNOWS MORE THAN HE SHOULD ABOUT MY AFFAIRS—HE WAS LEFT ALONE IN MY STUDY FOR SEVERAL MINUTES...
ROMERO
...OWING TO A STAFF MEMBER FAILING OUTRAGEOUSLY IN HIS DUTY—AND HE MAY EVEN KNOW THE DATE OF MY IMPORTANT MEETING
I KNOW THE PERSON RESPONSIBLE HAS BEEN DISMISSED, BUT I WANT THAT JOURNALIST PERSON CLOSELY WATCHED, HENRY
9903

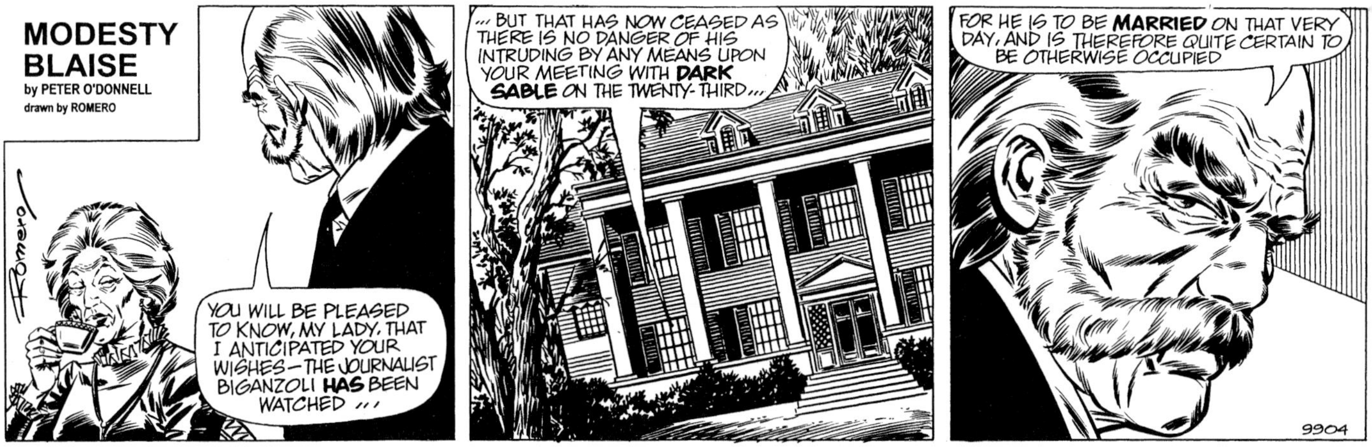
MODESTY BLAISE
by PETER O'DONNELL
drawn by ROMERO
YOU WILL BE PLEASED TO KNOW, MY LADY, THAT I ANTICIPATED YOUR WISHES—THE JOURNALIST BIGANZOLI **HAS** BEEN WATCHED ...
... BUT THAT HAS NOW CEASED AS THERE IS NO DANGER OF HIS INTRUDING BY ANY MEANS UPON YOUR MEETING WITH **DARK SABLE** ON THE TWENTY-THIRD ...
FOR HE IS TO BE **MARRIED** ON THAT VERY DAY, AND IS THEREFORE QUITE CERTAIN TO BE OTHERWISE OCCUPIED
9904

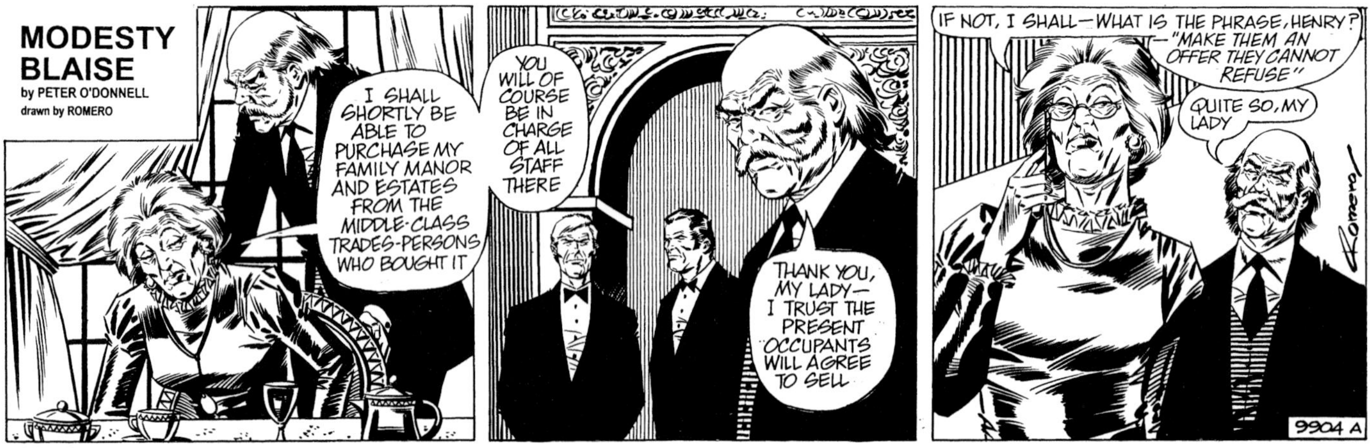
MODESTY BLAISE
by PETER O'DONNELL
drawn by ROMERO
I SHALL SHORTLY BE ABLE TO PURCHASE MY FAMILY MANOR AND ESTATES FROM THE MIDDLE-CLASS TRADES-PERSONS WHO BOUGHT IT
YOU WILL OF COURSE BE IN CHARGE OF ALL STAFF THERE
THANK YOU, MY LADY—I TRUST THE PRESENT OCCUPANTS WILL AGREE TO SELL
IF NOT, I SHALL—WHAT IS THE PHRASE, HENRY? —"MAKE THEM AN OFFER THEY CANNOT REFUSE"
QUITE SO, MY LADY
9904 A

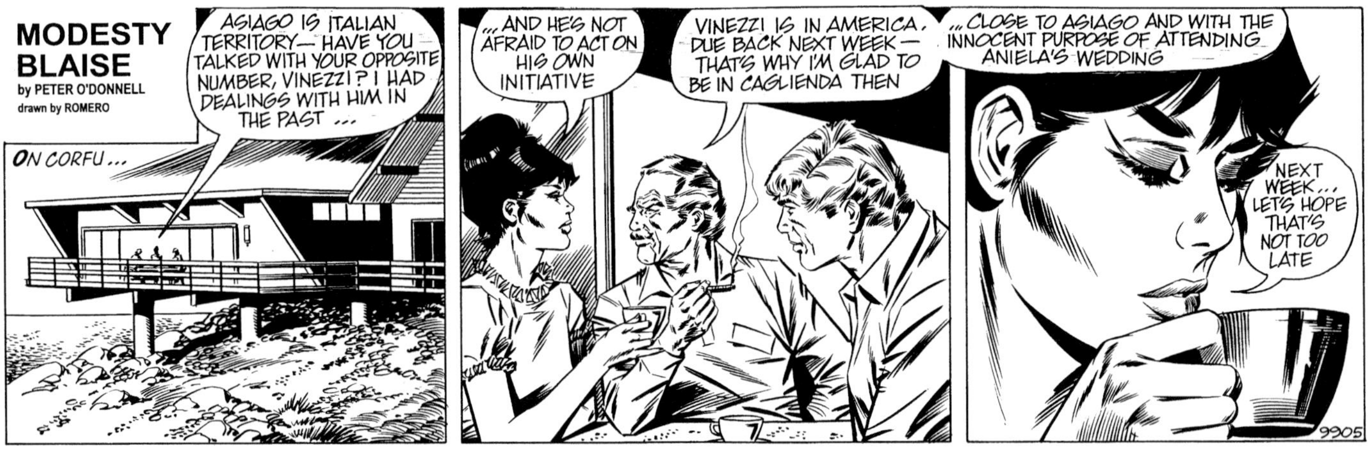
MODESTY BLAISE
by PETER O'DONNELL
drawn by ROMERO
ON CORFU ...
ASIAGO IS ITALIAN TERRITORY— HAVE YOU TALKED WITH YOUR OPPOSITE NUMBER, VINEZZI? I HAD DEALINGS WITH HIM IN THE PAST ...
... AND HE'S NOT AFRAID TO ACT ON HIS OWN INITIATIVE
VINEZZI IS IN AMERICA, DUE BACK NEXT WEEK—THAT'S WHY I'M GLAD TO BE IN CAGLIENDA THEN
... CLOSE TO ASIAGO AND WITH THE INNOCENT PURPOSE OF ATTENDING ANIELA'S WEDDING
NEXT WEEK ... LET'S HOPE THAT'S NOT TOO LATE
9905

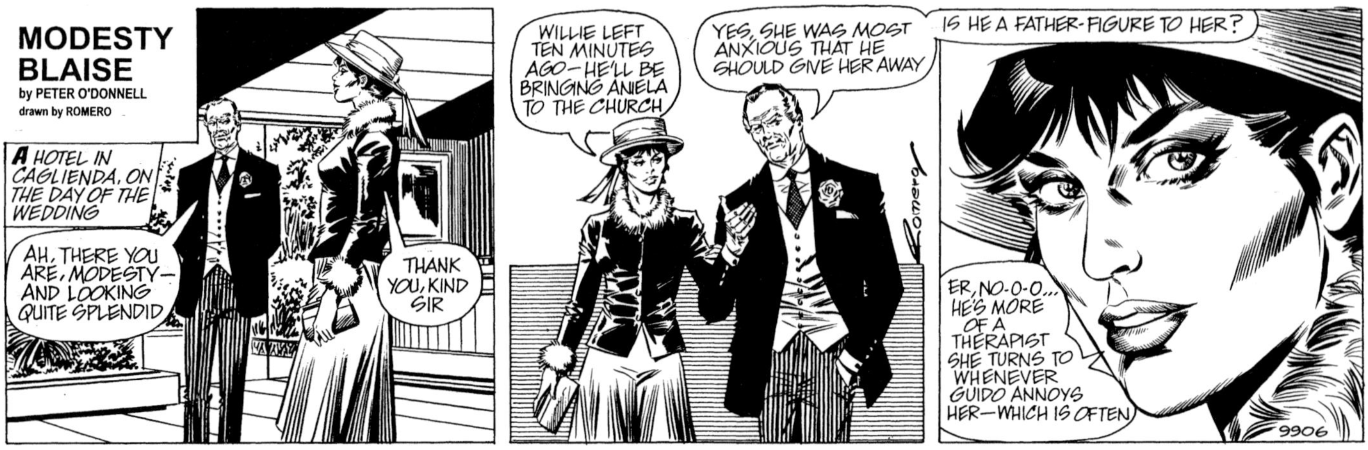
MODESTY BLAISE
by PETER O'DONNELL
drawn by ROMERO
A HOTEL IN CAGLIENDA, ON THE DAY OF THE WEDDING
AH, THERE YOU ARE, MODESTY—AND LOOKING QUITE SPLENDID
THANK YOU, KIND SIR
WILLIE LEFT TEN MINUTES AGO—HE'LL BE BRINGING ANIELA TO THE CHURCH
YES, SHE WAS MOST ANXIOUS THAT HE SHOULD GIVE HER AWAY
IS HE A FATHER-FIGURE TO HER?
ER, NO-O-O... HE'S MORE OF A THERAPIST SHE TURNS TO WHENEVER GUIDO ANNOYS HER—WHICH IS OFTEN
9906

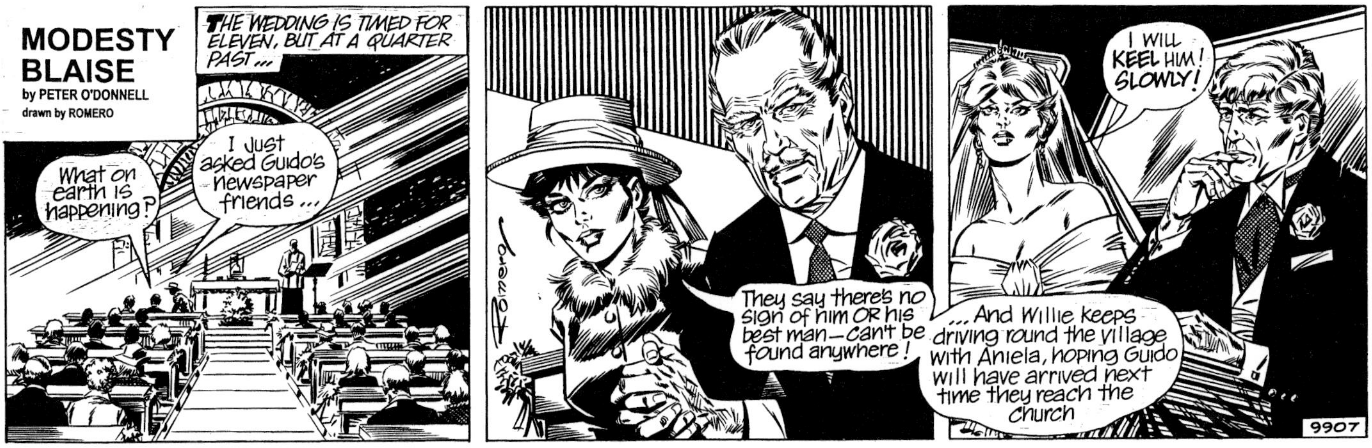
MODESTY BLAISE
by PETER O'DONNELL
drawn by ROMERO
THE WEDDING IS TIMED FOR ELEVEN, BUT AT A QUARTER PAST ...
What on earth is happening?
I just asked Guido's newspaper friends ...
They say there's no sign of him OR his best man—can't be found anywhere!
... And Willie keeps driving round the village with Aniela, hoping Guido will have arrived next time they reach the church
I WILL KEEL HIM! SLOWLY!
9907

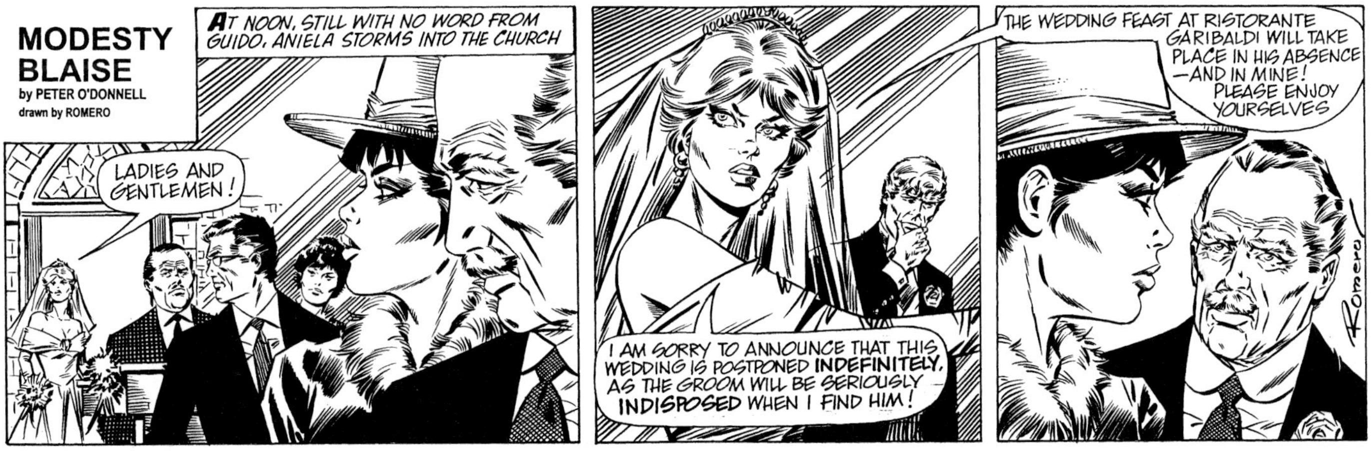
MODESTY BLAISE
by PETER O'DONNELL
drawn by ROMERO
AT NOON, STILL WITH NO WORD FROM GUIDO, ANIELA STORMS INTO THE CHURCH
LADIES AND GENTLEMEN!
I AM SORRY TO ANNOUNCE THAT THIS WEDDING IS POSTPONED INDEFINITELY, AS THE GROOM WILL BE SERIOUSLY INDISPOSED WHEN I FIND HIM!
THE WEDDING FEAST AT RISTORANTE GARIBALDI WILL TAKE PLACE IN HIS ABSENCE —AND IN MINE! PLEASE ENJOY YOURSELVES

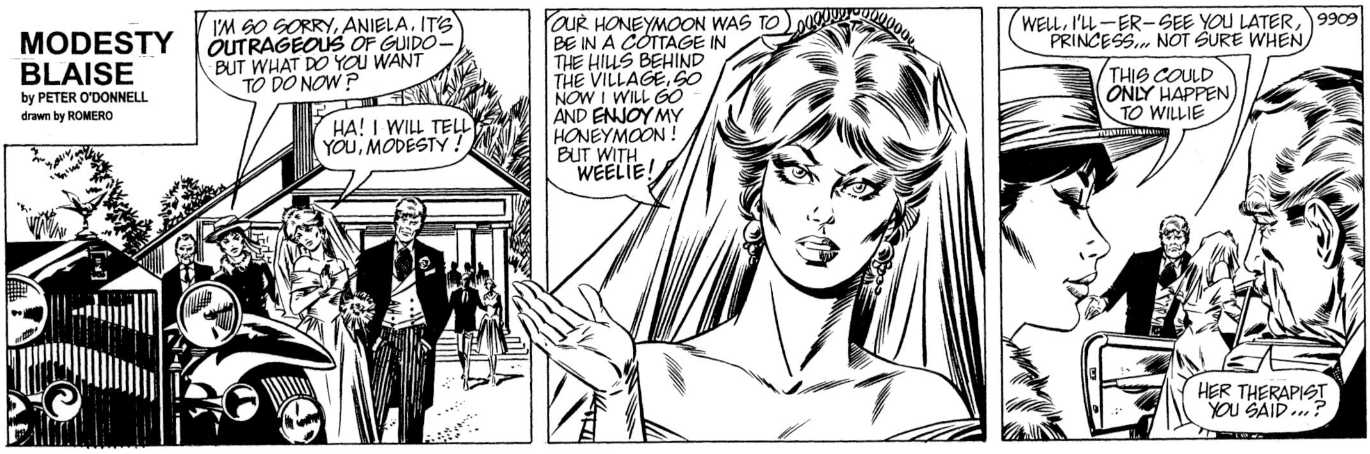
MODESTY BLAISE
by PETER O'DONNELL
drawn by ROMERO
I'M SO SORRY, ANIELA, IT'S OUTRAGEOUS OF GUIDO— BUT WHAT DO YOU WANT TO DO NOW?
HA! I WILL TELL YOU, MODESTY!
OUR HONEYMOON WAS TO BE IN A COTTAGE IN THE HILLS BEHIND THE VILLAGE, SO NOW I WILL GO AND ENJOY MY HONEYMOON! BUT WITH WEELIE!
9909
WELL, I'LL—ER—SEE YOU LATER, PRINCESS... NOT SURE WHEN
THIS COULD ONLY HAPPEN TO WILLIE
HER THERAPIST YOU SAID ...?

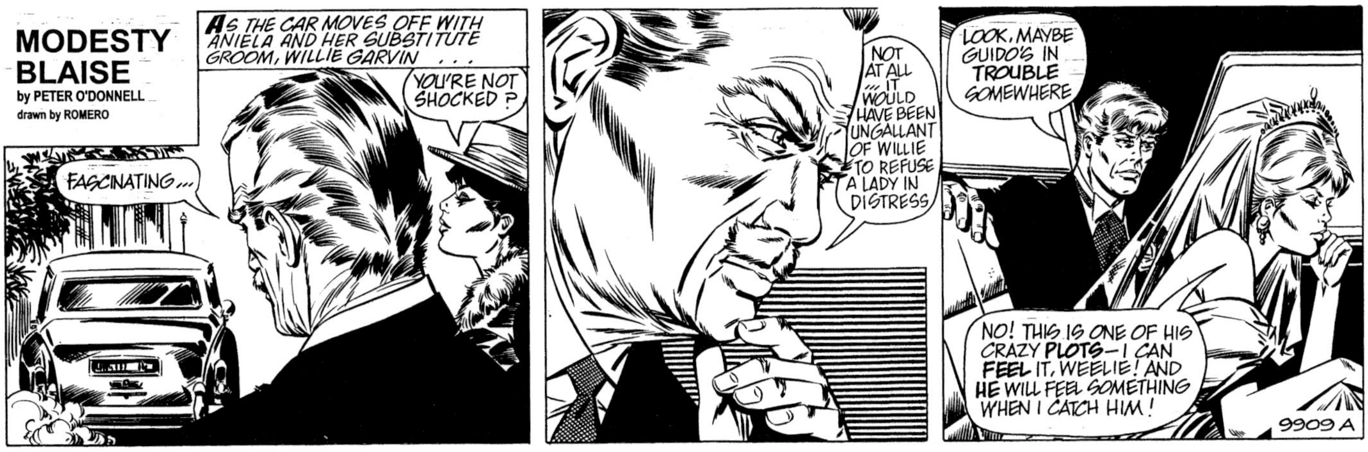
MODESTY BLAISE
by PETER O'DONNELL
drawn by ROMERO
AS THE CAR MOVES OFF WITH ANIELA AND HER SUBSTITUTE GROOM, WILLIE GARVIN . . .
YOU'RE NOT SHOCKED?
FASCINATING ...
NOT AT ALL ... IT WOULD HAVE BEEN UNGALLANT OF WILLIE TO REFUSE A LADY IN DISTRESS
LOOK, MAYBE GUIDO'S IN TROUBLE SOMEWHERE
NO! THIS IS ONE OF HIS CRAZY PLOTS—I CAN FEEL IT, WEELIE! AND HE WILL FEEL SOMETHING WHEN I CATCH HIM!
9909 A

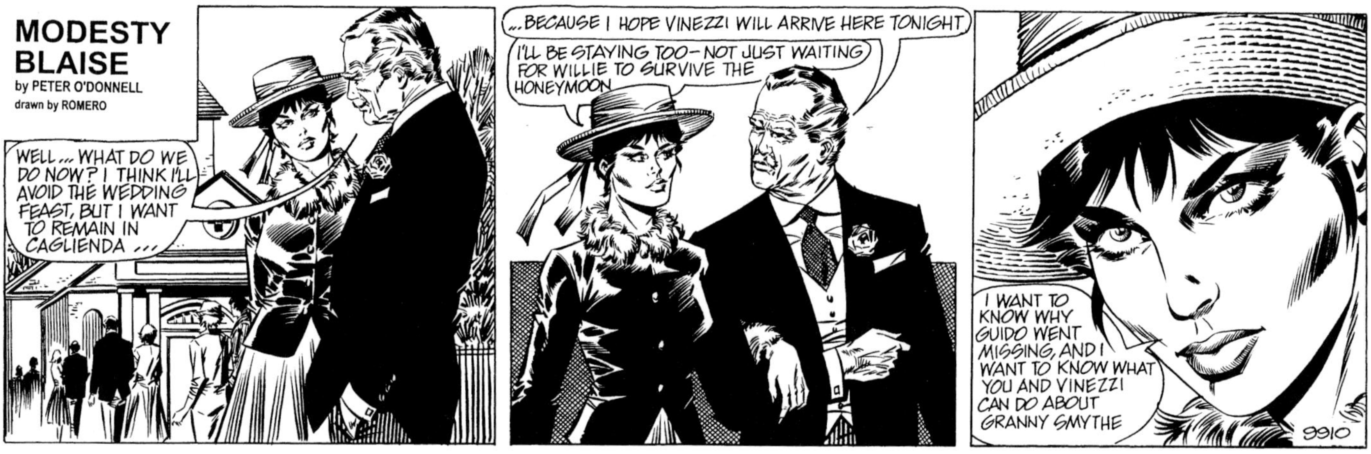
MODESTY BLAISE
by PETER O'DONNELL
drawn by ROMERO
WELL... WHAT DO WE DO NOW? I THINK I'LL AVOID THE WEDDING FEAST, BUT I WANT TO REMAIN IN CAGLIENDA...
...BECAUSE I HOPE VINEZZI WILL ARRIVE HERE TONIGHT
I'LL BE STAYING TOO—NOT JUST WAITING FOR WILLIE TO SURVIVE THE HONEYMOON
I WANT TO KNOW WHY GUIDO WENT MISSING, AND I WANT TO KNOW WHAT YOU AND VINEZZI CAN DO ABOUT GRANNY SMYTHE
9910

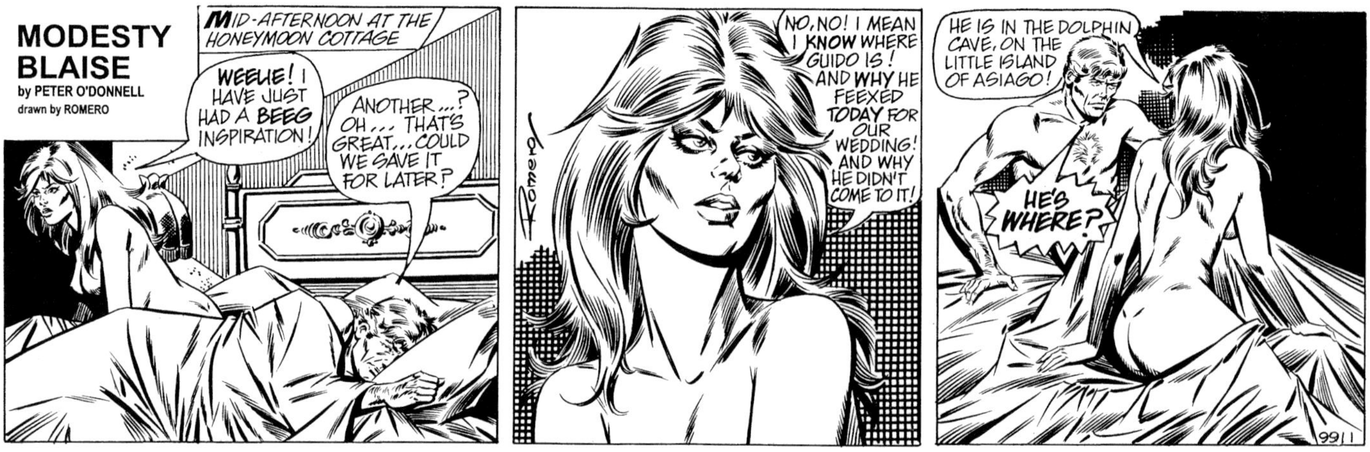
MODESTY BLAISE
by PETER O'DONNELL
drawn by ROMERO
MID-AFTERNOON AT THE HONEYMOON COTTAGE
WEELIE! I HAVE JUST HAD A BEEG INSPIRATION!
ANOTHER...? OH... THAT'S GREAT... COULD WE SAVE IT FOR LATER?
NO, NO! I MEAN I KNOW WHERE GUIDO IS! AND WHY HE FEEXED TODAY FOR OUR WEDDING! AND WHY HE DIDN'T COME TO IT!
HE IS IN THE DOLPHIN CAVE, ON THE LITTLE ISLAND OF ASIAGO!
HE'S WHERE?
9911

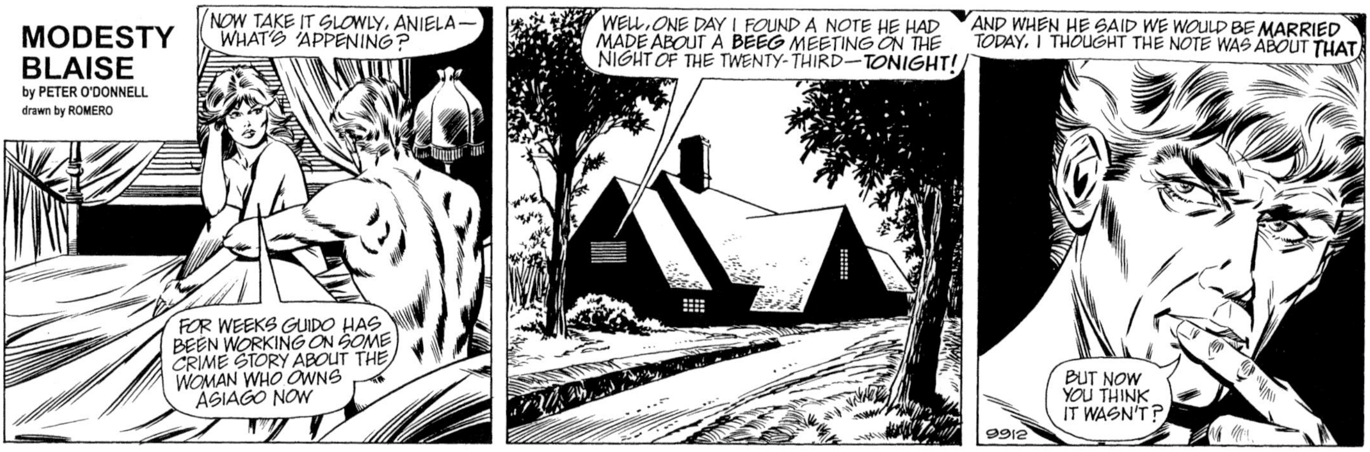
MODESTY BLAISE
by PETER O'DONNELL
drawn by ROMERO
NOW TAKE IT SLOWLY, ANIELA—WHAT'S 'APPENING?
FOR WEEKS GUIDO HAS BEEN WORKING ON SOME CRIME STORY ABOUT THE WOMAN WHO OWNS ASIAGO NOW
WELL, ONE DAY I FOUND A NOTE HE HAD MADE ABOUT A BEEG MEETING ON THE NIGHT OF THE TWENTY-THIRD—TONIGHT!
AND WHEN HE SAID WE WOULD BE MARRIED TODAY, I THOUGHT THE NOTE WAS ABOUT THAT
BUT NOW YOU THINK IT WASN'T?
9912

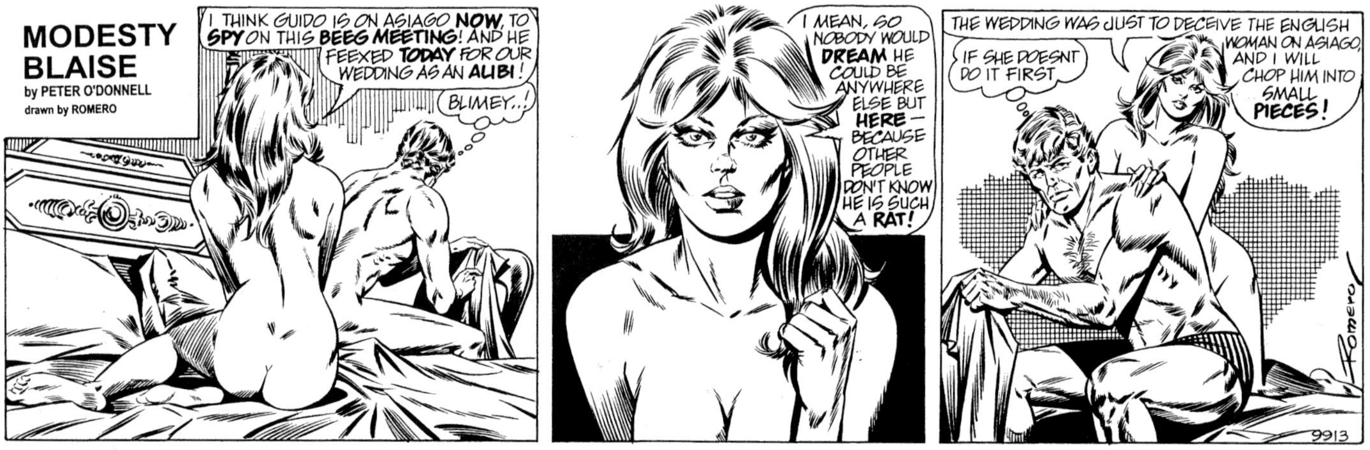
MODESTY BLAISE
by PETER O'DONNELL
drawn by ROMERO
I THINK GUIDO IS ON ASIAGO NOW, TO SPY ON THIS BEEG MEETING! AND HE FEEXED TODAY FOR OUR WEDDING AS AN ALIBI!
BLIMEY..!
I MEAN, SO NOBODY WOULD DREAM HE COULD BE ANYWHERE ELSE BUT HERE—BECAUSE OTHER PEOPLE DON'T KNOW HE IS SUCH A RAT!
THE WEDDING WAS JUST TO DECEIVE THE ENGLISH WOMAN ON ASIAGO, AND I WILL CHOP HIM INTO SMALL PIECES!
IF SHE DOESN'T DO IT FIRST
9913

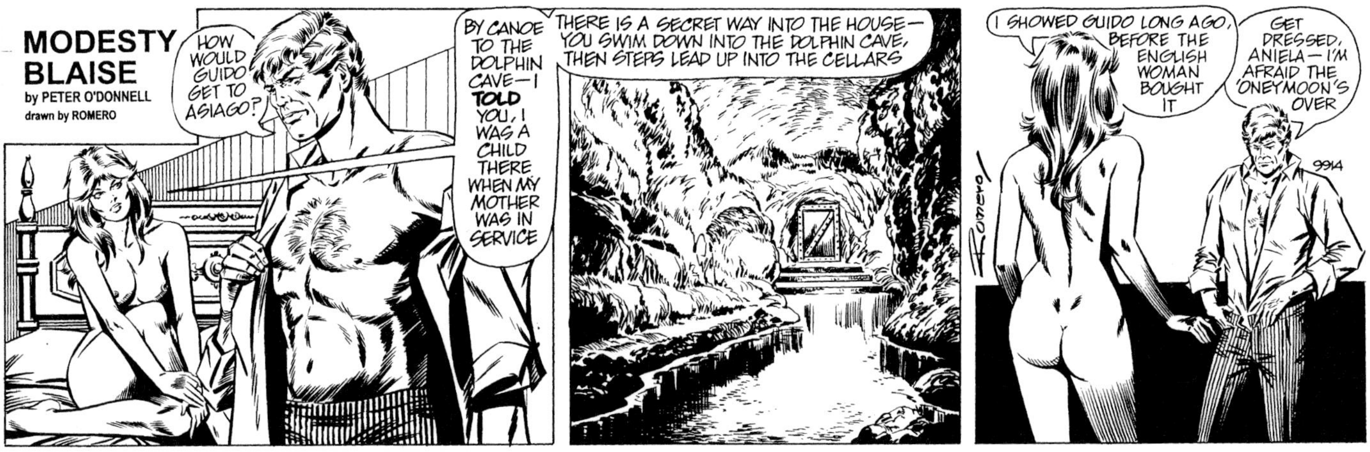
MODESTY BLAISE
by PETER O'DONNELL
drawn by ROMERO
HOW WOULD GUIDO GET TO ASIAGO?
BY CANOE TO THE DOLPHIN CAVE—I TOLD YOU, I WAS A CHILD THERE WHEN MY MOTHER WAS IN SERVICE
THERE IS A SECRET WAY INTO THE HOUSE—YOU SWIM DOWN INTO THE DOLPHIN CAVE, THEN STEPS LEAD UP INTO THE CELLARS
I SHOWED GUIDO LONG AGO, BEFORE THE ENGLISH WOMAN BOUGHT IT
GET DRESSED, ANIELA—I'M AFRAID THE 'ONEYMOON'S OVER
9914

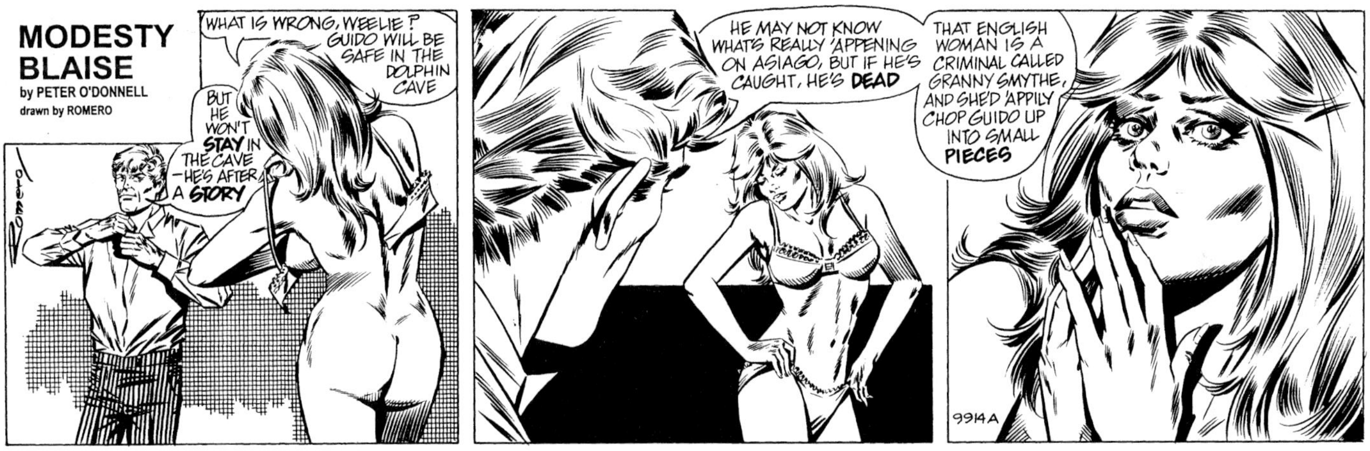
MODESTY BLAISE
by PETER O'DONNELL
drawn by ROMERO
WHAT IS WRONG, WEELIE? GUIDO WILL BE SAFE IN THE DOLPHIN CAVE
BUT HE WON'T STAY IN THE CAVE—HE'S AFTER A STORY
HE MAY NOT KNOW WHAT'S REALLY 'APPENING ON ASIAGO, BUT IF HE'S CAUGHT, HE'S DEAD
THAT ENGLISH WOMAN IS A CRIMINAL CALLED GRANNY SMYTHE, AND SHE'D 'APPILY CHOP GUIDO UP INTO SMALL PIECES
9914 A

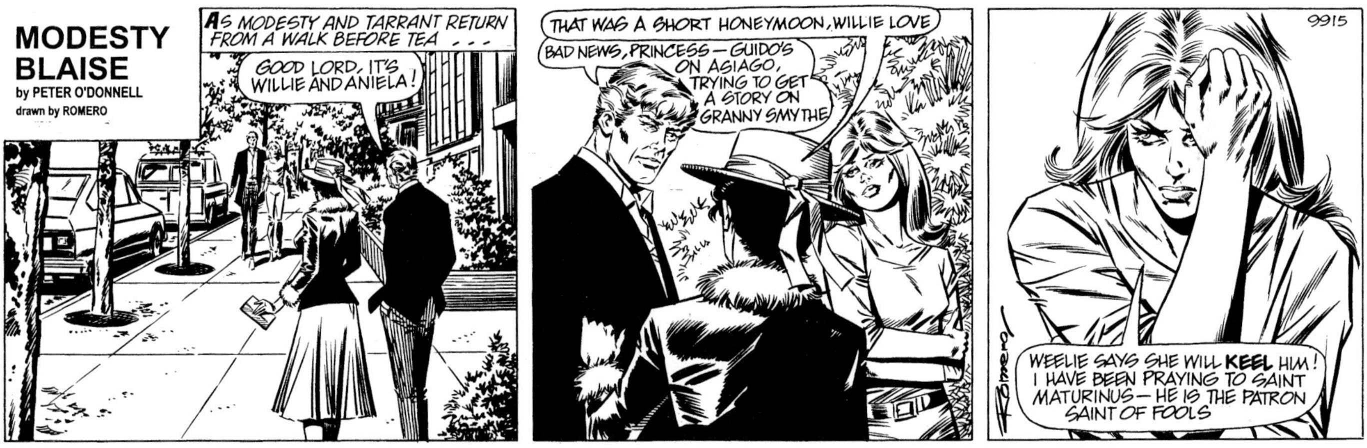
MODESTY BLAISE
by PETER O'DONNELL
drawn by ROMERO
AS MODESTY AND TARRANT RETURN FROM A WALK BEFORE TEA . . .
GOOD LORD, IT'S WILLIE AND ANIELA!
THAT WAS A SHORT HONEYMOON, WILLIE LOVE
BAD NEWS, PRINCESS—GUIDO'S ON ASIAGO, TRYING TO GET A STORY ON GRANNY SMYTHE
9915
WEELIE SAYS SHE WILL KEEL HIM! I HAVE BEEN PRAYING TO SAINT MATURINUS—HE IS THE PATRON SAINT OF FOOLS

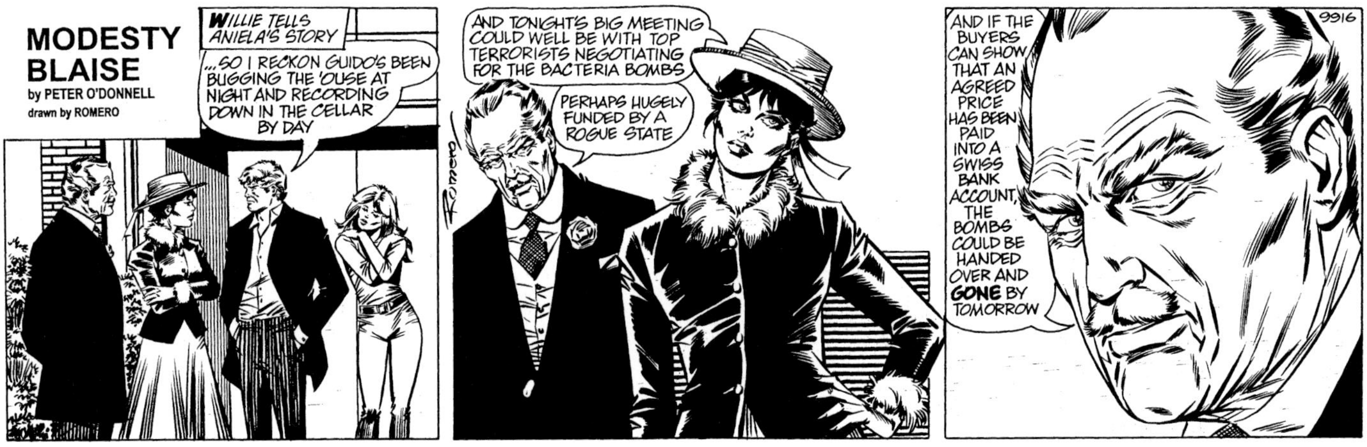
MODESTY BLAISE
by PETER O'DONNELL
drawn by ROMERO
WILLIE TELLS ANIELA'S STORY
...SO I RECKON GUIDO'S BEEN BUGGING THE 'OUSE AT NIGHT AND RECORDING DOWN IN THE CELLAR BY DAY
AND TONIGHT'S BIG MEETING COULD WELL BE WITH TOP TERRORISTS NEGOTIATING FOR THE BACTERIA BOMBS
PERHAPS HUGELY FUNDED BY A ROGUE STATE
AND IF THE BUYERS CAN SHOW THAT AN AGREED PRICE HAS BEEN PAID INTO A SWISS BANK ACCOUNT, THE BOMBS COULD BE HANDED OVER AND GONE BY TOMORROW
9916

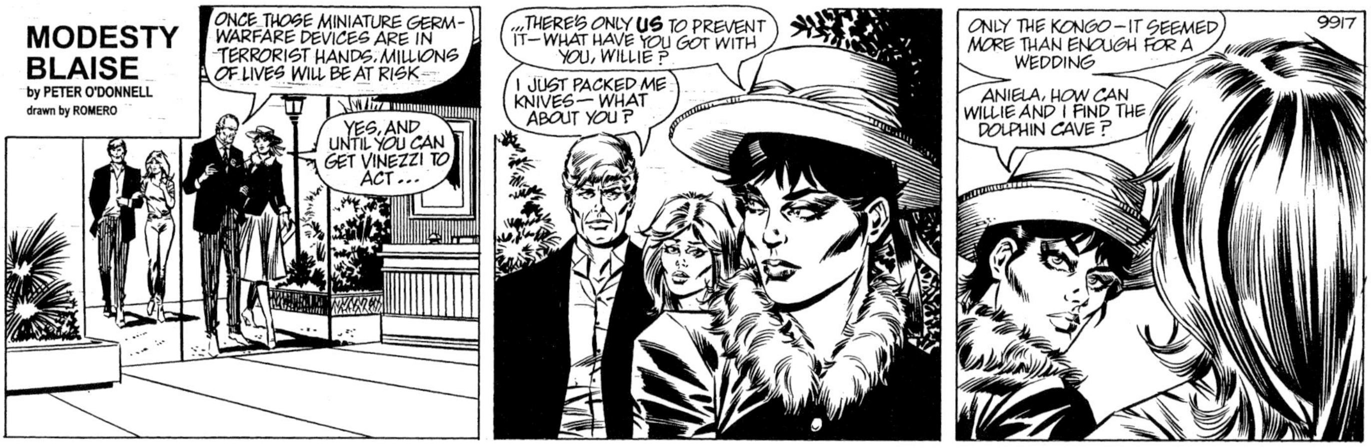
MODESTY BLAISE
by PETER O'DONNELL
drawn by ROMERO
ONCE THOSE MINIATURE GERM-WARFARE DEVICES ARE IN TERRORIST HANDS, MILLIONS OF LIVES WILL BE AT RISK
YES, AND UNTIL YOU CAN GET VINEZZI TO ACT...
...THERE'S ONLY US TO PREVENT IT—WHAT HAVE YOU GOT WITH YOU, WILLIE ?
I JUST PACKED ME KNIVES—WHAT ABOUT YOU ?
9917
ONLY THE KONGO—IT SEEMED MORE THAN ENOUGH FOR A WEDDING
ANIELA, HOW CAN WILLIE AND I FIND THE DOLPHIN CAVE ?

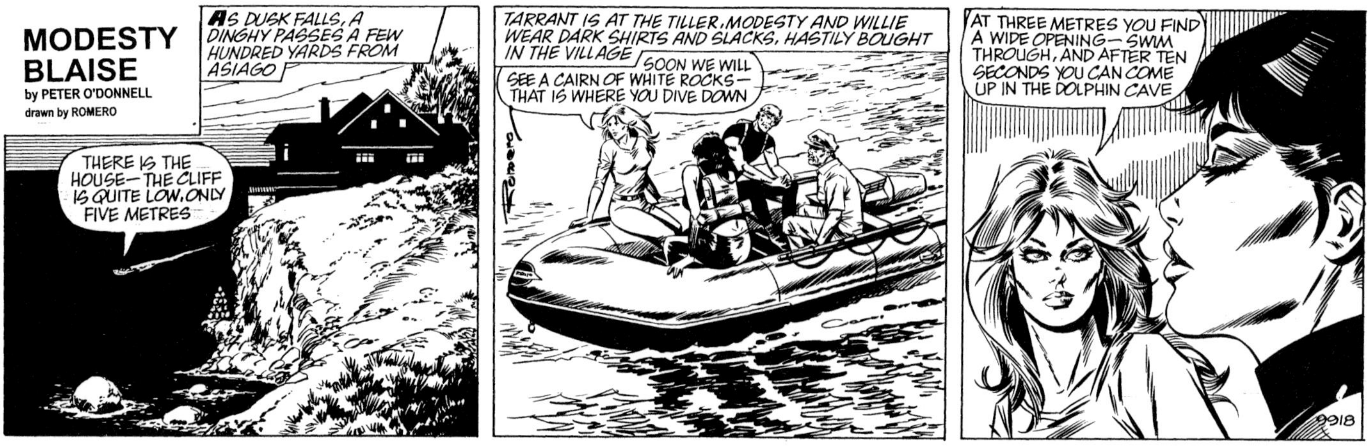
MODESTY BLAISE
by PETER O'DONNELL
drawn by ROMERO
AS DUSK FALLS, A DINGHY PASSES A FEW HUNDRED YARDS FROM ASIAGO
THERE IS THE HOUSE—THE CLIFF IS QUITE LOW, ONLY FIVE METRES
TARRANT IS AT THE TILLER, MODESTY AND WILLIE WEAR DARK SHIRTS AND SLACKS, HASTILY BOUGHT IN THE VILLAGE
SOON WE WILL SEE A CAIRN OF WHITE ROCKS—THAT IS WHERE YOU DIVE DOWN
AT THREE METRES YOU FIND A WIDE OPENING—SWIM THROUGH, AND AFTER TEN SECONDS YOU CAN COME UP IN THE DOLPHIN CAVE
9918

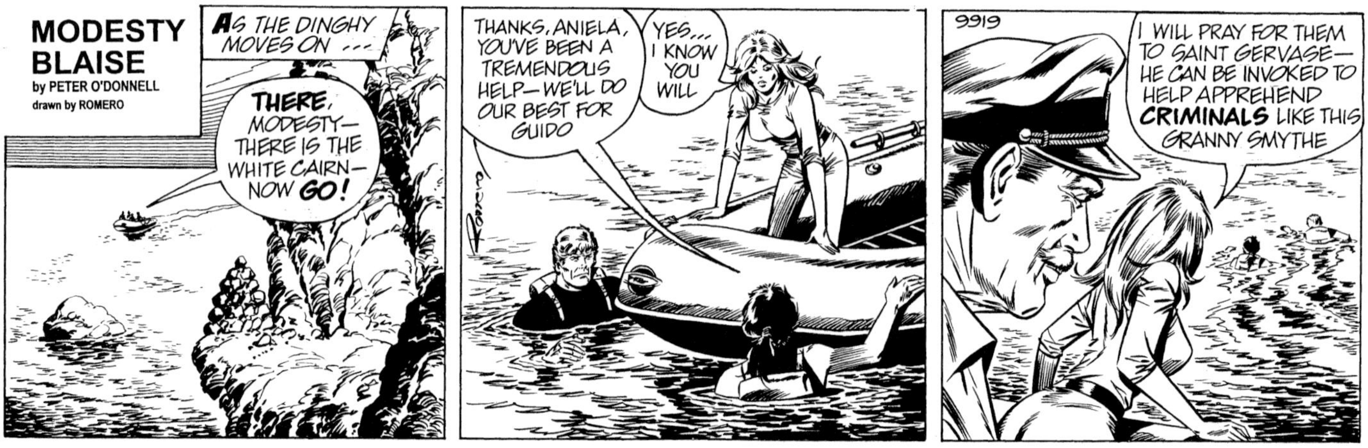
MODESTY BLAISE
by PETER O'DONNELL
drawn by ROMERO
AS THE DINGHY MOVES ON...
THERE, MODESTY—THERE IS THE WHITE CAIRN—NOW GO!
THANKS, ANIELA, YOU'VE BEEN A TREMENDOUS HELP—WE'LL DO OUR BEST FOR GUIDO
YES... I KNOW YOU WILL
9919
I WILL PRAY FOR THEM TO SAINT GERVASE—HE CAN BE INVOKED TO HELP APPREHEND CRIMINALS LIKE THIS GRANNY SMYTHE

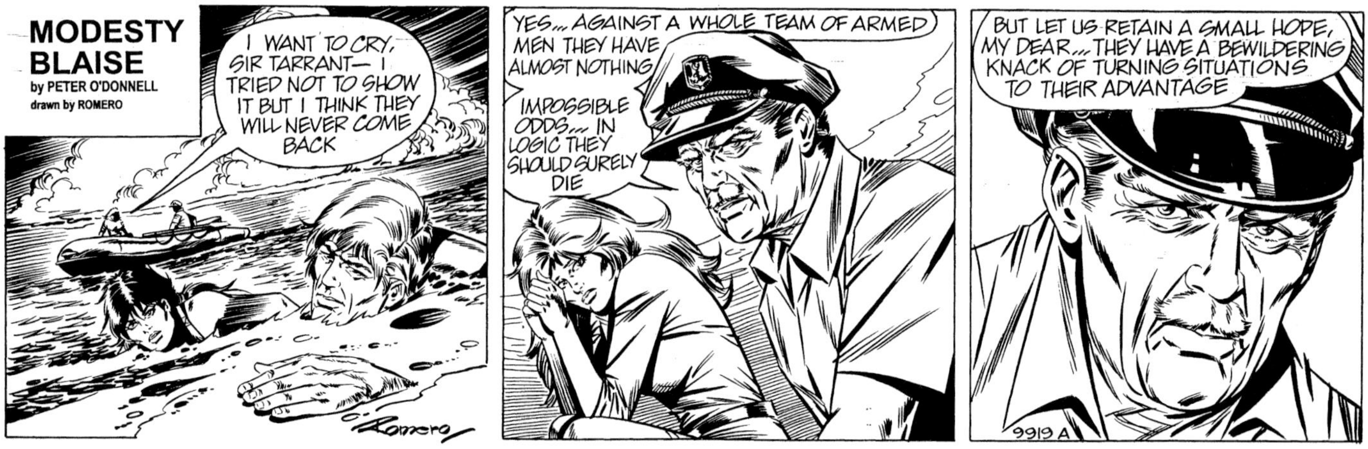
MODESTY BLAISE
by PETER O'DONNELL
drawn by ROMERO
I WANT TO CRY, SIR TARRANT—I TRIED NOT TO SHOW IT BUT I THINK THEY WILL NEVER COME BACK
Romero
YES... AGAINST A WHOLE TEAM OF ARMED MEN THEY HAVE ALMOST NOTHING
IMPOSSIBLE ODDS... IN LOGIC THEY SHOULD SURELY DIE
BUT LET US RETAIN A SMALL HOPE, MY DEAR... THEY HAVE A BEWILDERING KNACK OF TURNING SITUATIONS TO THEIR ADVANTAGE
9919 A

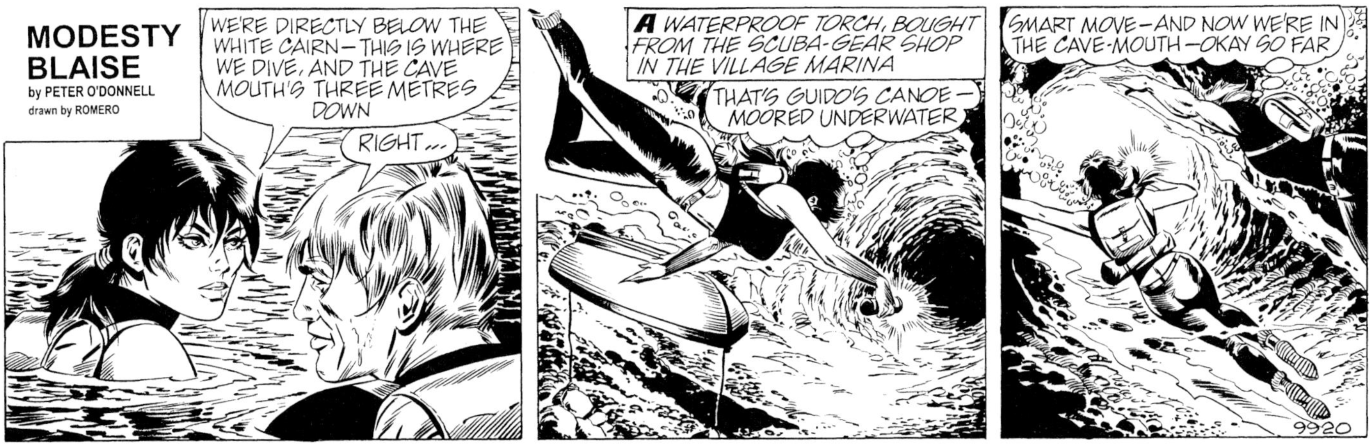
MODESTY BLAISE
by PETER O'DONNELL
drawn by ROMERO
WE'RE DIRECTLY BELOW THE WHITE CAIRN—THIS IS WHERE WE DIVE, AND THE CAVE MOUTH'S THREE METRES DOWN
RIGHT...
A WATERPROOF TORCH, BOUGHT FROM THE SCUBA-GEAR SHOP IN THE VILLAGE MARINA
THAT'S GUIDO'S CANOE—MOORED UNDERWATER
SMART MOVE—AND NOW WE'RE IN THE CAVE-MOUTH—OKAY SO FAR
9920

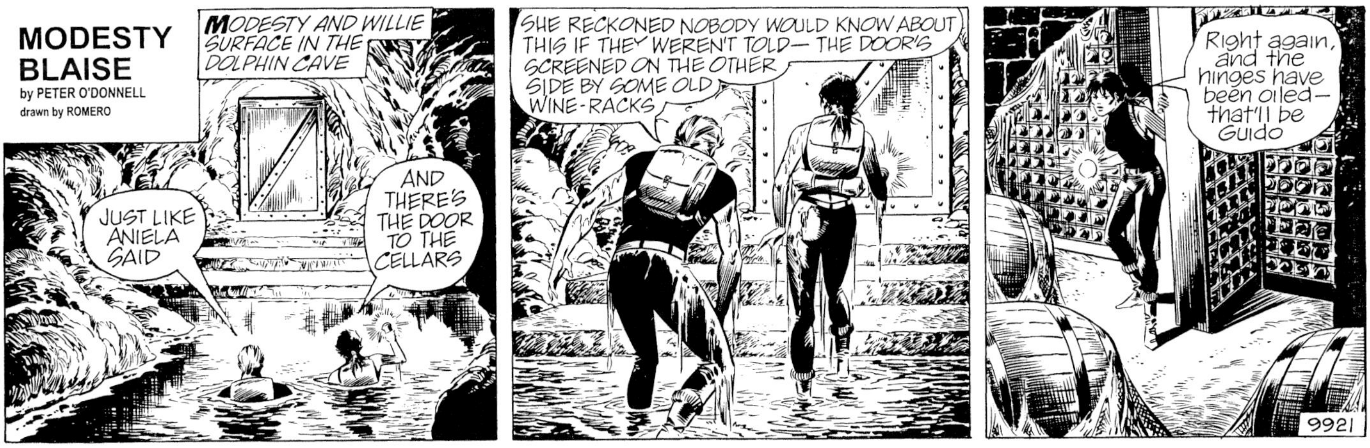
MODESTY BLAISE
by PETER O'DONNELL
drawn by ROMERO
MODESTY AND WILLIE SURFACE IN THE DOLPHIN CAVE
JUST LIKE ANIELA SAID
AND THERE'S THE DOOR TO THE CELLARS
SHE RECKONED NOBODY WOULD KNOW ABOUT THIS IF THEY WEREN'T TOLD—THE DOOR'S SCREENED ON THE OTHER SIDE BY SOME OLD WINE-RACKS
Right again, and the hinges have been oiled—that'll be Guido
9921

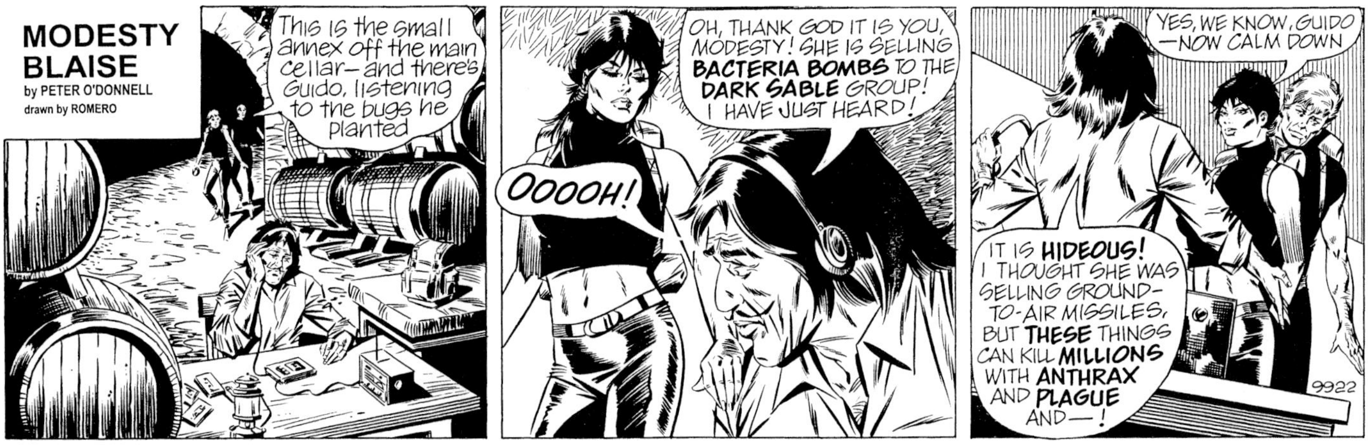
MODESTY BLAISE
by PETER O'DONNELL
drawn by ROMERO
This is the small annex off the main cellar—and there's Guido, listening to the bugs he planted
OH, THANK GOD IT IS YOU, MODESTY! SHE IS SELLING BACTERIA BOMBS TO THE DARK SABLE GROUP! I HAVE JUST HEARD!
OOOOH!
YES, WE KNOW, GUIDO—NOW CALM DOWN
IT IS HIDEOUS! I THOUGHT SHE WAS SELLING GROUND-TO-AIR MISSILES, BUT THESE THINGS CAN KILL MILLIONS WITH ANTHRAX AND PLAGUE AND—!
9922

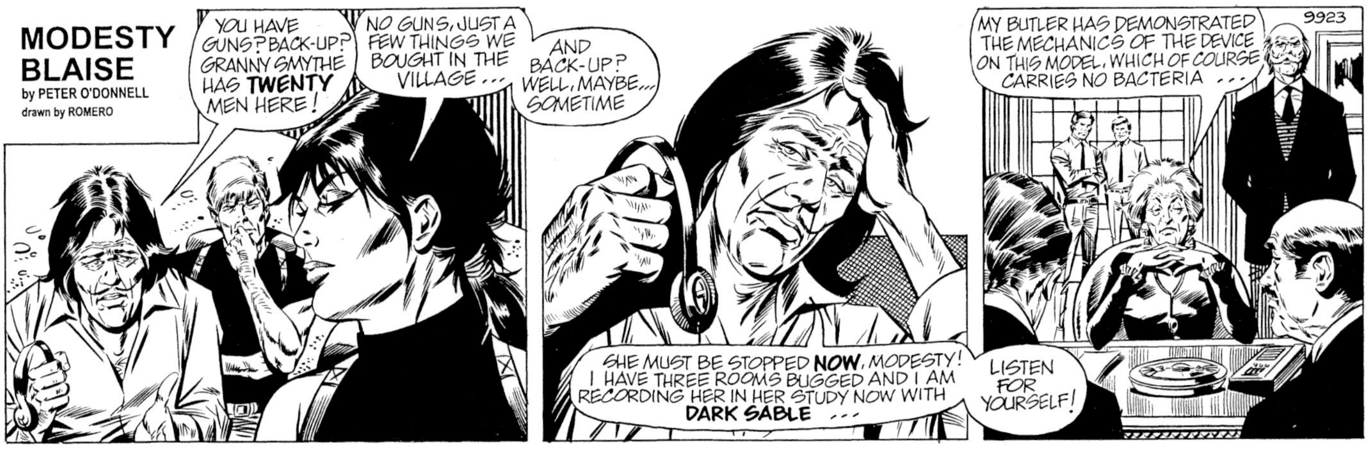
MODESTY BLAISE
by PETER O'DONNELL
drawn by ROMERO
YOU HAVE GUNS? BACK-UP? GRANNY SMYTHE HAS TWENTY MEN HERE!
NO GUNS, JUST A FEW THINGS WE BOUGHT IN THE VILLAGE...
AND BACK-UP? WELL, MAYBE... SOMETIME
SHE MUST BE STOPPED NOW, MODESTY! I HAVE THREE ROOMS BUGGED AND I AM RECORDING HER IN HER STUDY NOW WITH DARK SABLE...
LISTEN FOR YOURSELF!
MY BUTLER HAS DEMONSTRATED THE MECHANICS OF THE DEVICE ON THIS MODEL, WHICH OF COURSE CARRIES NO BACTERIA...
9923

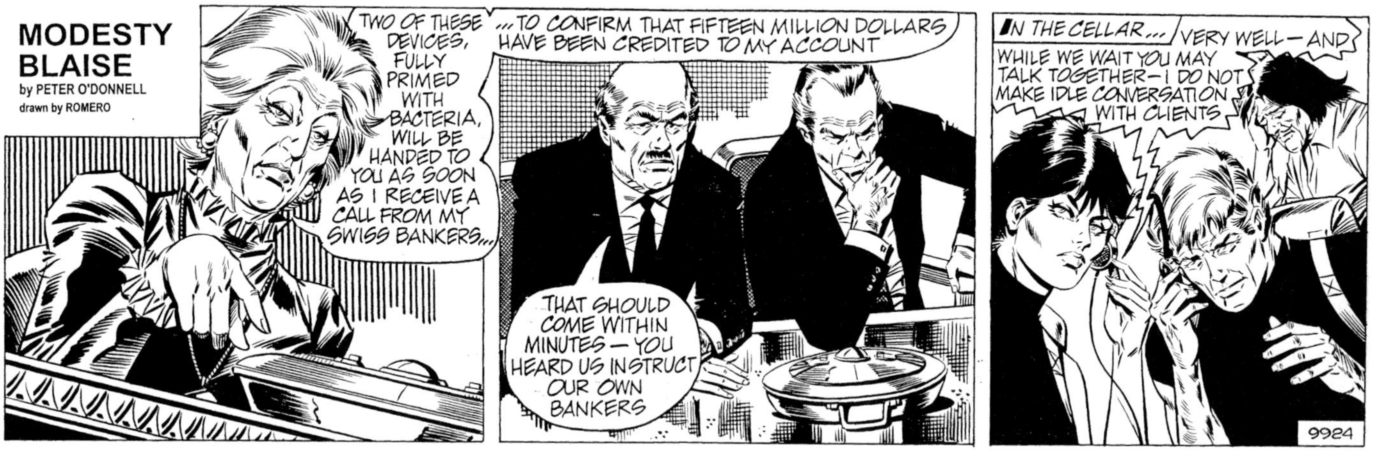
MODESTY BLAISE
by PETER O'DONNELL
drawn by ROMERO
TWO OF THESE DEVICES, FULLY PRIMED WITH BACTERIA, WILL BE HANDED TO YOU AS SOON AS I RECEIVE A CALL FROM MY SWISS BANKERS...
...TO CONFIRM THAT FIFTEEN MILLION DOLLARS HAVE BEEN CREDITED TO MY ACCOUNT
THAT SHOULD COME WITHIN MINUTES — YOU HEARD US INSTRUCT OUR OWN BANKERS
IN THE CELLAR...
VERY WELL — AND WHILE WE WAIT YOU MAY TALK TOGETHER — I DO NOT MAKE IDLE CONVERSATION WITH CLIENTS
9924

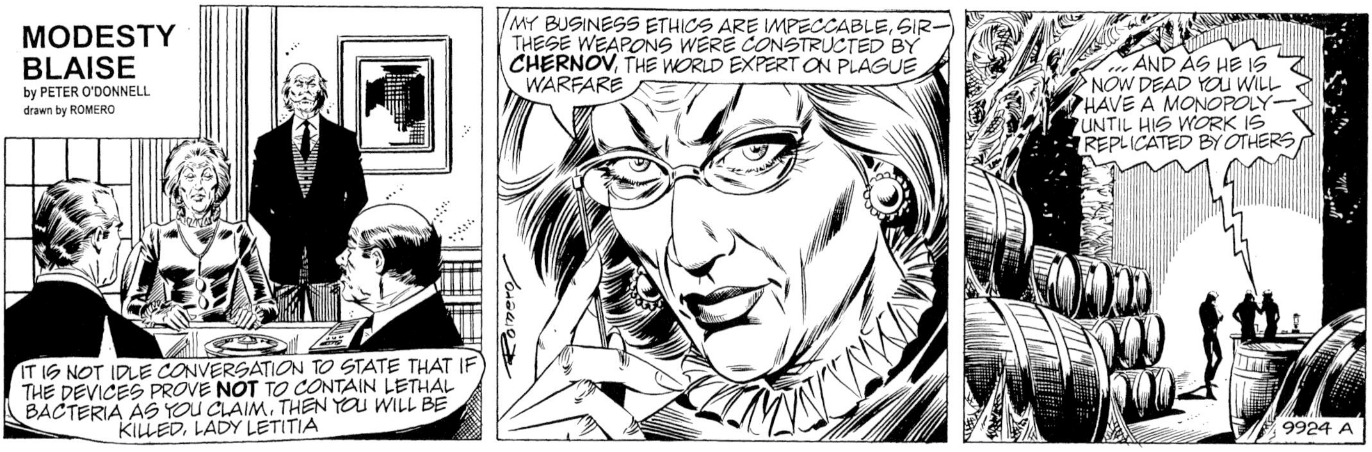
MODESTY BLAISE
by PETER O'DONNELL
drawn by ROMERO
IT IS NOT IDLE CONVERSATION TO STATE THAT IF THE DEVICES PROVE NOT TO CONTAIN LETHAL BACTERIA AS YOU CLAIM, THEN YOU WILL BE KILLED, LADY LETITIA
MY BUSINESS ETHICS ARE IMPECCABLE, SIR — THESE WEAPONS WERE CONSTRUCTED BY CHERNOV, THE WORLD EXPERT ON PLAGUE WARFARE
... AND AS HE IS NOW DEAD YOU WILL HAVE A MONOPOLY — UNTIL HIS WORK IS REPLICATED BY OTHERS
9924 A

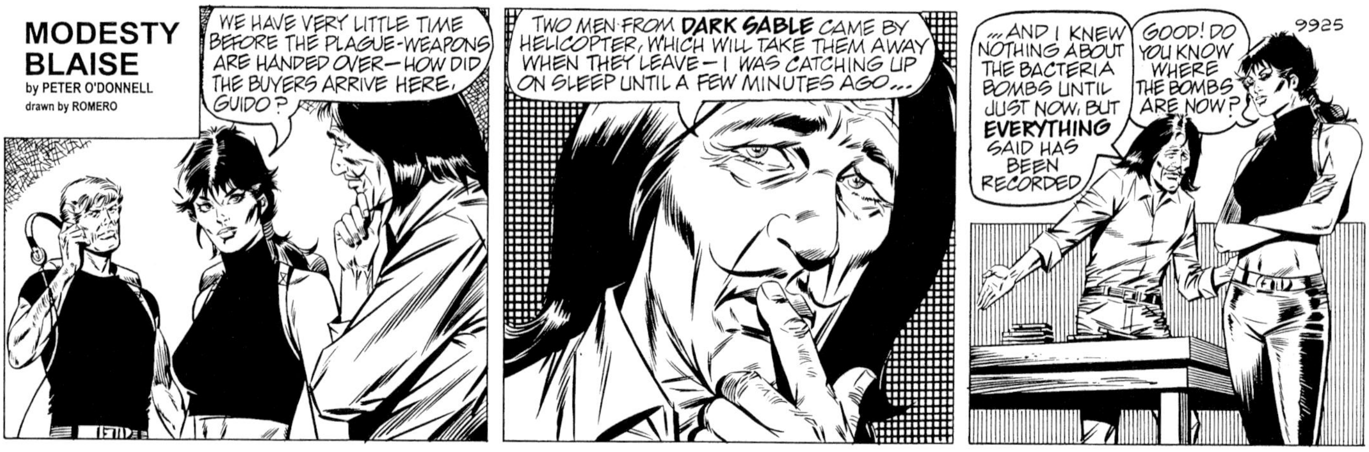
MODESTY BLAISE
by PETER O'DONNELL
drawn by ROMERO
WE HAVE VERY LITTLE TIME BEFORE THE PLAGUE-WEAPONS ARE HANDED OVER — HOW DID THE BUYERS ARRIVE HERE, GUIDO?
TWO MEN FROM DARK SABLE CAME BY HELICOPTER, WHICH WILL TAKE THEM AWAY WHEN THEY LEAVE — I WAS CATCHING UP ON SLEEP UNTIL A FEW MINUTES AGO...
...AND I KNEW NOTHING ABOUT THE BACTERIA BOMBS UNTIL JUST NOW, BUT EVERYTHING SAID HAS BEEN RECORDED
GOOD! DO YOU KNOW WHERE THE BOMBS ARE NOW?
9925

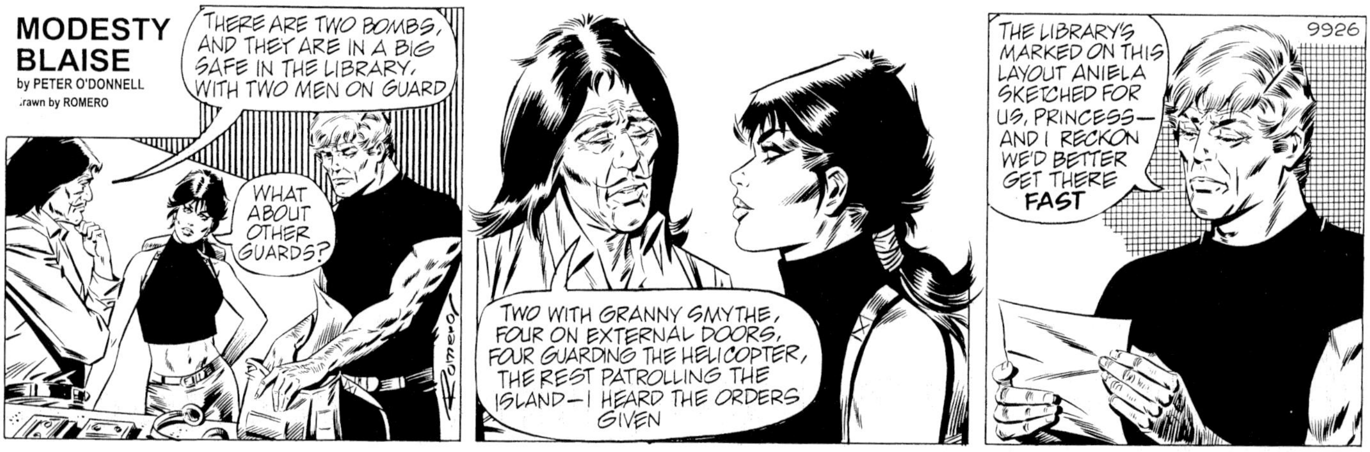
MODESTY BLAISE
by PETER O'DONNELL
drawn by ROMERO
THERE ARE TWO BOMBS, AND THEY ARE IN A BIG SAFE IN THE LIBRARY, WITH TWO MEN ON GUARD
WHAT ABOUT OTHER GUARDS?
TWO WITH GRANNY SMYTHE, FOUR ON EXTERNAL DOORS, FOUR GUARDING THE HELICOPTER, THE REST PATROLLING THE ISLAND — I HEARD THE ORDERS GIVEN
THE LIBRARY'S MARKED ON THIS LAYOUT ANIELA SKETCHED FOR US, PRINCESS — AND I RECKON WE'D BETTER GET THERE FAST
9926

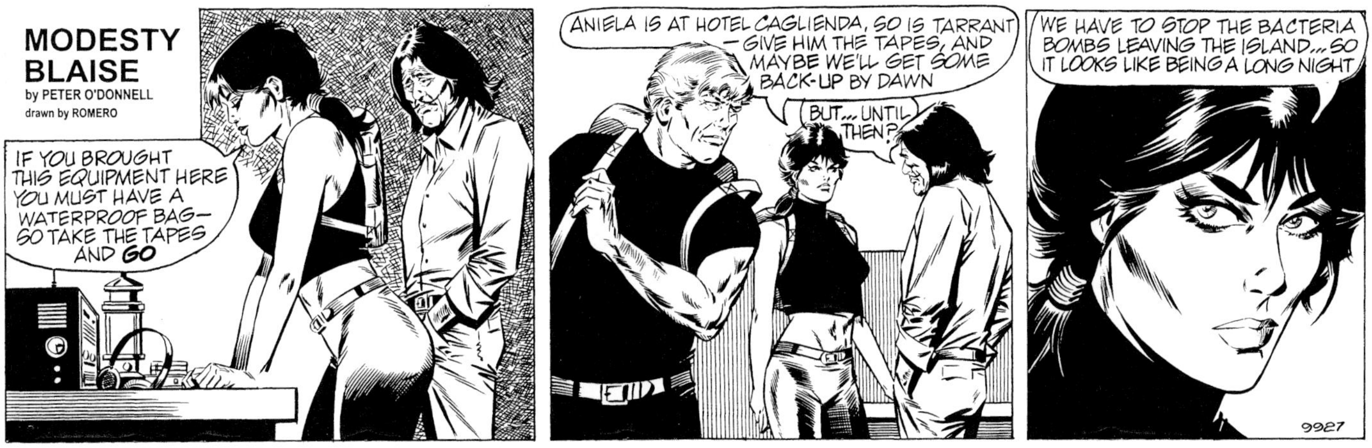
MODESTY BLAISE
by PETER O'DONNELL
drawn by ROMERO
IF YOU BROUGHT THIS EQUIPMENT HERE YOU MUST HAVE A WATERPROOF BAG— SO TAKE THE TAPES AND GO
ANIELA IS AT HOTEL CAGLIENDA, SO IS TARRANT — GIVE HIM THE TAPES, AND MAYBE WE'LL GET SOME BACK-UP BY DAWN
BUT... UNTIL THEN?
WE HAVE TO STOP THE BACTERIA BOMBS LEAVING THE ISLAND... SO IT LOOKS LIKE BEING A LONG NIGHT
9927

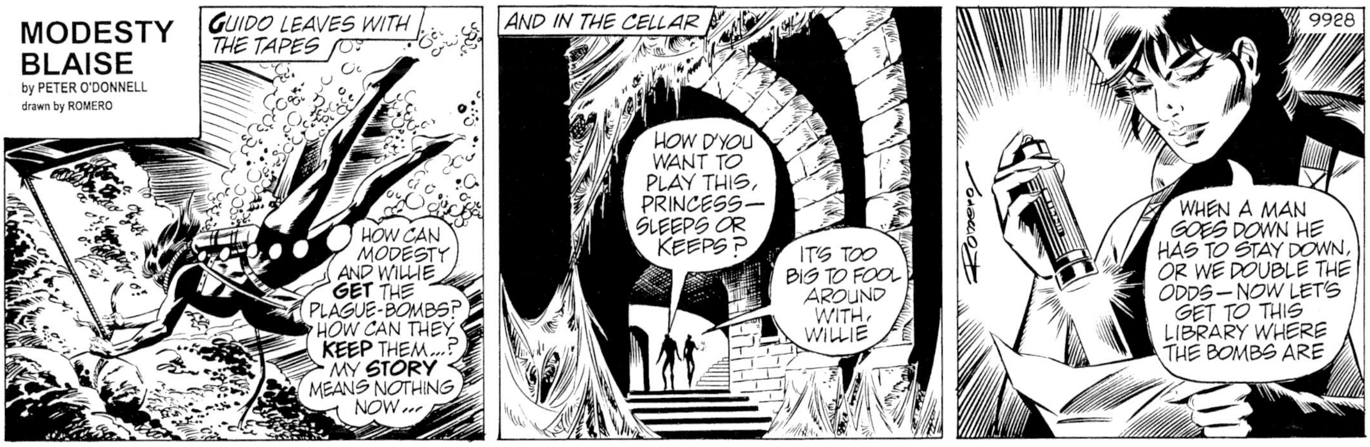
MODESTY BLAISE
by PETER O'DONNELL
drawn by ROMERO
GUIDO LEAVES WITH THE TAPES
HOW CAN MODESTY AND WILLIE GET THE PLAGUE-BOMBS? HOW CAN THEY KEEP THEM...? MY STORY MEANS NOTHING NOW...
AND IN THE CELLAR
HOW D'YOU WANT TO PLAY THIS, PRINCESS— SLEEPS OR KEEPS?
IT'S TOO BIG TO FOOL AROUND WITH, WILLIE
9928
WHEN A MAN GOES DOWN HE HAS TO STAY DOWN, OR WE DOUBLE THE ODDS — NOW LET'S GET TO THIS LIBRARY WHERE THE BOMBS ARE

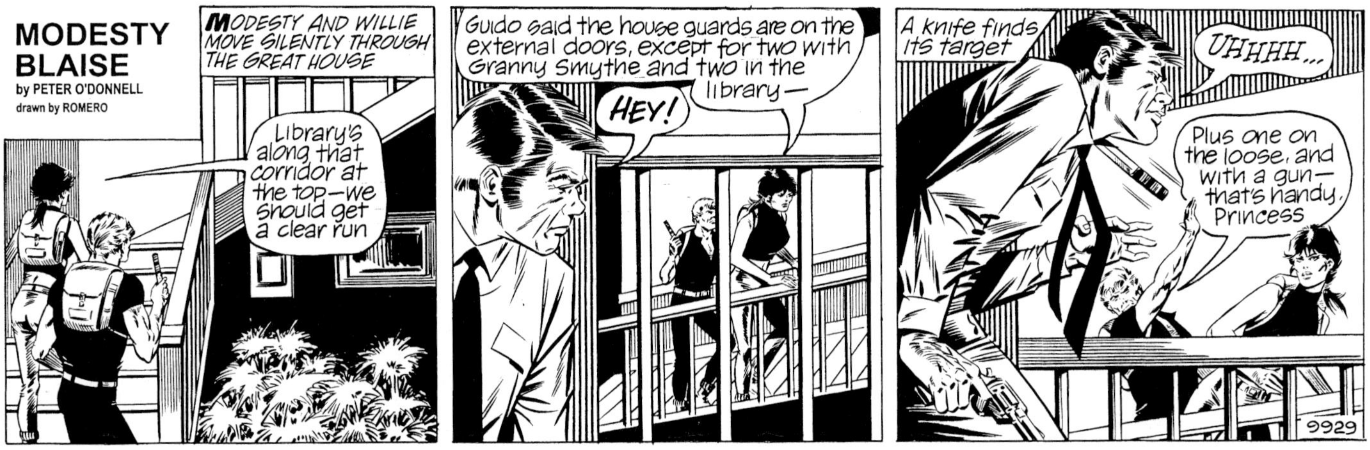
MODESTY BLAISE
by PETER O'DONNELL
drawn by ROMERO
MODESTY AND WILLIE MOVE SILENTLY THROUGH THE GREAT HOUSE
Library's along that corridor at the top—we should get a clear run
Guido said the house guards are on the external doors, except for two with Granny Smythe and two in the library—
HEY!
A knife finds its target
UHHHH...
Plus one on the loose, and with a gun— that's handy, Princess
9929

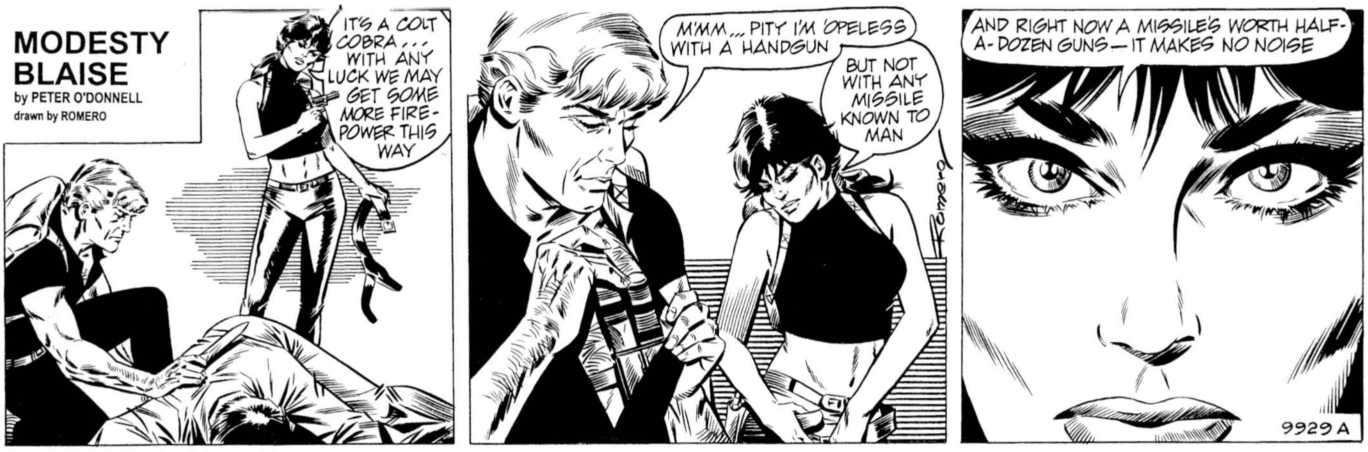
MODESTY BLAISE
by PETER O'DONNELL
drawn by ROMERO
IT'S A COLT COBRA... WITH ANY LUCK WE MAY GET SOME MORE FIRE-POWER THIS WAY
M'MM... PITY I'M 'OPELESS WITH A HANDGUN
BUT NOT WITH ANY MISSILE KNOWN TO MAN
AND RIGHT NOW A MISSILE'S WORTH HALF-A-DOZEN GUNS — IT MAKES NO NOISE
9929 A

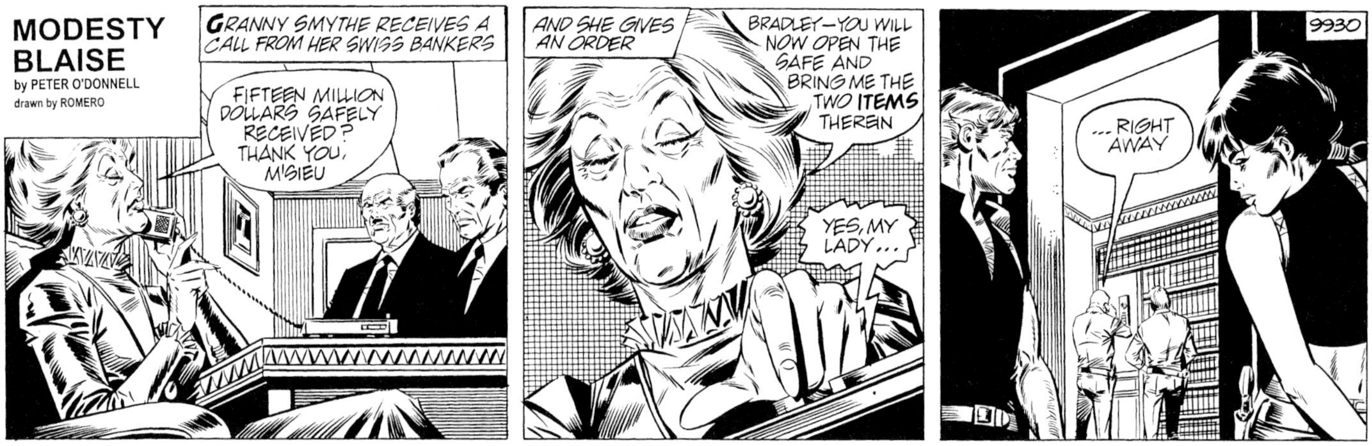
MODESTY BLAISE
by PETER O'DONNELL
drawn by ROMERO
GRANNY SMYTHE RECEIVES A CALL FROM HER SWISS BANKERS
FIFTEEN MILLION DOLLARS SAFELY RECEIVED? THANK YOU, M'SIEU
AND SHE GIVES AN ORDER
BRADLEY—YOU WILL NOW OPEN THE SAFE AND BRING ME THE TWO ITEMS THEREIN
YES, MY LADY...
9930
...RIGHT AWAY

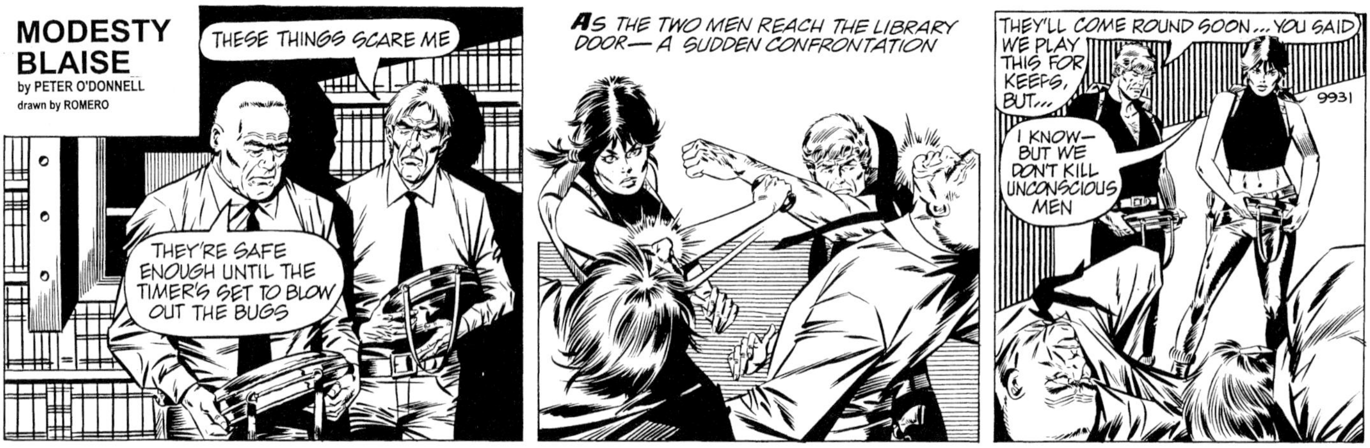
MODESTY BLAISE
by PETER O'DONNELL
drawn by ROMERO
THESE THINGS SCARE ME
THEY'RE SAFE ENOUGH UNTIL THE TIMER'S SET TO BLOW OUT THE BUGS
AS THE TWO MEN REACH THE LIBRARY DOOR— A SUDDEN CONFRONTATION
THEY'LL COME ROUND SOON... YOU SAID WE PLAY THIS FOR KEEPS, BUT...
9931
I KNOW— BUT WE DON'T KILL UNCONSCIOUS MEN

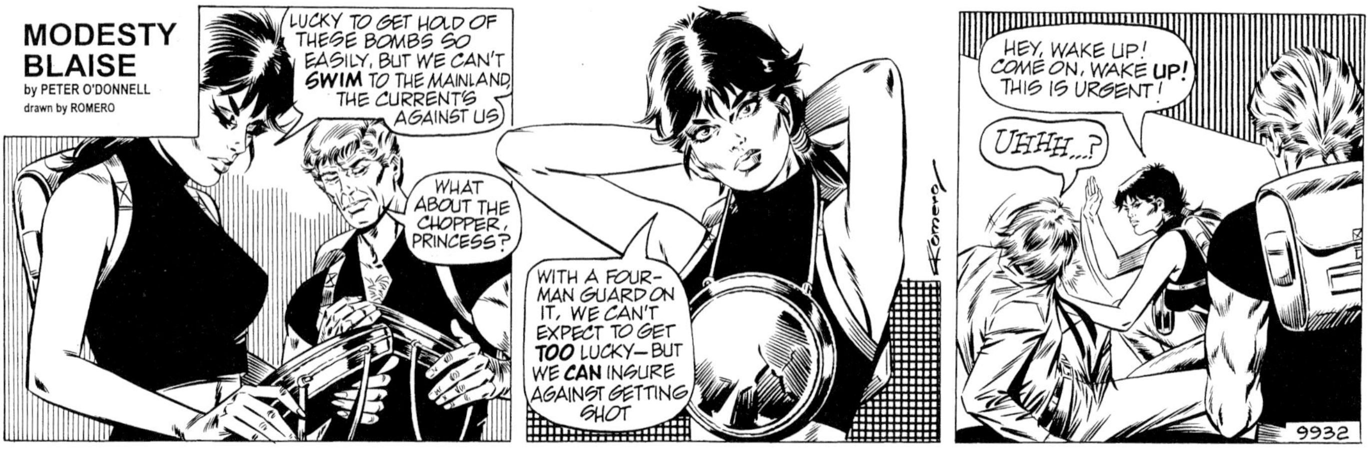
MODESTY BLAISE
by PETER O'DONNELL
drawn by ROMERO
LUCKY TO GET HOLD OF THESE BOMBS SO EASILY, BUT WE CAN'T SWIM TO THE MAINLAND, THE CURRENT'S AGAINST US
WHAT ABOUT THE CHOPPER, PRINCESS?
WITH A FOUR-MAN GUARD ON IT, WE CAN'T EXPECT TO GET TOO LUCKY— BUT WE CAN INSURE AGAINST GETTING SHOT
Romero
HEY, WAKE UP! COME ON, WAKE UP! THIS IS URGENT!
UHHH...?
9932

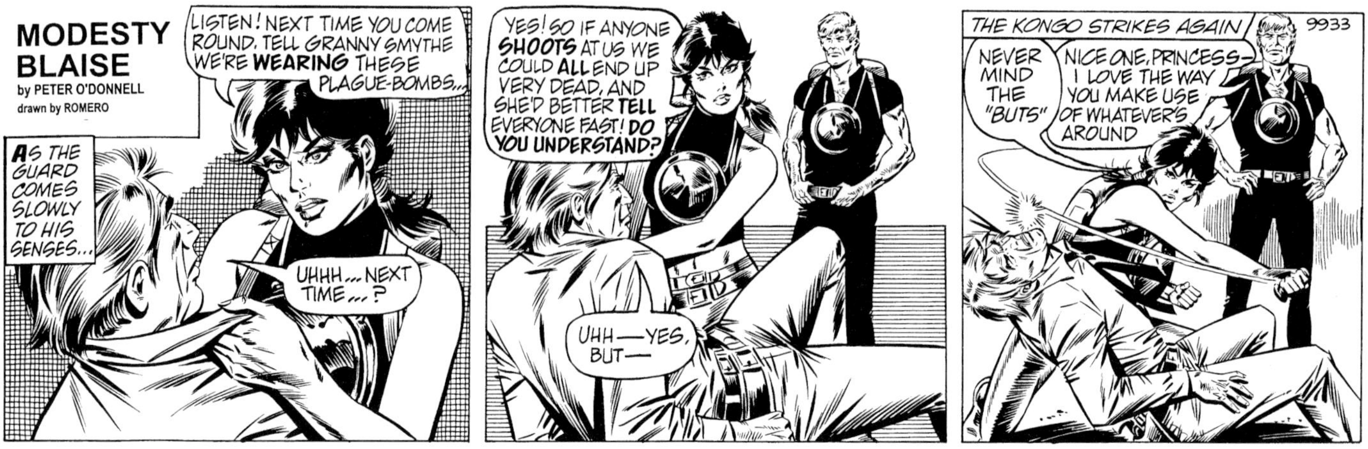
MODESTY BLAISE
by PETER O'DONNELL
drawn by ROMERO
AS THE GUARD COMES SLOWLY TO HIS SENSES...
LISTEN! NEXT TIME YOU COME ROUND, TELL GRANNY SMYTHE WE'RE WEARING THESE PLAGUE-BOMBS...
UHHH... NEXT TIME...?
YES! SO IF ANYONE SHOOTS AT US WE COULD ALL END UP VERY DEAD, AND SHE'D BETTER TELL EVERYONE FAST! DO YOU UNDERSTAND?
UHH—YES, BUT—
THE KONGO STRIKES AGAIN
9933
NEVER MIND THE "BUTS"
NICE ONE, PRINCESS— I LOVE THE WAY YOU MAKE USE OF WHATEVER'S AROUND

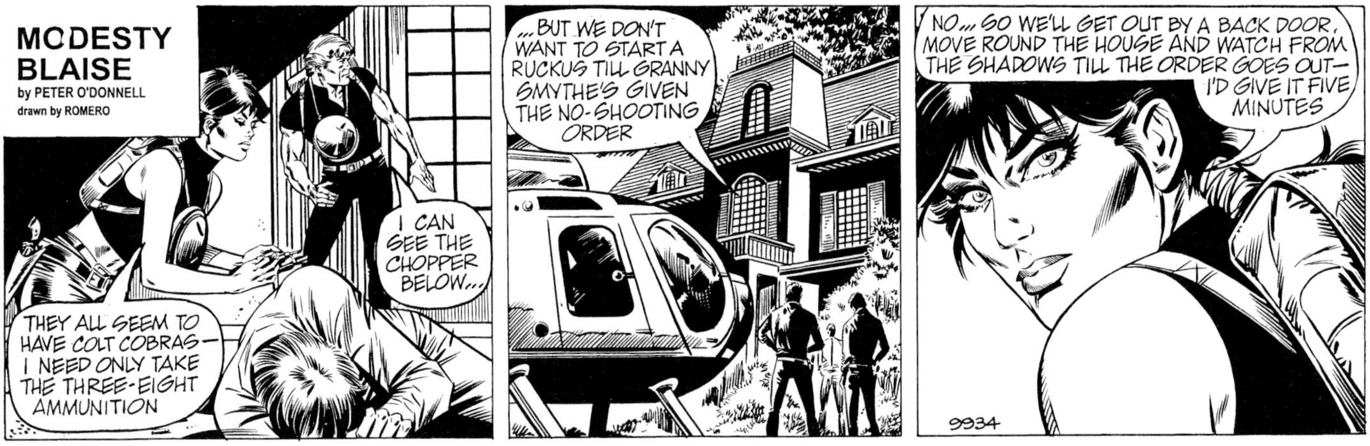
MODESTY BLAISE
by PETER O'DONNELL
drawn by ROMERO
I CAN SEE THE CHOPPER BELOW...
THEY ALL SEEM TO HAVE COLT COBRAS— I NEED ONLY TAKE THE THREE-EIGHT AMMUNITION
...BUT WE DON'T WANT TO START A RUCKUS TILL GRANNY SMYTHE'S GIVEN THE NO-SHOOTING ORDER
NO... SO WE'LL GET OUT BY A BACK DOOR, MOVE ROUND THE HOUSE AND WATCH FROM THE SHADOWS TILL THE ORDER GOES OUT— I'D GIVE IT FIVE MINUTES
9934

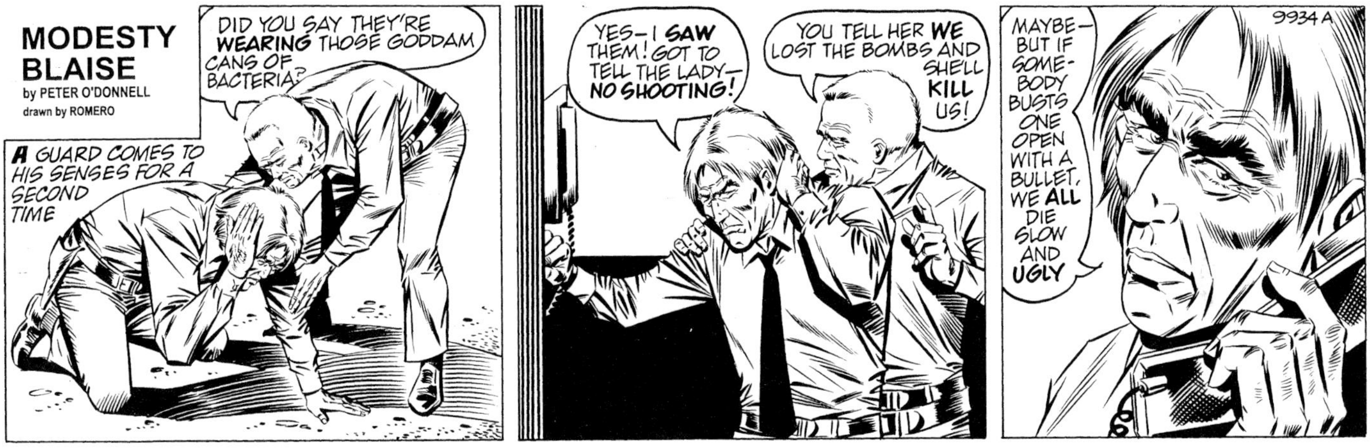
MODESTY BLAISE
by PETER O'DONNELL
drawn by ROMERO
A GUARD COMES TO HIS SENSES FOR A SECOND TIME
DID YOU SAY THEY'RE WEARING THOSE GODDAM CANS OF BACTERIA?
YES—I SAW THEM! GOT TO TELL THE LADY— NO SHOOTING!
YOU TELL HER WE LOST THE BOMBS AND SHE'LL KILL US!
9934 A
MAYBE— BUT IF SOME-BODY BUSTS ONE OPEN WITH A BULLET, WE ALL DIE SLOW AND UGLY

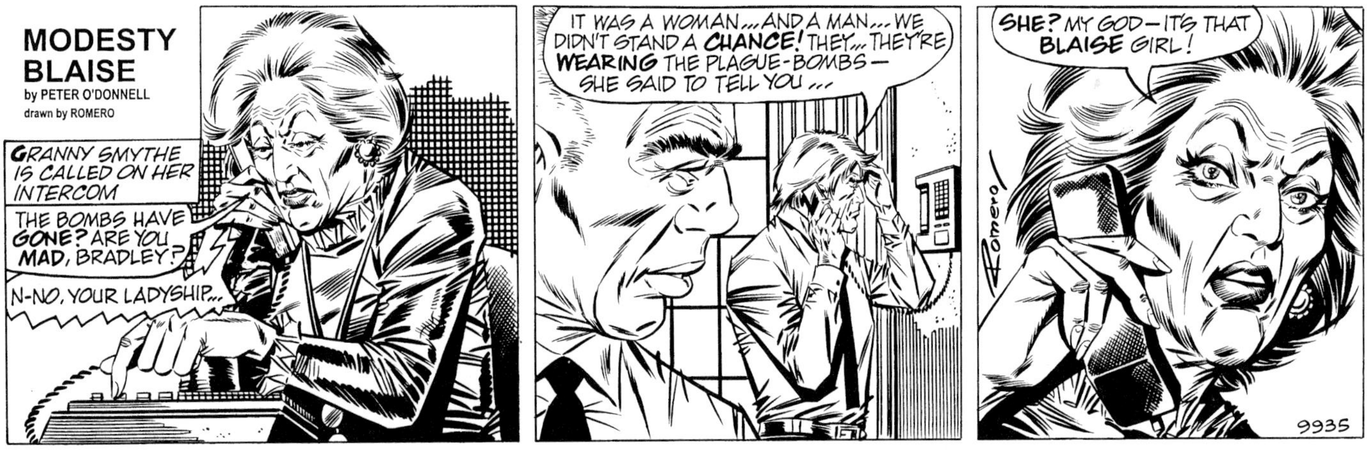
MODESTY BLAISE
by PETER O'DONNELL
drawn by ROMERO
GRANNY SMYTHE IS CALLED ON HER INTERCOM
THE BOMBS HAVE GONE? ARE YOU MAD, BRADLEY?
N-NO, YOUR LADYSHIP...
IT WAS A WOMAN... AND A MAN... WE DIDN'T STAND A CHANCE! THEY... THEY'RE WEARING THE PLAGUE-BOMBS— SHE SAID TO TELL YOU...
Romero
SHE? MY GOD—IT'S THAT BLAISE GIRL!
9935

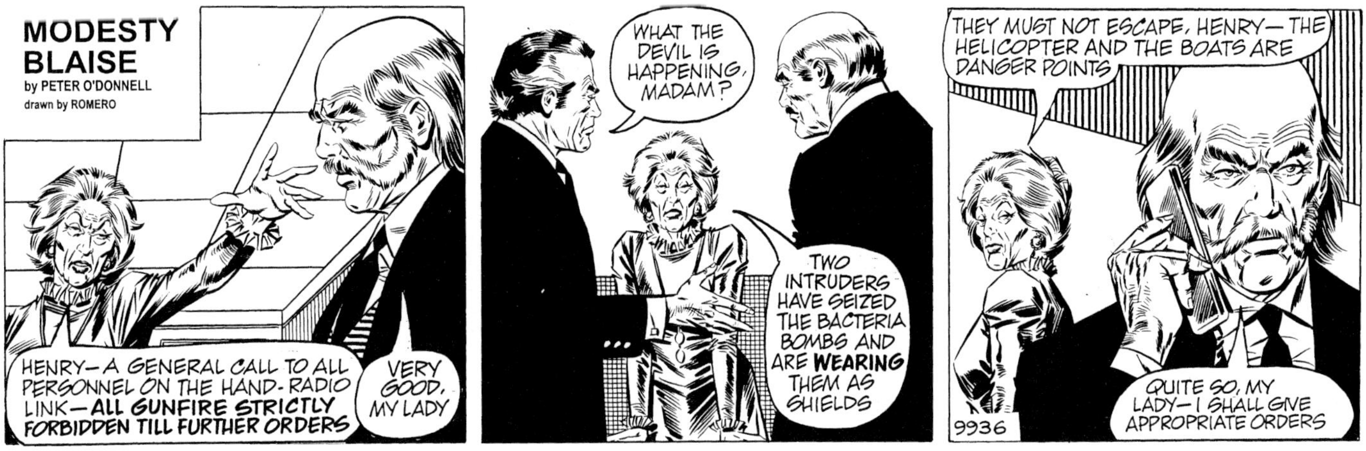
MODESTY BLAISE
by PETER O'DONNELL
drawn by ROMERO
HENRY—A GENERAL CALL TO ALL PERSONNEL ON THE HAND-RADIO LINK—ALL GUNFIRE STRICTLY FORBIDDEN TILL FURTHER ORDERS
VERY GOOD, MY LADY
WHAT THE DEVIL IS HAPPENING, MADAM?
TWO INTRUDERS HAVE SEIZED THE BACTERIA BOMBS AND ARE WEARING THEM AS SHIELDS
THEY MUST NOT ESCAPE, HENRY—THE HELICOPTER AND THE BOATS ARE DANGER POINTS
QUITE SO, MY LADY—I SHALL GIVE APPROPRIATE ORDERS
9936

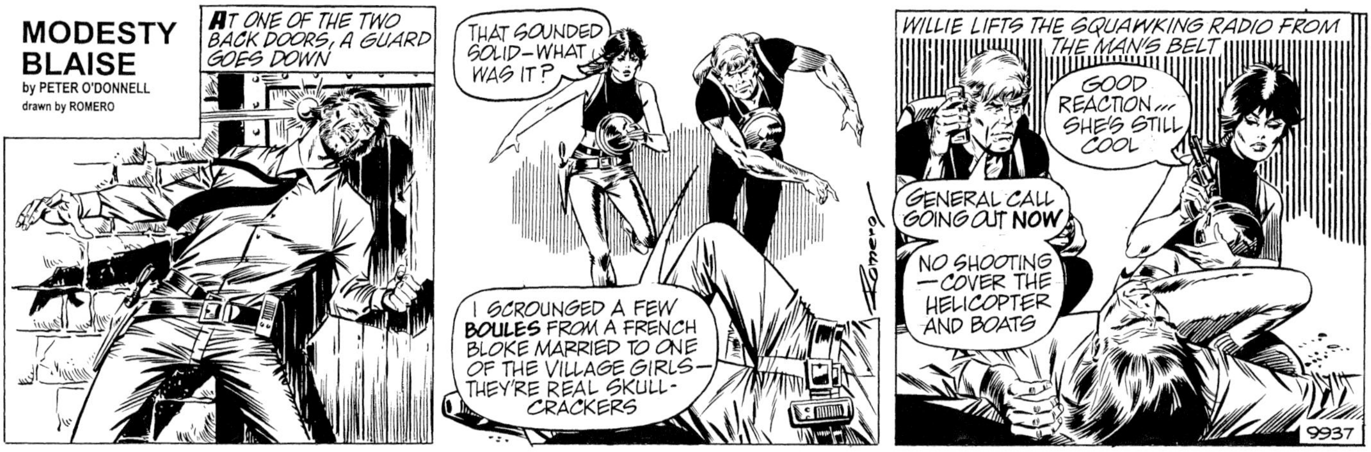
MODESTY BLAISE
by PETER O'DONNELL
drawn by ROMERO
AT ONE OF THE TWO BACK DOORS, A GUARD GOES DOWN
THAT SOUNDED SOLID—WHAT WAS IT?
I SCROUNGED A FEW BOULES FROM A FRENCH BLOKE MARRIED TO ONE OF THE VILLAGE GIRLS—THEY'RE REAL SKULL-CRACKERS
WILLIE LIFTS THE SQUAWKING RADIO FROM THE MAN'S BELT
GOOD REACTION... SHE'S STILL COOL
GENERAL CALL GOING OUT NOW
NO SHOOTING —COVER THE HELICOPTER AND BOATS
9937

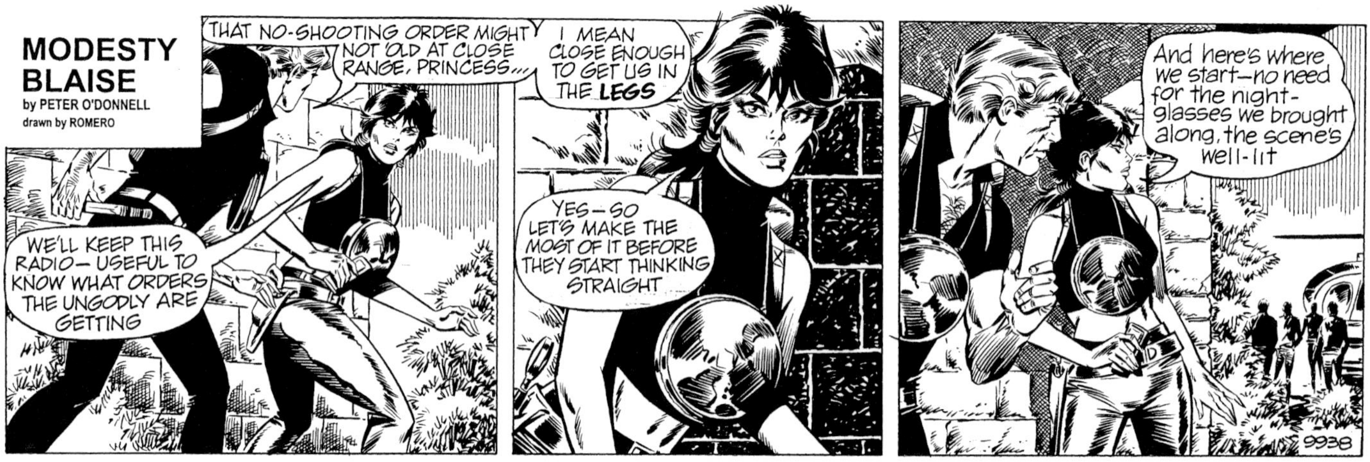
MODESTY BLAISE
by PETER O'DONNELL
drawn by ROMERO
THAT NO-SHOOTING ORDER MIGHT NOT 'OLD AT CLOSE RANGE, PRINCESS...
WE'LL KEEP THIS RADIO— USEFUL TO KNOW WHAT ORDERS THE UNGODLY ARE GETTING
I MEAN CLOSE ENOUGH TO GET US IN THE LEGS
YES—SO LET'S MAKE THE MOST OF IT BEFORE THEY START THINKING STRAIGHT
And here's where we start—no need for the night-glasses we brought along, the scene's well-lit
9938

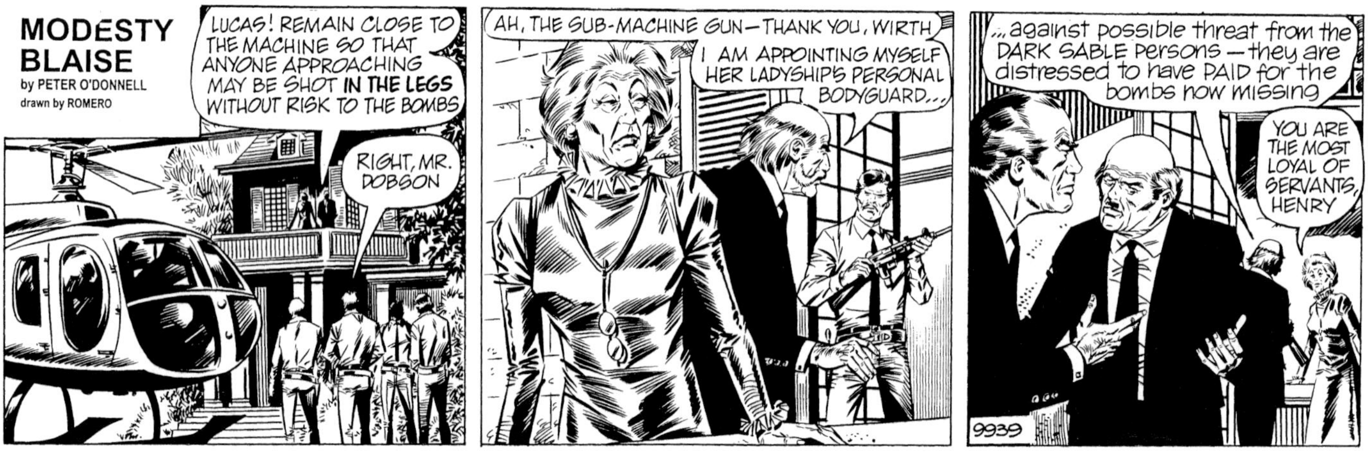
MODESTY BLAISE
by PETER O'DONNELL
drawn by ROMERO
LUCAS! REMAIN CLOSE TO THE MACHINE SO THAT ANYONE APPROACHING MAY BE SHOT IN THE LEGS WITHOUT RISK TO THE BOMBS
RIGHT, MR. DOBSON
AH, THE SUB-MACHINE GUN—THANK YOU, WIRTH
I AM APPOINTING MYSELF HER LADYSHIP'S PERSONAL BODYGUARD...
...against possible threat from the DARK SABLE persons —they are distressed to have PAID for the bombs now missing
YOU ARE THE MOST LOYAL OF SERVANTS, HENRY
9939

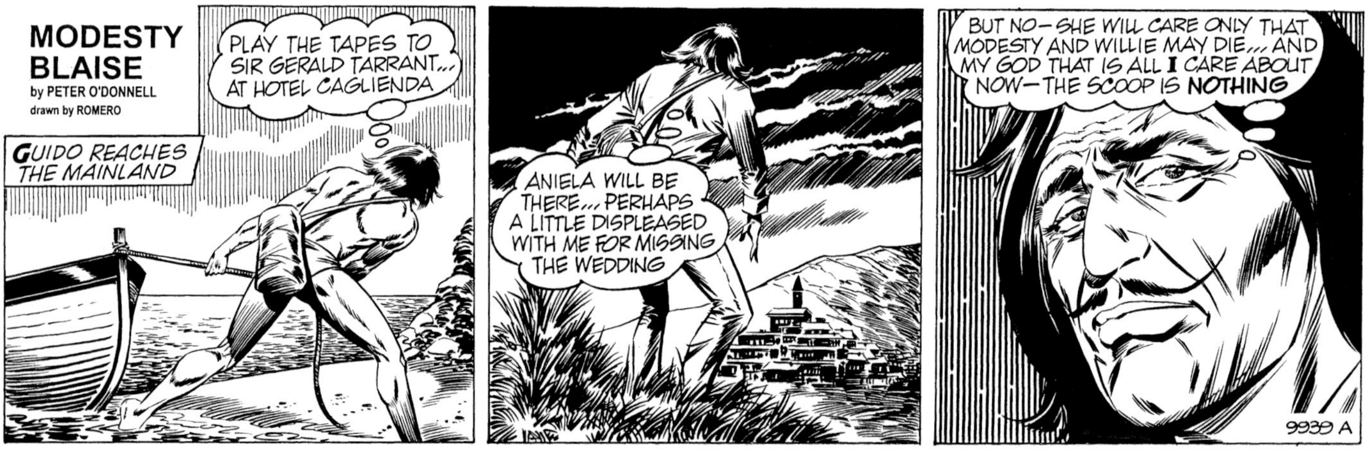
MODESTY BLAISE
by PETER O'DONNELL
drawn by ROMERO
PLAY THE TAPES TO SIR GERALD TARRANT... AT HOTEL CAGLIENDA
GUIDO REACHES THE MAINLAND
ANIELA WILL BE THERE... PERHAPS A LITTLE DISPLEASED WITH ME FOR MISSING THE WEDDING
BUT NO—SHE WILL CARE ONLY THAT MODESTY AND WILLIE MAY DIE... AND MY GOD THAT IS ALL I CARE ABOUT NOW—THE SCOOP IS NOTHING
9939 A

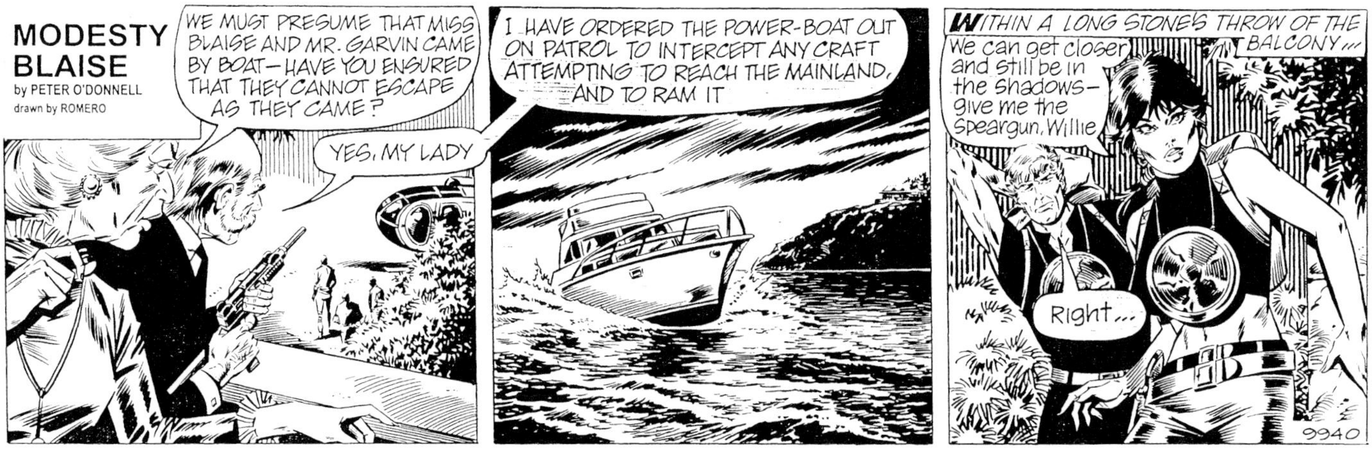
MODESTY BLAISE
by PETER O'DONNELL
drawn by ROMERO
WE MUST PRESUME THAT MISS BLAISE AND MR. GARVIN CAME BY BOAT—HAVE YOU ENSURED THAT THEY CANNOT ESCAPE AS THEY CAME?
YES, MY LADY
I HAVE ORDERED THE POWER-BOAT OUT ON PATROL TO INTERCEPT ANY CRAFT ATTEMPTING TO REACH THE MAINLAND, AND TO RAM IT
WITHIN A LONG STONE'S THROW OF THE BALCONY...
We can get closer and still be in the shadows—give me the Speargun, Willie
Right...
9940

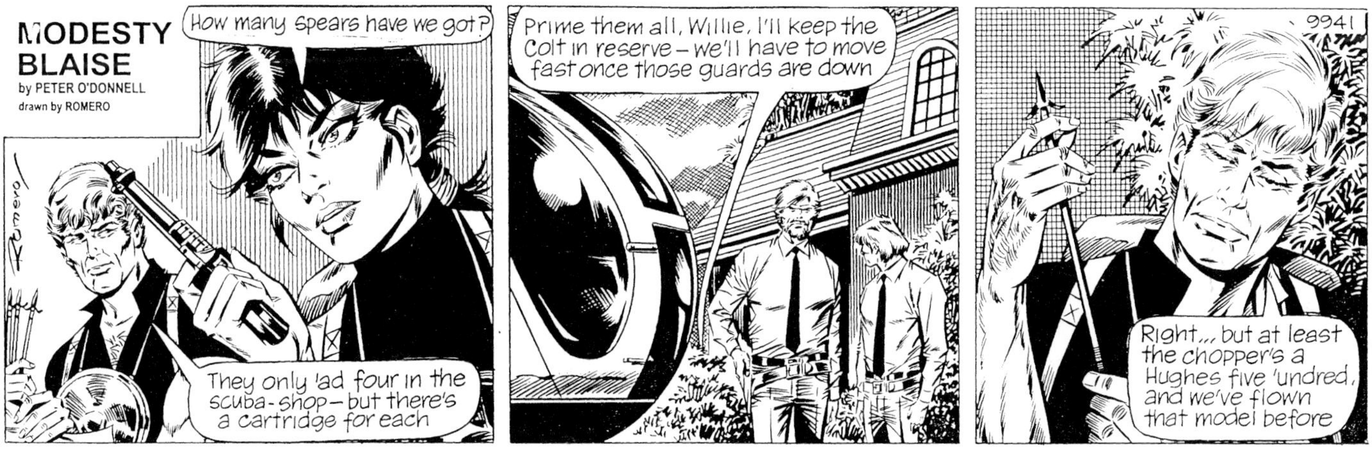
MODESTY BLAISE
by PETER O'DONNELL
drawn by ROMERO
How many spears have we got?
They only 'ad four in the scuba-shop—but there's a cartridge for each
Prime them all, Willie, I'll keep the Colt in reserve—we'll have to move fast once those guards are down
9941
Right... but at least the chopper's a Hughes five 'undred, and we've flown that model before

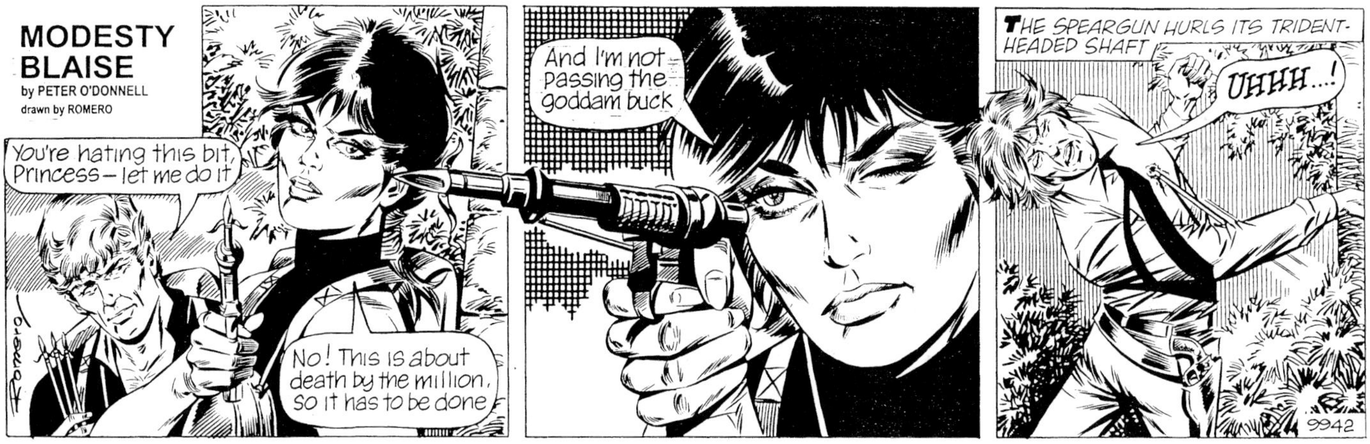
MODESTY BLAISE
by PETER O'DONNELL
drawn by ROMERO
You're hating this bit, Princess—let me do it
No! This is about death by the million, so it has to be done
And I'm not passing the goddam buck
THE SPEARGUN HURLS ITS TRIDENT-HEADED SHAFT
UHHH...!
9942

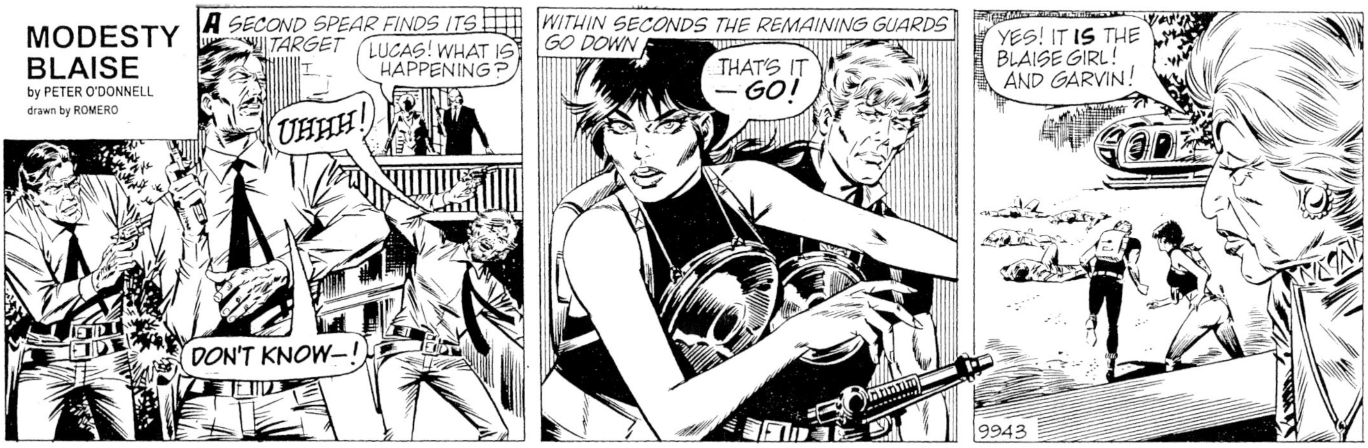
MODESTY BLAISE
by PETER O'DONNELL
drawn by ROMERO
A SECOND SPEAR FINDS ITS TARGET
LUCAS! WHAT IS HAPPENING?
UHHH!
DON'T KNOW—!
WITHIN SECONDS THE REMAINING GUARDS GO DOWN
THAT'S IT —GO!
YES! IT IS THE BLAISE GIRL! AND GARVIN!
9943

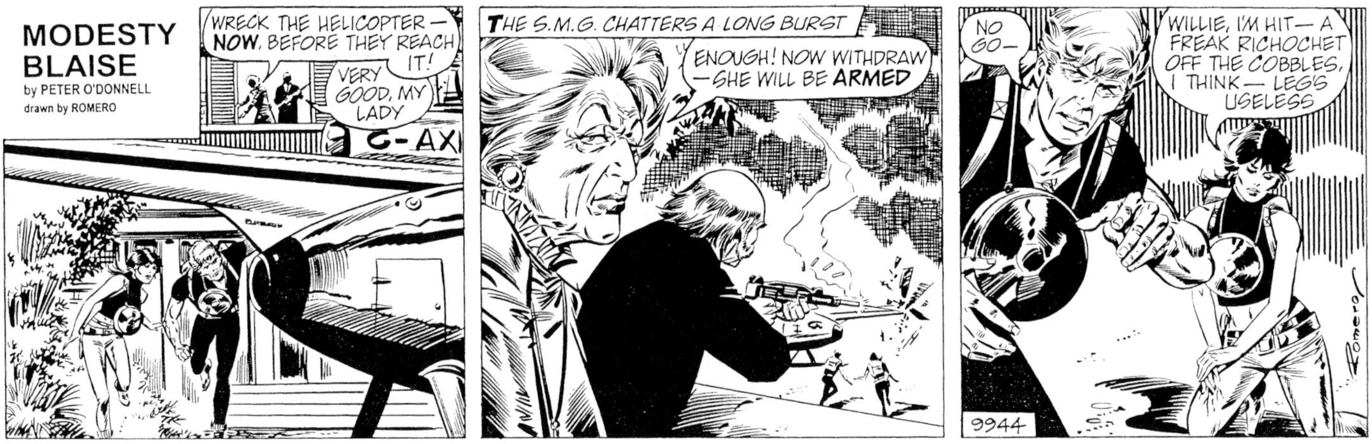
MODESTY BLAISE
by PETER O'DONNELL
drawn by ROMERO
WRECK THE HELICOPTER — NOW, BEFORE THEY REACH IT!
VERY GOOD, MY LADY
G-AX
THE S.M.G. CHATTERS A LONG BURST
ENOUGH! NOW WITHDRAW — SHE WILL BE ARMED
NO GO—
WILLIE, I'M HIT— A FREAK RICHOCHET OFF THE COBBLES, I THINK— LEG'S USELESS
Romero
9944

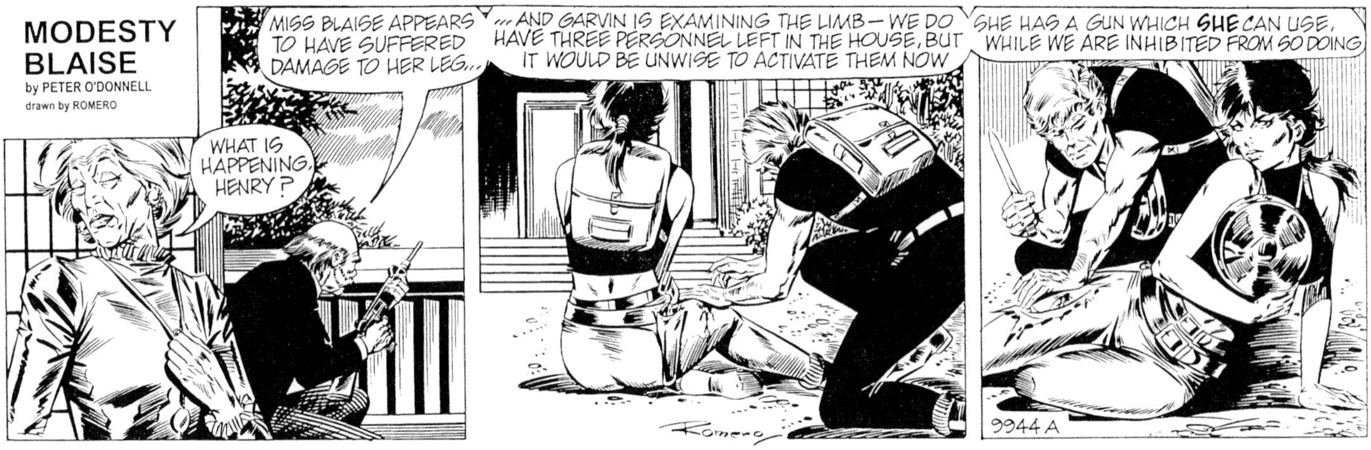
MODESTY BLAISE
by PETER O'DONNELL
drawn by ROMERO
WHAT IS HAPPENING, HENRY?
MISS BLAISE APPEARS TO HAVE SUFFERED DAMAGE TO HER LEG...
...AND GARVIN IS EXAMINING THE LIMB — WE DO HAVE THREE PERSONNEL LEFT IN THE HOUSE, BUT IT WOULD BE UNWISE TO ACTIVATE THEM NOW
SHE HAS A GUN WHICH SHE CAN USE, WHILE WE ARE INHIBITED FROM SO DOING
Romero
9944 A

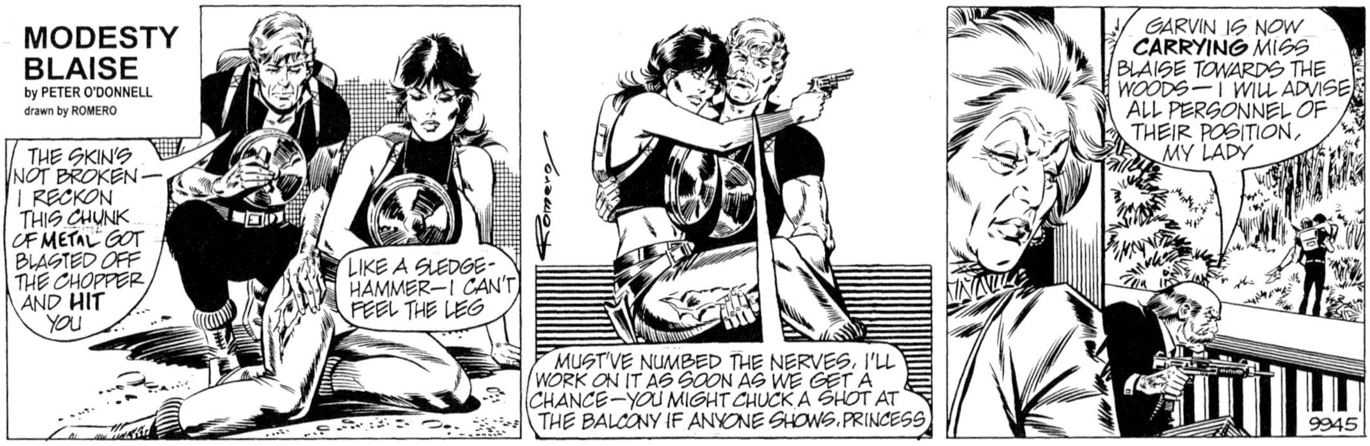
MODESTY BLAISE
by PETER O'DONNELL
drawn by ROMERO
THE SKIN'S NOT BROKEN — I RECKON THIS CHUNK OF METAL GOT BLASTED OFF THE CHOPPER AND HIT YOU
LIKE A SLEDGE-HAMMER— I CAN'T FEEL THE LEG
Romero
MUST'VE NUMBED THE NERVES. I'LL WORK ON IT AS SOON AS WE GET A CHANCE—YOU MIGHT CHUCK A SHOT AT THE BALCONY IF ANYONE SHOWS, PRINCESS
GARVIN IS NOW CARRYING MISS BLAISE TOWARDS THE WOODS — I WILL ADVISE ALL PERSONNEL OF THEIR POSITION, MY LADY
9945

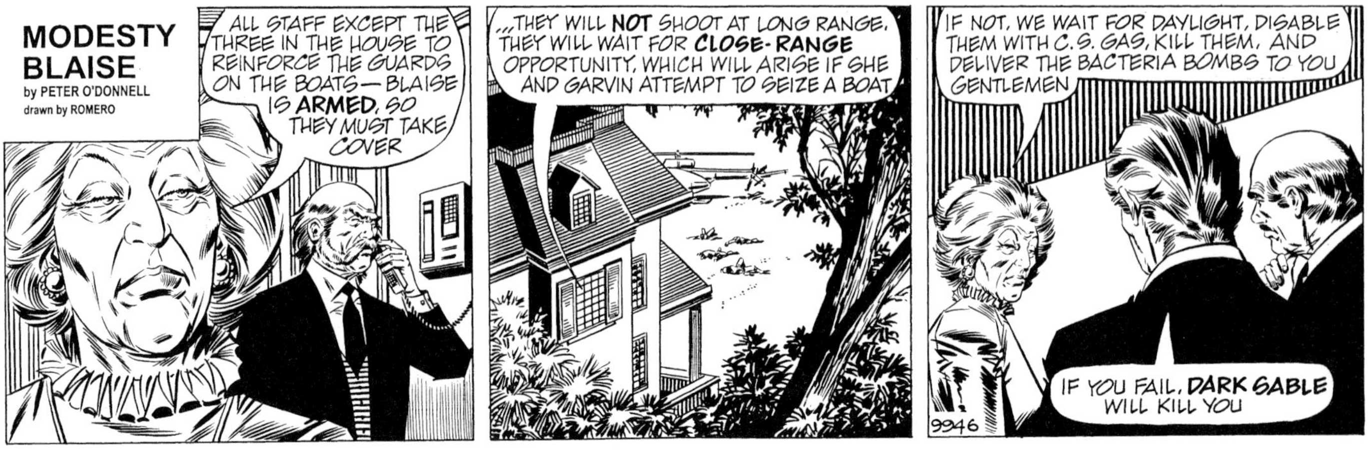
MODESTY BLAISE
by PETER O'DONNELL
drawn by ROMERO
ALL STAFF EXCEPT THE THREE IN THE HOUSE TO REINFORCE THE GUARDS ON THE BOATS — BLAISE IS ARMED, SO THEY MUST TAKE COVER
...THEY WILL NOT SHOOT AT LONG RANGE. THEY WILL WAIT FOR CLOSE-RANGE OPPORTUNITY, WHICH WILL ARISE IF SHE AND GARVIN ATTEMPT TO SEIZE A BOAT
IF NOT, WE WAIT FOR DAYLIGHT, DISABLE THEM WITH C.S. GAS, KILL THEM, AND DELIVER THE BACTERIA BOMBS TO YOU GENTLEMEN
IF YOU FAIL, DARK SABLE WILL KILL YOU
9946

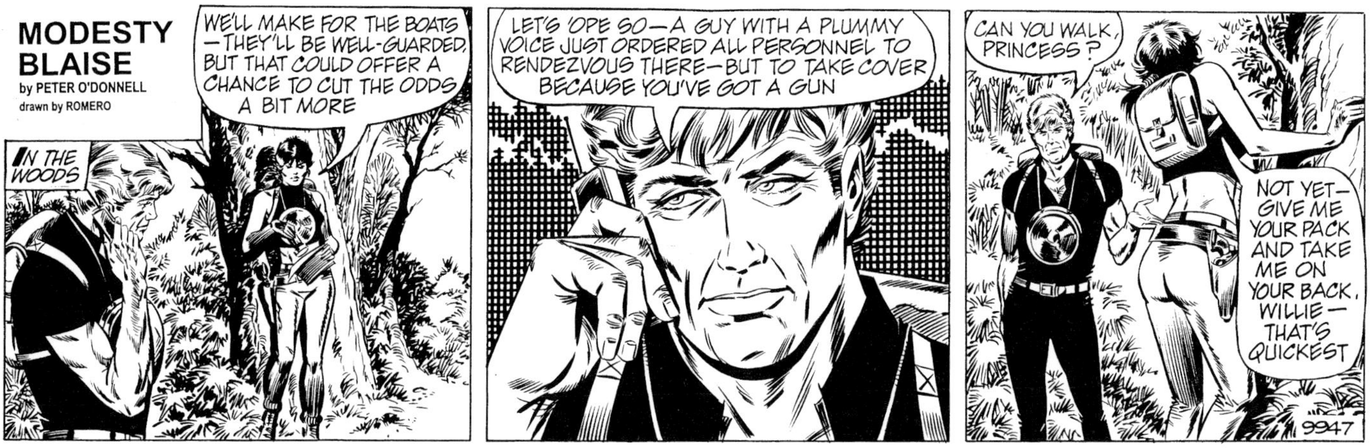
MODESTY BLAISE
by PETER O'DONNELL
drawn by ROMERO
IN THE WOODS
WE'LL MAKE FOR THE BOATS —THEY'LL BE WELL-GUARDED, BUT THAT COULD OFFER A CHANCE TO CUT THE ODDS A BIT MORE
LET'S 'OPE SO—A GUY WITH A PLUMMY VOICE JUST ORDERED ALL PERSONNEL TO RENDEZVOUS THERE—BUT TO TAKE COVER BECAUSE YOU'VE GOT A GUN
CAN YOU WALK, PRINCESS ?
NOT YET-GIVE ME YOUR PACK AND TAKE ME ON YOUR BACK, WILLIE—THAT'S QUICKEST
9947

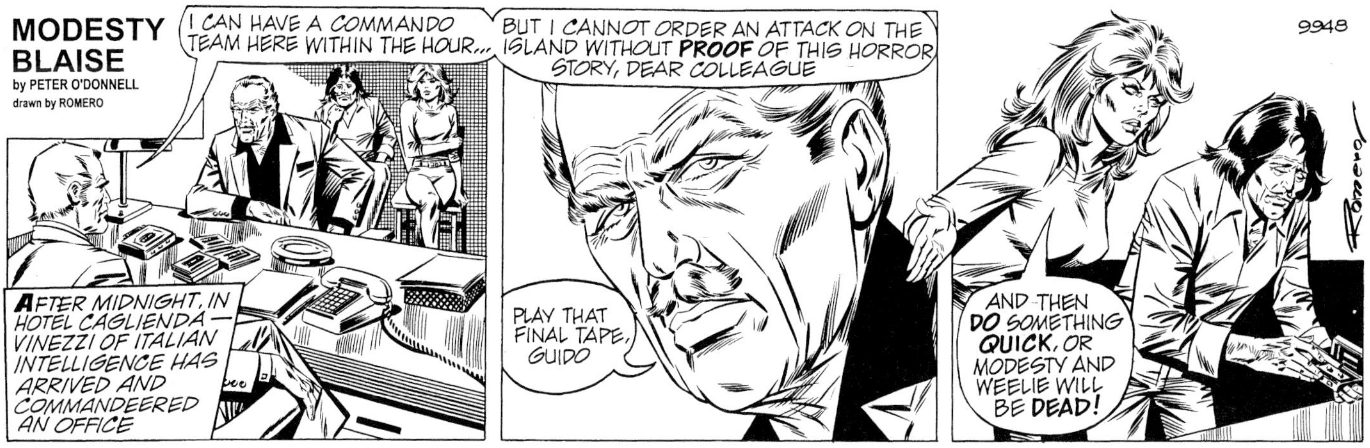
MODESTY BLAISE
by PETER O'DONNELL
drawn by ROMERO
AFTER MIDNIGHT, IN HOTEL CAGLIENDA—VINEZZI OF ITALIAN INTELLIGENCE HAS ARRIVED AND COMMANDEERED AN OFFICE
I CAN HAVE A COMMANDO TEAM HERE WITHIN THE HOUR...
BUT I CANNOT ORDER AN ATTACK ON THE ISLAND WITHOUT PROOF OF THIS HORROR STORY, DEAR COLLEAGUE
PLAY THAT FINAL TAPE, GUIDO
9948
AND THEN DO SOMETHING QUICK, OR MODESTY AND WEELIE WILL BE DEAD!
Romero

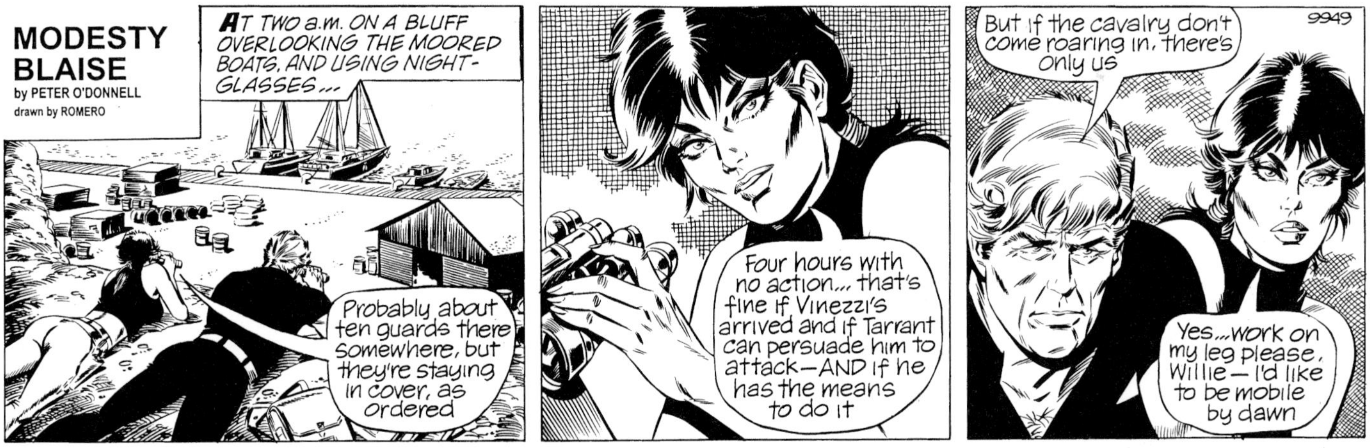
MODESTY BLAISE
by PETER O'DONNELL
drawn by ROMERO
AT TWO a.m. ON A BLUFF OVERLOOKING THE MOORED BOATS, AND USING NIGHT-GLASSES...
Probably about ten guards there somewhere, but they're staying in cover, as ordered
Four hours with no action... that's fine if Vinezzi's arrived and if Tarrant can persuade him to attack—AND if he has the means to do it
9949
But if the cavalry don't come roaring in, there's only us
Yes...work on my leg please, Willie—I'd like to be mobile by dawn

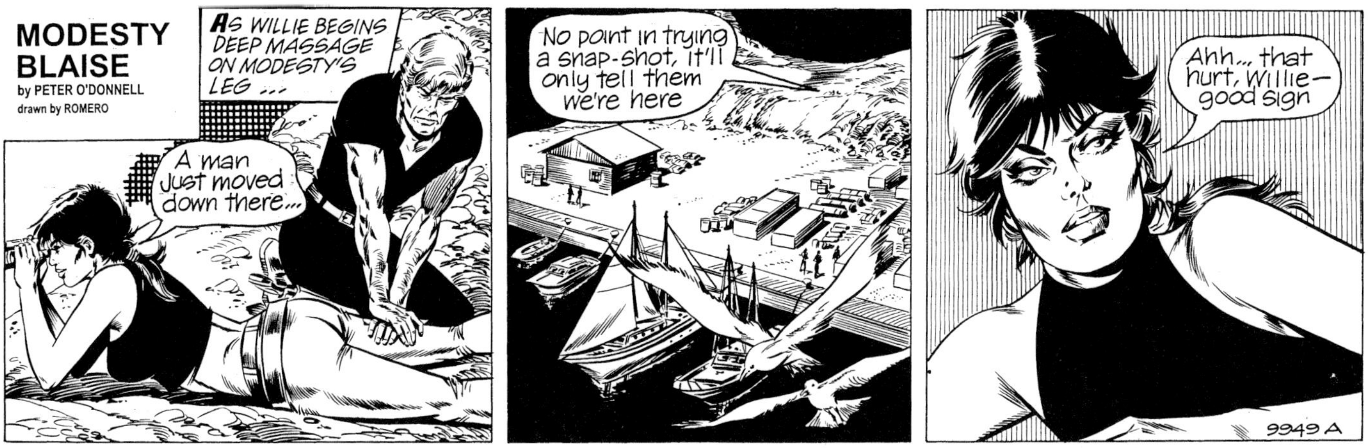
MODESTY BLAISE
by PETER O'DONNELL
drawn by ROMERO
AS WILLIE BEGINS DEEP MASSAGE ON MODESTY'S LEG ...
A man just moved down there...
No point in trying a snap-shot, it'll only tell them we're here
Ahh... that hurt, Willie—good sign
9949 A

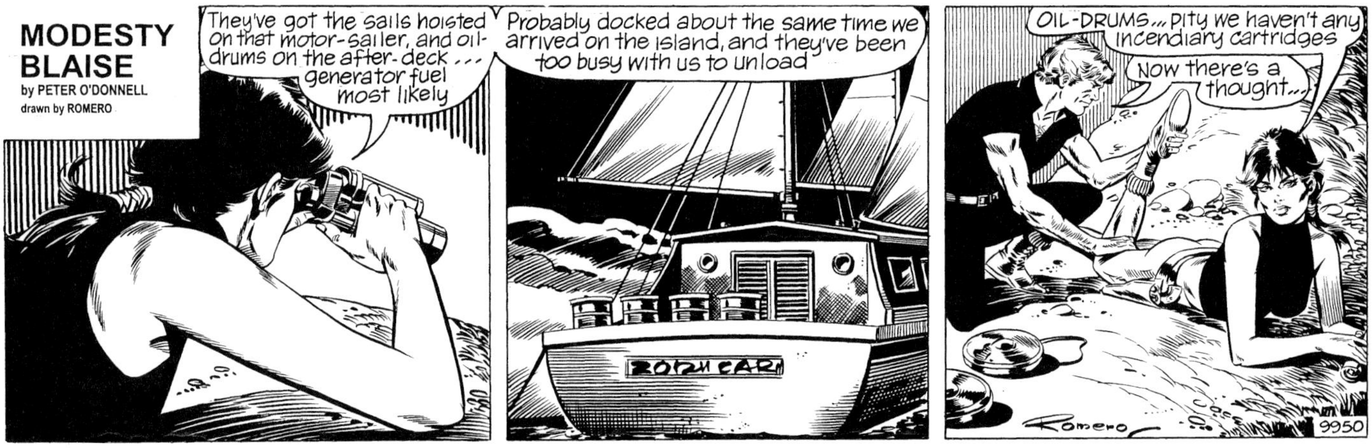
MODESTY BLAISE
by PETER O'DONNELL
drawn by ROMERO
They've got the sails hoisted on that motor-sailer, and oil-drums on the after-deck ... generator fuel most likely
Probably docked about the same time we arrived on the island, and they've been too busy with us to unload
OIL-DRUMS ... pity we haven't any incendiary cartridges
Now there's a thought ...
ROMERO
9950

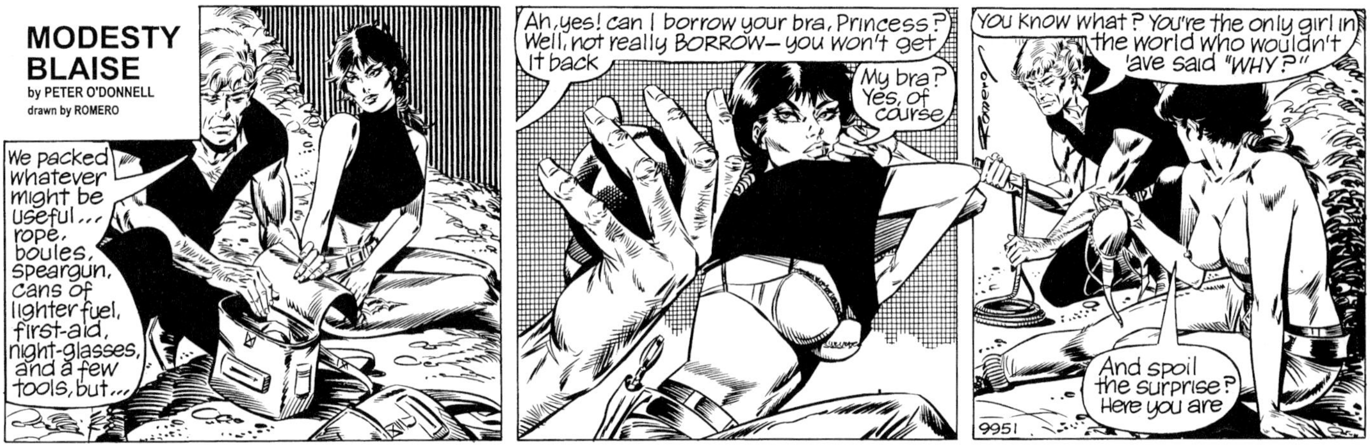
MODESTY BLAISE
by PETER O'DONNELL
drawn by ROMERO
We packed whatever might be useful ... rope, boules, speargun, cans of lighter-fuel, first-aid, night-glasses, and a few tools, but ...
Ah, yes! can I borrow your bra, Princess? Well, not really BORROW — you won't get it back
My bra? Yes, of course
You know what? You're the only girl in the world who wouldn't 'ave said "WHY?"
And spoil the surprise? Here you are
9951

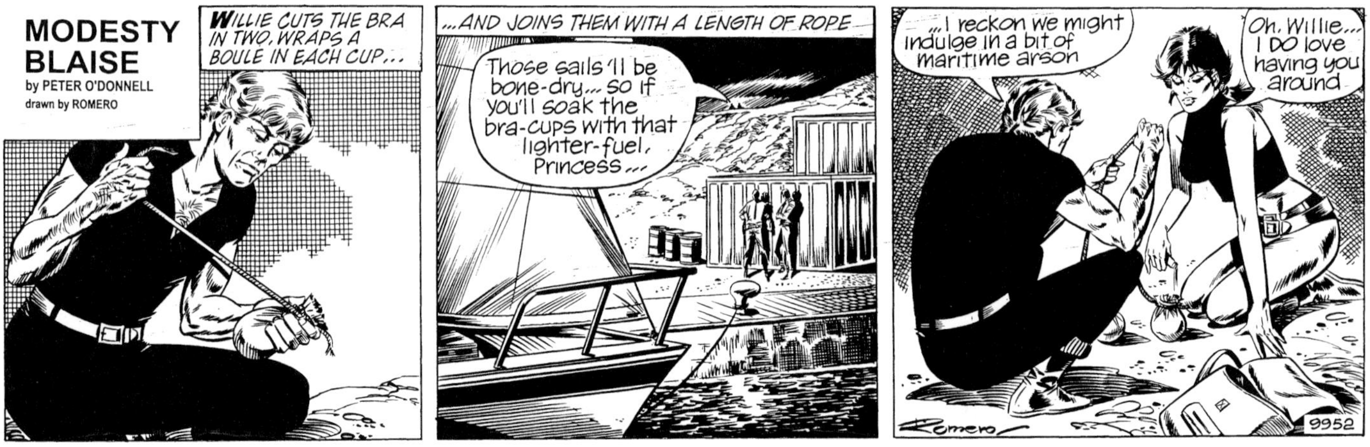
MODESTY BLAISE
by PETER O'DONNELL
drawn by ROMERO
WILLIE CUTS THE BRA IN TWO, WRAPS A BOULE IN EACH CUP ...
... AND JOINS THEM WITH A LENGTH OF ROPE
Those sails'll be bone-dry ... so if you'll soak the bra-cups with that lighter-fuel, Princess ...
... I reckon we might indulge in a bit of maritime arson
Oh, Willie ... I DO love having you around
ROMERO
9952

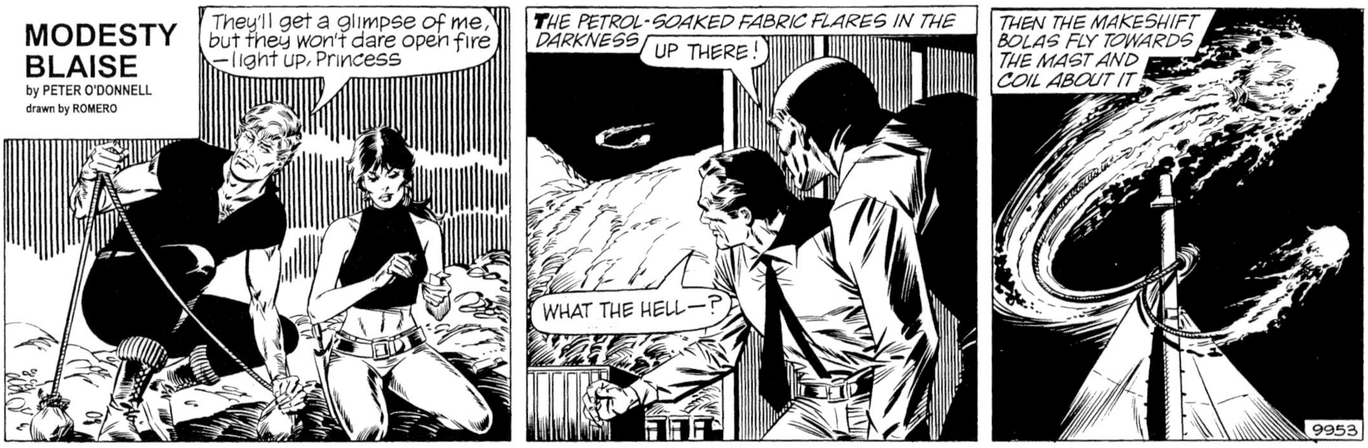
MODESTY BLAISE
by PETER O'DONNELL
drawn by ROMERO
They'll get a glimpse of me, but they won't dare open fire — light up, Princess
THE PETROL-SOAKED FABRIC FLARES IN THE DARKNESS
UP THERE!
WHAT THE HELL—?
THEN THE MAKESHIFT BOLAS FLY TOWARDS THE MAST AND COIL ABOUT IT
9953

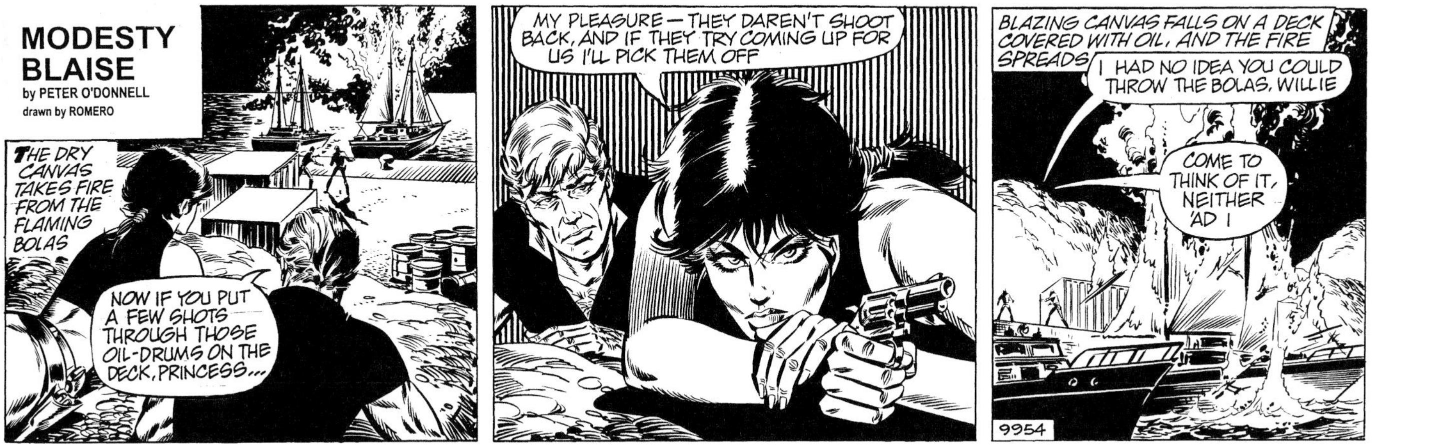
MODESTY BLAISE
by PETER O'DONNELL
drawn by ROMERO
THE DRY CANVAS TAKES FIRE FROM THE FLAMING BOLAS
NOW IF YOU PUT A FEW SHOTS THROUGH THOSE OIL-DRUMS ON THE DECK, PRINCESS...
MY PLEASURE — THEY DAREN'T SHOOT BACK, AND IF THEY TRY COMING UP FOR US I'LL PICK THEM OFF
BLAZING CANVAS FALLS ON A DECK COVERED WITH OIL, AND THE FIRE SPREADS
I HAD NO IDEA YOU COULD THROW THE BOLAS, WILLIE
COME TO THINK OF IT, NEITHER 'AD I
9954

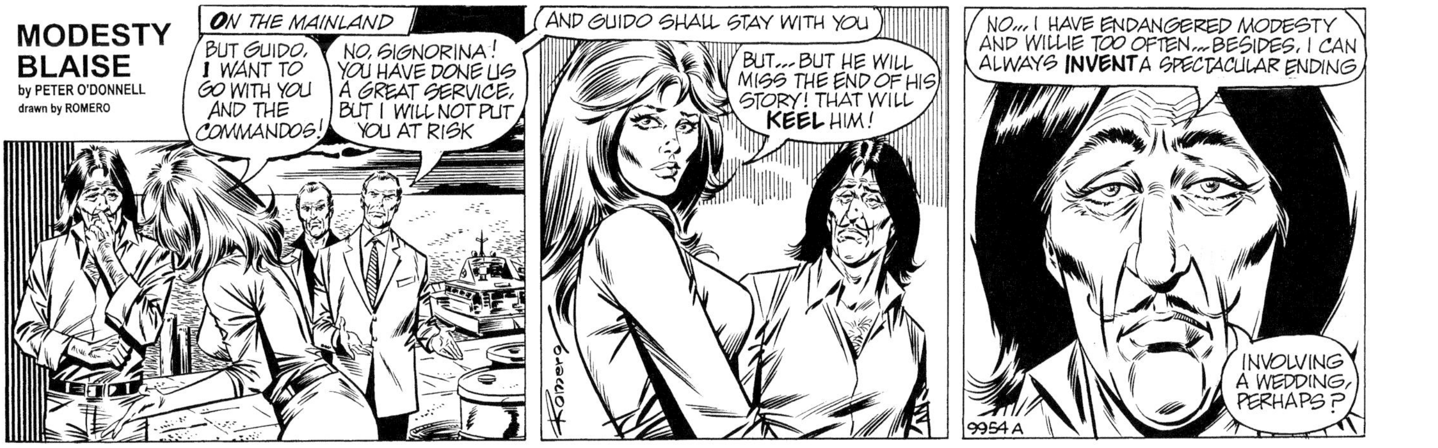
MODESTY BLAISE
by PETER O'DONNELL
drawn by ROMERO
ON THE MAINLAND
BUT GUIDO, I WANT TO GO WITH YOU AND THE COMMANDOS!
NO, SIGNORINA! YOU HAVE DONE US A GREAT SERVICE, BUT I WILL NOT PUT YOU AT RISK
AND GUIDO SHALL STAY WITH YOU
BUT... BUT HE WILL MISS THE END OF HIS STORY! THAT WILL KEEL HIM!
NO... I HAVE ENDANGERED MODESTY AND WILLIE TOO OFTEN... BESIDES, I CAN ALWAYS INVENT A SPECTACULAR ENDING
INVOLVING A WEDDING, PERHAPS?
9954 A

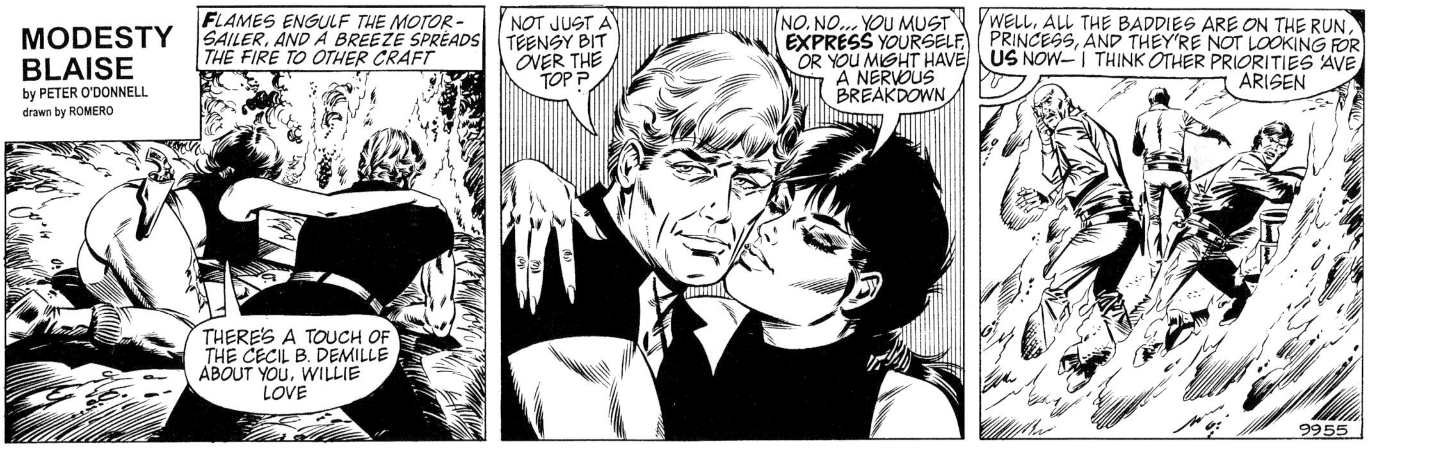
MODESTY BLAISE
by PETER O'DONNELL
drawn by ROMERO
FLAMES ENGULF THE MOTOR-SAILER, AND A BREEZE SPREADS THE FIRE TO OTHER CRAFT
THERE'S A TOUCH OF THE CECIL B. DEMILLE ABOUT YOU, WILLIE LOVE
NOT JUST A TEENSY BIT OVER THE TOP?
NO, NO... YOU MUST EXPRESS YOURSELF, OR YOU MIGHT HAVE A NERVOUS BREAKDOWN
WELL, ALL THE BADDIES ARE ON THE RUN, PRINCESS, AND THEY'RE NOT LOOKING FOR US NOW— I THINK OTHER PRIORITIES 'AVE ARISEN
9955

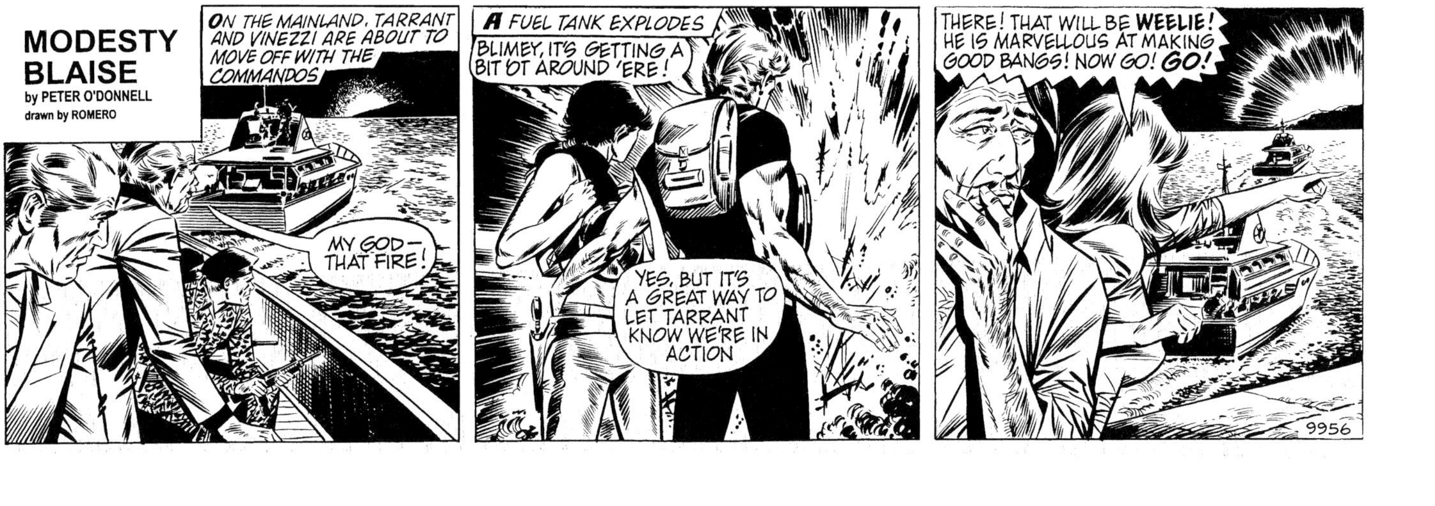
MODESTY BLAISE
by PETER O'DONNELL
drawn by ROMERO
ON THE MAINLAND, TARRANT AND VINEZZI ARE ABOUT TO MOVE OFF WITH THE COMMANDOS
MY GOD — THAT FIRE!
A FUEL TANK EXPLODES
BLIMEY, IT'S GETTING A BIT 'OT AROUND 'ERE!
YES, BUT IT'S A GREAT WAY TO LET TARRANT KNOW WE'RE IN ACTION
THERE! THAT WILL BE WEELIE! HE IS MARVELLOUS AT MAKING GOOD BANGS! NOW GO! GO!
9956

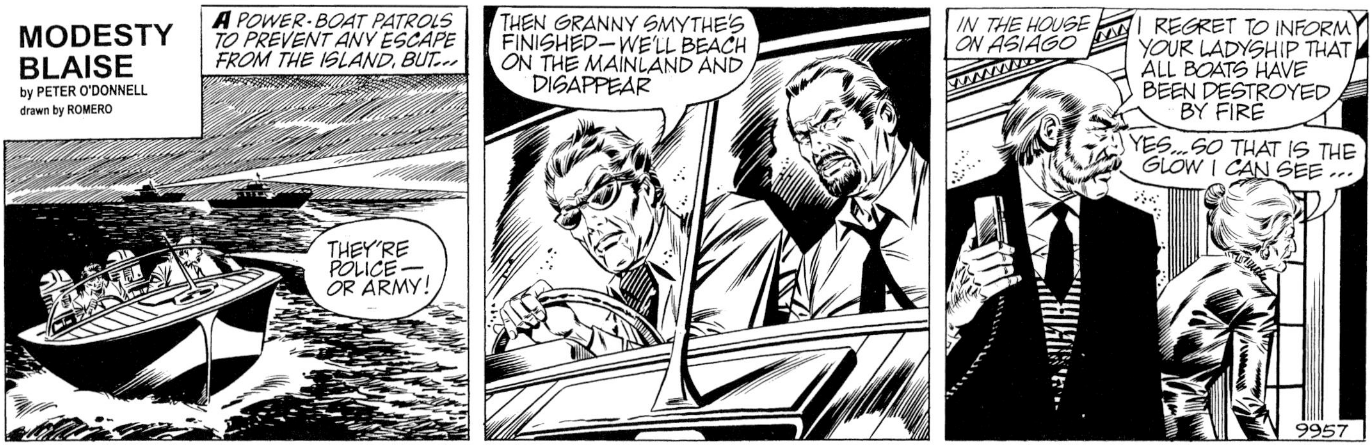
MODESTY BLAISE
by PETER O'DONNELL
drawn by ROMERO
A POWER-BOAT PATROLS TO PREVENT ANY ESCAPE FROM THE ISLAND, BUT...
THEY'RE POLICE — OR ARMY!
THEN GRANNY SMYTHE'S FINISHED — WE'LL BEACH ON THE MAINLAND AND DISAPPEAR
IN THE HOUSE ON ASIAGO
I REGRET TO INFORM YOUR LADYSHIP THAT ALL BOATS HAVE BEEN DESTROYED BY FIRE
YES... SO THAT IS THE GLOW I CAN SEE...
9957

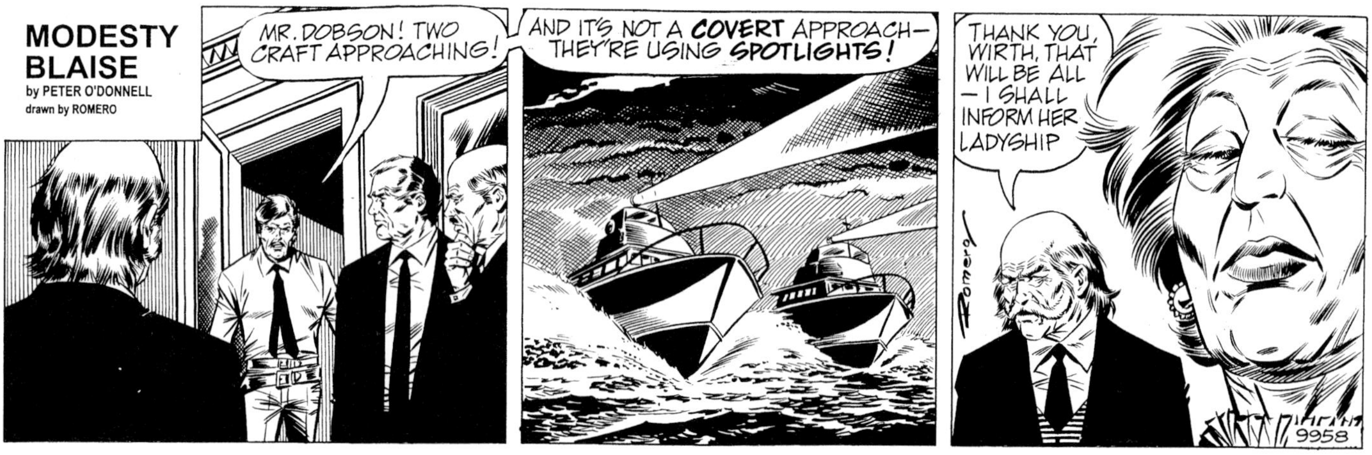
MODESTY BLAISE
by PETER O'DONNELL
drawn by ROMERO
MR. DOBSON! TWO CRAFT APPROACHING!
AND IT'S NOT A **COVERT** APPROACH — THEY'RE USING **SPOTLIGHTS**!
THANK YOU, WIRTH, THAT WILL BE ALL — I SHALL INFORM HER LADYSHIP
Romero
9958

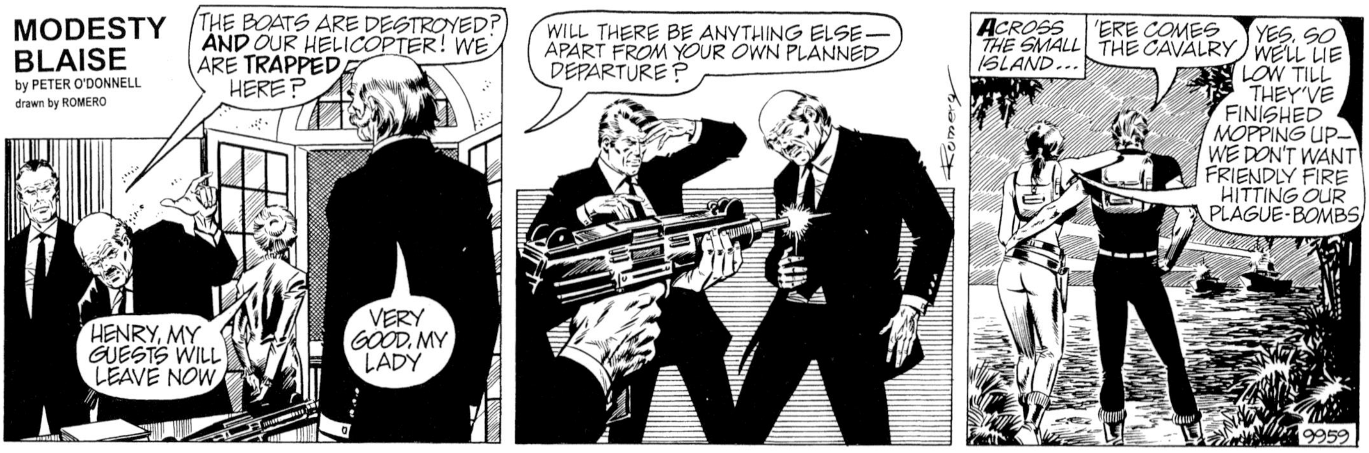
MODESTY BLAISE
by PETER O'DONNELL
drawn by ROMERO
THE BOATS ARE DESTROYED? **AND** OUR HELICOPTER! WE ARE **TRAPPED** HERE?
HENRY, MY GUESTS WILL LEAVE NOW
VERY GOOD, MY LADY
WILL THERE BE ANYTHING ELSE — APART FROM YOUR OWN PLANNED DEPARTURE?
Romero
ACROSS THE SMALL ISLAND...
'ERE COMES THE CAVALRY
YES, SO WE'LL LIE LOW TILL THEY'VE FINISHED MOPPING UP — WE DON'T WANT FRIENDLY FIRE HITTING OUR PLAGUE-BOMBS
9959

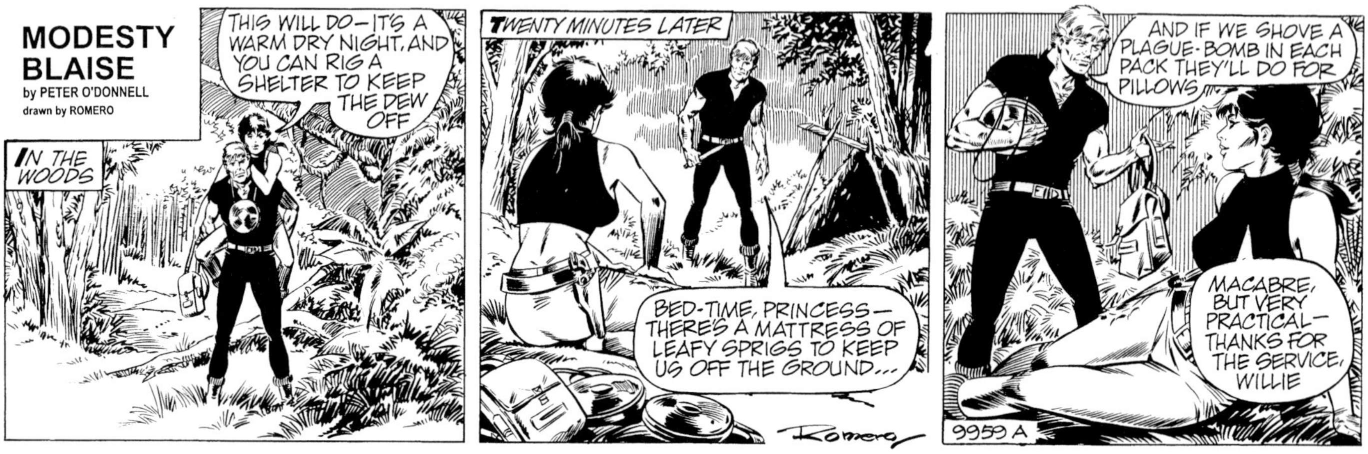
MODESTY BLAISE
by PETER O'DONNELL
drawn by ROMERO
THIS WILL DO — IT'S A WARM DRY NIGHT, AND YOU CAN RIG A SHELTER TO KEEP THE DEW OFF
IN THE WOODS
TWENTY MINUTES LATER
BED-TIME, PRINCESS — THERE'S A MATTRESS OF LEAFY SPRIGS TO KEEP US OFF THE GROUND...
Romero
AND IF WE SHOVE A PLAGUE-BOMB IN EACH PACK THEY'LL DO FOR PILLOWS
MACABRE, BUT VERY PRACTICAL — THANKS FOR THE SERVICE, WILLIE
9959 A

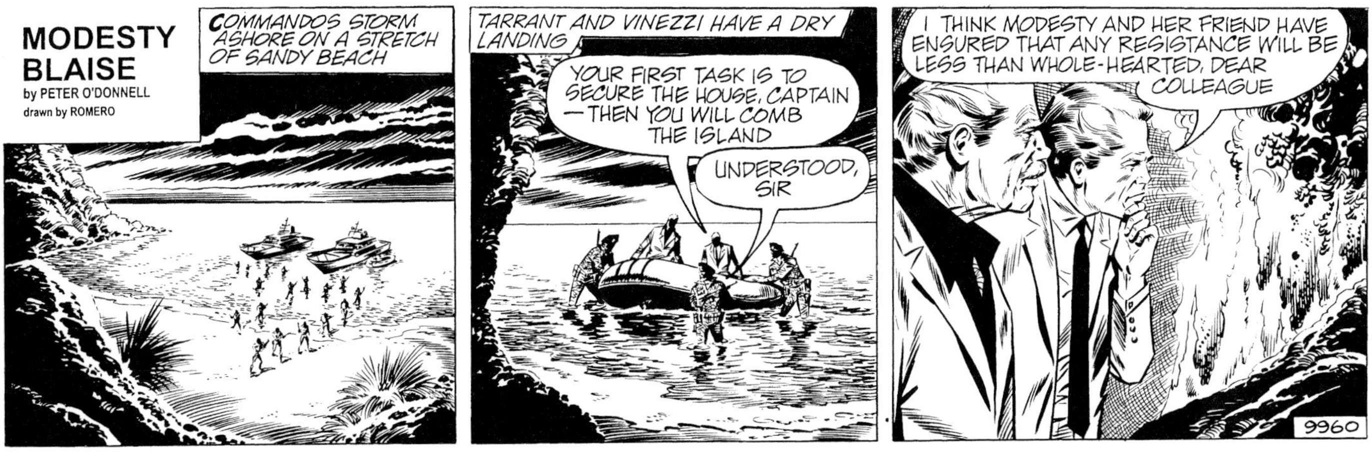
MODESTY BLAISE
by PETER O'DONNELL
drawn by ROMERO
COMMANDOS STORM ASHORE ON A STRETCH OF SANDY BEACH
TARRANT AND VINEZZI HAVE A DRY LANDING
YOUR FIRST TASK IS TO SECURE THE HOUSE, CAPTAIN — THEN YOU WILL COMB THE ISLAND
UNDERSTOOD, SIR
I THINK MODESTY AND HER FRIEND HAVE ENSURED THAT ANY RESISTANCE WILL BE LESS THAN WHOLE-HEARTED, DEAR COLLEAGUE
9960

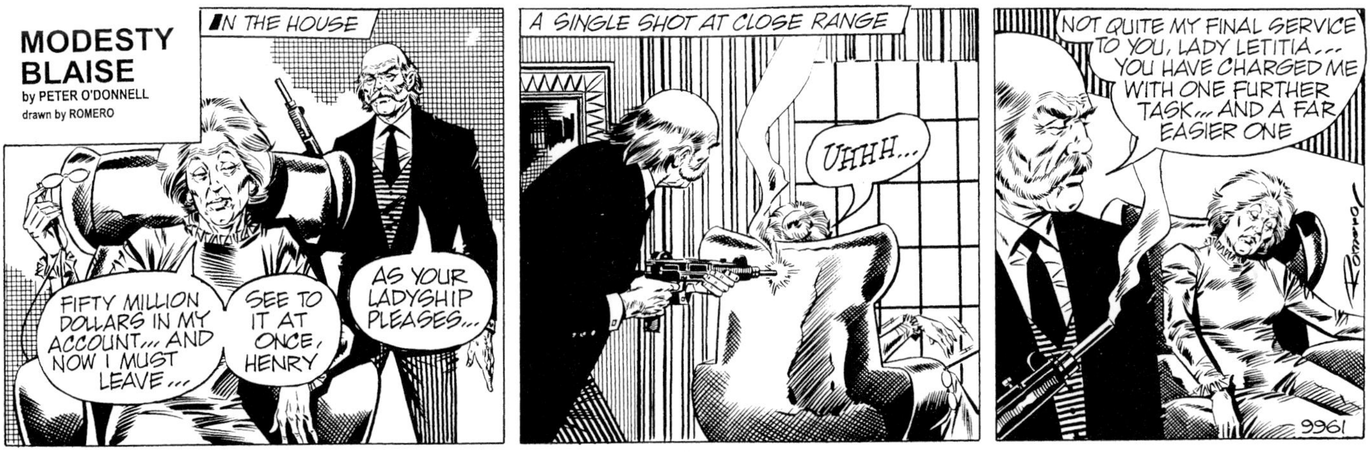
MODESTY BLAISE
by PETER O'DONNELL
drawn by ROMERO
IN THE HOUSE
FIFTY MILLION DOLLARS IN MY ACCOUNT,... AND NOW I MUST LEAVE...
SEE TO IT AT ONCE, HENRY
AS YOUR LADYSHIP PLEASES...
A SINGLE SHOT AT CLOSE RANGE
UHHH...
NOT QUITE MY FINAL SERVICE TO YOU, LADY LETITIA... YOU HAVE CHARGED ME WITH ONE FURTHER TASK... AND A FAR EASIER ONE
9961

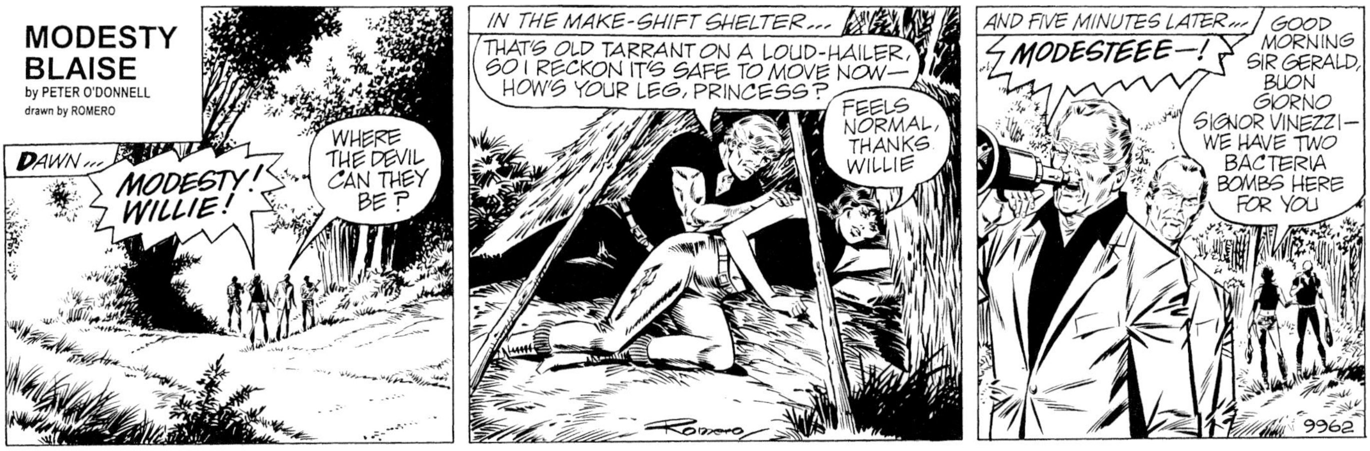
MODESTY BLAISE
by PETER O'DONNELL
drawn by ROMERO
DAWN...
MODESTY! WILLIE!
WHERE THE DEVIL CAN THEY BE?
IN THE MAKE-SHIFT SHELTER...
THAT'S OLD TARRANT ON A LOUD-HAILER, SO I RECKON IT'S SAFE TO MOVE NOW— HOW'S YOUR LEG, PRINCESS?
FEELS NORMAL, THANKS, WILLIE
AND FIVE MINUTES LATER...
MODESTEEE—!
GOOD MORNING SIR GERALD, BUON GIORNO SIGNOR VINEZZI— WE HAVE TWO BACTERIA BOMBS HERE FOR YOU
9962

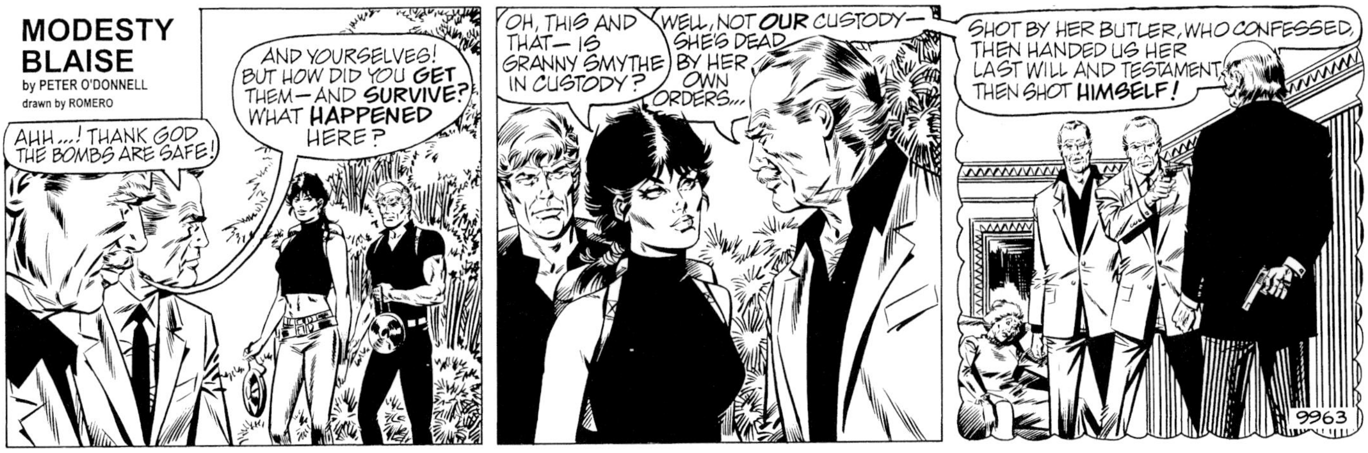
MODESTY BLAISE
by PETER O'DONNELL
drawn by ROMERO
AHH...! THANK GOD THE BOMBS ARE SAFE!
AND YOURSELVES! BUT HOW DID YOU GET THEM— AND SURVIVE? WHAT HAPPENED HERE?
OH, THIS AND THAT— IS GRANNY SMYTHE IN CUSTODY?
WELL, NOT OUR CUSTODY— SHE'S DEAD BY HER OWN ORDERS...
SHOT BY HER BUTLER, WHO CONFESSED, THEN HANDED US HER LAST WILL AND TESTAMENT, THEN SHOT HIMSELF!
9963

MODESTY BLAISE
by PETER O'DONNELL
drawn by ROMERO
A WEEK AFTER THE RETURN FROM ASIAGO, A POSTPONED WEDDING TAKES PLACE
I HOPE YOU DIDN'T SET TOO HIGH A STANDARD WHEN YOU HONEYMOONED WITH HER, WILLIE
I KNOW IT WAS BRIEF, BUT–
WHAT ARE YOU GOGGLING AT?
MESSAGE FROM VINEZZI, CAME AS WE LEFT THE 'OTEL. IT SAYS WE MIGHT LIKE TO KNOW...
...THAT GRANNY SMYTHE LEFT 'ER WHOLE FORTUNE TO ESTABLISH 'ER COUNTRY ESTATE AS A HOME FOR DISTRESSED GENTRY!
GENTRY...? AH, WELL, NOT FOR US THEN, WILLIE
9964

MODESTY BLAISE
by PETER O'DONNELL
drawn by ROMERO
WE MANAGED TO KEEP TWO PLAGUE-BOMBS SAFE, BUT THE GENIE'S OUT OF THE BOTTLE NOW...
SOMEBODY'S GOING TO REPLICATE CHERNOV'S WORK SOMETIME
THAT'S NOT OUR PROBLEM, SO LET'S FORGET IT, WILLIE
JUST REMEMBER WE'RE CHAMPION OPTIMISTS — SO TAKE ME SHOPPING IN ROME
PRINCESS, YOU'RE MY SOVEREIGN REMEDY— I CAN'T WAIT
9964 A

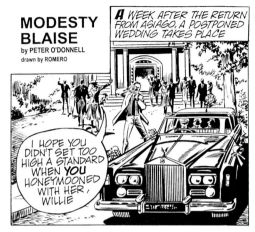

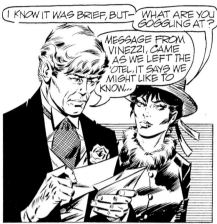

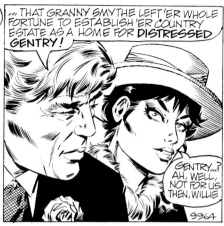

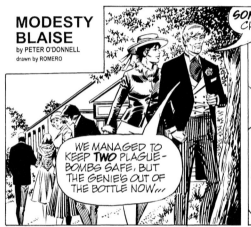

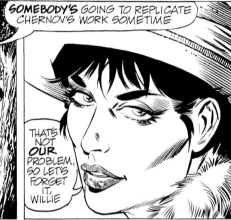

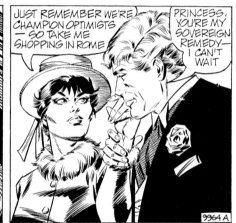

THE KILLING GAME

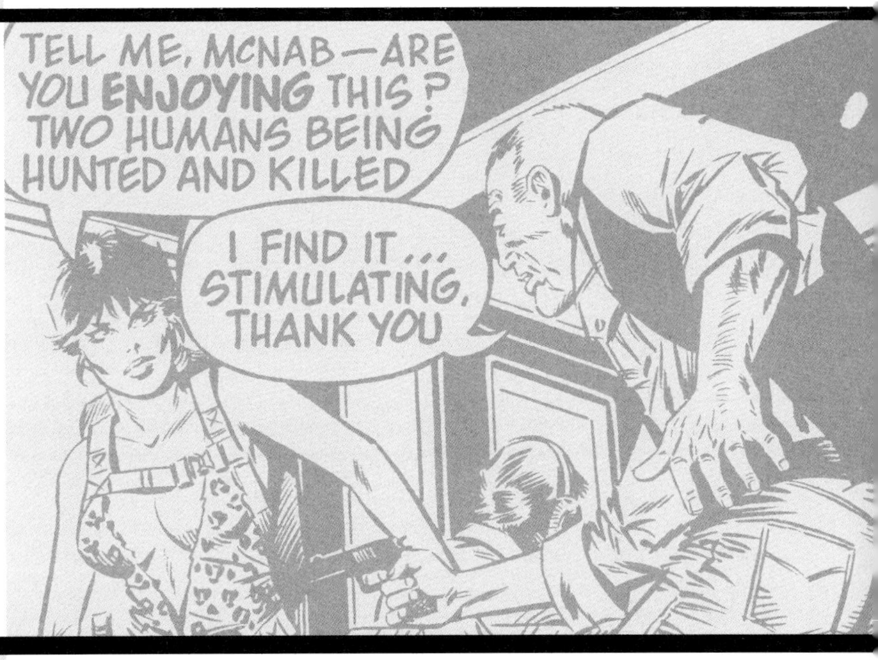
TELL ME, MCNAB—ARE YOU **ENJOYING** THIS? TWO HUMANS BEING HUNTED AND KILLED
I FIND IT... STIMULATING, THANK YOU

I'm on the top floor of a tall Georgian house in Brighton watching a young woman lying on the floor surrounded by pieces of rock and gravel. She's writhing around and grunting with effort.

I say I'm watching but really I'm listening. Do the noises she's making sound like Modesty Blaise climbing down a cliff face? The historic exterior of this house conceals a hi-tech interior. This is a radio studio, and the young woman so gamely wriggling around in the dust is Daphne Alexander, who plays our heroine in Radio 4's dramatizations of the Modesty novels. At this particular moment we're recreating a scene from *The Silver Mistress*, set in the Gorges du Tarn, where Modesty climbs down the side of a ravine to rescue Quinn who has slipped and lies injured on a ledge several feet below. The studio engineer and I are contemplating appropriate weather and wildlife to add to the sound picture. The local Griffon Vulture is frustratingly silent but buzzards are a possibility so we add a few distinctive cries. Peter often places his characters in glamorous and exotic locations but to make convincing radio you don't have to travel. The engineer makes a few adjustments to the mixing desk and with just the right amount of reverb this small, carpeted room is transformed into a deep gorge in the South of France. As a radio drama producer, whenever I read a Modesty story, whether in novel or strip form, I can't help imagining how it would sound. *The Killing Game* begins with the quintessentially English soundscape of a village fete in summer: song thrushes and chaffinches, the gentle laughter of folk enjoying simple pleasures, the thwack of a ball hitting a coconut. But soon the aural backdrop changes dramatically as we are transported to the rainforests of Indonesia. Perhaps, as you read, you too will be tempted to imagine the shrieking of parrots, the croaking of tree frogs, the low rumble of a cassowary or even the distant click of the tree kangaroo.

KATE MCALL

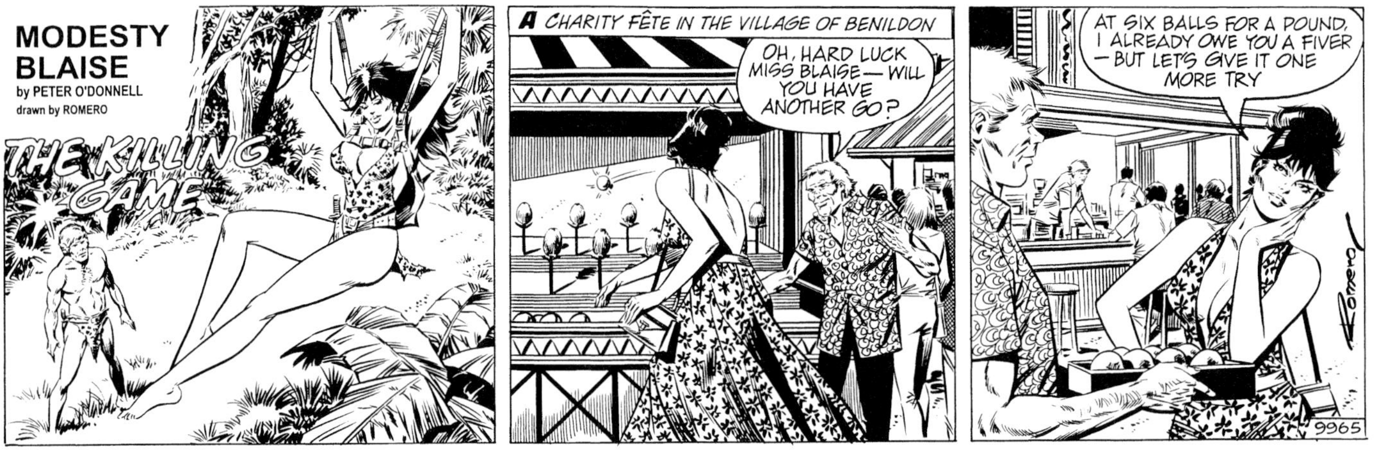
MODESTY BLAISE
by PETER O'DONNELL
drawn by ROMERO
THE KILLING GAME
A CHARITY FÊTE IN THE VILLAGE OF BENILDON
OH, HARD LUCK MISS BLAISE — WILL YOU HAVE ANOTHER GO?
AT SIX BALLS FOR A POUND, I ALREADY OWE YOU A FIVER — BUT LET'S GIVE IT ONE MORE TRY
9965

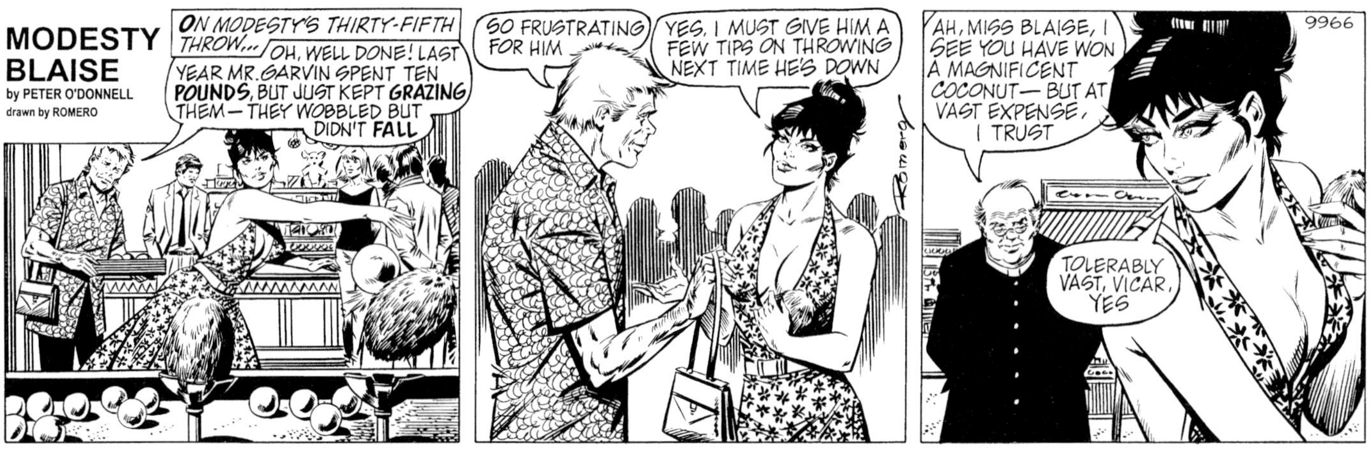
MODESTY BLAISE
by PETER O'DONNELL
drawn by ROMERO
ON MODESTY'S THIRTY-FIFTH THROW...
OH, WELL DONE! LAST YEAR MR. GARVIN SPENT TEN POUNDS, BUT JUST KEPT GRAZING THEM — THEY WOBBLED BUT DIDN'T FALL
SO FRUSTRATING FOR HIM
YES, I MUST GIVE HIM A FEW TIPS ON THROWING NEXT TIME HE'S DOWN
9966
AH, MISS BLAISE, I SEE YOU HAVE WON A MAGNIFICENT COCONUT — BUT AT VAST EXPENSE, I TRUST
TOLERABLY VAST, VICAR, YES

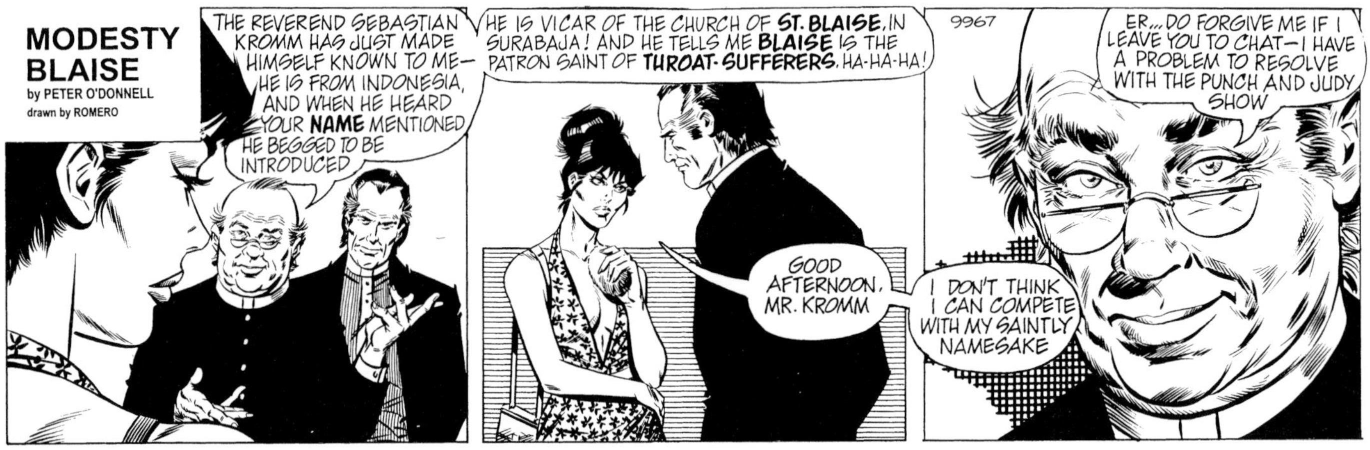
MODESTY BLAISE
by PETER O'DONNELL
drawn by ROMERO
THE REVEREND SEBASTIAN KROMM HAS JUST MADE HIMSELF KNOWN TO ME — HE IS FROM INDONESIA, AND WHEN HE HEARD YOUR NAME MENTIONED HE BEGGED TO BE INTRODUCED
HE IS VICAR OF THE CHURCH OF ST. BLAISE, IN SURABAJA! AND HE TELLS ME BLAISE IS THE PATRON SAINT OF THROAT-SUFFERERS, HA-HA-HA!
GOOD AFTERNOON, MR. KROMM
I DON'T THINK I CAN COMPETE WITH MY SAINTLY NAMESAKE
9967
ER... DO FORGIVE ME IF I LEAVE YOU TO CHAT — I HAVE A PROBLEM TO RESOLVE WITH THE PUNCH AND JUDY SHOW

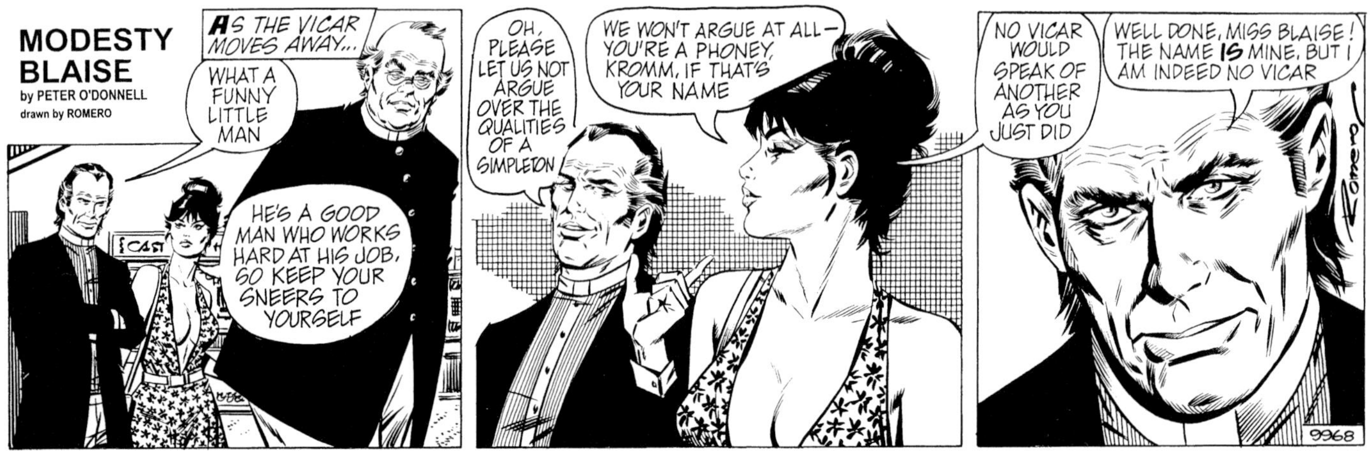
MODESTY BLAISE
by PETER O'DONNELL
drawn by ROMERO
AS THE VICAR MOVES AWAY...
WHAT A FUNNY LITTLE MAN
HE'S A GOOD MAN WHO WORKS HARD AT HIS JOB, SO KEEP YOUR SNEERS TO YOURSELF
OH, PLEASE LET US NOT ARGUE OVER THE QUALITIES OF A SIMPLETON
WE WON'T ARGUE AT ALL — YOU'RE A PHONEY, KROMM, IF THAT'S YOUR NAME
NO VICAR WOULD SPEAK OF ANOTHER AS YOU JUST DID
WELL DONE, MISS BLAISE! THE NAME IS MINE, BUT I AM INDEED NO VICAR
9968

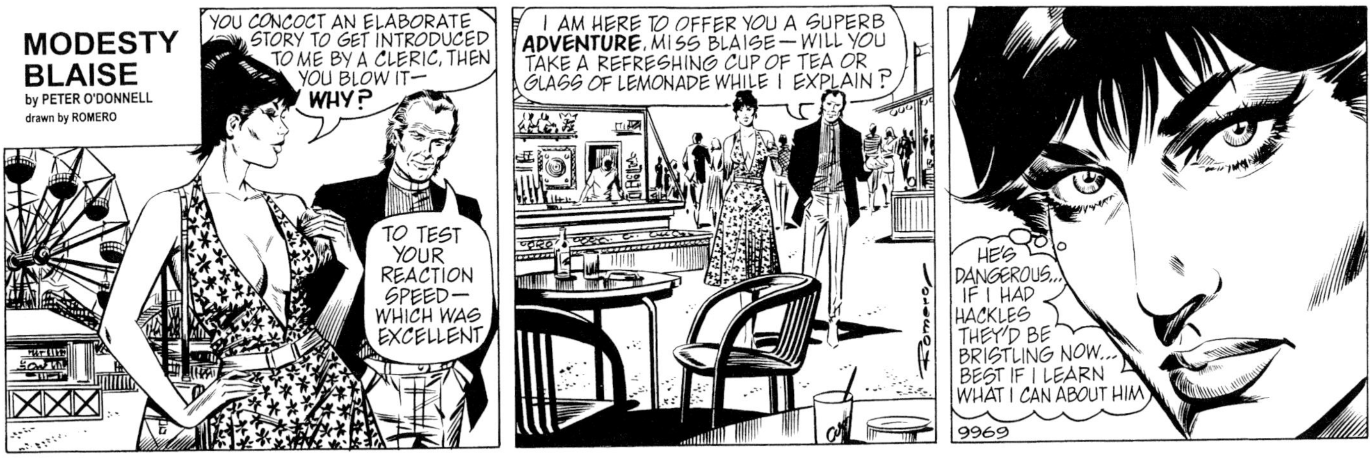
MODESTY BLAISE
by PETER O'DONNELL
drawn by ROMERO
YOU CONCOCT AN ELABORATE STORY TO GET INTRODUCED TO ME BY A CLERIC, THEN YOU BLOW IT— **WHY?**
TO TEST YOUR REACTION SPEED—WHICH WAS EXCELLENT
I AM HERE TO OFFER YOU A SUPERB **ADVENTURE**, MISS BLAISE— WILL YOU TAKE A REFRESHING CUP OF TEA OR GLASS OF LEMONADE WHILE I EXPLAIN?
HE'S DANGEROUS... IF I HAD HACKLES THEY'D BE BRISTLING NOW... BEST IF I LEARN WHAT I CAN ABOUT HIM
9969

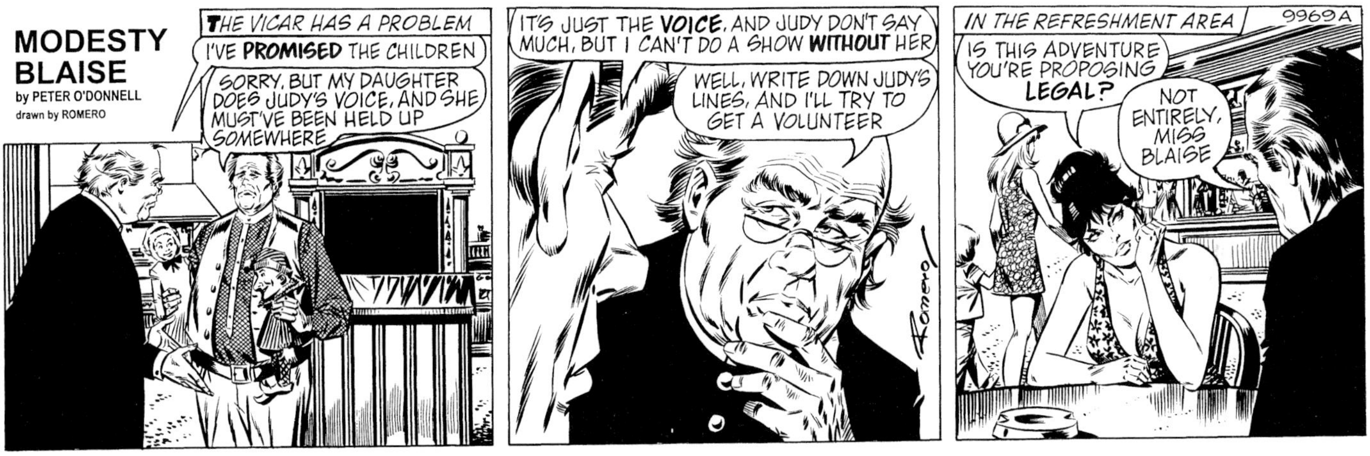
MODESTY BLAISE
by PETER O'DONNELL
drawn by ROMERO
THE VICAR HAS A PROBLEM
I'VE **PROMISED** THE CHILDREN
SORRY, BUT MY DAUGHTER DOES JUDY'S VOICE, AND SHE MUST'VE BEEN HELD UP SOMEWHERE
IT'S JUST THE **VOICE**, AND JUDY DON'T SAY MUCH, BUT I CAN'T DO A SHOW **WITHOUT** HER
WELL, WRITE DOWN JUDY'S LINES, AND I'LL TRY TO GET A VOLUNTEER
IN THE REFRESHMENT AREA
9969A
IS THIS ADVENTURE YOU'RE PROPOSING **LEGAL?**
NOT ENTIRELY, MISS BLAISE

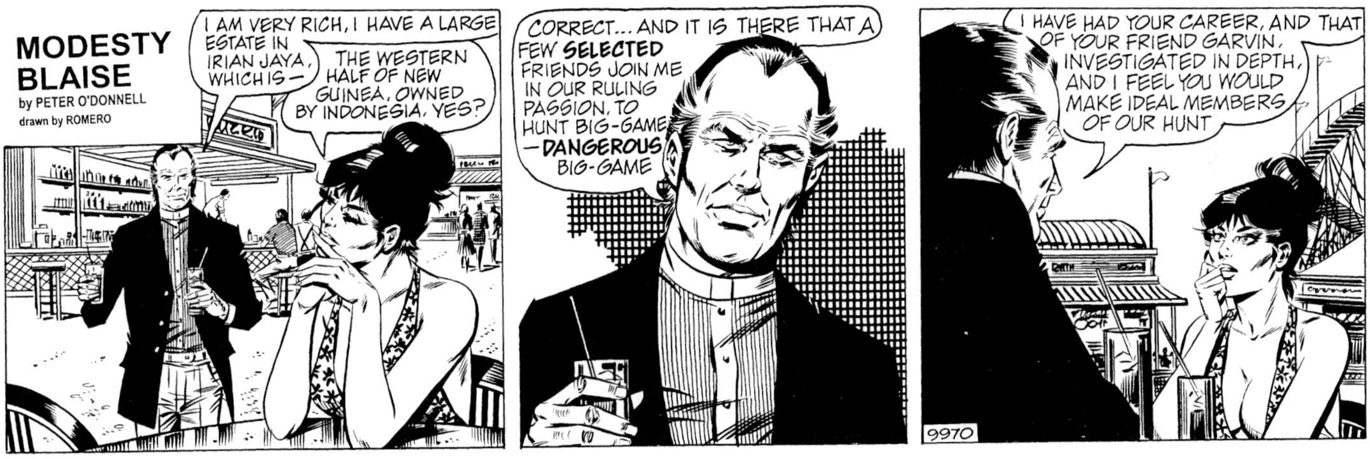
MODESTY BLAISE
by PETER O'DONNELL
drawn by ROMERO
I AM VERY RICH, I HAVE A LARGE ESTATE IN IRIAN JAYA, WHICH IS—
THE WESTERN HALF OF NEW GUINEA, OWNED BY INDONESIA, YES?
CORRECT... AND IT IS THERE THAT A FEW **SELECTED** FRIENDS JOIN ME IN OUR RULING PASSION, TO HUNT BIG-GAME —**DANGEROUS** BIG-GAME
I HAVE HAD YOUR CAREER, AND THAT OF YOUR FRIEND GARVIN, INVESTIGATED IN DEPTH, AND I FEEL YOU WOULD MAKE IDEAL MEMBERS OF OUR HUNT
9970

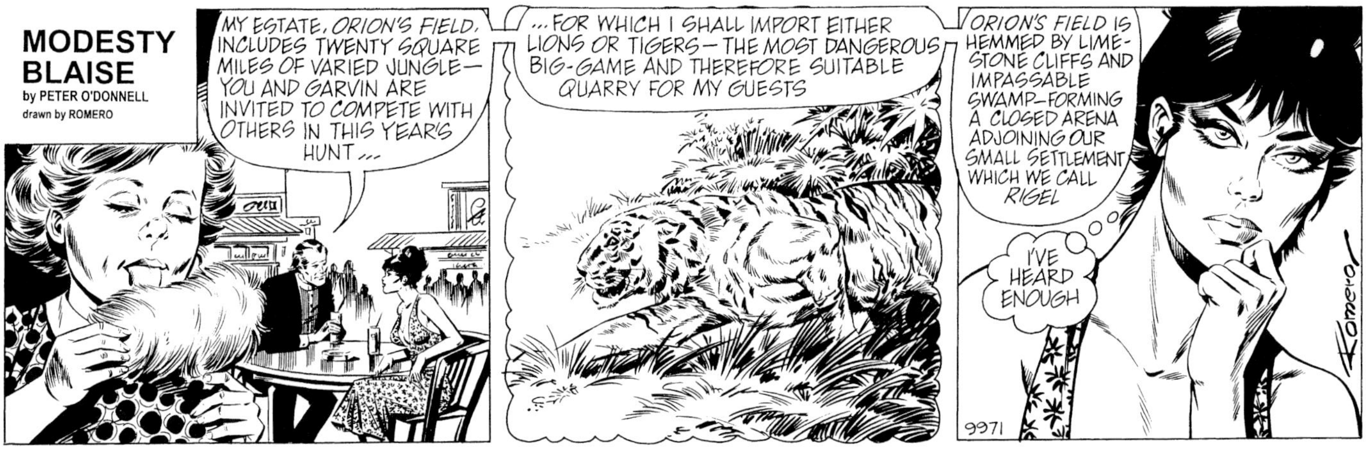
MODESTY BLAISE
by PETER O'DONNELL
drawn by ROMERO
MY ESTATE, *ORION'S FIELD*, INCLUDES TWENTY SQUARE MILES OF VARIED JUNGLE— YOU AND GARVIN ARE INVITED TO COMPETE WITH OTHERS IN THIS YEAR'S HUNT...
...FOR WHICH I SHALL IMPORT EITHER LIONS OR TIGERS— THE MOST DANGEROUS BIG-GAME AND THEREFORE SUITABLE QUARRY FOR MY GUESTS
ORION'S FIELD IS HEMMED BY LIME-STONE CLIFFS AND IMPASSABLE SWAMP—FORMING A CLOSED ARENA ADJOINING OUR SMALL SETTLEMENT WHICH WE CALL *RIGEL*
I'VE HEARD ENOUGH
9971

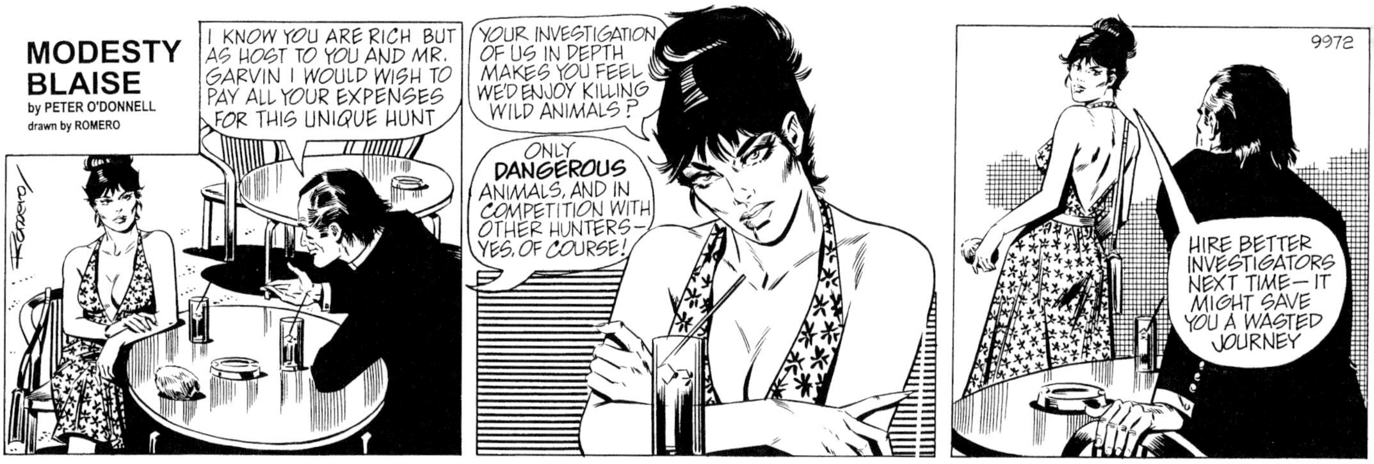
MODESTY BLAISE
by PETER O'DONNELL
drawn by ROMERO
I KNOW YOU ARE RICH BUT AS HOST TO YOU AND MR. GARVIN I WOULD WISH TO PAY ALL YOUR EXPENSES FOR THIS UNIQUE HUNT
YOUR INVESTIGATION OF US IN DEPTH MAKES YOU FEEL WE'D ENJOY KILLING WILD ANIMALS?
ONLY **DANGEROUS** ANIMALS, AND IN COMPETITION WITH OTHER HUNTERS- YES, OF COURSE!
9972
HIRE BETTER INVESTIGATORS NEXT TIME—IT MIGHT SAVE YOU A WASTED JOURNEY

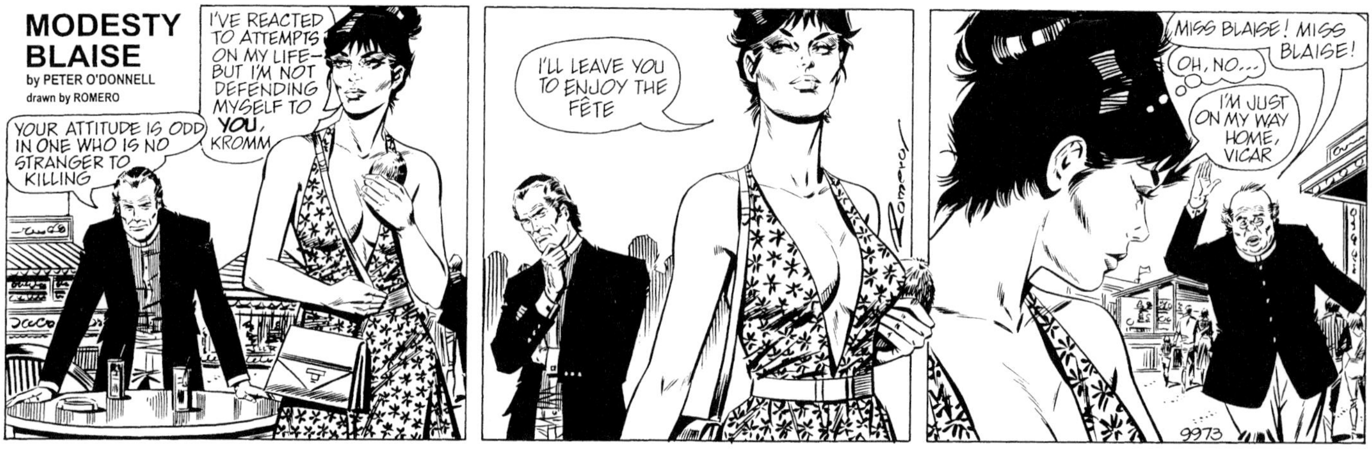
MODESTY BLAISE
by PETER O'DONNELL
drawn by ROMERO
YOUR ATTITUDE IS ODD IN ONE WHO IS NO STRANGER TO KILLING
I'VE REACTED TO ATTEMPTS ON MY LIFE- BUT I'M NOT DEFENDING MYSELF TO **YOU**, KROMM
I'LL LEAVE YOU TO ENJOY THE FÊTE
MISS BLAISE! MISS BLAISE!
OH, NO...
I'M JUST ON MY WAY HOME, VICAR
9973

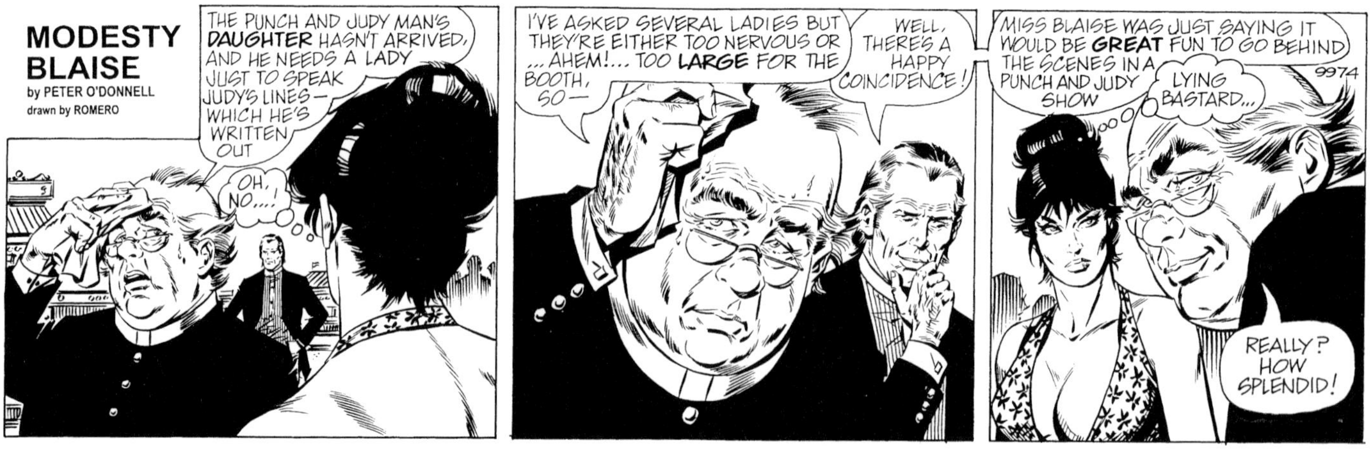
MODESTY BLAISE
by PETER O'DONNELL
drawn by ROMERO
THE PUNCH AND JUDY MAN'S **DAUGHTER** HASN'T ARRIVED, AND HE NEEDS A LADY JUST TO SPEAK JUDY'S LINES— WHICH HE'S WRITTEN OUT
OH, NO...!
I'VE ASKED SEVERAL LADIES BUT THEY'RE EITHER TOO NERVOUS OR ... AHEM!... TOO **LARGE** FOR THE BOOTH, SO—
WELL, THERE'S A HAPPY COINCIDENCE!
MISS BLAISE WAS JUST SAYING IT WOULD BE **GREAT** FUN TO GO BEHIND THE SCENES IN A PUNCH AND JUDY SHOW
LYING BASTARD...
9974
REALLY? HOW SPLENDID!

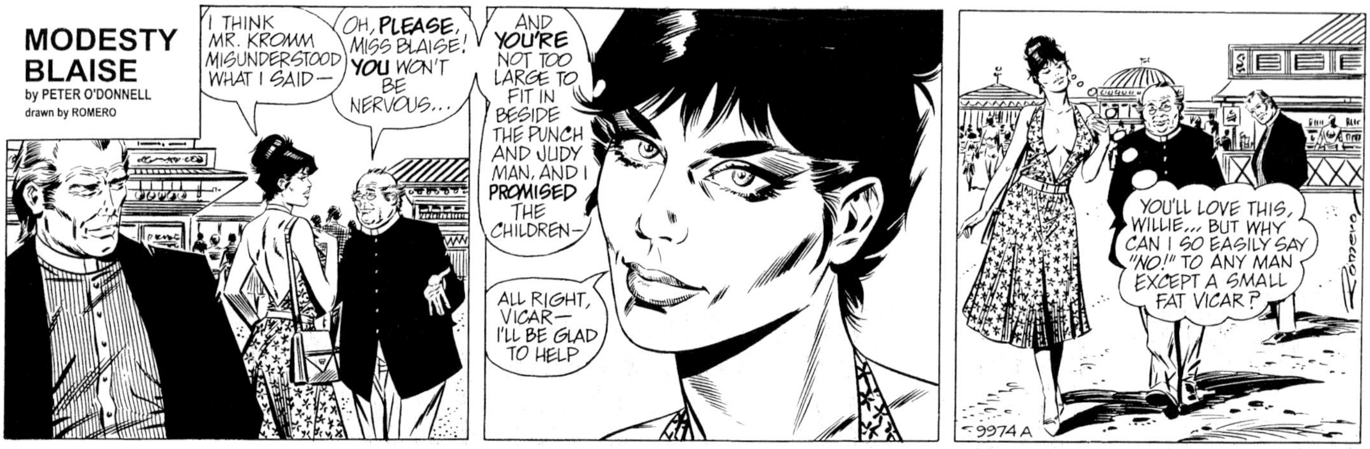
MODESTY BLAISE
by PETER O'DONNELL
drawn by ROMERO
I THINK MR. KROMM MISUNDERSTOOD WHAT I SAID—
OH, **PLEASE**, MISS BLAISE! **YOU** WON'T BE NERVOUS...
AND **YOU'RE** NOT TOO LARGE TO FIT IN BESIDE THE PUNCH AND JUDY MAN, AND I **PROMISED** THE CHILDREN—
ALL RIGHT, VICAR— I'LL BE GLAD TO HELP
YOU'LL LOVE THIS, WILLIE... BUT WHY CAN I SO EASILY SAY "NO!" TO ANY MAN EXCEPT A SMALL FAT VICAR?
9974 A

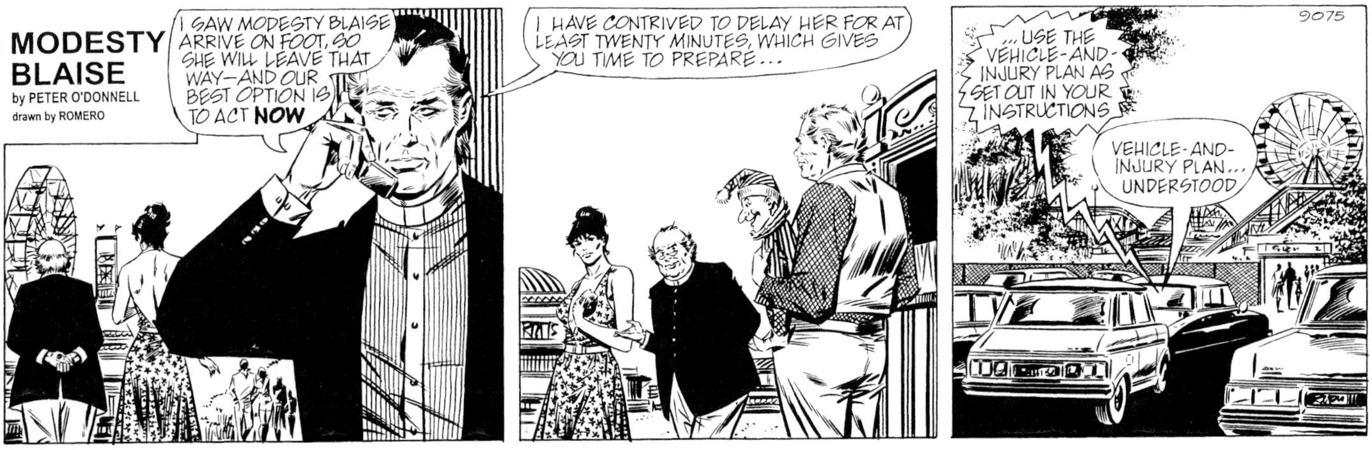
MODESTY BLAISE
by PETER O'DONNELL
drawn by ROMERO
I SAW MODESTY BLAISE ARRIVE ON FOOT, SO SHE WILL LEAVE THAT WAY—AND OUR BEST OPTION IS TO ACT **NOW**
I HAVE CONTRIVED TO DELAY HER FOR AT LEAST TWENTY MINUTES, WHICH GIVES YOU TIME TO PREPARE . . .
9075
. . . USE THE VEHICLE-AND-INJURY PLAN AS SET OUT IN YOUR INSTRUCTIONS
VEHICLE-AND-INJURY PLAN . . . UNDERSTOOD

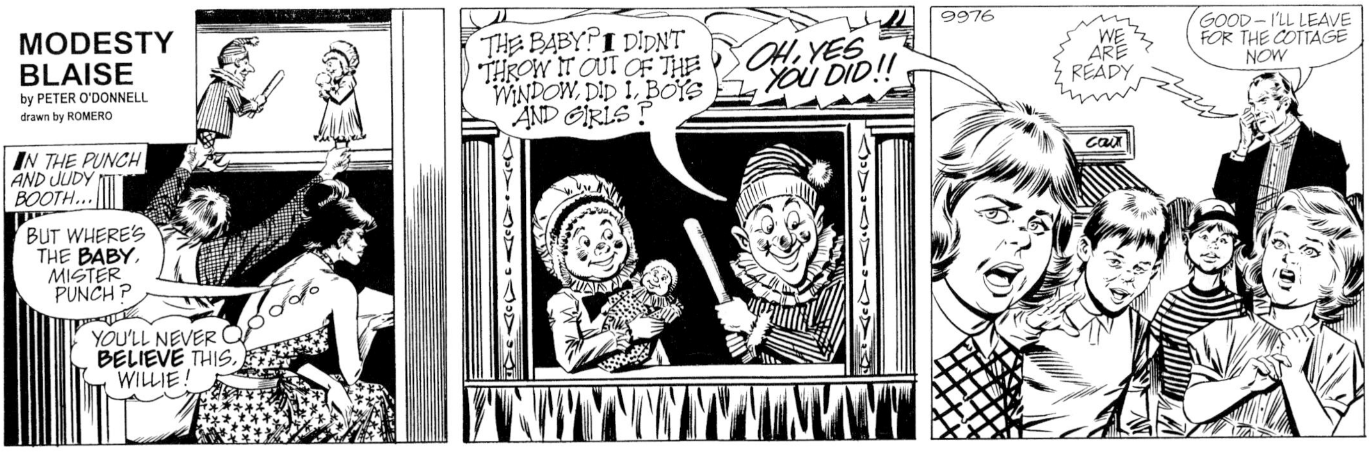
MODESTY BLAISE
by PETER O'DONNELL
drawn by ROMERO
IN THE PUNCH AND JUDY BOOTH . . .
BUT WHERE'S THE **BABY**, MISTER PUNCH?
YOU'LL NEVER **BELIEVE** THIS, WILLIE!
THE BABY? I DIDN'T THROW IT OUT OF THE WINDOW, DID I, BOYS AND GIRLS?
OH, YES YOU DID!!
9976
WE ARE READY
GOOD—I'LL LEAVE FOR THE COTTAGE NOW

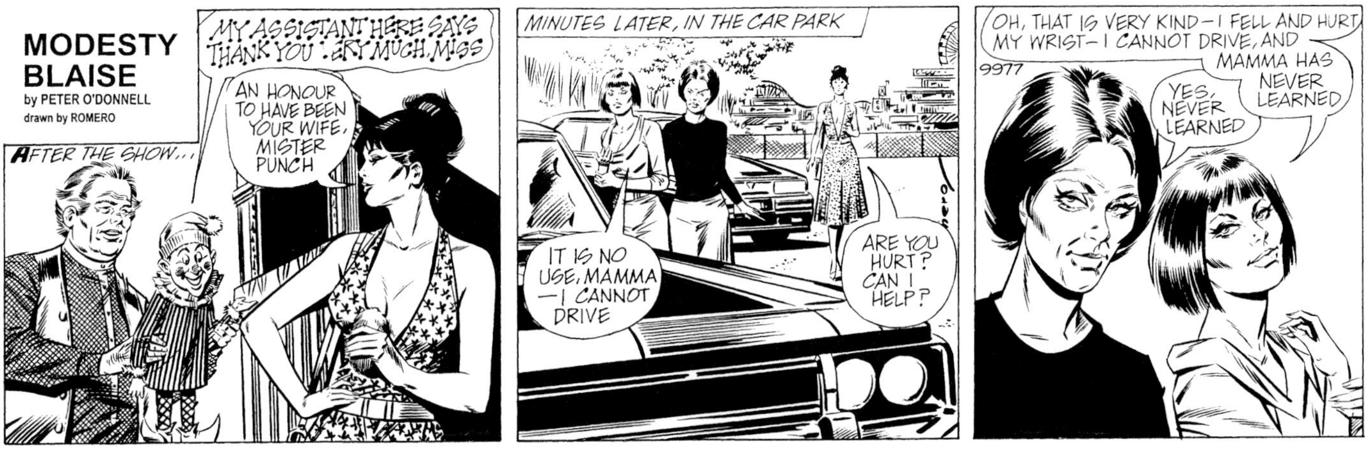
MODESTY BLAISE
by PETER O'DONNELL
drawn by ROMERO
AFTER THE SHOW . . .
MY ASSISTANT HERE SAYS THANK YOU .ERY MUCH, MISS
AN HONOUR TO HAVE BEEN YOUR WIFE, MISTER PUNCH
MINUTES LATER, IN THE CAR PARK
IT IS NO USE, MAMMA—I CANNOT DRIVE
ARE YOU HURT? CAN I HELP?
OH, THAT IS VERY KIND—I FELL AND HURT MY WRIST—I CANNOT DRIVE, AND MAMMA HAS NEVER LEARNED
9977
YES, NEVER LEARNED

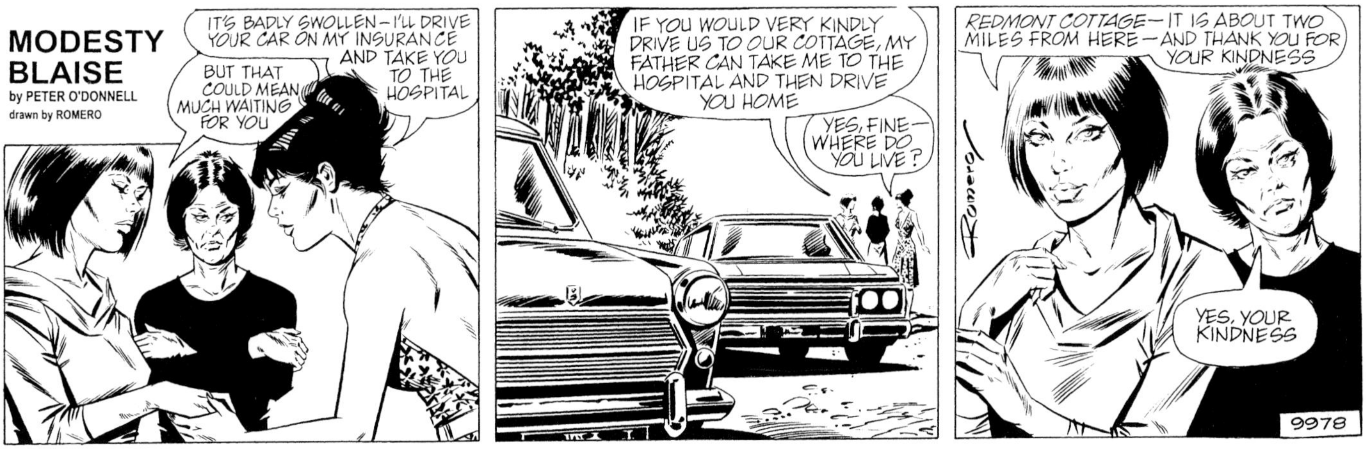
MODESTY BLAISE
by PETER O'DONNELL
drawn by ROMERO
IT'S BADLY SWOLLEN—I'LL DRIVE YOUR CAR ON MY INSURANCE AND TAKE YOU TO THE HOSPITAL
BUT THAT COULD MEAN MUCH WAITING FOR YOU
IF YOU WOULD VERY KINDLY DRIVE US TO OUR COTTAGE, MY FATHER CAN TAKE ME TO THE HOSPITAL AND THEN DRIVE YOU HOME
YES, FINE—WHERE DO YOU LIVE?
REDMONT COTTAGE—IT IS ABOUT TWO MILES FROM HERE—AND THANK YOU FOR YOUR KINDNESS
YES, YOUR KINDNESS
ROMERO
9978

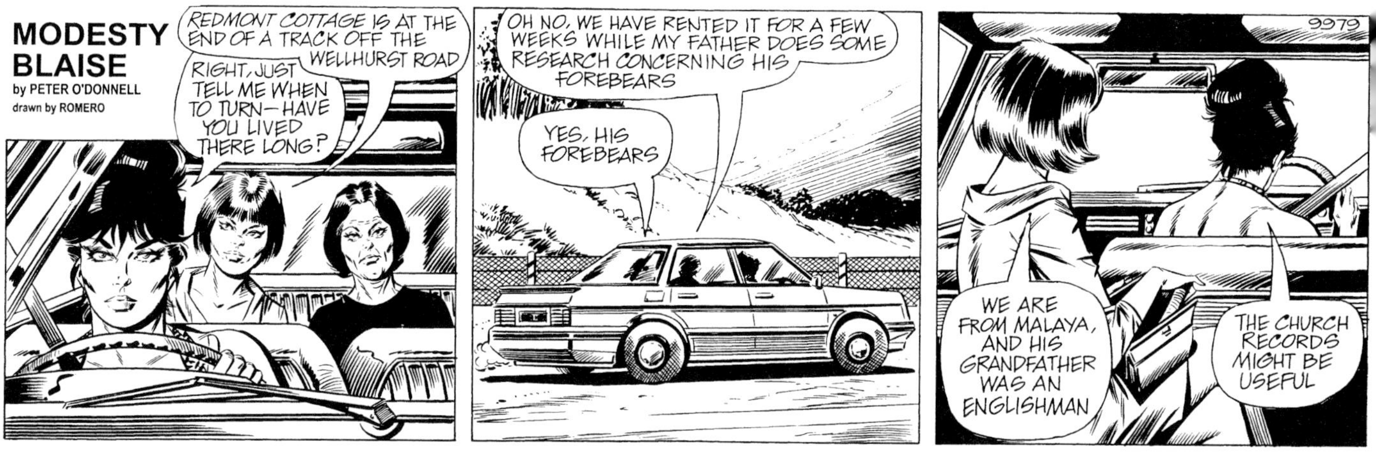
MODESTY BLAISE
by PETER O'DONNELL
drawn by ROMERO
REDMONT COTTAGE IS AT THE END OF A TRACK OFF THE WELLHURST ROAD
RIGHT, JUST TELL ME WHEN TO TURN—HAVE YOU LIVED THERE LONG?
OH NO, WE HAVE RENTED IT FOR A FEW WEEKS WHILE MY FATHER DOES SOME RESEARCH CONCERNING HIS FOREBEARS
YES, HIS FOREBEARS
9979
WE ARE FROM MALAYA, AND HIS GRANDFATHER WAS AN ENGLISHMAN
THE CHURCH RECORDS MIGHT BE USEFUL

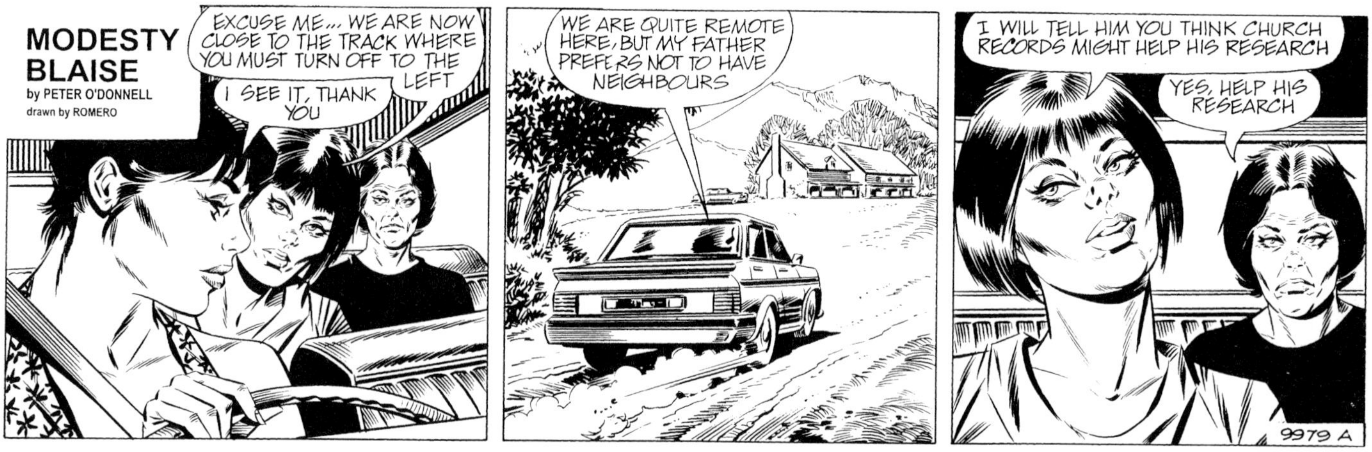
MODESTY BLAISE
by PETER O'DONNELL
drawn by ROMERO
EXCUSE ME... WE ARE NOW CLOSE TO THE TRACK WHERE YOU MUST TURN OFF TO THE LEFT
I SEE IT, THANK YOU
WE ARE QUITE REMOTE HERE, BUT MY FATHER PREFERS NOT TO HAVE NEIGHBOURS
I WILL TELL HIM YOU THINK CHURCH RECORDS MIGHT HELP HIS RESEARCH
YES, HELP HIS RESEARCH
9979 A

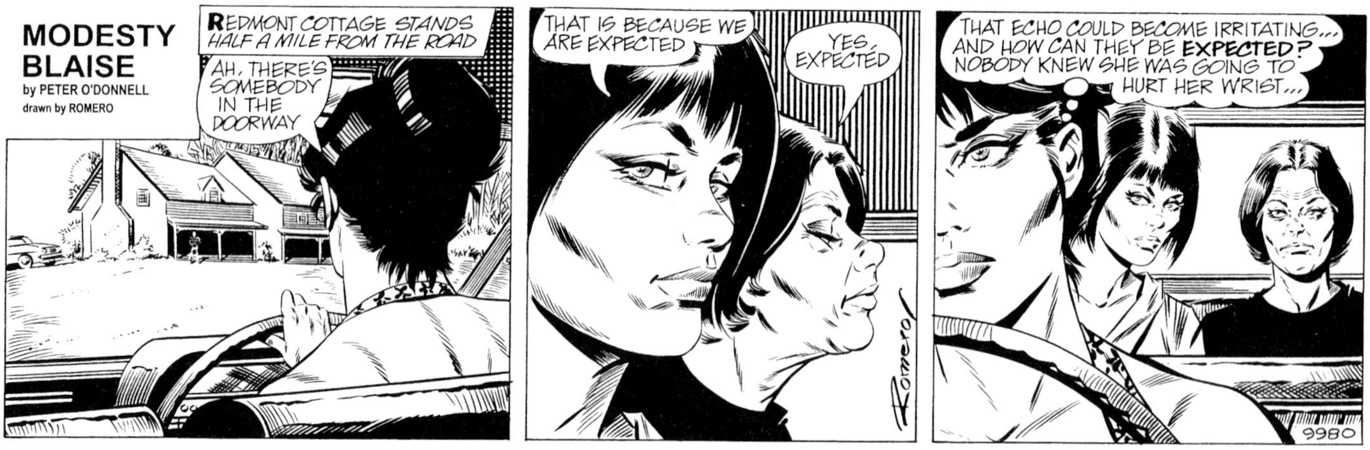
MODESTY BLAISE
by PETER O'DONNELL
drawn by ROMERO
REDMONT COTTAGE STANDS HALF A MILE FROM THE ROAD
AH, THERE'S SOMEBODY IN THE DOORWAY
THAT IS BECAUSE WE ARE EXPECTED
YES, EXPECTED
Romero
THAT ECHO COULD BECOME IRRITATING... AND HOW CAN THEY BE **EXPECTED?** NOBODY KNEW SHE WAS GOING TO HURT HER WRIST...
9980

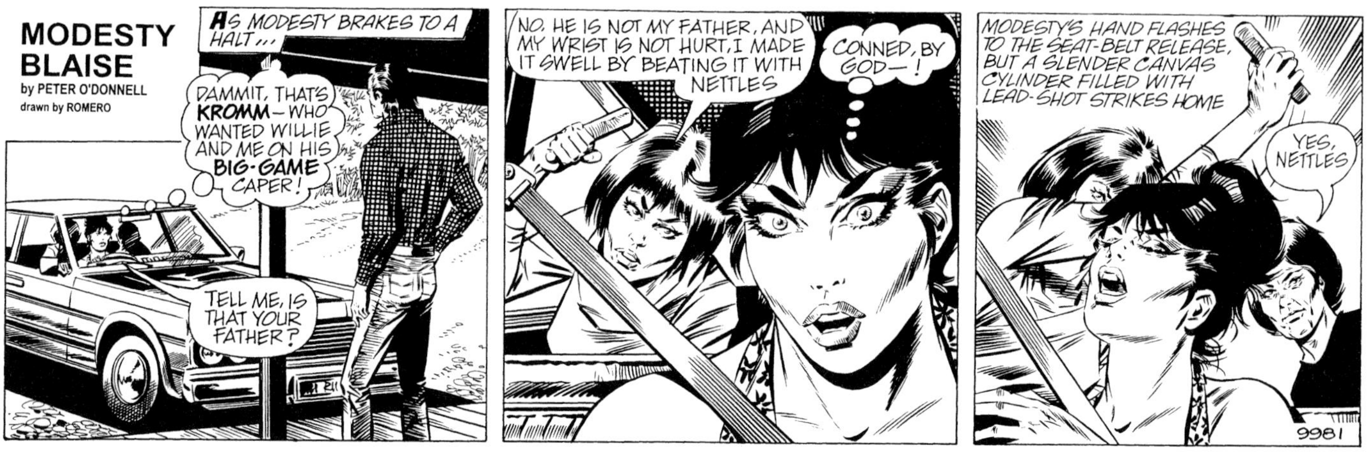
MODESTY BLAISE
by PETER O'DONNELL
drawn by ROMERO
AS MODESTY BRAKES TO A HALT...
DAMMIT, THAT'S **KROMM**—WHO WANTED WILLIE AND ME ON HIS **BIG-GAME** CAPER!
TELL ME, IS THAT YOUR FATHER?
NO, HE IS NOT MY FATHER, AND MY WRIST IS NOT HURT, I MADE IT SWELL BY BEATING IT WITH NETTLES
CONNED, BY GOD—!
MODESTY'S HAND FLASHES TO THE SEAT-BELT RELEASE, BUT A SLENDER CANVAS CYLINDER FILLED WITH LEAD-SHOT STRIKES HOME
YES, NETTLES
9981

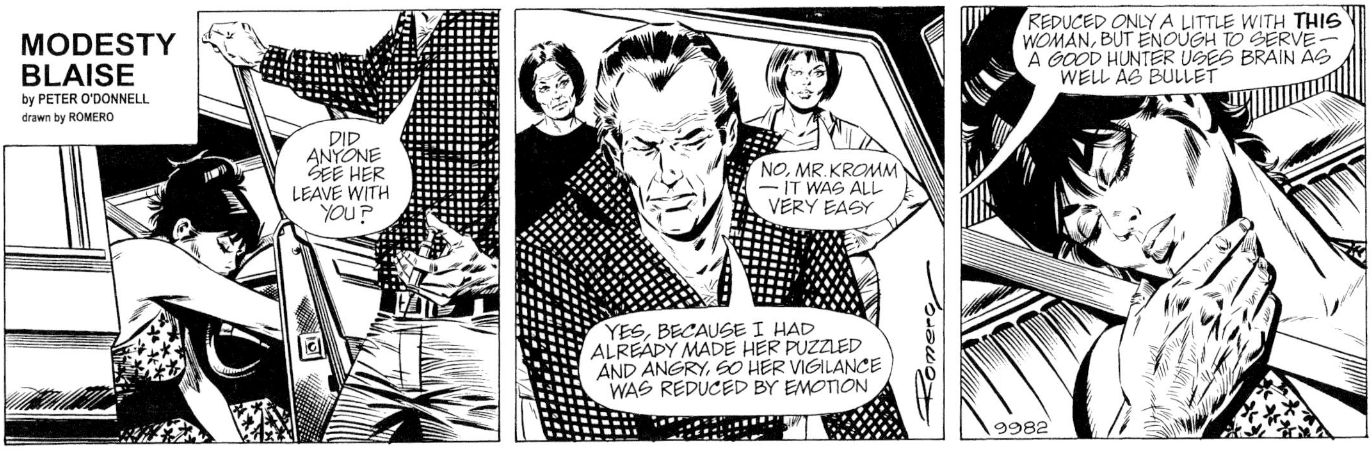
MODESTY BLAISE
by PETER O'DONNELL
drawn by ROMERO
DID ANYONE SEE HER LEAVE WITH YOU?
NO, MR. KROMM — IT WAS ALL VERY EASY
YES, BECAUSE I HAD ALREADY MADE HER PUZZLED AND ANGRY, SO HER VIGILANCE WAS REDUCED BY EMOTION
Romero
REDUCED ONLY A LITTLE WITH THIS WOMAN, BUT ENOUGH TO SERVE — A GOOD HUNTER USES BRAIN AS WELL AS BULLET
9982

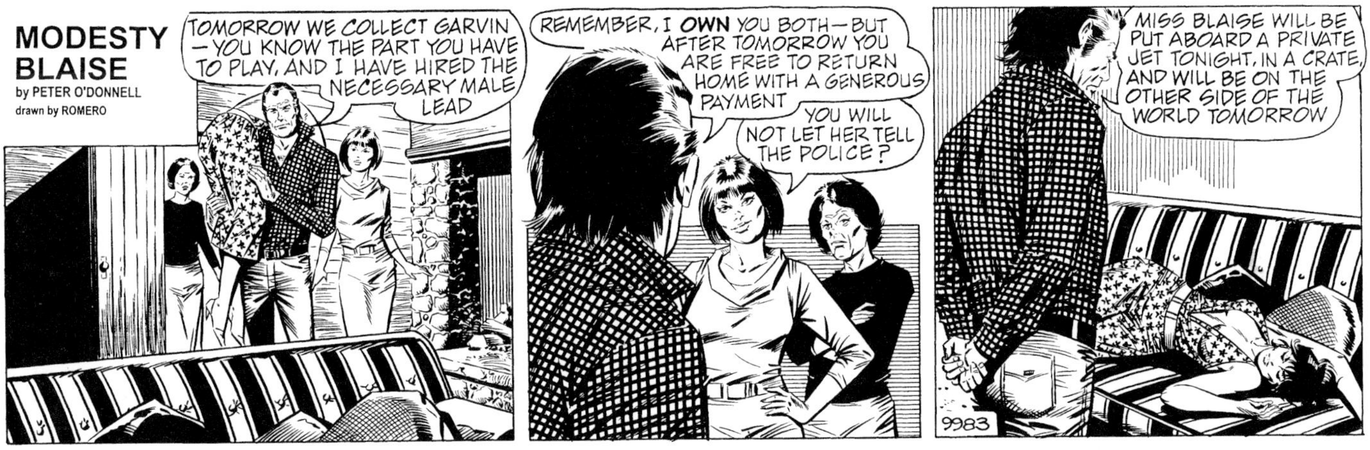
MODESTY BLAISE
by PETER O'DONNELL
drawn by ROMERO
TOMORROW WE COLLECT GARVIN — YOU KNOW THE PART YOU HAVE TO PLAY, AND I HAVE HIRED THE NECESSARY MALE LEAD
REMEMBER, I OWN YOU BOTH — BUT AFTER TOMORROW YOU ARE FREE TO RETURN HOME WITH A GENEROUS PAYMENT
YOU WILL NOT LET HER TELL THE POLICE?
MISS BLAISE WILL BE PUT ABOARD A PRIVATE JET TONIGHT, IN A CRATE, AND WILL BE ON THE OTHER SIDE OF THE WORLD TOMORROW
9983

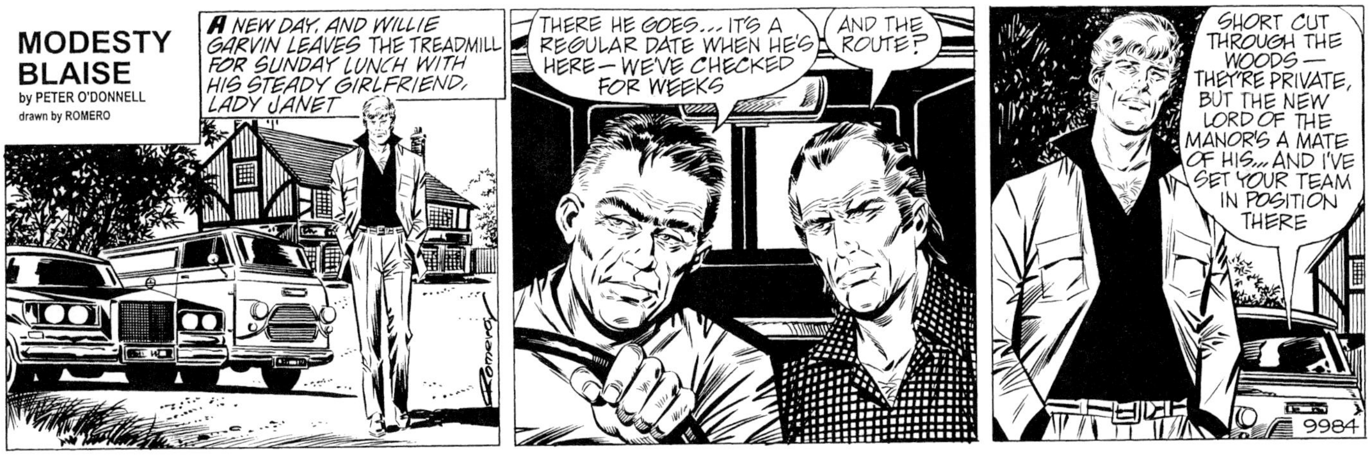
MODESTY BLAISE
by PETER O'DONNELL
drawn by ROMERO
A NEW DAY, AND WILLIE GARVIN LEAVES THE TREADMILL FOR SUNDAY LUNCH WITH HIS STEADY GIRLFRIEND, LADY JANET
Romero
THERE HE GOES... IT'S A REGULAR DATE WHEN HE'S HERE — WE'VE CHECKED FOR WEEKS
AND THE ROUTE?
SHORT CUT THROUGH THE WOODS — THEY'RE PRIVATE, BUT THE NEW LORD OF THE MANOR'S A MATE OF HIS... AND I'VE SET YOUR TEAM IN POSITION THERE
9984

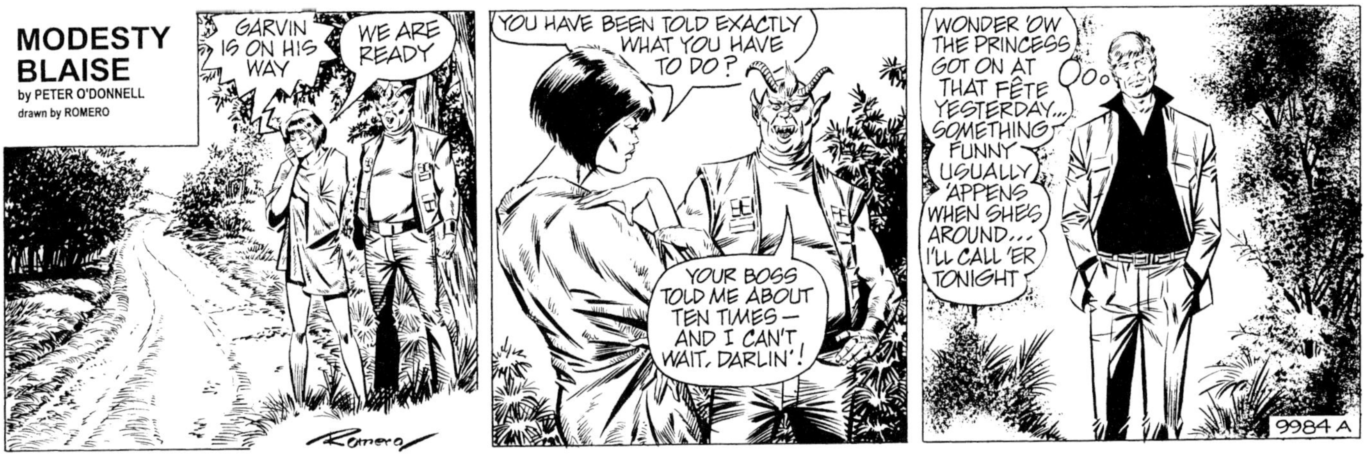
MODESTY BLAISE
by PETER O'DONNELL
drawn by ROMERO
GARVIN IS ON HIS WAY
WE ARE READY
Romero
YOU HAVE BEEN TOLD EXACTLY WHAT YOU HAVE TO DO?
YOUR BOSS TOLD ME ABOUT TEN TIMES — AND I CAN'T WAIT, DARLIN'!
WONDER 'OW THE PRINCESS GOT ON AT THAT FÊTE YESTERDAY... SOMETHING FUNNY USUALLY 'APPENS WHEN SHE'S AROUND... I'LL CALL 'ER TONIGHT
9984 A

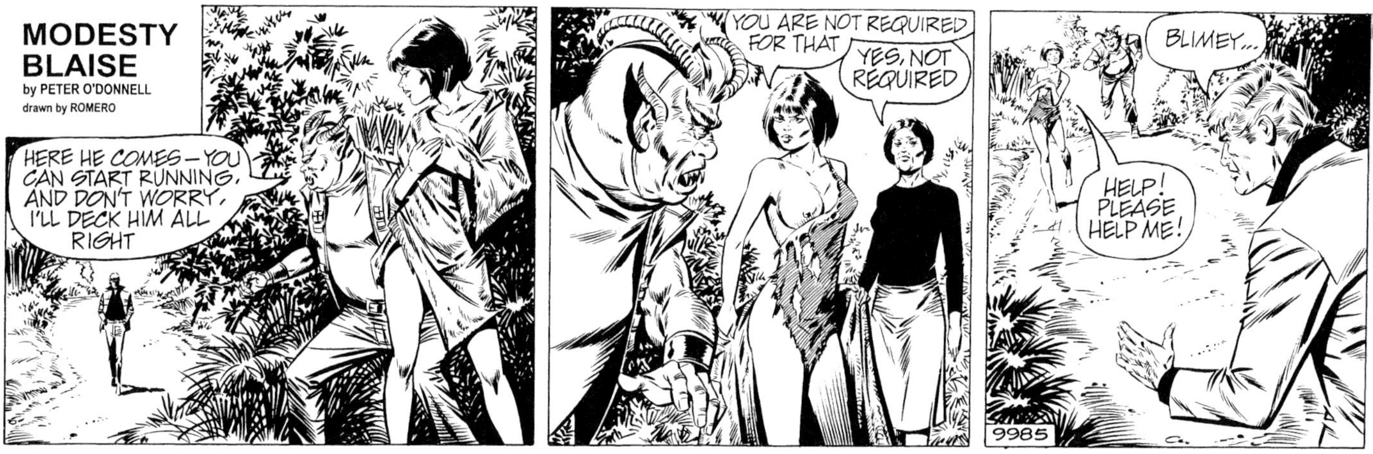
MODESTY BLAISE
by PETER O'DONNELL
drawn by ROMERO
HERE HE COMES—YOU CAN START RUNNING, AND DON'T WORRY, I'LL DECK HIM ALL RIGHT
YOU ARE NOT REQUIRED FOR THAT
YES, NOT REQUIRED
BLIMEY...
HELP! PLEASE HELP ME!
9985

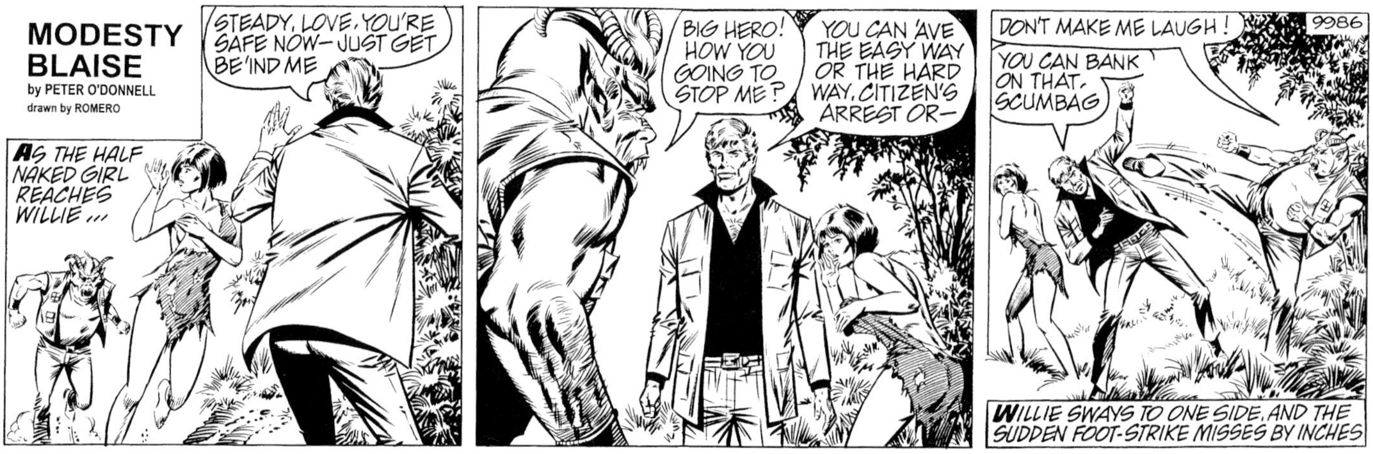
MODESTY BLAISE
by PETER O'DONNELL
drawn by ROMERO
AS THE HALF NAKED GIRL REACHES WILLIE...
STEADY, LOVE, YOU'RE SAFE NOW—JUST GET BE'IND ME
BIG HERO! HOW YOU GOING TO STOP ME?
YOU CAN 'AVE THE EASY WAY OR THE HARD WAY. CITIZEN'S ARREST OR—
DON'T MAKE ME LAUGH!
YOU CAN BANK ON THAT, SCUMBAG
9986
WILLIE SWAYS TO ONE SIDE, AND THE SUDDEN FOOT-STRIKE MISSES BY INCHES

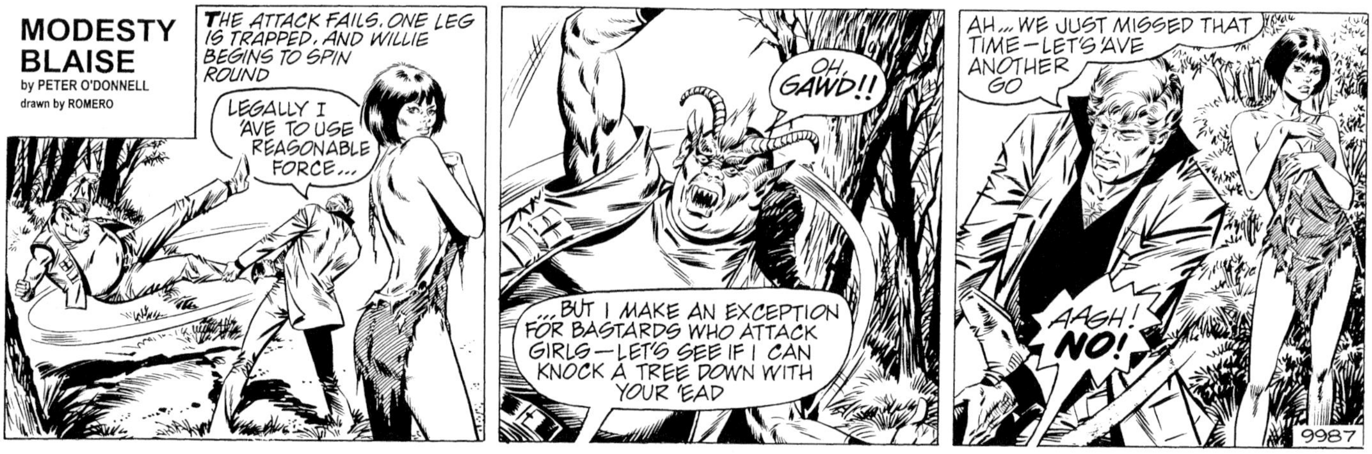
MODESTY BLAISE
by PETER O'DONNELL
drawn by ROMERO
THE ATTACK FAILS. ONE LEG IS TRAPPED, AND WILLIE BEGINS TO SPIN ROUND
LEGALLY I 'AVE TO USE REASONABLE FORCE...
OH, GAWD!!
...BUT I MAKE AN EXCEPTION FOR BASTARDS WHO ATTACK GIRLS—LET'S SEE IF I CAN KNOCK A TREE DOWN WITH YOUR 'EAD
AH... WE JUST MISSED THAT TIME—LET'S 'AVE ANOTHER GO
AAGH! NO!
9987

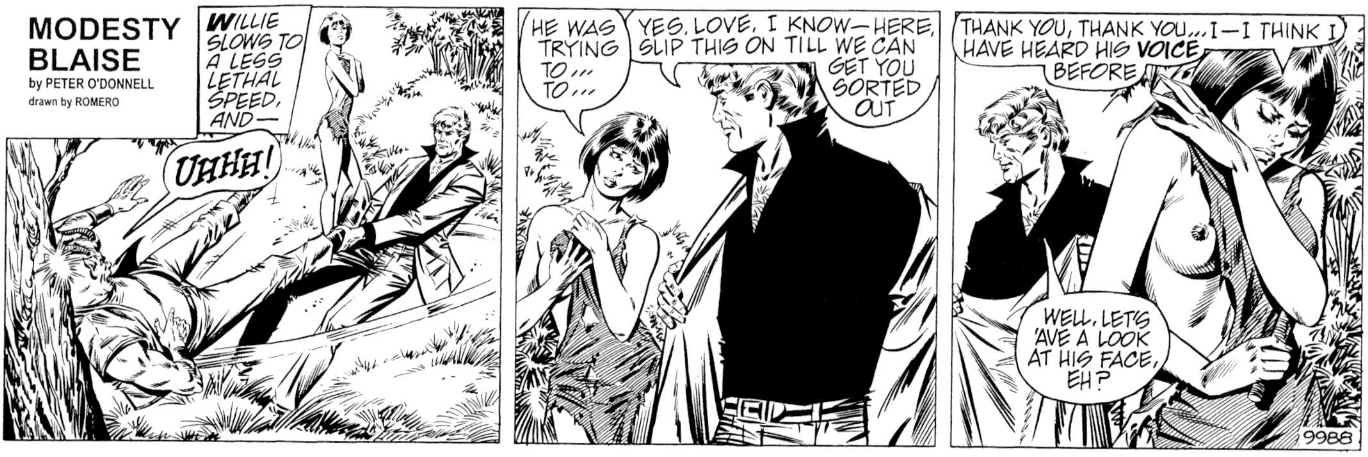
MODESTY BLAISE
by PETER O'DONNELL
drawn by ROMERO
WILLIE SLOWS TO A LESS LETHAL SPEED, AND—
UHHH!
HE WAS TRYING TO... TO...
YES, LOVE, I KNOW—HERE, SLIP THIS ON TILL WE CAN GET YOU SORTED OUT
THANK YOU, THANK YOU... I—I THINK I HAVE HEARD HIS VOICE BEFORE
WELL, LET'S 'AVE A LOOK AT HIS FACE, EH?
9988

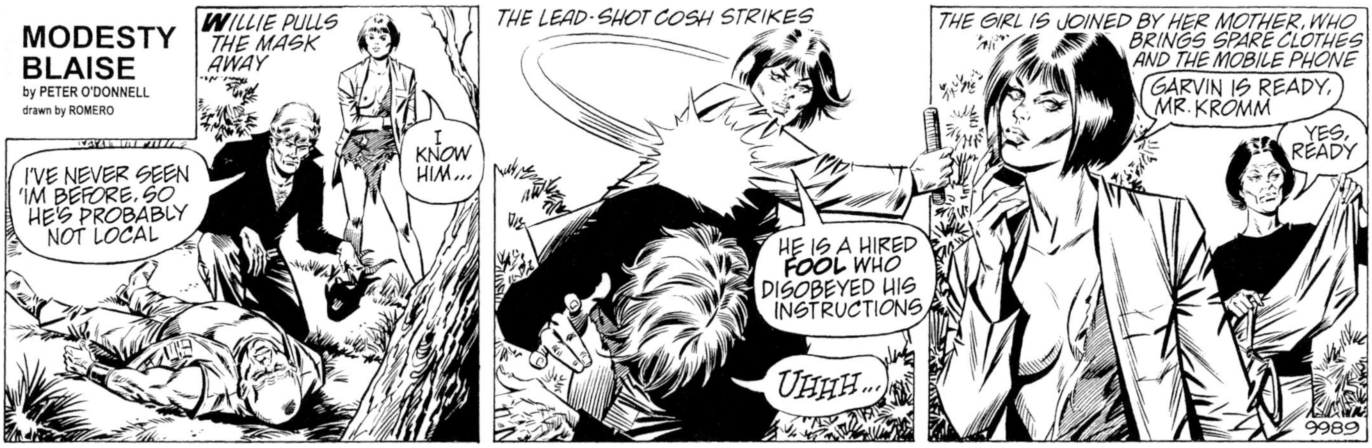
MODESTY BLAISE
by PETER O'DONNELL
drawn by ROMERO
WILLIE PULLS THE MASK AWAY
I'VE NEVER SEEN 'IM BEFORE, SO HE'S PROBABLY NOT LOCAL
I KNOW HIM...
THE LEAD-SHOT COSH STRIKES
HE IS A HIRED FOOL WHO DISOBEYED HIS INSTRUCTIONS
UHHH...
THE GIRL IS JOINED BY HER MOTHER, WHO BRINGS SPARE CLOTHES AND THE MOBILE PHONE
GARVIN IS READY, MR. KROMM
YES, READY
9989

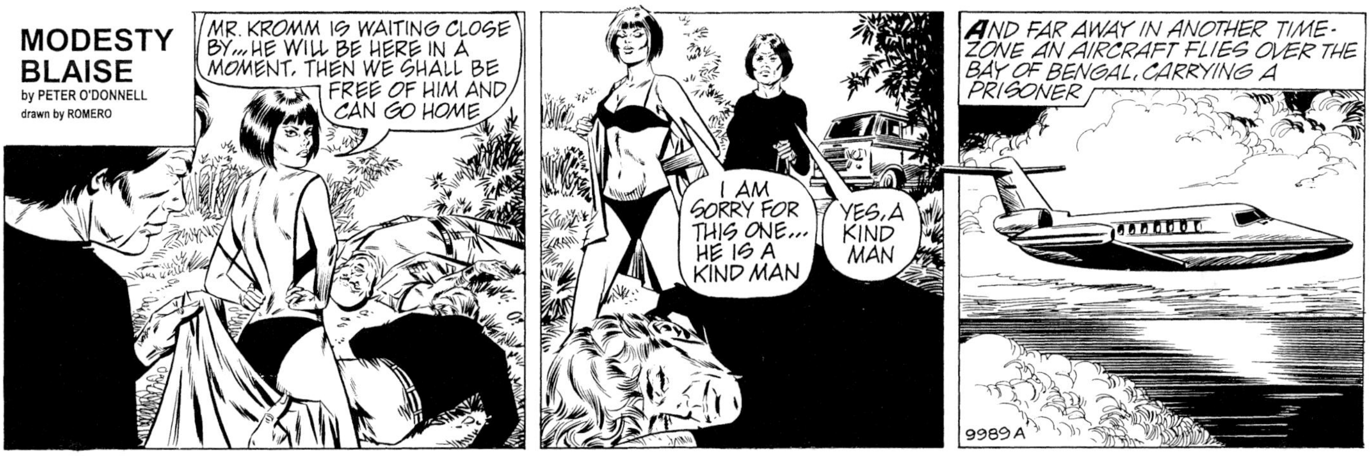
MODESTY BLAISE
by PETER O'DONNELL
drawn by ROMERO
MR. KROMM IS WAITING CLOSE BY... HE WILL BE HERE IN A MOMENT. THEN WE SHALL BE FREE OF HIM AND CAN GO HOME
I AM SORRY FOR THIS ONE... HE IS A KIND MAN
YES, A KIND MAN
AND FAR AWAY IN ANOTHER TIME-ZONE AN AIRCRAFT FLIES OVER THE BAY OF BENGAL, CARRYING A PRISONER
9989 A

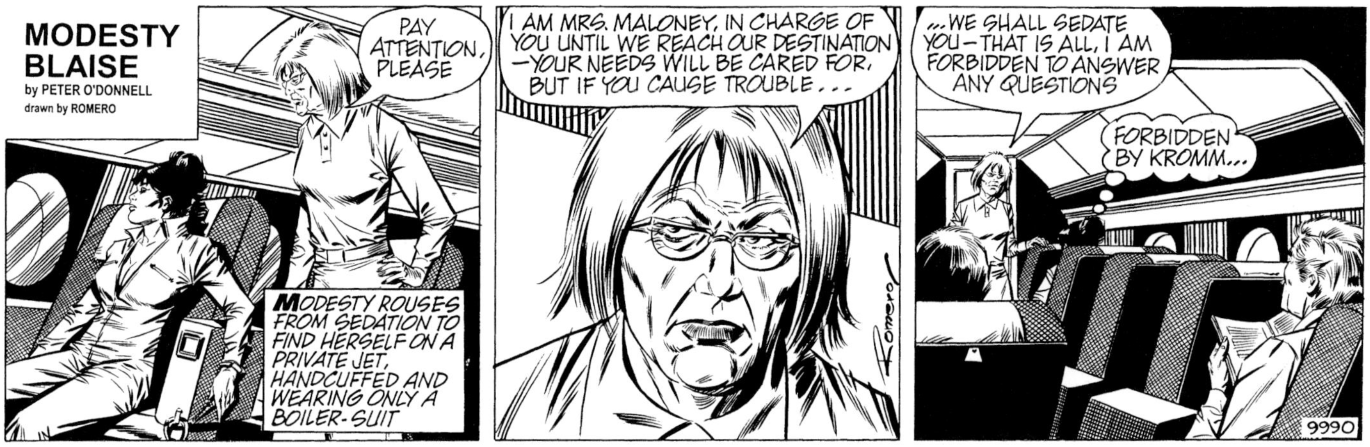
MODESTY BLAISE
by PETER O'DONNELL
drawn by ROMERO
PAY ATTENTION, PLEASE
MODESTY ROUSES FROM SEDATION TO FIND HERSELF ON A PRIVATE JET, HANDCUFFED AND WEARING ONLY A BOILER-SUIT
I AM MRS. MALONEY, IN CHARGE OF YOU UNTIL WE REACH OUR DESTINATION —YOUR NEEDS WILL BE CARED FOR, BUT IF YOU CAUSE TROUBLE...
Romero
...WE SHALL SEDATE YOU—THAT IS ALL. I AM FORBIDDEN TO ANSWER ANY QUESTIONS
FORBIDDEN BY KROMM...
9990

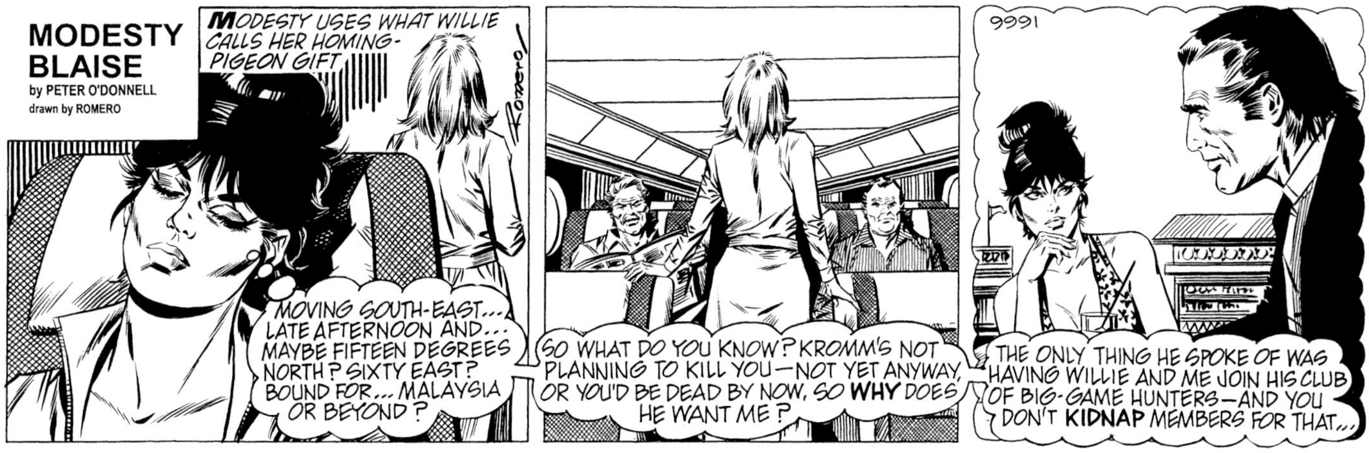
MODESTY BLAISE
by PETER O'DONNELL
drawn by ROMERO
MODESTY USES WHAT WILLIE CALLS HER HOMING-PIGEON GIFT
Romero
MOVING SOUTH-EAST... LATE AFTERNOON AND... MAYBE FIFTEEN DEGREES NORTH? SIXTY EAST? BOUND FOR... MALAYSIA OR BEYOND?
SO WHAT DO YOU KNOW? KROMM'S NOT PLANNING TO KILL YOU—NOT YET ANYWAY, OR YOU'D BE DEAD BY NOW, SO WHY DOES HE WANT ME?
9991
THE ONLY THING HE SPOKE OF WAS HAVING WILLIE AND ME JOIN HIS CLUB OF BIG-GAME HUNTERS—AND YOU DON'T KIDNAP MEMBERS FOR THAT...

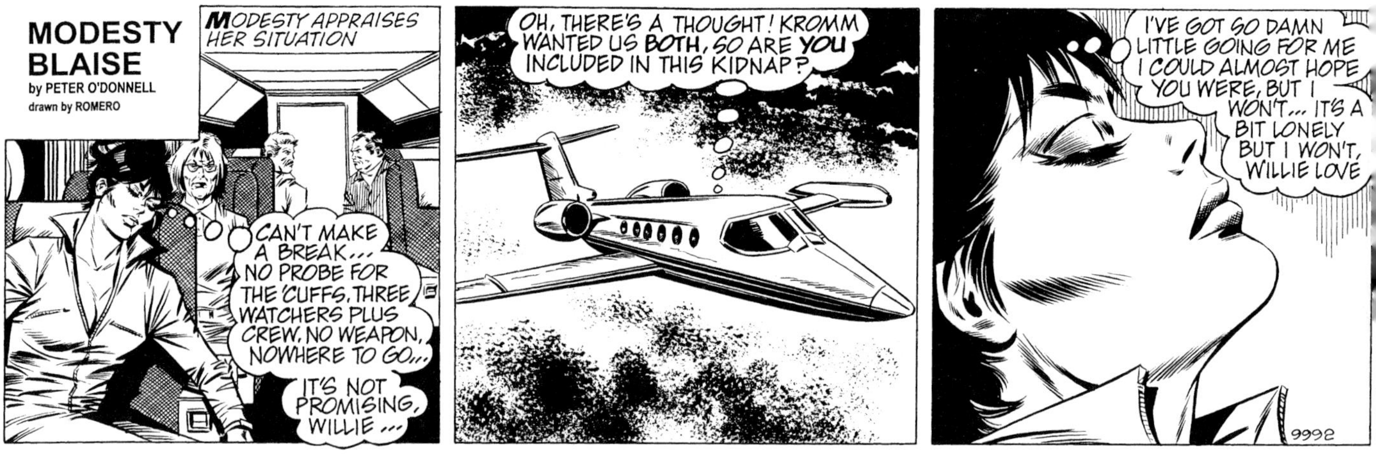
MODESTY BLAISE
by PETER O'DONNELL
drawn by ROMERO
MODESTY APPRAISES HER SITUATION
CAN'T MAKE A BREAK... NO PROBE FOR THE 'CUFFS. THREE WATCHERS PLUS CREW. NO WEAPON, NOWHERE TO GO...
IT'S NOT PROMISING, WILLIE...
OH, THERE'S A THOUGHT! KROMM WANTED US BOTH, SO ARE YOU INCLUDED IN THIS KIDNAP?
I'VE GOT SO DAMN LITTLE GOING FOR ME I COULD ALMOST HOPE YOU WERE, BUT I WON'T... IT'S A BIT LONELY BUT I WON'T, WILLIE LOVE
9992

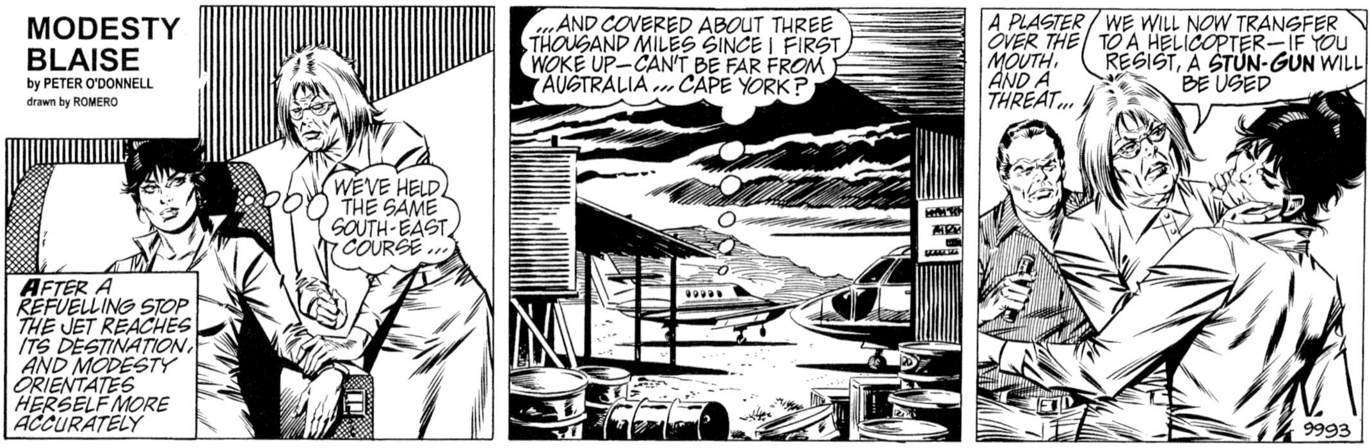
MODESTY BLAISE
by PETER O'DONNELL
drawn by ROMERO
AFTER A REFUELLING STOP THE JET REACHES ITS DESTINATION, AND MODESTY ORIENTATES HERSELF MORE ACCURATELY
WE'VE HELD THE SAME SOUTH-EAST COURSE...
...AND COVERED ABOUT THREE THOUSAND MILES SINCE I FIRST WOKE UP—CAN'T BE FAR FROM AUSTRALIA... CAPE YORK?
A PLASTER OVER THE MOUTH, AND A THREAT...
WE WILL NOW TRANSFER TO A HELICOPTER—IF YOU RESIST, A STUN-GUN WILL BE USED
9993

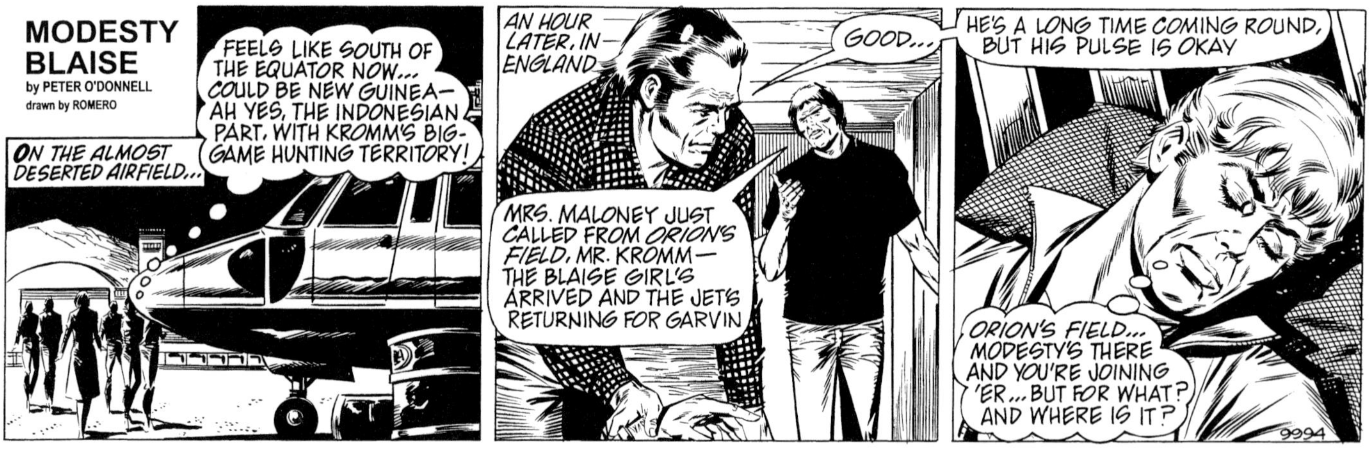
MODESTY BLAISE
by PETER O'DONNELL
drawn by ROMERO
ON THE ALMOST DESERTED AIRFIELD...
FEELS LIKE SOUTH OF THE EQUATOR NOW... COULD BE NEW GUINEA— AH YES, THE INDONESIAN PART, WITH KROMM'S BIG-GAME HUNTING TERRITORY!
AN HOUR LATER, IN ENGLAND
MRS. MALONEY JUST CALLED FROM ORION'S FIELD, MR. KROMM— THE BLAISE GIRL'S ARRIVED AND THE JET'S RETURNING FOR GARVIN
GOOD...
HE'S A LONG TIME COMING ROUND, BUT HIS PULSE IS OKAY
ORION'S FIELD... MODESTY'S THERE AND YOU'RE JOINING 'ER... BUT FOR WHAT? AND WHERE IS IT?
9994

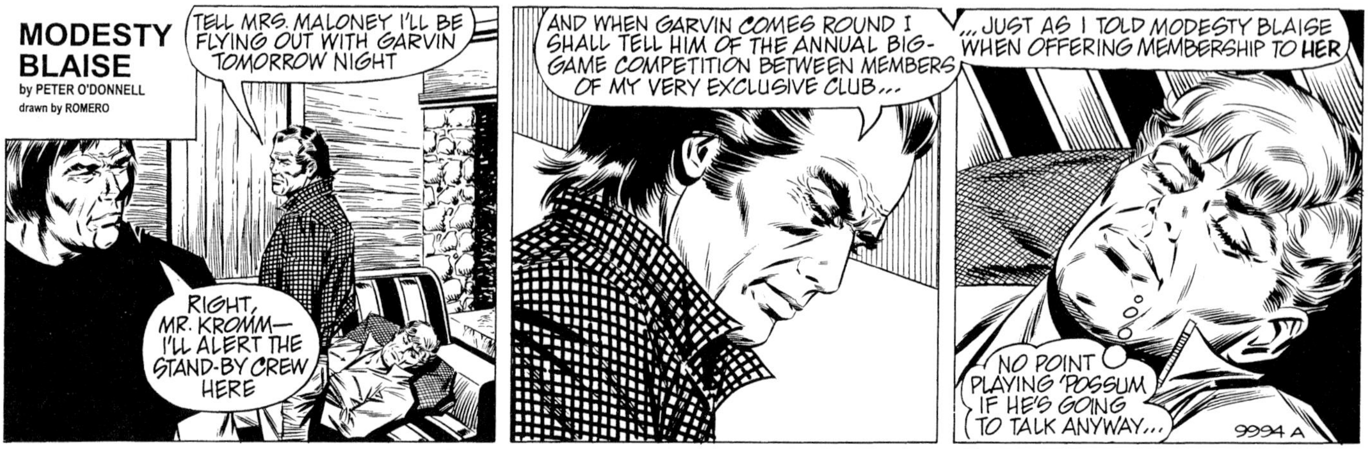
MODESTY BLAISE
by PETER O'DONNELL
drawn by ROMERO
TELL MRS. MALONEY I'LL BE FLYING OUT WITH GARVIN TOMORROW NIGHT
RIGHT, MR. KROMM— I'LL ALERT THE STAND-BY CREW HERE
AND WHEN GARVIN COMES ROUND I SHALL TELL HIM OF THE ANNUAL BIG-GAME COMPETITION BETWEEN MEMBERS OF MY VERY EXCLUSIVE CLUB...
...JUST AS I TOLD MODESTY BLAISE WHEN OFFERING MEMBERSHIP TO HER
NO POINT PLAYING 'POSSUM IF HE'S GOING TO TALK ANYWAY...
9994 A

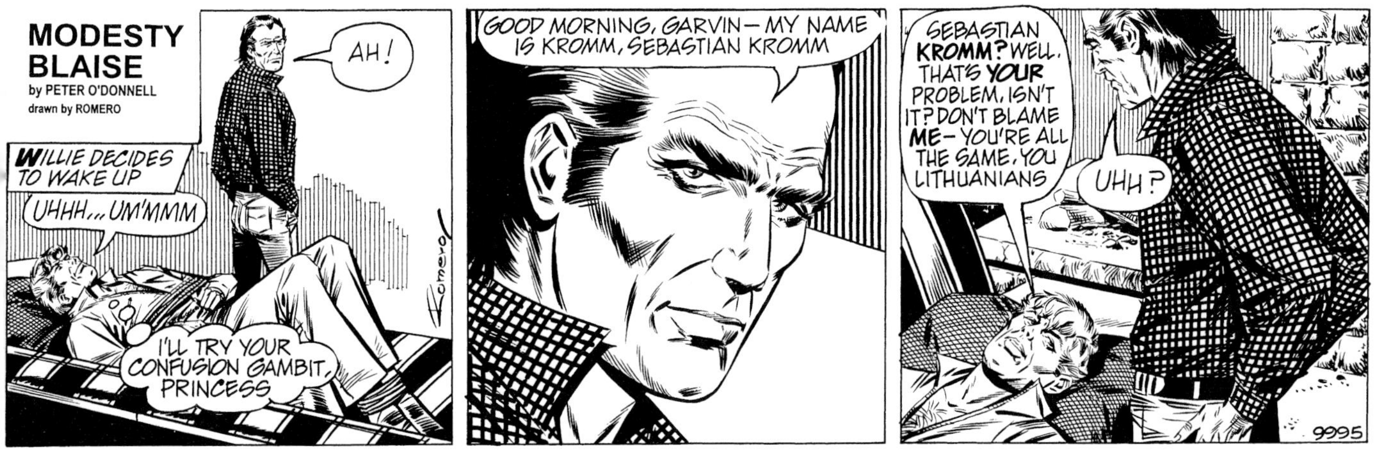
MODESTY BLAISE
by PETER O'DONNELL
drawn by ROMERO
AH!
WILLIE DECIDES TO WAKE UP
UHHH... UM'MMM
I'LL TRY YOUR CONFUSION GAMBIT, PRINCESS
GOOD MORNING, GARVIN — MY NAME IS KROMM, SEBASTIAN KROMM
SEBASTIAN KROMM? WELL, THAT'S YOUR PROBLEM, ISN'T IT? DON'T BLAME ME — YOU'RE ALL THE SAME, YOU LITHUANIANS
UHH?
9995

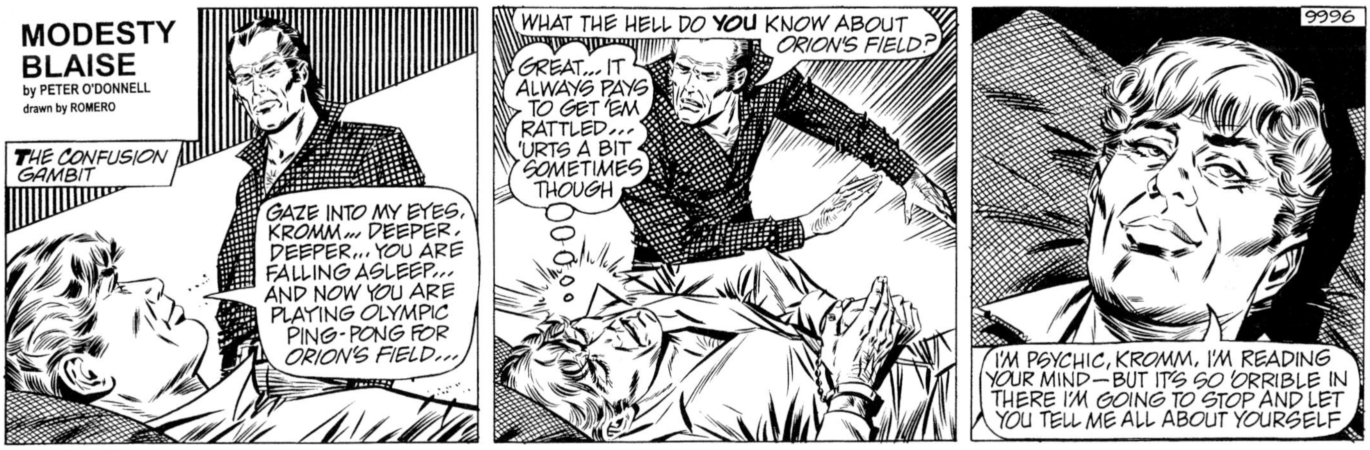
MODESTY BLAISE
by PETER O'DONNELL
drawn by ROMERO
THE CONFUSION GAMBIT
GAZE INTO MY EYES, KROMM... DEEPER, DEEPER... YOU ARE FALLING ASLEEP... AND NOW YOU ARE PLAYING OLYMPIC PING-PONG FOR ORION'S FIELD...
WHAT THE HELL DO YOU KNOW ABOUT ORION'S FIELD?
GREAT... IT ALWAYS PAYS TO GET 'EM RATTLED... 'URTS A BIT SOMETIMES THOUGH
9996
I'M PSYCHIC, KROMM, I'M READING YOUR MIND — BUT IT'S SO 'ORRIBLE IN THERE I'M GOING TO STOP AND LET YOU TELL ME ALL ABOUT YOURSELF

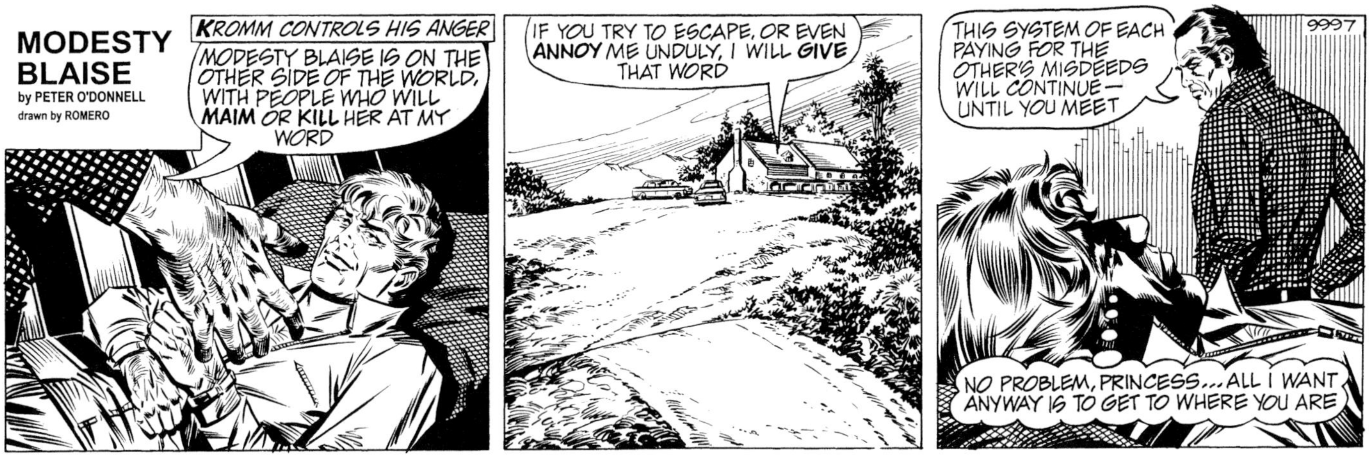
MODESTY BLAISE
by PETER O'DONNELL
drawn by ROMERO
KROMM CONTROLS HIS ANGER
MODESTY BLAISE IS ON THE OTHER SIDE OF THE WORLD, WITH PEOPLE WHO WILL MAIM OR KILL HER AT MY WORD
IF YOU TRY TO ESCAPE, OR EVEN ANNOY ME UNDULY, I WILL GIVE THAT WORD
9997
THIS SYSTEM OF EACH PAYING FOR THE OTHER'S MISDEEDS WILL CONTINUE — UNTIL YOU MEET
NO PROBLEM, PRINCESS... ALL I WANT ANYWAY IS TO GET TO WHERE YOU ARE

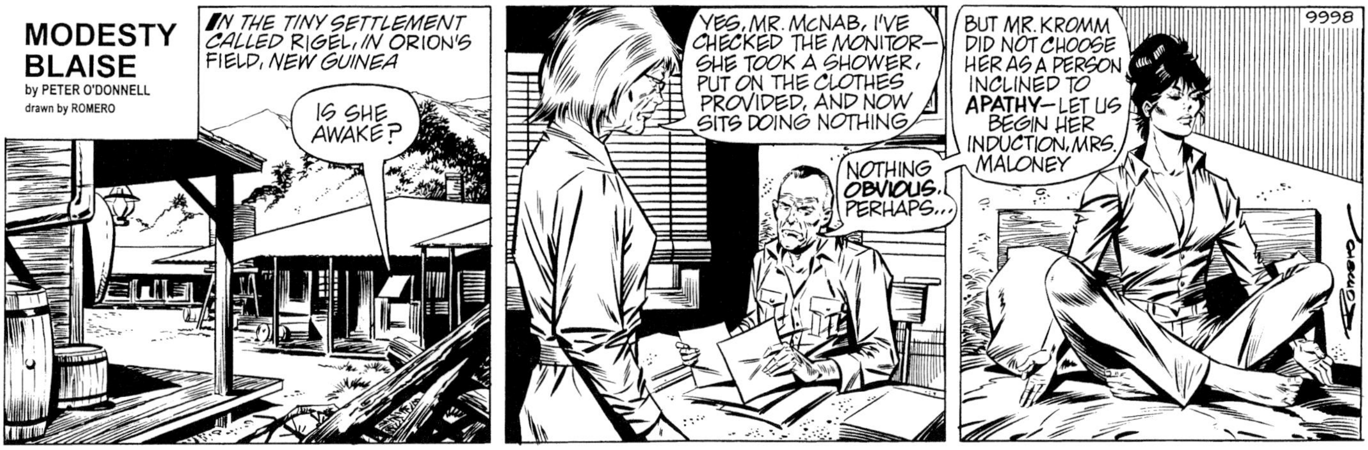
MODESTY BLAISE
by PETER O'DONNELL
drawn by ROMERO
IN THE TINY SETTLEMENT CALLED RIGEL, IN ORION'S FIELD, NEW GUINEA
IS SHE AWAKE?
YES, MR. McNAB, I'VE CHECKED THE MONITOR — SHE TOOK A SHOWER, PUT ON THE CLOTHES PROVIDED, AND NOW SITS DOING NOTHING
NOTHING OBVIOUS, PERHAPS...
9998
BUT MR. KROMM DID NOT CHOOSE HER AS A PERSON INCLINED TO APATHY — LET US BEGIN HER INDUCTION, MRS. MALONEY

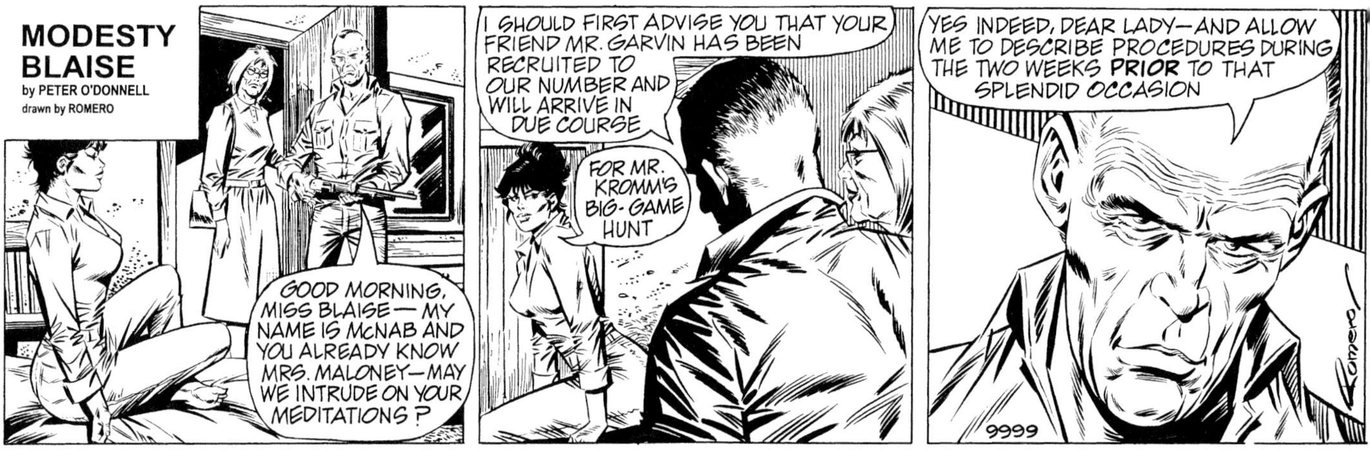
MODESTY BLAISE
by PETER O'DONNELL
drawn by ROMERO
GOOD MORNING, MISS BLAISE — MY NAME IS McNAB AND YOU ALREADY KNOW MRS. MALONEY — MAY WE INTRUDE ON YOUR MEDITATIONS ?
I SHOULD FIRST ADVISE YOU THAT YOUR FRIEND MR. GARVIN HAS BEEN RECRUITED TO OUR NUMBER AND WILL ARRIVE IN DUE COURSE
FOR MR. KROMM'S BIG-GAME HUNT
YES INDEED, DEAR LADY — AND ALLOW ME TO DESCRIBE PROCEDURES DURING THE TWO WEEKS PRIOR TO THAT SPLENDID OCCASION
Romero
9999

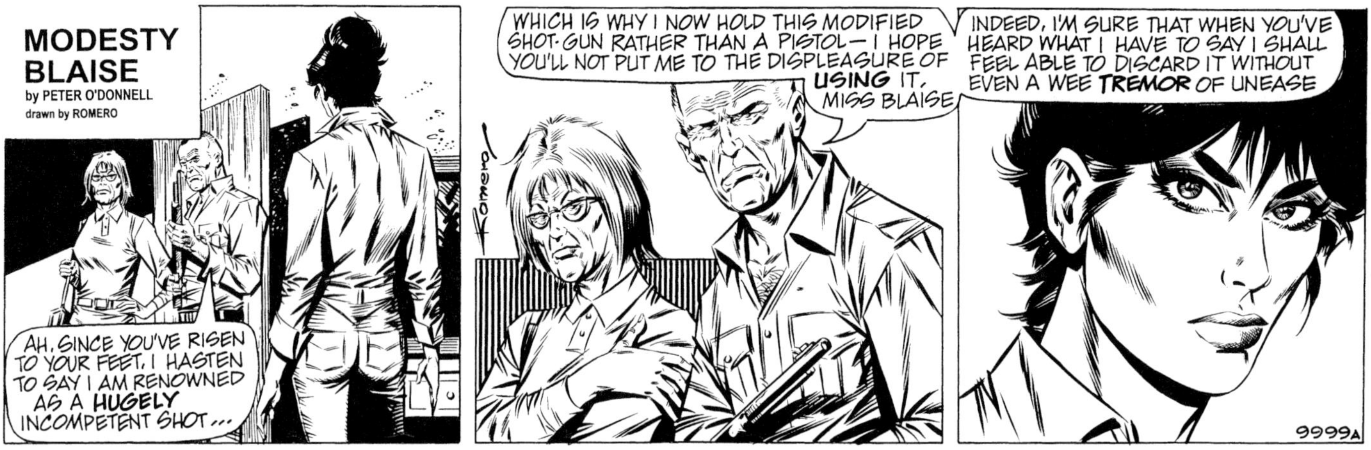
MODESTY BLAISE
by PETER O'DONNELL
drawn by ROMERO
AH, SINCE YOU'VE RISEN TO YOUR FEET, I HASTEN TO SAY I AM RENOWNED AS A HUGELY INCOMPETENT SHOT ...
WHICH IS WHY I NOW HOLD THIS MODIFIED SHOT-GUN RATHER THAN A PISTOL — I HOPE YOU'LL NOT PUT ME TO THE DISPLEASURE OF USING IT, MISS BLAISE
Romero
INDEED, I'M SURE THAT WHEN YOU'VE HEARD WHAT I HAVE TO SAY I SHALL FEEL ABLE TO DISCARD IT WITHOUT EVEN A WEE TREMOR OF UNEASE
9999A

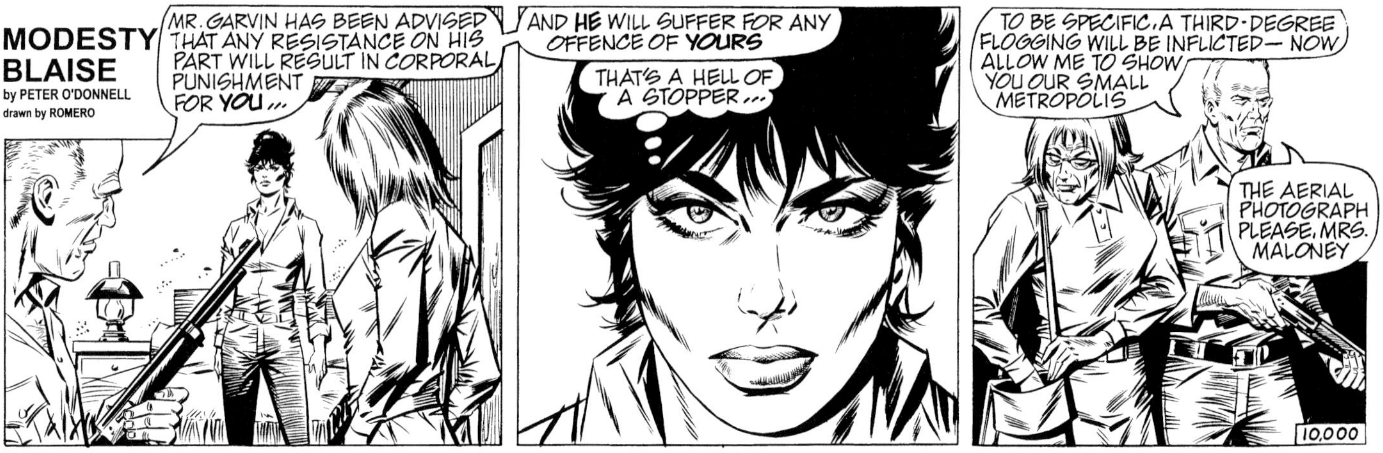
MODESTY BLAISE
by PETER O'DONNELL
drawn by ROMERO
MR. GARVIN HAS BEEN ADVISED THAT ANY RESISTANCE ON HIS PART WILL RESULT IN CORPORAL PUNISHMENT FOR YOU ...
AND HE WILL SUFFER FOR ANY OFFENCE OF YOURS
THAT'S A HELL OF A STOPPER ...
TO BE SPECIFIC, A THIRD-DEGREE FLOGGING WILL BE INFLICTED — NOW ALLOW ME TO SHOW YOU OUR SMALL METROPOLIS
THE AERIAL PHOTOGRAPH PLEASE, MRS. MALONEY
10,000

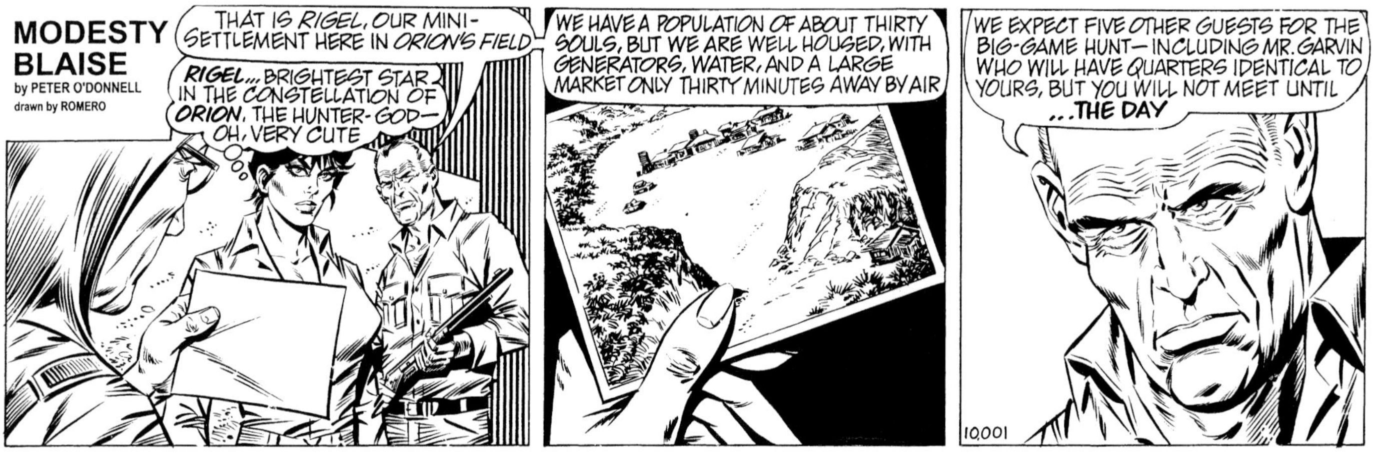
MODESTY BLAISE
by PETER O'DONNELL
drawn by ROMERO
THAT IS RIGEL, OUR MINI-SETTLEMENT HERE IN ORION'S FIELD
RIGEL ... BRIGHTEST STAR IN THE CONSTELLATION OF ORION, THE HUNTER-GOD — OH, VERY CUTE
WE HAVE A POPULATION OF ABOUT THIRTY SOULS, BUT WE ARE WELL HOUSED, WITH GENERATORS, WATER, AND A LARGE MARKET ONLY THIRTY MINUTES AWAY BY AIR
WE EXPECT FIVE OTHER GUESTS FOR THE BIG-GAME HUNT — INCLUDING MR. GARVIN WHO WILL HAVE QUARTERS IDENTICAL TO YOURS, BUT YOU WILL NOT MEET UNTIL ... THE DAY
10,001

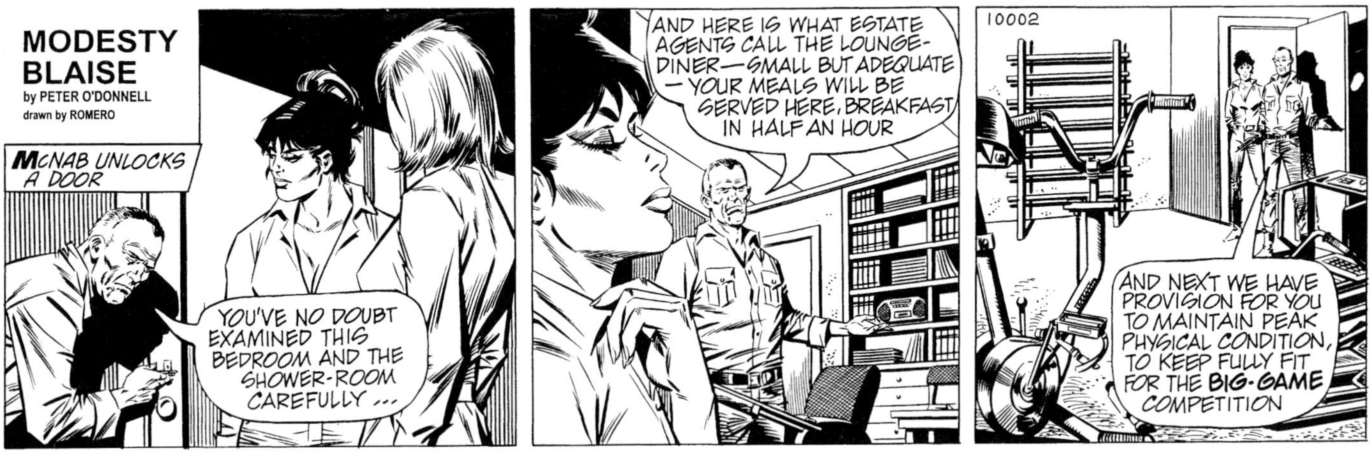
MODESTY BLAISE
by PETER O'DONNELL
drawn by ROMERO
McNAB UNLOCKS A DOOR
YOU'VE NO DOUBT EXAMINED THIS BEDROOM AND THE SHOWER-ROOM CAREFULLY ...
AND HERE IS WHAT ESTATE AGENTS CALL THE LOUNGE-DINER — SMALL BUT ADEQUATE — YOUR MEALS WILL BE SERVED HERE, BREAKFAST IN HALF AN HOUR
10002
AND NEXT WE HAVE PROVISION FOR YOU TO MAINTAIN PEAK PHYSICAL CONDITION, TO KEEP FULLY FIT FOR THE BIG-GAME COMPETITION

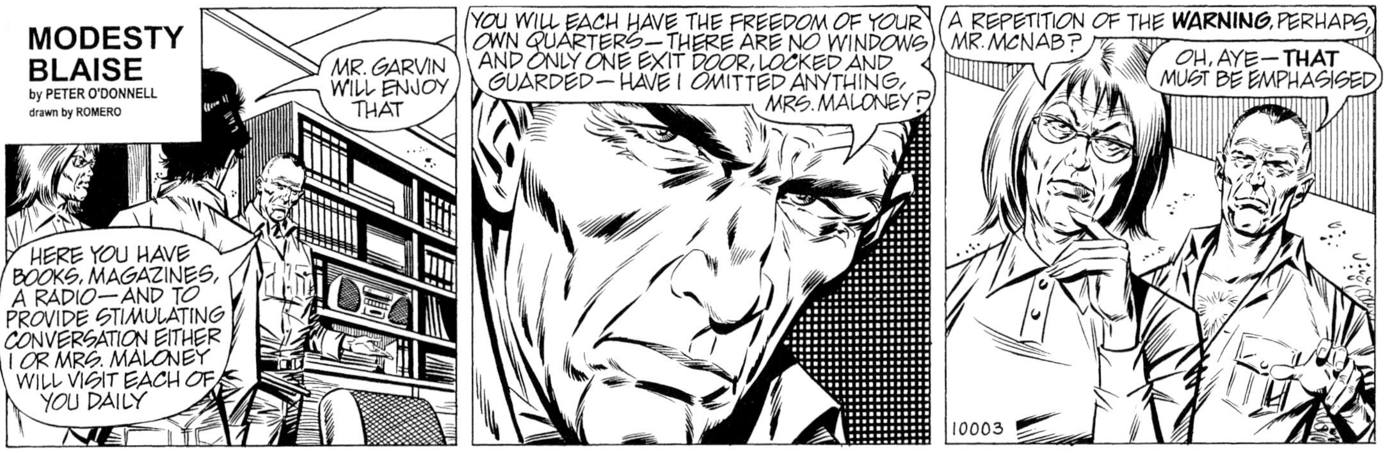
MODESTY BLAISE
by PETER O'DONNELL
drawn by ROMERO
MR. GARVIN WILL ENJOY THAT
HERE YOU HAVE BOOKS, MAGAZINES, A RADIO — AND TO PROVIDE STIMULATING CONVERSATION EITHER I OR MRS. MALONEY WILL VISIT EACH OF YOU DAILY
YOU WILL EACH HAVE THE FREEDOM OF YOUR OWN QUARTERS — THERE ARE NO WINDOWS AND ONLY ONE EXIT DOOR, LOCKED AND GUARDED — HAVE I OMITTED ANYTHING, MRS. MALONEY?
A REPETITION OF THE WARNING, PERHAPS, MR. McNAB?
OH, AYE — THAT MUST BE EMPHASISED
10003

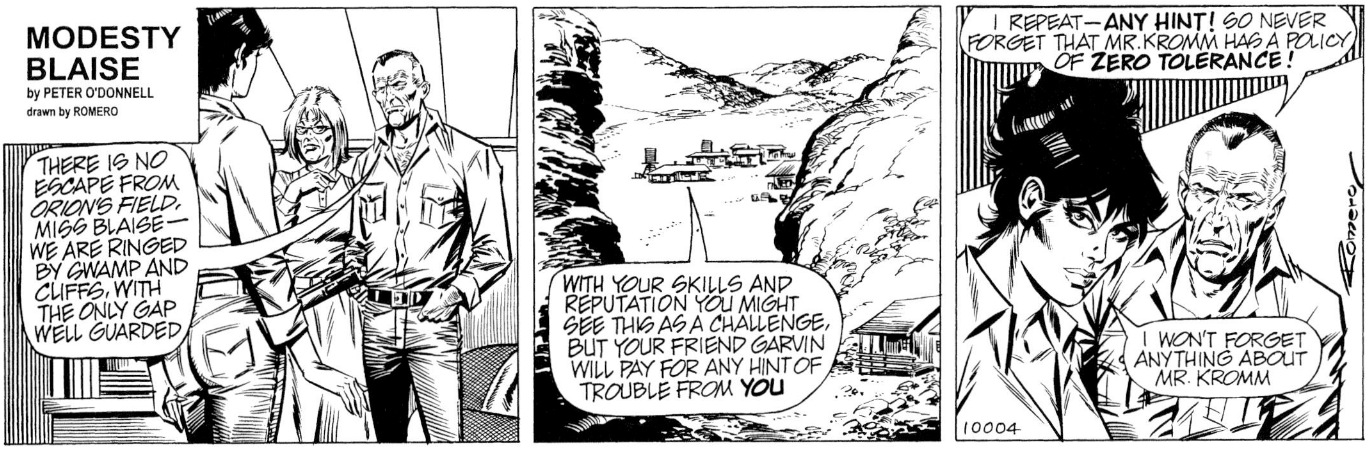
MODESTY BLAISE
by PETER O'DONNELL
drawn by ROMERO
THERE IS NO ESCAPE FROM ORION'S FIELD, MISS BLAISE — WE ARE RINGED BY SWAMP AND CLIFFS, WITH THE ONLY GAP WELL GUARDED
WITH YOUR SKILLS AND REPUTATION YOU MIGHT SEE THIS AS A CHALLENGE, BUT YOUR FRIEND GARVIN WILL PAY FOR ANY HINT OF TROUBLE FROM YOU
I REPEAT — ANY HINT! SO NEVER FORGET THAT MR. KROMM HAS A POLICY OF ZERO TOLERANCE!
I WON'T FORGET ANYTHING ABOUT MR. KROMM
Romero
10004

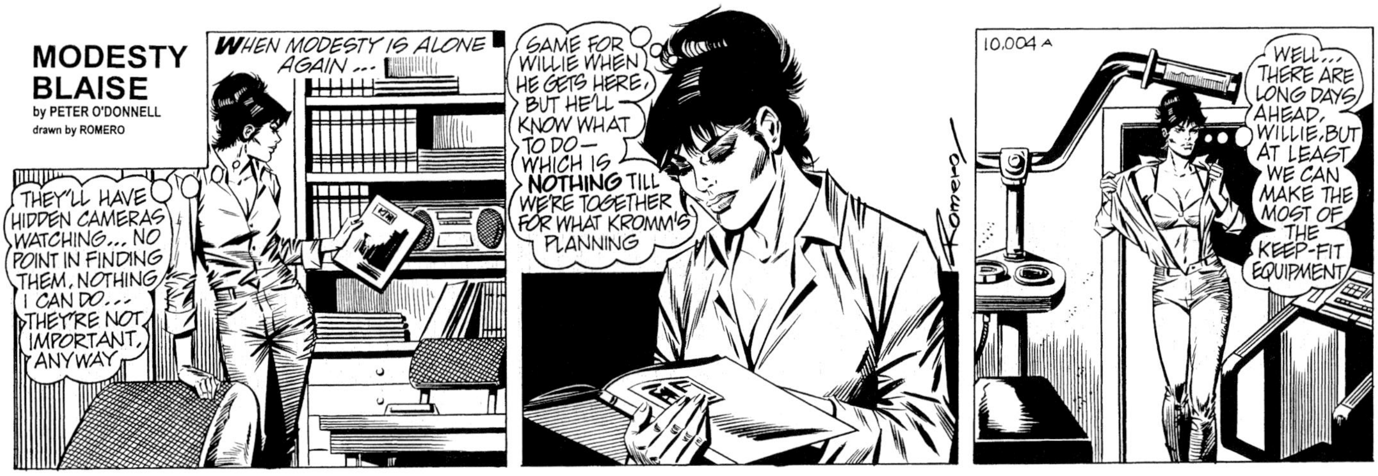
MODESTY BLAISE
by PETER O'DONNELL
drawn by ROMERO
WHEN MODESTY IS ALONE AGAIN ...
THEY'LL HAVE HIDDEN CAMERAS WATCHING... NO POINT IN FINDING THEM, NOTHING I CAN DO... THEY'RE NOT IMPORTANT, ANYWAY
SAME FOR WILLIE WHEN HE GETS HERE, BUT HE'LL KNOW WHAT TO DO — WHICH IS NOTHING TILL WE'RE TOGETHER FOR WHAT KROMM'S PLANNING
Romero
10,004 A
WELL... THERE ARE LONG DAYS AHEAD, WILLIE, BUT AT LEAST WE CAN MAKE THE MOST OF THE KEEP-FIT EQUIPMENT

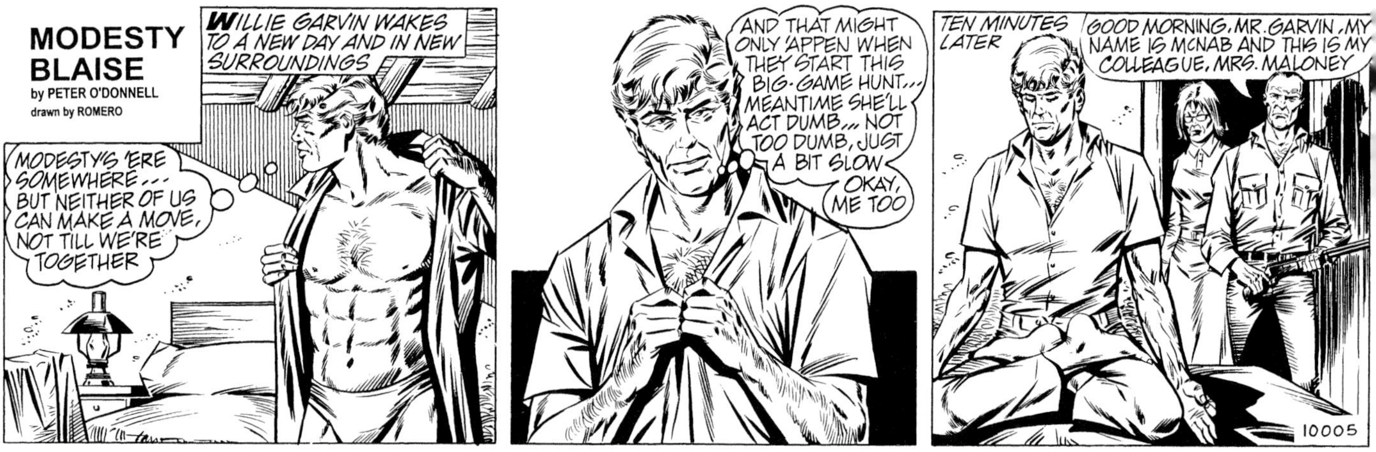
MODESTY BLAISE
by PETER O'DONNELL
drawn by ROMERO
WILLIE GARVIN WAKES TO A NEW DAY AND IN NEW SURROUNDINGS
MODESTY'S 'ERE SOMEWHERE... BUT NEITHER OF US CAN MAKE A MOVE, NOT TILL WE'RE TOGETHER
AND THAT MIGHT ONLY 'APPEN WHEN THEY START THIS BIG-GAME HUNT... MEANTIME SHE'LL ACT DUMB... NOT TOO DUMB, JUST A BIT SLOW
OKAY, ME TOO
TEN MINUTES LATER
GOOD MORNING, MR. GARVIN, MY NAME IS MCNAB AND THIS IS MY COLLEAGUE, MRS. MALONEY
10005

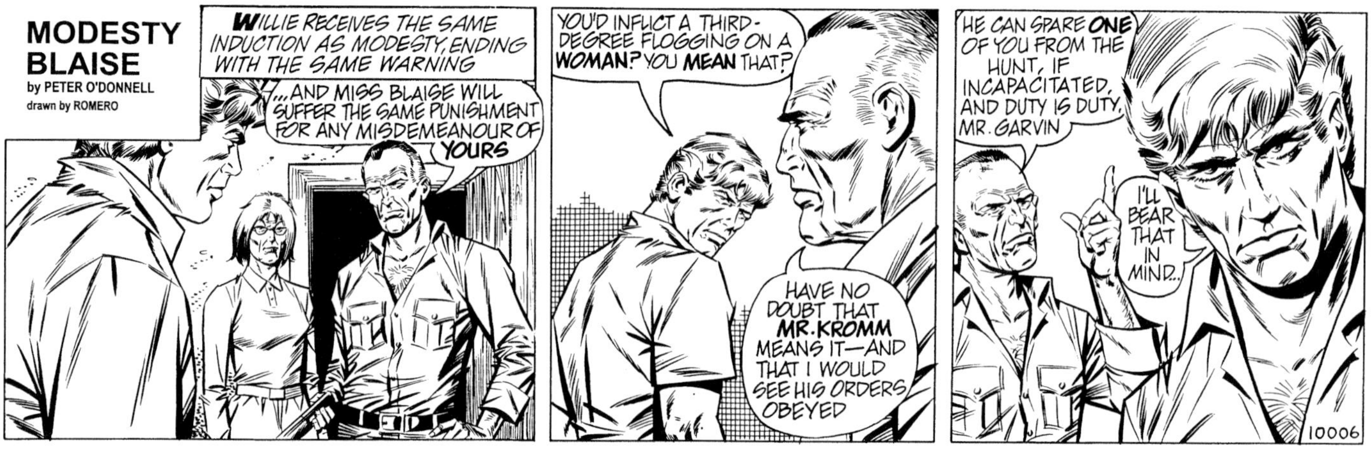
MODESTY BLAISE
by PETER O'DONNELL
drawn by ROMERO
WILLIE RECEIVES THE SAME INDUCTION AS MODESTY, ENDING WITH THE SAME WARNING
...AND MISS BLAISE WILL SUFFER THE SAME PUNISHMENT FOR ANY MISDEMEANOUR OF YOURS
YOU'D INFLICT A THIRD-DEGREE FLOGGING ON A WOMAN? YOU MEAN THAT?
HAVE NO DOUBT THAT MR. KROMM MEANS IT—AND THAT I WOULD SEE HIS ORDERS OBEYED
HE CAN SPARE ONE OF YOU FROM THE HUNT, IF INCAPACITATED, AND DUTY IS DUTY, MR. GARVIN
I'LL BEAR THAT IN MIND...
10006

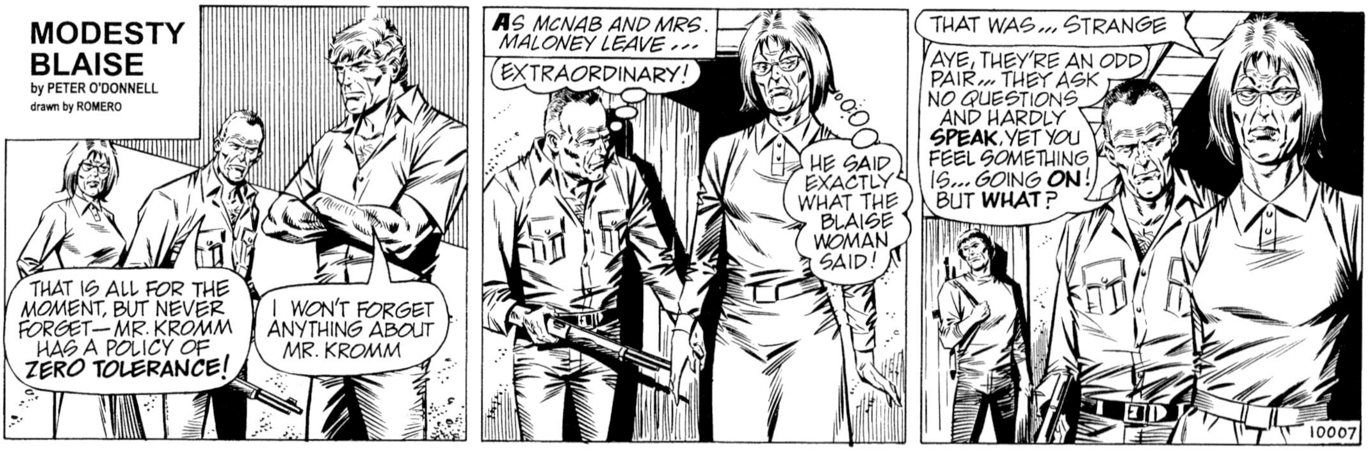
MODESTY BLAISE
by PETER O'DONNELL
drawn by ROMERO
THAT IS ALL FOR THE MOMENT, BUT NEVER FORGET—MR. KROMM HAS A POLICY OF ZERO TOLERANCE!
I WON'T FORGET ANYTHING ABOUT MR. KROMM
AS MCNAB AND MRS. MALONEY LEAVE...
EXTRAORDINARY!
HE SAID EXACTLY WHAT THE BLAISE WOMAN SAID!
THAT WAS... STRANGE
AYE, THEY'RE AN ODD PAIR... THEY ASK NO QUESTIONS AND HARDLY SPEAK, YET YOU FEEL SOMETHING IS... GOING ON! BUT WHAT?
10007

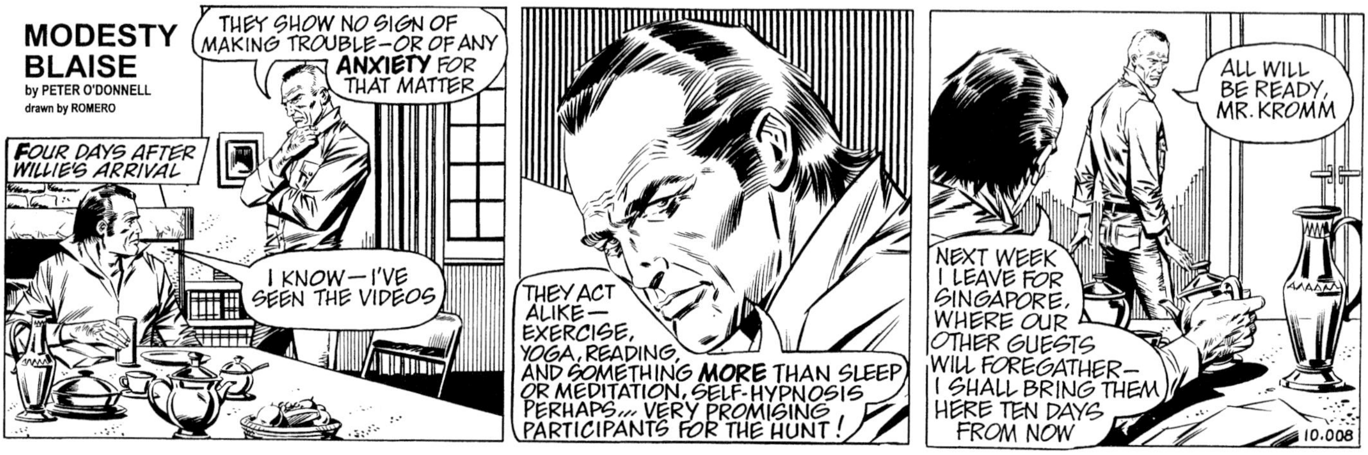
MODESTY BLAISE
by PETER O'DONNELL
drawn by ROMERO
THEY SHOW NO SIGN OF MAKING TROUBLE—OR OF ANY ANXIETY FOR THAT MATTER
FOUR DAYS AFTER WILLIE'S ARRIVAL
I KNOW—I'VE SEEN THE VIDEOS
THEY ACT ALIKE—EXERCISE, YOGA, READING, AND SOMETHING MORE THAN SLEEP OR MEDITATION. SELF-HYPNOSIS PERHAPS... VERY PROMISING PARTICIPANTS FOR THE HUNT!
ALL WILL BE READY, MR. KROMM
NEXT WEEK I LEAVE FOR SINGAPORE, WHERE OUR OTHER GUESTS WILL FOREGATHER—I SHALL BRING THEM HERE TEN DAYS FROM NOW
10.008

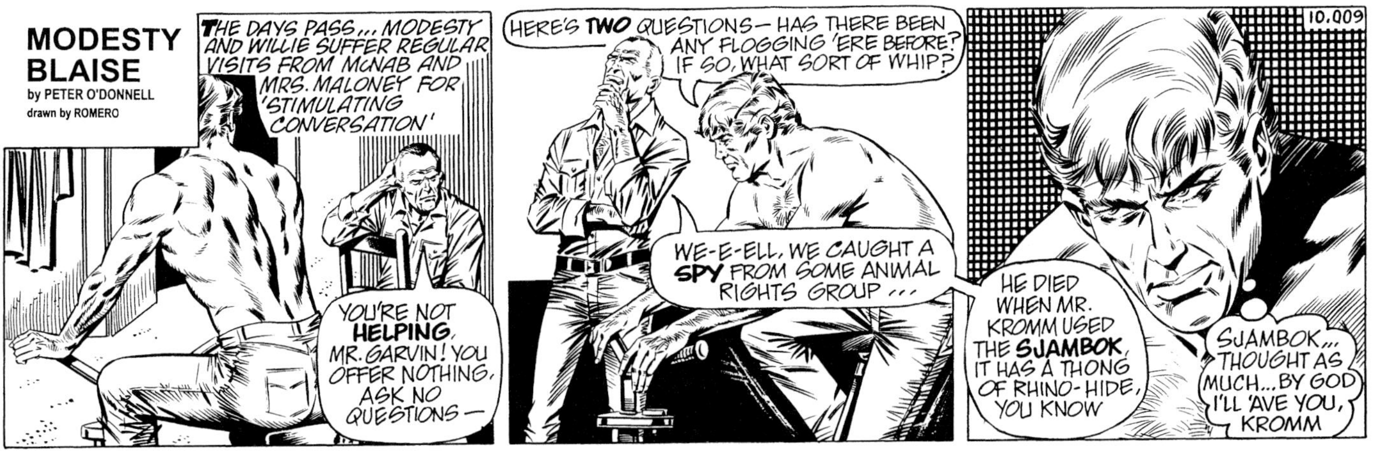
MODESTY BLAISE
by PETER O'DONNELL
drawn by ROMERO
THE DAYS PASS... MODESTY AND WILLIE SUFFER REGULAR VISITS FROM McNAB AND MRS. MALONEY FOR 'STIMULATING CONVERSATION'
YOU'RE NOT HELPING, MR. GARVIN! YOU OFFER NOTHING, ASK NO QUESTIONS —
HERE'S TWO QUESTIONS — HAS THERE BEEN ANY FLOGGING 'ERE BEFORE? IF SO, WHAT SORT OF WHIP?
WE-E-ELL, WE CAUGHT A SPY FROM SOME ANIMAL RIGHTS GROUP...
10.009
HE DIED WHEN MR. KROMM USED THE SJAMBOK, IT HAS A THONG OF RHINO-HIDE, YOU KNOW
SJAMBOK... THOUGHT AS MUCH... BY GOD I'LL 'AVE YOU, KROMM

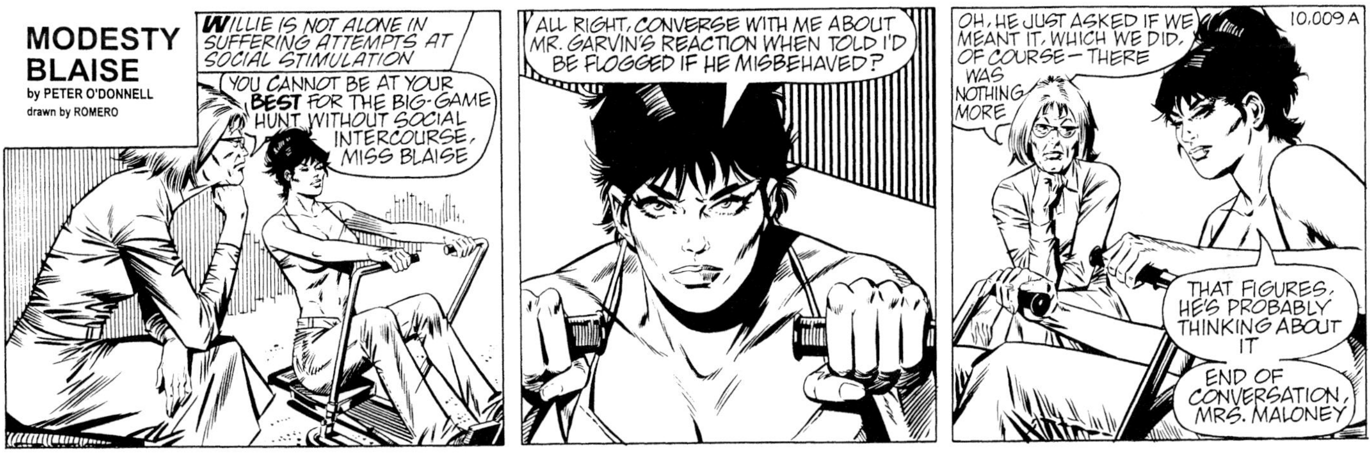
MODESTY BLAISE
by PETER O'DONNELL
drawn by ROMERO
WILLIE IS NOT ALONE IN SUFFERING ATTEMPTS AT SOCIAL STIMULATION
YOU CANNOT BE AT YOUR BEST FOR THE BIG-GAME HUNT WITHOUT SOCIAL INTERCOURSE, MISS BLAISE
ALL RIGHT, CONVERSE WITH ME ABOUT MR. GARVIN'S REACTION WHEN TOLD I'D BE FLOGGED IF HE MISBEHAVED?
10.009 A
OH, HE JUST ASKED IF WE MEANT IT, WHICH WE DID, OF COURSE — THERE WAS NOTHING MORE
THAT FIGURES, HE'S PROBABLY THINKING ABOUT IT
END OF CONVERSATION, MRS. MALONEY

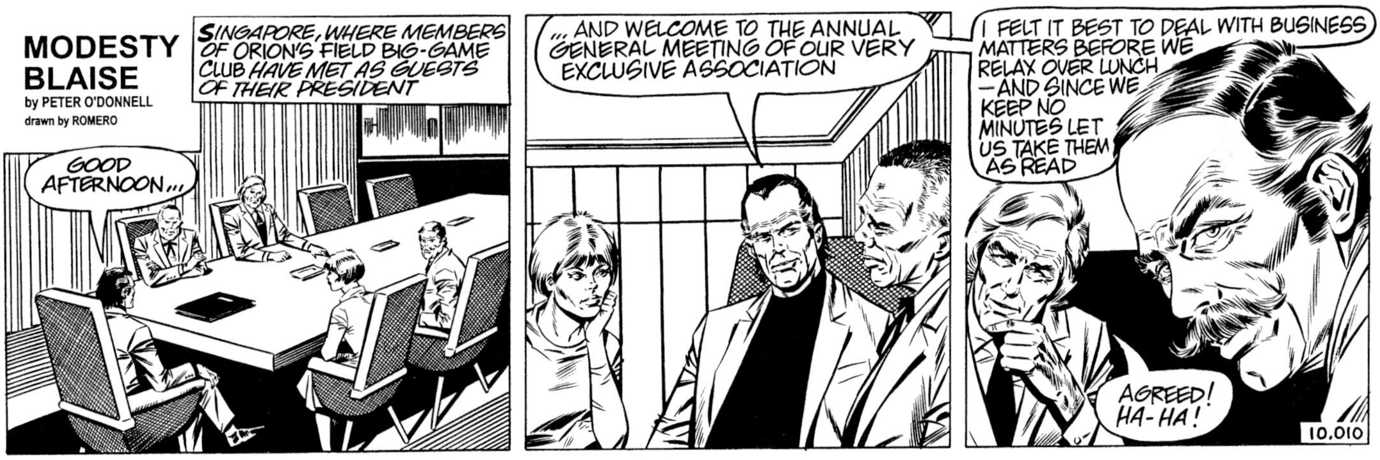
MODESTY BLAISE
by PETER O'DONNELL
drawn by ROMERO
SINGAPORE, WHERE MEMBERS OF ORION'S FIELD BIG-GAME CLUB HAVE MET AS GUESTS OF THEIR PRESIDENT
GOOD AFTERNOON...
...AND WELCOME TO THE ANNUAL GENERAL MEETING OF OUR VERY EXCLUSIVE ASSOCIATION
I FELT IT BEST TO DEAL WITH BUSINESS MATTERS BEFORE WE RELAX OVER LUNCH — AND SINCE WE KEEP NO MINUTES LET US TAKE THEM AS READ
AGREED! HA-HA!
10.010

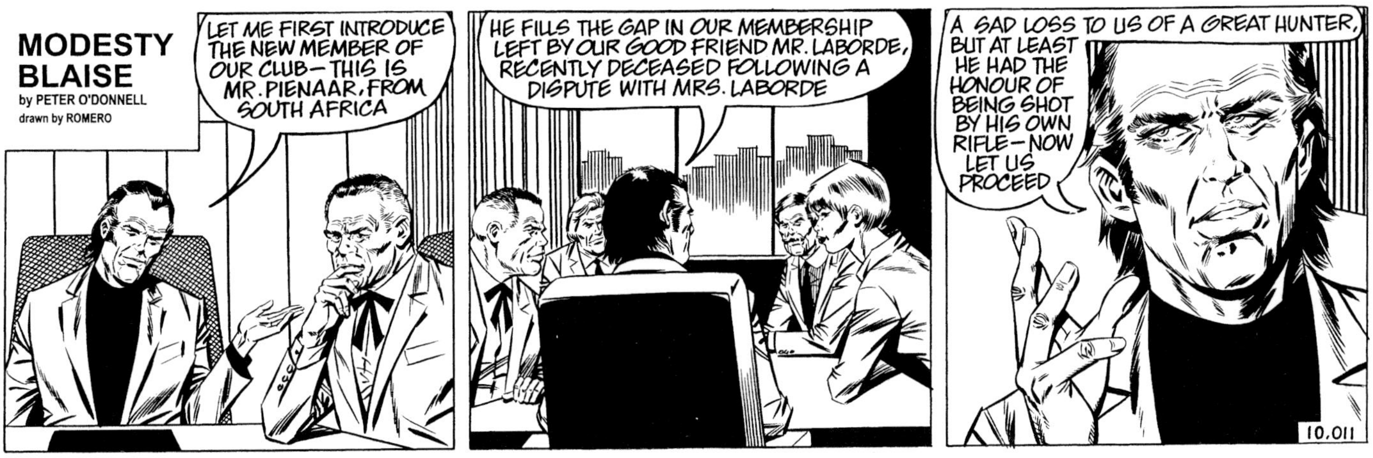
MODESTY BLAISE
by PETER O'DONNELL
drawn by ROMERO
LET ME FIRST INTRODUCE THE NEW MEMBER OF OUR CLUB — THIS IS MR. PIENAAR, FROM SOUTH AFRICA
HE FILLS THE GAP IN OUR MEMBERSHIP LEFT BY OUR GOOD FRIEND MR. LABORDE, RECENTLY DECEASED FOLLOWING A DISPUTE WITH MRS. LABORDE
A SAD LOSS TO US OF A GREAT HUNTER, BUT AT LEAST HE HAD THE HONOUR OF BEING SHOT BY HIS OWN RIFLE — NOW LET US PROCEED
10.011

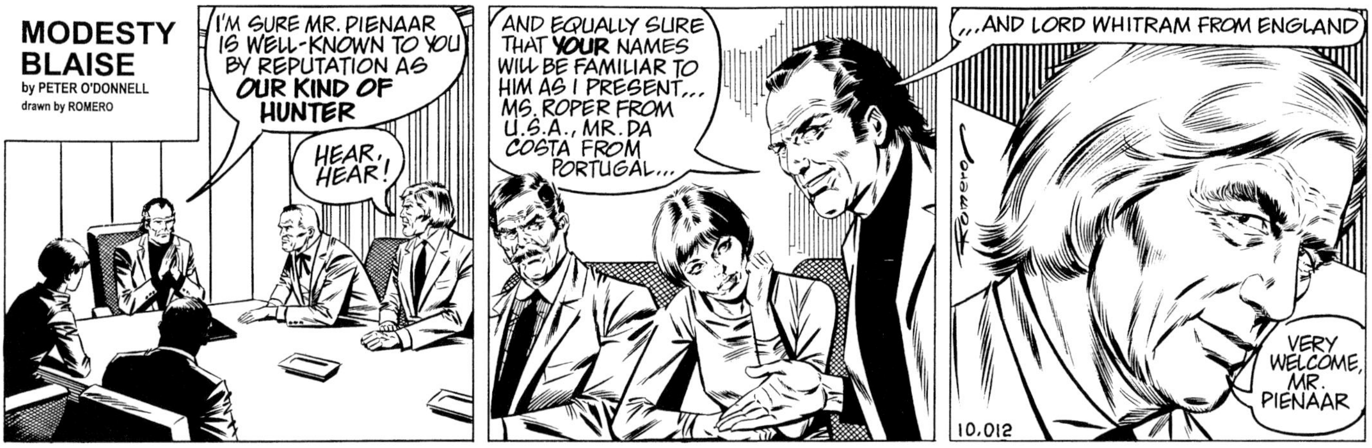
MODESTY BLAISE
by PETER O'DONNELL
drawn by ROMERO
I'M SURE MR. PIENAAR IS WELL-KNOWN TO YOU BY REPUTATION AS **OUR KIND OF HUNTER**
HEAR, HEAR!
AND EQUALLY SURE THAT **YOUR** NAMES WILL BE FAMILIAR TO HIM AS I PRESENT... MS. ROPER FROM U.S.A., MR. DA COSTA FROM PORTUGAL...
...AND LORD WHITRAM FROM ENGLAND
VERY WELCOME, MR. PIENAAR
ROMERO
10,012

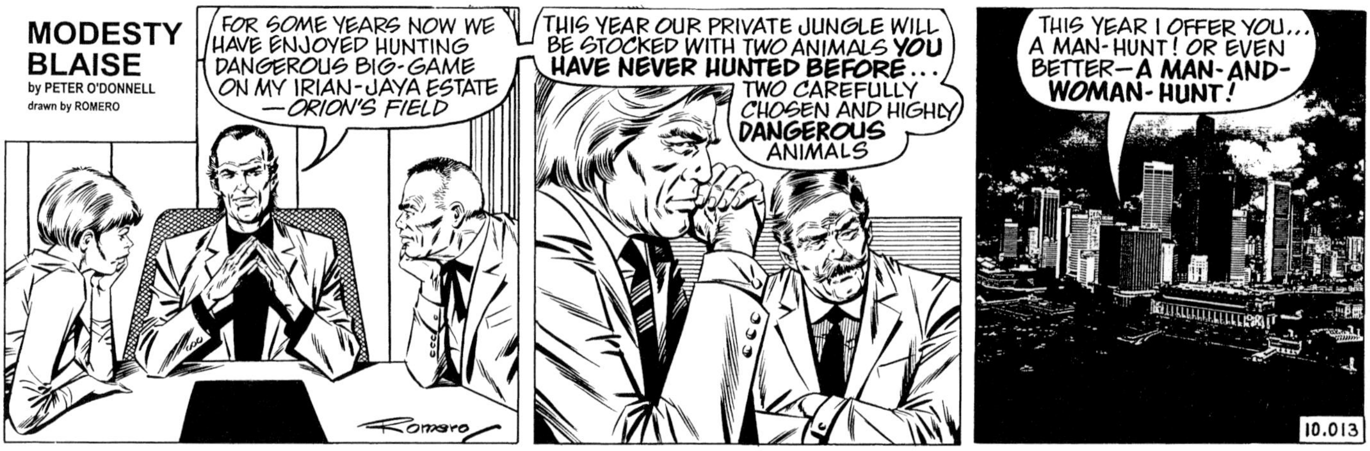
MODESTY BLAISE
by PETER O'DONNELL
drawn by ROMERO
FOR SOME YEARS NOW WE HAVE ENJOYED HUNTING DANGEROUS BIG-GAME ON MY IRIAN-JAYA ESTATE —*ORION'S FIELD*
ROMERO
THIS YEAR OUR PRIVATE JUNGLE WILL BE STOCKED WITH TWO ANIMALS **YOU HAVE NEVER HUNTED BEFORE**...
TWO CAREFULLY CHOSEN AND HIGHLY **DANGEROUS** ANIMALS
THIS YEAR I OFFER YOU... A MAN-HUNT! OR EVEN BETTER—**A MAN-AND-WOMAN-HUNT!**
10,013

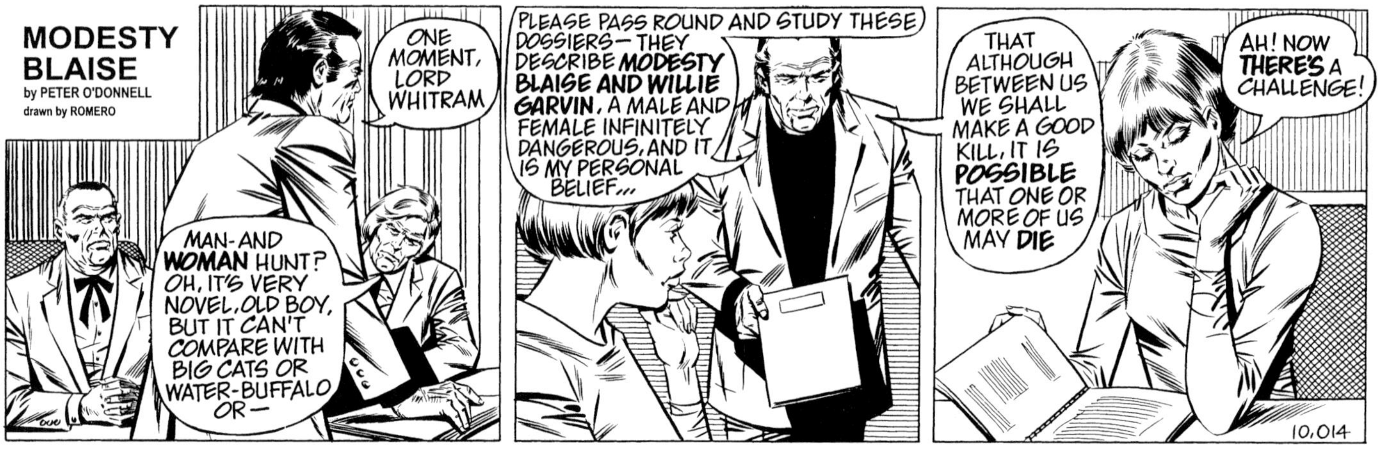
MODESTY BLAISE
by PETER O'DONNELL
drawn by ROMERO
MAN-AND **WOMAN** HUNT? OH, IT'S VERY NOVEL, OLD BOY, BUT IT CAN'T COMPARE WITH BIG CATS OR WATER-BUFFALO OR—
ONE MOMENT, LORD WHITRAM
PLEASE PASS ROUND AND STUDY THESE DOSSIERS— THEY DESCRIBE **MODESTY BLAISE AND WILLIE GARVIN**, A MALE AND FEMALE INFINITELY DANGEROUS, AND IT IS MY PERSONAL BELIEF...
THAT ALTHOUGH BETWEEN US WE SHALL MAKE A GOOD KILL, IT IS **POSSIBLE** THAT ONE OR MORE OF US MAY **DIE**
AH! NOW **THERE'S** A CHALLENGE!
10,014

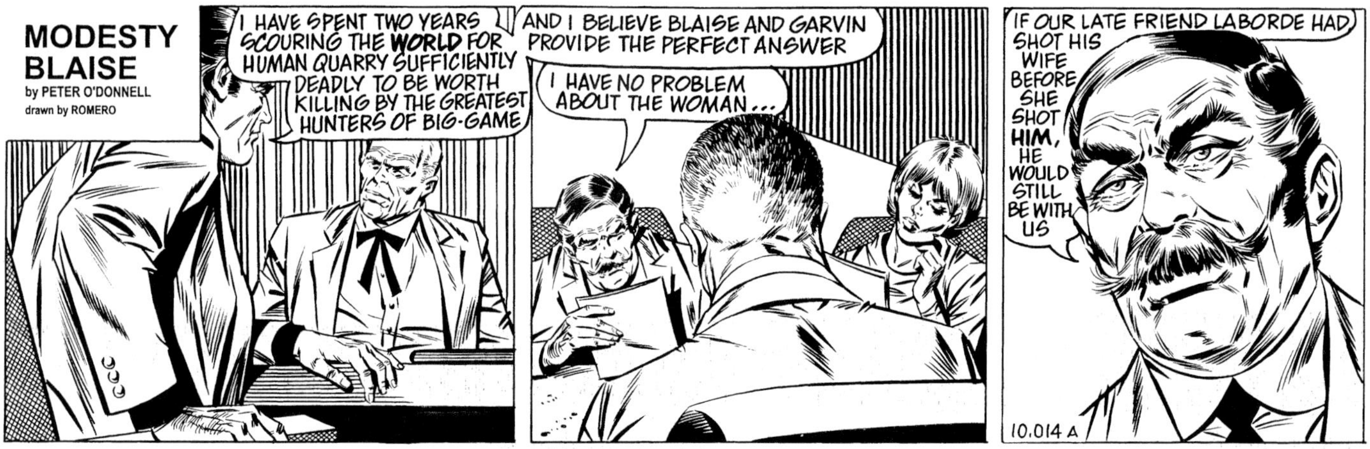
MODESTY BLAISE
by PETER O'DONNELL
drawn by ROMERO
I HAVE SPENT TWO YEARS SCOURING THE **WORLD** FOR HUMAN QUARRY SUFFICIENTLY DEADLY TO BE WORTH KILLING BY THE GREATEST HUNTERS OF BIG-GAME
AND I BELIEVE BLAISE AND GARVIN PROVIDE THE PERFECT ANSWER
I HAVE NO PROBLEM ABOUT THE WOMAN...
IF OUR LATE FRIEND LABORDE HAD SHOT HIS WIFE BEFORE SHE SHOT **HIM**, HE WOULD STILL BE WITH US
10,014 A

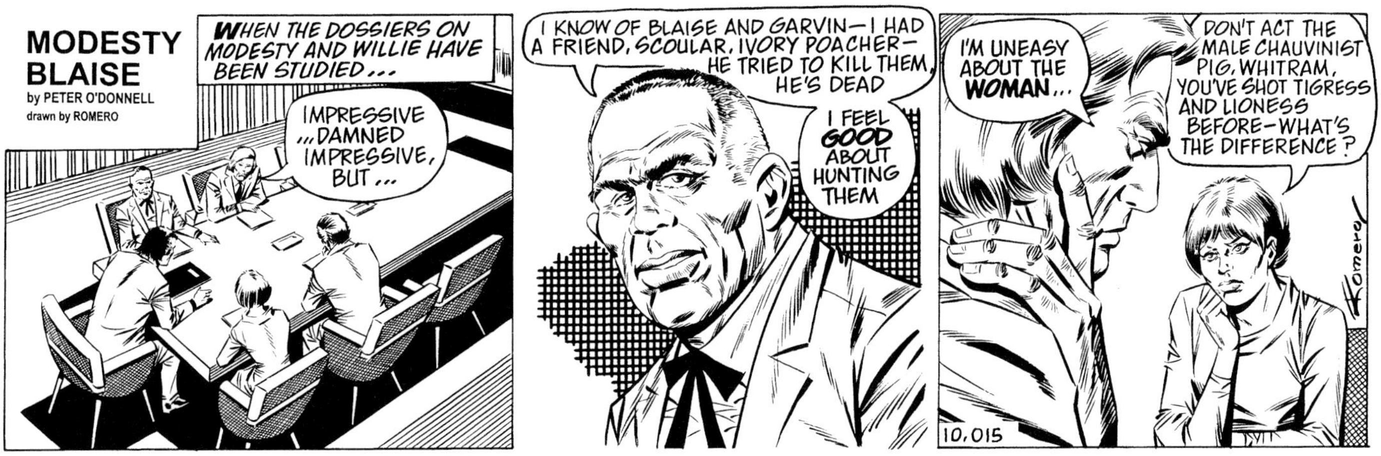
MODESTY BLAISE
by PETER O'DONNELL
drawn by ROMERO
WHEN THE DOSSIERS ON MODESTY AND WILLIE HAVE BEEN STUDIED...
IMPRESSIVE ...DAMNED IMPRESSIVE, BUT...
I KNOW OF BLAISE AND GARVIN—I HAD A FRIEND, SCOULAR, IVORY POACHER—HE TRIED TO KILL THEM. HE'S DEAD
I FEEL GOOD ABOUT HUNTING THEM
I'M UNEASY ABOUT THE WOMAN...
DON'T ACT THE MALE CHAUVINIST PIG, WHITRAM, YOU'VE SHOT TIGRESS AND LIONESS BEFORE—WHAT'S THE DIFFERENCE?
Romero
10,015

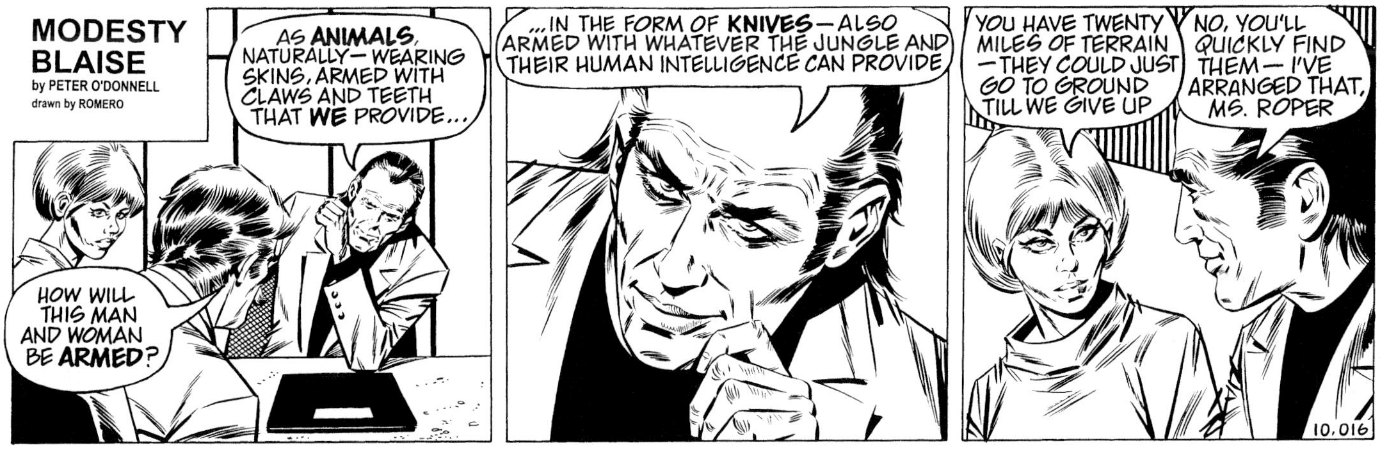
MODESTY BLAISE
by PETER O'DONNELL
drawn by ROMERO
HOW WILL THIS MAN AND WOMAN BE ARMED?
AS ANIMALS, NATURALLY—WEARING SKINS, ARMED WITH CLAWS AND TEETH THAT WE PROVIDE...
...IN THE FORM OF KNIVES—ALSO ARMED WITH WHATEVER THE JUNGLE AND THEIR HUMAN INTELLIGENCE CAN PROVIDE
YOU HAVE TWENTY MILES OF TERRAIN—THEY COULD JUST GO TO GROUND TILL WE GIVE UP
NO, YOU'LL QUICKLY FIND THEM—I'VE ARRANGED THAT, MS. ROPER
10,016

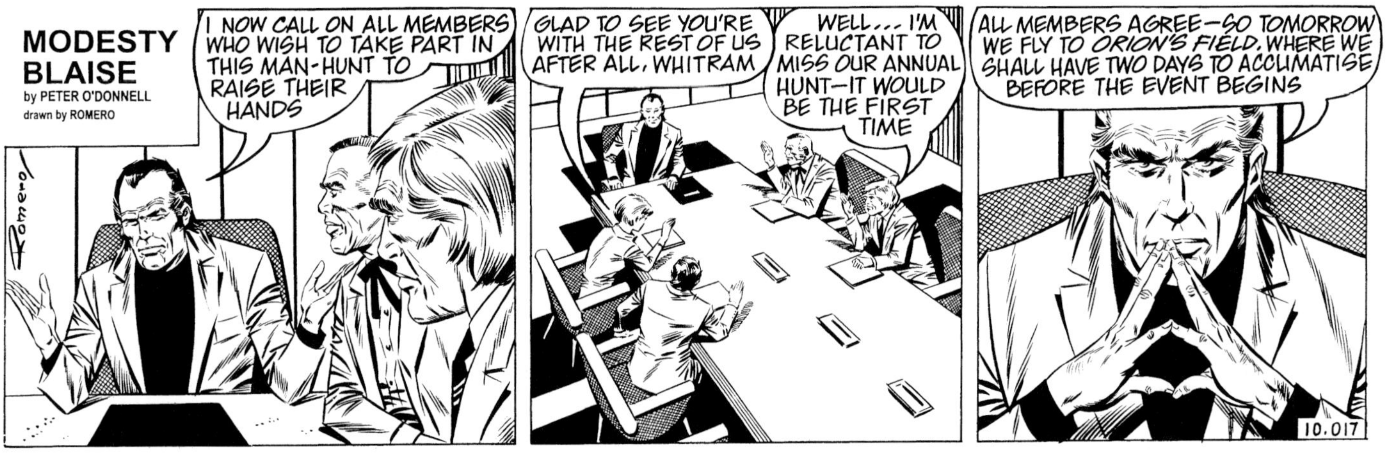
MODESTY BLAISE
by PETER O'DONNELL
drawn by ROMERO
I NOW CALL ON ALL MEMBERS WHO WISH TO TAKE PART IN THIS MAN-HUNT TO RAISE THEIR HANDS
Romero
GLAD TO SEE YOU'RE WITH THE REST OF US AFTER ALL, WHITRAM
WELL... I'M RELUCTANT TO MISS OUR ANNUAL HUNT—IT WOULD BE THE FIRST TIME
ALL MEMBERS AGREE—SO TOMORROW WE FLY TO ORION'S FIELD, WHERE WE SHALL HAVE TWO DAYS TO ACCLIMATISE BEFORE THE EVENT BEGINS
10,017

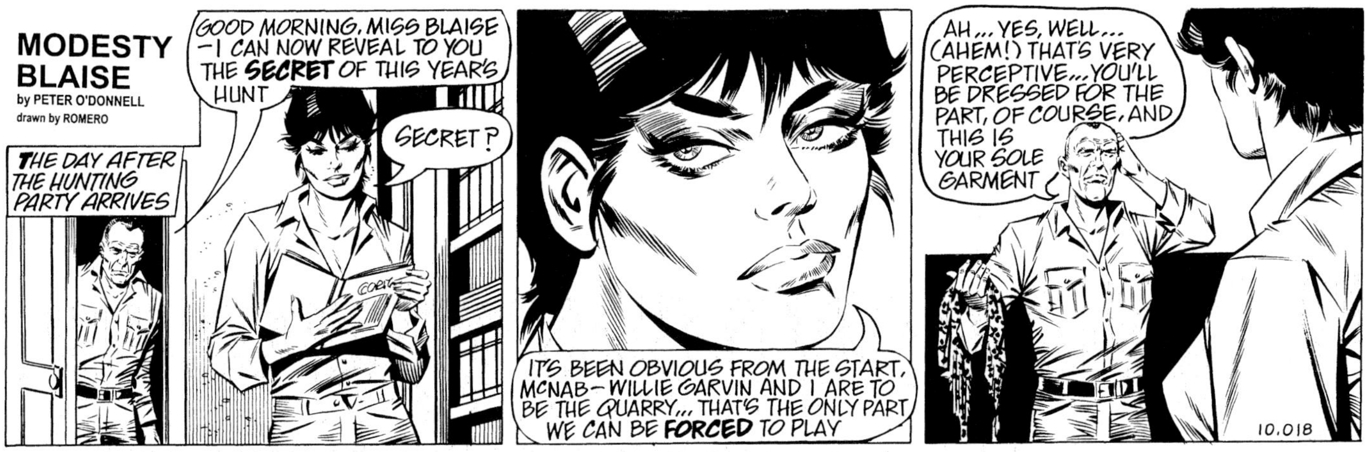
MODESTY BLAISE
by PETER O'DONNELL
drawn by ROMERO
THE DAY AFTER THE HUNTING PARTY ARRIVES
GOOD MORNING, MISS BLAISE—I CAN NOW REVEAL TO YOU THE SECRET OF THIS YEAR'S HUNT
SECRET?
IT'S BEEN OBVIOUS FROM THE START, McNAB—WILLIE GARVIN AND I ARE TO BE THE QUARRY... THAT'S THE ONLY PART WE CAN BE FORCED TO PLAY
AH... YES, WELL... (AHEM!) THAT'S VERY PERCEPTIVE... YOU'LL BE DRESSED FOR THE PART, OF COURSE, AND THIS IS YOUR SOLE GARMENT
10,018

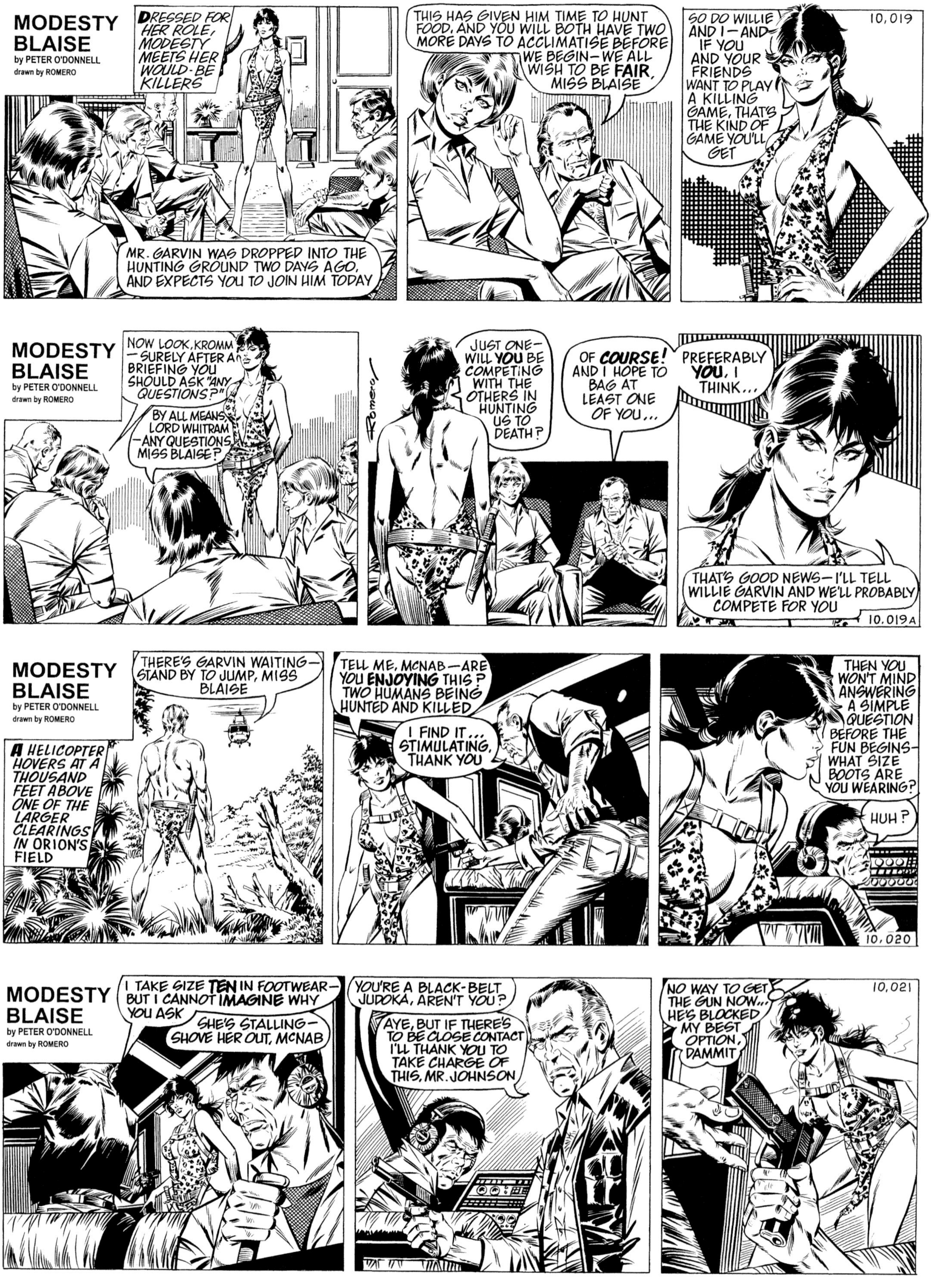
MODESTY BLAISE
by PETER O'DONNELL
drawn by ROMERO
DRESSED FOR HER ROLE, MODESTY MEETS HER WOULD-BE KILLERS
MR. GARVIN WAS DROPPED INTO THE HUNTING GROUND TWO DAYS AGO, AND EXPECTS YOU TO JOIN HIM TODAY
THIS HAS GIVEN HIM TIME TO HUNT FOOD, AND YOU WILL BOTH HAVE TWO MORE DAYS TO ACCLIMATISE BEFORE WE BEGIN—WE ALL WISH TO BE FAIR, MISS BLAISE
10,019
SO DO WILLIE AND I—AND IF YOU AND YOUR FRIENDS WANT TO PLAY A KILLING GAME, THAT'S THE KIND OF GAME YOU'LL GET
MODESTY BLAISE
by PETER O'DONNELL
drawn by ROMERO
NOW LOOK, KROMM—SURELY AFTER A BRIEFING YOU SHOULD ASK "ANY QUESTIONS?"
BY ALL MEANS, LORD WHITRAM—ANY QUESTIONS, MISS BLAISE?
JUST ONE—WILL YOU BE COMPETING WITH THE OTHERS IN HUNTING US TO DEATH?
OF COURSE! AND I HOPE TO BAG AT LEAST ONE OF YOU...
PREFERABLY YOU, I THINK...
THAT'S GOOD NEWS—I'LL TELL WILLIE GARVIN AND WE'LL PROBABLY COMPETE FOR YOU
10,019A
MODESTY BLAISE
by PETER O'DONNELL
drawn by ROMERO
THERE'S GARVIN WAITING—STAND BY TO JUMP, MISS BLAISE
A HELICOPTER HOVERS AT A THOUSAND FEET ABOVE ONE OF THE LARGER CLEARINGS IN ORION'S FIELD
TELL ME, MCNAB—ARE YOU ENJOYING THIS? TWO HUMANS BEING HUNTED AND KILLED
I FIND IT... STIMULATING, THANK YOU
THEN YOU WON'T MIND ANSWERING A SIMPLE QUESTION BEFORE THE FUN BEGINS—WHAT SIZE BOOTS ARE YOU WEARING?
HUH?
10,020
MODESTY BLAISE
by PETER O'DONNELL
drawn by ROMERO
I TAKE SIZE TEN IN FOOTWEAR—BUT I CANNOT IMAGINE WHY YOU ASK
SHE'S STALLING—SHOVE HER OUT, MCNAB
YOU'RE A BLACK-BELT JUDOKA, AREN'T YOU?
AYE, BUT IF THERE'S TO BE CLOSE CONTACT I'LL THANK YOU TO TAKE CHARGE OF THIS, MR. JOHNSON
10,021
NO WAY TO GET THE GUN NOW... HE'S BLOCKED MY BEST OPTION, DAMMIT

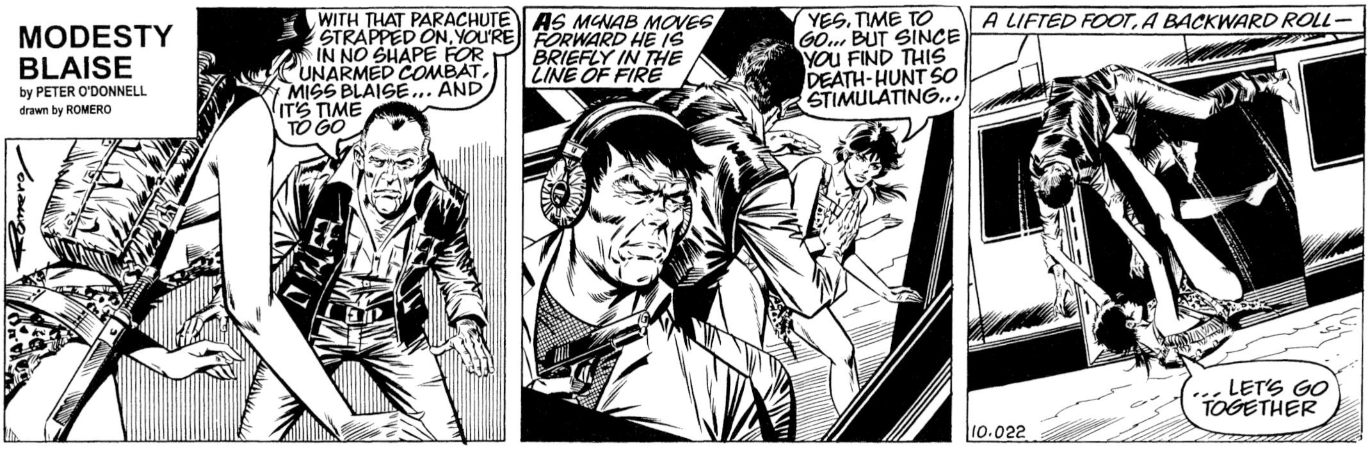
MODESTY BLAISE
by PETER O'DONNELL
drawn by ROMERO
WITH THAT PARACHUTE STRAPPED ON, YOU'RE IN NO SHAPE FOR UNARMED COMBAT, MISS BLAISE ... AND IT'S TIME TO GO
AS McNAB MOVES FORWARD HE IS BRIEFLY IN THE LINE OF FIRE
YES, TIME TO GO... BUT SINCE YOU FIND THIS DEATH-HUNT SO STIMULATING...
A LIFTED FOOT, A BACKWARD ROLL—
... LET'S GO TOGETHER
10.022

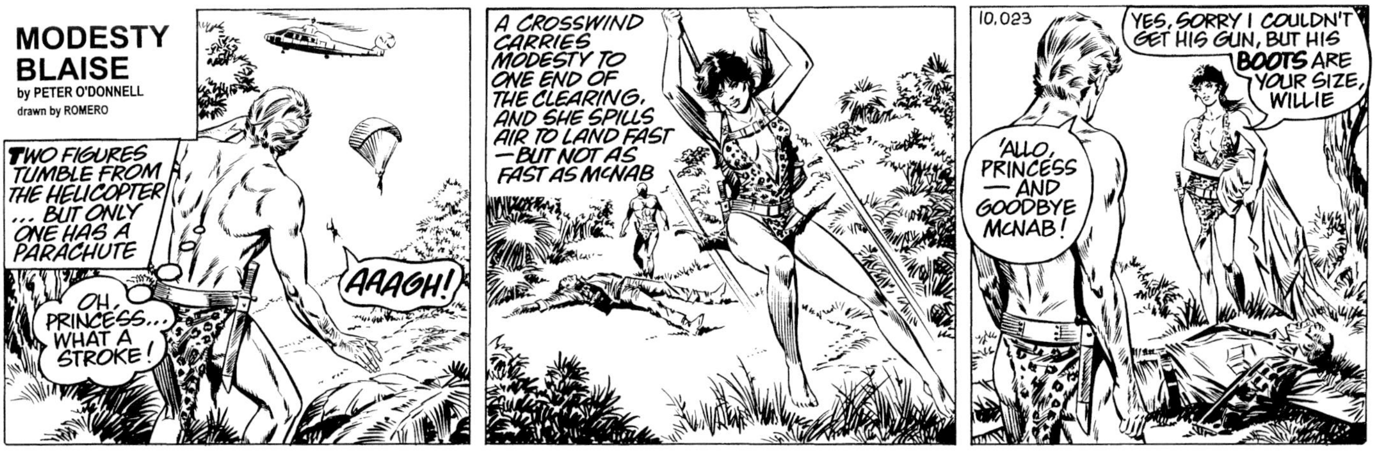
MODESTY BLAISE
by PETER O'DONNELL
drawn by ROMERO
TWO FIGURES TUMBLE FROM THE HELICOPTER ... BUT ONLY ONE HAS A PARACHUTE
AAAGH!
OH, PRINCESS... WHAT A STROKE!
A CROSSWIND CARRIES MODESTY TO ONE END OF THE CLEARING, AND SHE SPILLS AIR TO LAND FAST —BUT NOT AS FAST AS McNAB
10.023
YES, SORRY I COULDN'T GET HIS GUN, BUT HIS BOOTS ARE YOUR SIZE, WILLIE
'ALLO, PRINCESS — AND GOODBYE McNAB!

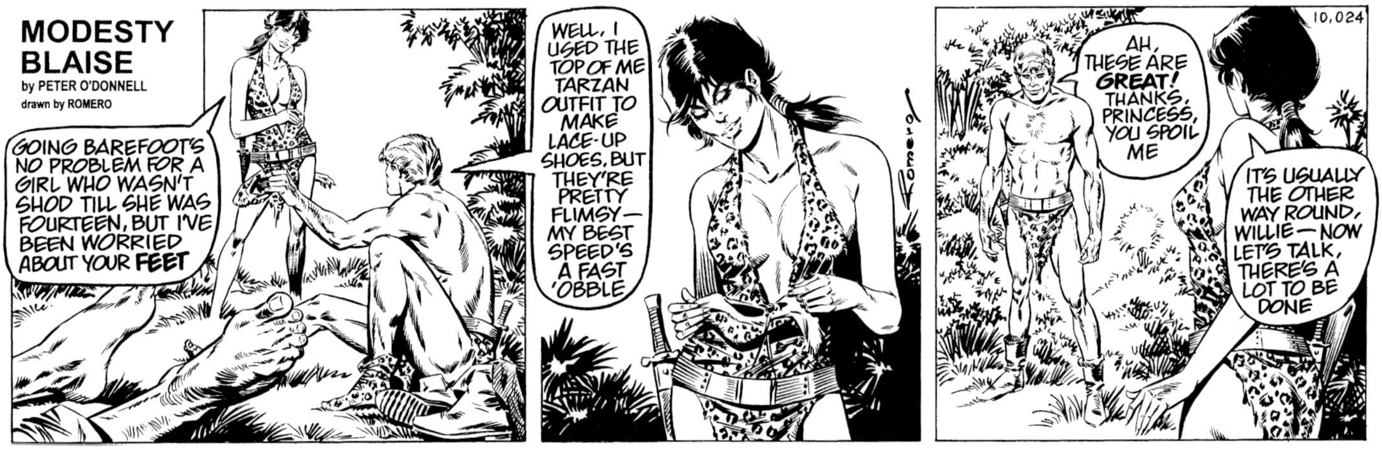
MODESTY BLAISE
by PETER O'DONNELL
drawn by ROMERO
GOING BAREFOOT'S NO PROBLEM FOR A GIRL WHO WASN'T SHOD TILL SHE WAS FOURTEEN, BUT I'VE BEEN WORRIED ABOUT YOUR FEET
WELL, I USED THE TOP OF ME TARZAN OUTFIT TO MAKE LACE-UP SHOES, BUT THEY'RE PRETTY FLIMSY— MY BEST SPEED'S A FAST 'OBBLE
10.024
AH, THESE ARE GREAT! THANKS, PRINCESS, YOU SPOIL ME
IT'S USUALLY THE OTHER WAY ROUND, WILLIE— NOW LET'S TALK, THERE'S A LOT TO BE DONE

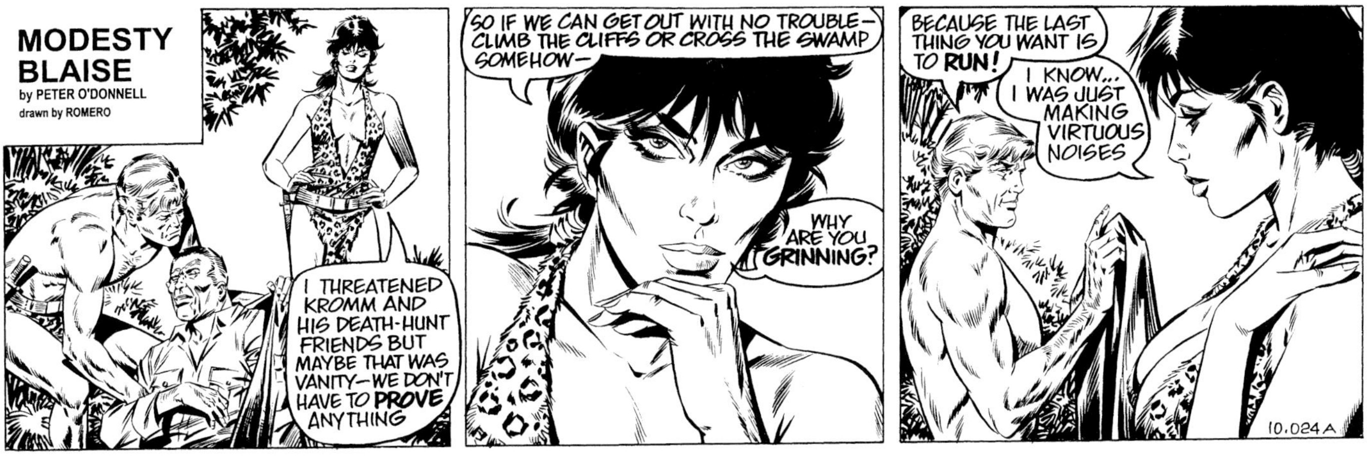
MODESTY BLAISE
by PETER O'DONNELL
drawn by ROMERO
I THREATENED KROMM AND HIS DEATH-HUNT FRIENDS BUT MAYBE THAT WAS VANITY—WE DON'T HAVE TO PROVE ANYTHING
SO IF WE CAN GET OUT WITH NO TROUBLE— CLIMB THE CLIFFS OR CROSS THE SWAMP SOMEHOW—
WHY ARE YOU GRINNING?
BECAUSE THE LAST THING YOU WANT IS TO RUN!
I KNOW... I WAS JUST MAKING VIRTUOUS NOISES
10.024 A

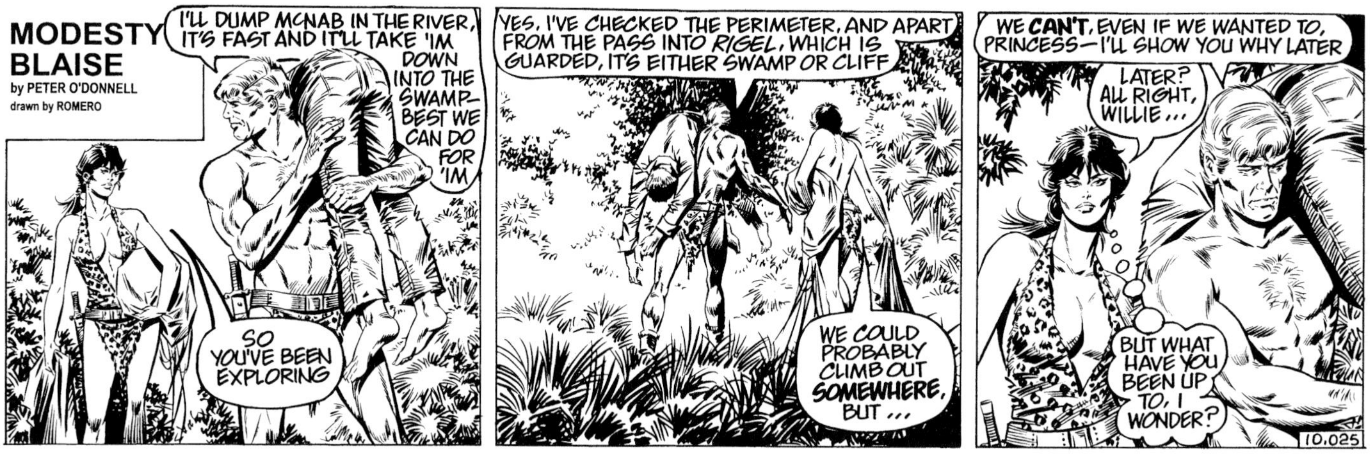
MODESTY BLAISE
by PETER O'DONNELL
drawn by ROMERO
I'LL DUMP MCNAB IN THE RIVER, IT'S FAST AND IT'LL TAKE 'IM DOWN INTO THE SWAMP- BEST WE CAN DO FOR 'IM
SO YOU'VE BEEN EXPLORING
YES, I'VE CHECKED THE PERIMETER, AND APART FROM THE PASS INTO RIGEL, WHICH IS GUARDED, IT'S EITHER SWAMP OR CLIFF
WE COULD PROBABLY CLIMB OUT SOMEWHERE, BUT ...
WE CAN'T, EVEN IF WE WANTED TO, PRINCESS—I'LL SHOW YOU WHY LATER
LATER? ALL RIGHT, WILLIE ...
BUT WHAT HAVE YOU BEEN UP TO, I WONDER?
10,025

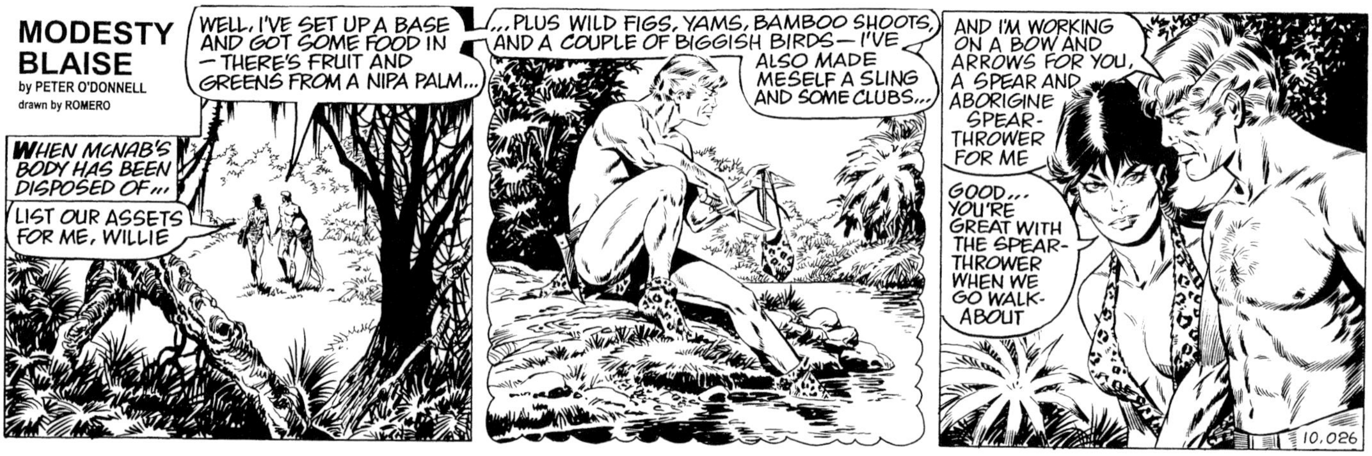
MODESTY BLAISE
by PETER O'DONNELL
drawn by ROMERO
WHEN MCNAB'S BODY HAS BEEN DISPOSED OF ...
LIST OUR ASSETS FOR ME, WILLIE
WELL, I'VE SET UP A BASE AND GOT SOME FOOD IN —THERE'S FRUIT AND GREENS FROM A NIPA PALM ...
... PLUS WILD FIGS, YAMS, BAMBOO SHOOTS, AND A COUPLE OF BIGGISH BIRDS— I'VE ALSO MADE MESELF A SLING AND SOME CLUBS ...
AND I'M WORKING ON A BOW AND ARROWS FOR YOU, A SPEAR AND ABORIGINE SPEAR-THROWER FOR ME
GOOD ... YOU'RE GREAT WITH THE SPEAR-THROWER WHEN WE GO WALK-ABOUT
10,026

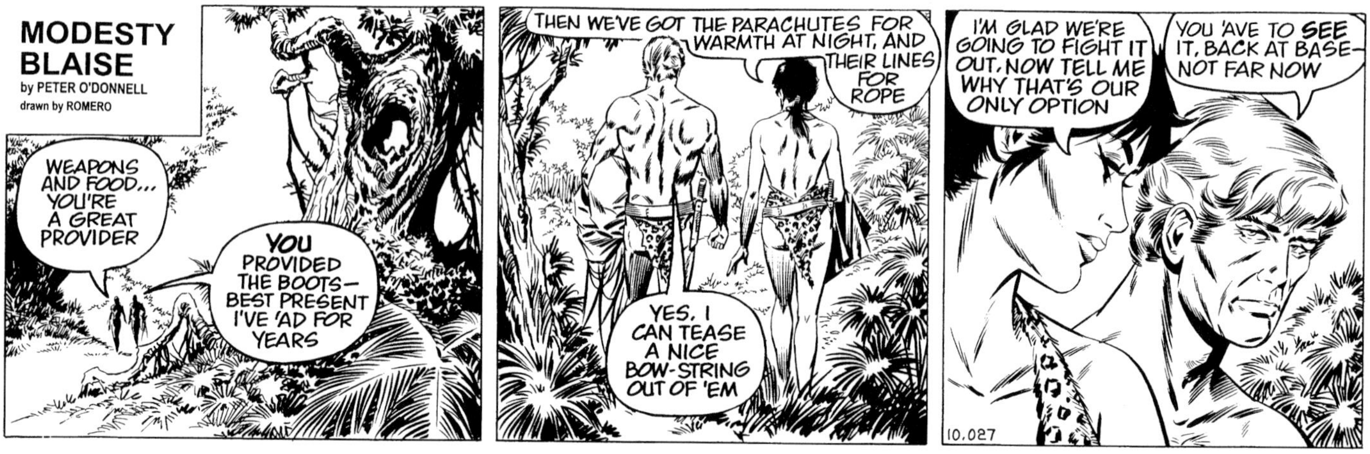
MODESTY BLAISE
by PETER O'DONNELL
drawn by ROMERO
WEAPONS AND FOOD ... YOU'RE A GREAT PROVIDER
YOU PROVIDED THE BOOTS— BEST PRESENT I'VE 'AD FOR YEARS
THEN WE'VE GOT THE PARACHUTES FOR WARMTH AT NIGHT, AND THEIR LINES FOR ROPE
YES, I CAN TEASE A NICE BOW-STRING OUT OF 'EM
I'M GLAD WE'RE GOING TO FIGHT IT OUT. NOW TELL ME WHY THAT'S OUR ONLY OPTION
YOU 'AVE TO SEE IT, BACK AT BASE- NOT FAR NOW
10,027

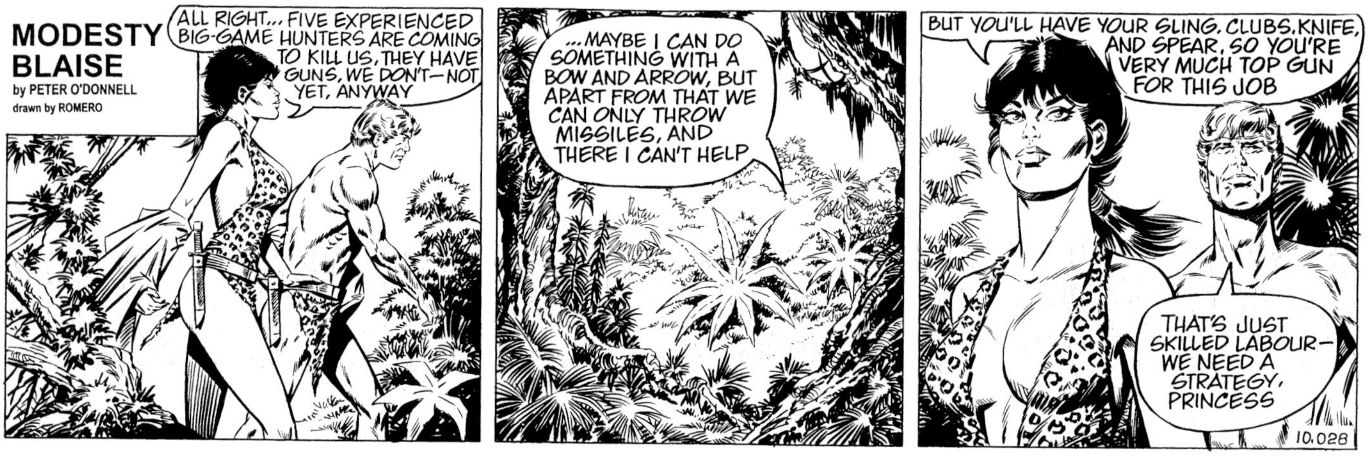
MODESTY BLAISE
by PETER O'DONNELL
drawn by ROMERO
ALL RIGHT ... FIVE EXPERIENCED BIG-GAME HUNTERS ARE COMING TO KILL US. THEY HAVE GUNS, WE DON'T—NOT YET, ANYWAY
... MAYBE I CAN DO SOMETHING WITH A BOW AND ARROW, BUT APART FROM THAT WE CAN ONLY THROW MISSILES, AND THERE I CAN'T HELP
BUT YOU'LL HAVE YOUR SLING, CLUBS, KNIFE, AND SPEAR, SO YOU'RE VERY MUCH TOP GUN FOR THIS JOB
THAT'S JUST SKILLED LABOUR— WE NEED A STRATEGY, PRINCESS
10,028

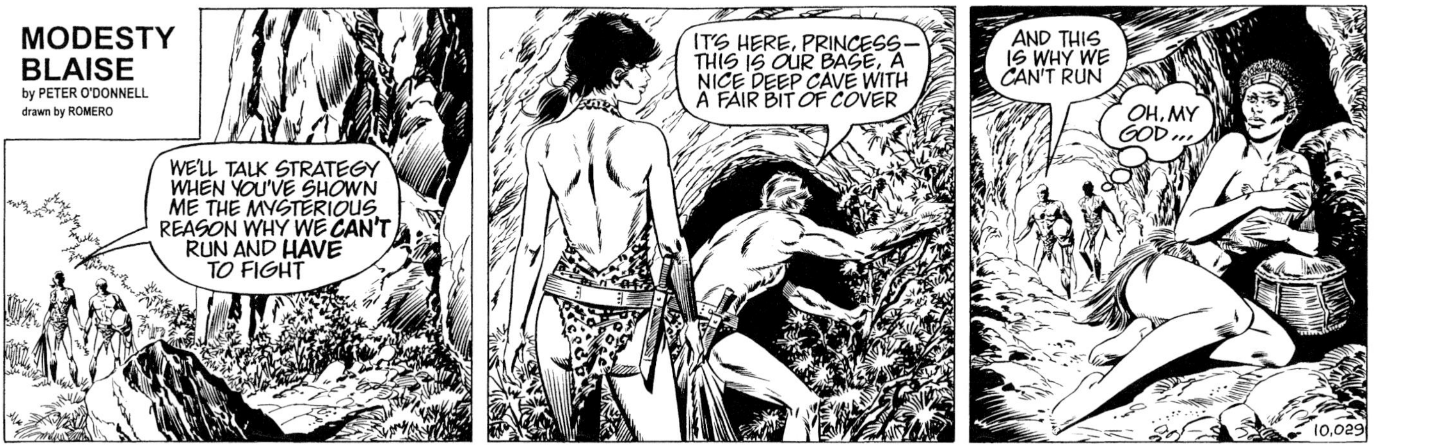
MODESTY BLAISE
by PETER O'DONNELL
drawn by ROMERO
WE'LL TALK STRATEGY WHEN YOU'VE SHOWN ME THE MYSTERIOUS REASON WHY WE **CAN'T** RUN AND **HAVE** TO FIGHT
IT'S HERE, PRINCESS— THIS IS OUR BASE, A NICE DEEP CAVE WITH A FAIR BIT OF COVER
AND THIS IS WHY WE CAN'T RUN
OH, MY GOD...
10,029

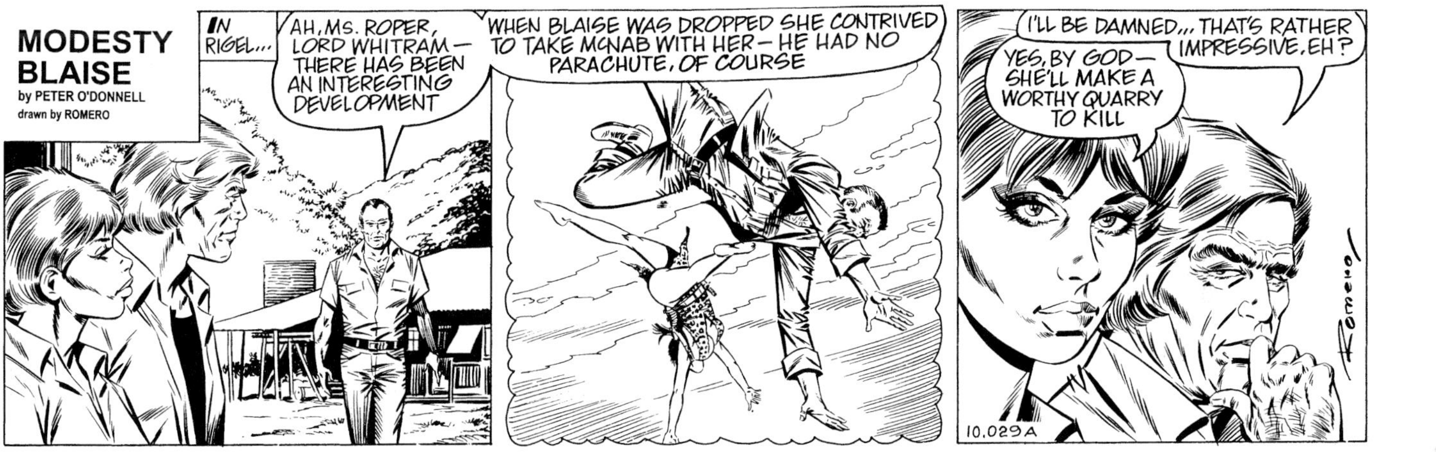
MODESTY BLAISE
by PETER O'DONNELL
drawn by ROMERO
IN RIGEL...
AH, MS. ROPER, LORD WHITRAM— THERE HAS BEEN AN INTERESTING DEVELOPMENT
WHEN BLAISE WAS DROPPED SHE CONTRIVED TO TAKE McNAB WITH HER— HE HAD NO PARACHUTE, OF COURSE
I'LL BE DAMNED... THAT'S RATHER IMPRESSIVE, EH?
YES, BY GOD— SHE'LL MAKE A WORTHY QUARRY TO KILL
Romero
10,029A

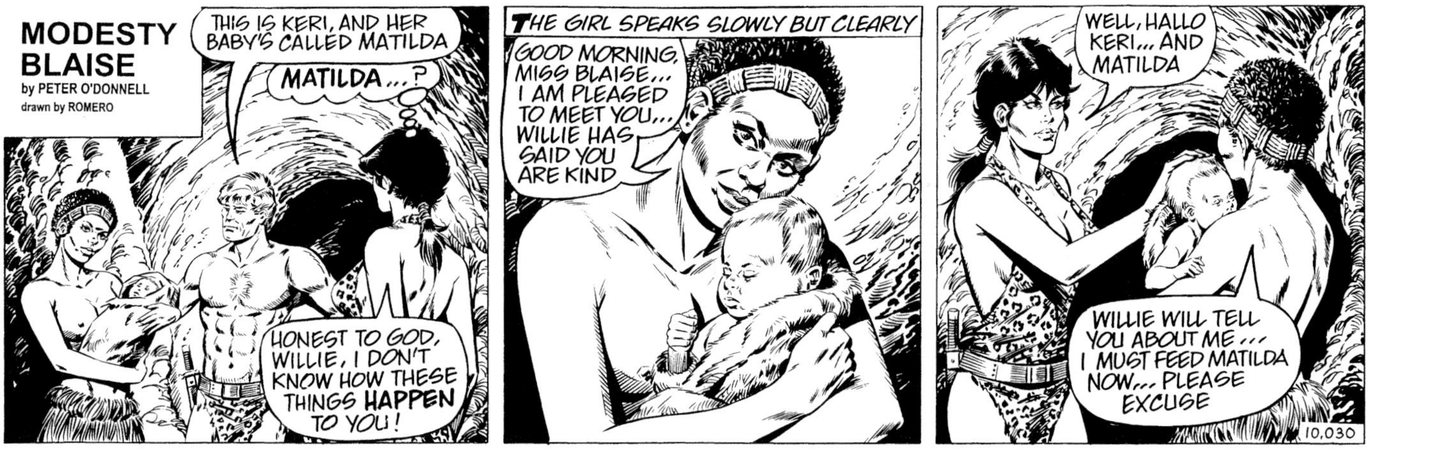
MODESTY BLAISE
by PETER O'DONNELL
drawn by ROMERO
THIS IS KERI, AND HER BABY'S CALLED MATILDA
MATILDA...?
HONEST TO GOD, WILLIE, I DON'T KNOW HOW THESE THINGS **HAPPEN** TO YOU!
THE GIRL SPEAKS SLOWLY BUT CLEARLY
GOOD MORNING, MISS BLAISE... I AM PLEASED TO MEET YOU... WILLIE HAS SAID YOU ARE KIND
WELL, HALLO KERI... AND MATILDA
WILLIE WILL TELL YOU ABOUT ME... I MUST FEED MATILDA NOW... PLEASE EXCUSE
10,030

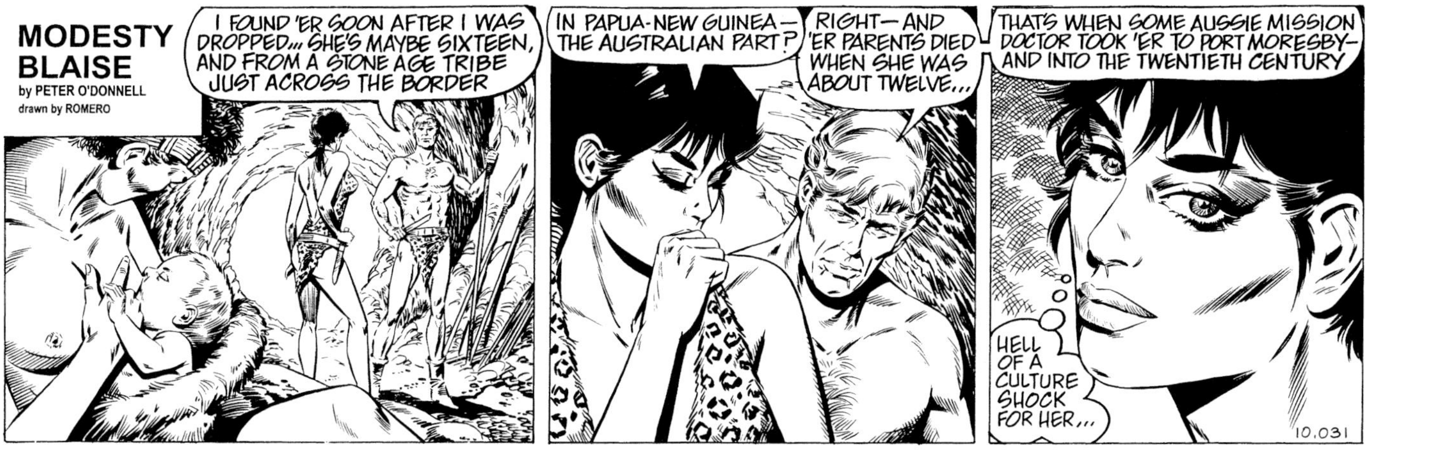
MODESTY BLAISE
by PETER O'DONNELL
drawn by ROMERO
I FOUND 'ER SOON AFTER I WAS DROPPED... SHE'S MAYBE SIXTEEN, AND FROM A STONE AGE TRIBE JUST ACROSS THE BORDER
IN PAPUA-NEW GUINEA— THE AUSTRALIAN PART?
RIGHT— AND 'ER PARENTS DIED WHEN SHE WAS ABOUT TWELVE...
THAT'S WHEN SOME AUSSIE MISSION DOCTOR TOOK 'ER TO PORT MORESBY— AND INTO THE TWENTIETH CENTURY
HELL OF A CULTURE SHOCK FOR HER...
10,031

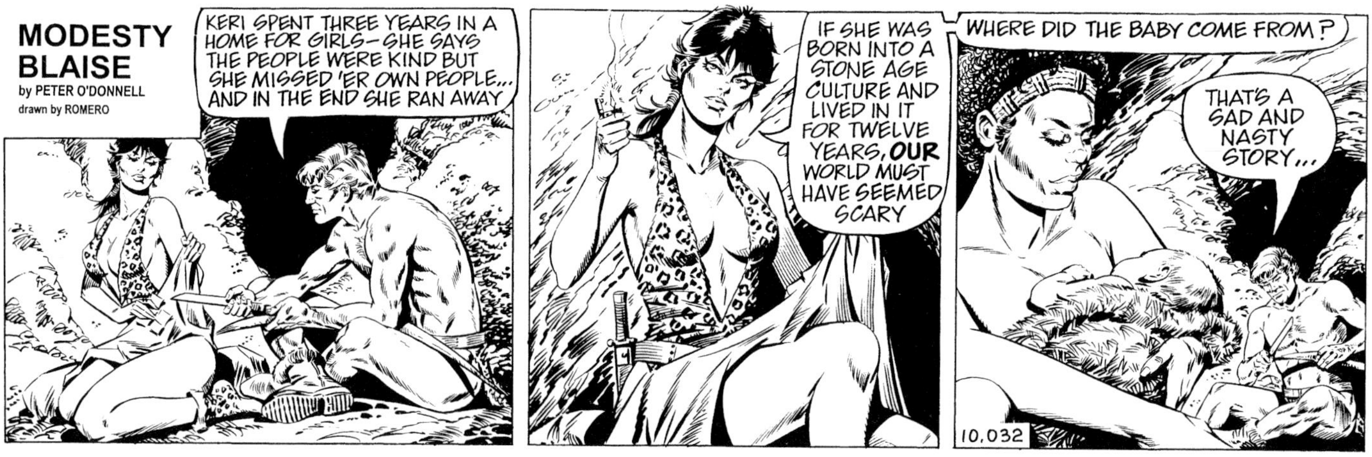
MODESTY BLAISE
by PETER O'DONNELL
drawn by ROMERO
KERI SPENT THREE YEARS IN A HOME FOR GIRLS—SHE SAYS THE PEOPLE WERE KIND BUT SHE MISSED 'ER OWN PEOPLE... AND IN THE END SHE RAN AWAY
IF SHE WAS BORN INTO A STONE AGE CULTURE AND LIVED IN IT FOR TWELVE YEARS, **OUR** WORLD MUST HAVE SEEMED SCARY
WHERE DID THE BABY COME FROM?
THAT'S A SAD AND NASTY STORY...
10,032

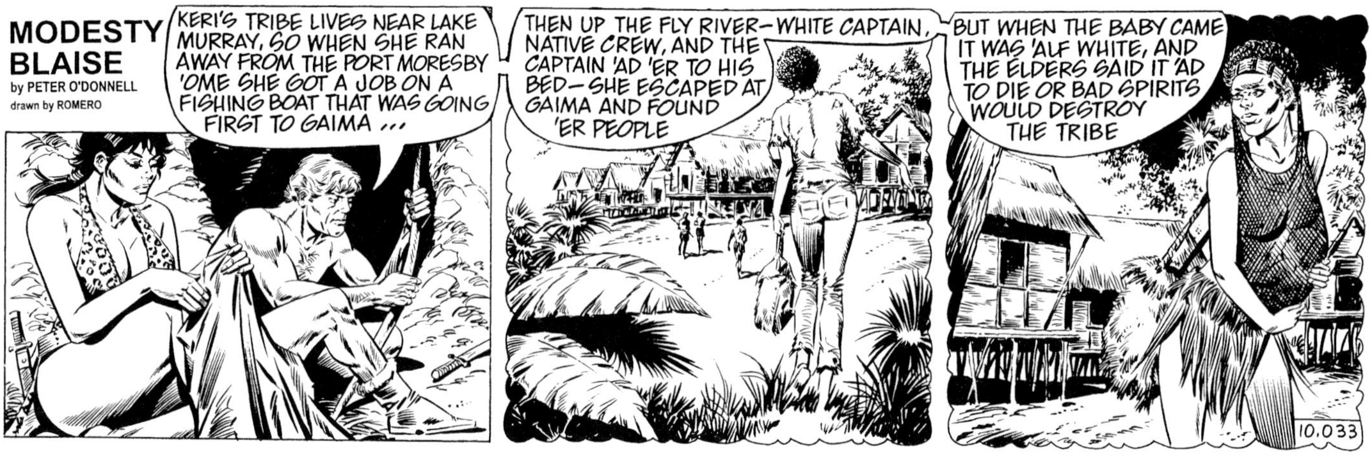
MODESTY BLAISE
by PETER O'DONNELL
drawn by ROMERO
KERI'S TRIBE LIVES NEAR LAKE MURRAY, SO WHEN SHE RAN AWAY FROM THE PORT MORESBY 'OME SHE GOT A JOB ON A FISHING BOAT THAT WAS GOING FIRST TO GAIMA ...
THEN UP THE FLY RIVER—WHITE CAPTAIN, NATIVE CREW, AND THE CAPTAIN 'AD 'ER TO HIS BED—SHE ESCAPED AT GAIMA AND FOUND 'ER PEOPLE
BUT WHEN THE BABY CAME IT WAS 'ALF WHITE, AND THE ELDERS SAID IT 'AD TO DIE OR BAD SPIRITS WOULD DESTROY THE TRIBE
10,033

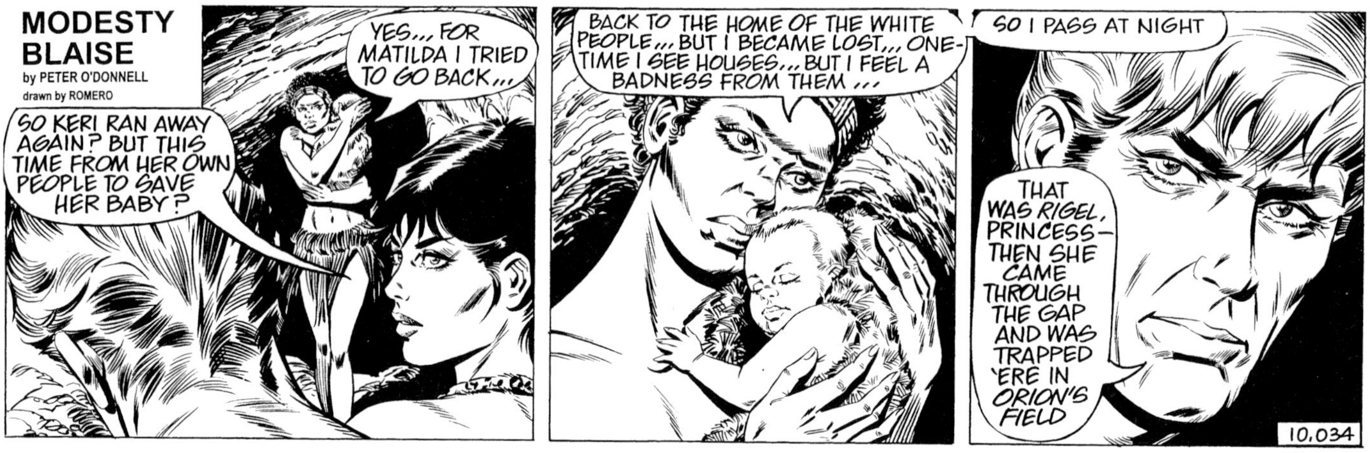
MODESTY BLAISE
by PETER O'DONNELL
drawn by ROMERO
SO KERI RAN AWAY AGAIN? BUT THIS TIME FROM HER OWN PEOPLE TO SAVE HER BABY?
YES... FOR MATILDA I TRIED TO GO BACK...
BACK TO THE HOME OF THE WHITE PEOPLE... BUT I BECAME LOST... ONE-TIME I SEE HOUSES... BUT I FEEL A BADNESS FROM THEM ...
SO I PASS AT NIGHT
THAT WAS *RIGEL*, PRINCESS—THEN SHE CAME THROUGH THE GAP AND WAS TRAPPED 'ERE IN *ORION'S FIELD*
10,034

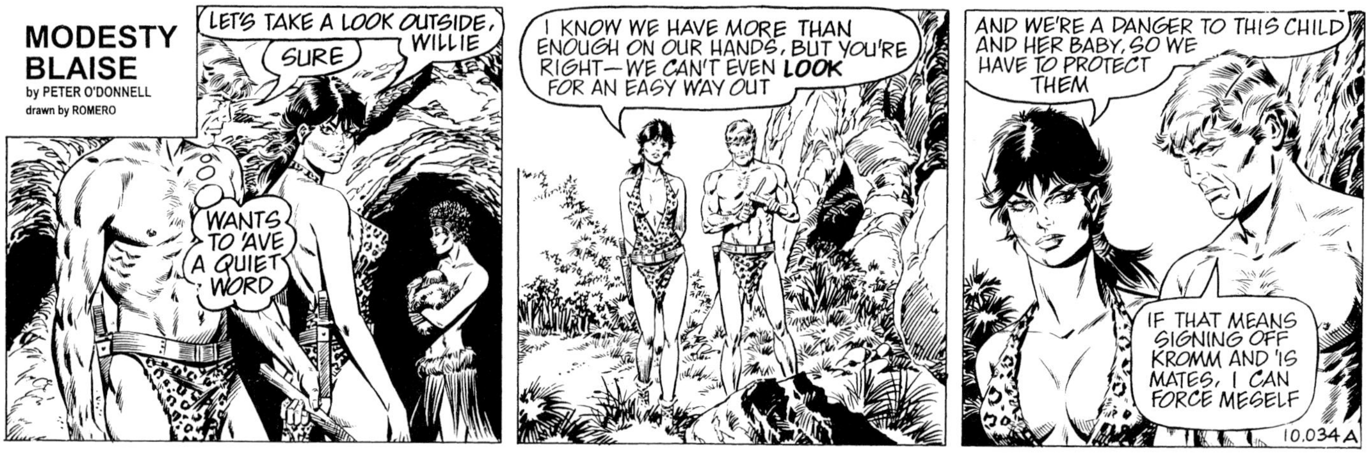
MODESTY BLAISE
by PETER O'DONNELL
drawn by ROMERO
LET'S TAKE A LOOK OUTSIDE, WILLIE
SURE
WANTS TO 'AVE A QUIET WORD
I KNOW WE HAVE MORE THAN ENOUGH ON OUR HANDS, BUT YOU'RE RIGHT—WE CAN'T EVEN **LOOK** FOR AN EASY WAY OUT
AND WE'RE A DANGER TO THIS CHILD AND HER BABY, SO WE HAVE TO PROTECT THEM
IF THAT MEANS SIGNING OFF KROMM AND 'IS MATES, I CAN FORCE MESELF
10.034 A

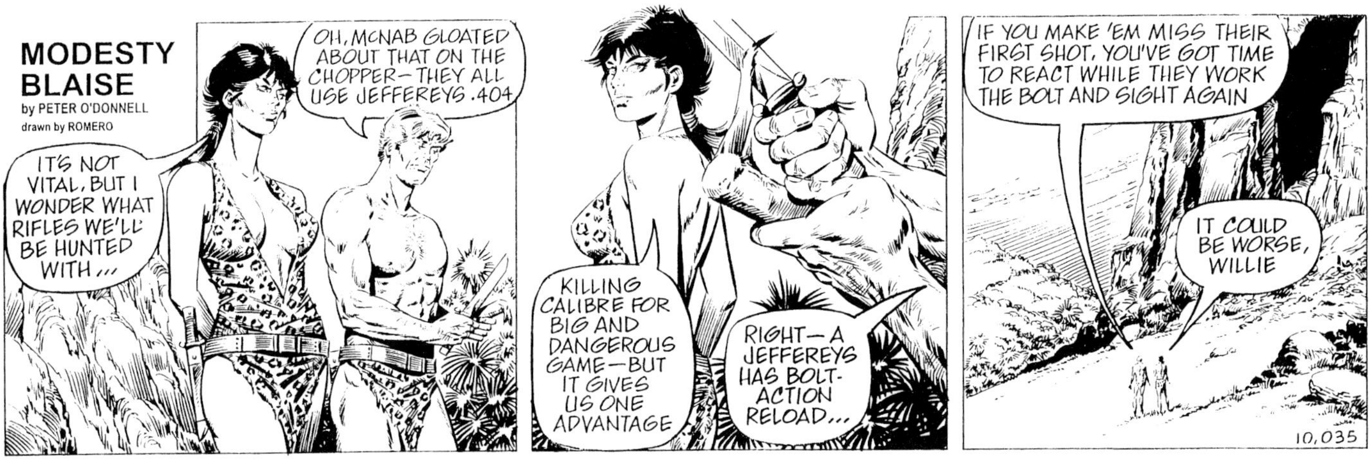
MODESTY BLAISE
by PETER O'DONNELL
drawn by ROMERO
IT'S NOT VITAL, BUT I WONDER WHAT RIFLES WE'LL BE HUNTED WITH ...
OH, McNAB GLOATED ABOUT THAT ON THE CHOPPER—THEY ALL USE JEFFEREYS .404
KILLING CALIBRE FOR BIG AND DANGEROUS GAME—BUT IT GIVES US ONE ADVANTAGE
RIGHT—A JEFFEREYS HAS BOLT-ACTION RELOAD ...
IF YOU MAKE 'EM MISS THEIR FIRST SHOT, YOU'VE GOT TIME TO REACT WHILE THEY WORK THE BOLT AND SIGHT AGAIN
IT COULD BE WORSE, WILLIE
10,035

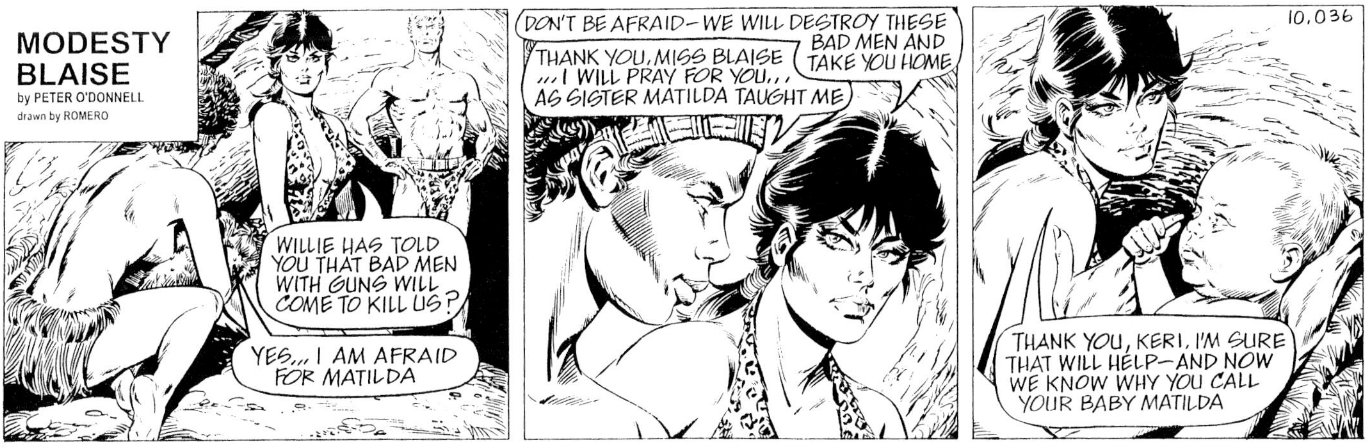
MODESTY BLAISE
by PETER O'DONNELL
drawn by ROMERO
WILLIE HAS TOLD YOU THAT BAD MEN WITH GUNS WILL COME TO KILL US?
YES ... I AM AFRAID FOR MATILDA
DON'T BE AFRAID—WE WILL DESTROY THESE BAD MEN AND TAKE YOU HOME
THANK YOU, MISS BLAISE ... I WILL PRAY FOR YOU ... AS SISTER MATILDA TAUGHT ME
10,036
THANK YOU, KERI, I'M SURE THAT WILL HELP—AND NOW WE KNOW WHY YOU CALL YOUR BABY MATILDA

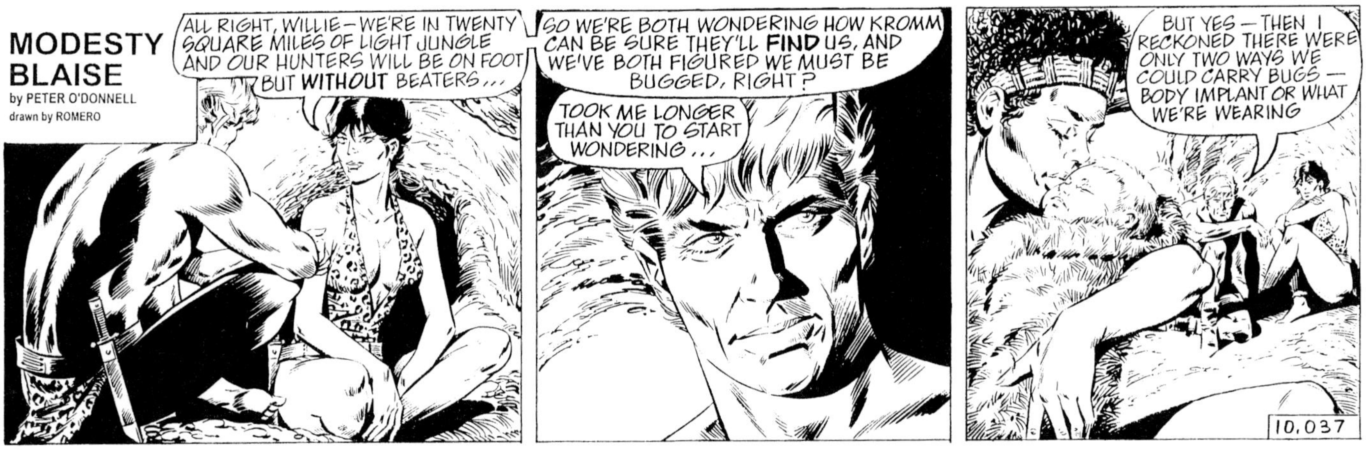
MODESTY BLAISE
by PETER O'DONNELL
drawn by ROMERO
ALL RIGHT, WILLIE—WE'RE IN TWENTY SQUARE MILES OF LIGHT JUNGLE AND OUR HUNTERS WILL BE ON FOOT
BUT WITHOUT BEATERS ...
SO WE'RE BOTH WONDERING HOW KROMM CAN BE SURE THEY'LL FIND US, AND WE'VE BOTH FIGURED WE MUST BE BUGGED, RIGHT?
TOOK ME LONGER THAN YOU TO START WONDERING ...
BUT YES—THEN I RECKONED THERE WERE ONLY TWO WAYS WE COULD CARRY BUGS—BODY IMPLANT OR WHAT WE'RE WEARING
10,037

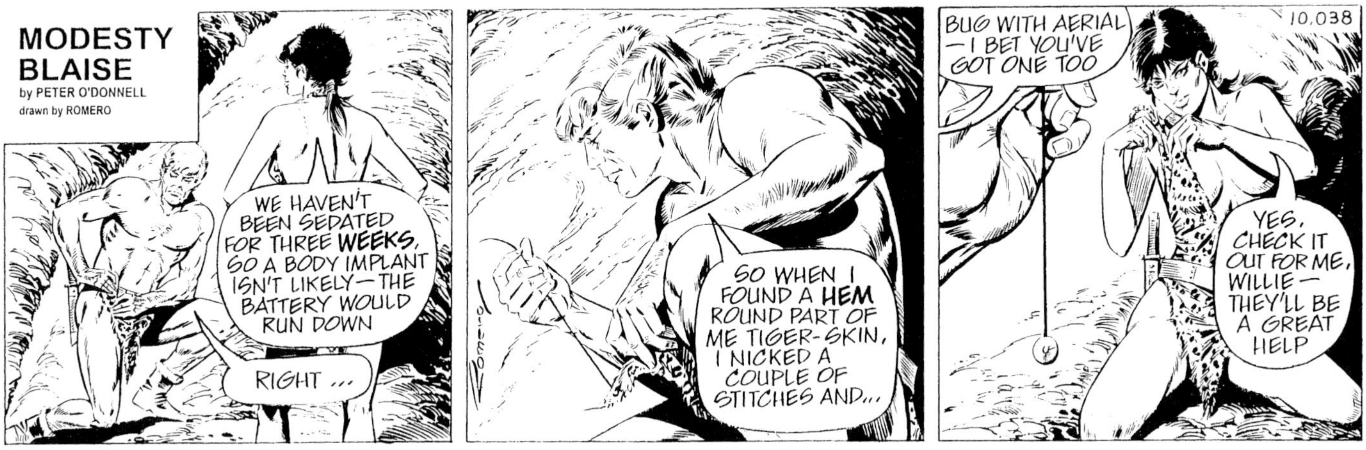
MODESTY BLAISE
by PETER O'DONNELL
drawn by ROMERO
WE HAVEN'T BEEN SEDATED FOR THREE WEEKS, SO A BODY IMPLANT ISN'T LIKELY—THE BATTERY WOULD RUN DOWN
RIGHT ...
SO WHEN I FOUND A HEM ROUND PART OF ME TIGER-SKIN, I NICKED A COUPLE OF STITCHES AND ...
10,038
BUG WITH AERIAL—I BET YOU'VE GOT ONE TOO
YES, CHECK IT OUT FOR ME, WILLIE—THEY'LL BE A GREAT HELP

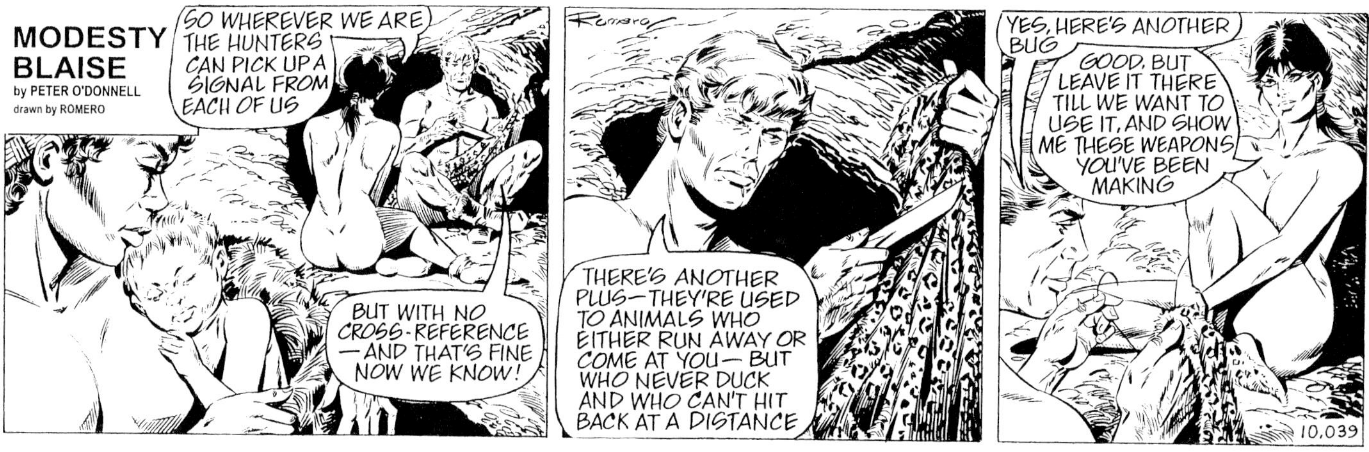
MODESTY BLAISE
by PETER O'DONNELL
drawn by ROMERO
SO WHEREVER WE ARE THE HUNTERS CAN PICK UP A SIGNAL FROM EACH OF US
BUT WITH NO CROSS-REFERENCE —AND THAT'S FINE NOW WE KNOW!
THERE'S ANOTHER PLUS—THEY'RE USED TO ANIMALS WHO EITHER RUN AWAY OR COME AT YOU— BUT WHO NEVER DUCK AND WHO CAN'T HIT BACK AT A DISTANCE
YES, HERE'S ANOTHER BUG
GOOD, BUT LEAVE IT THERE TILL WE WANT TO USE IT, AND SHOW ME THESE WEAPONS YOU'VE BEEN MAKING
10,039

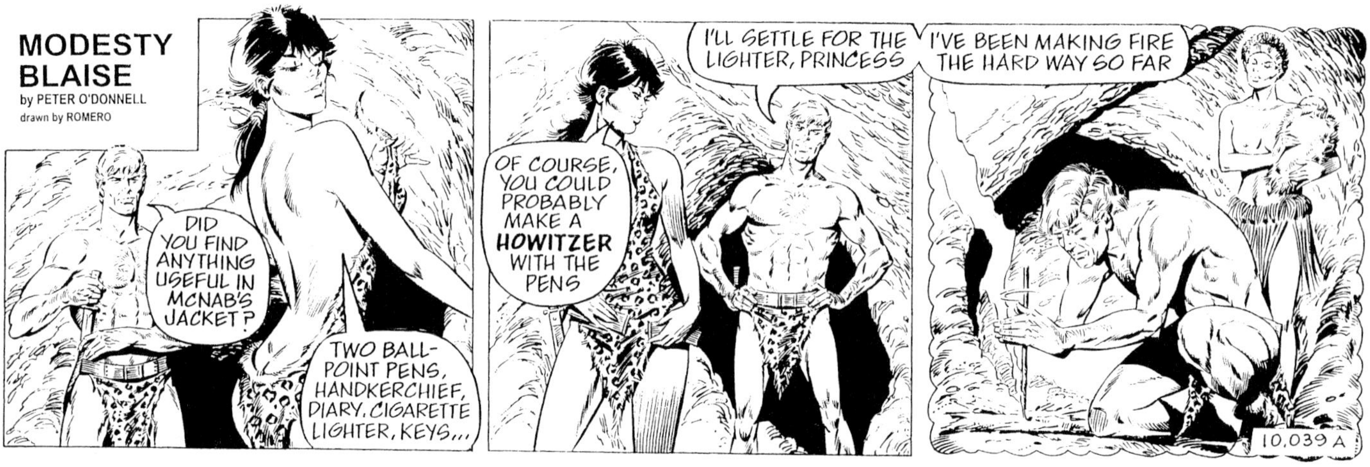
MODESTY BLAISE
by PETER O'DONNELL
drawn by ROMERO
DID YOU FIND ANYTHING USEFUL IN MCNAB'S JACKET?
TWO BALL-POINT PENS, HANDKERCHIEF, DIARY, CIGARETTE LIGHTER, KEYS...
OF COURSE, YOU COULD PROBABLY MAKE A HOWITZER WITH THE PENS
I'LL SETTLE FOR THE LIGHTER, PRINCESS
I'VE BEEN MAKING FIRE THE HARD WAY SO FAR
10,039 A

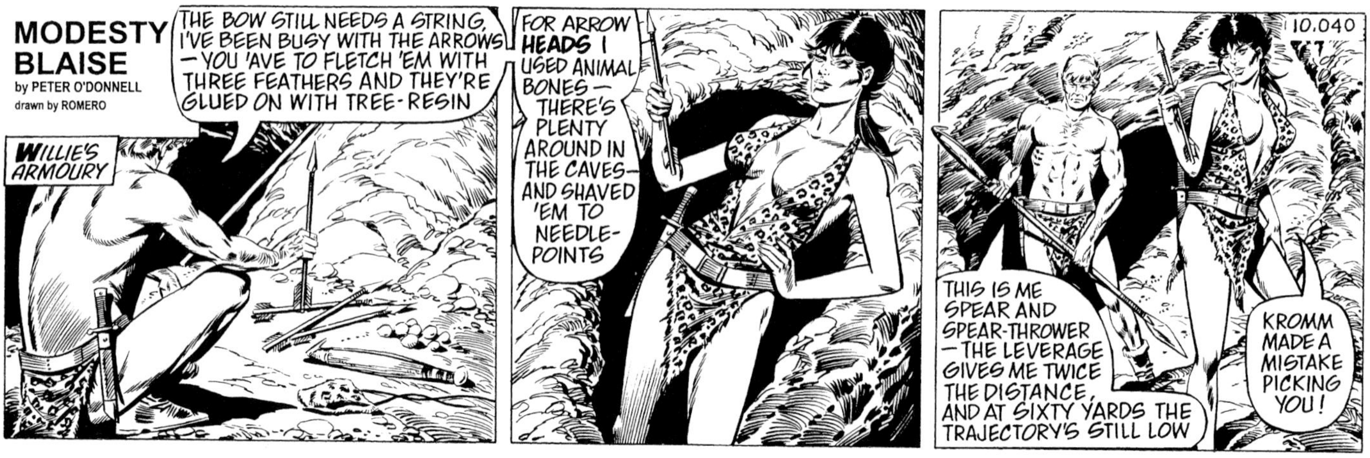
MODESTY BLAISE
by PETER O'DONNELL
drawn by ROMERO
THE BOW STILL NEEDS A STRING, I'VE BEEN BUSY WITH THE ARROWS —YOU 'AVE TO FLETCH 'EM WITH THREE FEATHERS AND THEY'RE GLUED ON WITH TREE-RESIN
WILLIE'S ARMOURY
FOR ARROW HEADS I USED ANIMAL BONES—THERE'S PLENTY AROUND IN THE CAVES—AND SHAVED 'EM TO NEEDLE-POINTS
10,040
THIS IS ME SPEAR AND SPEAR-THROWER —THE LEVERAGE GIVES ME TWICE THE DISTANCE, AND AT SIXTY YARDS THE TRAJECTORY'S STILL LOW
KROMM MADE A MISTAKE PICKING YOU!

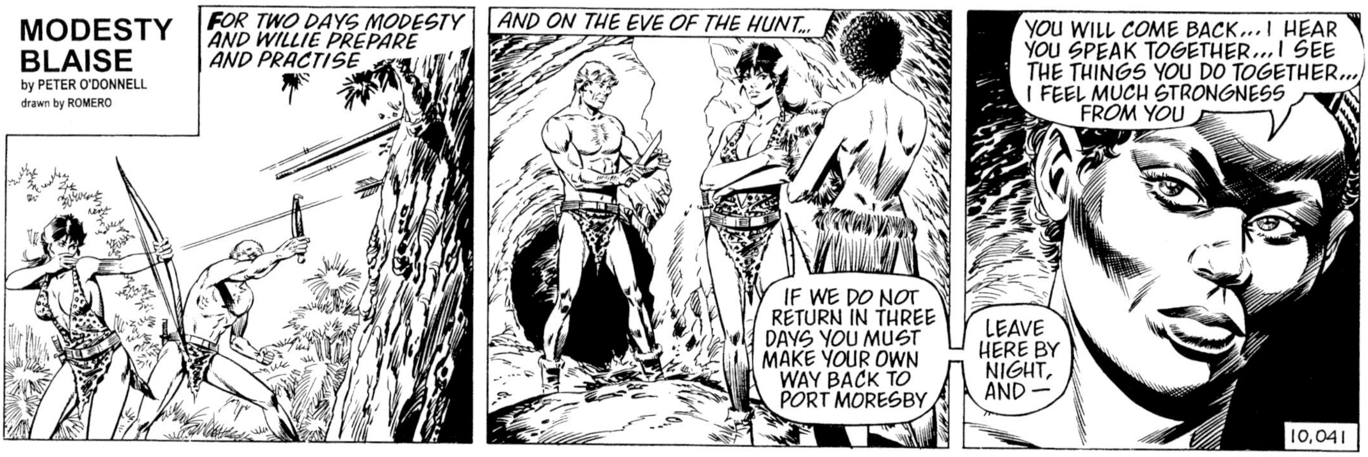
MODESTY BLAISE
by PETER O'DONNELL
drawn by ROMERO
FOR TWO DAYS MODESTY AND WILLIE PREPARE AND PRACTISE
AND ON THE EVE OF THE HUNT...
IF WE DO NOT RETURN IN THREE DAYS YOU MUST MAKE YOUR OWN WAY BACK TO PORT MORESBY
LEAVE HERE BY NIGHT, AND—
YOU WILL COME BACK... I HEAR YOU SPEAK TOGETHER... I SEE THE THINGS YOU DO TOGETHER... I FEEL MUCH STRONGNESS FROM YOU
10,041

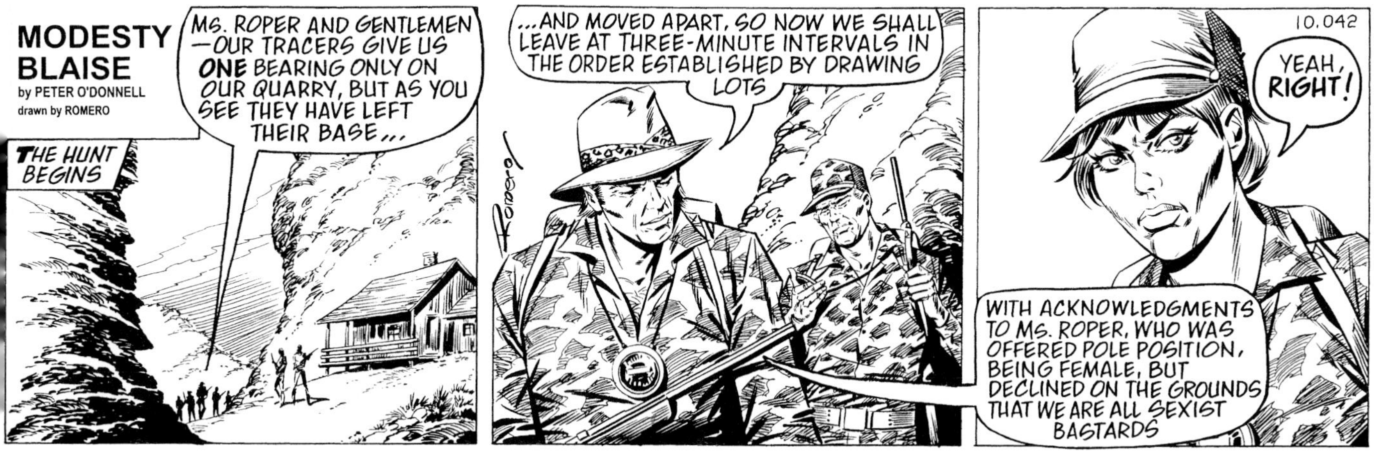
MODESTY BLAISE
by PETER O'DONNELL
drawn by ROMERO
THE HUNT BEGINS
MS. ROPER AND GENTLEMEN —OUR TRACERS GIVE US ONE BEARING ONLY ON OUR QUARRY, BUT AS YOU SEE THEY HAVE LEFT THEIR BASE...
...AND MOVED APART, SO NOW WE SHALL LEAVE AT THREE-MINUTE INTERVALS IN THE ORDER ESTABLISHED BY DRAWING LOTS
10,042
YEAH, RIGHT!
WITH ACKNOWLEDGMENTS TO MS. ROPER, WHO WAS OFFERED POLE POSITION, BEING FEMALE, BUT DECLINED ON THE GROUNDS THAT WE ARE ALL SEXIST BASTARDS

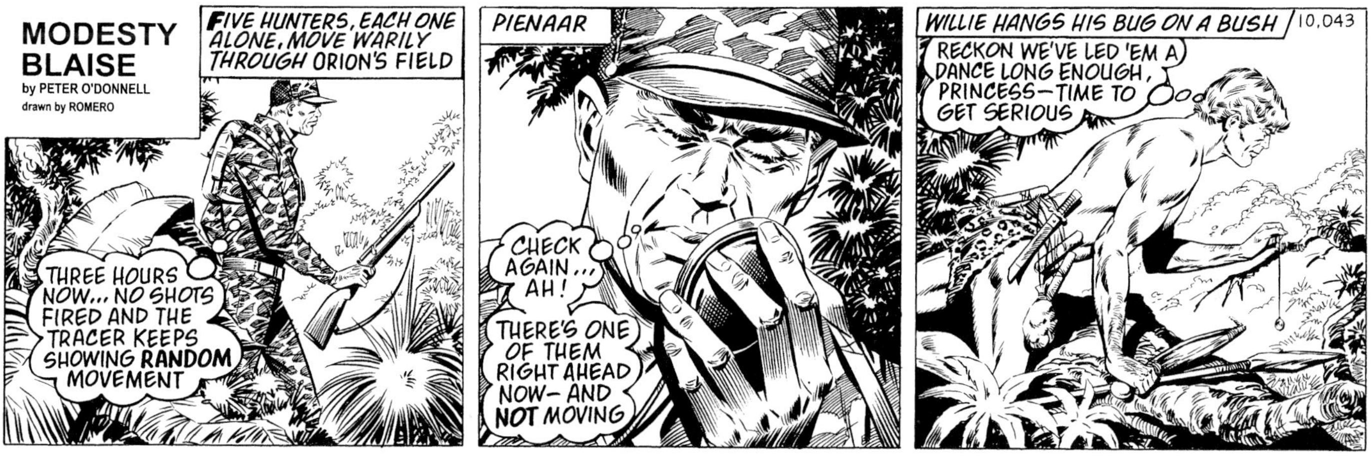
MODESTY BLAISE
by PETER O'DONNELL
drawn by ROMERO
FIVE HUNTERS, EACH ONE ALONE, MOVE WARILY THROUGH ORION'S FIELD
THREE HOURS NOW... NO SHOTS FIRED AND THE TRACER KEEPS SHOWING RANDOM MOVEMENT
PIENAAR
CHECK AGAIN... AH!
THERE'S ONE OF THEM RIGHT AHEAD NOW— AND NOT MOVING
WILLIE HANGS HIS BUG ON A BUSH
10,043
RECKON WE'VE LED 'EM A DANCE LONG ENOUGH, PRINCESS—TIME TO GET SERIOUS

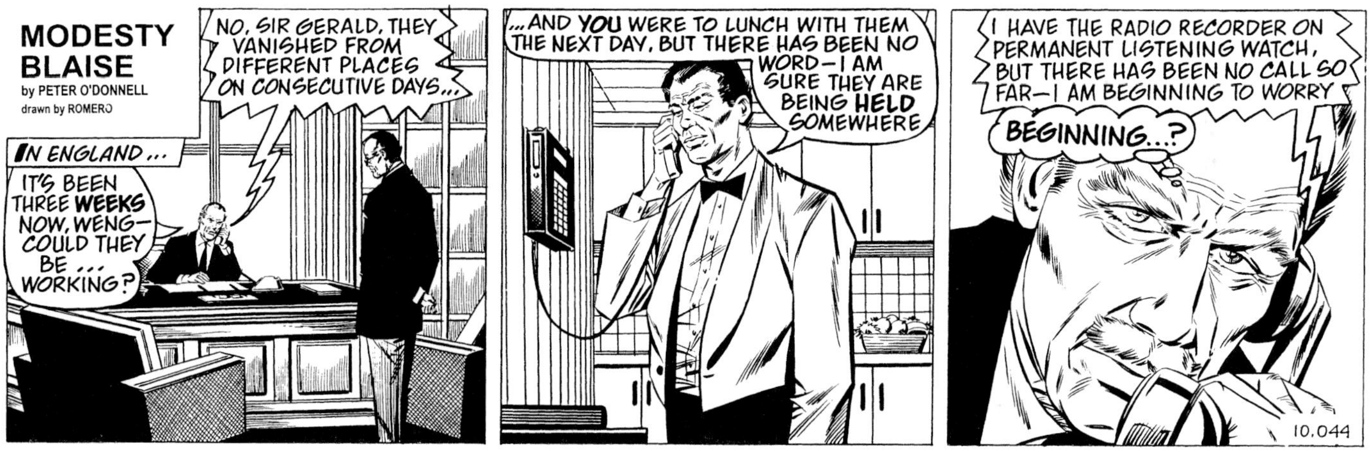
MODESTY BLAISE
by PETER O'DONNELL
drawn by ROMERO
NO, SIR GERALD, THEY VANISHED FROM DIFFERENT PLACES ON CONSECUTIVE DAYS...
IN ENGLAND...
IT'S BEEN THREE WEEKS NOW, WENG- COULD THEY BE ... WORKING?
...AND YOU WERE TO LUNCH WITH THEM THE NEXT DAY, BUT THERE HAS BEEN NO WORD—I AM SURE THEY ARE BEING HELD SOMEWHERE
I HAVE THE RADIO RECORDER ON PERMANENT LISTENING WATCH, BUT THERE HAS BEEN NO CALL SO FAR—I AM BEGINNING TO WORRY
BEGINNING...?
10,044

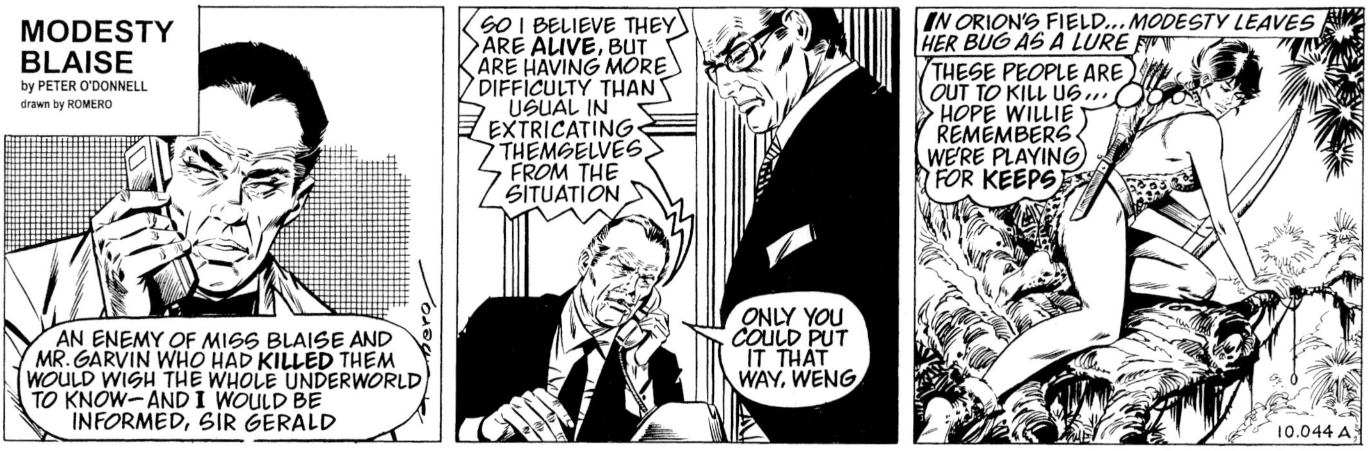
MODESTY BLAISE
by PETER O'DONNELL
drawn by ROMERO
AN ENEMY OF MISS BLAISE AND MR. GARVIN WHO HAD KILLED THEM WOULD WISH THE WHOLE UNDERWORLD TO KNOW—AND I WOULD BE INFORMED, SIR GERALD
SO I BELIEVE THEY ARE ALIVE, BUT ARE HAVING MORE DIFFICULTY THAN USUAL IN EXTRICATING THEMSELVES FROM THE SITUATION
ONLY YOU COULD PUT IT THAT WAY, WENG
IN ORION'S FIELD... MODESTY LEAVES HER BUG AS A LURE
THESE PEOPLE ARE OUT TO KILL US... HOPE WILLIE REMEMBERS WE'RE PLAYING FOR KEEPS
10,044 A

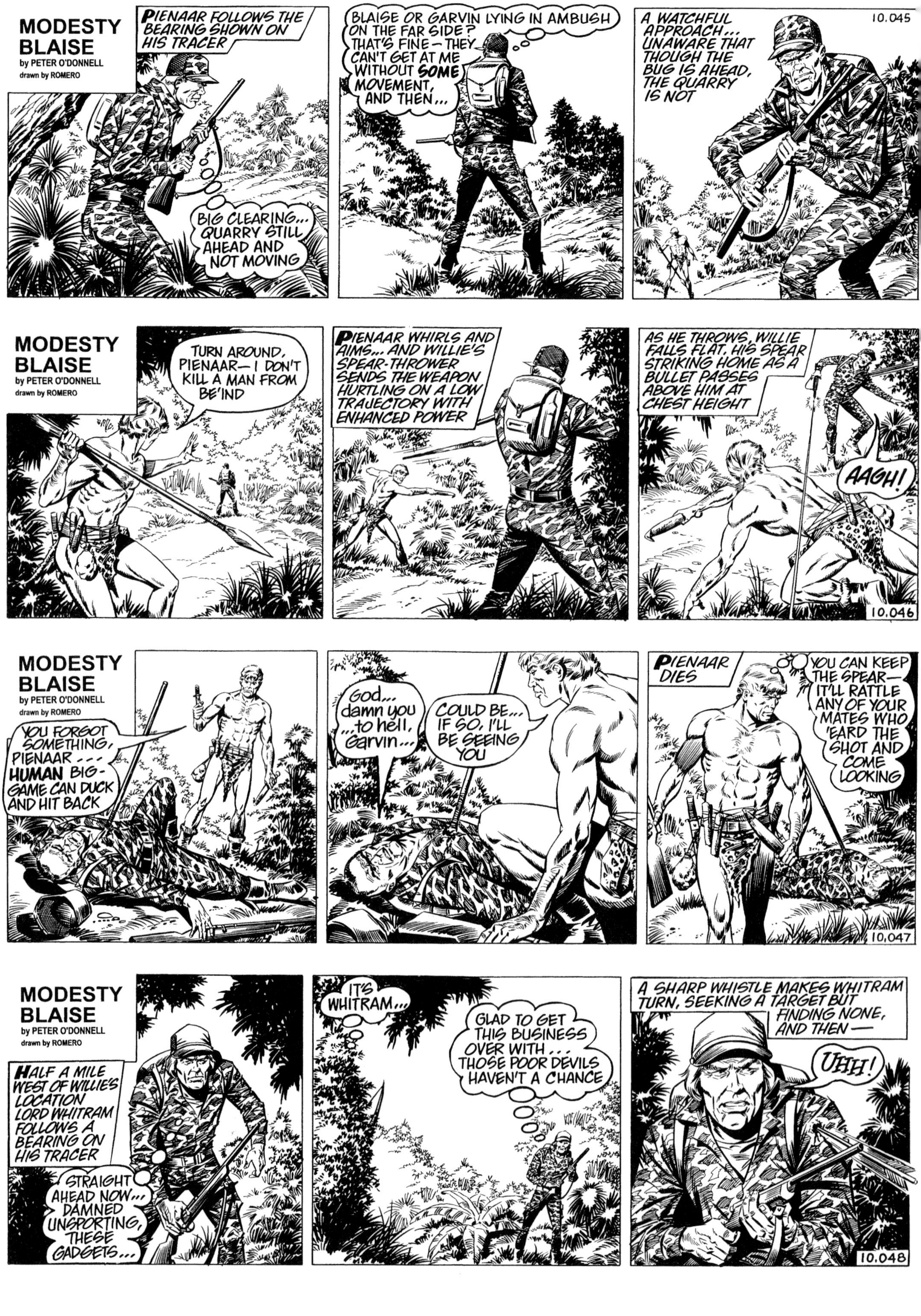

MODESTY BLAISE
by PETER O'DONNELL
drawn by ROMERO
PIENAAR FOLLOWS THE BEARING SHOWN ON HIS TRACER
BIG CLEARING... QUARRY STILL AHEAD AND NOT MOVING
BLAISE OR GARVIN LYING IN AMBUSH ON THE FAR SIDE? THAT'S FINE – THEY CAN'T GET AT ME WITHOUT SOME MOVEMENT, AND THEN...
10.045
A WATCHFUL APPROACH... UNAWARE THAT THOUGH THE BUG IS AHEAD, THE QUARRY IS NOT
MODESTY BLAISE
by PETER O'DONNELL
drawn by ROMERO
TURN AROUND, PIENAAR— I DON'T KILL A MAN FROM BE'IND
PIENAAR WHIRLS AND AIMS... AND WILLIE'S SPEAR-THROWER SENDS THE WEAPON HURTLING ON A LOW TRAJECTORY WITH ENHANCED POWER
AS HE THROWS, WILLIE FALLS FLAT. HIS SPEAR STRIKING HOME AS A BULLET PASSES ABOVE HIM AT CHEST HEIGHT
AAGH!
10.046
MODESTY BLAISE
by PETER O'DONNELL
drawn by ROMERO
YOU FORGOT SOMETHING, PIENAAR... HUMAN BIG-GAME CAN DUCK AND HIT BACK
God... damn you ...to hell, Garvin...
COULD BE... IF SO, I'LL BE SEEING YOU
PIENAAR DIES
YOU CAN KEEP THE SPEAR— IT'LL RATTLE ANY OF YOUR MATES WHO 'EARD THE SHOT AND COME LOOKING
10.047
MODESTY BLAISE
by PETER O'DONNELL
drawn by ROMERO
HALF A MILE WEST OF WILLIE'S LOCATION LORD WHITRAM FOLLOWS A BEARING ON HIS TRACER
STRAIGHT AHEAD NOW... DAMNED UNSPORTING, THESE GADGETS...
IT'S WHITRAM...
GLAD TO GET THIS BUSINESS OVER WITH... THOSE POOR DEVILS HAVEN'T A CHANCE
A SHARP WHISTLE MAKES WHITRAM TURN, SEEKING A TARGET BUT FINDING NONE, AND THEN—
UHH!
10.048

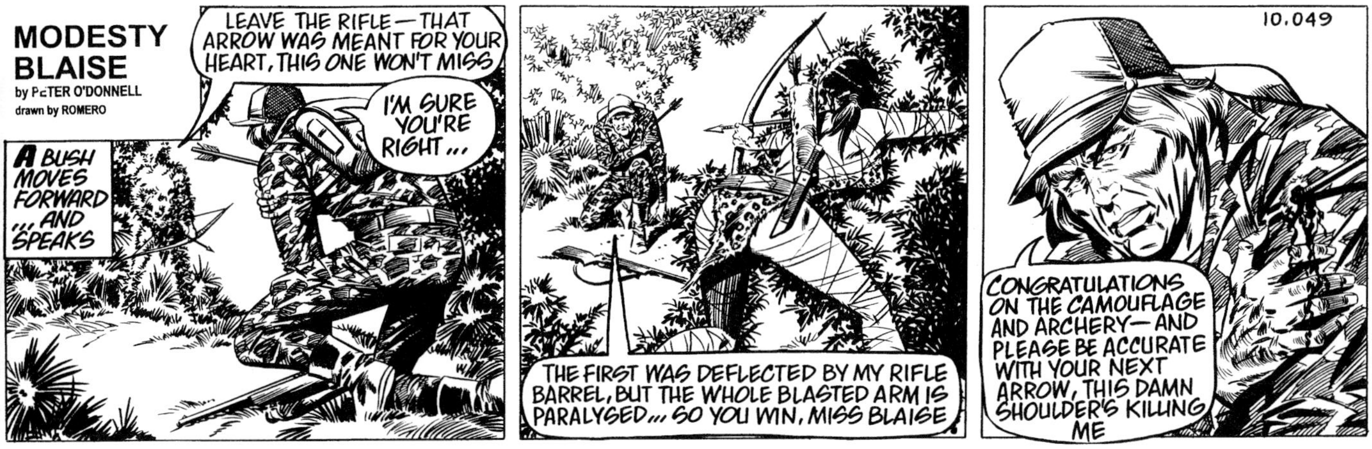
MODESTY BLAISE
by PETER O'DONNELL
drawn by ROMERO
A BUSH MOVES FORWARD ... AND SPEAKS
LEAVE THE RIFLE — THAT ARROW WAS MEANT FOR YOUR HEART, THIS ONE WON'T MISS
I'M SURE YOU'RE RIGHT ...
THE FIRST WAS DEFLECTED BY MY RIFLE BARREL, BUT THE WHOLE BLASTED ARM IS PARALYSED ... SO YOU WIN, MISS BLAISE
10,049
CONGRATULATIONS ON THE CAMOUFLAGE AND ARCHERY — AND PLEASE BE ACCURATE WITH YOUR NEXT ARROW, THIS DAMN SHOULDER'S KILLING ME

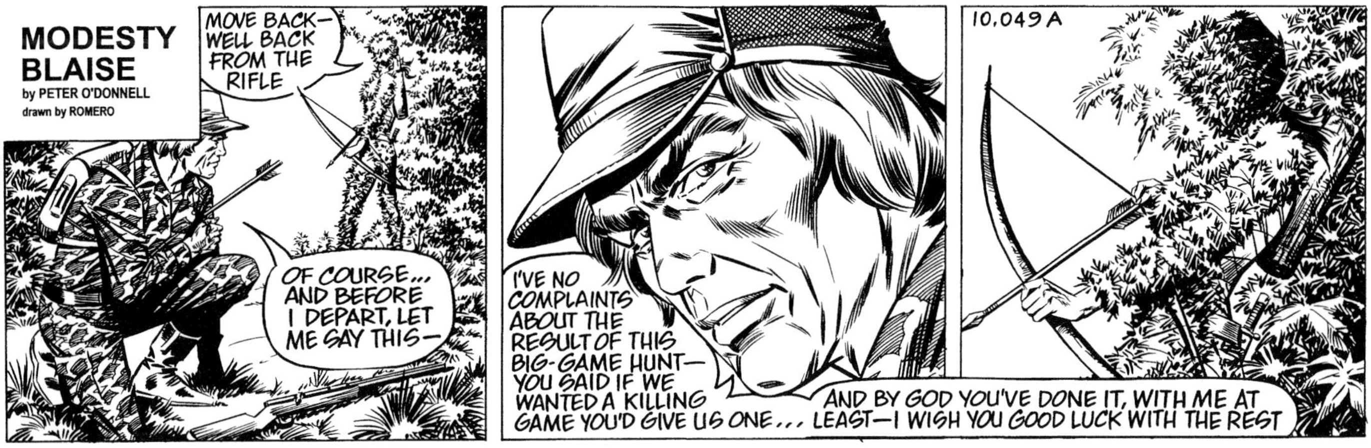
MODESTY BLAISE
by PETER O'DONNELL
drawn by ROMERO
MOVE BACK — WELL BACK FROM THE RIFLE
OF COURSE ... AND BEFORE I DEPART, LET ME SAY THIS —
I'VE NO COMPLAINTS ABOUT THE RESULT OF THIS BIG-GAME HUNT — YOU SAID IF WE WANTED A KILLING GAME YOU'D GIVE US ONE ...
10,049 A
AND BY GOD YOU'VE DONE IT, WITH ME AT LEAST — I WISH YOU GOOD LUCK WITH THE REST

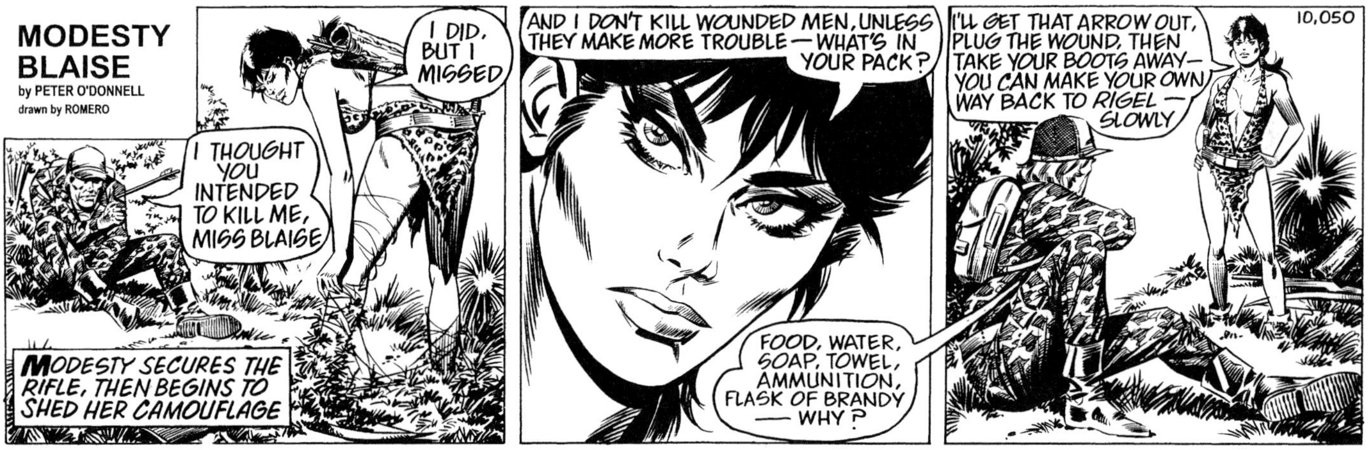
MODESTY BLAISE
by PETER O'DONNELL
drawn by ROMERO
I THOUGHT YOU INTENDED TO KILL ME, MISS BLAISE
I DID, BUT I MISSED
MODESTY SECURES THE RIFLE, THEN BEGINS TO SHED HER CAMOUFLAGE
AND I DON'T KILL WOUNDED MEN, UNLESS THEY MAKE MORE TROUBLE — WHAT'S IN YOUR PACK?
FOOD, WATER, SOAP, TOWEL, AMMUNITION, FLASK OF BRANDY — WHY?
10,050
I'LL GET THAT ARROW OUT, PLUG THE WOUND, THEN TAKE YOUR BOOTS AWAY — YOU CAN MAKE YOUR OWN WAY BACK TO RIGEL — SLOWLY

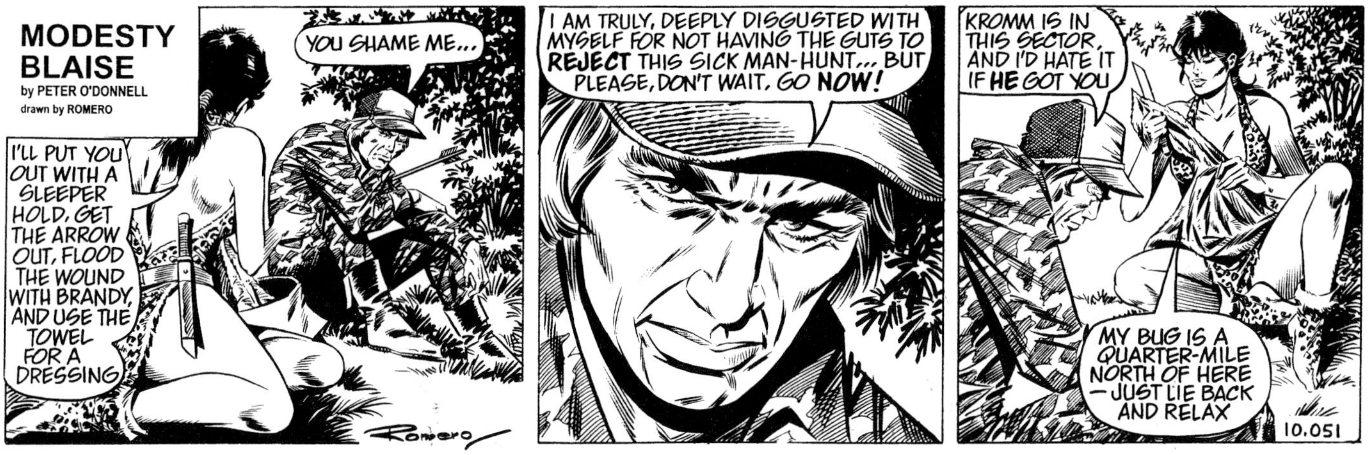
MODESTY BLAISE
by PETER O'DONNELL
drawn by ROMERO
I'LL PUT YOU OUT WITH A SLEEPER HOLD, GET THE ARROW OUT, FLOOD THE WOUND WITH BRANDY, AND USE THE TOWEL FOR A DRESSING
YOU SHAME ME ...
Romero
I AM TRULY, DEEPLY DISGUSTED WITH MYSELF FOR NOT HAVING THE GUTS TO REJECT THIS SICK MAN-HUNT ... BUT PLEASE, DON'T WAIT, GO NOW!
KROMM IS IN THIS SECTOR, AND I'D HATE IT IF HE GOT YOU
MY BUG IS A QUARTER-MILE NORTH OF HERE — JUST LIE BACK AND RELAX
10,051

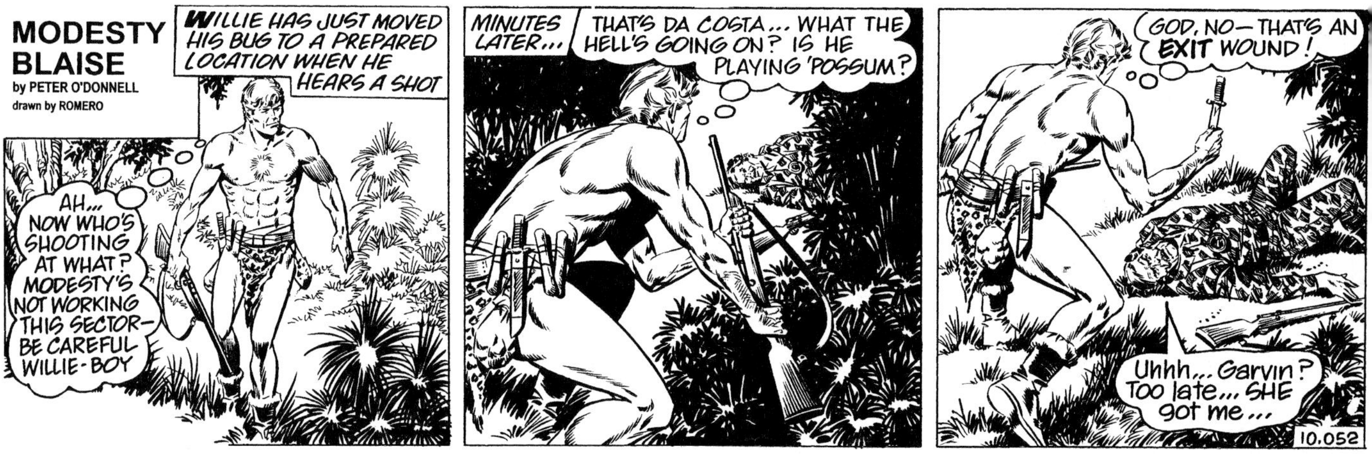
MODESTY BLAISE
by PETER O'DONNELL
drawn by ROMERO
WILLIE HAS JUST MOVED HIS BUG TO A PREPARED LOCATION WHEN HE HEARS A SHOT
AH... NOW WHO'S SHOOTING AT WHAT? MODESTY'S NOT WORKING THIS SECTOR– BE CAREFUL WILLIE-BOY
MINUTES LATER...
THAT'S DA COSTA... WHAT THE HELL'S GOING ON? IS HE PLAYING 'POSSUM?
GOD, NO– THAT'S AN EXIT WOUND!
Uhhh... Garvin? Too late... SHE got me...
10,052

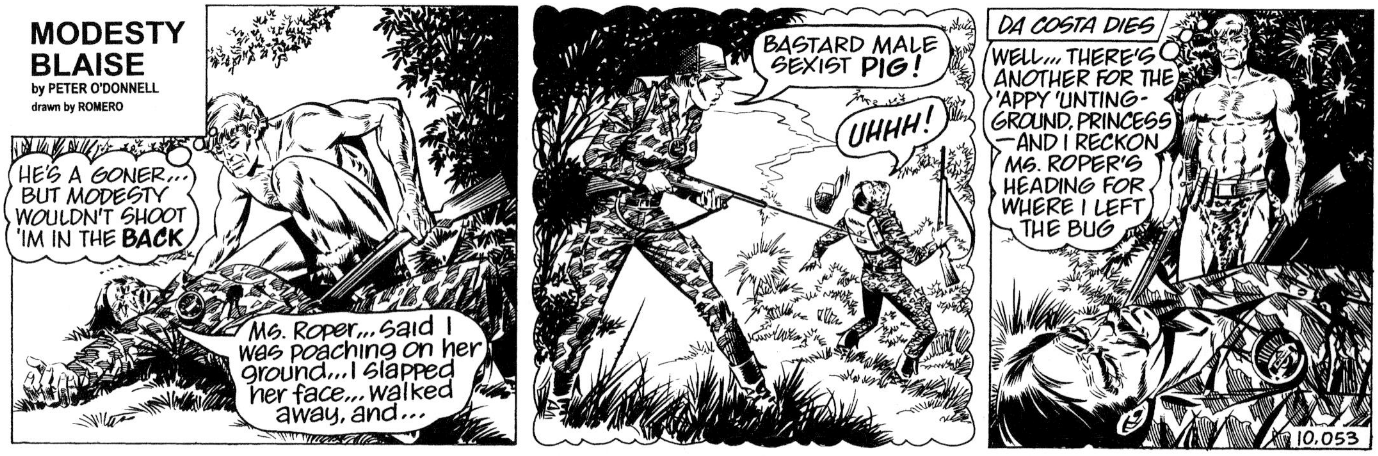
MODESTY BLAISE
by PETER O'DONNELL
drawn by ROMERO
HE'S A GONER... BUT MODESTY WOULDN'T SHOOT 'IM IN THE BACK
Ms. Roper... said I was poaching on her ground... I slapped her face... walked away, and...
BASTARD MALE SEXIST PIG!
UHHH!
DA COSTA DIES
WELL... THERE'S ANOTHER FOR THE 'APPY 'UNTING-GROUND, PRINCESS –AND I RECKON MS. ROPER'S HEADING FOR WHERE I LEFT THE BUG
10,053

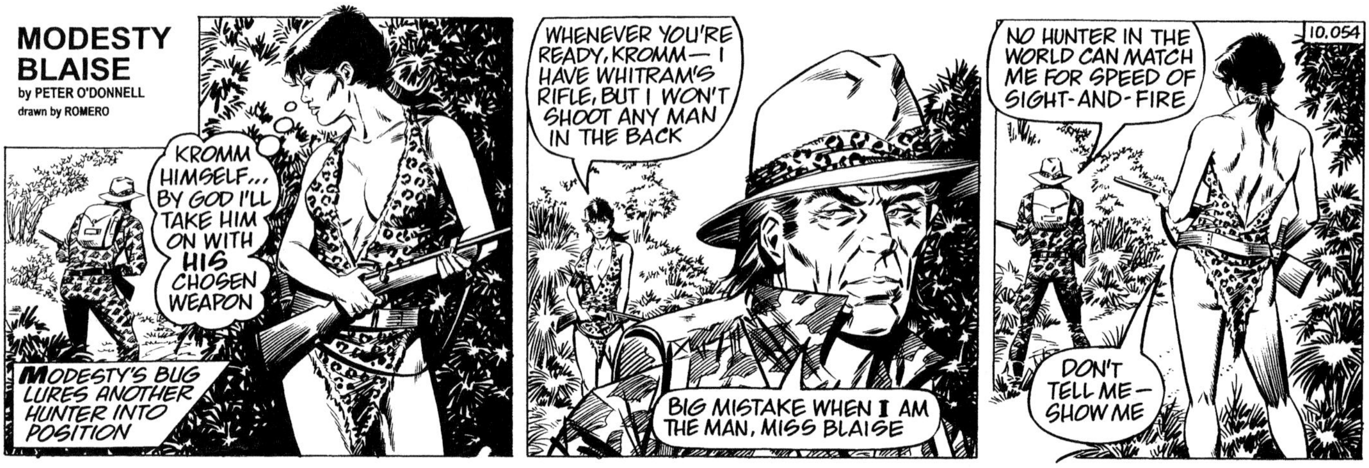
MODESTY BLAISE
by PETER O'DONNELL
drawn by ROMERO
KROMM HIMSELF... BY GOD I'LL TAKE HIM ON WITH HIS CHOSEN WEAPON
MODESTY'S BUG LURES ANOTHER HUNTER INTO POSITION
WHENEVER YOU'RE READY, KROMM– I HAVE WHITRAM'S RIFLE, BUT I WON'T SHOOT ANY MAN IN THE BACK
BIG MISTAKE WHEN I AM THE MAN, MISS BLAISE
10,054
NO HUNTER IN THE WORLD CAN MATCH ME FOR SPEED OF SIGHT-AND-FIRE
DON'T TELL ME– SHOW ME

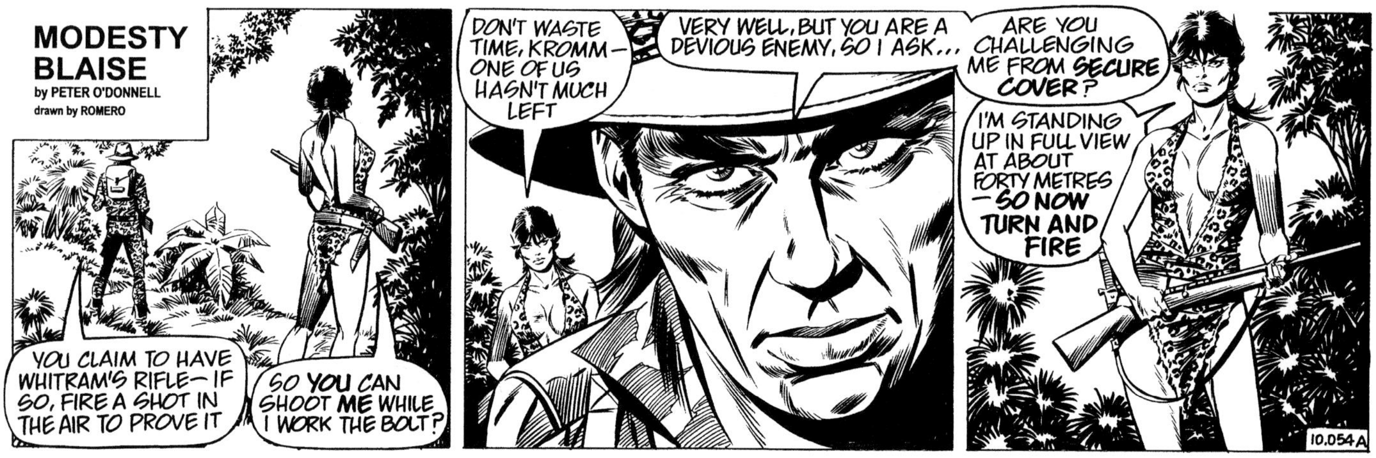
MODESTY BLAISE
by PETER O'DONNELL
drawn by ROMERO
YOU CLAIM TO HAVE WHITRAM'S RIFLE– IF SO, FIRE A SHOT IN THE AIR TO PROVE IT
SO YOU CAN SHOOT ME WHILE I WORK THE BOLT?
DON'T WASTE TIME, KROMM– ONE OF US HASN'T MUCH LEFT
VERY WELL, BUT YOU ARE A DEVIOUS ENEMY, SO I ASK...
ARE YOU CHALLENGING ME FROM SECURE COVER?
I'M STANDING UP IN FULL VIEW AT ABOUT FORTY METRES –SO NOW TURN AND FIRE
10,054A

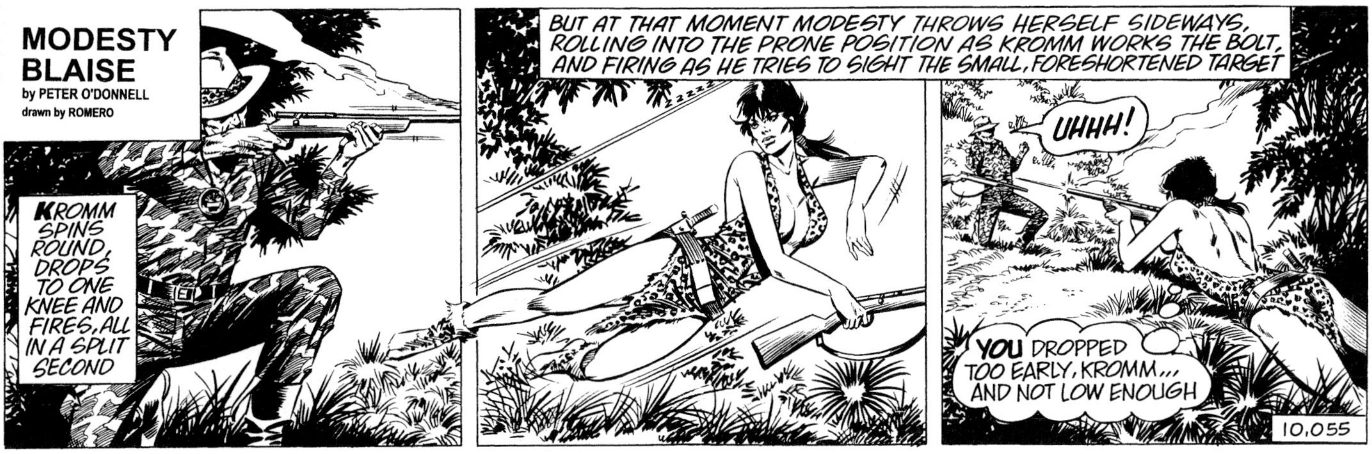

MODESTY BLAISE
by PETER O'DONNELL
drawn by ROMERO
KROMM SPINS ROUND, DROPS TO ONE KNEE AND FIRES, ALL IN A SPLIT SECOND
BUT AT THAT MOMENT MODESTY THROWS HERSELF SIDEWAYS, ROLLING INTO THE PRONE POSITION AS KROMM WORKS THE BOLT, AND FIRING AS HE TRIES TO SIGHT THE SMALL, FORESHORTENED TARGET
UHHH!
YOU DROPPED TOO EARLY, KROMM... AND NOT LOW ENOUGH
10,055

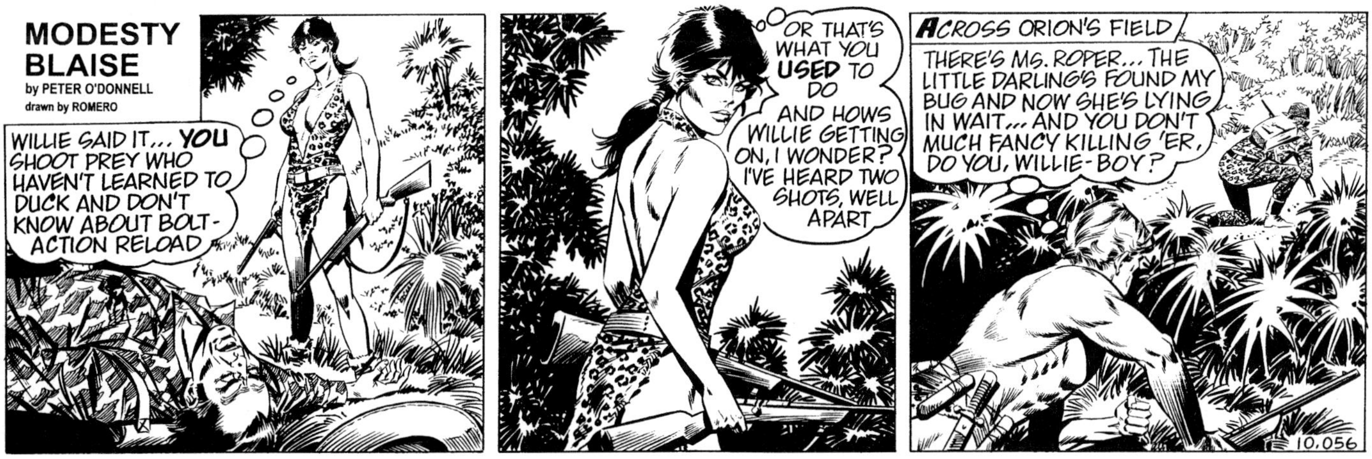

MODESTY BLAISE
by PETER O'DONNELL
drawn by ROMERO
WILLIE SAID IT... YOU SHOOT PREY WHO HAVEN'T LEARNED TO DUCK AND DON'T KNOW ABOUT BOLT-ACTION RELOAD
OR THAT'S WHAT YOU USED TO DO
AND HOWS WILLIE GETTING ON, I WONDER? I'VE HEARD TWO SHOTS, WELL APART
ACROSS ORION'S FIELD
THERE'S MS. ROPER... THE LITTLE DARLING'S FOUND MY BUG AND NOW SHE'S LYING IN WAIT... AND YOU DON'T MUCH FANCY KILLING 'ER, DO YOU, WILLIE-BOY?
10,056

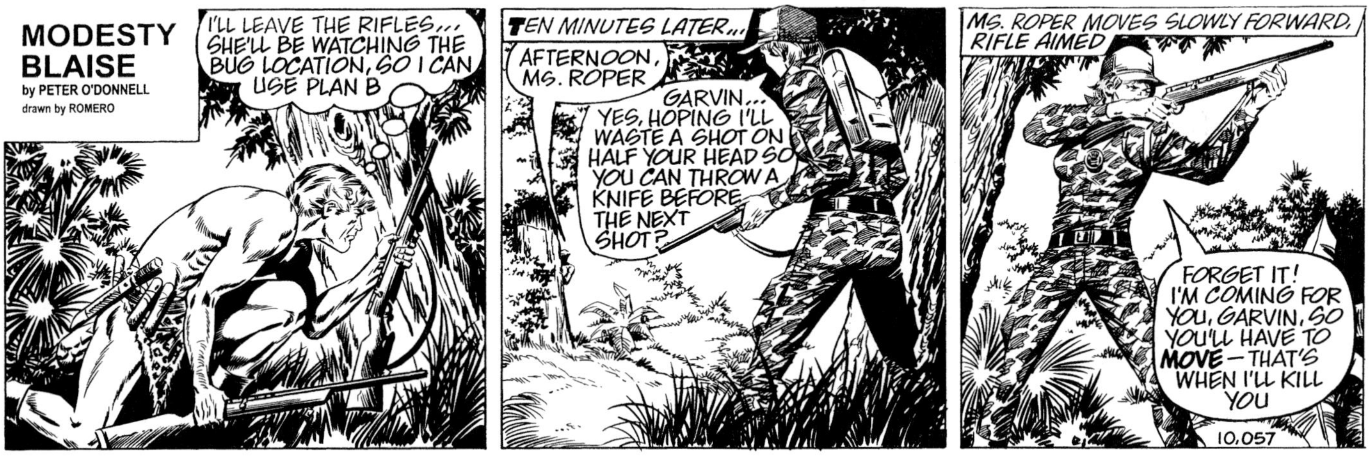

MODESTY BLAISE
by PETER O'DONNELL
drawn by ROMERO
I'LL LEAVE THE RIFLES... SHE'LL BE WATCHING THE BUG LOCATION, SO I CAN USE PLAN B
TEN MINUTES LATER...
AFTERNOON, MS. ROPER
GARVIN... YES, HOPING I'LL WASTE A SHOT ON HALF YOUR HEAD SO YOU CAN THROW A KNIFE BEFORE THE NEXT SHOT?
MS. ROPER MOVES SLOWLY FORWARD, RIFLE AIMED
FORGET IT! I'M COMING FOR YOU, GARVIN, SO YOU'LL HAVE TO MOVE—THAT'S WHEN I'LL KILL YOU
10,057

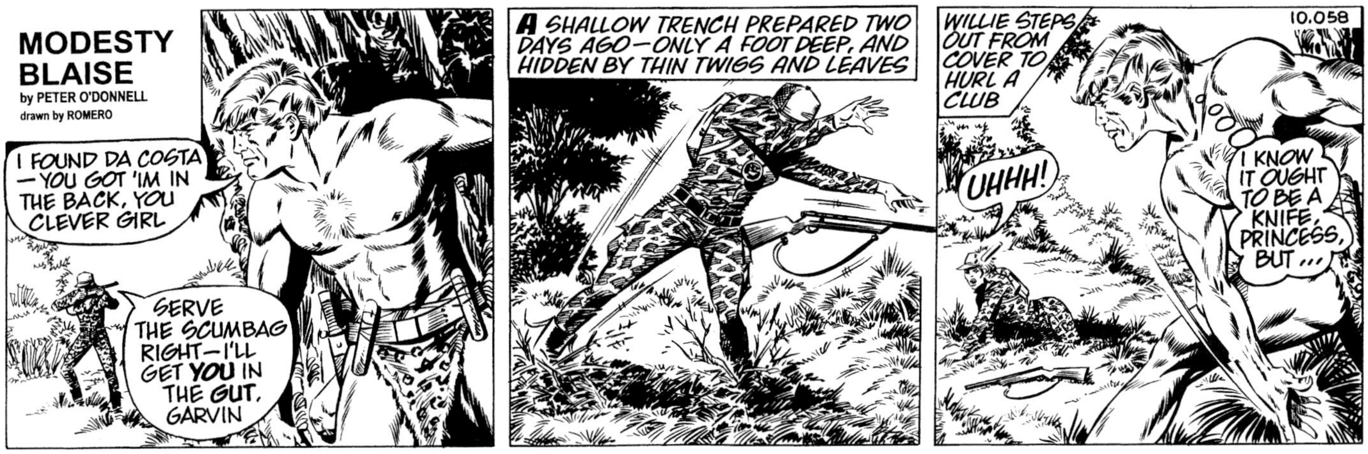

MODESTY BLAISE
by PETER O'DONNELL
drawn by ROMERO
I FOUND DA COSTA—YOU GOT 'IM IN THE BACK, YOU CLEVER GIRL
SERVE THE SCUMBAG RIGHT—I'LL GET YOU IN THE GUT, GARVIN
A SHALLOW TRENCH PREPARED TWO DAYS AGO—ONLY A FOOT DEEP, AND HIDDEN BY THIN TWIGS AND LEAVES
10,058
WILLIE STEPS OUT FROM COVER TO HURL A CLUB
UHHH!
I KNOW IT OUGHT TO BE A KNIFE, PRINCESS, BUT...

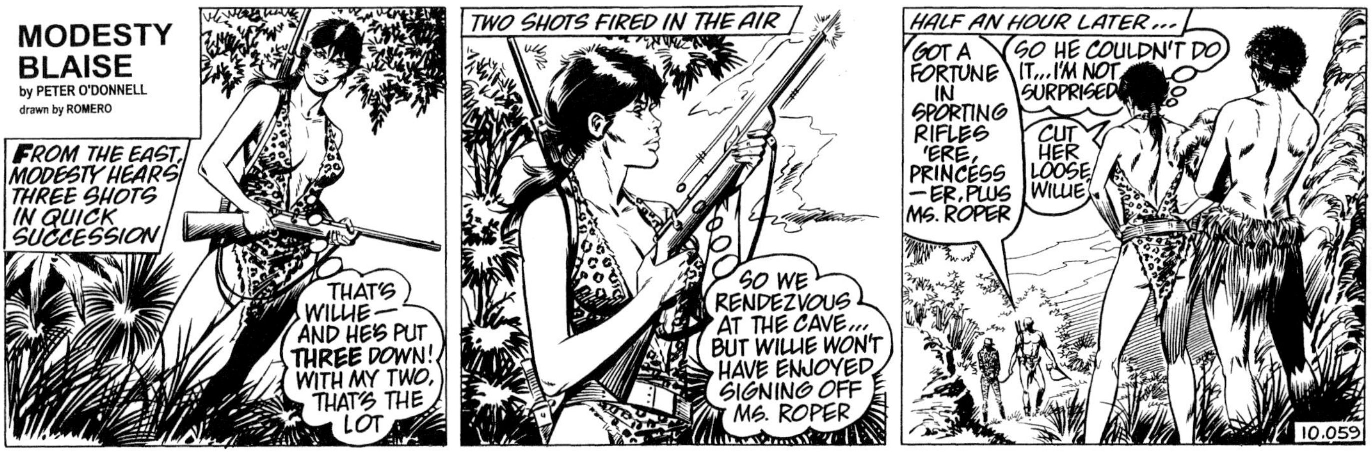
MODESTY BLAISE
by PETER O'DONNELL
drawn by ROMERO
FROM THE EAST, MODESTY HEARS THREE SHOTS IN QUICK SUCCESSION
THAT'S WILLIE— AND HE'S PUT THREE DOWN! WITH MY TWO, THAT'S THE LOT
TWO SHOTS FIRED IN THE AIR
SO WE RENDEZVOUS AT THE CAVE... BUT WILLIE WON'T HAVE ENJOYED SIGNING OFF MS. ROPER
HALF AN HOUR LATER...
GOT A FORTUNE IN SPORTING RIFLES 'ERE, PRINCESS —ER, PLUS MS. ROPER
SO HE COULDN'T DO IT... I'M NOT SURPRISED
CUT HER LOOSE, WILLIE
10.059

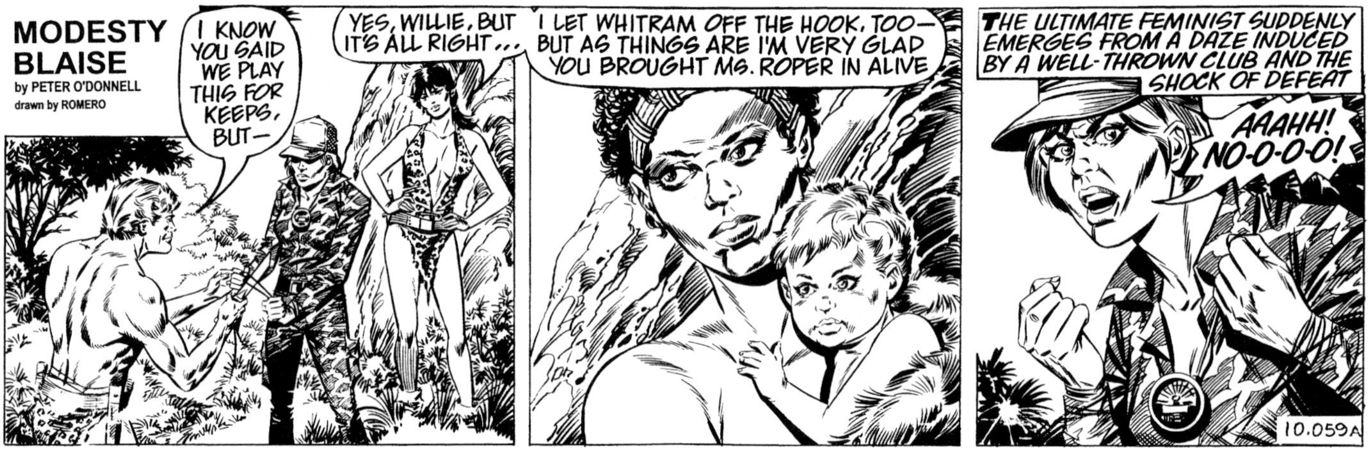
MODESTY BLAISE
by PETER O'DONNELL
drawn by ROMERO
I KNOW YOU SAID WE PLAY THIS FOR KEEPS, BUT—
YES, WILLIE, BUT IT'S ALL RIGHT...
I LET WHITRAM OFF THE HOOK, TOO— BUT AS THINGS ARE I'M VERY GLAD YOU BROUGHT MS. ROPER IN ALIVE
THE ULTIMATE FEMINIST SUDDENLY EMERGES FROM A DAZE INDUCED BY A WELL-THROWN CLUB AND THE SHOCK OF DEFEAT
AAAHH! NO-O-O-O!
10.059A

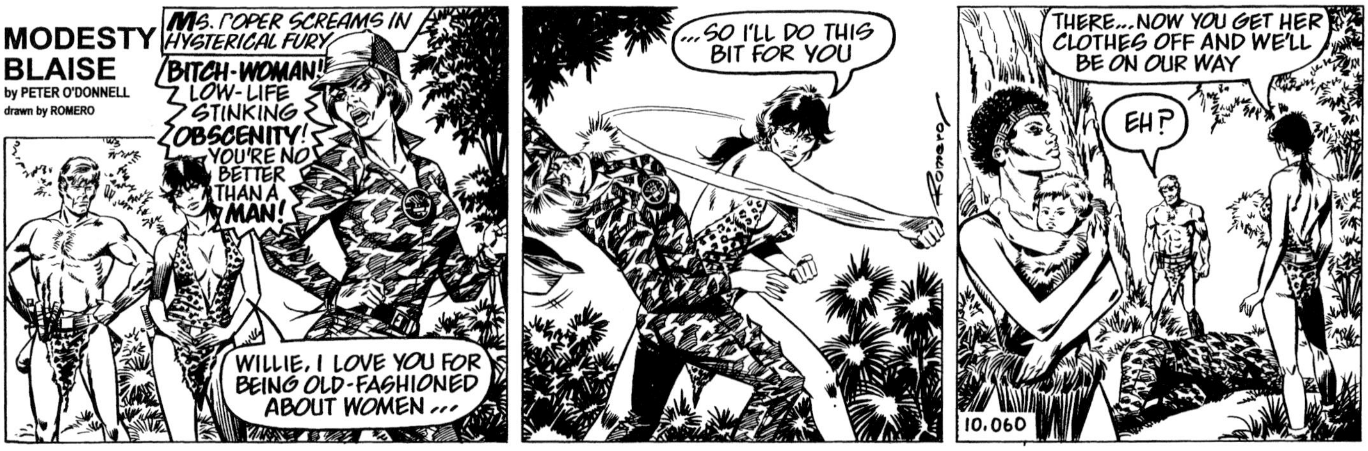
MODESTY BLAISE
by PETER O'DONNELL
drawn by ROMERO
MS. ROPER SCREAMS IN HYSTERICAL FURY
BITCH-WOMAN! LOW-LIFE STINKING OBSCENITY! YOU'RE NO BETTER THAN A MAN!
WILLIE, I LOVE YOU FOR BEING OLD-FASHIONED ABOUT WOMEN...
...SO I'LL DO THIS BIT FOR YOU
Romero
THERE... NOW YOU GET HER CLOTHES OFF AND WE'LL BE ON OUR WAY
EH?
10.060

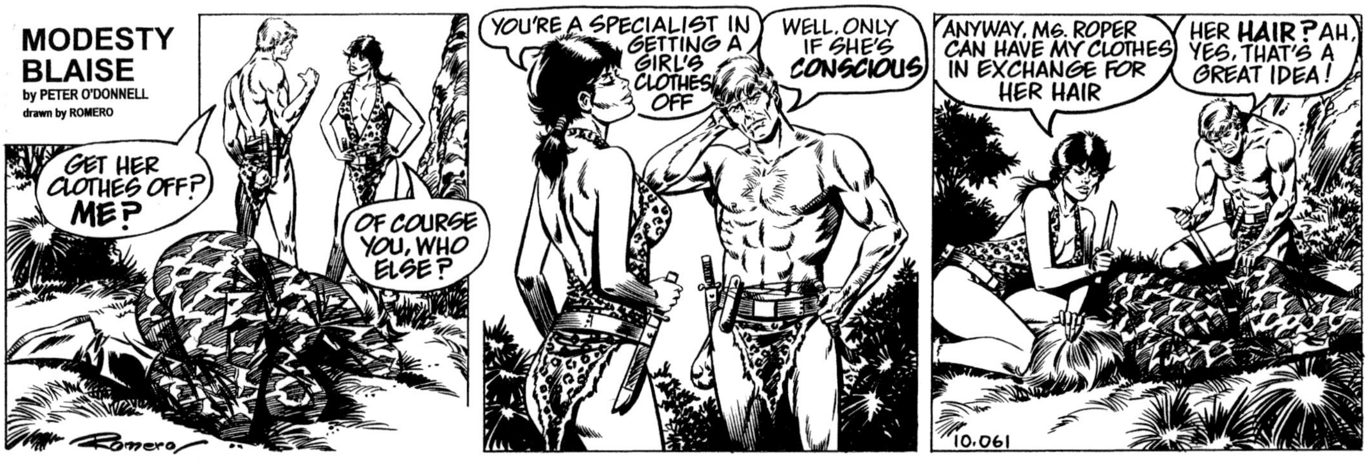
MODESTY BLAISE
by PETER O'DONNELL
drawn by ROMERO
GET HER CLOTHES OFF? ME?
OF COURSE YOU, WHO ELSE?
Romero
YOU'RE A SPECIALIST IN GETTING A GIRL'S CLOTHES OFF
WELL, ONLY IF SHE'S CONSCIOUS
ANYWAY, MS. ROPER CAN HAVE MY CLOTHES IN EXCHANGE FOR HER HAIR
HER HAIR? AH, YES, THAT'S A GREAT IDEA!
10.061

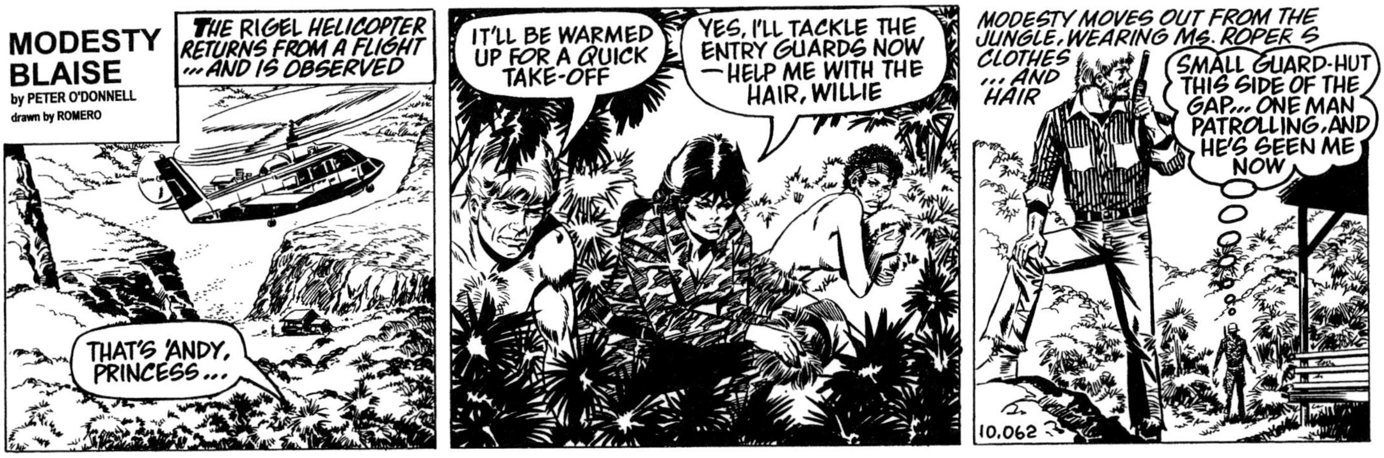
MODESTY BLAISE
by PETER O'DONNELL
drawn by ROMERO
THE RIGEL HELICOPTER RETURNS FROM A FLIGHT ... AND IS OBSERVED
THAT'S 'ANDY, PRINCESS...
IT'LL BE WARMED UP FOR A QUICK TAKE-OFF
YES, I'LL TACKLE THE ENTRY GUARDS NOW —HELP ME WITH THE HAIR, WILLIE
MODESTY MOVES OUT FROM THE JUNGLE, WEARING MS. ROPER'S CLOTHES ... AND HAIR
SMALL GUARD-HUT THIS SIDE OF THE GAP... ONE MAN PATROLLING, AND HE'S SEEN ME NOW
10.062

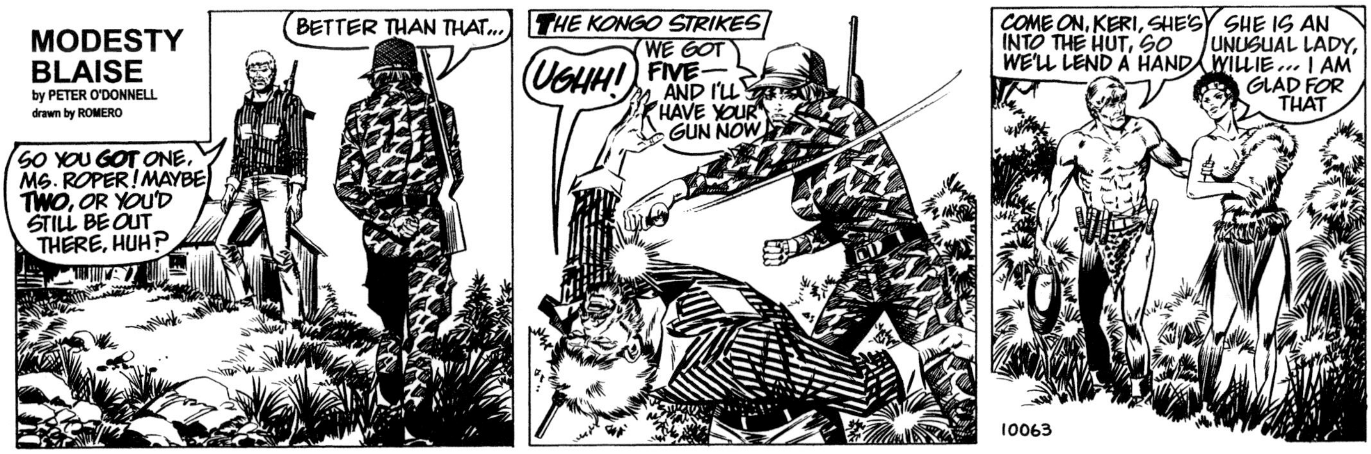
MODESTY BLAISE
by PETER O'DONNELL
drawn by ROMERO
SO YOU GOT ONE, MS. ROPER! MAYBE TWO, OR YOU'D STILL BE OUT THERE, HUH?
BETTER THAN THAT...
THE KONGO STRIKES
UGHH!
WE GOT FIVE— AND I'LL HAVE YOUR GUN NOW
COME ON, KERI, SHE'S INTO THE HUT, SO WE'LL LEND A HAND
SHE IS AN UNUSUAL LADY, WILLIE... I AM GLAD FOR THAT
10063

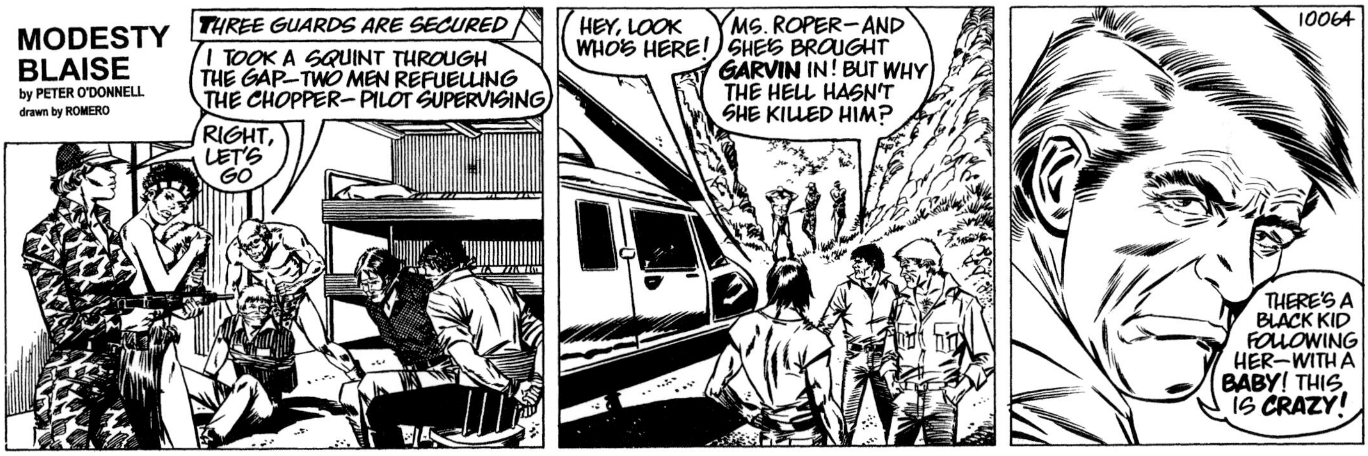
MODESTY BLAISE
by PETER O'DONNELL
drawn by ROMERO
THREE GUARDS ARE SECURED
I TOOK A SQUINT THROUGH THE GAP—TWO MEN REFUELLING THE CHOPPER—PILOT SUPERVISING
RIGHT, LET'S GO
HEY, LOOK WHO'S HERE!
MS. ROPER—AND SHE'S BROUGHT GARVIN IN! BUT WHY THE HELL HASN'T SHE KILLED HIM?
10064
THERE'S A BLACK KID FOLLOWING HER—WITH A BABY! THIS IS CRAZY!

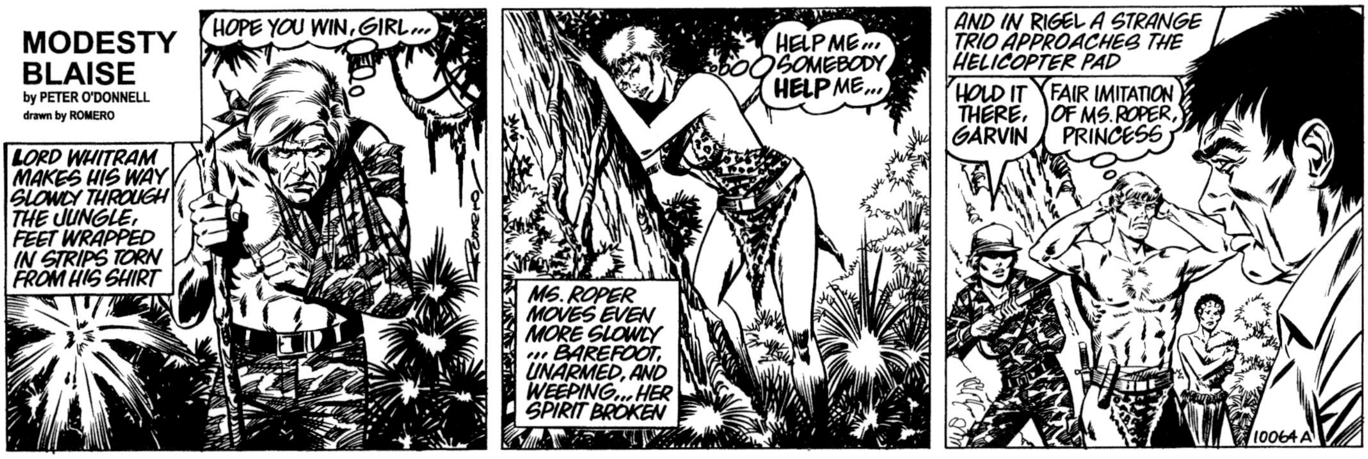
MODESTY BLAISE
by PETER O'DONNELL
drawn by ROMERO
HOPE YOU WIN, GIRL...
LORD WHITRAM MAKES HIS WAY SLOWLY THROUGH THE JUNGLE, FEET WRAPPED IN STRIPS TORN FROM HIS SHIRT
HELP ME... SOMEBODY HELP ME...
MS. ROPER MOVES EVEN MORE SLOWLY ... BAREFOOT, UNARMED, AND WEEPING... HER SPIRIT BROKEN
AND IN RIGEL A STRANGE TRIO APPROACHES THE HELICOPTER PAD
HOLD IT THERE, GARVIN
FAIR IMITATION OF MS. ROPER, PRINCESS
10064 A

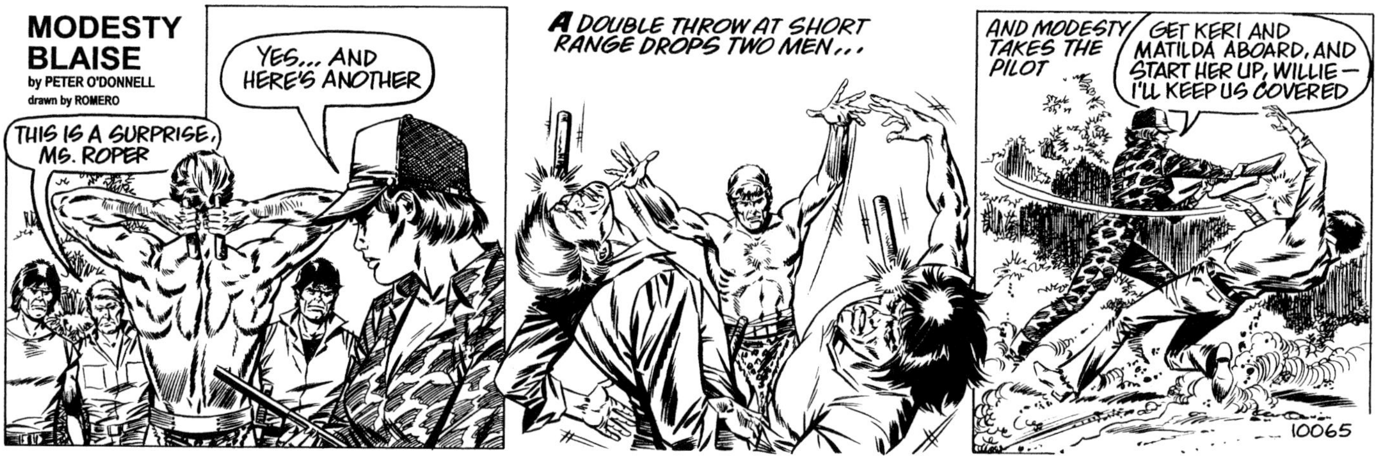
MODESTY BLAISE
by PETER O'DONNELL
drawn by ROMERO
THIS IS A SURPRISE, MS. ROPER
YES... AND HERE'S ANOTHER
A DOUBLE THROW AT SHORT RANGE DROPS TWO MEN...
AND MODESTY TAKES THE PILOT
GET KERI AND MATILDA ABOARD, AND START HER UP, WILLIE — I'LL KEEP US COVERED
10065

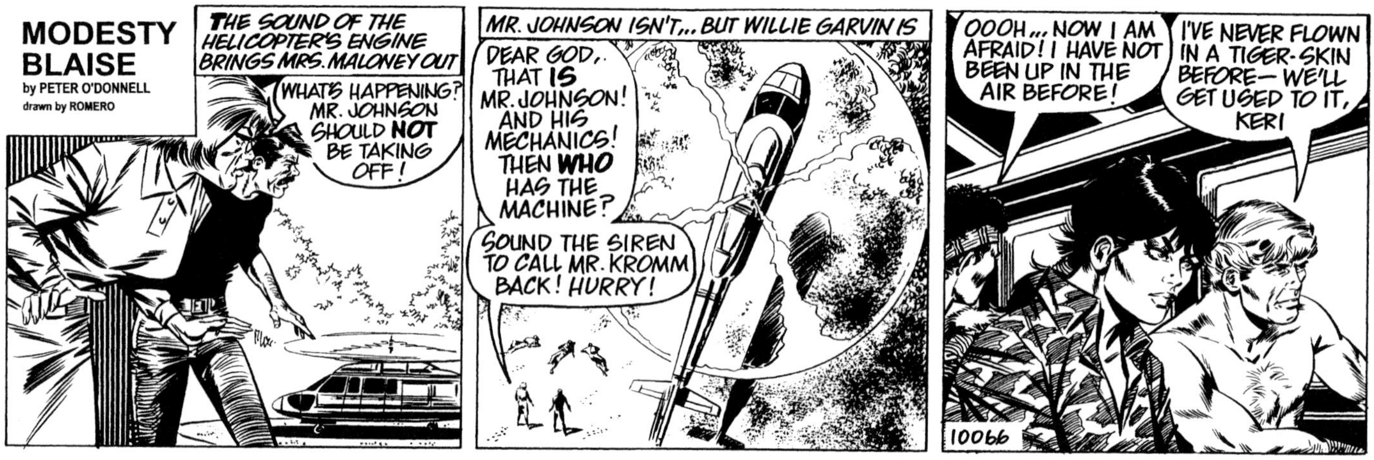
MODESTY BLAISE
by PETER O'DONNELL
drawn by ROMERO
THE SOUND OF THE HELICOPTER'S ENGINE BRINGS MRS. MALONEY OUT
WHAT'S HAPPENING? MR. JOHNSON SHOULD NOT BE TAKING OFF!
MR. JOHNSON ISN'T... BUT WILLIE GARVIN IS
DEAR GOD, THAT IS MR. JOHNSON! AND HIS MECHANICS! THEN WHO HAS THE MACHINE?
SOUND THE SIREN TO CALL MR. KROMM BACK! HURRY!
OOOH... NOW I AM AFRAID! I HAVE NOT BEEN UP IN THE AIR BEFORE!
I'VE NEVER FLOWN IN A TIGER-SKIN BEFORE — WE'LL GET USED TO IT, KERI
10066

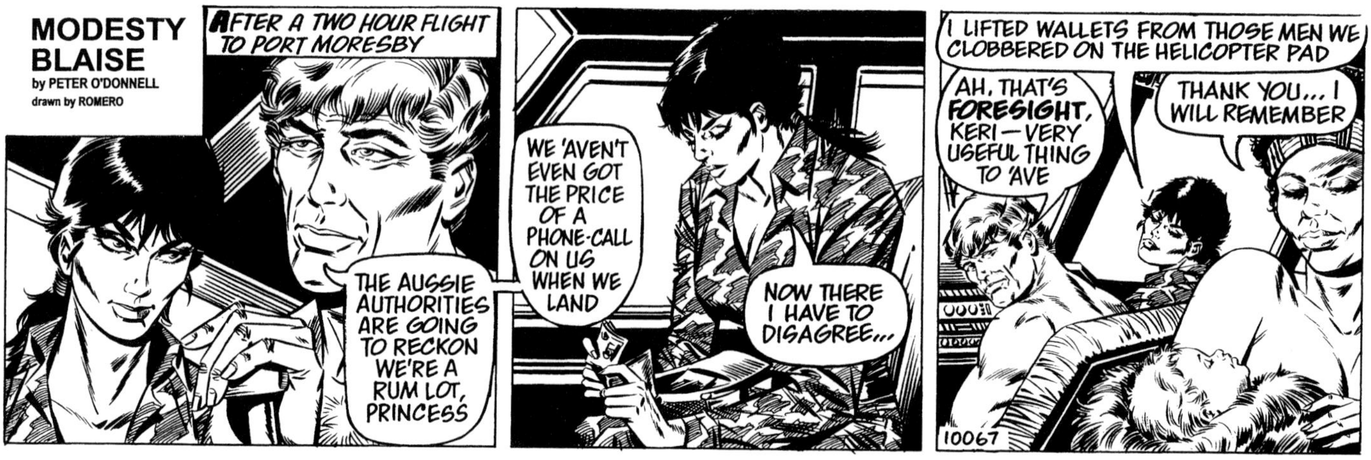
MODESTY BLAISE
by PETER O'DONNELL
drawn by ROMERO
AFTER A TWO HOUR FLIGHT TO PORT MORESBY
THE AUSSIE AUTHORITIES ARE GOING TO RECKON WE'RE A RUM LOT, PRINCESS
WE 'AVEN'T EVEN GOT THE PRICE OF A PHONE-CALL ON US WHEN WE LAND
NOW THERE I HAVE TO DISAGREE...
I LIFTED WALLETS FROM THOSE MEN WE CLOBBERED ON THE HELICOPTER PAD
AH, THAT'S FORESIGHT, KERI — VERY USEFUL THING TO 'AVE
THANK YOU... I WILL REMEMBER
10067

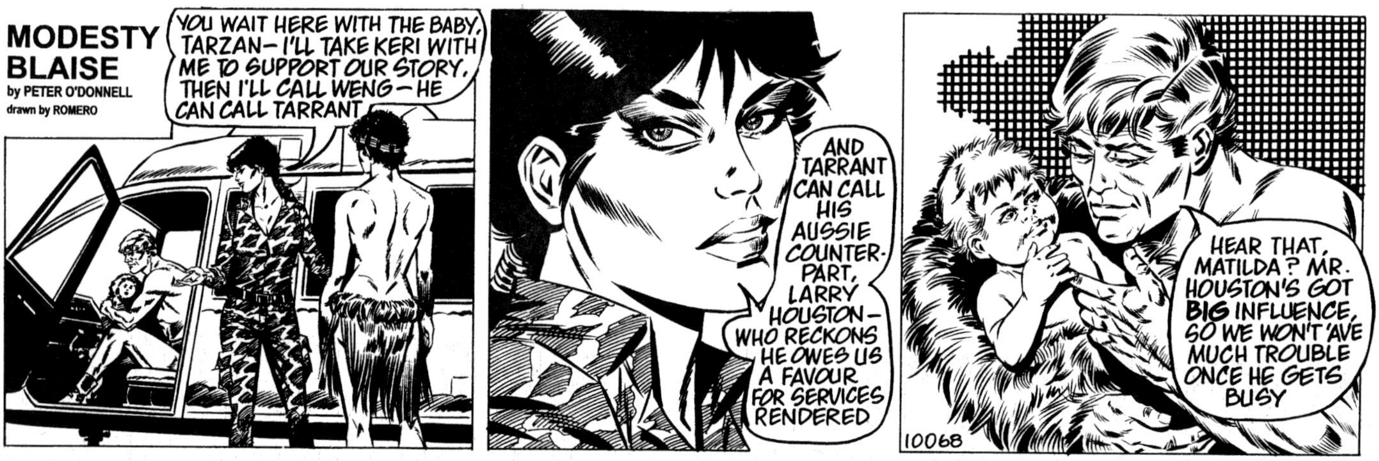
MODESTY BLAISE
by PETER O'DONNELL
drawn by ROMERO
YOU WAIT HERE WITH THE BABY, TARZAN — I'LL TAKE KERI WITH ME TO SUPPORT OUR STORY, THEN I'LL CALL WENG — HE CAN CALL TARRANT
AND TARRANT CAN CALL HIS AUSSIE COUNTER-PART, LARRY HOUSTON — WHO RECKONS HE OWES US A FAVOUR FOR SERVICES RENDERED
HEAR THAT, MATILDA? MR. HOUSTON'S GOT BIG INFLUENCE, SO WE WON'T 'AVE MUCH TROUBLE ONCE HE GETS BUSY
10068

MODESTY BLAISE
by PETER O'DONNELL
drawn by ROMERO
FOUR DAYS AFTER THE MAN-HUNT...
IT'S A LOVELY 'OME FOR YOU AND MATILDA, SO YOU WON'T RUN AWAY AGAIN, KERI, EH?
NO...
I WILL STAY, AND LEARN, AND WORK HARD FOR MY BABY... I HOPE YOU AND MISS BLAISE FLY HOME SAFE, WILLIE
THANKS, KERI — I'LL WRITE TO YOU
WHY DID YOU WANT ME TO DO THAT BIT?
BECAUSE SHE ADORES YOU, DIDN'T YOU KNOW? SOMETIMES YOU'RE DOPEY IN A VERY NICE WAY, WILLIE LOVE
10069

MODESTY BLAISE
by PETER O'DONNELL
drawn by ROMERO
YOU FOUND KERI, YOU LOOKED AFTER HER AND HER BABY— OF COURSE SHE THINKS YOU'RE WONDERFUL, AND THERE'S SOMETHING I DIDN'T SAY BEFORE...
...IN CASE YOU LOOKED HORRIFIED AND HURT HER FEELINGS — SHE'S RENAMED MATILDA AFTER YOU
ROMERO
ME? BUT YOU CAN'T CALL A GIRL WILLIE!
WHY NOT? KERI WAS BORN INTO A STONE AGE TRIBE WHERE MAYBE NAMES DON'T HAVE GENDER — ANYWAY, WHAT'S IN A NAME?
GOOD QUESTION... LET'S GO 'OME, PRINCESS
10069 A

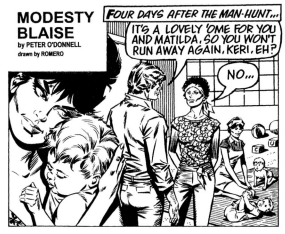

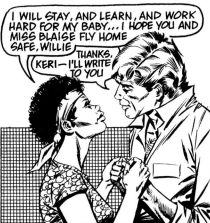

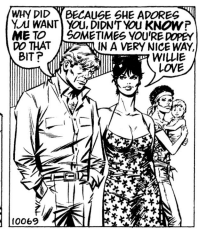

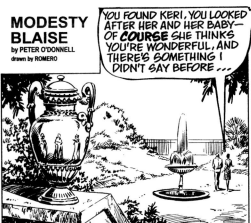

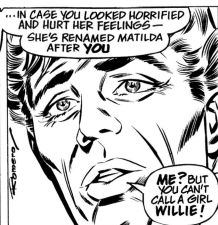

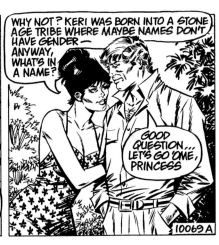

THE ZOMBIE

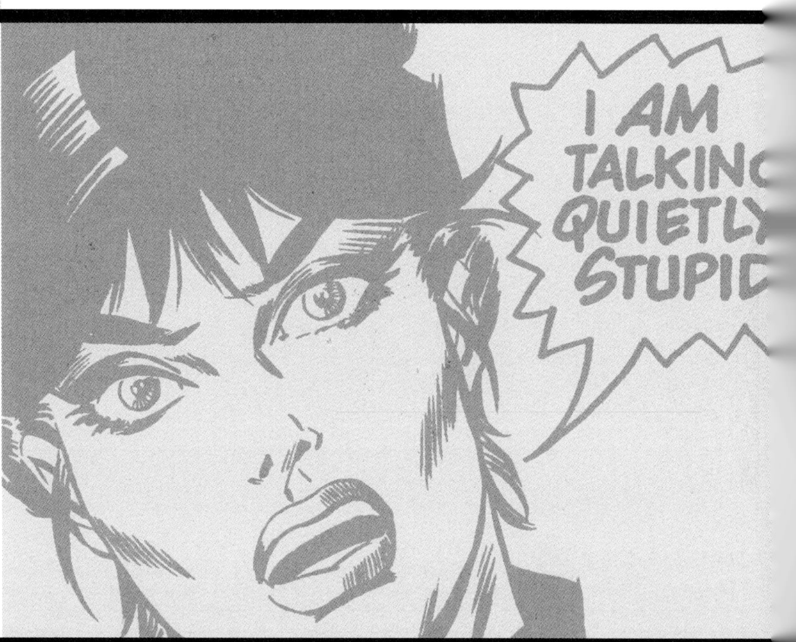
I AM TALKING QUIETLY STUPID

It has truly been a pleasure and an honour to return to Modesty Blaise, this time as an introducer to two delicious stories - a very different experience to playing Modesty in the BBC Radio 4 dramatisations.

The Zombie is a charming romp of veteran car runs and racehorses. It evokes one of my favourite genres- sci-fi- and gives us villains who have been raised to resemble computers. Leda is an interesting female character in her own right, who eventually melts thanks to Modesty's most seductive of lovers, Danny Chavasse. Peter O'Donnell ingeniously creates a fascinating parallel between two strong female characters: Leda as the weaker, dark version of Modesty - both experienced fighters raised by brilliant professors (a dark genius jealous of Einstein, in Leda's case). Unlike Modesty, Leda has been taught self-suppression. Modesty on the other hand is a liberated force of nature.

I particularly love how Peter always mixes the action with hilarity. In 'The Zombie' the scene of pretend improvised dialogue Modesty devises with Danny to confuse their attackers - "calm down Millicent, you know what the doctor said" and "you forgot to take your Valium my treasure"- are particular delights. It also strikes me yet again how finely drawn and unique a heroine Peter O'Donnell has created: her fierce loyalty to humans and love of animals (I do wish I could visit that donkey sanctuary in Tangiers) are particularly poignant.

Amidst lots of evidence of Peter's feminism, one of the minders here is told off for calling Modesty "bird" and is ordered to sit in the back seat while Lady Modesty drives him where she chooses. Supremely satisfying.

DAPHNE ALEXANDER

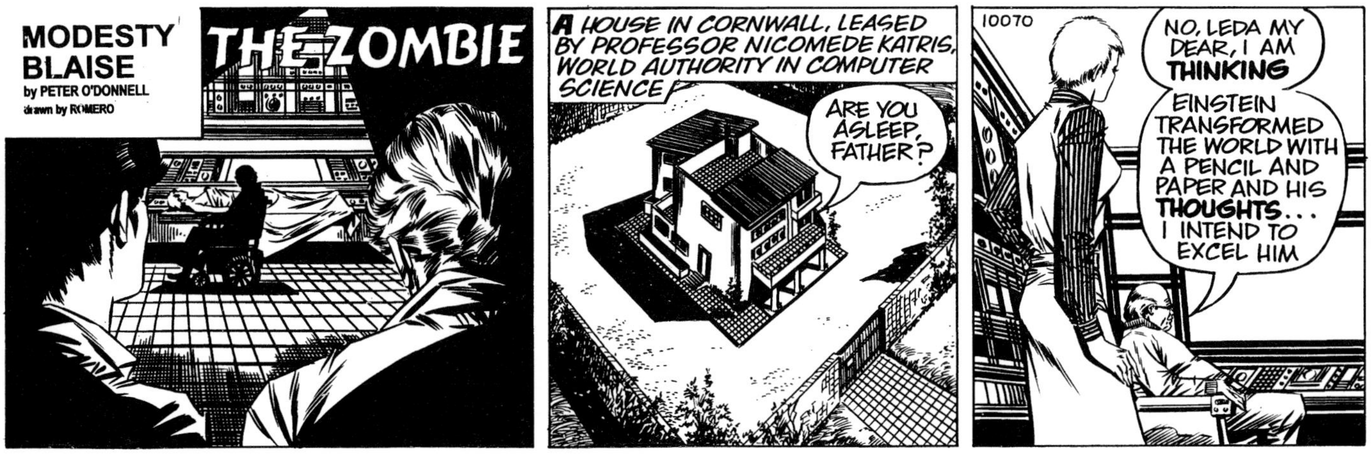
MODESTY BLAISE
by PETER O'DONNELL
drawn by ROMERO
THE ZOMBIE
A HOUSE IN CORNWALL, LEASED BY PROFESSOR NICOMEDE KATRIS, WORLD AUTHORITY IN COMPUTER SCIENCE
ARE YOU ASLEEP, FATHER?
10070
NO, LEDA MY DEAR, I AM THINKING
EINSTEIN TRANSFORMED THE WORLD WITH A PENCIL AND PAPER AND HIS THOUGHTS... I INTEND TO EXCEL HIM

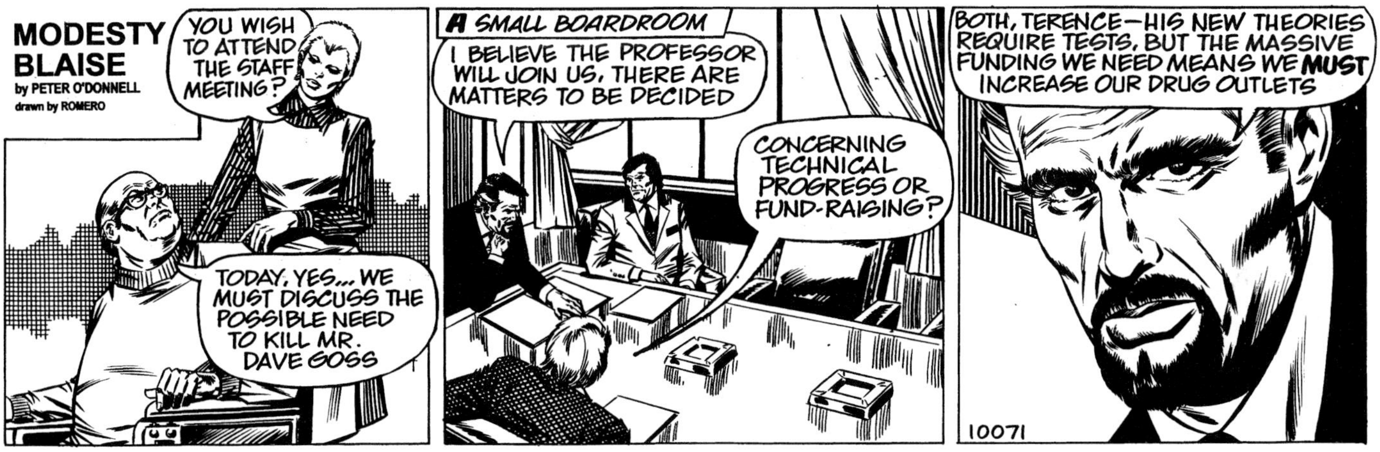
MODESTY BLAISE
by PETER O'DONNELL
drawn by ROMERO
YOU WISH TO ATTEND THE STAFF MEETING?
TODAY, YES... WE MUST DISCUSS THE POSSIBLE NEED TO KILL MR. DAVE GOSS
A SMALL BOARDROOM
I BELIEVE THE PROFESSOR WILL JOIN US, THERE ARE MATTERS TO BE DECIDED
CONCERNING TECHNICAL PROGRESS OR FUND-RAISING?
BOTH, TERENCE—HIS NEW THEORIES REQUIRE TESTS, BUT THE MASSIVE FUNDING WE NEED MEANS WE MUST INCREASE OUR DRUG OUTLETS
10071

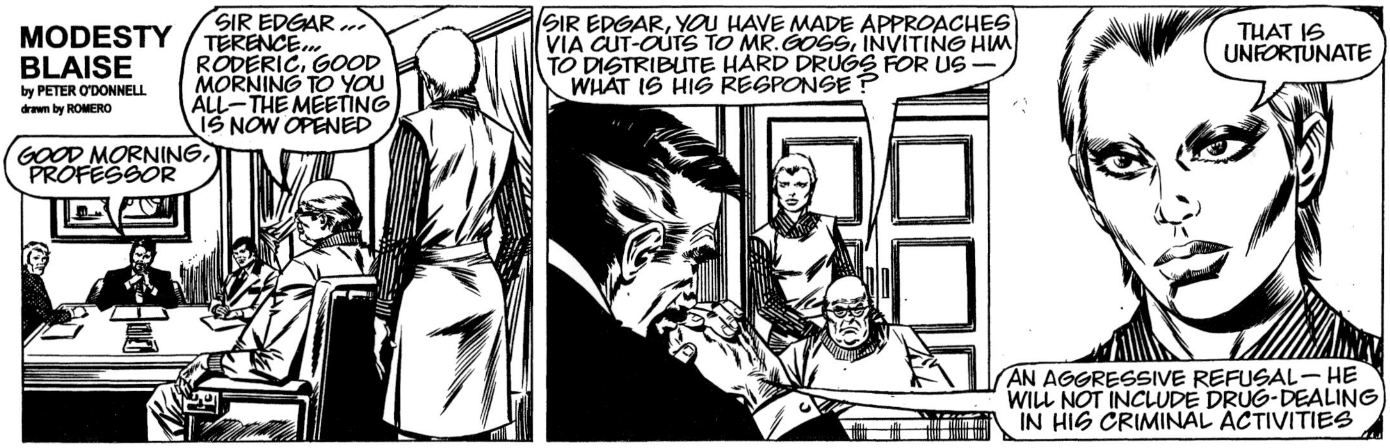
MODESTY BLAISE
by PETER O'DONNELL
drawn by ROMERO
SIR EDGAR... TERENCE... RODERIC, GOOD MORNING TO YOU ALL—THE MEETING IS NOW OPENED
GOOD MORNING, PROFESSOR
SIR EDGAR, YOU HAVE MADE APPROACHES VIA CUT-OUTS TO MR. GOSS, INVITING HIM TO DISTRIBUTE HARD DRUGS FOR US — WHAT IS HIS RESPONSE?
AN AGGRESSIVE REFUSAL — HE WILL NOT INCLUDE DRUG-DEALING IN HIS CRIMINAL ACTIVITIES
THAT IS UNFORTUNATE

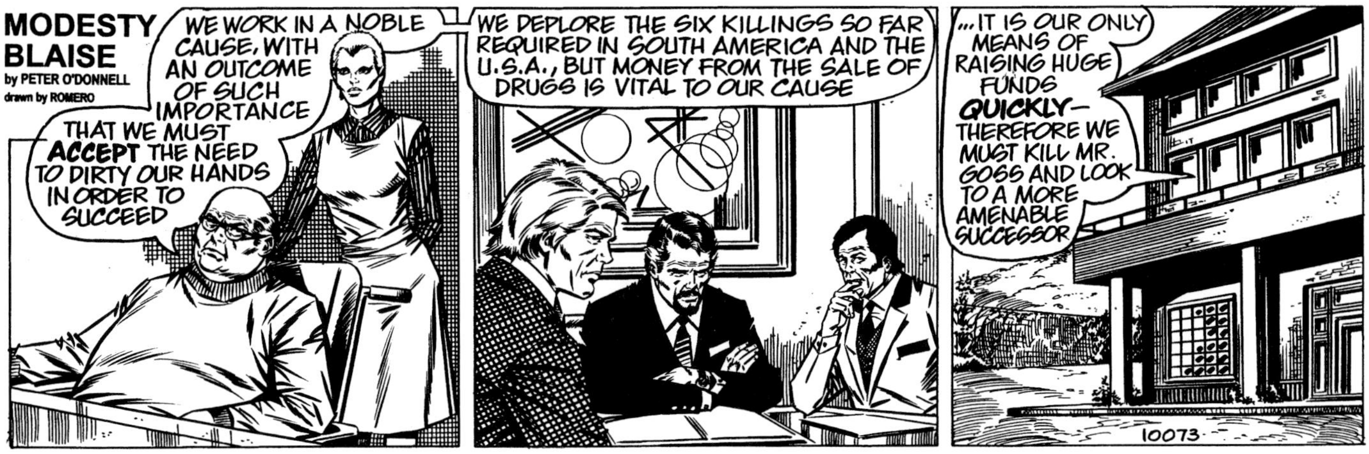
MODESTY BLAISE
by PETER O'DONNELL
drawn by ROMERO
WE WORK IN A NOBLE CAUSE, WITH AN OUTCOME OF SUCH IMPORTANCE
THAT WE MUST ACCEPT THE NEED TO DIRTY OUR HANDS IN ORDER TO SUCCEED
WE DEPLORE THE SIX KILLINGS SO FAR REQUIRED IN SOUTH AMERICA AND THE U.S.A., BUT MONEY FROM THE SALE OF DRUGS IS VITAL TO OUR CAUSE
...IT IS OUR ONLY MEANS OF RAISING HUGE FUNDS QUICKLY—
THEREFORE WE MUST KILL MR. GOSS AND LOOK TO A MORE AMENABLE SUCCESSOR
10073

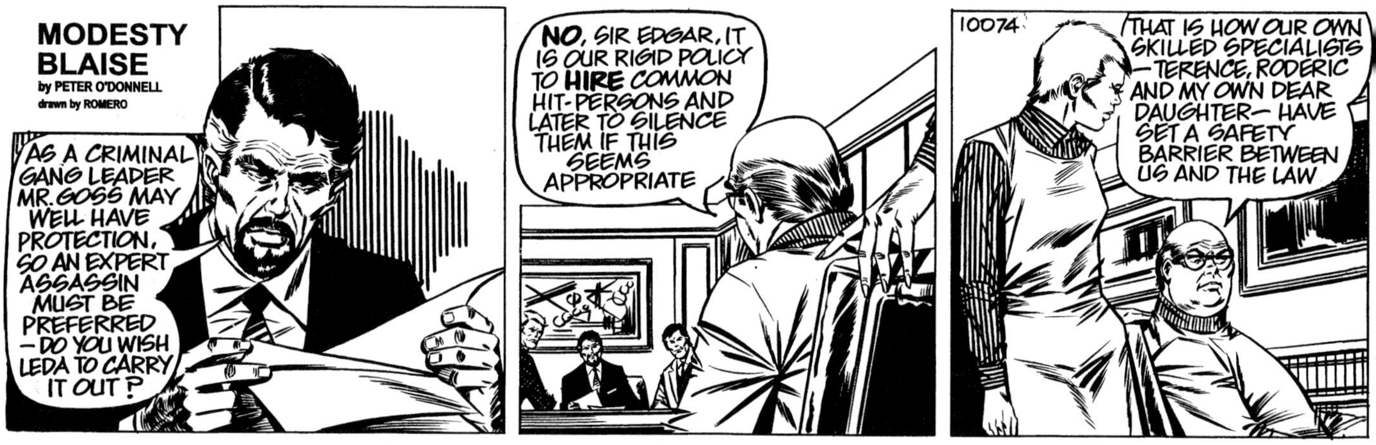
MODESTY BLAISE
by PETER O'DONNELL
drawn by ROMERO
AS A CRIMINAL GANG LEADER MR. GOSS MAY WELL HAVE PROTECTION, SO AN EXPERT ASSASSIN MUST BE PREFERRED — DO YOU WISH LEDA TO CARRY IT OUT?
NO, SIR EDGAR, IT IS OUR RIGID POLICY TO HIRE COMMON HIT-PERSONS AND LATER TO SILENCE THEM IF THIS SEEMS APPROPRIATE
10074
THAT IS HOW OUR OWN SKILLED SPECIALISTS — TERENCE, RODERIC AND MY OWN DEAR DAUGHTER — HAVE SET A SAFETY BARRIER BETWEEN US AND THE LAW

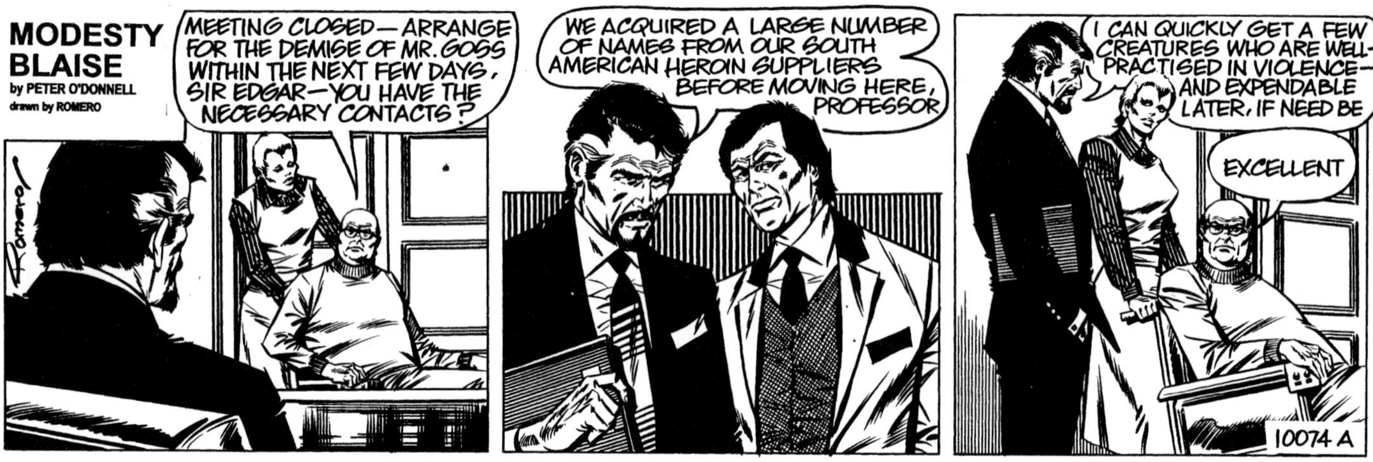
MODESTY BLAISE
by PETER O'DONNELL
drawn by ROMERO
MEETING CLOSED — ARRANGE FOR THE DEMISE OF MR. GOSS WITHIN THE NEXT FEW DAYS, SIR EDGAR — YOU HAVE THE NECESSARY CONTACTS?
Romero
WE ACQUIRED A LARGE NUMBER OF NAMES FROM OUR SOUTH AMERICAN HEROIN SUPPLIERS BEFORE MOVING HERE, PROFESSOR
I CAN QUICKLY GET A FEW CREATURES WHO ARE WELL-PRACTISED IN VIOLENCE — AND EXPENDABLE LATER, IF NEED BE
EXCELLENT
10074 A

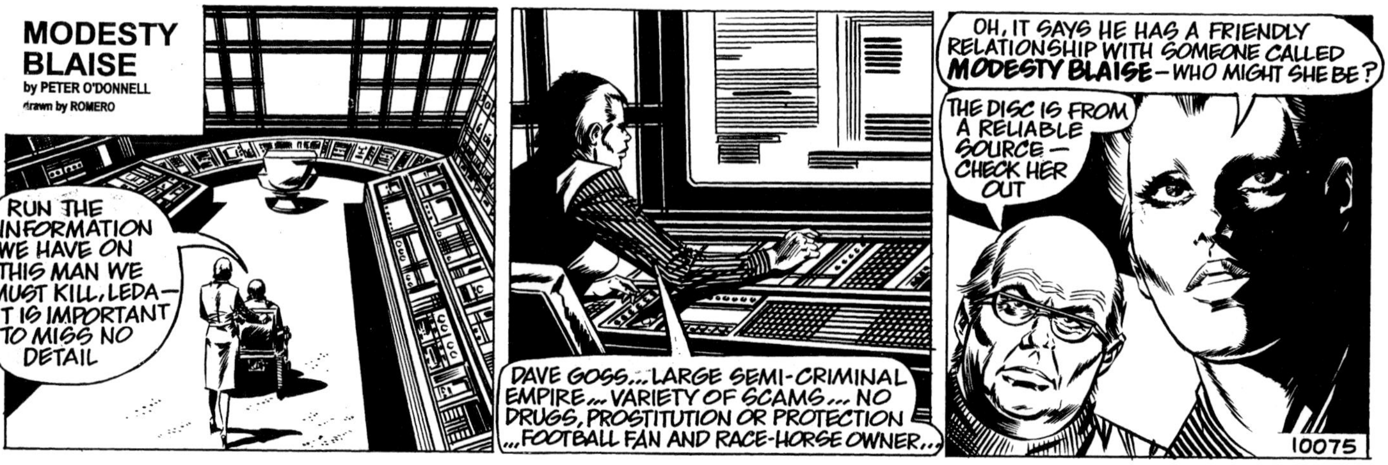
MODESTY BLAISE
by PETER O'DONNELL
drawn by ROMERO
RUN THE INFORMATION WE HAVE ON THIS MAN WE MUST KILL, LEDA — IT IS IMPORTANT TO MISS NO DETAIL
DAVE GOSS... LARGE SEMI-CRIMINAL EMPIRE... VARIETY OF SCAMS... NO DRUGS, PROSTITUTION OR PROTECTION ...FOOTBALL FAN AND RACE-HORSE OWNER...
OH, IT SAYS HE HAS A FRIENDLY RELATIONSHIP WITH SOMEONE CALLED MODESTY BLAISE — WHO MIGHT SHE BE?
THE DISC IS FROM A RELIABLE SOURCE — CHECK HER OUT
10075

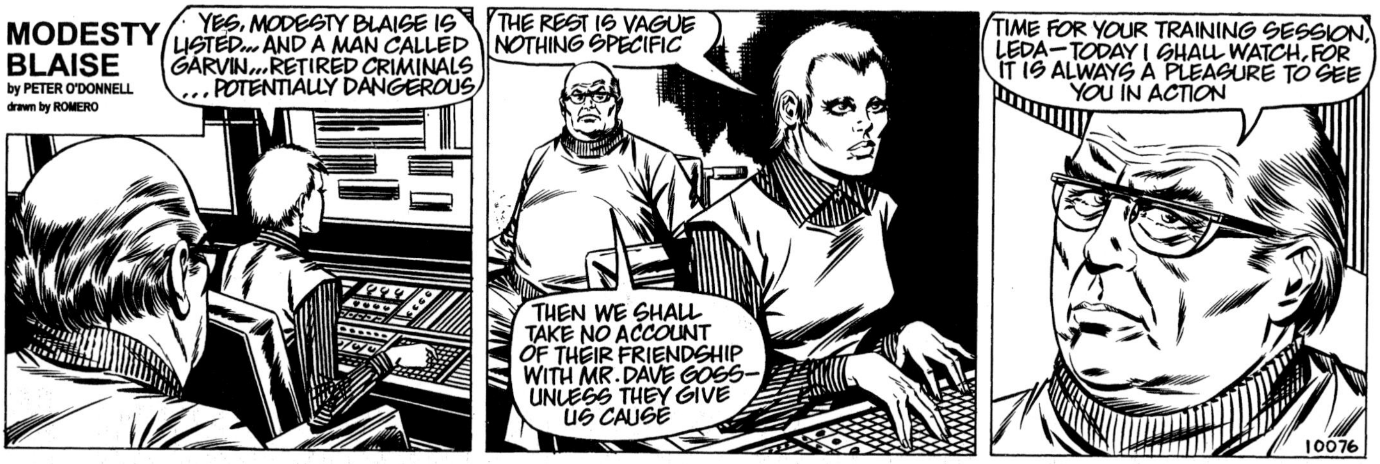
MODESTY BLAISE
by PETER O'DONNELL
drawn by ROMERO
YES, MODESTY BLAISE IS LISTED... AND A MAN CALLED GARVIN... RETIRED CRIMINALS ... POTENTIALLY DANGEROUS
THE REST IS VAGUE NOTHING SPECIFIC
THEN WE SHALL TAKE NO ACCOUNT OF THEIR FRIENDSHIP WITH MR. DAVE GOSS — UNLESS THEY GIVE US CAUSE
TIME FOR YOUR TRAINING SESSION, LEDA — TODAY I SHALL WATCH, FOR IT IS ALWAYS A PLEASURE TO SEE YOU IN ACTION
10076

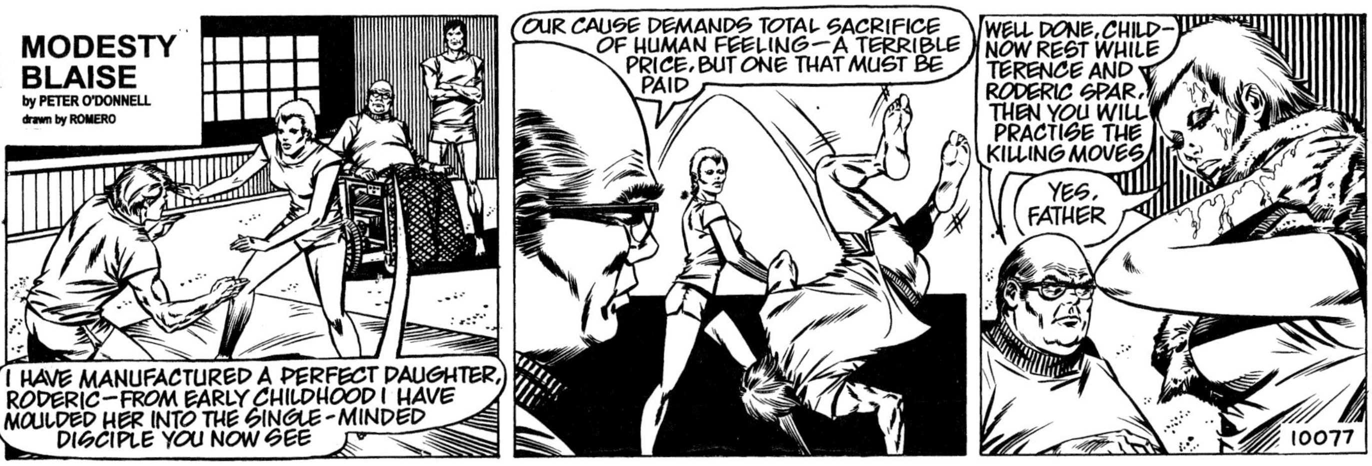
MODESTY BLAISE
by PETER O'DONNELL
drawn by ROMERO
I HAVE MANUFACTURED A PERFECT DAUGHTER, RODERIC—FROM EARLY CHILDHOOD I HAVE MOULDED HER INTO THE SINGLE-MINDED DISCIPLE YOU NOW SEE
OUR CAUSE DEMANDS TOTAL SACRIFICE OF HUMAN FEELING—A TERRIBLE PRICE, BUT ONE THAT MUST BE PAID
WELL DONE, CHILD—NOW REST WHILE TERENCE AND RODERIC SPAR. THEN YOU WILL PRACTISE THE KILLING MOVES
YES, FATHER
10077

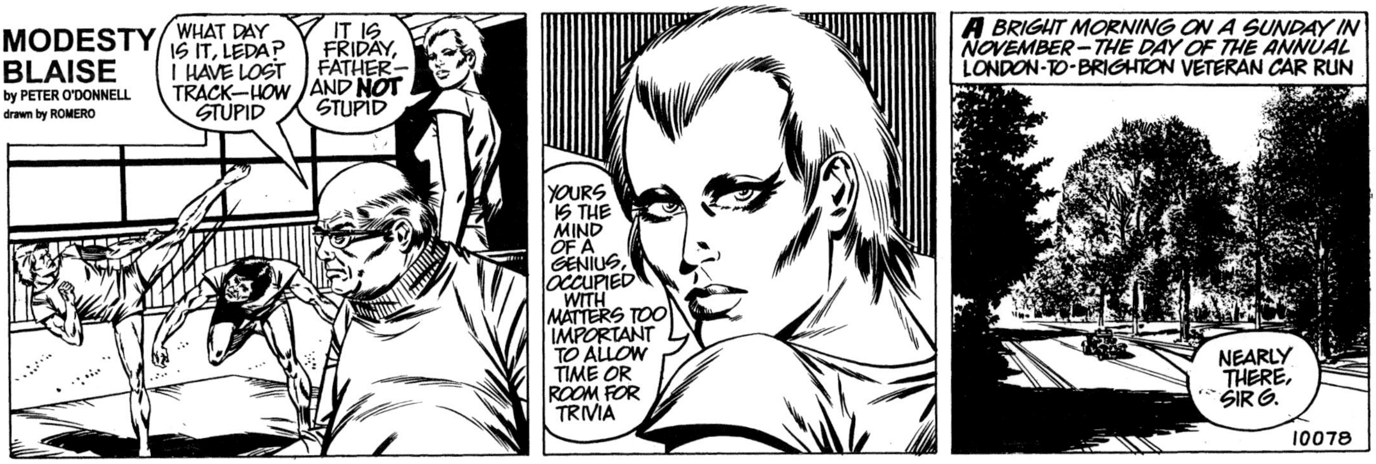
MODESTY BLAISE
by PETER O'DONNELL
drawn by ROMERO
WHAT DAY IS IT, LEDA? I HAVE LOST TRACK—HOW STUPID
IT IS FRIDAY, FATHER—AND NOT STUPID
YOURS IS THE MIND OF A GENIUS, OCCUPIED WITH MATTERS TOO IMPORTANT TO ALLOW TIME OR ROOM FOR TRIVIA
A BRIGHT MORNING ON A SUNDAY IN NOVEMBER—THE DAY OF THE ANNUAL LONDON-TO-BRIGHTON VETERAN CAR RUN
NEARLY THERE, SIR G.
10078

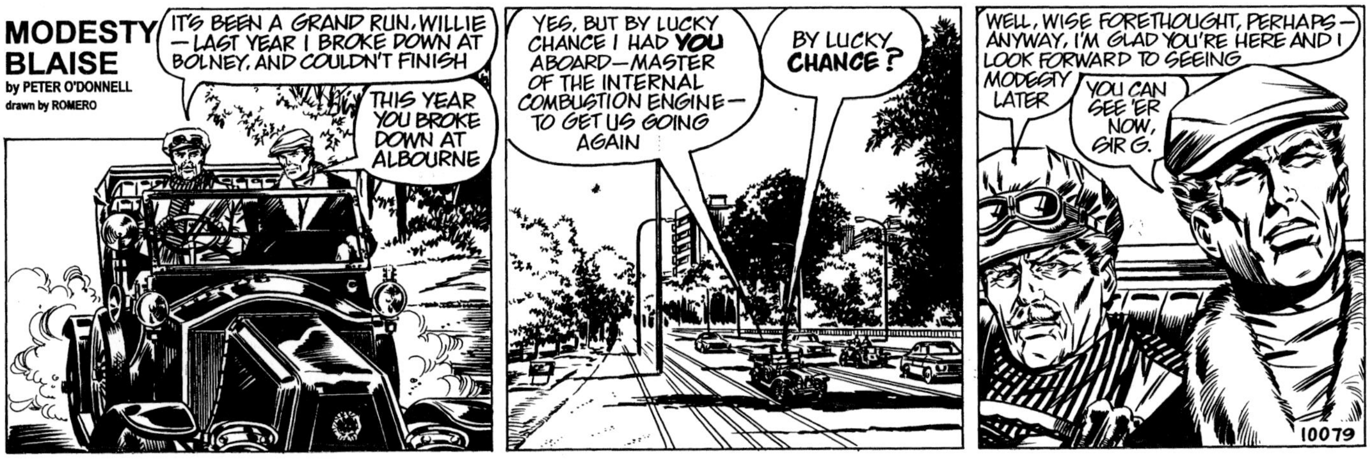
MODESTY BLAISE
by PETER O'DONNELL
drawn by ROMERO
IT'S BEEN A GRAND RUN, WILLIE—LAST YEAR I BROKE DOWN AT BOLNEY, AND COULDN'T FINISH
THIS YEAR YOU BROKE DOWN AT ALBOURNE
YES, BUT BY LUCKY CHANCE I HAD YOU ABOARD—MASTER OF THE INTERNAL COMBUSTION ENGINE—TO GET US GOING AGAIN
BY LUCKY CHANCE?
WELL, WISE FORETHOUGHT, PERHAPS—ANYWAY, I'M GLAD YOU'RE HERE AND I LOOK FORWARD TO SEEING MODESTY LATER
YOU CAN SEE 'ER NOW, SIR G.
10079

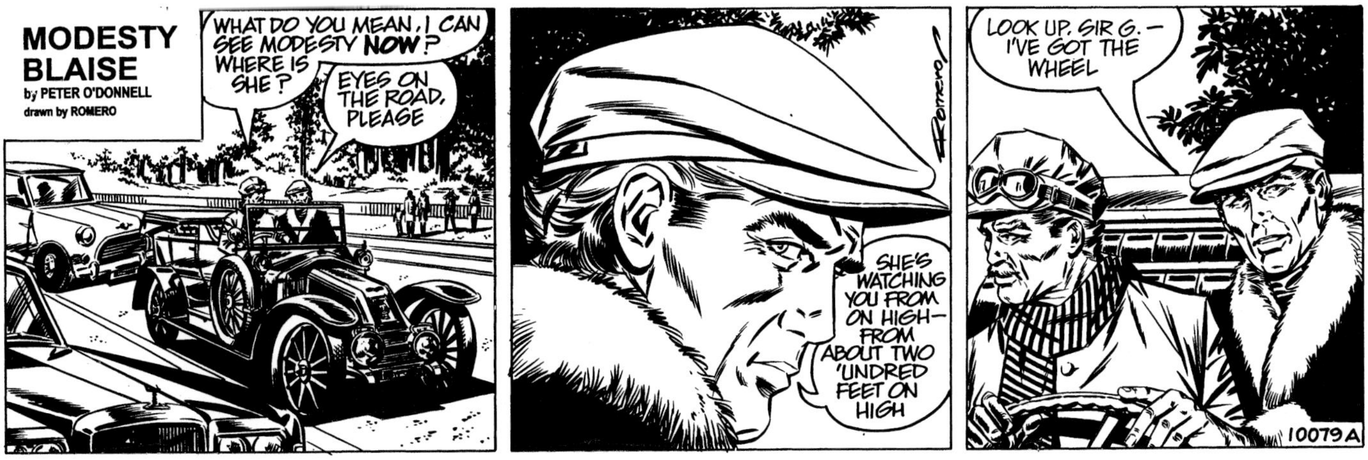
MODESTY BLAISE
by PETER O'DONNELL
drawn by ROMERO
WHAT DO YOU MEAN, I CAN SEE MODESTY NOW? WHERE IS SHE?
EYES ON THE ROAD, PLEASE
SHE'S WATCHING YOU FROM ON HIGH—FROM ABOUT TWO 'UNDRED FEET ON HIGH
LOOK UP, SIR G.—I'VE GOT THE WHEEL
10079 A

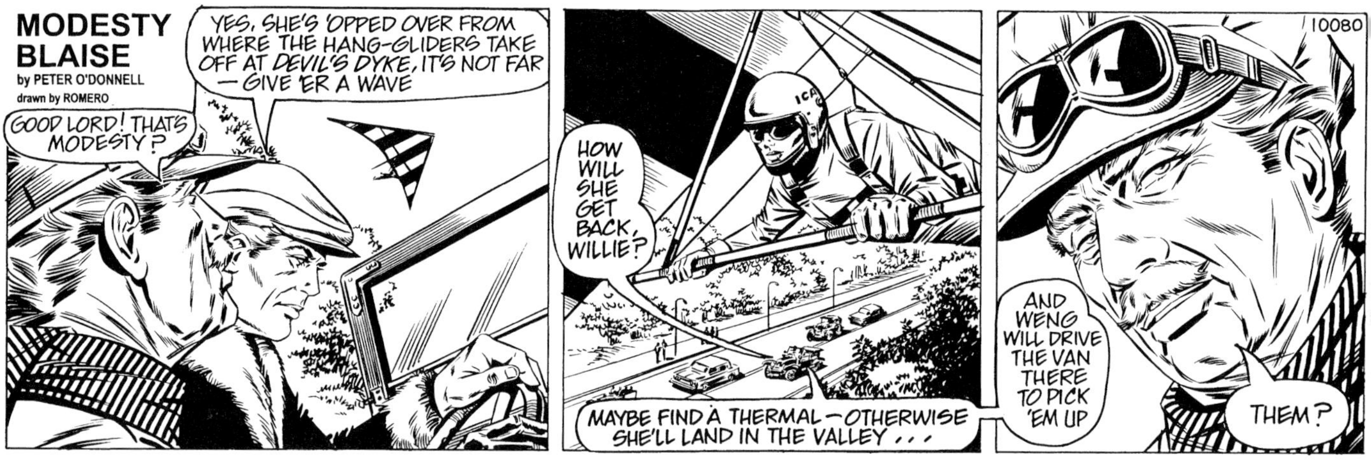
MODESTY BLAISE
by PETER O'DONNELL
drawn by ROMERO
GOOD LORD! THAT'S MODESTY?
YES, SHE'S 'OPPED OVER FROM WHERE THE HANG-GLIDERS TAKE OFF AT DEVIL'S DYKE, IT'S NOT FAR — GIVE 'ER A WAVE
HOW WILL SHE GET BACK, WILLIE?
MAYBE FIND A THERMAL — OTHERWISE SHE'LL LAND IN THE VALLEY . . .
AND WENG WILL DRIVE THE VAN THERE TO PICK 'EM UP
THEM?
10080

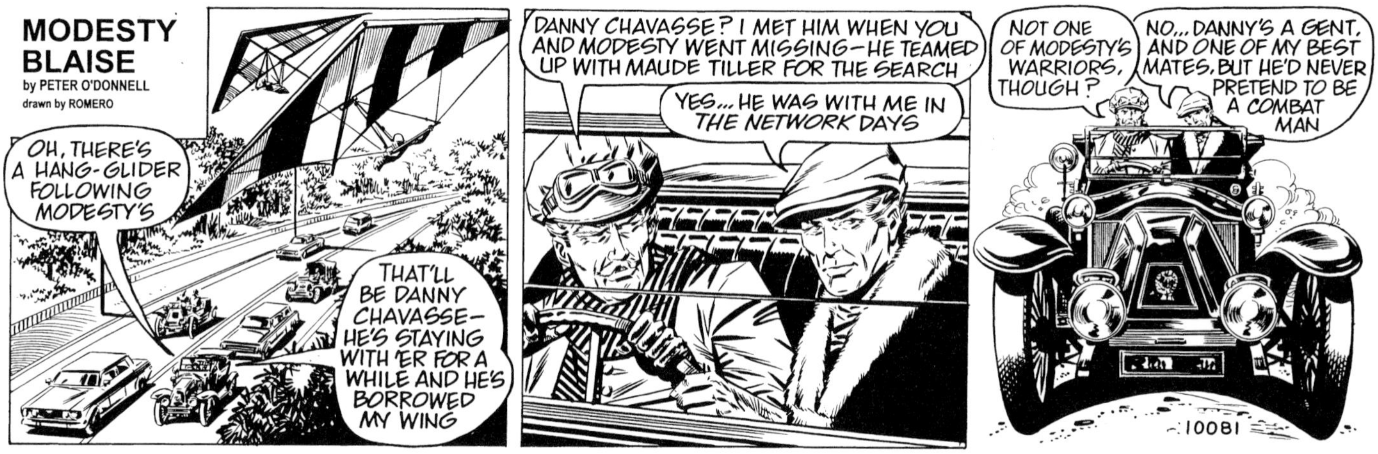
MODESTY BLAISE
by PETER O'DONNELL
drawn by ROMERO
OH, THERE'S A HANG-GLIDER FOLLOWING MODESTY'S
THAT'LL BE DANNY CHAVASSE — HE'S STAYING WITH 'ER FOR A WHILE AND HE'S BORROWED MY WING
DANNY CHAVASSE? I MET HIM WHEN YOU AND MODESTY WENT MISSING — HE TEAMED UP WITH MAUDE TILLER FOR THE SEARCH
YES... HE WAS WITH ME IN THE NETWORK DAYS
NOT ONE OF MODESTY'S WARRIORS, THOUGH?
NO... DANNY'S A GENT, AND ONE OF MY BEST MATES, BUT HE'D NEVER PRETEND TO BE A COMBAT MAN
10081

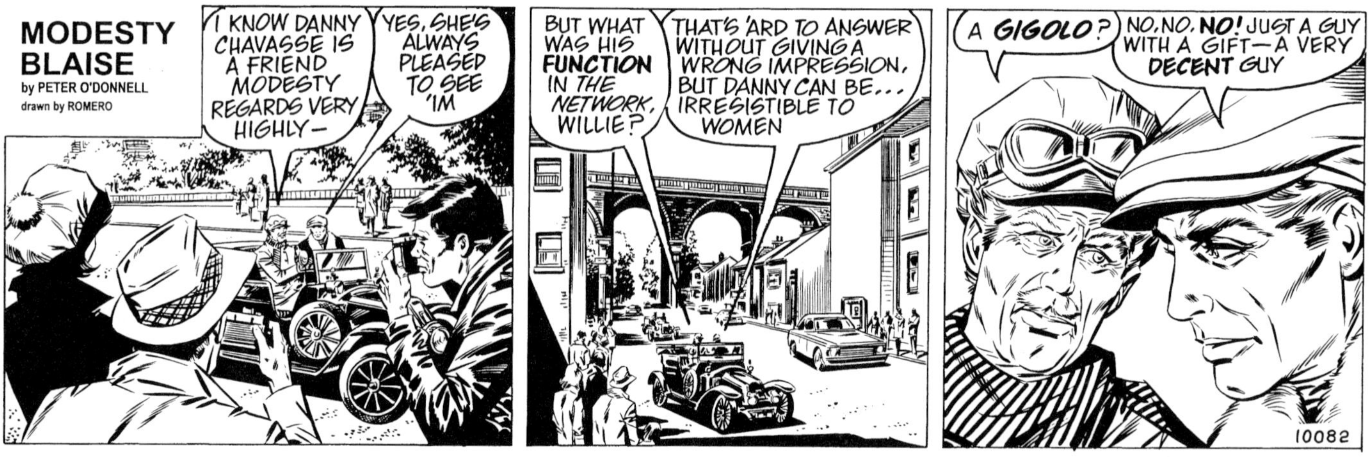
MODESTY BLAISE
by PETER O'DONNELL
drawn by ROMERO
I KNOW DANNY CHAVASSE IS A FRIEND MODESTY REGARDS VERY HIGHLY —
YES, SHE'S ALWAYS PLEASED TO SEE 'IM
BUT WHAT WAS HIS FUNCTION IN THE NETWORK, WILLIE?
THAT'S 'ARD TO ANSWER WITHOUT GIVING A WRONG IMPRESSION, BUT DANNY CAN BE... IRRESISTIBLE TO WOMEN
A GIGOLO?
NO, NO, NO! JUST A GUY WITH A GIFT — A VERY DECENT GUY
10082

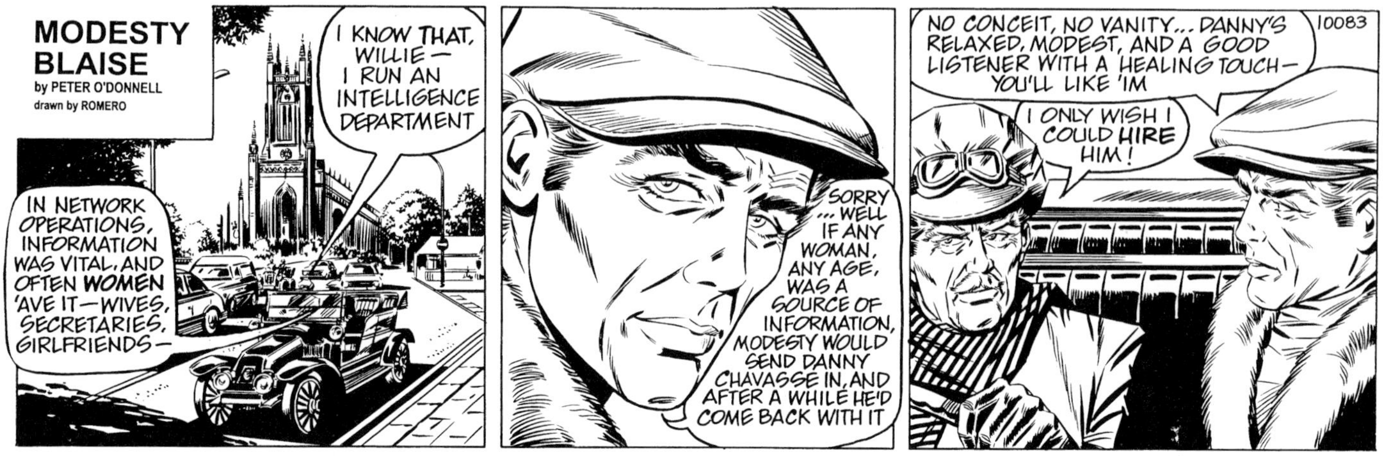
MODESTY BLAISE
by PETER O'DONNELL
drawn by ROMERO
IN NETWORK OPERATIONS, INFORMATION WAS VITAL, AND OFTEN WOMEN 'AVE IT — WIVES, SECRETARIES, GIRLFRIENDS —
I KNOW THAT, WILLIE — I RUN AN INTELLIGENCE DEPARTMENT
SORRY... WELL IF ANY WOMAN, ANY AGE, WAS A SOURCE OF INFORMATION, MODESTY WOULD SEND DANNY CHAVASSE IN, AND AFTER A WHILE HE'D COME BACK WITH IT
NO CONCEIT, NO VANITY... DANNY'S RELAXED, MODEST, AND A GOOD LISTENER WITH A HEALING TOUCH — YOU'LL LIKE 'IM
I ONLY WISH I COULD HIRE HIM!
10083

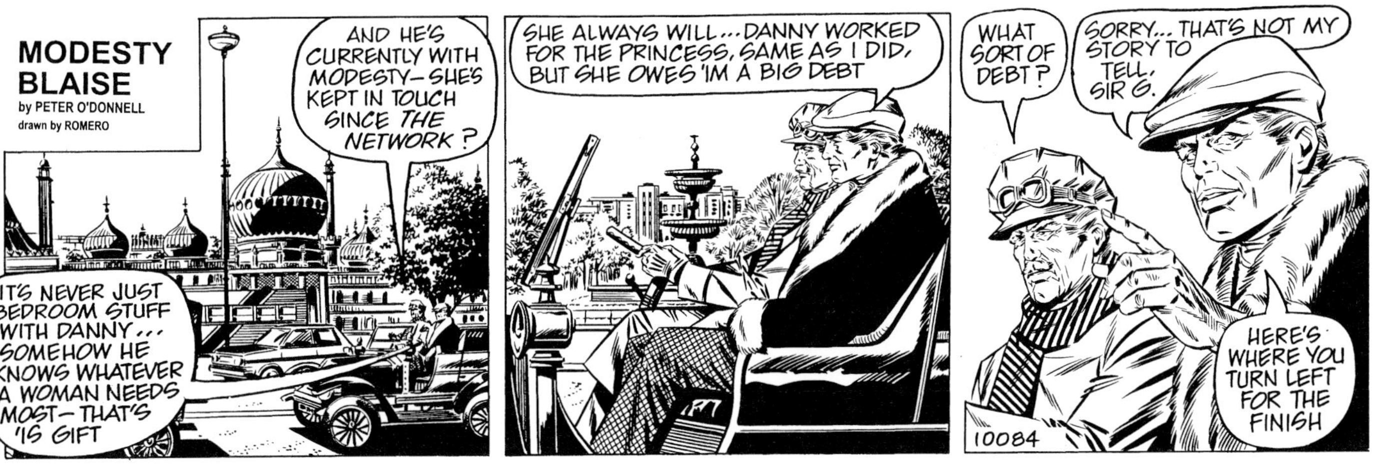
MODESTY BLAISE
by PETER O'DONNELL
drawn by ROMERO
AND HE'S CURRENTLY WITH MODESTY— SHE'S KEPT IN TOUCH SINCE THE NETWORK ?
IT'S NEVER JUST BEDROOM STUFF WITH DANNY... SOMEHOW HE KNOWS WHATEVER A WOMAN NEEDS MOST— THAT'S 'IS GIFT
SHE ALWAYS WILL... DANNY WORKED FOR THE PRINCESS, SAME AS I DID, BUT SHE OWES 'IM A BIG DEBT
WHAT SORT OF DEBT ?
SORRY... THAT'S NOT MY STORY TO TELL, SIR G.
HERE'S WHERE YOU TURN LEFT FOR THE FINISH
10084

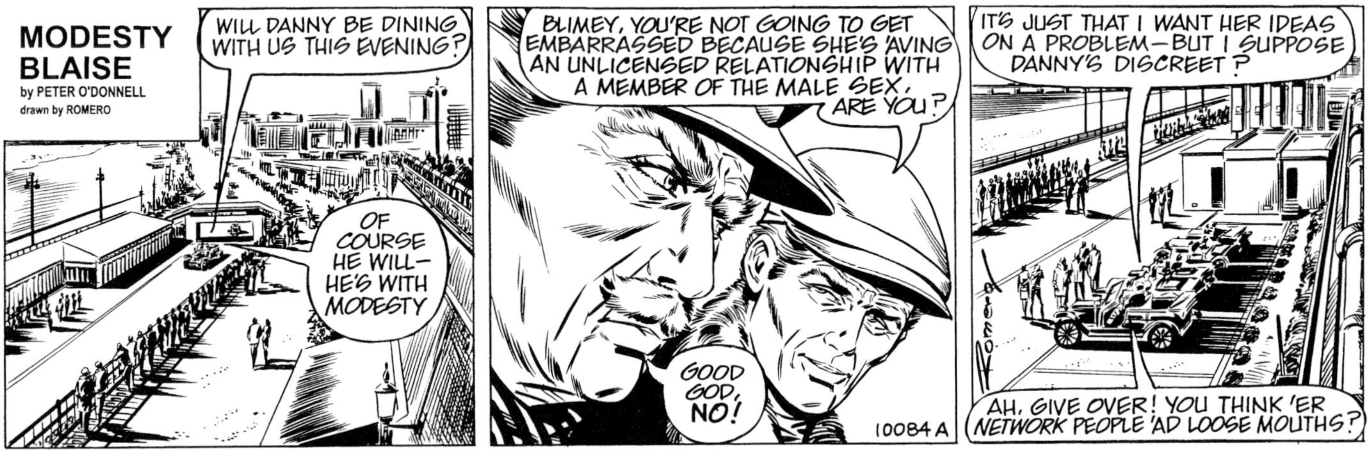
MODESTY BLAISE
by PETER O'DONNELL
drawn by ROMERO
WILL DANNY BE DINING WITH US THIS EVENING?
OF COURSE HE WILL— HE'S WITH MODESTY
BLIMEY, YOU'RE NOT GOING TO GET EMBARRASSED BECAUSE SHE'S 'AVING AN UNLICENSED RELATIONSHIP WITH A MEMBER OF THE MALE SEX, ARE YOU ?
GOOD GOD, NO!
10084 A
IT'S JUST THAT I WANT HER IDEAS ON A PROBLEM— BUT I SUPPOSE DANNY'S DISCREET ?
AH, GIVE OVER! YOU THINK 'ER NETWORK PEOPLE 'AD LOOSE MOUTHS?

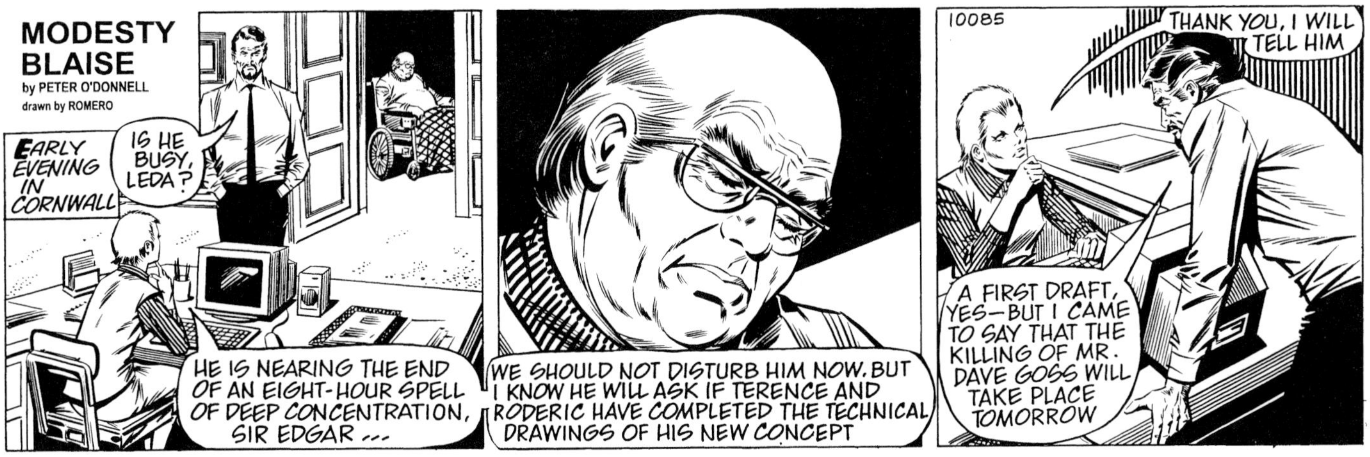
MODESTY BLAISE
by PETER O'DONNELL
drawn by ROMERO
EARLY EVENING IN CORNWALL
IS HE BUSY, LEDA ?
HE IS NEARING THE END OF AN EIGHT-HOUR SPELL OF DEEP CONCENTRATION, SIR EDGAR ...
WE SHOULD NOT DISTURB HIM NOW. BUT I KNOW HE WILL ASK IF TERENCE AND RODERIC HAVE COMPLETED THE TECHNICAL DRAWINGS OF HIS NEW CONCEPT
10085
THANK YOU, I WILL TELL HIM
A FIRST DRAFT, YES— BUT I CAME TO SAY THAT THE KILLING OF MR. DAVE GOSS WILL TAKE PLACE TOMORROW

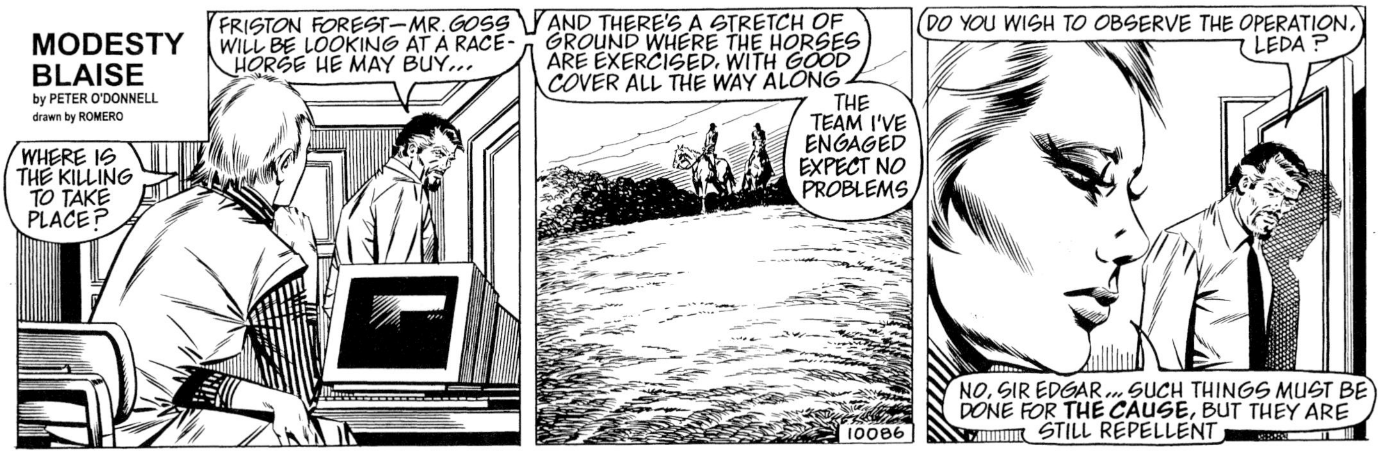
MODESTY BLAISE
by PETER O'DONNELL
drawn by ROMERO
WHERE IS THE KILLING TO TAKE PLACE?
FRISTON FOREST— MR. GOSS WILL BE LOOKING AT A RACE-HORSE HE MAY BUY...
AND THERE'S A STRETCH OF GROUND WHERE THE HORSES ARE EXERCISED, WITH GOOD COVER ALL THE WAY ALONG
THE TEAM I'VE ENGAGED EXPECT NO PROBLEMS
10086
DO YOU WISH TO OBSERVE THE OPERATION, LEDA ?
NO, SIR EDGAR... SUCH THINGS MUST BE DONE FOR THE CAUSE, BUT THEY ARE STILL REPELLENT

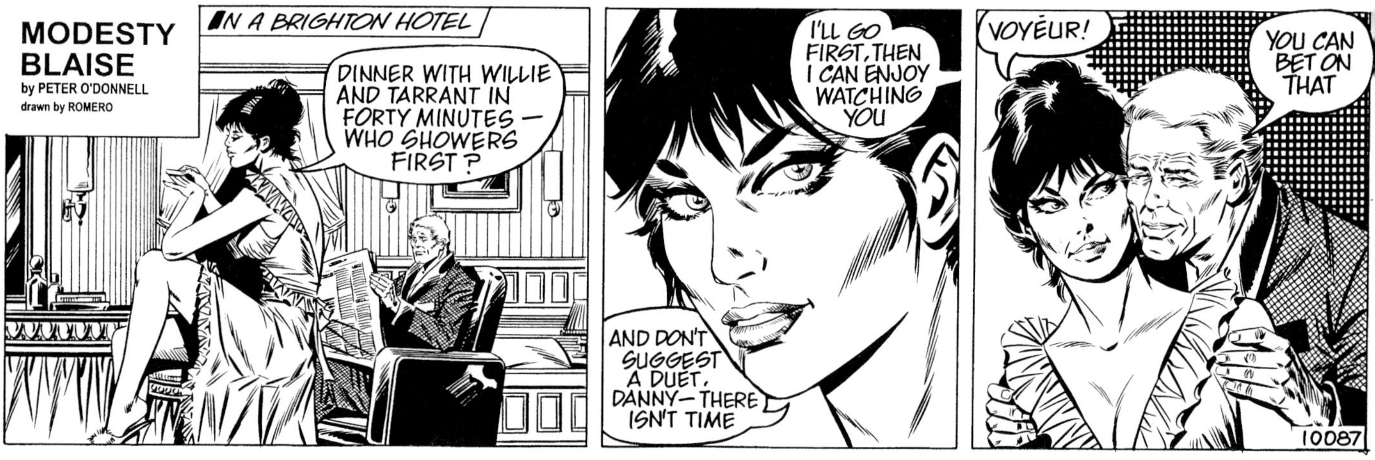
MODESTY BLAISE
by PETER O'DONNELL
drawn by ROMERO
IN A BRIGHTON HOTEL
DINNER WITH WILLIE AND TARRANT IN FORTY MINUTES — WHO SHOWERS FIRST?
I'LL GO FIRST, THEN I CAN ENJOY WATCHING YOU
AND DON'T SUGGEST A DUET, DANNY— THERE ISN'T TIME
VOYEUR!
YOU CAN BET ON THAT
10087

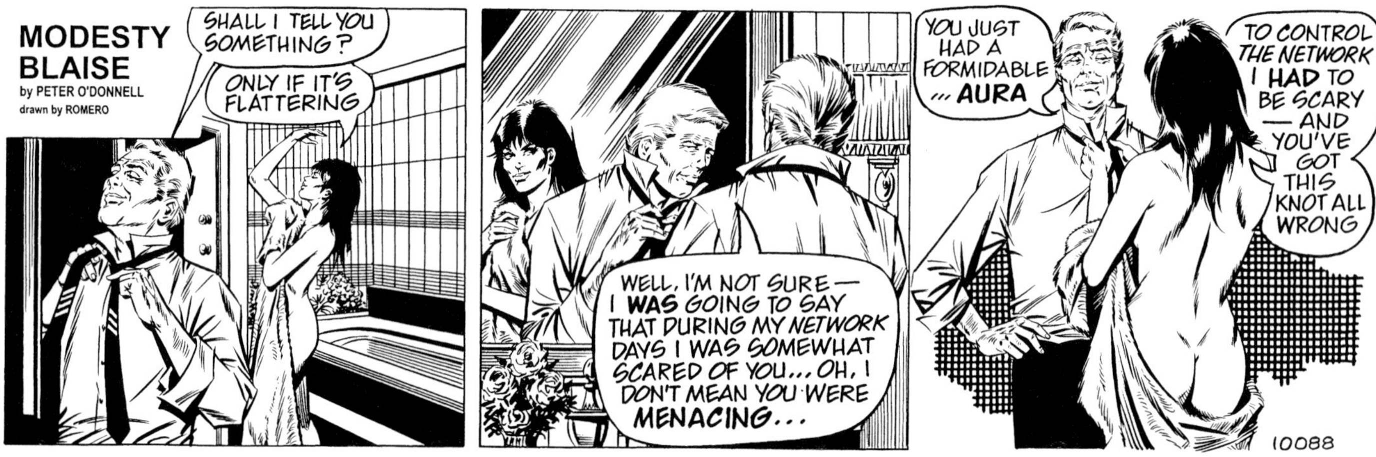
MODESTY BLAISE
by PETER O'DONNELL
drawn by ROMERO
SHALL I TELL YOU SOMETHING?
ONLY IF IT'S FLATTERING
WELL, I'M NOT SURE — I WAS GOING TO SAY THAT DURING MY NETWORK DAYS I WAS SOMEWHAT SCARED OF YOU... OH, I DON'T MEAN YOU WERE MENACING...
YOU JUST HAD A FORMIDABLE ... AURA
TO CONTROL THE NETWORK I HAD TO BE SCARY — AND YOU'VE GOT THIS KNOT ALL WRONG
10088

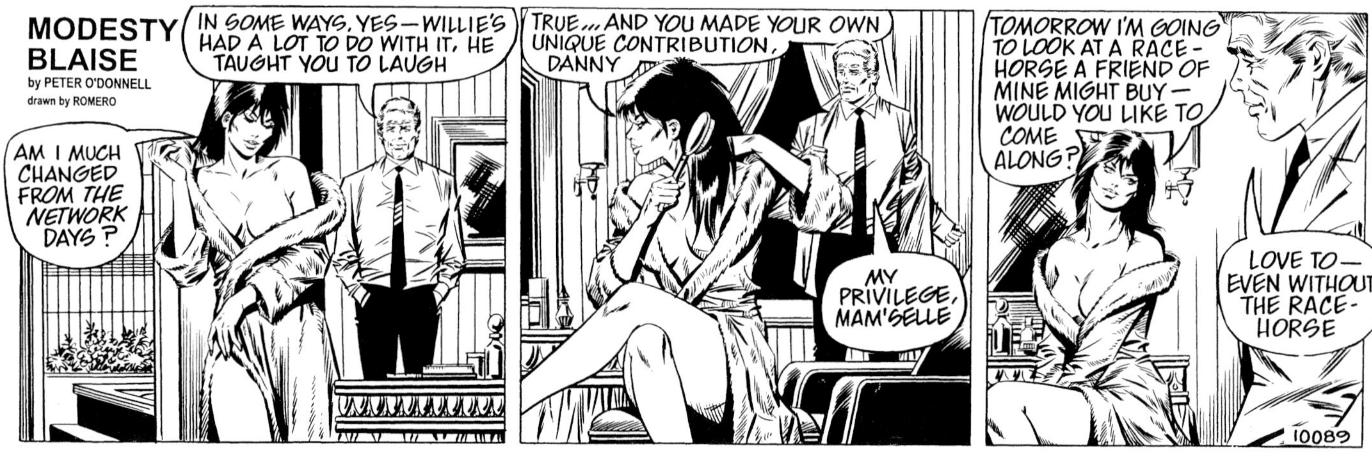
MODESTY BLAISE
by PETER O'DONNELL
drawn by ROMERO
AM I MUCH CHANGED FROM THE NETWORK DAYS?
IN SOME WAYS, YES— WILLIE'S HAD A LOT TO DO WITH IT, HE TAUGHT YOU TO LAUGH
TRUE... AND YOU MADE YOUR OWN UNIQUE CONTRIBUTION, DANNY
MY PRIVILEGE, MAM'SELLE
TOMORROW I'M GOING TO LOOK AT A RACE-HORSE A FRIEND OF MINE MIGHT BUY — WOULD YOU LIKE TO COME ALONG?
LOVE TO— EVEN WITHOUT THE RACE-HORSE
10089

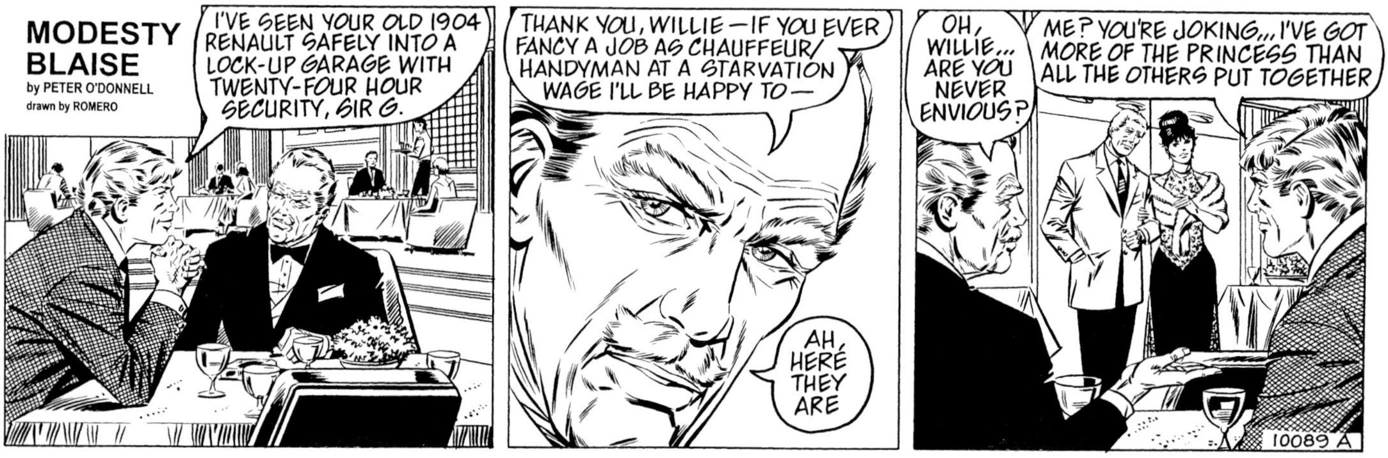
MODESTY BLAISE
by PETER O'DONNELL
drawn by ROMERO
I'VE SEEN YOUR OLD 1904 RENAULT SAFELY INTO A LOCK-UP GARAGE WITH TWENTY-FOUR HOUR SECURITY, SIR G.
THANK YOU, WILLIE — IF YOU EVER FANCY A JOB AS CHAUFFEUR/HANDYMAN AT A STARVATION WAGE I'LL BE HAPPY TO —
AH, HERE THEY ARE
OH, WILLIE... ARE YOU NEVER ENVIOUS?
ME? YOU'RE JOKING... I'VE GOT MORE OF THE PRINCESS THAN ALL THE OTHERS PUT TOGETHER
10089 A

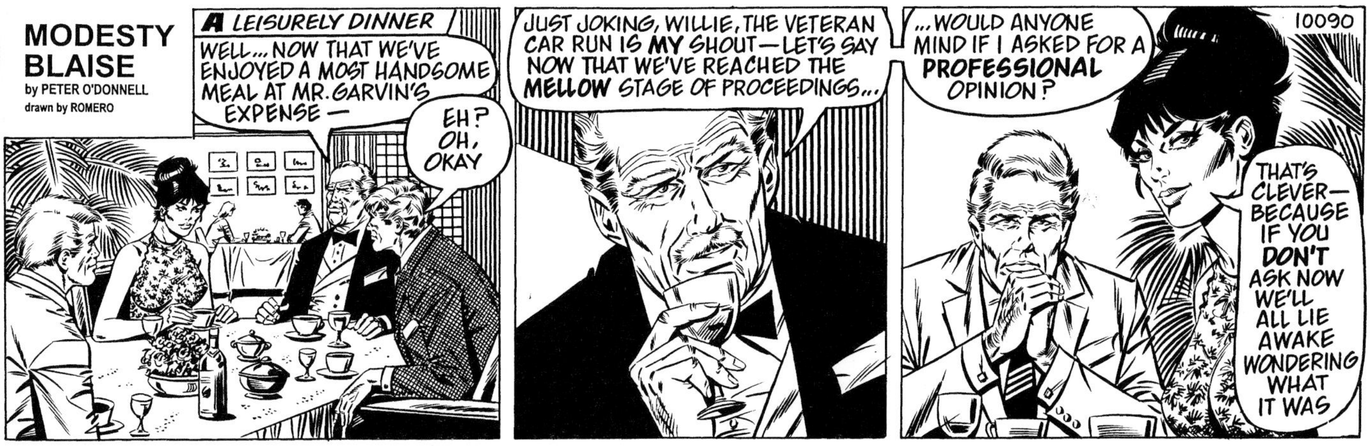
MODESTY BLAISE
by PETER O'DONNELL
drawn by ROMERO
A LEISURELY DINNER
WELL... NOW THAT WE'VE ENJOYED A MOST HANDSOME MEAL AT MR. GARVIN'S EXPENSE —
EH? OH, OKAY
JUST JOKING, WILLIE, THE VETERAN CAR RUN IS MY SHOUT — LET'S SAY NOW THAT WE'VE REACHED THE MELLOW STAGE OF PROCEEDINGS...
...WOULD ANYONE MIND IF I ASKED FOR A PROFESSIONAL OPINION?
THAT'S CLEVER — BECAUSE IF YOU DON'T ASK NOW WE'LL ALL LIE AWAKE WONDERING WHAT IT WAS
10090

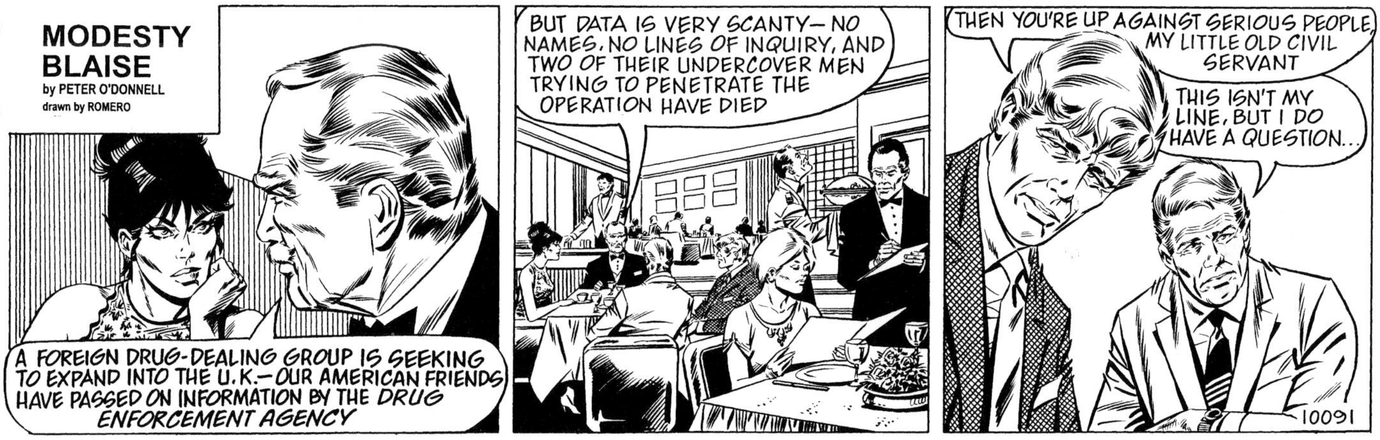
MODESTY BLAISE
by PETER O'DONNELL
drawn by ROMERO
A FOREIGN DRUG-DEALING GROUP IS SEEKING TO EXPAND INTO THE U.K. — OUR AMERICAN FRIENDS HAVE PASSED ON INFORMATION BY THE DRUG ENFORCEMENT AGENCY
BUT DATA IS VERY SCANTY — NO NAMES, NO LINES OF INQUIRY, AND TWO OF THEIR UNDERCOVER MEN TRYING TO PENETRATE THE OPERATION HAVE DIED
THEN YOU'RE UP AGAINST SERIOUS PEOPLE, MY LITTLE OLD CIVIL SERVANT
THIS ISN'T MY LINE, BUT I DO HAVE A QUESTION...
10091

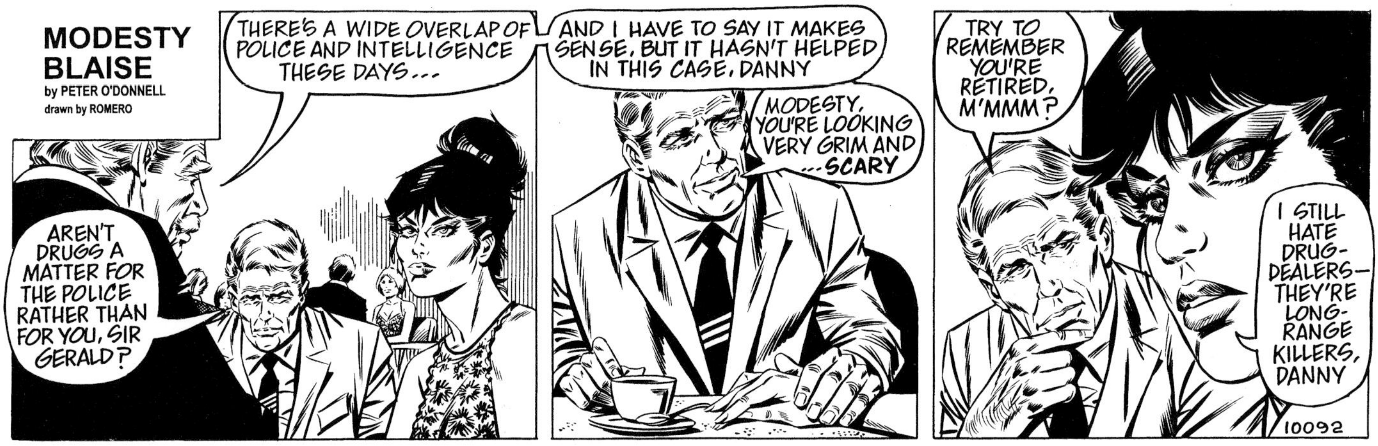
MODESTY BLAISE
by PETER O'DONNELL
drawn by ROMERO
AREN'T DRUGS A MATTER FOR THE POLICE RATHER THAN FOR YOU, SIR GERALD?
THERE'S A WIDE OVERLAP OF POLICE AND INTELLIGENCE THESE DAYS...
AND I HAVE TO SAY IT MAKES SENSE, BUT IT HASN'T HELPED IN THIS CASE, DANNY
MODESTY, YOU'RE LOOKING VERY GRIM AND ...SCARY
TRY TO REMEMBER YOU'RE RETIRED, M'MMM?
I STILL HATE DRUG-DEALERS — THEY'RE LONG-RANGE KILLERS, DANNY
10092

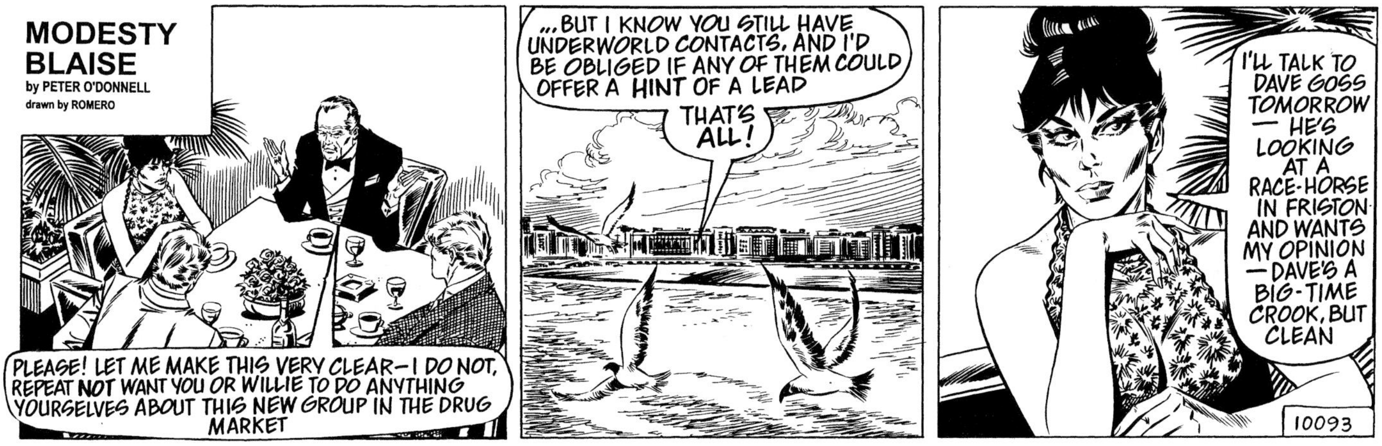
MODESTY BLAISE
by PETER O'DONNELL
drawn by ROMERO
PLEASE! LET ME MAKE THIS VERY CLEAR — I DO NOT, REPEAT NOT WANT YOU OR WILLIE TO DO ANYTHING YOURSELVES ABOUT THIS NEW GROUP IN THE DRUG MARKET
...BUT I KNOW YOU STILL HAVE UNDERWORLD CONTACTS, AND I'D BE OBLIGED IF ANY OF THEM COULD OFFER A HINT OF A LEAD
THAT'S ALL!
I'LL TALK TO DAVE GOSS TOMORROW — HE'S LOOKING AT A RACE-HORSE IN FRISTON AND WANTS MY OPINION — DAVE'S A BIG-TIME CROOK, BUT CLEAN
10093

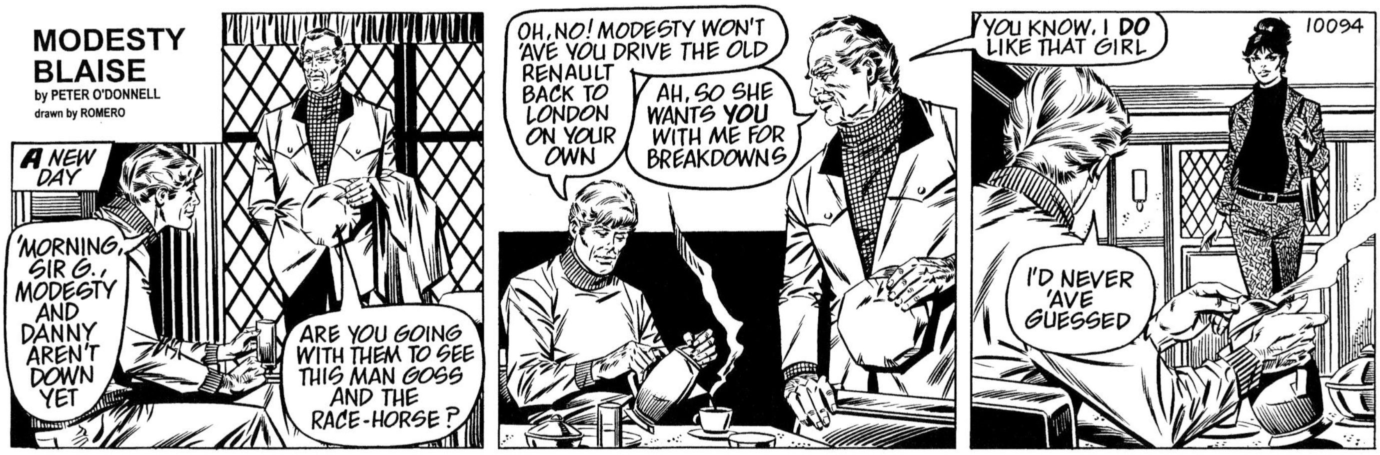
MODESTY BLAISE
by PETER O'DONNELL
drawn by ROMERO
A NEW DAY
'MORNING, SIR G., MODESTY AND DANNY AREN'T DOWN YET
ARE YOU GOING WITH THEM TO SEE THIS MAN GOSS AND THE RACE-HORSE?
OH, NO! MODESTY WON'T 'AVE YOU DRIVE THE OLD RENAULT BACK TO LONDON ON YOUR OWN
AH, SO SHE WANTS YOU WITH ME FOR BREAKDOWNS
YOU KNOW, I DO LIKE THAT GIRL
I'D NEVER 'AVE GUESSED
10094

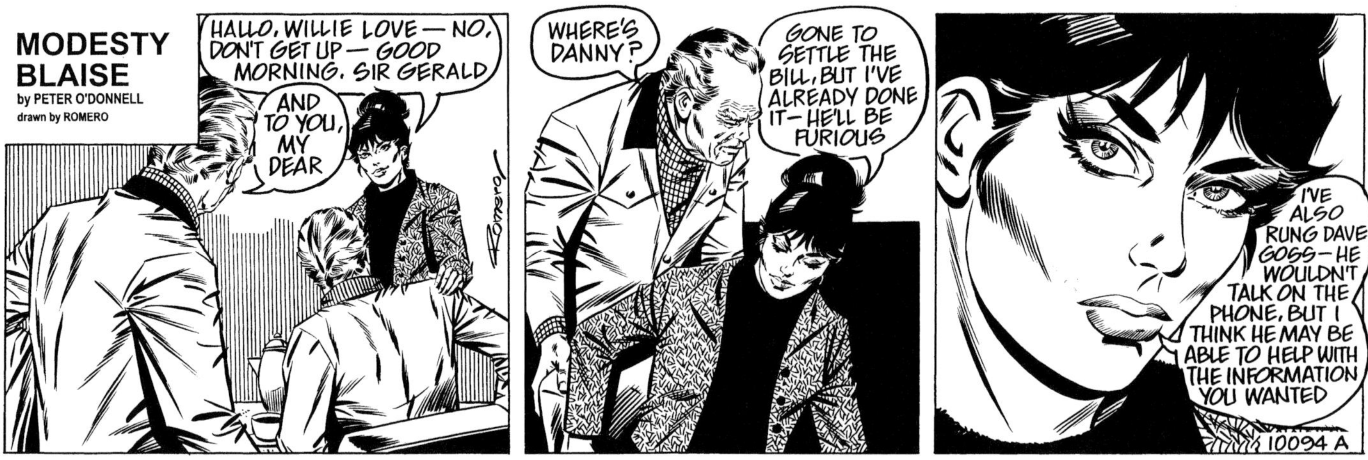
MODESTY BLAISE
by PETER O'DONNELL
drawn by ROMERO
HALLO, WILLIE LOVE — NO, DON'T GET UP — GOOD MORNING, SIR GERALD
AND TO YOU, MY DEAR
Romero
WHERE'S DANNY?
GONE TO SETTLE THE BILL, BUT I'VE ALREADY DONE IT — HE'LL BE FURIOUS
I'VE ALSO RUNG DAVE GOSS — HE WOULDN'T TALK ON THE PHONE, BUT I THINK HE MAY BE ABLE TO HELP WITH THE INFORMATION YOU WANTED
10094 A

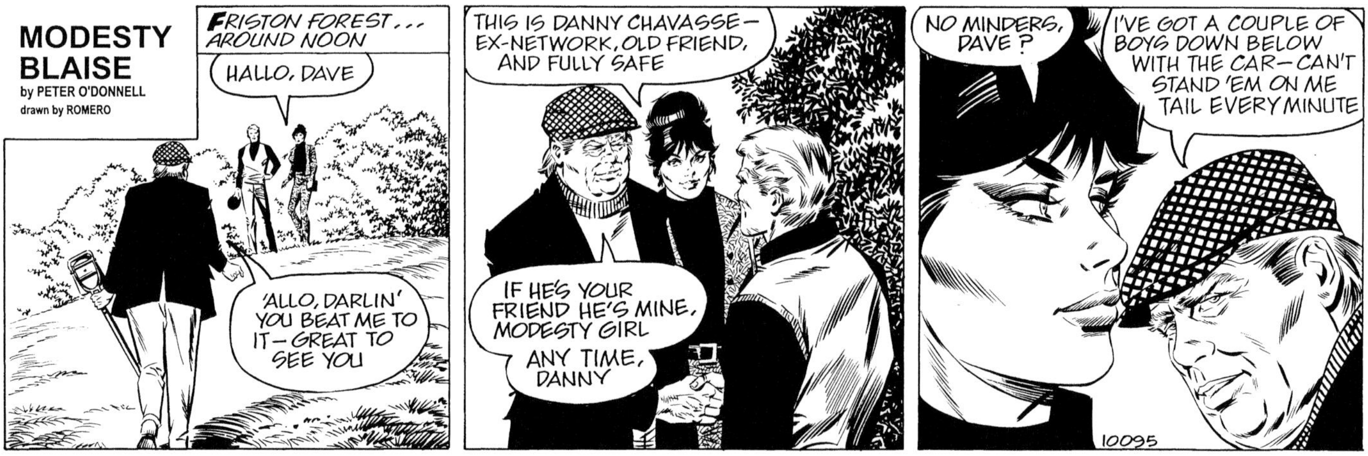
MODESTY BLAISE
by PETER O'DONNELL
drawn by ROMERO
FRISTON FOREST... AROUND NOON
HALLO, DAVE
'ALLO, DARLIN' YOU BEAT ME TO IT — GREAT TO SEE YOU
THIS IS DANNY CHAVASSE — EX-NETWORK, OLD FRIEND, AND FULLY SAFE
IF HE'S YOUR FRIEND HE'S MINE, MODESTY GIRL
ANY TIME, DANNY
NO MINDERS, DAVE?
I'VE GOT A COUPLE OF BOYS DOWN BELOW WITH THE CAR — CAN'T STAND 'EM ON ME TAIL EVERY MINUTE
10095

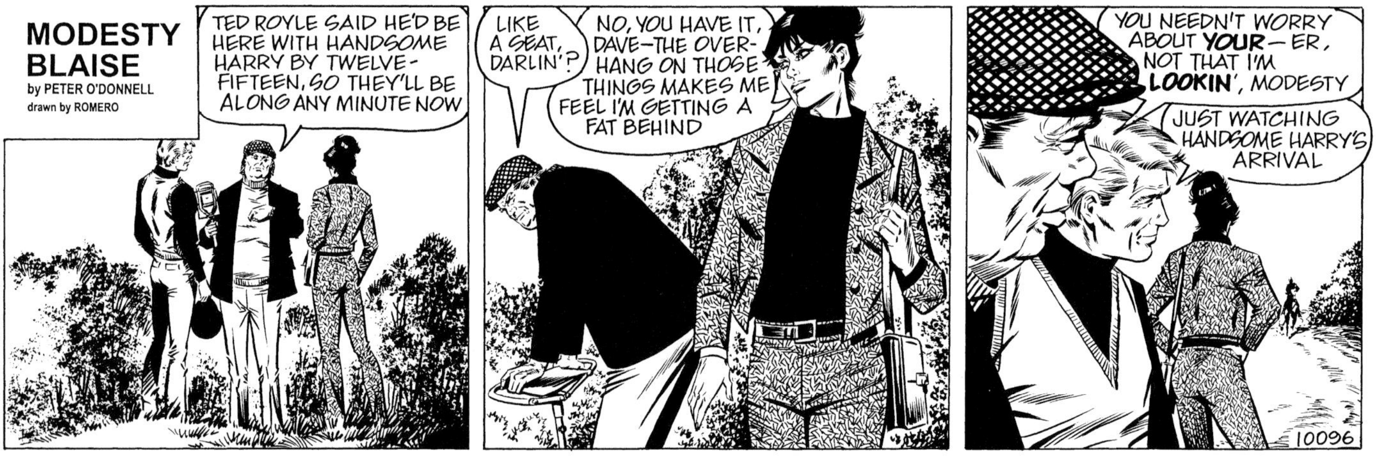
MODESTY BLAISE
by PETER O'DONNELL
drawn by ROMERO
TED ROYLE SAID HE'D BE HERE WITH HANDSOME HARRY BY TWELVE-FIFTEEN, SO THEY'LL BE ALONG ANY MINUTE NOW
LIKE A SEAT, DARLIN'?
NO, YOU HAVE IT, DAVE — THE OVER-HANG ON THOSE THINGS MAKES ME FEEL I'M GETTING A FAT BEHIND
YOU NEEDN'T WORRY ABOUT YOUR — ER, NOT THAT I'M LOOKIN', MODESTY
JUST WATCHING HANDSOME HARRY'S ARRIVAL
10096

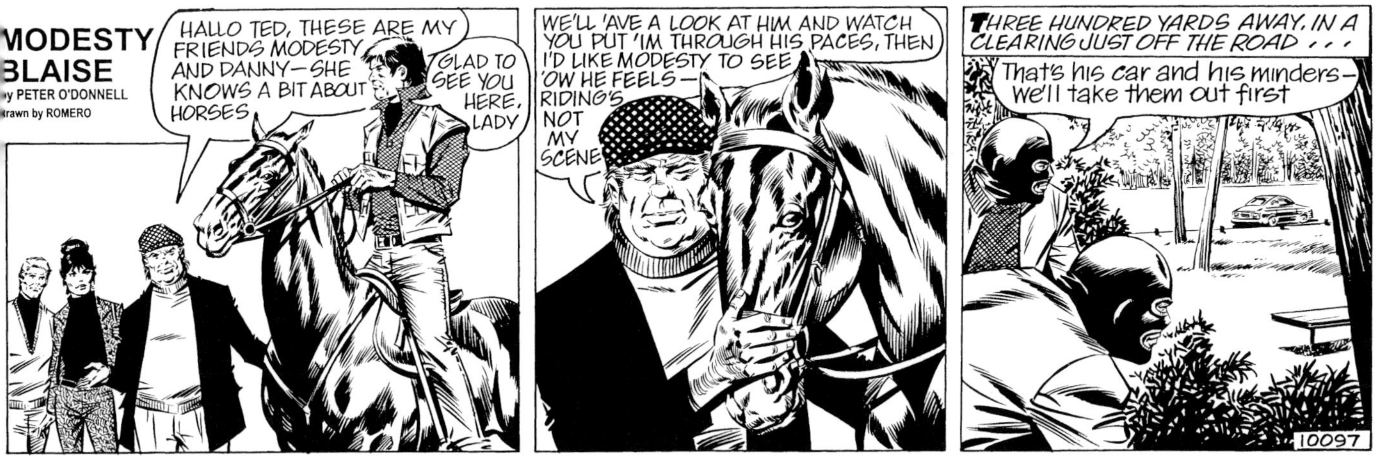
MODESTY BLAISE
by PETER O'DONNELL
drawn by ROMERO
HALLO TED, THESE ARE MY FRIENDS MODESTY AND DANNY—SHE KNOWS A BIT ABOUT HORSES
GLAD TO SEE YOU HERE, LADY
WE'LL 'AVE A LOOK AT HIM AND WATCH YOU PUT 'IM THROUGH HIS PACES, THEN I'D LIKE MODESTY TO SEE 'OW HE FEELS—RIDING'S NOT MY SCENE
THREE HUNDRED YARDS AWAY, IN A CLEARING JUST OFF THE ROAD . . .
That's his car and his minders—we'll take them out first
10097

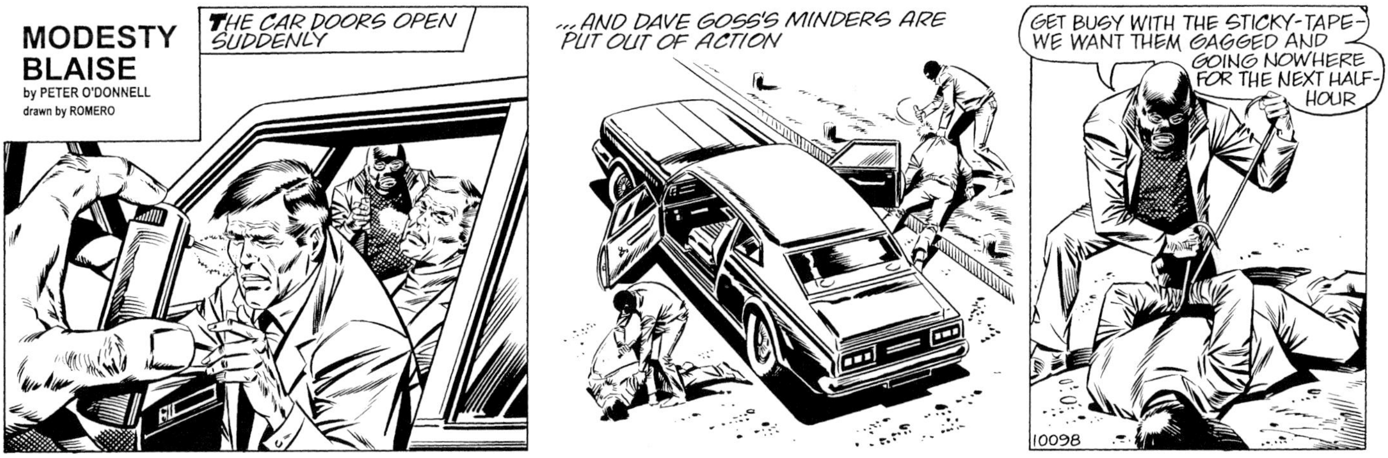
MODESTY BLAISE
by PETER O'DONNELL
drawn by ROMERO
THE CAR DOORS OPEN SUDDENLY
...AND DAVE GOSS'S MINDERS ARE PUT OUT OF ACTION
GET BUSY WITH THE STICKY-TAPE—WE WANT THEM GAGGED AND GOING NOWHERE FOR THE NEXT HALF-HOUR
10098

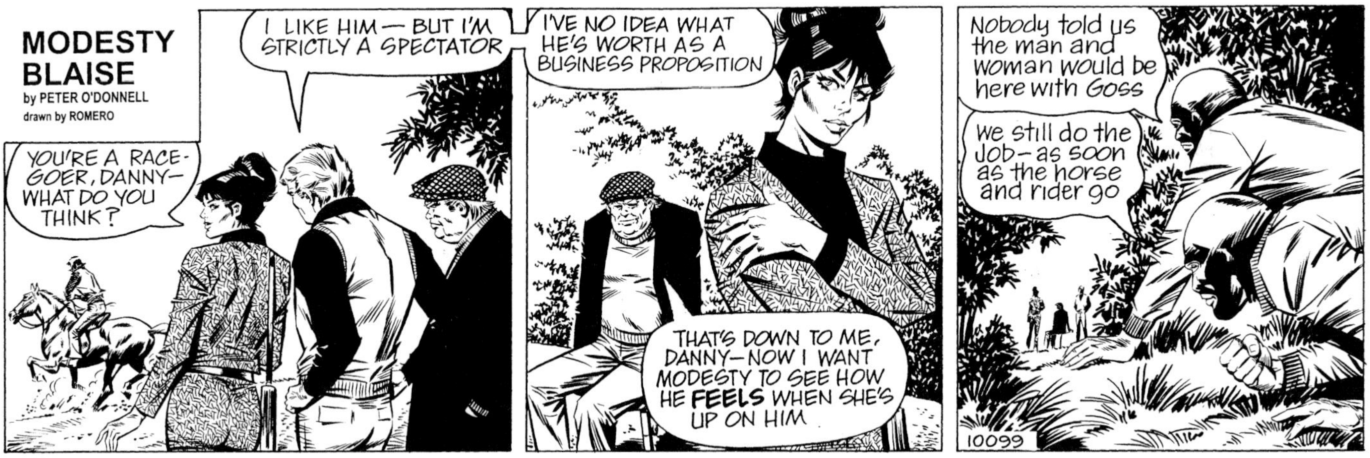
MODESTY BLAISE
by PETER O'DONNELL
drawn by ROMERO
YOU'RE A RACE-GOER, DANNY—WHAT DO YOU THINK?
I LIKE HIM—BUT I'M STRICTLY A SPECTATOR
I'VE NO IDEA WHAT HE'S WORTH AS A BUSINESS PROPOSITION
THAT'S DOWN TO ME, DANNY—NOW I WANT MODESTY TO SEE HOW HE FEELS WHEN SHE'S UP ON HIM
Nobody told us the man and woman would be here with Goss
We still do the job—as soon as the horse and rider go
10099

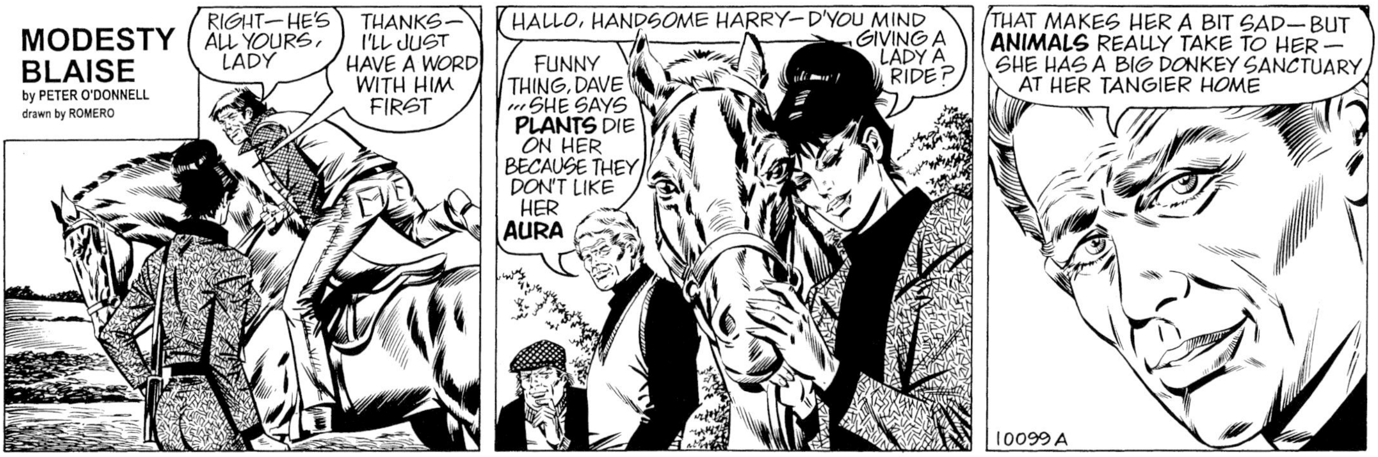
MODESTY BLAISE
by PETER O'DONNELL
drawn by ROMERO
RIGHT—HE'S ALL YOURS, LADY
THANKS—I'LL JUST HAVE A WORD WITH HIM FIRST
HALLO, HANDSOME HARRY—D'YOU MIND GIVING A LADY A RIDE?
FUNNY THING, DAVE ...SHE SAYS PLANTS DIE ON HER BECAUSE THEY DON'T LIKE HER AURA
THAT MAKES HER A BIT SAD—BUT ANIMALS REALLY TAKE TO HER—SHE HAS A BIG DONKEY SANCTUARY AT HER TANGIER HOME
10099 A

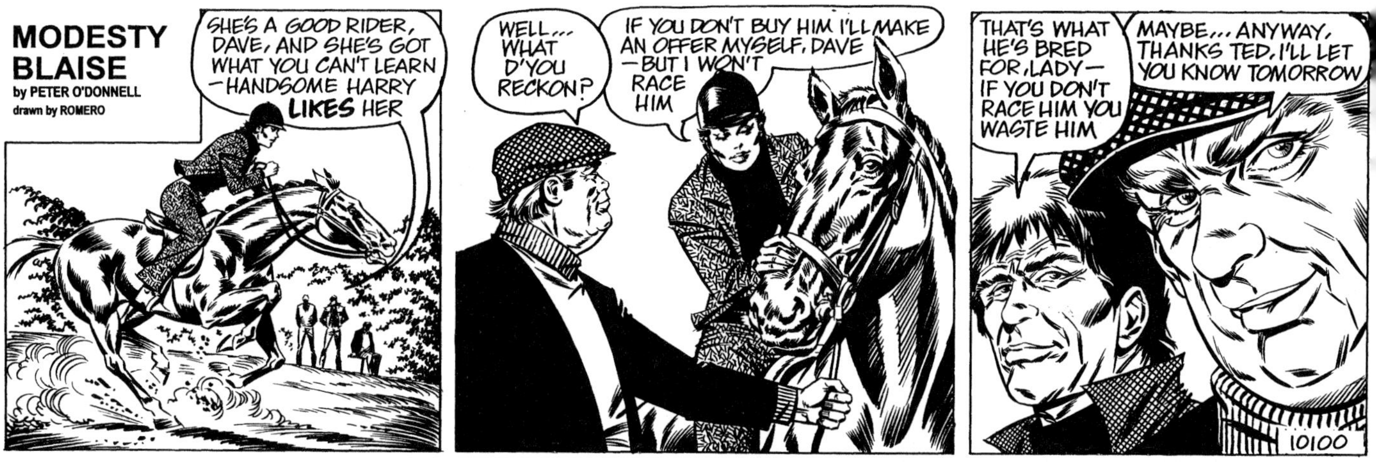
MODESTY BLAISE
by PETER O'DONNELL
drawn by ROMERO
SHE'S A GOOD RIDER, DAVE, AND SHE'S GOT WHAT YOU CAN'T LEARN —HANDSOME HARRY LIKES HER
WELL... WHAT D'YOU RECKON?
IF YOU DON'T BUY HIM I'LL MAKE AN OFFER MYSELF, DAVE —BUT I WON'T RACE HIM
THAT'S WHAT HE'S BRED FOR, LADY— IF YOU DON'T RACE HIM YOU WASTE HIM
MAYBE... ANYWAY, THANKS TED, I'LL LET YOU KNOW TOMORROW
10100

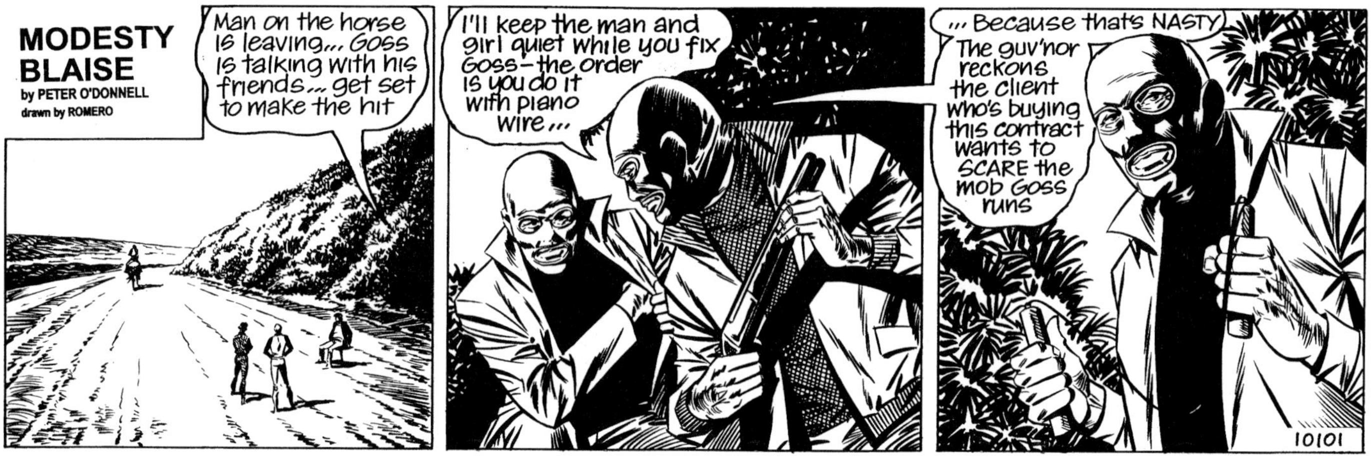
MODESTY BLAISE
by PETER O'DONNELL
drawn by ROMERO
Man on the horse is leaving... Goss is talking with his friends... get set to make the hit
I'll keep the man and girl quiet while you fix Goss—the order is you do it with piano wire...
...Because that's NASTY
The guv'nor reckons the client who's buying this contract wants to SCARE the mob Goss runs
10101

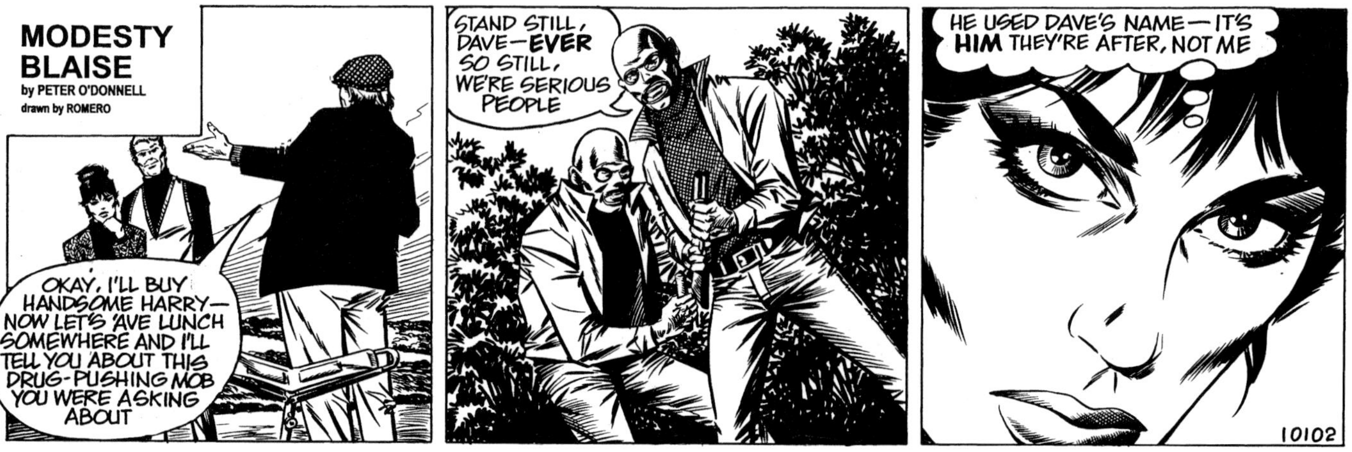
MODESTY BLAISE
by PETER O'DONNELL
drawn by ROMERO
OKAY, I'LL BUY HANDSOME HARRY— NOW LET'S 'AVE LUNCH SOMEWHERE AND I'LL TELL YOU ABOUT THIS DRUG-PUSHING MOB YOU WERE ASKING ABOUT
STAND STILL, DAVE—EVER SO STILL, WE'RE SERIOUS PEOPLE
HE USED DAVE'S NAME—IT'S HIM THEY'RE AFTER, NOT ME
10102

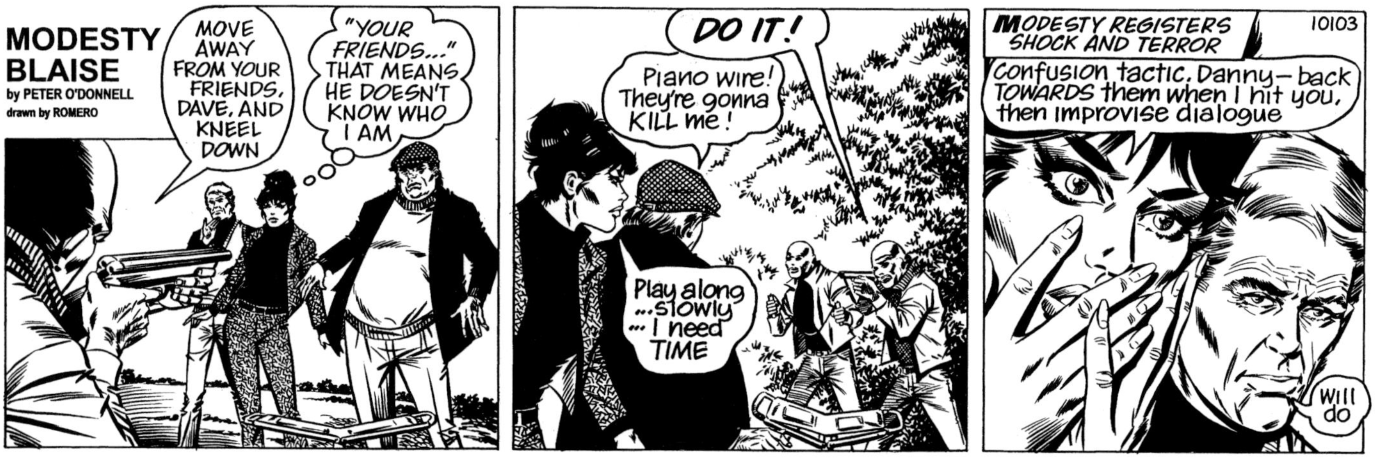
MODESTY BLAISE
by PETER O'DONNELL
drawn by ROMERO
MOVE AWAY FROM YOUR FRIENDS, DAVE, AND KNEEL DOWN
"YOUR FRIENDS..." THAT MEANS HE DOESN'T KNOW WHO I AM
DO IT!
Piano wire! They're gonna KILL me!
Play along ...slowly ...I need TIME
MODESTY REGISTERS SHOCK AND TERROR
10103
Confusion tactic, Danny—back TOWARDS them when I hit you, then improvise dialogue
Will do

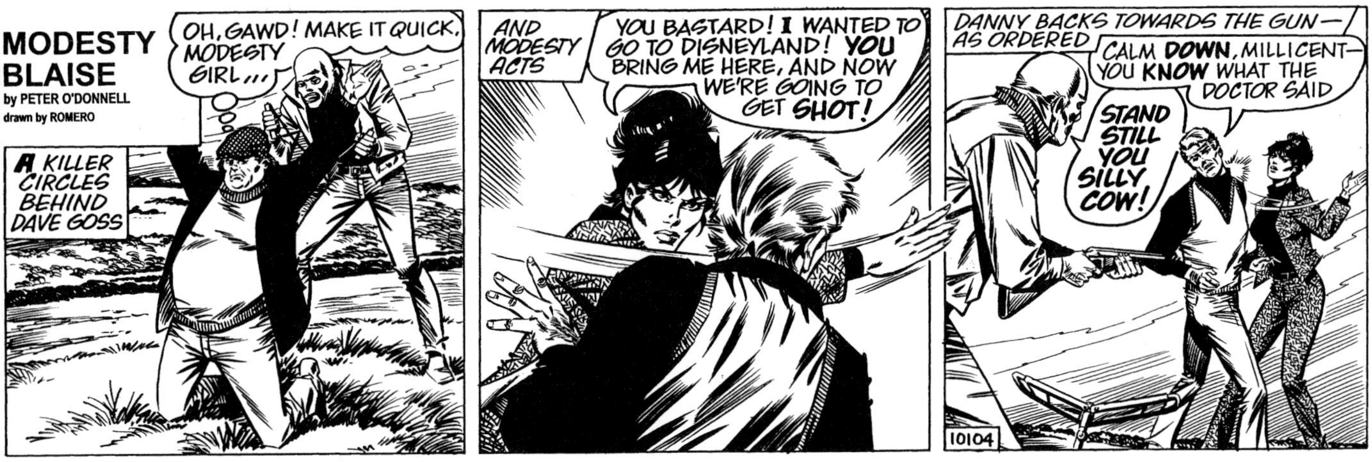
MODESTY BLAISE
by PETER O'DONNELL
drawn by ROMERO
A KILLER CIRCLES BEHIND DAVE GOSS
OH, GAWD! MAKE IT QUICK, MODESTY GIRL...
AND MODESTY ACTS
YOU BASTARD! I WANTED TO GO TO DISNEYLAND! YOU BRING ME HERE, AND NOW WE'RE GOING TO GET SHOT!
DANNY BACKS TOWARDS THE GUN— AS ORDERED
CALM DOWN, MILLICENT— YOU KNOW WHAT THE DOCTOR SAID
STAND STILL YOU SILLY COW!
10104

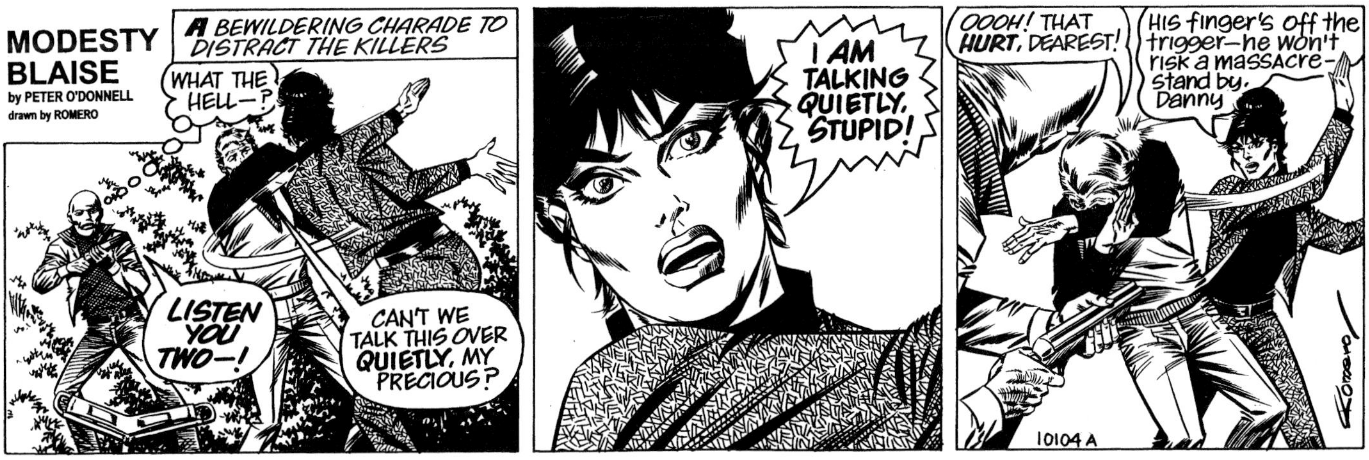
MODESTY BLAISE
by PETER O'DONNELL
drawn by ROMERO
A BEWILDERING CHARADE TO DISTRACT THE KILLERS
WHAT THE HELL—?
LISTEN YOU TWO—!
CAN'T WE TALK THIS OVER QUIETLY, MY PRECIOUS?
I AM TALKING QUIETLY, STUPID!
OOOH! THAT HURT, DEAREST!
His finger's off the trigger—he won't risk a massacre—stand by, Danny
10104 A

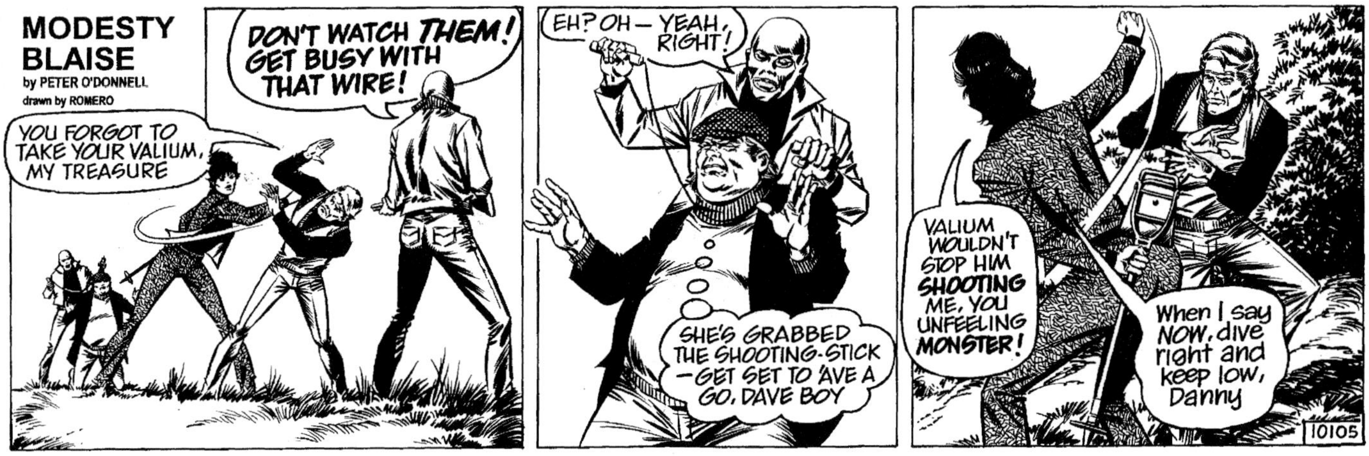
MODESTY BLAISE
by PETER O'DONNELL
drawn by ROMERO
DON'T WATCH THEM! GET BUSY WITH THAT WIRE!
YOU FORGOT TO TAKE YOUR VALIUM, MY TREASURE
EH? OH — YEAH, RIGHT!
SHE'S GRABBED THE SHOOTING-STICK —GET SET TO 'AVE A GO, DAVE BOY
VALIUM WOULDN'T STOP HIM SHOOTING ME, YOU UNFEELING MONSTER!
When I say NOW, dive right and keep low, Danny
10105

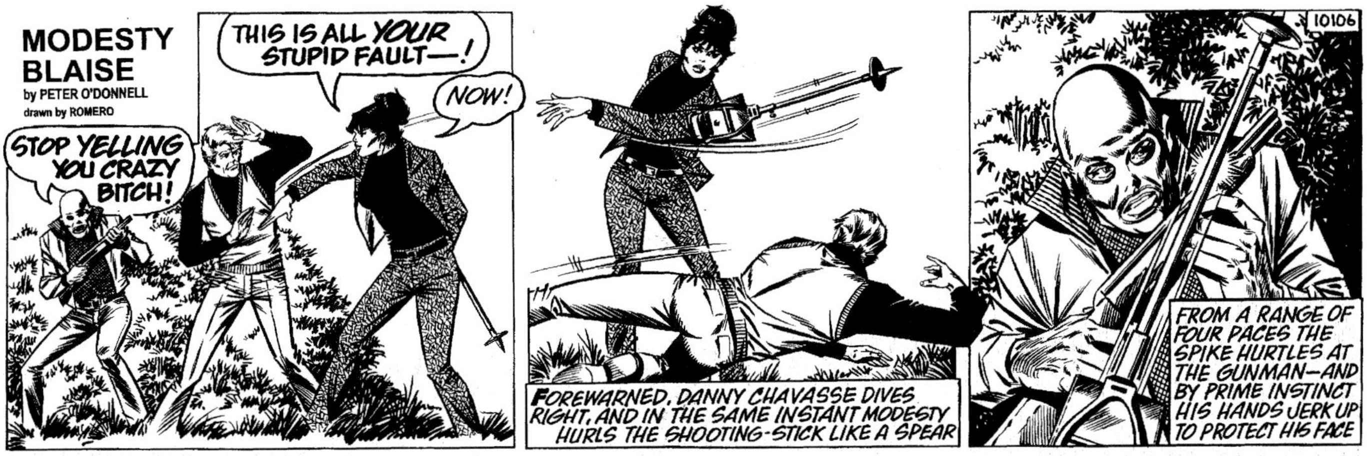
MODESTY BLAISE
by PETER O'DONNELL
drawn by ROMERO
THIS IS ALL YOUR STUPID FAULT—!
STOP YELLING YOU CRAZY BITCH!
NOW!
FOREWARNED, DANNY CHAVASSE DIVES RIGHT, AND IN THE SAME INSTANT MODESTY HURLS THE SHOOTING-STICK LIKE A SPEAR
10106
FROM A RANGE OF FOUR PACES THE SPIKE HURTLES AT THE GUNMAN—AND BY PRIME INSTINCT HIS HANDS JERK UP TO PROTECT HIS FACE

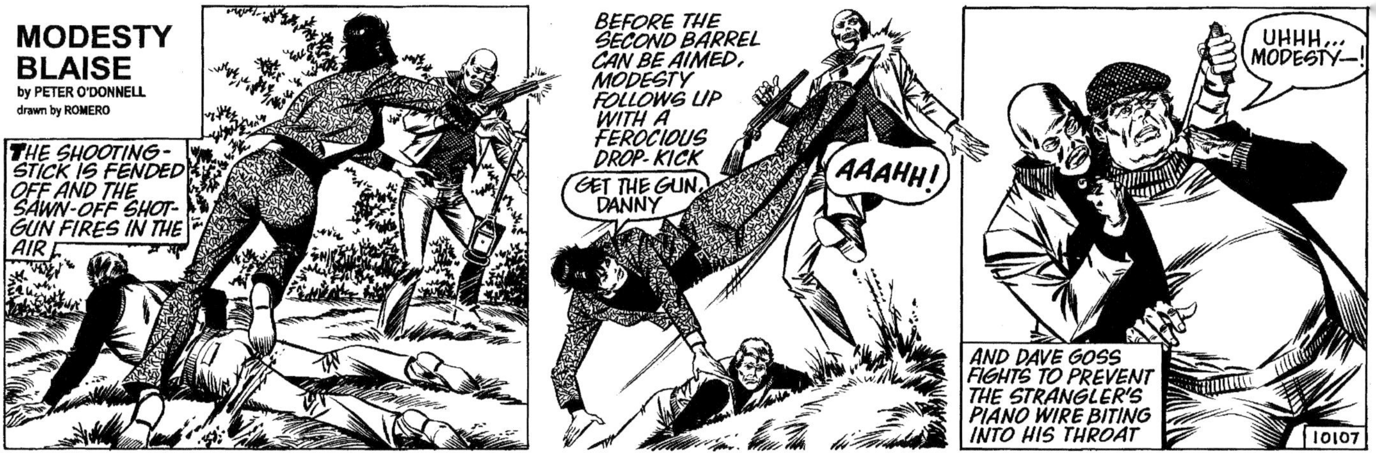
MODESTY BLAISE
by PETER O'DONNELL
drawn by ROMERO
THE SHOOTING-STICK IS FENDED OFF AND THE SAWN-OFF SHOT-GUN FIRES IN THE AIR
BEFORE THE SECOND BARREL CAN BE AIMED, MODESTY FOLLOWS UP WITH A FEROCIOUS DROP-KICK
GET THE GUN, DANNY
AAAHH!
UHHH... MODESTY—!
AND DAVE GOSS FIGHTS TO PREVENT THE STRANGLER'S PIANO WIRE BITING INTO HIS THROAT
10107

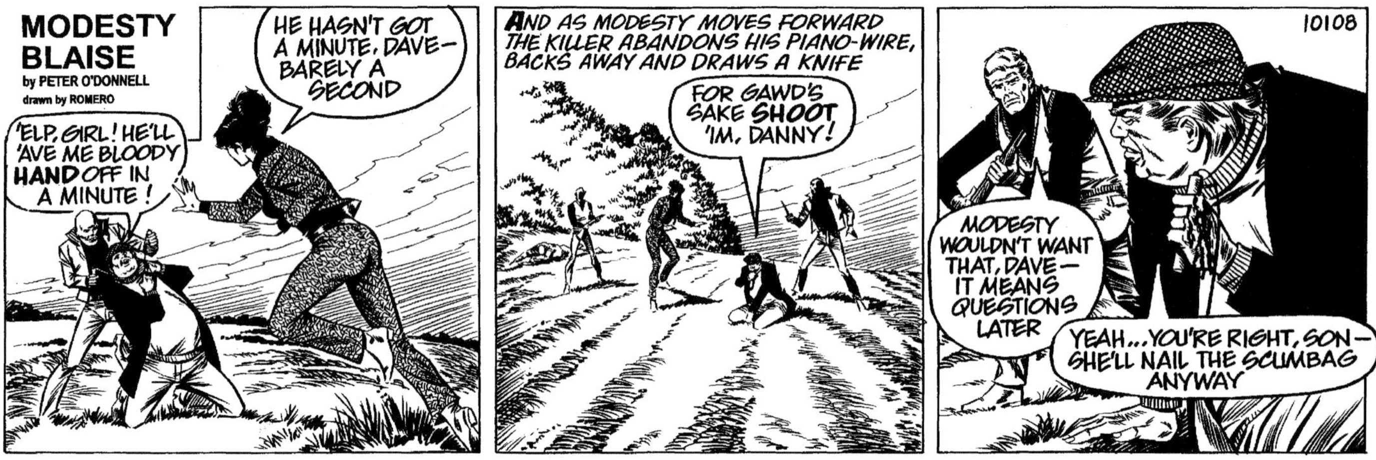
MODESTY BLAISE
by PETER O'DONNELL
drawn by ROMERO
'ELP, GIRL! HE'LL 'AVE ME BLOODY HAND OFF IN A MINUTE!
HE HASN'T GOT A MINUTE, DAVE— BARELY A SECOND
AND AS MODESTY MOVES FORWARD THE KILLER ABANDONS HIS PIANO-WIRE, BACKS AWAY AND DRAWS A KNIFE
FOR GAWD'S SAKE SHOOT 'IM, DANNY!
10108
MODESTY WOULDN'T WANT THAT, DAVE— IT MEANS QUESTIONS LATER
YEAH... YOU'RE RIGHT, SON— SHE'LL NAIL THE SCUMBAG ANYWAY

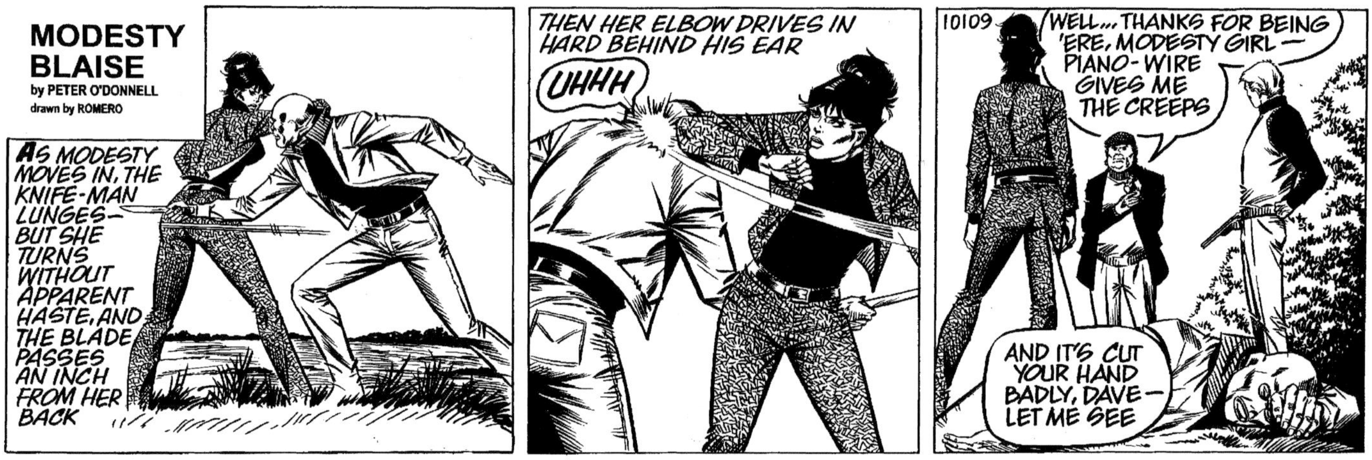
MODESTY BLAISE
by PETER O'DONNELL
drawn by ROMERO
AS MODESTY MOVES IN, THE KNIFE-MAN LUNGES— BUT SHE TURNS WITHOUT APPARENT HASTE, AND THE BLADE PASSES AN INCH FROM HER BACK
THEN HER ELBOW DRIVES IN HARD BEHIND HIS EAR
UHHH
10109
WELL... THANKS FOR BEING 'ERE, MODESTY GIRL— PIANO-WIRE GIVES ME THE CREEPS
AND IT'S CUT YOUR HAND BADLY, DAVE— LET ME SEE

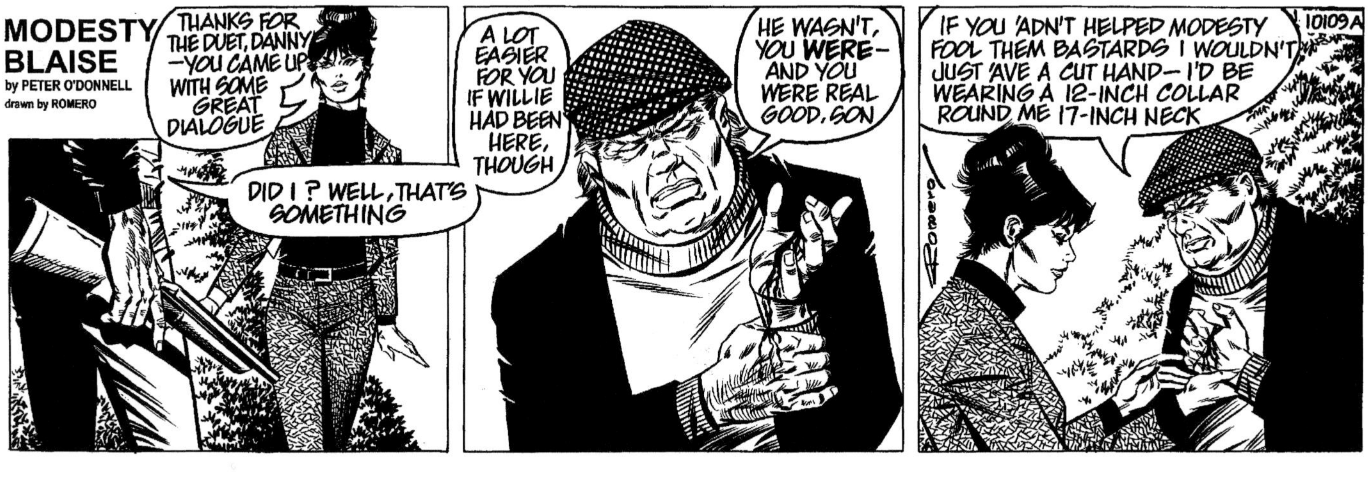
MODESTY BLAISE
by PETER O'DONNELL
drawn by ROMERO
THANKS FOR THE DUET, DANNY —YOU CAME UP WITH SOME GREAT DIALOGUE
DID I? WELL, THAT'S SOMETHING
A LOT EASIER FOR YOU IF WILLIE HAD BEEN HERE, THOUGH
HE WASN'T, YOU WERE— AND YOU WERE REAL GOOD, SON
10109 A
IF YOU 'ADN'T HELPED MODESTY FOOL THEM BASTARDS I WOULDN'T JUST 'AVE A CUT HAND— I'D BE WEARING A 12-INCH COLLAR ROUND ME 17-INCH NECK

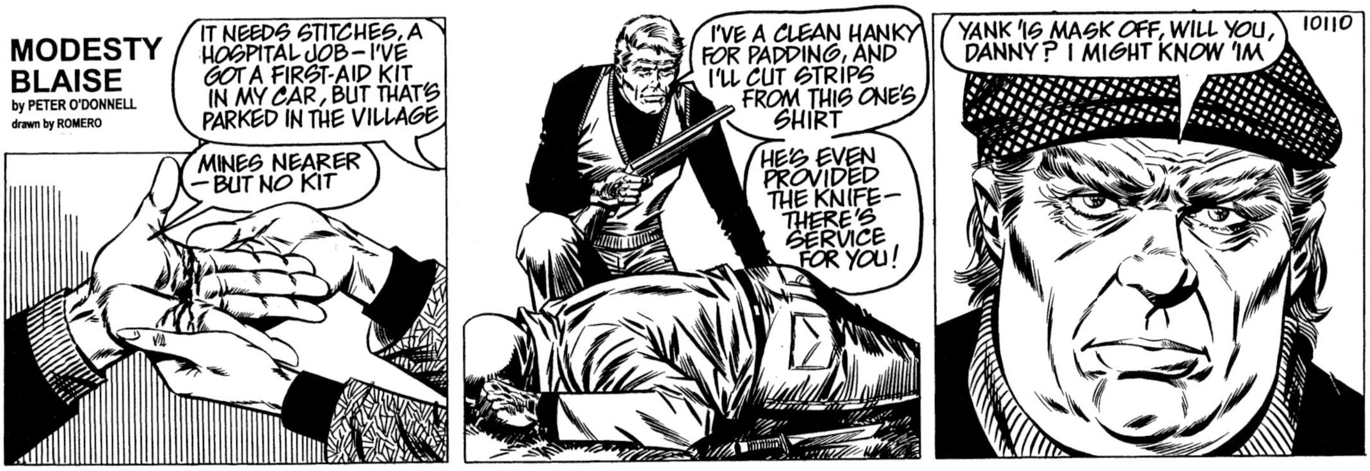
MODESTY BLAISE
by PETER O'DONNELL
drawn by ROMERO
IT NEEDS STITCHES, A HOSPITAL JOB—I'VE GOT A FIRST-AID KIT IN MY CAR, BUT THAT'S PARKED IN THE VILLAGE
MINES NEARER —BUT NO KIT
I'VE A CLEAN HANKY FOR PADDING, AND I'LL CUT STRIPS FROM THIS ONE'S SHIRT
HE'S EVEN PROVIDED THE KNIFE— THERE'S SERVICE FOR YOU!
10110
YANK 'IS MASK OFF, WILL YOU, DANNY? I MIGHT KNOW 'IM

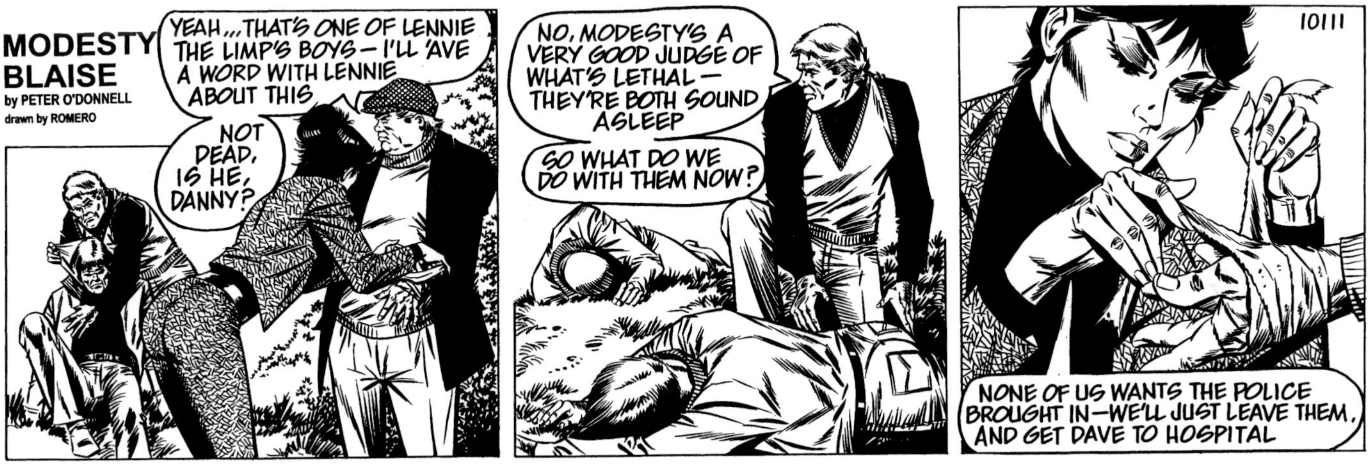
MODESTY BLAISE
by PETER O'DONNELL
drawn by ROMERO
YEAH... THAT'S ONE OF LENNIE THE LIMP'S BOYS—I'LL 'AVE A WORD WITH LENNIE ABOUT THIS
NOT DEAD, IS HE, DANNY?
NO, MODESTY'S A VERY GOOD JUDGE OF WHAT'S LETHAL— THEY'RE BOTH SOUND ASLEEP
SO WHAT DO WE DO WITH THEM NOW?
10111
NONE OF US WANTS THE POLICE BROUGHT IN—WE'LL JUST LEAVE THEM, AND GET DAVE TO HOSPITAL

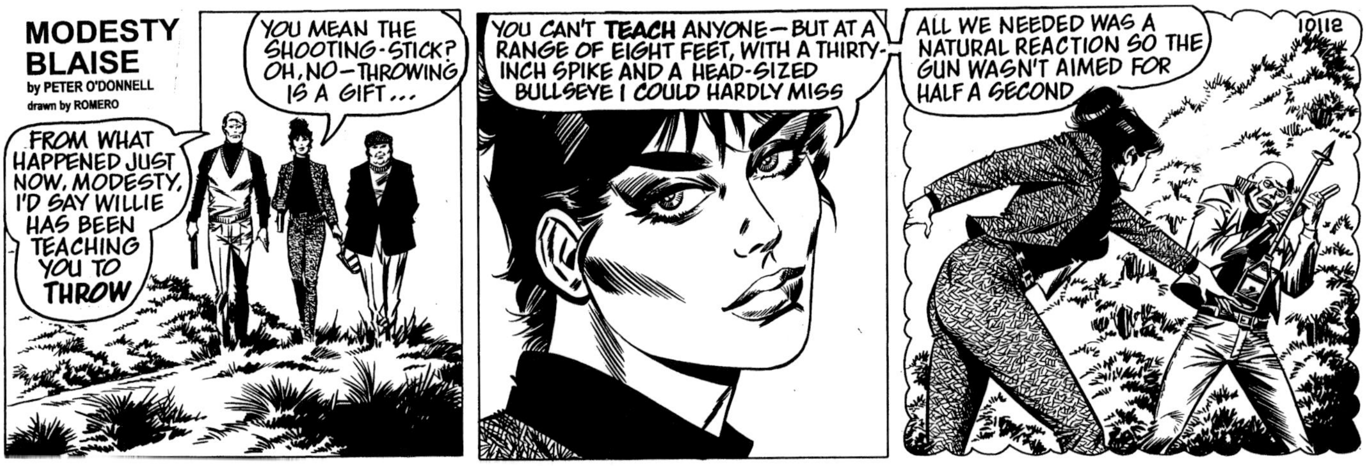
MODESTY BLAISE
by PETER O'DONNELL
drawn by ROMERO
FROM WHAT HAPPENED JUST NOW, MODESTY, I'D SAY WILLIE HAS BEEN TEACHING YOU TO THROW
YOU MEAN THE SHOOTING-STICK? OH, NO—THROWING IS A GIFT...
YOU CAN'T TEACH ANYONE—BUT AT A RANGE OF EIGHT FEET, WITH A THIRTY-INCH SPIKE AND A HEAD-SIZED BULLSEYE I COULD HARDLY MISS
10112
ALL WE NEEDED WAS A NATURAL REACTION SO THE GUN WASN'T AIMED FOR HALF A SECOND

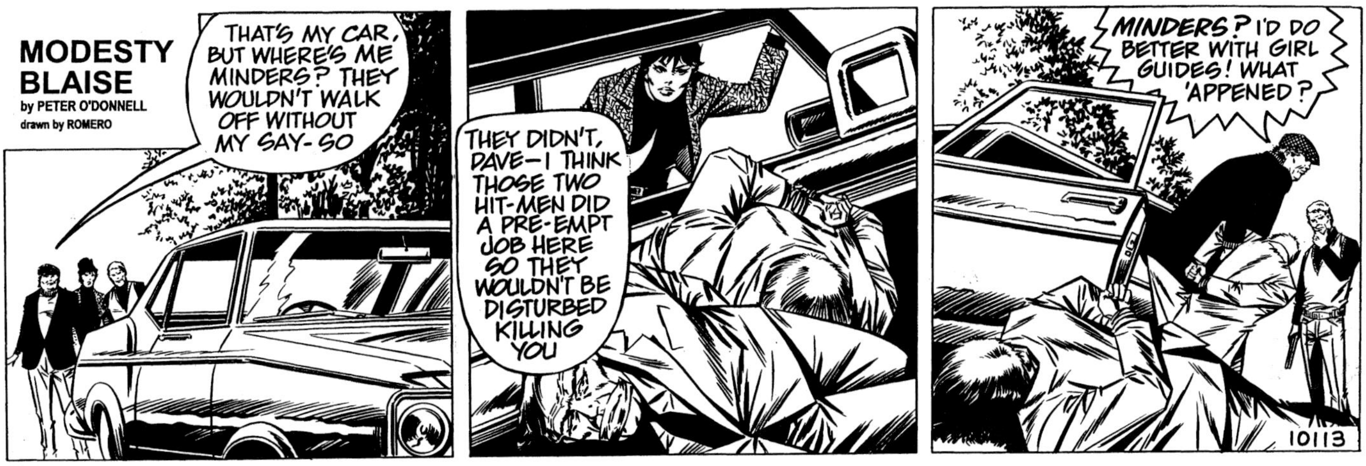
MODESTY BLAISE
by PETER O'DONNELL
drawn by ROMERO
THAT'S MY CAR, BUT WHERE'S ME MINDERS? THEY WOULDN'T WALK OFF WITHOUT MY SAY-SO
THEY DIDN'T, DAVE—I THINK THOSE TWO HIT-MEN DID A PRE-EMPT JOB HERE SO THEY WOULDN'T BE DISTURBED KILLING YOU
MINDERS? I'D DO BETTER WITH GIRL GUIDES! WHAT 'APPENED?
10113

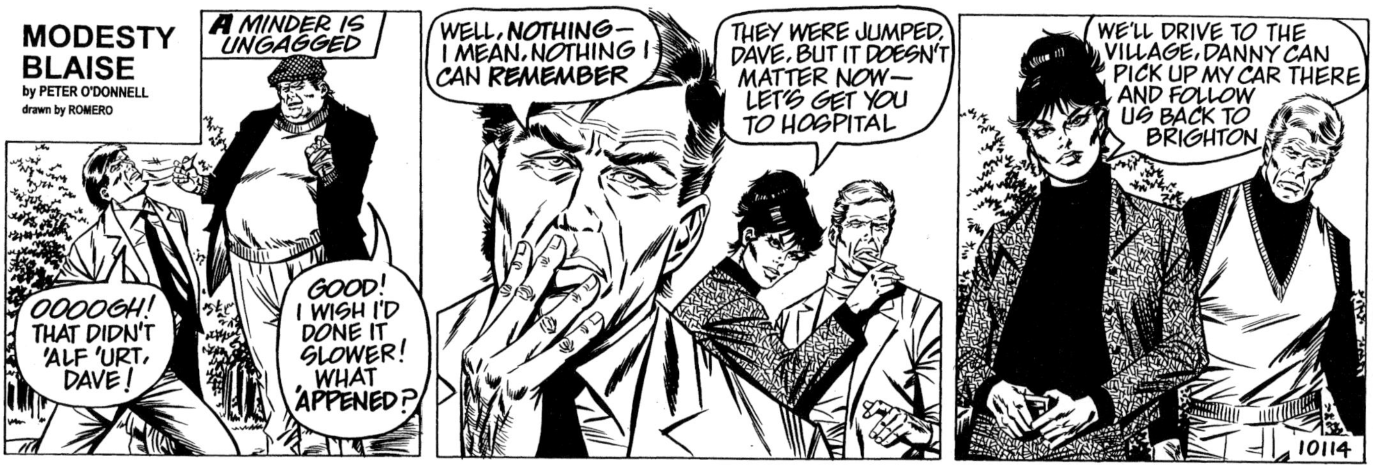
MODESTY BLAISE
by PETER O'DONNELL
drawn by ROMERO
A MINDER IS UNGAGGED
OOOOGH! THAT DIDN'T 'ALF 'URT, DAVE!
GOOD! I WISH I'D DONE IT SLOWER! WHAT 'APPENED?
WELL, NOTHING— I MEAN, NOTHING I CAN REMEMBER
THEY WERE JUMPED, DAVE, BUT IT DOESN'T MATTER NOW— LET'S GET YOU TO HOSPITAL
WE'LL DRIVE TO THE VILLAGE, DANNY CAN PICK UP MY CAR THERE AND FOLLOW US BACK TO BRIGHTON
10114

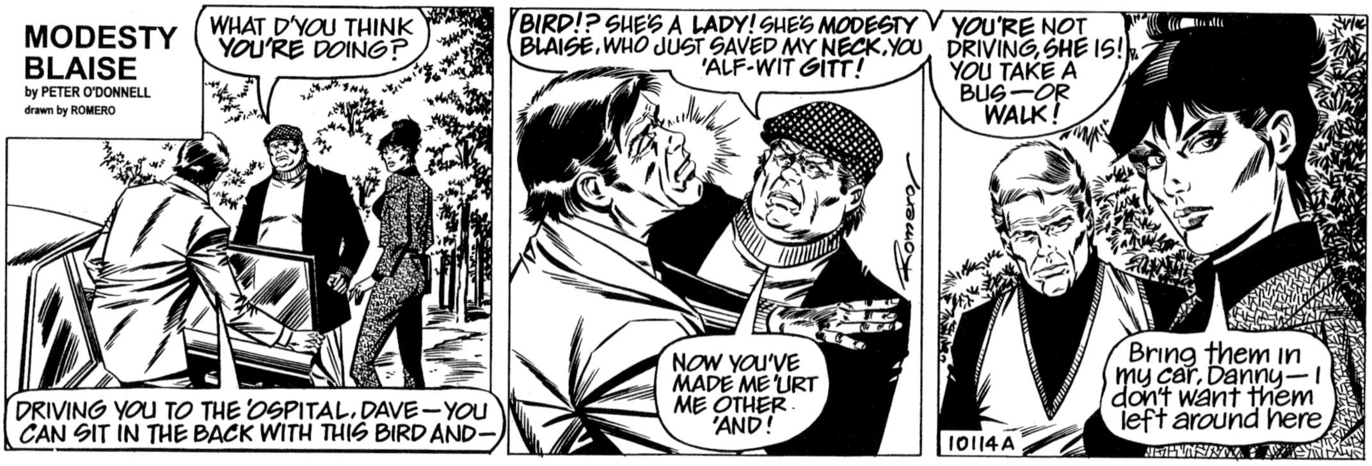
MODESTY BLAISE
by PETER O'DONNELL
drawn by ROMERO
WHAT D'YOU THINK YOU'RE DOING?
DRIVING YOU TO THE 'OSPITAL, DAVE—YOU CAN SIT IN THE BACK WITH THIS BIRD AND—
BIRD!? SHE'S A LADY! SHE'S MODESTY BLAISE, WHO JUST SAVED MY NECK, YOU 'ALF-WIT GITT!
NOW YOU'VE MADE ME 'URT ME OTHER 'AND!
Romero
YOU'RE NOT DRIVING, SHE IS! YOU TAKE A BUS—OR WALK!
Bring them in my car, Danny—I don't want them left around here
10114 A

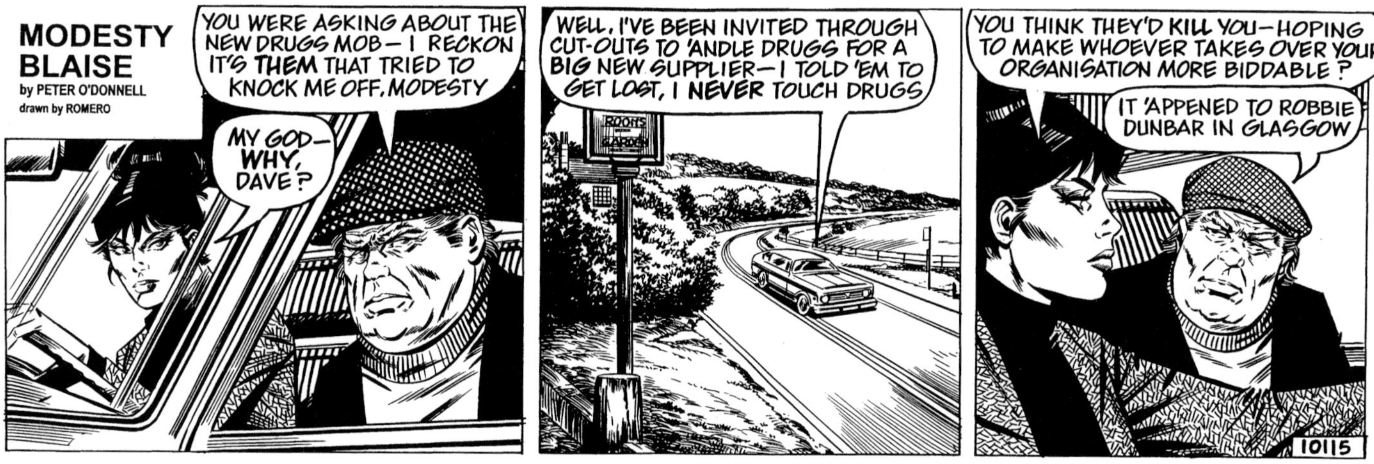
MODESTY BLAISE
by PETER O'DONNELL
drawn by ROMERO
YOU WERE ASKING ABOUT THE NEW DRUGS MOB— I RECKON IT'S THEM THAT TRIED TO KNOCK ME OFF, MODESTY
MY GOD— WHY, DAVE?
WELL, I'VE BEEN INVITED THROUGH CUT-OUTS TO 'ANDLE DRUGS FOR A BIG NEW SUPPLIER—I TOLD 'EM TO GET LOST, I NEVER TOUCH DRUGS
ROOMS
GARDEN
YOU THINK THEY'D KILL YOU—HOPING TO MAKE WHOEVER TAKES OVER YOUR ORGANISATION MORE BIDDABLE?
IT 'APPENED TO ROBBIE DUNBAR IN GLASGOW
10115

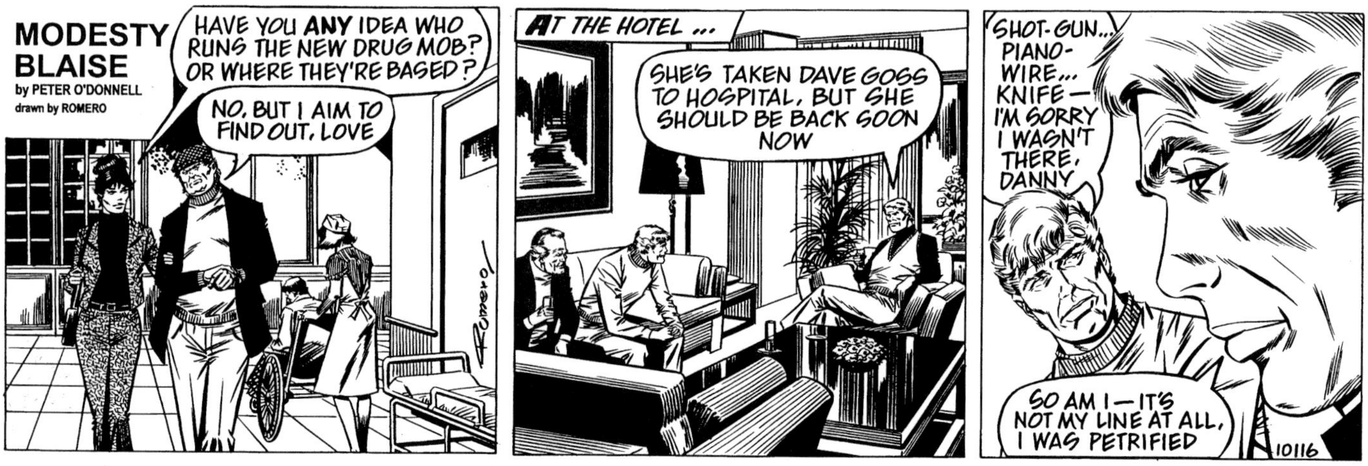
MODESTY BLAISE
by PETER O'DONNELL
drawn by ROMERO
HAVE YOU ANY IDEA WHO RUNS THE NEW DRUG MOB? OR WHERE THEY'RE BASED?
NO, BUT I AIM TO FIND OUT, LOVE
Romero
AT THE HOTEL ...
SHE'S TAKEN DAVE GOSS TO HOSPITAL, BUT SHE SHOULD BE BACK SOON NOW
SHOT-GUN... PIANO-WIRE... KNIFE— I'M SORRY I WASN'T THERE, DANNY
SO AM I—IT'S NOT MY LINE AT ALL, I WAS PETRIFIED
10116

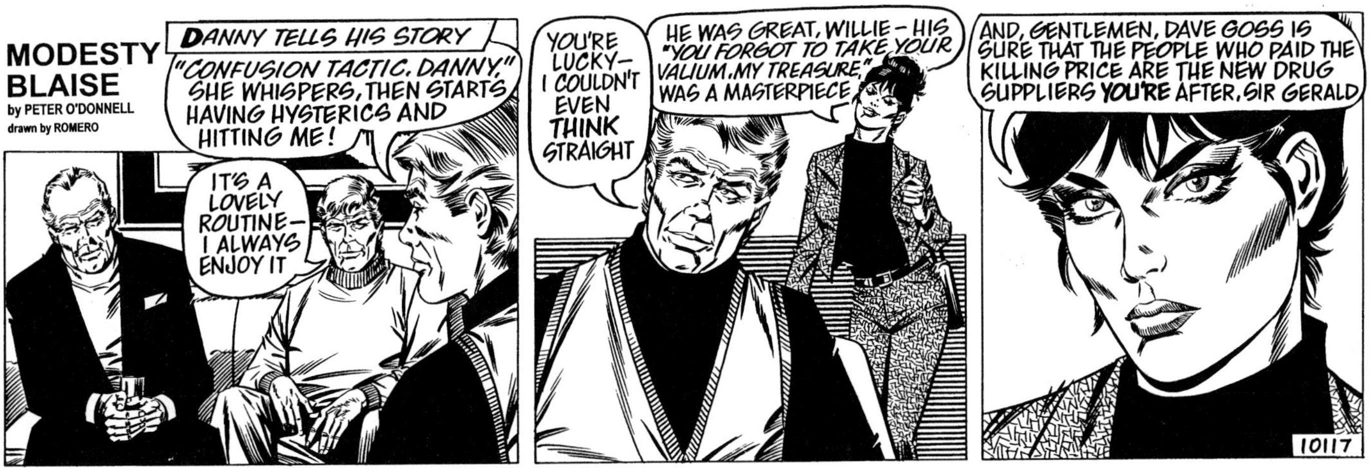
MODESTY BLAISE
by PETER O'DONNELL
drawn by ROMERO
DANNY TELLS HIS STORY
"CONFUSION TACTIC, DANNY," SHE WHISPERS, THEN STARTS HAVING HYSTERICS AND HITTING ME!
IT'S A LOVELY ROUTINE— I ALWAYS ENJOY IT
YOU'RE LUCKY— I COULDN'T EVEN THINK STRAIGHT
HE WAS GREAT, WILLIE— HIS "YOU FORGOT TO TAKE YOUR VALIUM, MY TREASURE," WAS A MASTERPIECE
AND, GENTLEMEN, DAVE GOSS IS SURE THAT THE PEOPLE WHO PAID THE KILLING PRICE ARE THE NEW DRUG SUPPLIERS YOU'RE AFTER, SIR GERALD
10117

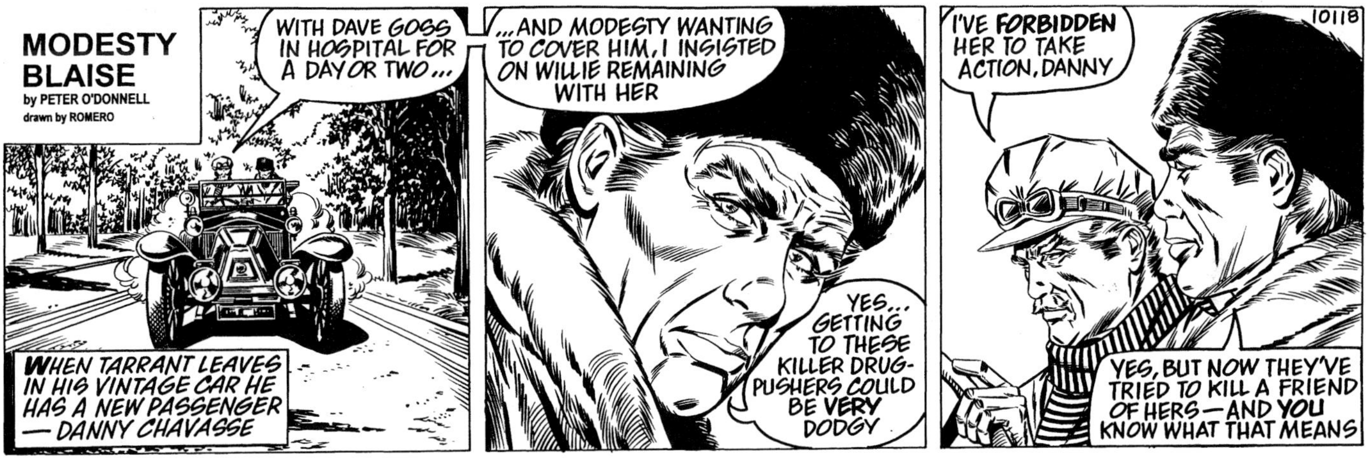
MODESTY BLAISE
by PETER O'DONNELL
drawn by ROMERO
WITH DAVE GOSS IN HOSPITAL FOR A DAY OR TWO...
WHEN TARRANT LEAVES IN HIS VINTAGE CAR HE HAS A NEW PASSENGER — DANNY CHAVASSE
...AND MODESTY WANTING TO COVER HIM, I INSISTED ON WILLIE REMAINING WITH HER
YES... GETTING TO THESE KILLER DRUG-PUSHERS COULD BE VERY DODGY
10118
I'VE FORBIDDEN HER TO TAKE ACTION, DANNY
YES, BUT NOW THEY'VE TRIED TO KILL A FRIEND OF HERS— AND YOU KNOW WHAT THAT MEANS

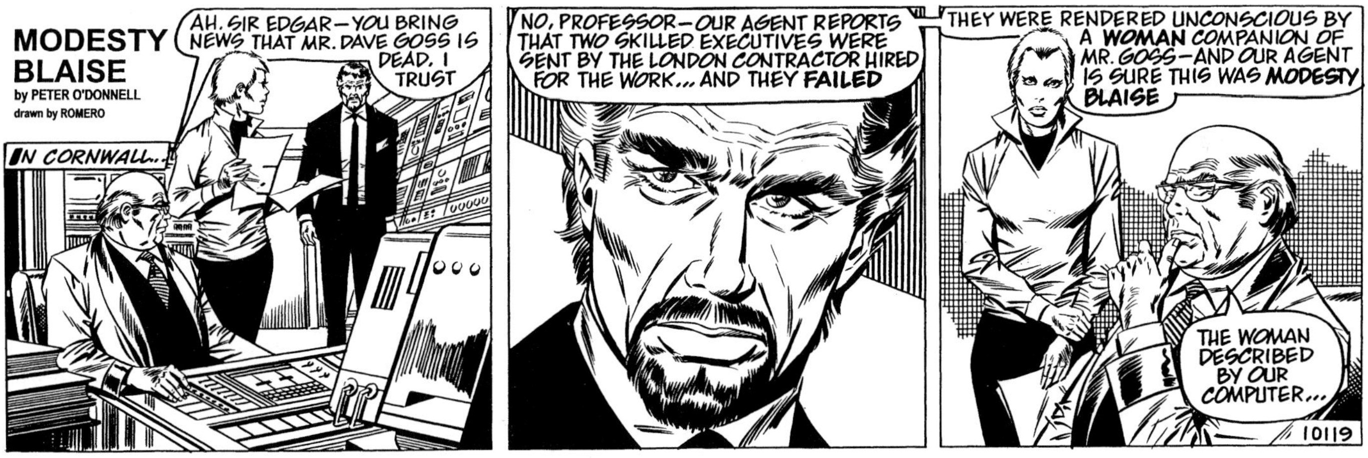
MODESTY BLAISE
by PETER O'DONNELL
drawn by ROMERO
IN CORNWALL...
AH, SIR EDGAR— YOU BRING NEWS THAT MR. DAVE GOSS IS DEAD, I TRUST
NO, PROFESSOR— OUR AGENT REPORTS THAT TWO SKILLED EXECUTIVES WERE SENT BY THE LONDON CONTRACTOR HIRED FOR THE WORK... AND THEY FAILED
THEY WERE RENDERED UNCONSCIOUS BY A WOMAN COMPANION OF MR. GOSS— AND OUR AGENT IS SURE THIS WAS MODESTY BLAISE
THE WOMAN DESCRIBED BY OUR COMPUTER...
10119

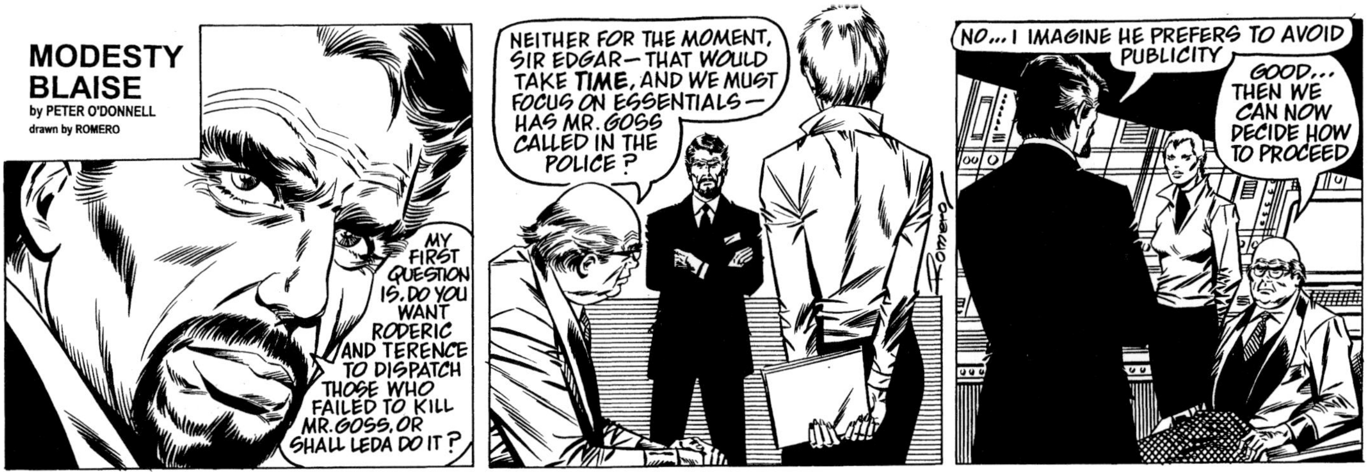
MODESTY BLAISE
by PETER O'DONNELL
drawn by ROMERO
MY FIRST QUESTION IS, DO YOU WANT RODERIC AND TERENCE TO DISPATCH THOSE WHO FAILED TO KILL MR. GOSS, OR SHALL LEDA DO IT?
NEITHER FOR THE MOMENT, SIR EDGAR— THAT WOULD TAKE TIME, AND WE MUST FOCUS ON ESSENTIALS— HAS MR. GOSS CALLED IN THE POLICE?
Romero
NO... I IMAGINE HE PREFERS TO AVOID PUBLICITY
GOOD... THEN WE CAN NOW DECIDE HOW TO PROCEED

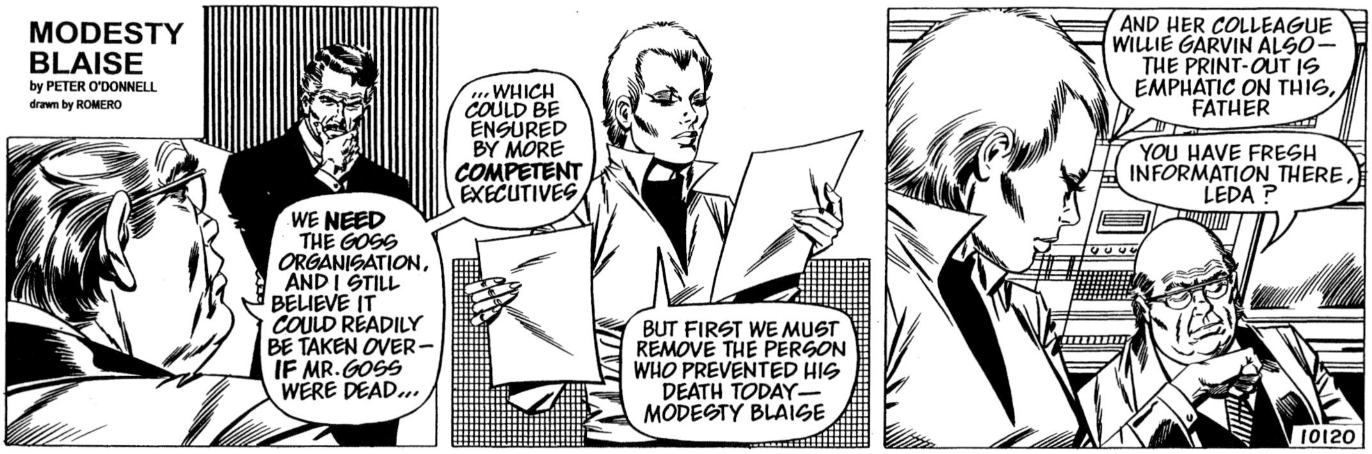
MODESTY BLAISE
by PETER O'DONNELL
drawn by ROMERO
WE NEED THE GOSS ORGANISATION, AND I STILL BELIEVE IT COULD READILY BE TAKEN OVER—IF MR. GOSS WERE DEAD...
...WHICH COULD BE ENSURED BY MORE COMPETENT EXECUTIVES
BUT FIRST WE MUST REMOVE THE PERSON WHO PREVENTED HIS DEATH TODAY—MODESTY BLAISE
AND HER COLLEAGUE WILLIE GARVIN ALSO—THE PRINT-OUT IS EMPHATIC ON THIS, FATHER
YOU HAVE FRESH INFORMATION THERE, LEDA ?
10120

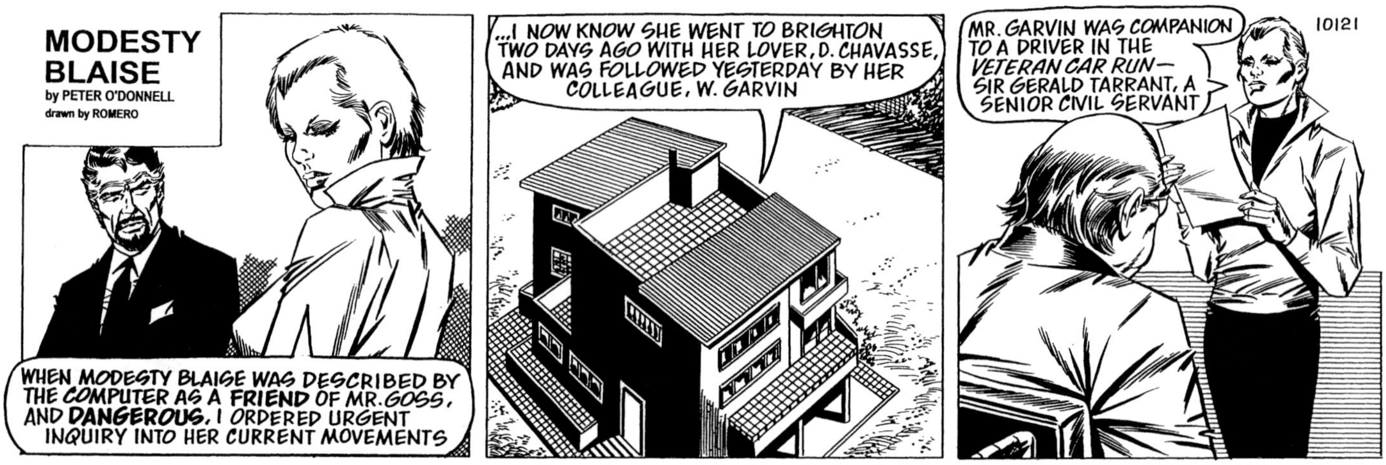
MODESTY BLAISE
by PETER O'DONNELL
drawn by ROMERO
WHEN MODESTY BLAISE WAS DESCRIBED BY THE COMPUTER AS A FRIEND OF MR. GOSS, AND DANGEROUS, I ORDERED URGENT INQUIRY INTO HER CURRENT MOVEMENTS
...I NOW KNOW SHE WENT TO BRIGHTON TWO DAYS AGO WITH HER LOVER, D. CHAVASSE, AND WAS FOLLOWED YESTERDAY BY HER COLLEAGUE, W. GARVIN
MR. GARVIN WAS COMPANION TO A DRIVER IN THE VETERAN CAR RUN—SIR GERALD TARRANT, A SENIOR CIVIL SERVANT
10121

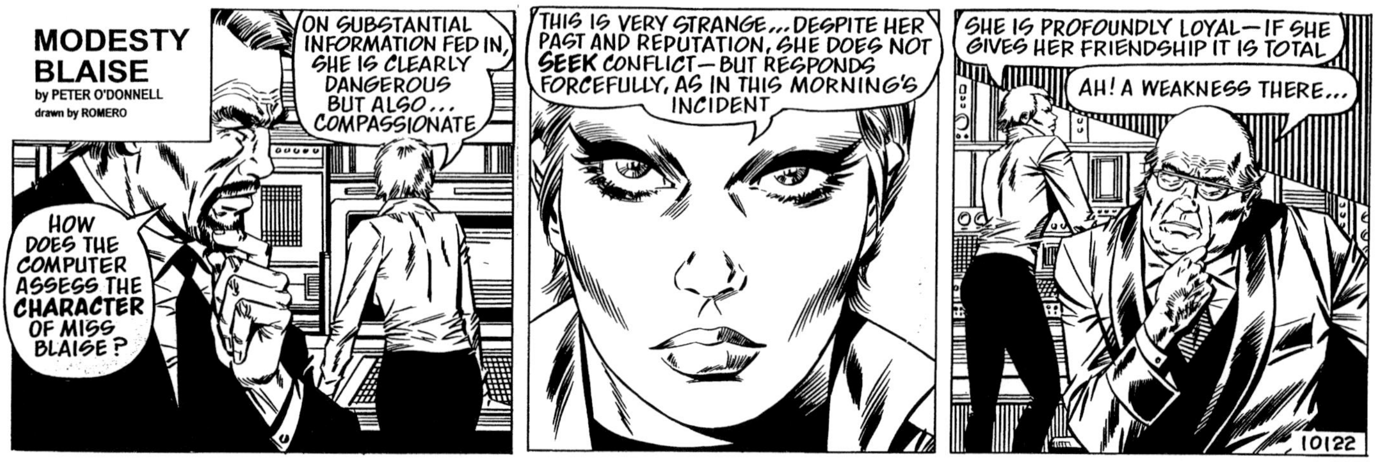
MODESTY BLAISE
by PETER O'DONNELL
drawn by ROMERO
HOW DOES THE COMPUTER ASSESS THE CHARACTER OF MISS BLAISE ?
ON SUBSTANTIAL INFORMATION FED IN, SHE IS CLEARLY DANGEROUS BUT ALSO... COMPASSIONATE
THIS IS VERY STRANGE,... DESPITE HER PAST AND REPUTATION, SHE DOES NOT SEEK CONFLICT—BUT RESPONDS FORCEFULLY, AS IN THIS MORNING'S INCIDENT
SHE IS PROFOUNDLY LOYAL—IF SHE GIVES HER FRIENDSHIP IT IS TOTAL
AH! A WEAKNESS THERE...
10122

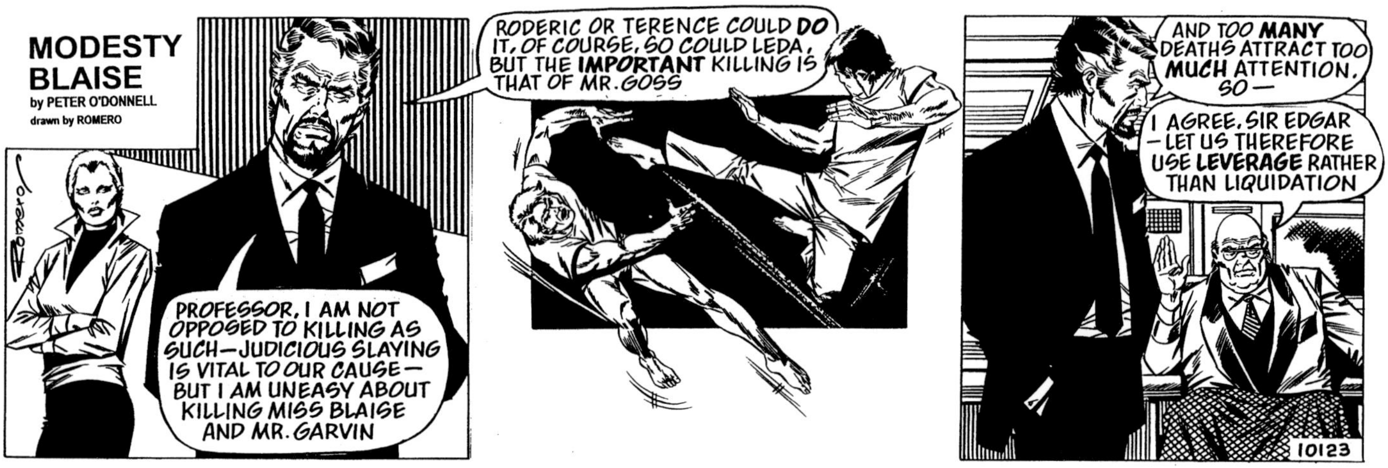
MODESTY BLAISE
by PETER O'DONNELL
drawn by ROMERO
ROMERO
PROFESSOR, I AM NOT OPPOSED TO KILLING AS SUCH—JUDICIOUS SLAYING IS VITAL TO OUR CAUSE—BUT I AM UNEASY ABOUT KILLING MISS BLAISE AND MR. GARVIN
RODERIC OR TERENCE COULD DO IT, OF COURSE, SO COULD LEDA, BUT THE IMPORTANT KILLING IS THAT OF MR. GOSS
AND TOO MANY DEATHS ATTRACT TOO MUCH ATTENTION. SO—
I AGREE, SIR EDGAR—LET US THEREFORE USE LEVERAGE RATHER THAN LIQUIDATION
10123

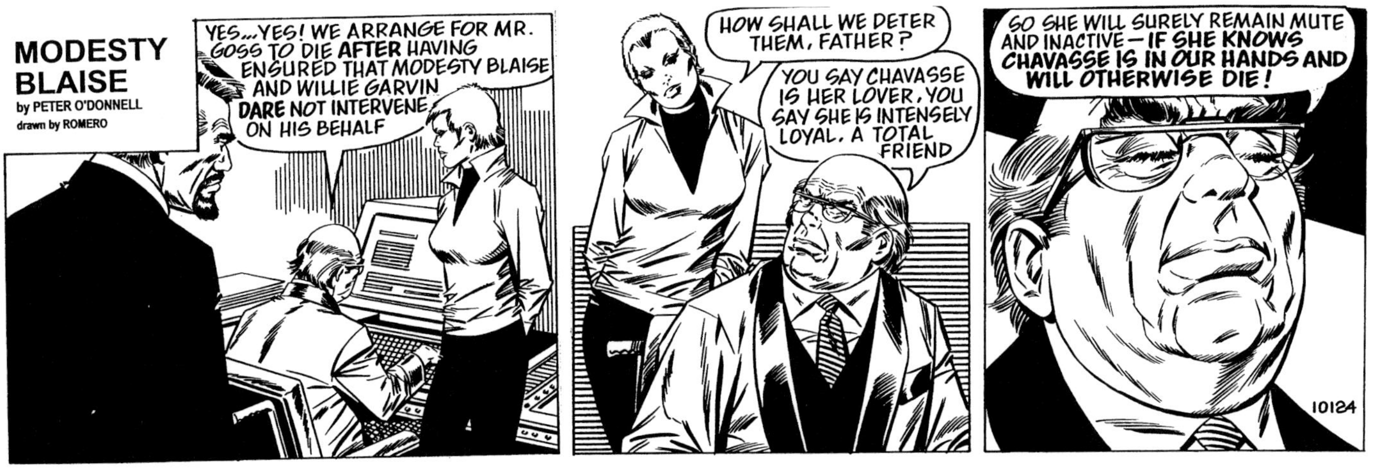
MODESTY BLAISE
by PETER O'DONNELL
drawn by ROMERO
YES...YES! WE ARRANGE FOR MR. GOSS TO DIE **AFTER** HAVING ENSURED THAT MODESTY BLAISE AND WILLIE GARVIN **DARE** NOT INTERVENE ON HIS BEHALF
HOW SHALL WE DETER THEM, FATHER?
YOU SAY CHAVASSE IS HER LOVER, YOU SAY SHE IS INTENSELY LOYAL, A TOTAL FRIEND
SO SHE WILL SURELY REMAIN MUTE AND INACTIVE — **IF SHE KNOWS CHAVASSE IS IN OUR HANDS AND WILL OTHERWISE DIE!**
10124

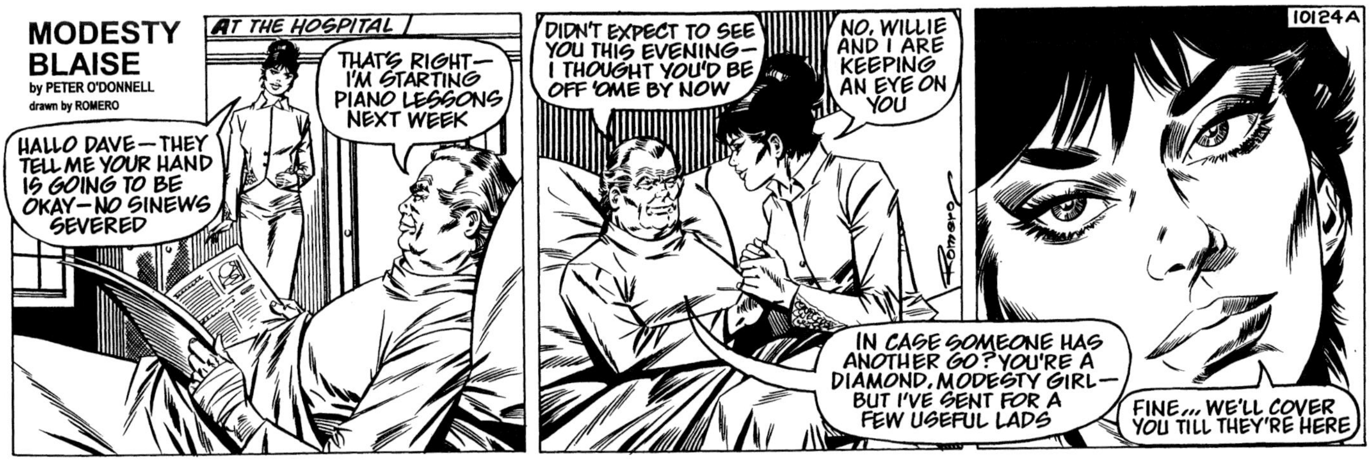
MODESTY BLAISE
by PETER O'DONNELL
drawn by ROMERO
AT THE HOSPITAL
HALLO DAVE — THEY TELL ME YOUR HAND IS GOING TO BE OKAY — NO SINEWS SEVERED
THAT'S RIGHT — I'M STARTING PIANO LESSONS NEXT WEEK
DIDN'T EXPECT TO SEE YOU THIS EVENING — I THOUGHT YOU'D BE OFF 'OME BY NOW
NO, WILLIE AND I ARE KEEPING AN EYE ON YOU
10124 A
IN CASE SOMEONE HAS ANOTHER GO? YOU'RE A DIAMOND, MODESTY GIRL — BUT I'VE SENT FOR A FEW USEFUL LADS
FINE... WE'LL COVER YOU TILL THEY'RE HERE

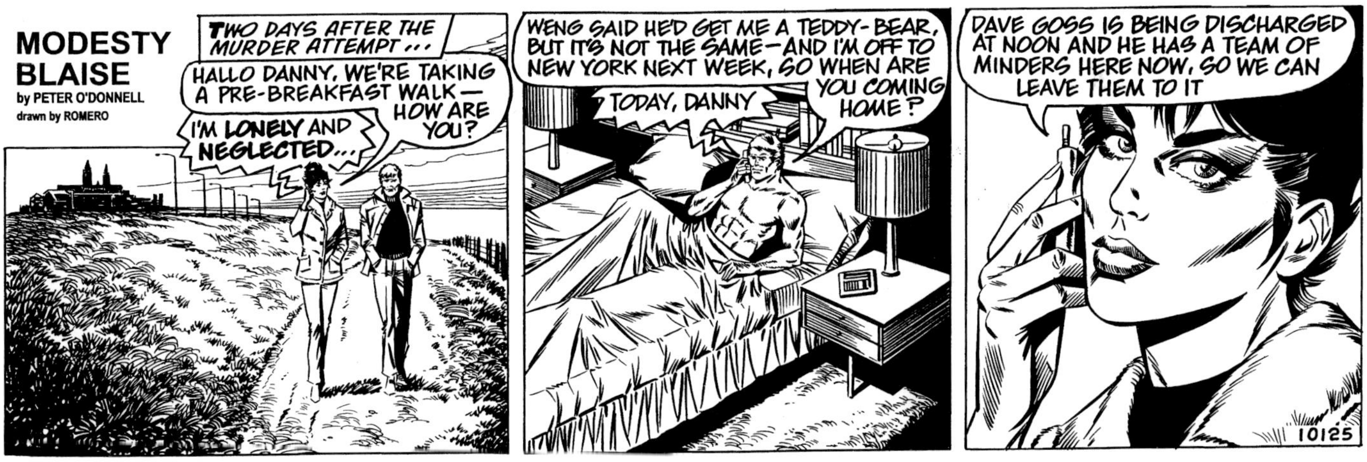
MODESTY BLAISE
by PETER O'DONNELL
drawn by ROMERO
TWO DAYS AFTER THE MURDER ATTEMPT...
HALLO DANNY, WE'RE TAKING A PRE-BREAKFAST WALK — HOW ARE YOU?
I'M **LONELY** AND **NEGLECTED**...
WENG SAID HE'D GET ME A TEDDY-BEAR, BUT IT'S NOT THE SAME — AND I'M OFF TO NEW YORK NEXT WEEK, SO WHEN ARE YOU COMING HOME?
TODAY, DANNY
DAVE GOSS IS BEING DISCHARGED AT NOON AND HE HAS A TEAM OF MINDERS HERE NOW, SO WE CAN LEAVE THEM TO IT
10125

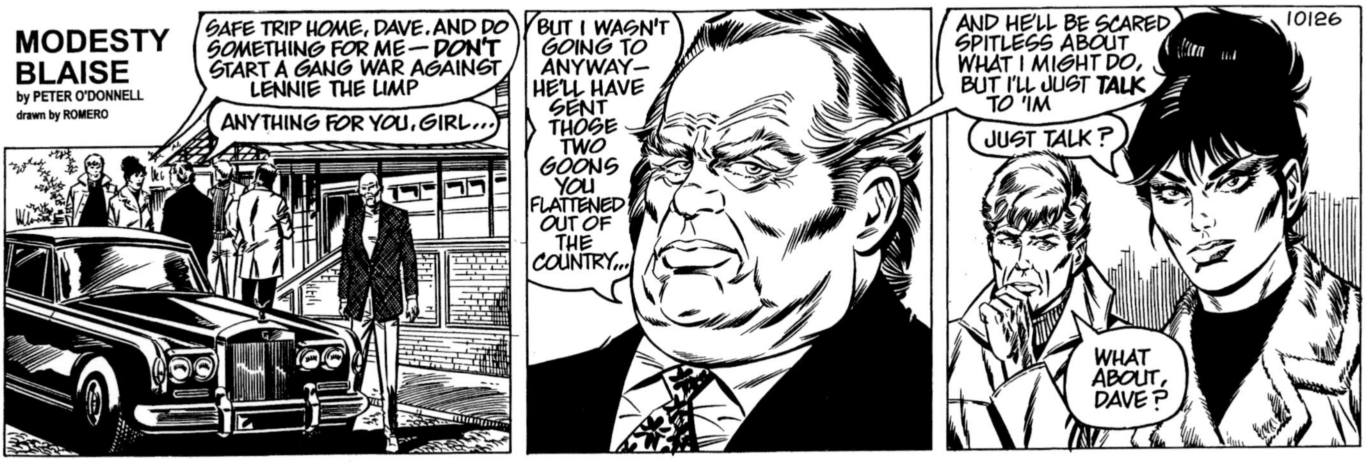
MODESTY BLAISE
by PETER O'DONNELL
drawn by ROMERO
SAFE TRIP HOME, DAVE. AND DO SOMETHING FOR ME — **DON'T** START A GANG WAR AGAINST LENNIE THE LIMP
ANYTHING FOR YOU, GIRL...
BUT I WASN'T GOING TO ANYWAY — HE'LL HAVE SENT THOSE TWO GOONS YOU FLATTENED OUT OF THE COUNTRY...
10126
AND HE'LL BE SCARED SPITLESS ABOUT WHAT I MIGHT DO, BUT I'LL JUST **TALK** TO 'IM
JUST TALK?
WHAT ABOUT, DAVE?

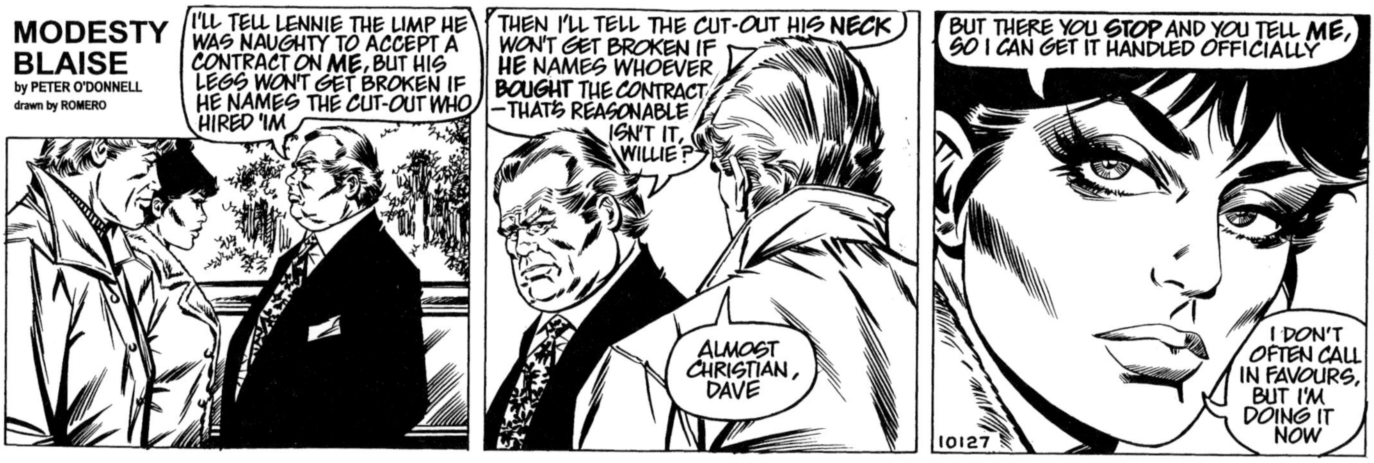
MODESTY BLAISE
by PETER O'DONNELL
drawn by ROMERO
I'LL TELL LENNIE THE LIMP HE WAS NAUGHTY TO ACCEPT A CONTRACT ON **ME**, BUT HIS LEGS WON'T GET BROKEN IF HE NAMES THE CUT-OUT WHO HIRED 'IM
THEN I'LL TELL THE CUT-OUT HIS **NECK** WON'T GET BROKEN IF **HE** NAMES WHOEVER **BOUGHT** THE CONTRACT —THAT'S REASONABLE ISN'T IT, WILLIE?
ALMOST CHRISTIAN, DAVE
BUT THERE YOU **STOP** AND YOU TELL **ME**, SO I CAN GET IT HANDLED OFFICIALLY
I DON'T OFTEN CALL IN FAVOURS, BUT I'M DOING IT NOW
10127

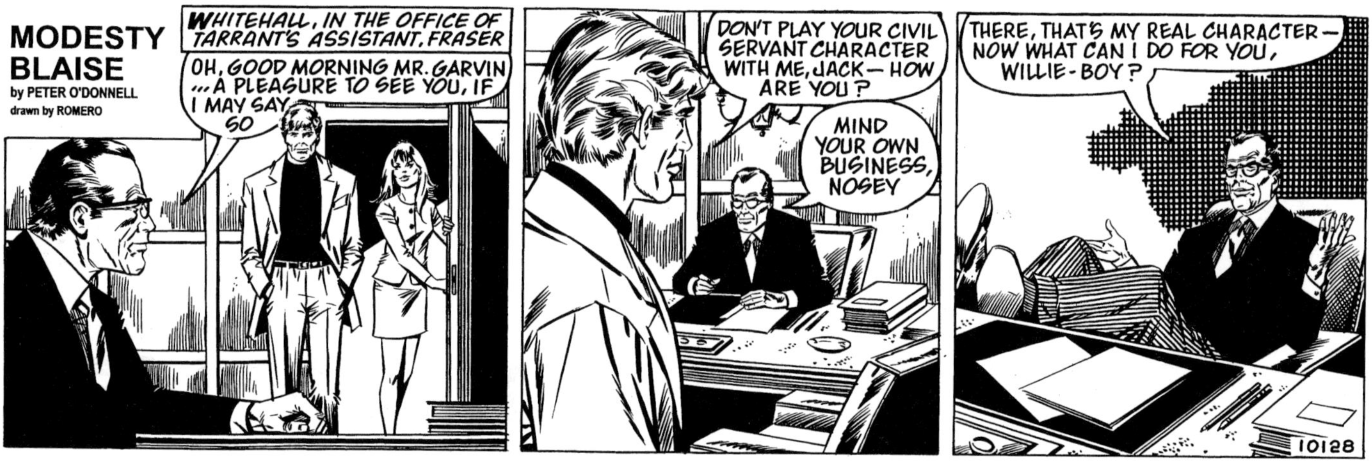
MODESTY BLAISE
by PETER O'DONNELL
drawn by ROMERO
WHITEHALL, IN THE OFFICE OF TARRANT'S ASSISTANT, FRASER
OH, GOOD MORNING MR. GARVIN ... A PLEASURE TO SEE YOU, IF I MAY SAY SO
DON'T PLAY YOUR CIVIL SERVANT CHARACTER WITH ME, JACK— HOW ARE YOU?
MIND YOUR OWN BUSINESS, NOSEY
THERE, THAT'S MY REAL CHARACTER— NOW WHAT CAN I DO FOR YOU, WILLIE-BOY?
10128

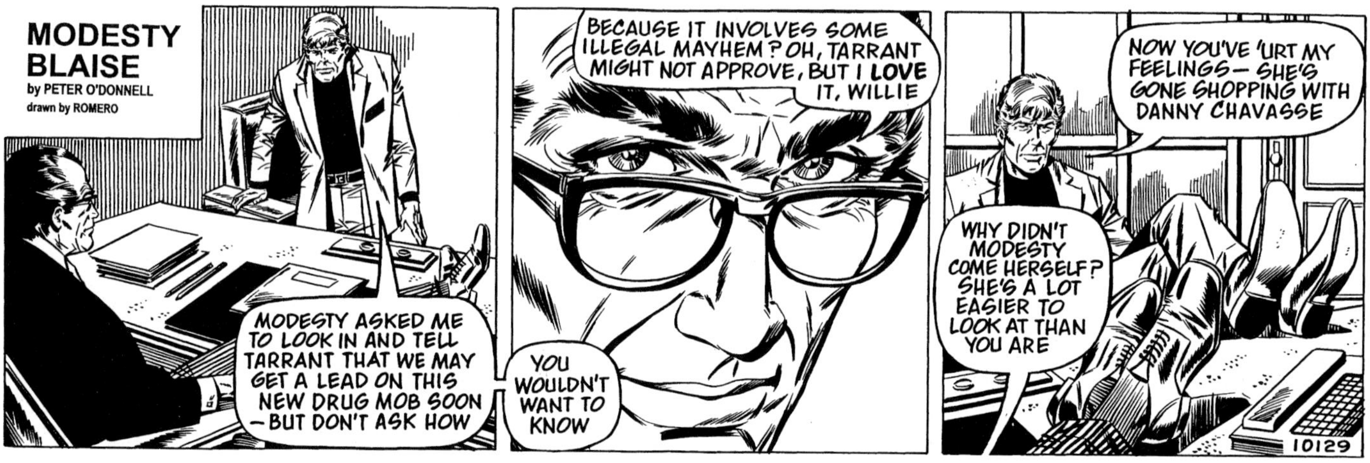
MODESTY BLAISE
by PETER O'DONNELL
drawn by ROMERO
MODESTY ASKED ME TO LOOK IN AND TELL TARRANT THAT WE MAY GET A LEAD ON THIS NEW DRUG MOB SOON —BUT DON'T ASK HOW
YOU WOULDN'T WANT TO KNOW
BECAUSE IT INVOLVES SOME ILLEGAL MAYHEM? OH, TARRANT MIGHT NOT APPROVE, BUT I **LOVE** IT, WILLIE
WHY DIDN'T MODESTY COME HERSELF? SHE'S A LOT EASIER TO LOOK AT THAN YOU ARE
NOW YOU'VE 'URT MY FEELINGS— SHE'S GONE SHOPPING WITH DANNY CHAVASSE
10129

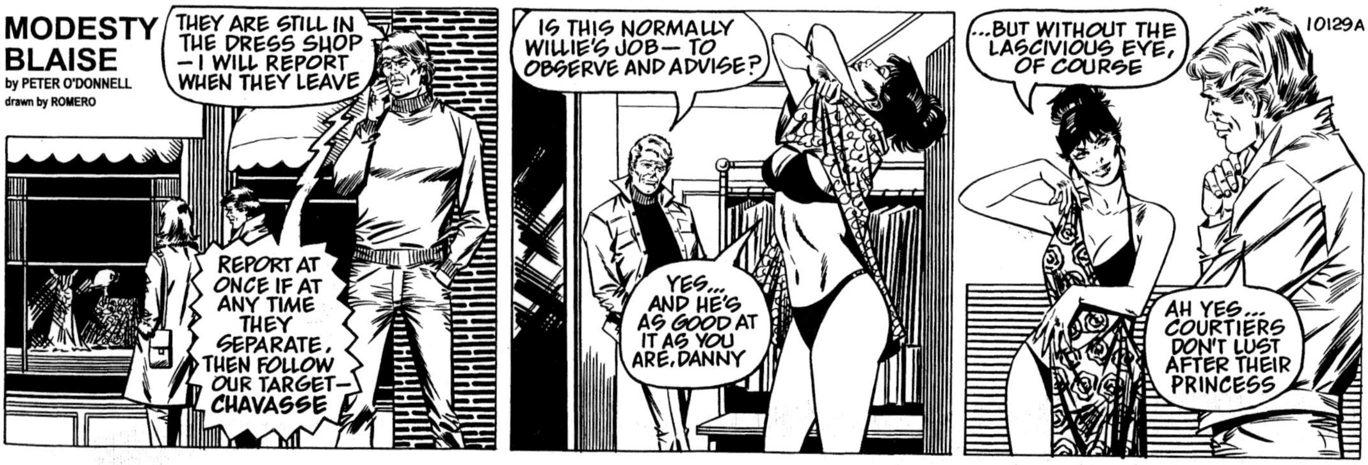
MODESTY BLAISE
by PETER O'DONNELL
drawn by ROMERO
THEY ARE STILL IN THE DRESS SHOP —I WILL REPORT WHEN THEY LEAVE
REPORT AT ONCE IF AT ANY TIME THEY SEPARATE, THEN FOLLOW OUR TARGET— **CHAVASSE**
IS THIS NORMALLY WILLIE'S JOB— TO OBSERVE AND ADVISE?
YES... AND HE'S AS GOOD AT IT AS YOU ARE, DANNY
10129A
...BUT WITHOUT THE LASCIVIOUS EYE, OF COURSE
AH YES... COURTIERS DON'T LUST AFTER THEIR PRINCESS

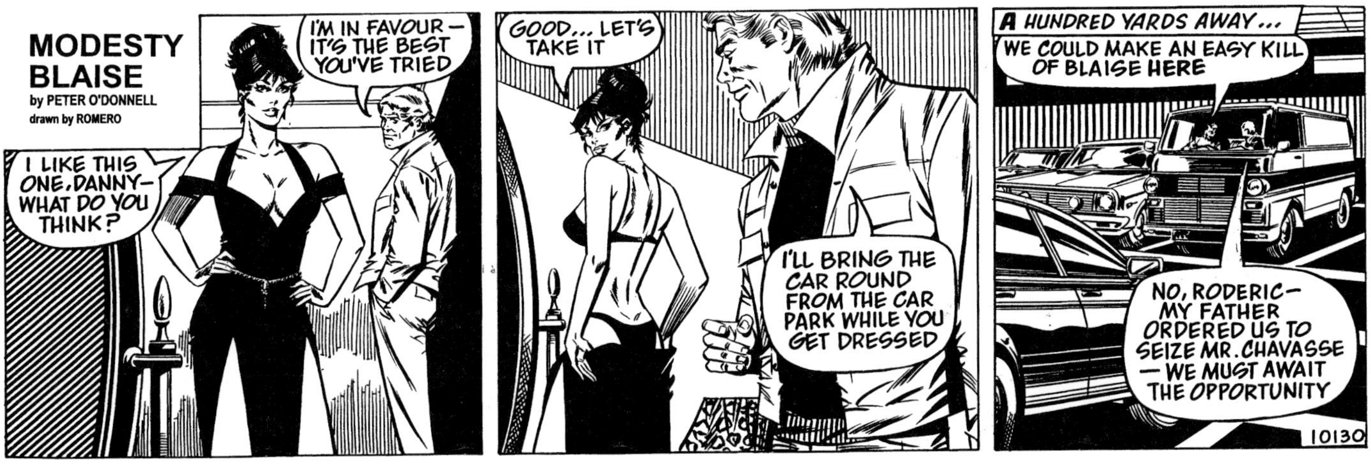
MODESTY BLAISE
by PETER O'DONNELL
drawn by ROMERO
I LIKE THIS ONE, DANNY— WHAT DO YOU THINK?
I'M IN FAVOUR— IT'S THE BEST YOU'VE TRIED
GOOD... LET'S TAKE IT
I'LL BRING THE CAR ROUND FROM THE CAR PARK WHILE YOU GET DRESSED
A HUNDRED YARDS AWAY...
WE COULD MAKE AN EASY KILL OF BLAISE HERE
NO, RODERIC— MY FATHER ORDERED US TO SEIZE MR. CHAVASSE —WE MUST AWAIT THE OPPORTUNITY
10130

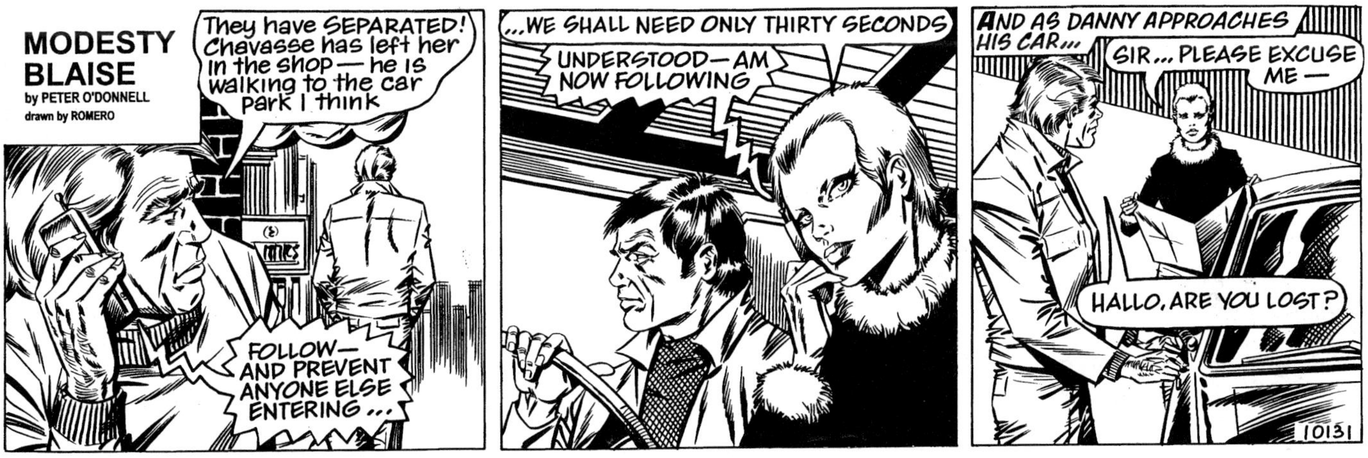
MODESTY BLAISE
by PETER O'DONNELL
drawn by ROMERO
They have SEPARATED! Chavasse has left her in the shop — he is walking to the car park I think
FOLLOW— AND PREVENT ANYONE ELSE ENTERING...
...WE SHALL NEED ONLY THIRTY SECONDS
UNDERSTOOD—AM NOW FOLLOWING
AND AS DANNY APPROACHES HIS CAR...
SIR... PLEASE EXCUSE ME —
HALLO, ARE YOU LOST?
10131

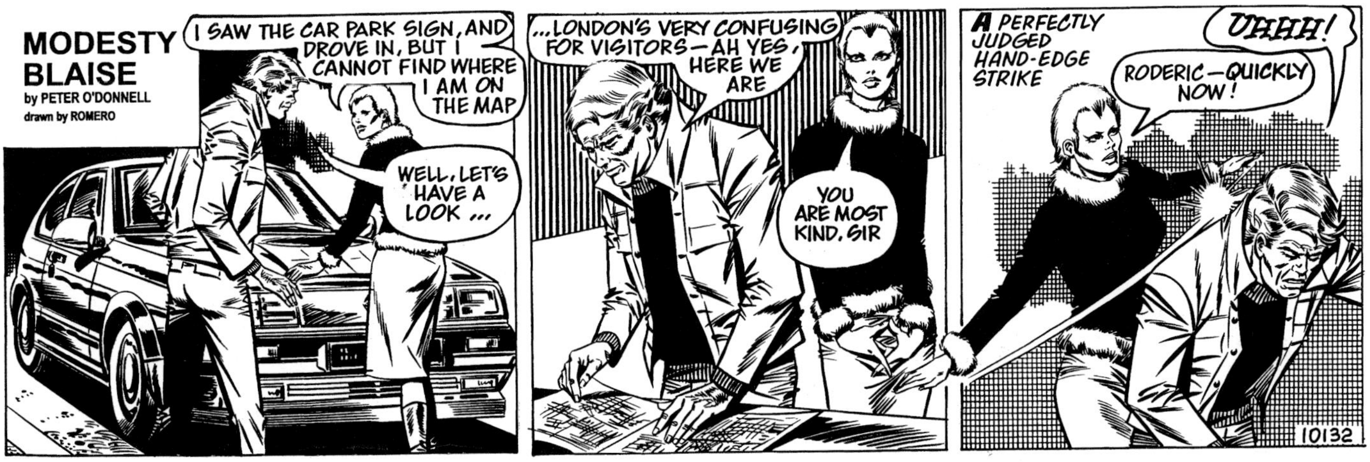
MODESTY BLAISE
by PETER O'DONNELL
drawn by ROMERO
I SAW THE CAR PARK SIGN, AND DROVE IN, BUT I CANNOT FIND WHERE I AM ON THE MAP
WELL, LET'S HAVE A LOOK...
...LONDON'S VERY CONFUSING FOR VISITORS—AH YES, HERE WE ARE
YOU ARE MOST KIND, SIR
A PERFECTLY JUDGED HAND-EDGE STRIKE
UHHH!
RODERIC—QUICKLY NOW!
10132

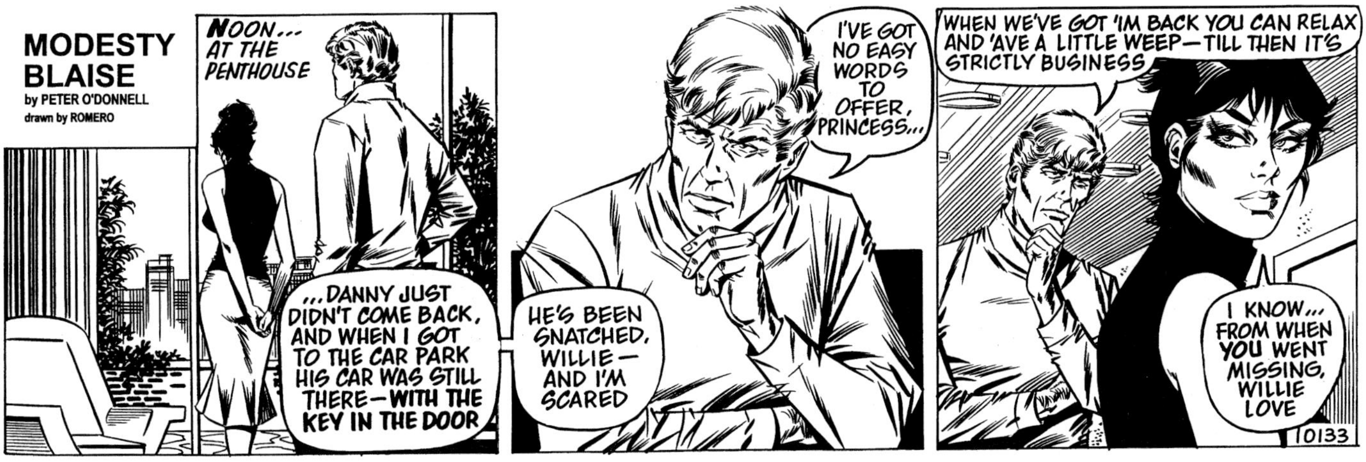
MODESTY BLAISE
by PETER O'DONNELL
drawn by ROMERO
NOON... AT THE PENTHOUSE
...DANNY JUST DIDN'T COME BACK, AND WHEN I GOT TO THE CAR PARK HIS CAR WAS STILL THERE—WITH THE KEY IN THE DOOR
HE'S BEEN SNATCHED, WILLIE— AND I'M SCARED
I'VE GOT NO EASY WORDS TO OFFER, PRINCESS...
WHEN WE'VE GOT 'IM BACK YOU CAN RELAX AND 'AVE A LITTLE WEEP—TILL THEN IT'S STRICTLY BUSINESS
I KNOW... FROM WHEN YOU WENT MISSING, WILLIE LOVE
10133

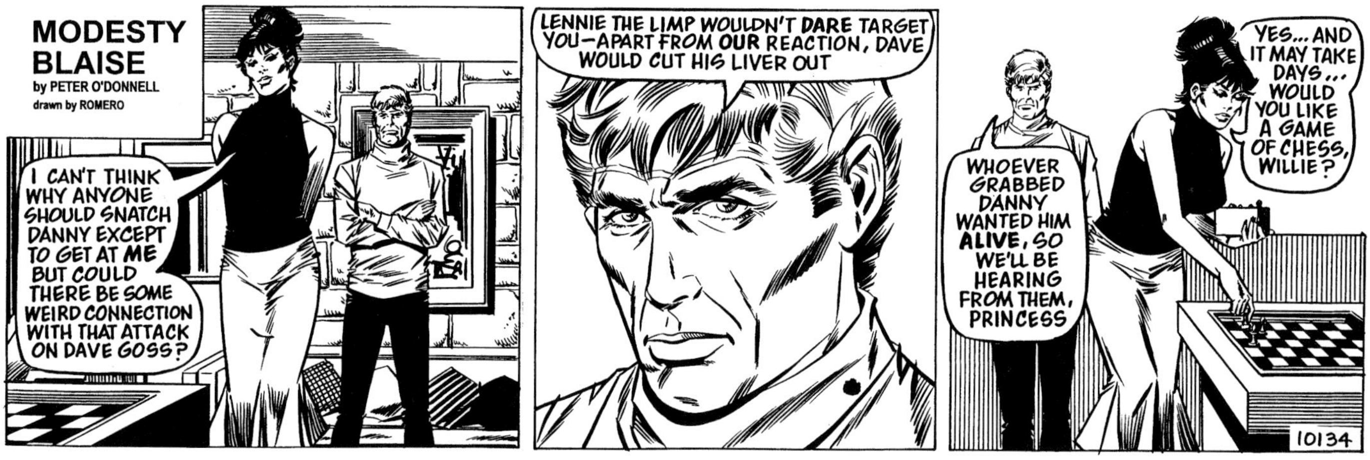
MODESTY BLAISE
by PETER O'DONNELL
drawn by ROMERO
I CAN'T THINK WHY ANYONE SHOULD SNATCH DANNY EXCEPT TO GET AT ME BUT COULD THERE BE SOME WEIRD CONNECTION WITH THAT ATTACK ON DAVE GOSS?
LENNIE THE LIMP WOULDN'T DARE TARGET YOU—APART FROM OUR REACTION, DAVE WOULD CUT HIS LIVER OUT
WHOEVER GRABBED DANNY WANTED HIM ALIVE, SO WE'LL BE HEARING FROM THEM, PRINCESS
YES... AND IT MAY TAKE DAYS... WOULD YOU LIKE A GAME OF CHESS, WILLIE?
10134

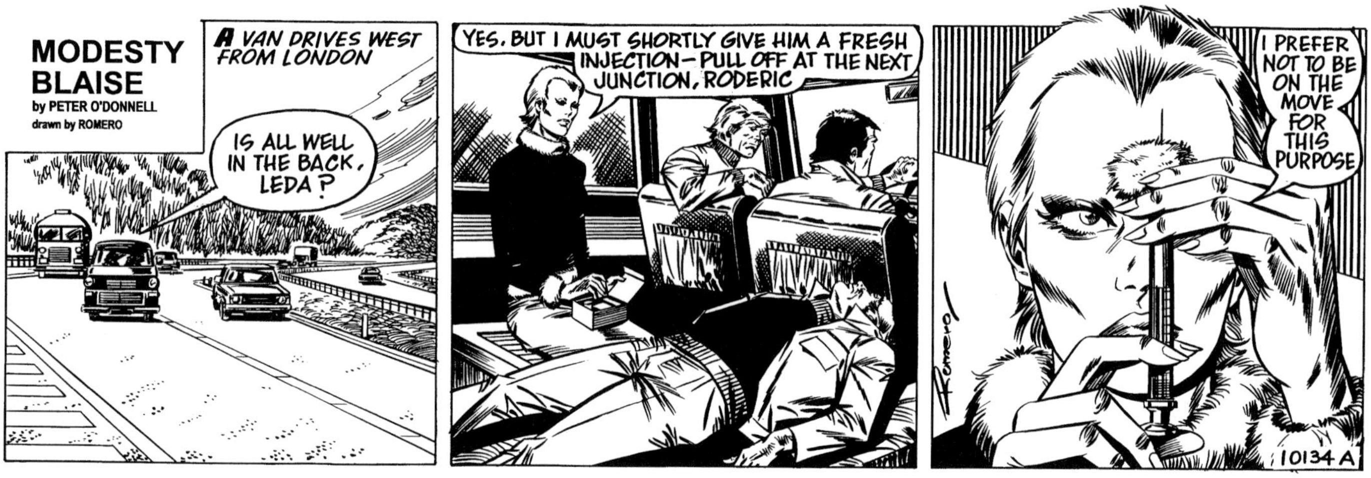
MODESTY BLAISE
by PETER O'DONNELL
drawn by ROMERO
A VAN DRIVES WEST FROM LONDON
IS ALL WELL IN THE BACK, LEDA?
YES. BUT I MUST SHORTLY GIVE HIM A FRESH INJECTION—PULL OFF AT THE NEXT JUNCTION, RODERIC
I PREFER NOT TO BE ON THE MOVE FOR THIS PURPOSE
Romero
10134 A

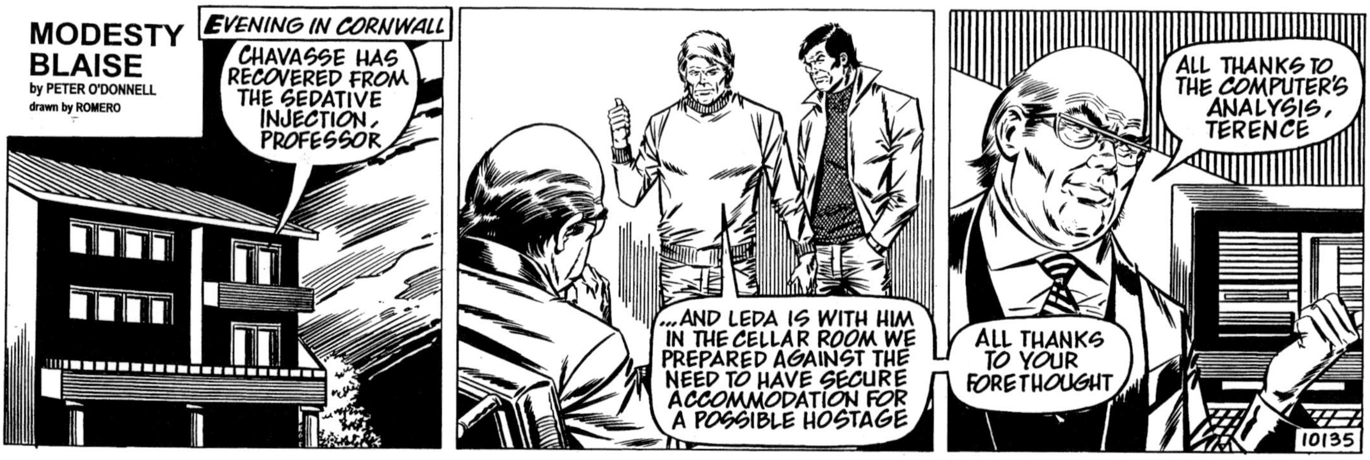
MODESTY BLAISE
by PETER O'DONNELL
drawn by ROMERO
EVENING IN CORNWALL
CHAVASSE HAS RECOVERED FROM THE SEDATIVE INJECTION, PROFESSOR
...AND LEDA IS WITH HIM IN THE CELLAR ROOM WE PREPARED AGAINST THE NEED TO HAVE SECURE ACCOMMODATION FOR A POSSIBLE HOSTAGE
ALL THANKS TO YOUR FORETHOUGHT
ALL THANKS TO THE COMPUTER'S ANALYSIS, TERENCE
10135

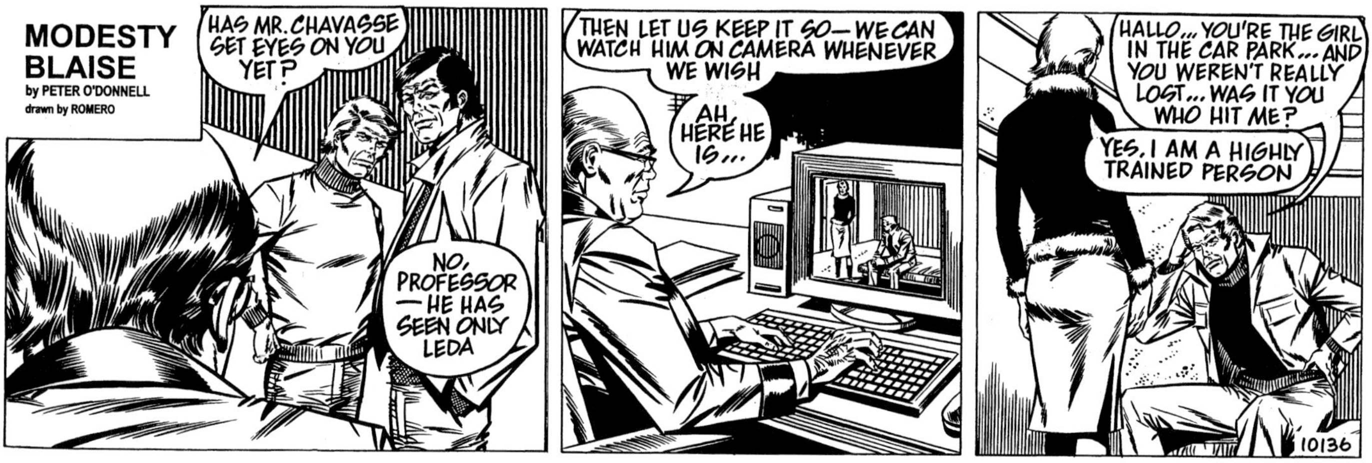
MODESTY BLAISE
by PETER O'DONNELL
drawn by ROMERO
HAS MR. CHAVASSE SET EYES ON YOU YET?
NO, PROFESSOR—HE HAS SEEN ONLY LEDA
THEN LET US KEEP IT SO—WE CAN WATCH HIM ON CAMERA WHENEVER WE WISH
AH, HERE HE IS...
HALLO... YOU'RE THE GIRL IN THE CAR PARK... AND YOU WEREN'T REALLY LOST... WAS IT YOU WHO HIT ME?
YES. I AM A HIGHLY TRAINED PERSON
10136

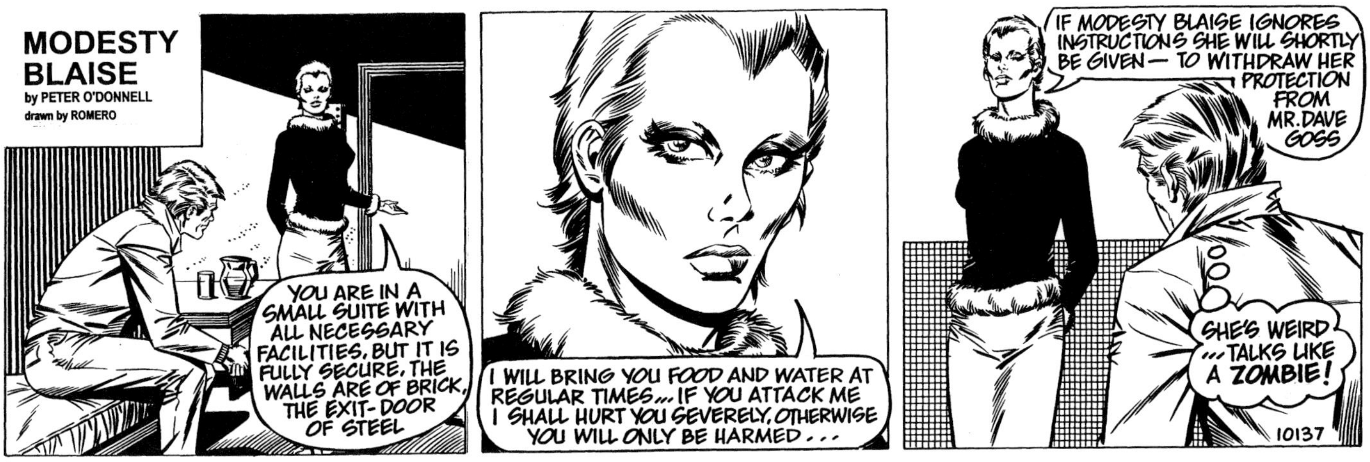
MODESTY BLAISE
by PETER O'DONNELL
drawn by ROMERO
YOU ARE IN A SMALL SUITE WITH ALL NECESSARY FACILITIES, BUT IT IS FULLY SECURE. THE WALLS ARE OF BRICK, THE EXIT-DOOR OF STEEL
I WILL BRING YOU FOOD AND WATER AT REGULAR TIMES... IF YOU ATTACK ME I SHALL HURT YOU SEVERELY. OTHERWISE YOU WILL ONLY BE HARMED . . .
IF MODESTY BLAISE IGNORES INSTRUCTIONS SHE WILL SHORTLY BE GIVEN — TO WITHDRAW HER PROTECTION FROM MR. DAVE GOSS
SHE'S WEIRD ... TALKS LIKE A ZOMBIE!
10137

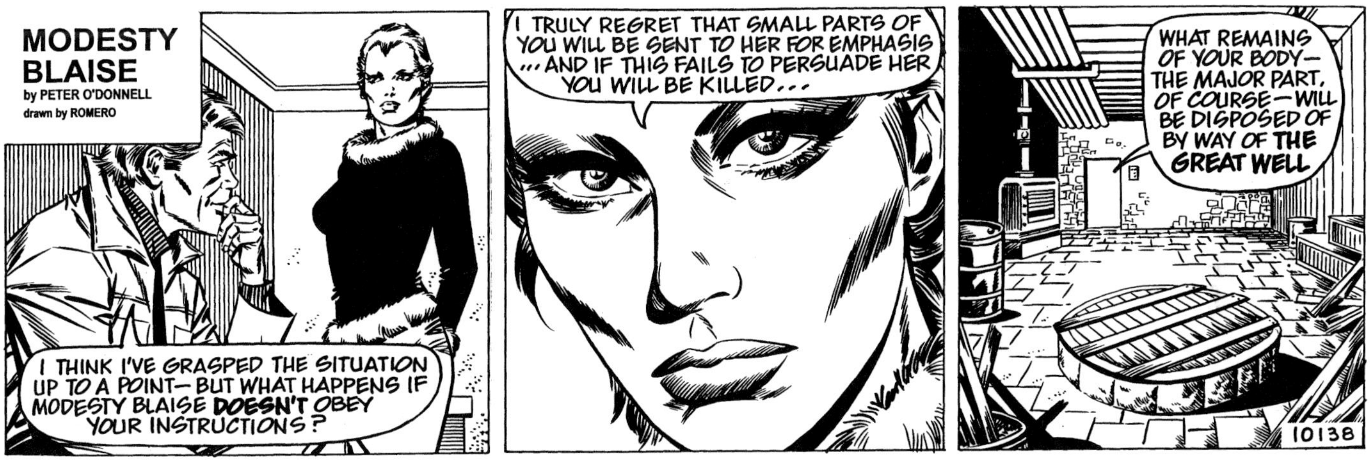
MODESTY BLAISE
by PETER O'DONNELL
drawn by ROMERO
I THINK I'VE GRASPED THE SITUATION UP TO A POINT— BUT WHAT HAPPENS IF MODESTY BLAISE DOESN'T OBEY YOUR INSTRUCTIONS?
I TRULY REGRET THAT SMALL PARTS OF YOU WILL BE SENT TO HER FOR EMPHASIS ... AND IF THIS FAILS TO PERSUADE HER YOU WILL BE KILLED . . .
WHAT REMAINS OF YOUR BODY— THE MAJOR PART, OF COURSE— WILL BE DISPOSED OF BY WAY OF THE GREAT WELL
10138

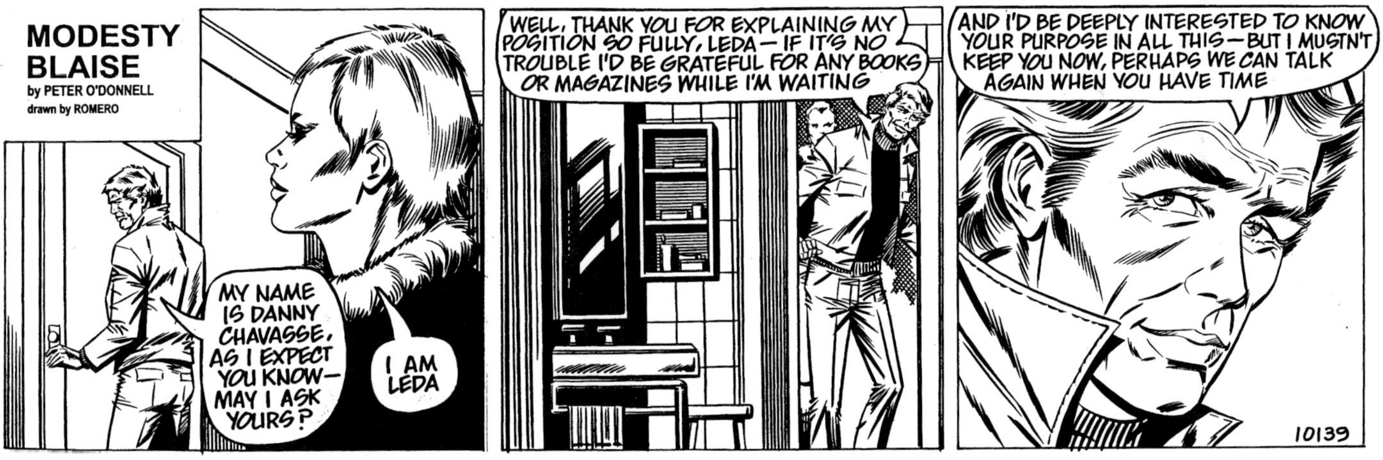
MODESTY BLAISE
by PETER O'DONNELL
drawn by ROMERO
MY NAME IS DANNY CHAVASSE, AS I EXPECT YOU KNOW— MAY I ASK YOURS?
I AM LEDA
WELL, THANK YOU FOR EXPLAINING MY POSITION SO FULLY, LEDA— IF IT'S NO TROUBLE I'D BE GRATEFUL FOR ANY BOOKS OR MAGAZINES WHILE I'M WAITING
AND I'D BE DEEPLY INTERESTED TO KNOW YOUR PURPOSE IN ALL THIS— BUT I MUSTN'T KEEP YOU NOW. PERHAPS WE CAN TALK AGAIN WHEN YOU HAVE TIME
10139

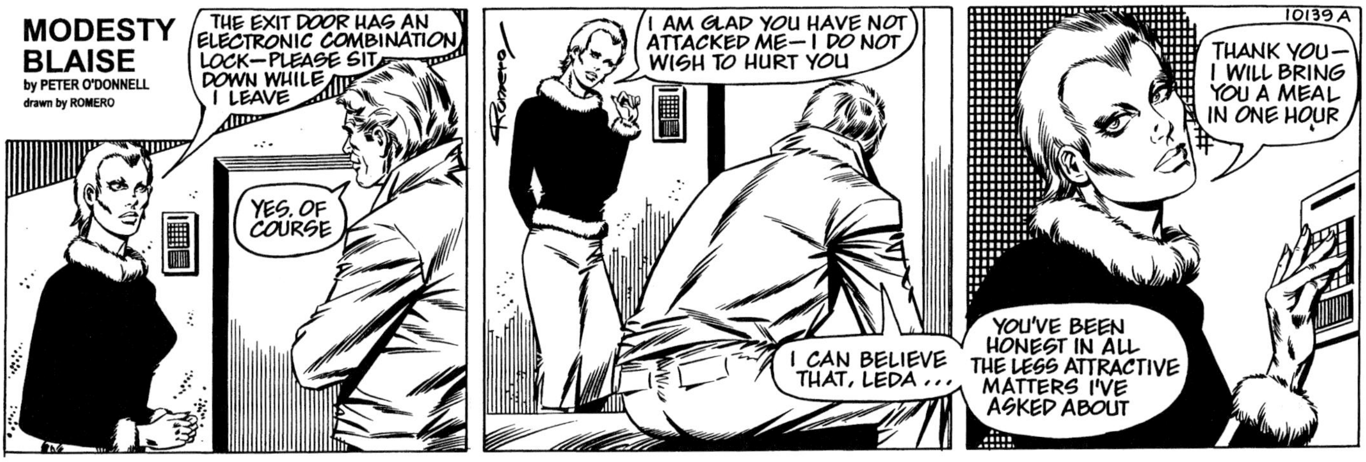
MODESTY BLAISE
by PETER O'DONNELL
drawn by ROMERO
THE EXIT DOOR HAS AN ELECTRONIC COMBINATION LOCK— PLEASE SIT DOWN WHILE I LEAVE
YES, OF COURSE
I AM GLAD YOU HAVE NOT ATTACKED ME— I DO NOT WISH TO HURT YOU
I CAN BELIEVE THAT, LEDA . . .
YOU'VE BEEN HONEST IN ALL THE LESS ATTRACTIVE MATTERS I'VE ASKED ABOUT
THANK YOU— I WILL BRING YOU A MEAL IN ONE HOUR
10139 A

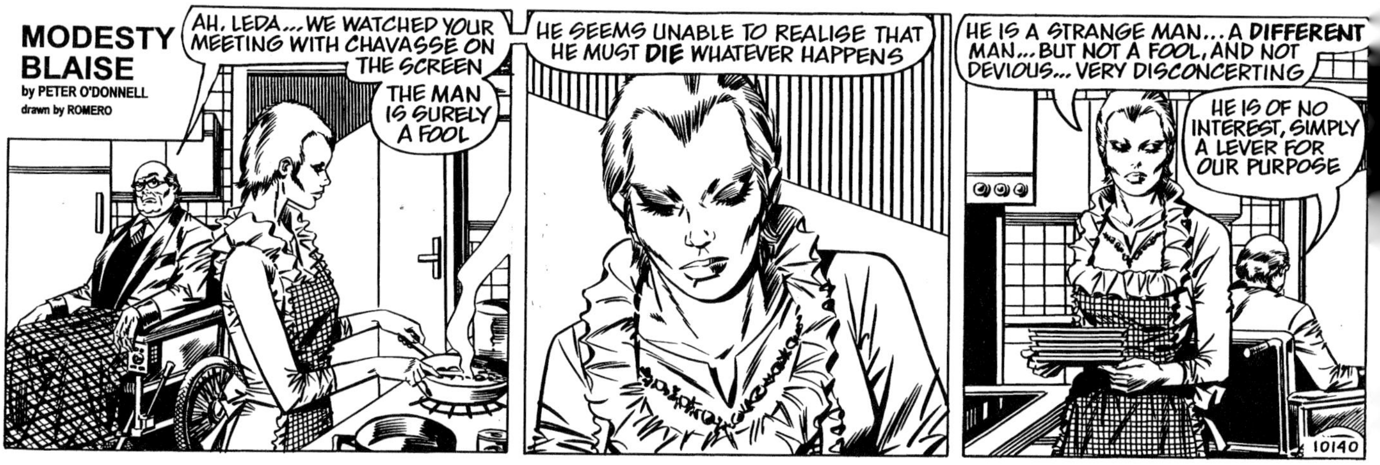
MODESTY BLAISE
by PETER O'DONNELL
drawn by ROMERO
AH, LEDA... WE WATCHED YOUR MEETING WITH CHAVASSE ON THE SCREEN
THE MAN IS SURELY A FOOL
HE SEEMS UNABLE TO REALISE THAT HE MUST DIE WHATEVER HAPPENS
HE IS A STRANGE MAN... A DIFFERENT MAN... BUT NOT A FOOL, AND NOT DEVIOUS... VERY DISCONCERTING
HE IS OF NO INTEREST, SIMPLY A LEVER FOR OUR PURPOSE
10140

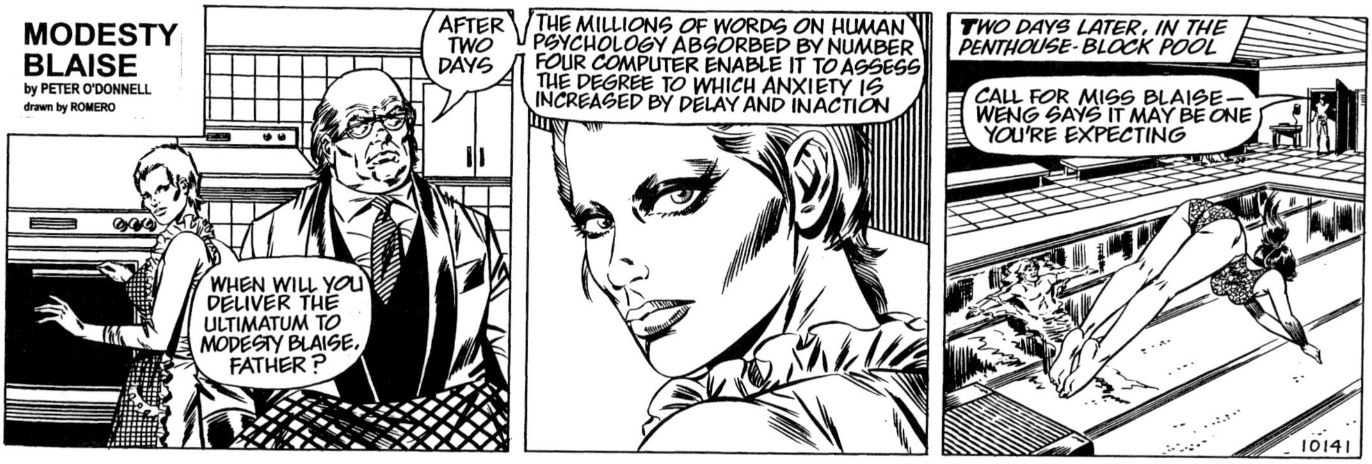
MODESTY BLAISE
by PETER O'DONNELL
drawn by ROMERO
AFTER TWO DAYS
WHEN WILL YOU DELIVER THE ULTIMATUM TO MODESTY BLAISE, FATHER?
THE MILLIONS OF WORDS ON HUMAN PSYCHOLOGY ABSORBED BY NUMBER FOUR COMPUTER ENABLE IT TO ASSESS THE DEGREE TO WHICH ANXIETY IS INCREASED BY DELAY AND INACTION
TWO DAYS LATER, IN THE PENTHOUSE-BLOCK POOL
CALL FOR MISS BLAISE— WENG SAYS IT MAY BE ONE YOU'RE EXPECTING
10141

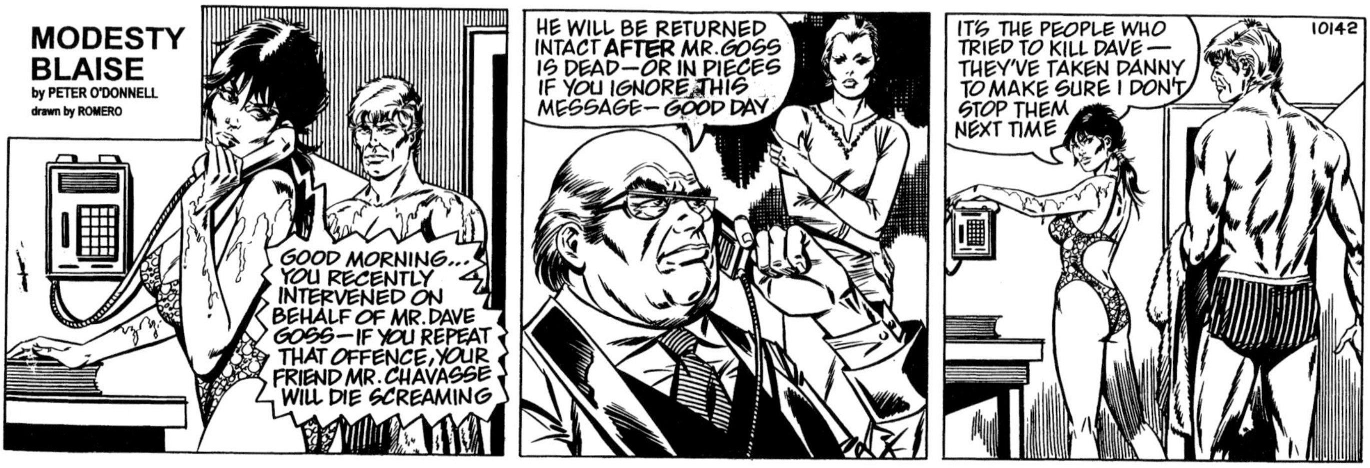
MODESTY BLAISE
by PETER O'DONNELL
drawn by ROMERO
GOOD MORNING... YOU RECENTLY INTERVENED ON BEHALF OF MR. DAVE GOSS—IF YOU REPEAT THAT OFFENCE, YOUR FRIEND MR. CHAVASSE WILL DIE SCREAMING
HE WILL BE RETURNED INTACT AFTER MR. GOSS IS DEAD—OR IN PIECES IF YOU IGNORE THIS MESSAGE—GOOD DAY
10142
IT'S THE PEOPLE WHO TRIED TO KILL DAVE— THEY'VE TAKEN DANNY TO MAKE SURE I DON'T STOP THEM NEXT TIME

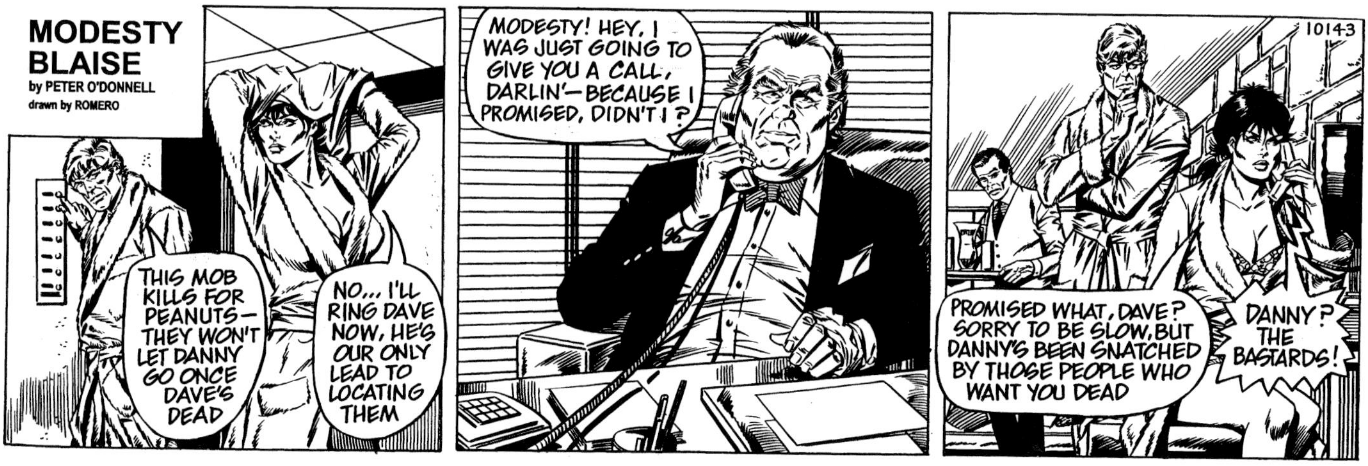
MODESTY BLAISE
by PETER O'DONNELL
drawn by ROMERO
THIS MOB KILLS FOR PEANUTS— THEY WON'T LET DANNY GO ONCE DAVE'S DEAD
NO... I'LL RING DAVE NOW, HE'S OUR ONLY LEAD TO LOCATING THEM
MODESTY! HEY, I WAS JUST GOING TO GIVE YOU A CALL, DARLIN'—BECAUSE I PROMISED, DIDN'T I?
10143
PROMISED WHAT, DAVE? SORRY TO BE SLOW, BUT DANNY'S BEEN SNATCHED BY THOSE PEOPLE WHO WANT YOU DEAD
DANNY? THE BASTARDS!

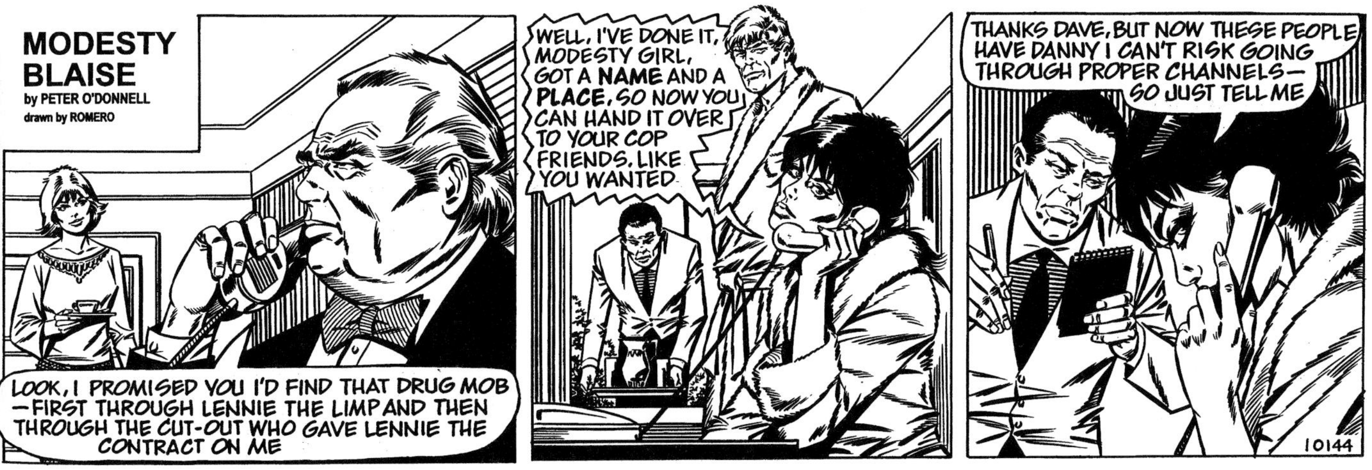
MODESTY BLAISE
by PETER O'DONNELL
drawn by ROMERO
LOOK, I PROMISED YOU I'D FIND THAT DRUG MOB —FIRST THROUGH LENNIE THE LIMP AND THEN THROUGH THE CUT-OUT WHO GAVE LENNIE THE CONTRACT ON ME
WELL, I'VE DONE IT, MODESTY GIRL, GOT A NAME AND A PLACE, SO NOW YOU CAN HAND IT OVER TO YOUR COP FRIENDS, LIKE YOU WANTED
THANKS DAVE, BUT NOW THESE PEOPLE HAVE DANNY I CAN'T RISK GOING THROUGH PROPER CHANNELS— SO JUST TELL ME
10144

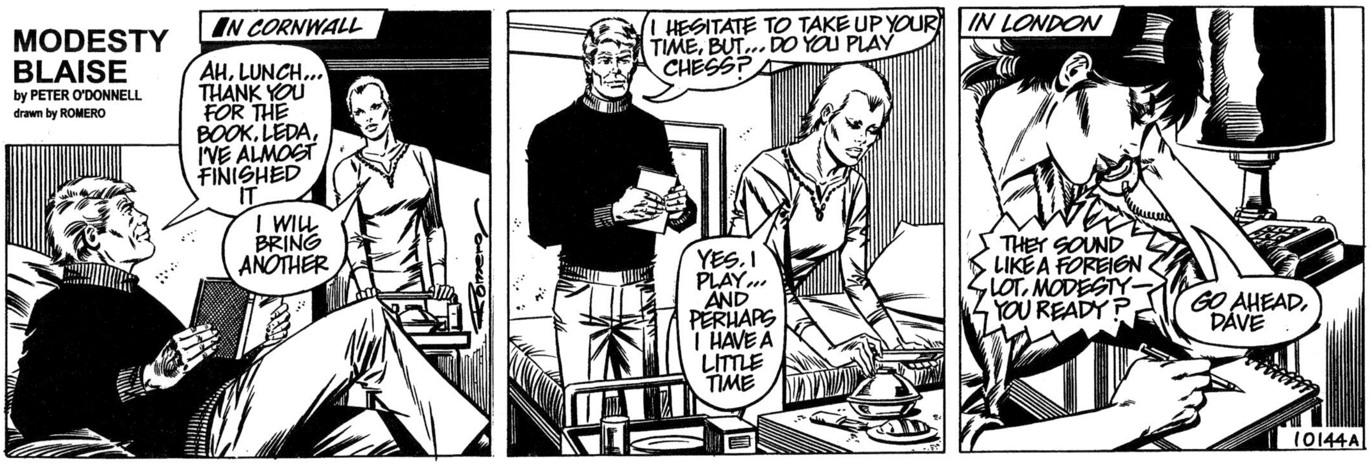
MODESTY BLAISE
by PETER O'DONNELL
drawn by ROMERO
IN CORNWALL
AH, LUNCH... THANK YOU FOR THE BOOK, LEDA, I'VE ALMOST FINISHED IT
I WILL BRING ANOTHER
I HESITATE TO TAKE UP YOUR TIME, BUT... DO YOU PLAY CHESS?
YES, I PLAY... AND PERHAPS I HAVE A LITTLE TIME
IN LONDON
THEY SOUND LIKE A FOREIGN LOT, MODESTY— YOU READY?
GO AHEAD, DAVE
10144A

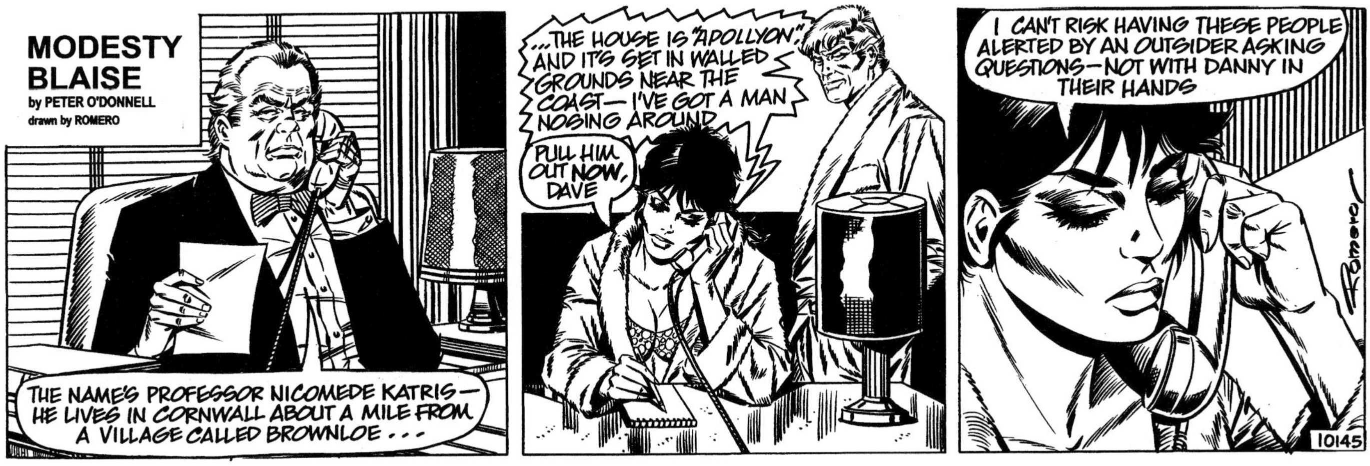
MODESTY BLAISE
by PETER O'DONNELL
drawn by ROMERO
THE NAME'S PROFESSOR NICOMEDE KATRIS— HE LIVES IN CORNWALL ABOUT A MILE FROM A VILLAGE CALLED BROWNLOE . . .
...THE HOUSE IS "APOLLYON", AND IT'S SET IN WALLED GROUNDS NEAR THE COAST— I'VE GOT A MAN NOSING AROUND
PULL HIM OUT NOW, DAVE
I CAN'T RISK HAVING THESE PEOPLE ALERTED BY AN OUTSIDER ASKING QUESTIONS—NOT WITH DANNY IN THEIR HANDS
10145

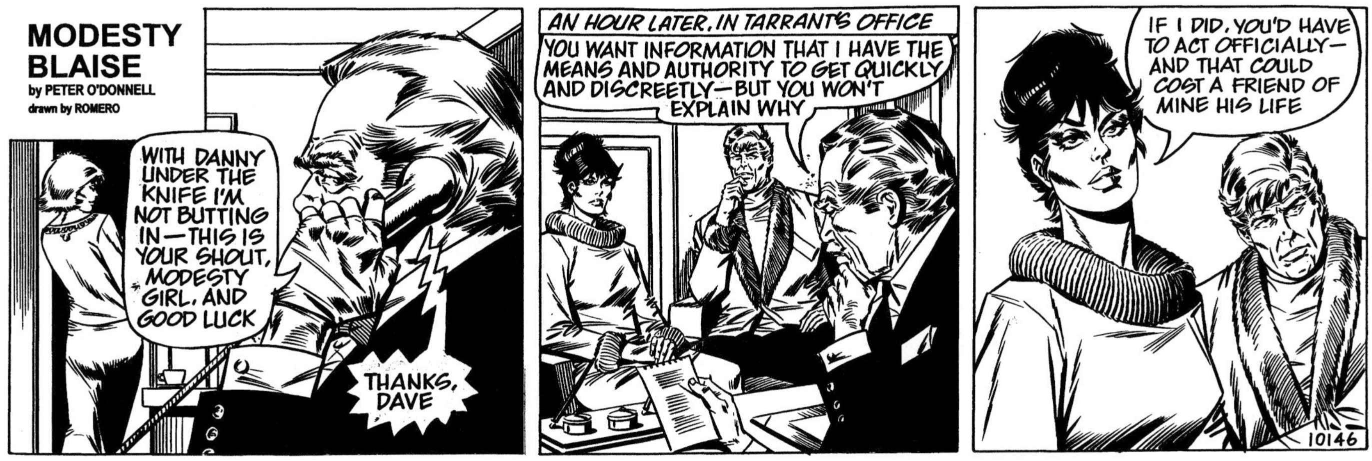
MODESTY BLAISE
by PETER O'DONNELL
drawn by ROMERO
WITH DANNY UNDER THE KNIFE I'M NOT BUTTING IN—THIS IS YOUR SHOUT, MODESTY GIRL, AND GOOD LUCK
THANKS, DAVE
AN HOUR LATER, IN TARRANT'S OFFICE
YOU WANT INFORMATION THAT I HAVE THE MEANS AND AUTHORITY TO GET QUICKLY AND DISCREETLY—BUT YOU WON'T EXPLAIN WHY
IF I DID, YOU'D HAVE TO ACT OFFICIALLY— AND THAT COULD COST A FRIEND OF MINE HIS LIFE
10146

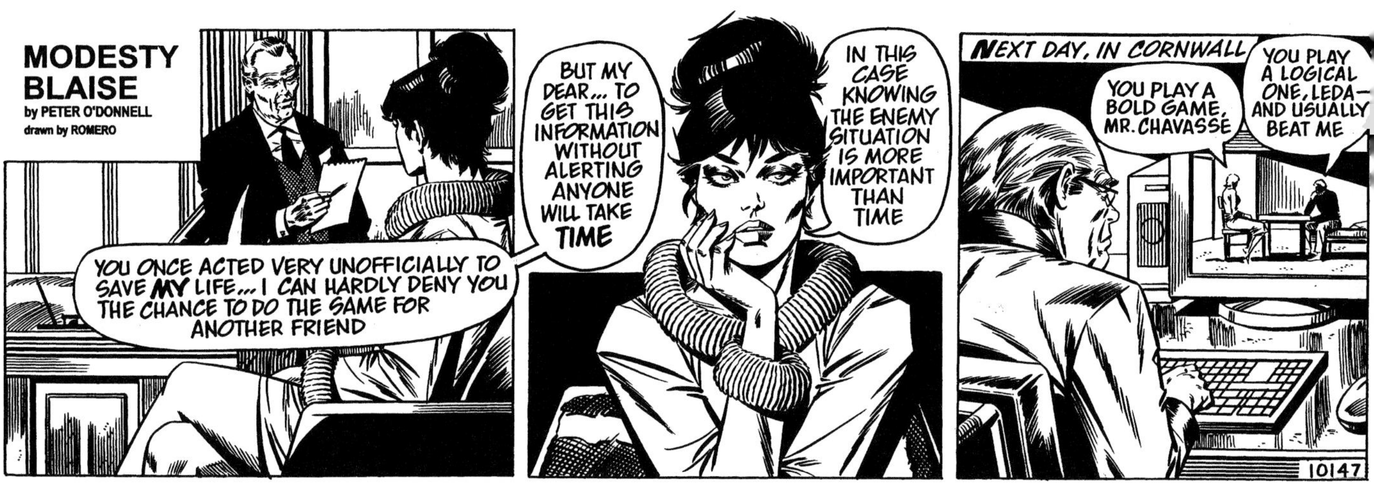
MODESTY BLAISE
by PETER O'DONNELL
drawn by ROMERO
YOU ONCE ACTED VERY UNOFFICIALLY TO SAVE MY LIFE... I CAN HARDLY DENY YOU THE CHANCE TO DO THE SAME FOR ANOTHER FRIEND
BUT MY DEAR... TO GET THIS INFORMATION WITHOUT ALERTING ANYONE WILL TAKE TIME
IN THIS CASE KNOWING THE ENEMY SITUATION IS MORE IMPORTANT THAN TIME
NEXT DAY, IN CORNWALL
YOU PLAY A BOLD GAME, MR. CHAVASSE
YOU PLAY A LOGICAL ONE, LEDA— AND USUALLY BEAT ME
10147

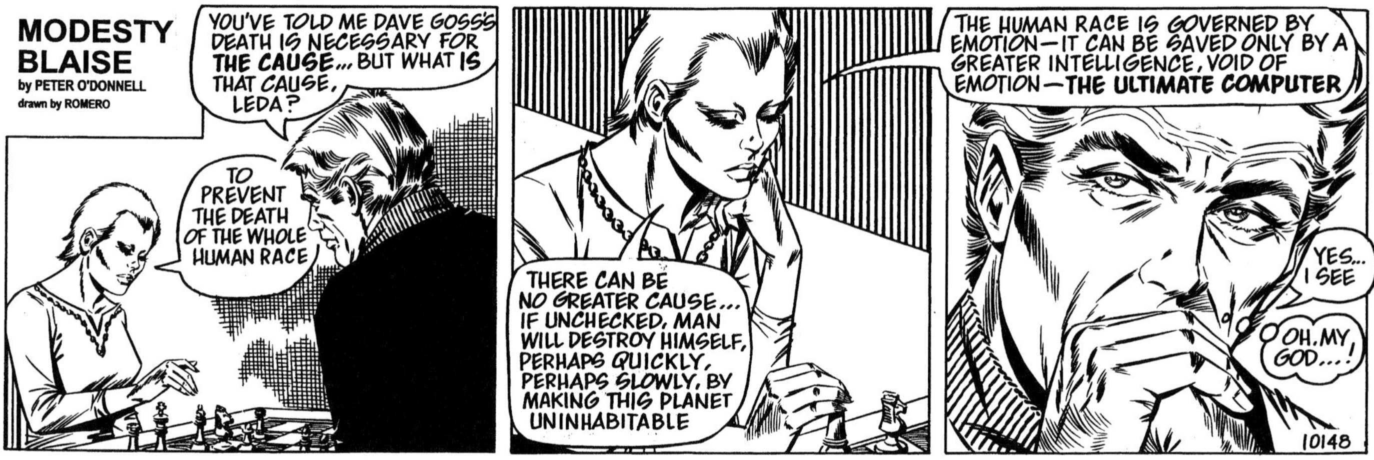
MODESTY BLAISE
by PETER O'DONNELL
drawn by ROMERO
YOU'VE TOLD ME DAVE GOSS'S DEATH IS NECESSARY FOR THE CAUSE... BUT WHAT IS THAT CAUSE, LEDA?
TO PREVENT THE DEATH OF THE WHOLE HUMAN RACE
THERE CAN BE NO GREATER CAUSE... IF UNCHECKED, MAN WILL DESTROY HIMSELF, PERHAPS QUICKLY, PERHAPS SLOWLY, BY MAKING THIS PLANET UNINHABITABLE
THE HUMAN RACE IS GOVERNED BY EMOTION—IT CAN BE SAVED ONLY BY A GREATER INTELLIGENCE, VOID OF EMOTION—THE ULTIMATE COMPUTER
YES... I SEE
OH, MY GOD...!
10148

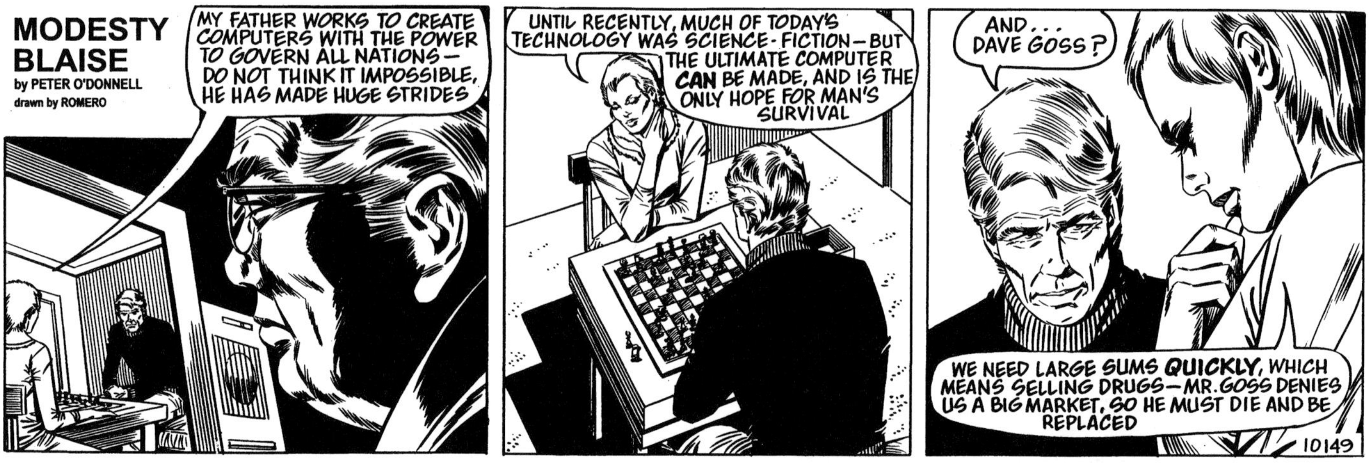
MODESTY BLAISE
by PETER O'DONNELL
drawn by ROMERO
MY FATHER WORKS TO CREATE COMPUTERS WITH THE POWER TO GOVERN ALL NATIONS— DO NOT THINK IT IMPOSSIBLE, HE HAS MADE HUGE STRIDES
UNTIL RECENTLY, MUCH OF TODAY'S TECHNOLOGY WAS SCIENCE-FICTION—BUT THE ULTIMATE COMPUTER CAN BE MADE, AND IS THE ONLY HOPE FOR MAN'S SURVIVAL
AND... DAVE GOSS?
WE NEED LARGE SUMS QUICKLY, WHICH MEANS SELLING DRUGS—MR. GOSS DENIES US A BIG MARKET, SO HE MUST DIE AND BE REPLACED
10149

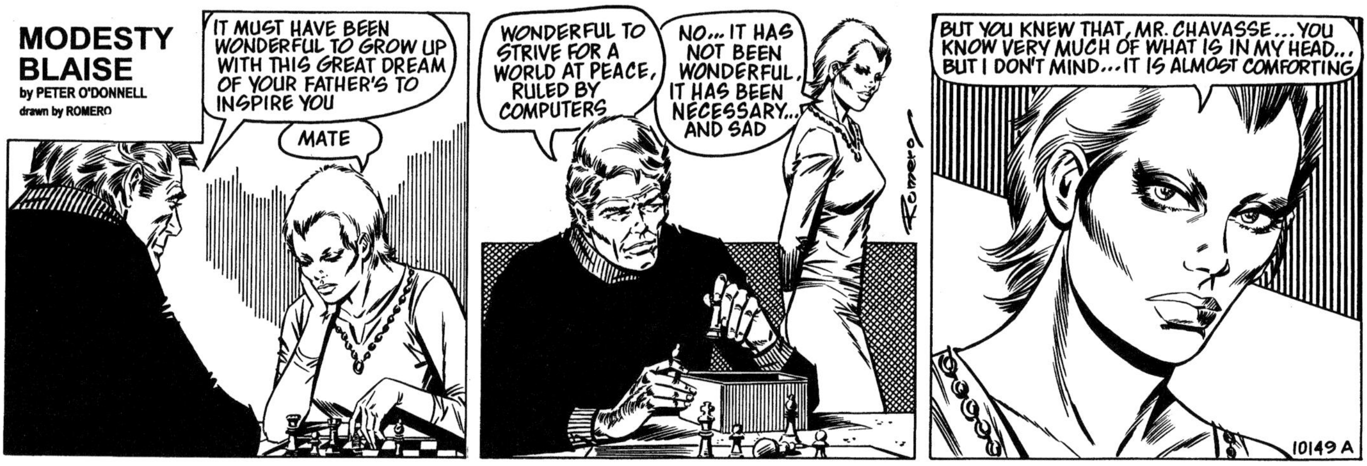
MODESTY BLAISE
by PETER O'DONNELL
drawn by ROMERO
IT MUST HAVE BEEN WONDERFUL TO GROW UP WITH THIS GREAT DREAM OF YOUR FATHER'S TO INSPIRE YOU
MATE
WONDERFUL TO STRIVE FOR A WORLD AT PEACE, RULED BY COMPUTERS
NO... IT HAS NOT BEEN WONDERFUL, IT HAS BEEN NECESSARY... AND SAD
Romero
BUT YOU KNEW THAT, MR. CHAVASSE... YOU KNOW VERY MUCH OF WHAT IS IN MY HEAD... BUT I DON'T MIND... IT IS ALMOST COMFORTING
10149 A

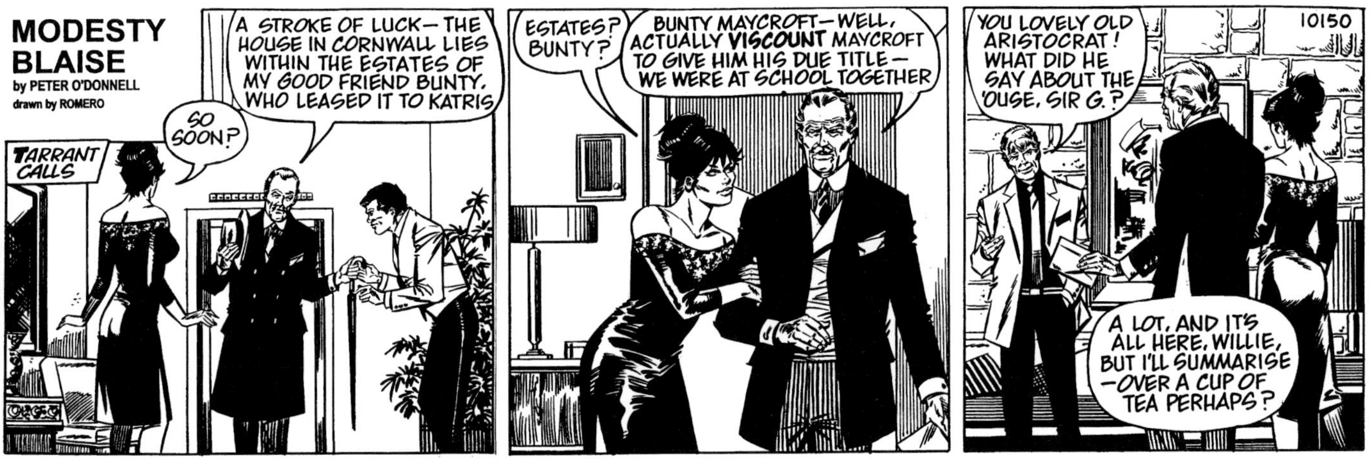
MODESTY BLAISE
by PETER O'DONNELL
drawn by ROMERO
TARRANT CALLS
A STROKE OF LUCK—THE HOUSE IN CORNWALL LIES WITHIN THE ESTATES OF MY GOOD FRIEND BUNTY, WHO LEASED IT TO KATRIS
SO SOON?
ESTATES? BUNTY?
BUNTY MAYCROFT—WELL, ACTUALLY **VISCOUNT** MAYCROFT TO GIVE HIM HIS DUE TITLE—WE WERE AT SCHOOL TOGETHER
10150
YOU LOVELY OLD ARISTOCRAT! WHAT DID HE SAY ABOUT THE 'OUSE, SIR G.?
A LOT, AND IT'S ALL HERE, WILLIE, BUT I'LL SUMMARISE—OVER A CUP OF TEA PERHAPS?

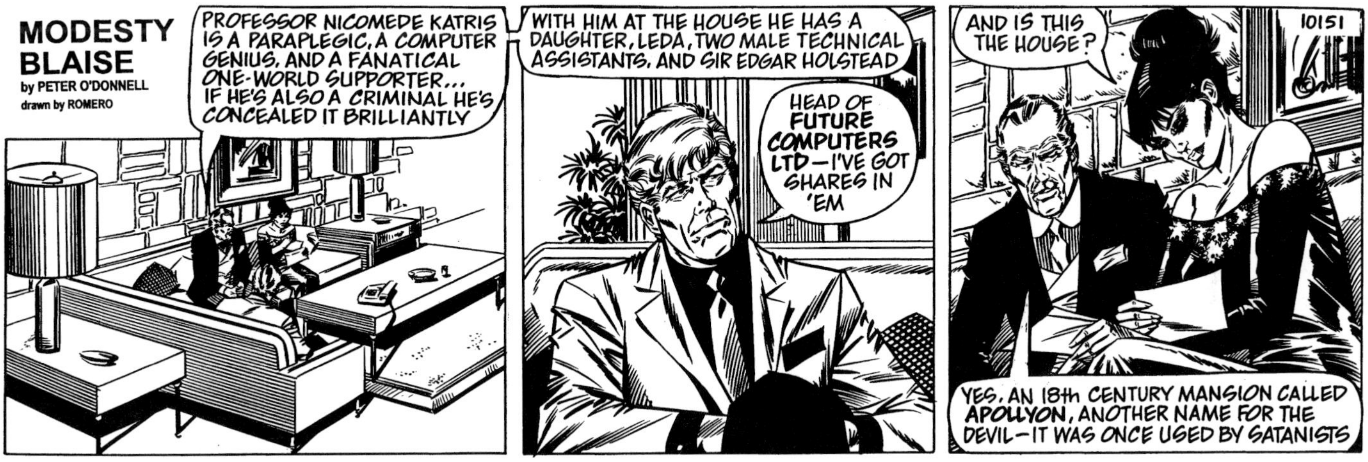
MODESTY BLAISE
by PETER O'DONNELL
drawn by ROMERO
PROFESSOR NICOMEDE KATRIS IS A PARAPLEGIC, A COMPUTER GENIUS, AND A FANATICAL ONE-WORLD SUPPORTER... IF HE'S ALSO A CRIMINAL HE'S CONCEALED IT BRILLIANTLY
WITH HIM AT THE HOUSE HE HAS A DAUGHTER, LEDA, TWO MALE TECHNICAL ASSISTANTS, AND SIR EDGAR HOLSTEAD
HEAD OF **FUTURE COMPUTERS LTD**—I'VE GOT SHARES IN 'EM
10151
AND IS THIS THE HOUSE?
YES, AN 18th CENTURY MANSION CALLED **APOLLYON**, ANOTHER NAME FOR THE DEVIL—IT WAS ONCE USED BY SATANISTS

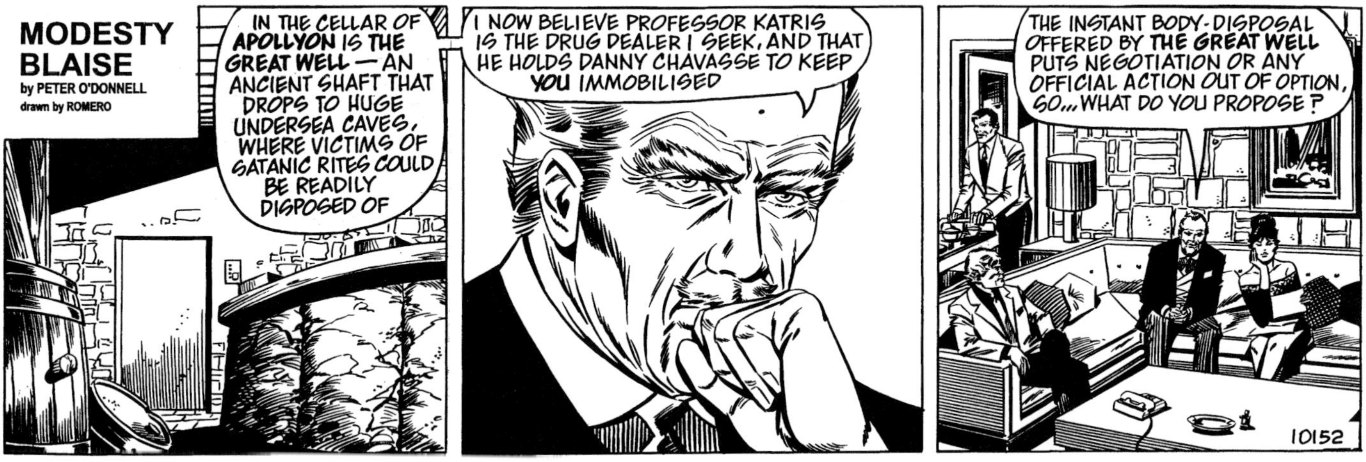
MODESTY BLAISE
by PETER O'DONNELL
drawn by ROMERO
IN THE CELLAR OF **APOLLYON** IS **THE GREAT WELL**—AN ANCIENT SHAFT THAT DROPS TO HUGE UNDERSEA CAVES, WHERE VICTIMS OF SATANIC RITES COULD BE READILY DISPOSED OF
I NOW BELIEVE PROFESSOR KATRIS IS THE DRUG DEALER I SEEK, AND THAT HE HOLDS DANNY CHAVASSE TO KEEP **YOU** IMMOBILISED
THE INSTANT BODY-DISPOSAL OFFERED BY **THE GREAT WELL** PUTS NEGOTIATION OR ANY OFFICIAL ACTION OUT OF OPTION, SO... WHAT DO YOU PROPOSE?
10152

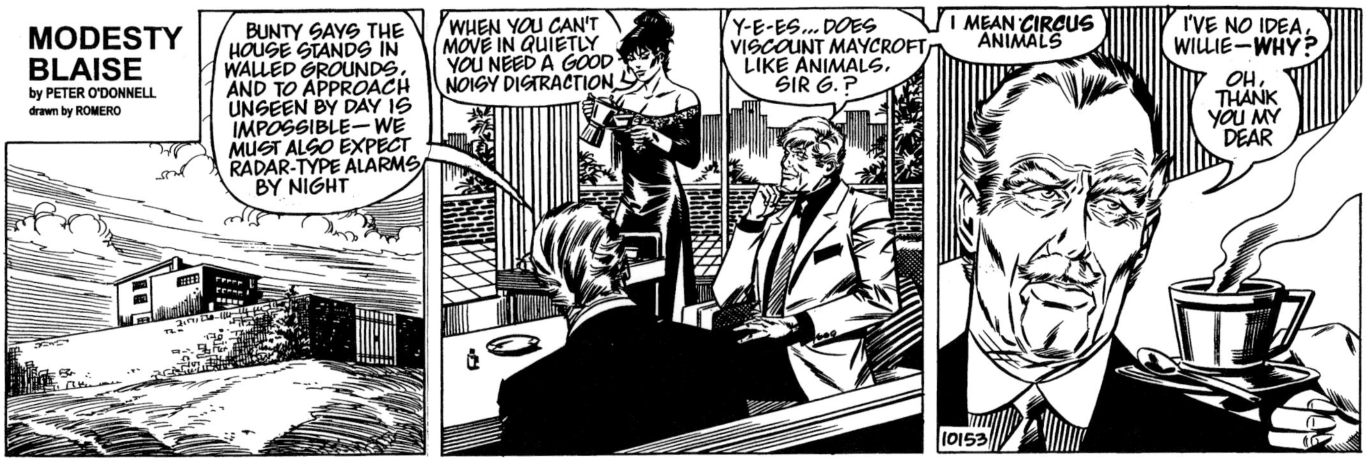
MODESTY BLAISE
by PETER O'DONNELL
drawn by ROMERO
BUNTY SAYS THE HOUSE STANDS IN WALLED GROUNDS, AND TO APPROACH UNSEEN BY DAY IS IMPOSSIBLE—WE MUST ALSO EXPECT RADAR-TYPE ALARMS BY NIGHT
WHEN YOU CAN'T MOVE IN QUIETLY YOU NEED A GOOD NOISY DISTRACTION
Y-E-ES... DOES VISCOUNT MAYCROFT LIKE ANIMALS, SIR G.?
I MEAN **CIRCUS** ANIMALS
I'VE NO IDEA, WILLIE—**WHY?**
OH, THANK YOU MY DEAR
10153

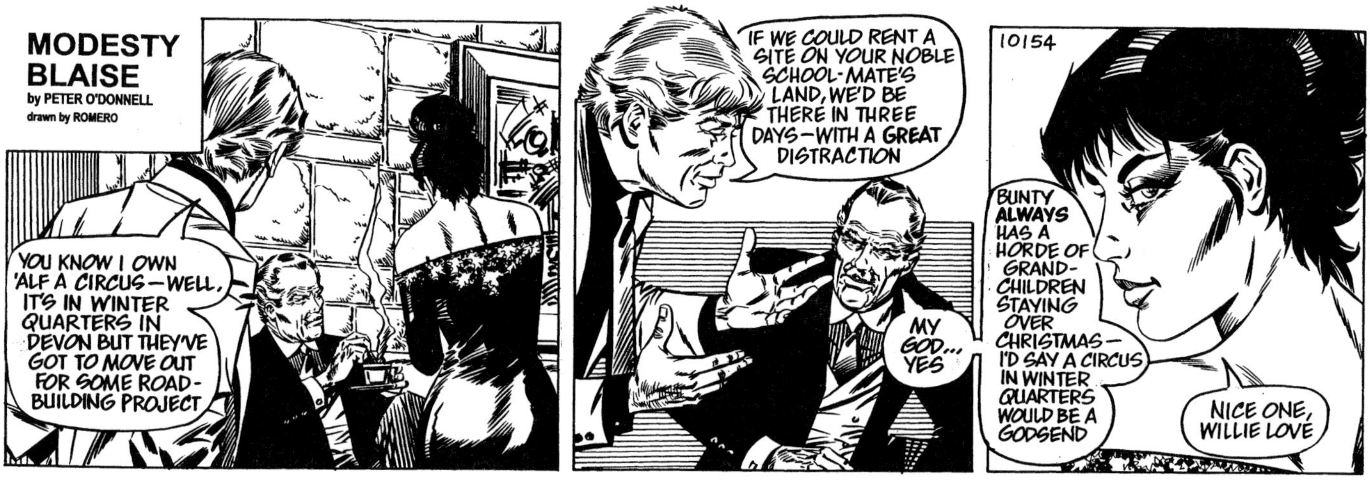
MODESTY BLAISE
by PETER O'DONNELL
drawn by ROMERO
YOU KNOW I OWN 'ALF A CIRCUS—WELL, IT'S IN WINTER QUARTERS IN DEVON BUT THEY'VE GOT TO MOVE OUT FOR SOME ROAD-BUILDING PROJECT
IF WE COULD RENT A SITE ON YOUR NOBLE SCHOOL-MATE'S LAND, WE'D BE THERE IN THREE DAYS—WITH A GREAT DISTRACTION
MY GOD... YES
10154
BUNTY ALWAYS HAS A HORDE OF GRAND-CHILDREN STAYING OVER CHRISTMAS—I'D SAY A CIRCUS IN WINTER QUARTERS WOULD BE A GODSEND
NICE ONE, WILLIE LOVE

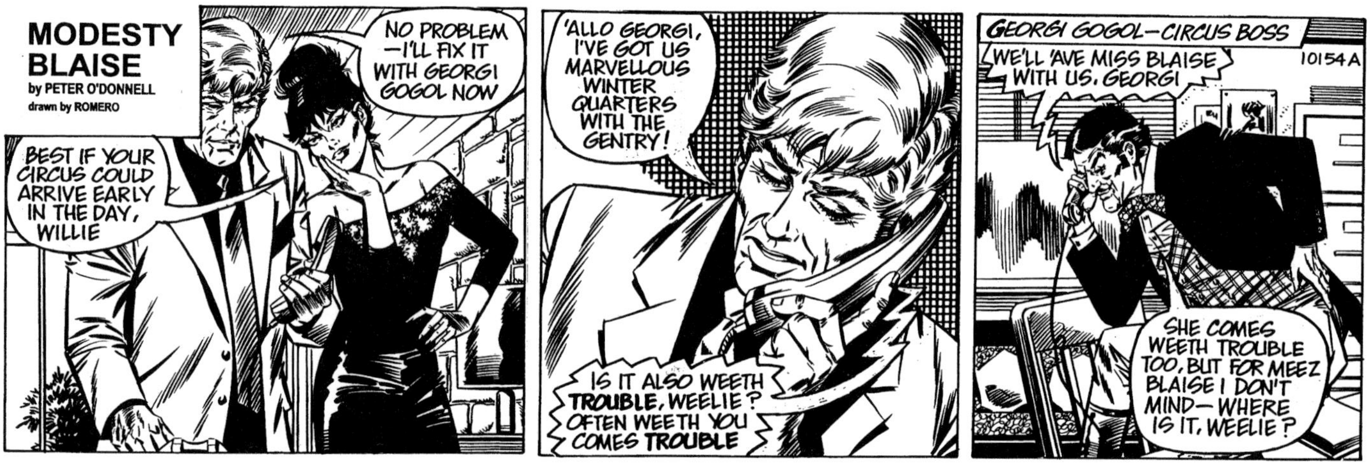
MODESTY BLAISE
by PETER O'DONNELL
drawn by ROMERO
BEST IF YOUR CIRCUS COULD ARRIVE EARLY IN THE DAY, WILLIE
NO PROBLEM —I'LL FIX IT WITH GEORGI GOGOL NOW
'ALLO GEORGI, I'VE GOT US MARVELLOUS WINTER QUARTERS WITH THE GENTRY!
IS IT ALSO WEETH TROUBLE, WEELIE? OFTEN WEETH YOU COMES TROUBLE
GEORGI GOGOL—CIRCUS BOSS
10154A
WE'LL 'AVE MISS BLAISE WITH US, GEORGI
SHE COMES WEETH TROUBLE TOO, BUT FOR MEEZ BLAISE I DON'T MIND—WHERE IS IT, WEELIE?

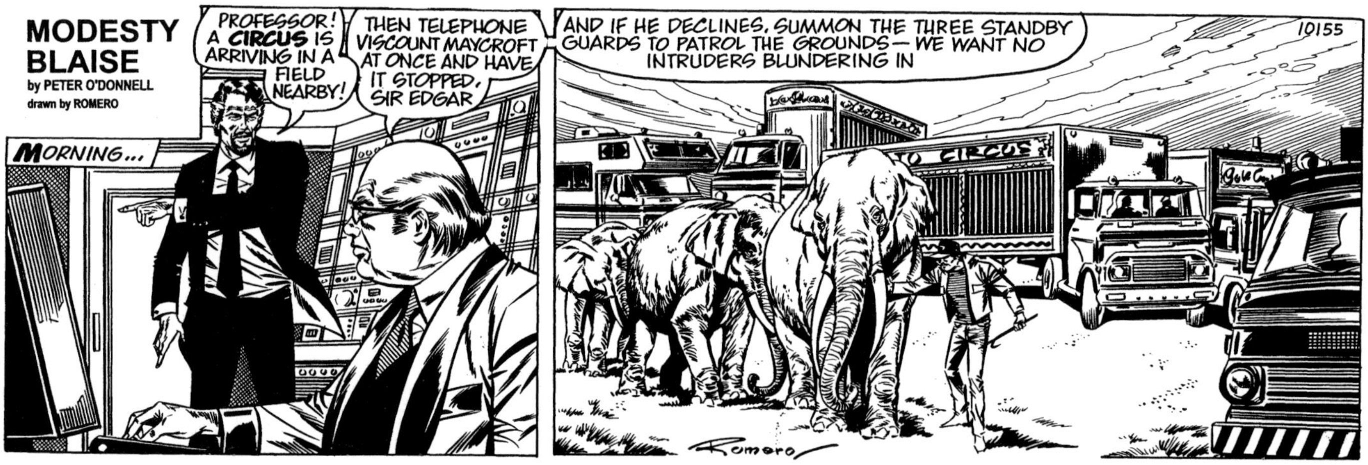
MODESTY BLAISE
by PETER O'DONNELL
drawn by ROMERO
MORNING...
PROFESSOR! A CIRCUS IS ARRIVING IN A FIELD NEARBY!
THEN TELEPHONE VISCOUNT MAYCROFT AT ONCE AND HAVE IT STOPPED, SIR EDGAR
AND IF HE DECLINES, SUMMON THE THREE STANDBY GUARDS TO PATROL THE GROUNDS—WE WANT NO INTRUDERS BLUNDERING IN
10155
CIRCUS
Romero

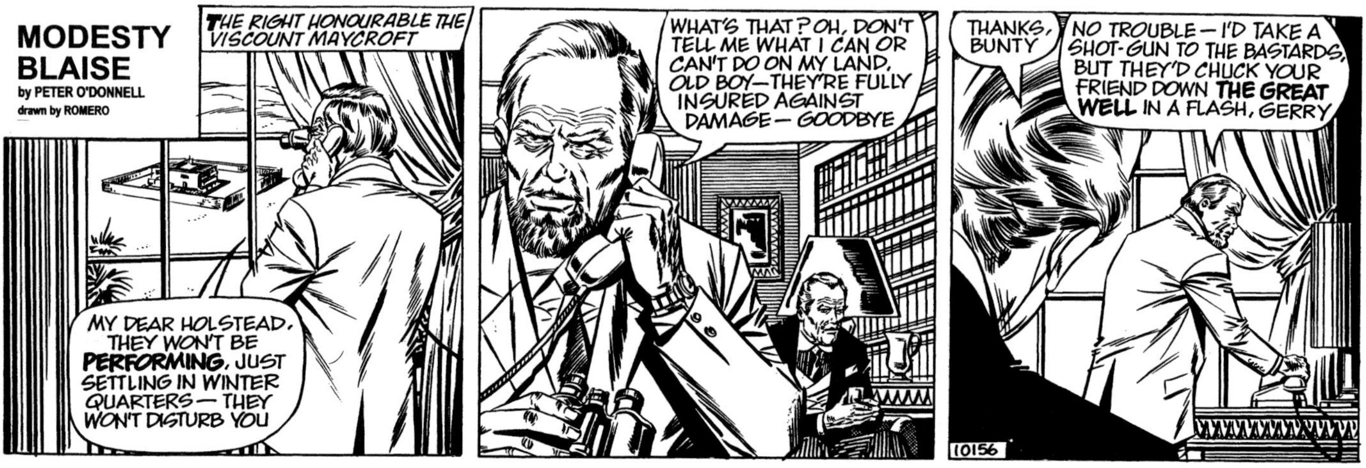
MODESTY BLAISE
by PETER O'DONNELL
drawn by ROMERO
THE RIGHT HONOURABLE THE VISCOUNT MAYCROFT
MY DEAR HOLSTEAD, THEY WON'T BE PERFORMING, JUST SETTLING IN WINTER QUARTERS—THEY WON'T DISTURB YOU
WHAT'S THAT? OH, DON'T TELL ME WHAT I CAN OR CAN'T DO ON MY LAND, OLD BOY—THEY'RE FULLY INSURED AGAINST DAMAGE—GOODBYE
THANKS, BUNTY
NO TROUBLE—I'D TAKE A SHOT-GUN TO THE BASTARDS, BUT THEY'D CHUCK YOUR FRIEND DOWN THE GREAT WELL IN A FLASH, GERRY
10156

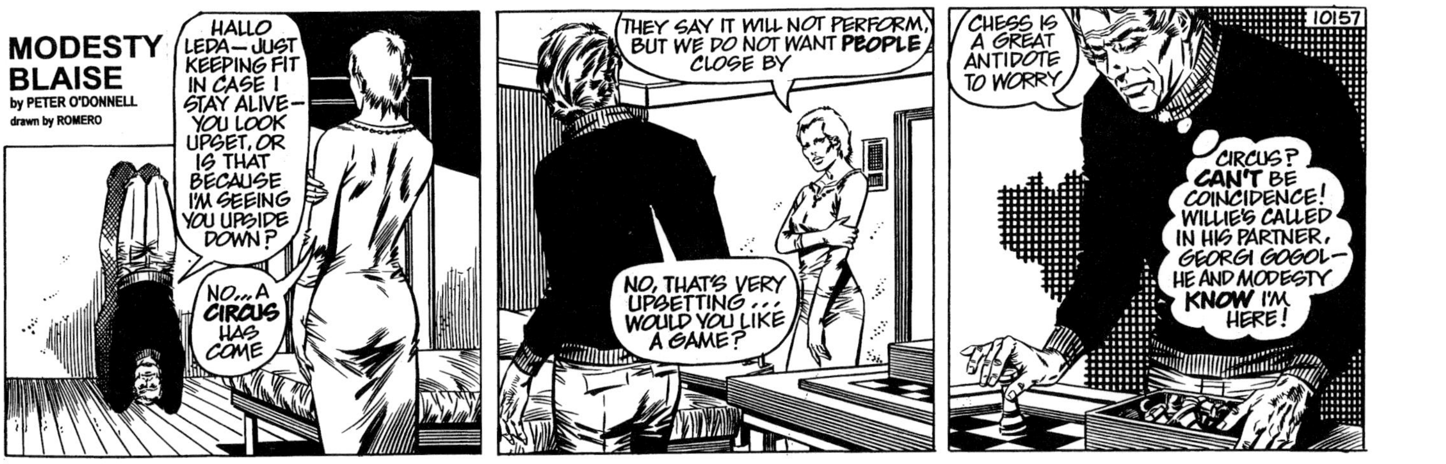
MODESTY BLAISE
by PETER O'DONNELL
drawn by ROMERO
HALLO LEDA—JUST KEEPING FIT IN CASE I STAY ALIVE—YOU LOOK UPSET, OR IS THAT BECAUSE I'M SEEING YOU UPSIDE DOWN?
NO... A CIRCUS HAS COME
THEY SAY IT WILL NOT PERFORM, BUT WE DO NOT WANT PEOPLE CLOSE BY
NO, THAT'S VERY UPSETTING... WOULD YOU LIKE A GAME?
10157
CHESS IS A GREAT ANTIDOTE TO WORRY
CIRCUS? CAN'T BE COINCIDENCE! WILLIE'S CALLED IN HIS PARTNER, GEORGI GOGOL—HE AND MODESTY KNOW I'M HERE!

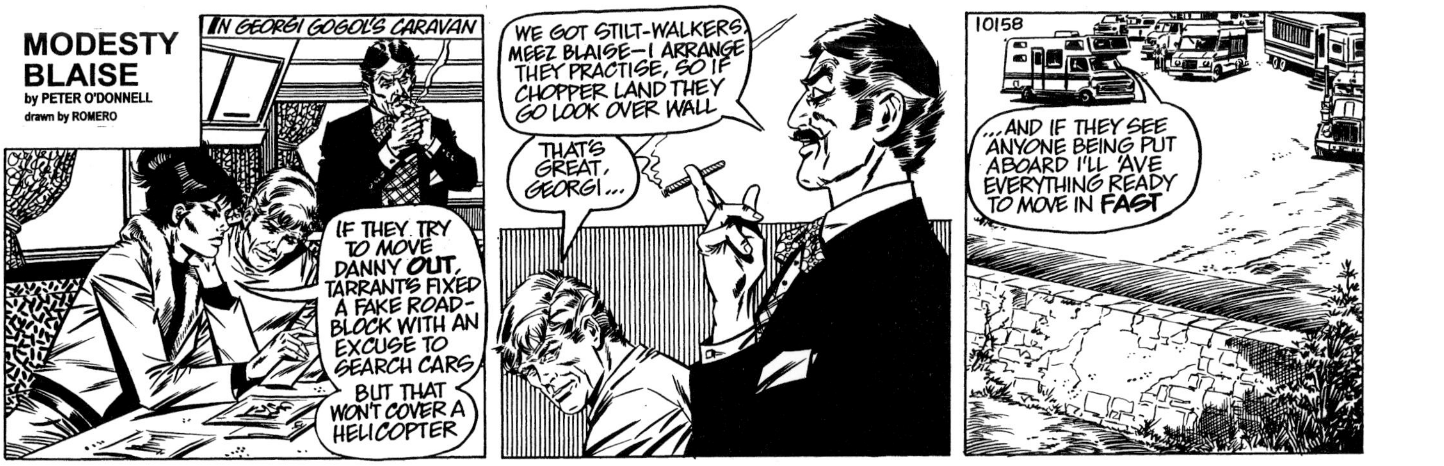
MODESTY BLAISE
by PETER O'DONNELL
drawn by ROMERO
IN GEORGI GOGOL'S CARAVAN
IF THEY TRY TO MOVE DANNY OUT, TARRANT'S FIXED A FAKE ROAD-BLOCK WITH AN EXCUSE TO SEARCH CARS
BUT THAT WON'T COVER A HELICOPTER
WE GOT STILT-WALKERS, MEEZ BLAISE—I ARRANGE THEY PRACTISE, SO IF CHOPPER LAND THEY GO LOOK OVER WALL
THAT'S GREAT, GEORGI...
10158
...AND IF THEY SEE ANYONE BEING PUT ABOARD I'LL 'AVE EVERYTHING READY TO MOVE IN FAST

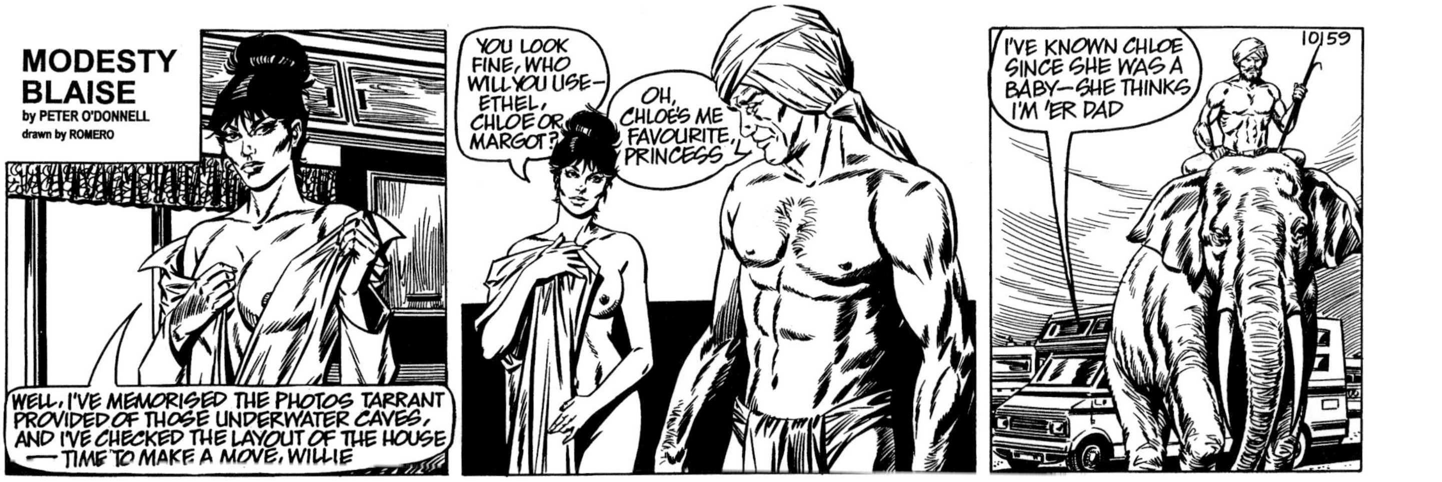
MODESTY BLAISE
by PETER O'DONNELL
drawn by ROMERO
WELL, I'VE MEMORISED THE PHOTOS TARRANT PROVIDED OF THOSE UNDERWATER CAVES, AND I'VE CHECKED THE LAYOUT OF THE HOUSE—TIME TO MAKE A MOVE, WILLIE
YOU LOOK FINE, WHO WILL YOU USE—ETHEL, CHLOE OR MARGOT?
OH, CHLOE'S ME FAVOURITE, PRINCESS
10159
I'VE KNOWN CHLOE SINCE SHE WAS A BABY—SHE THINKS I'M 'ER DAD

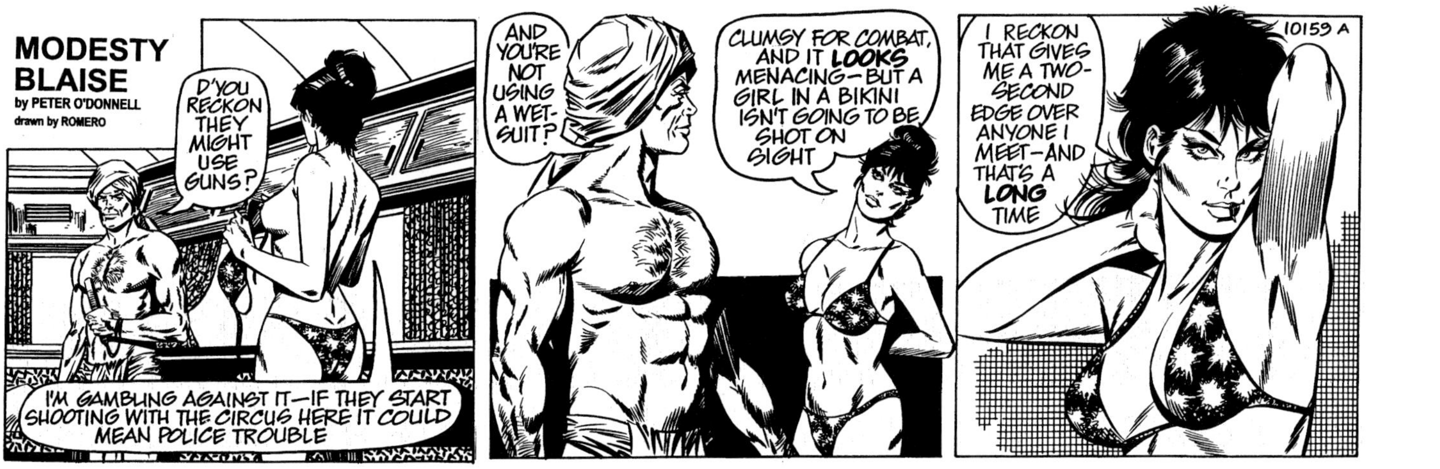
MODESTY BLAISE
by PETER O'DONNELL
drawn by ROMERO
D'YOU RECKON THEY MIGHT USE GUNS?
I'M GAMBLING AGAINST IT—IF THEY START SHOOTING WITH THE CIRCUS HERE IT COULD MEAN POLICE TROUBLE
AND YOU'RE NOT USING A WET-SUIT?
CLUMSY FOR COMBAT, AND IT LOOKS MENACING—BUT A GIRL IN A BIKINI ISN'T GOING TO BE SHOT ON SIGHT
10159 A
I RECKON THAT GIVES ME A TWO-SECOND EDGE OVER ANYONE I MEET—AND THAT'S A LONG TIME

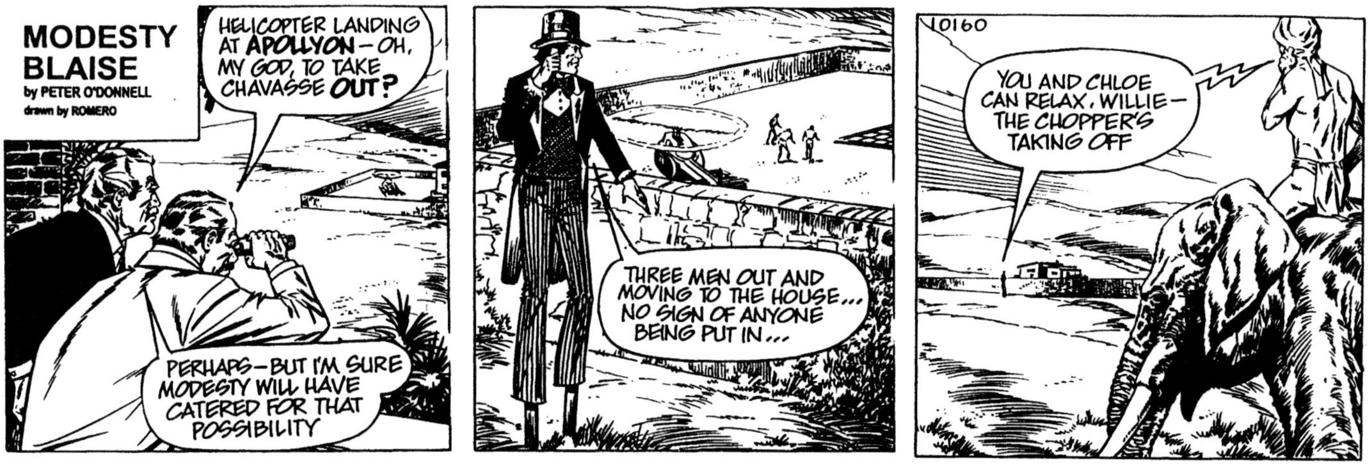
MODESTY BLAISE
by PETER O'DONNELL
drawn by ROMERO
HELICOPTER LANDING AT APOLLYON — OH, MY GOD, TO TAKE CHAVASSE OUT?
PERHAPS—BUT I'M SURE MODESTY WILL HAVE CATERED FOR THAT POSSIBILITY
THREE MEN OUT AND MOVING TO THE HOUSE... NO SIGN OF ANYONE BEING PUT IN...
10160
YOU AND CHLOE CAN RELAX, WILLIE— THE CHOPPER'S TAKING OFF

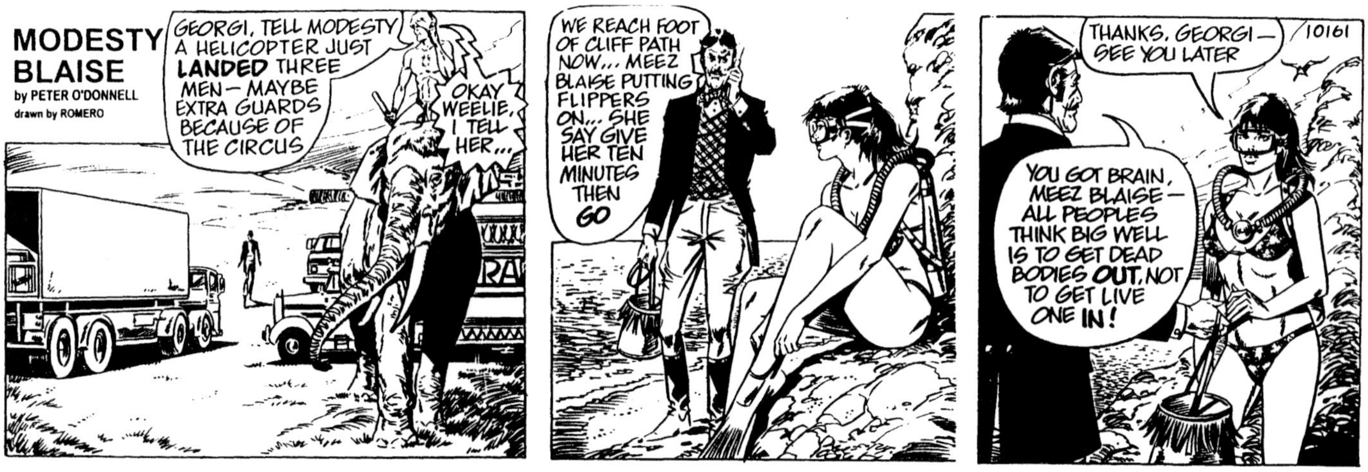
MODESTY BLAISE
by PETER O'DONNELL
drawn by ROMERO
GEORGI, TELL MODESTY A HELICOPTER JUST LANDED THREE MEN—MAYBE EXTRA GUARDS BECAUSE OF THE CIRCUS
OKAY WEELIE, I TELL HER...
WE REACH FOOT OF CLIFF PATH NOW... MEEZ BLAISE PUTTING FLIPPERS ON... SHE SAY GIVE HER TEN MINUTES THEN GO
THANKS, GEORGI— SEE YOU LATER
10161
YOU GOT BRAIN, MEEZ BLAISE— ALL PEOPLES THINK BIG WELL IS TO GET DEAD BODIES OUT, NOT TO GET LIVE ONE IN!

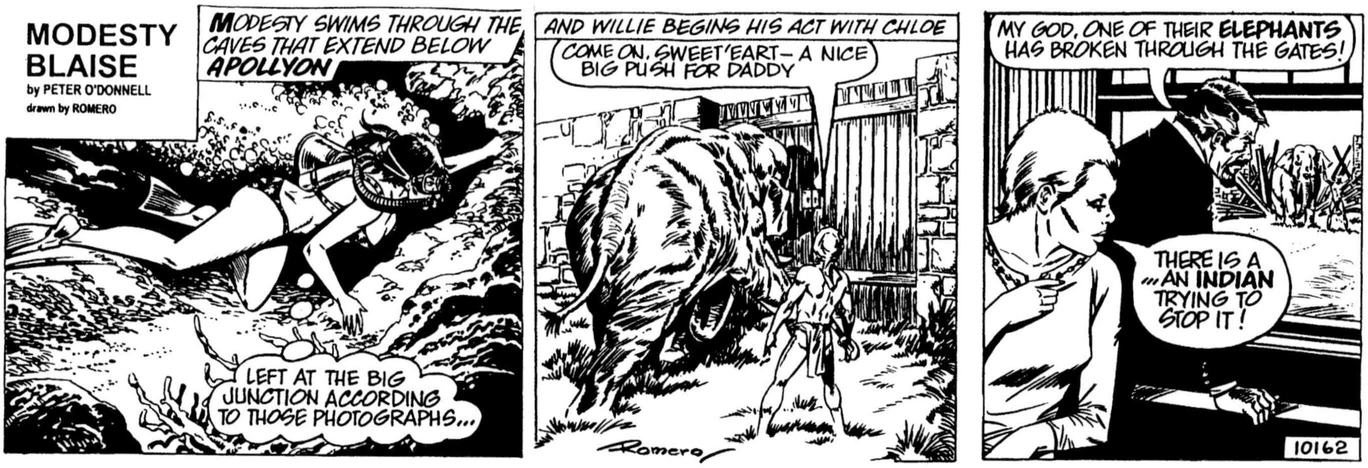
MODESTY BLAISE
by PETER O'DONNELL
drawn by ROMERO
MODESTY SWIMS THROUGH THE CAVES THAT EXTEND BELOW APOLLYON
LEFT AT THE BIG JUNCTION ACCORDING TO THOSE PHOTOGRAPHS...
AND WILLIE BEGINS HIS ACT WITH CHLOE
COME ON, SWEET'EART— A NICE BIG PUSH FOR DADDY
Romero
MY GOD, ONE OF THEIR ELEPHANTS HAS BROKEN THROUGH THE GATES!
THERE IS A ...AN INDIAN TRYING TO STOP IT!
10162

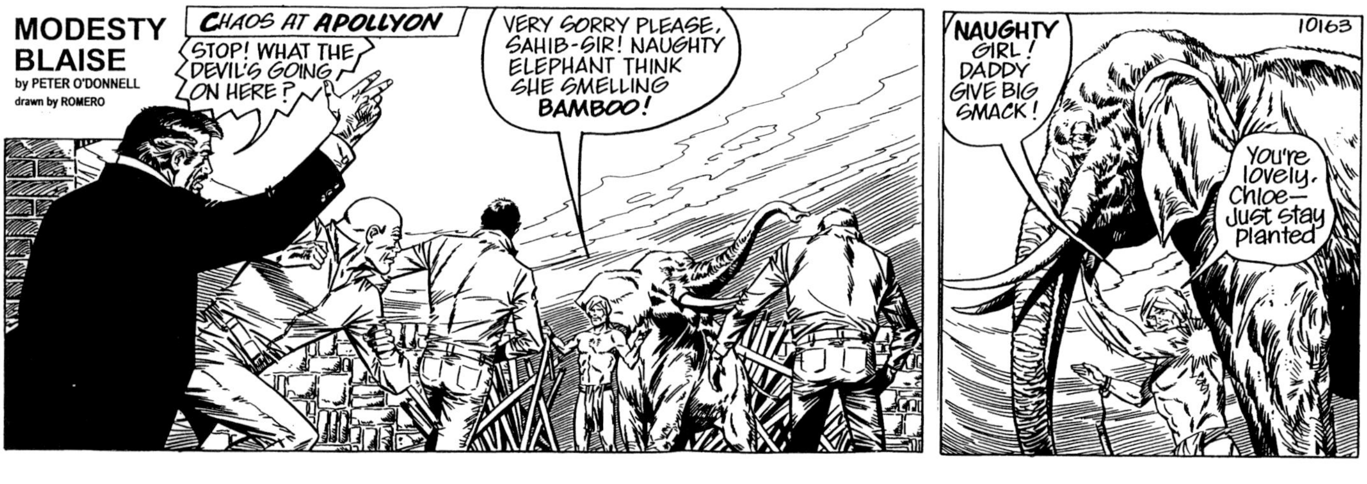
MODESTY BLAISE
by PETER O'DONNELL
drawn by ROMERO
CHAOS AT APOLLYON
STOP! WHAT THE DEVIL'S GOING ON HERE?
VERY SORRY PLEASE, SAHIB-SIR! NAUGHTY ELEPHANT THINK SHE SMELLING BAMBOO!
10163
NAUGHTY GIRL! DADDY GIVE BIG SMACK!
You're lovely, Chloe— Just stay planted

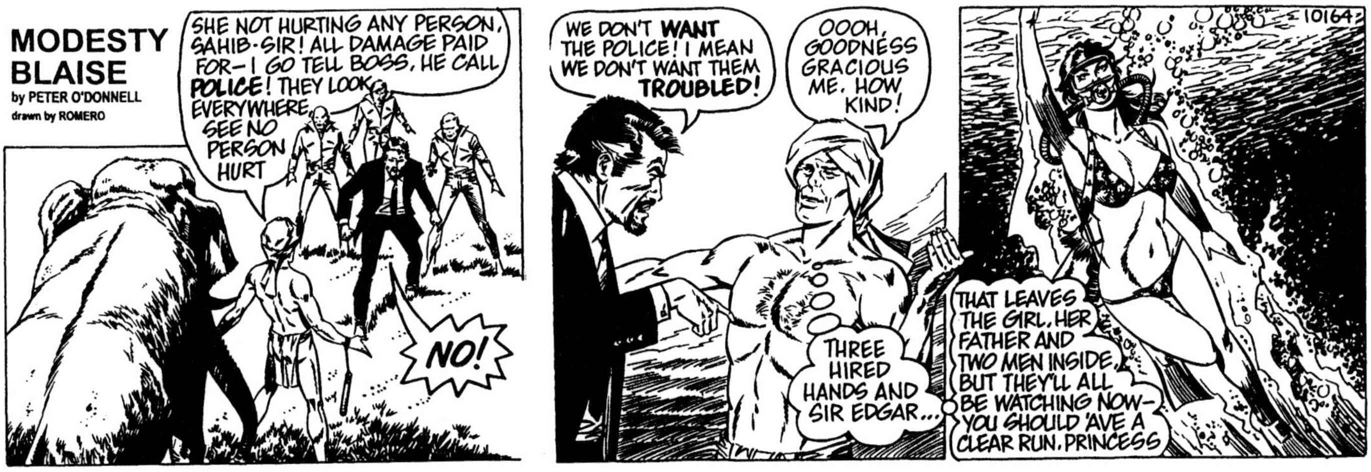
MODESTY BLAISE
by PETER O'DONNELL
drawn by ROMERO
SHE NOT HURTING ANY PERSON, SAHIB-SIR! ALL DAMAGE PAID FOR– I GO TELL BOSS, HE CALL POLICE! THEY LOOK EVERYWHERE, SEE NO PERSON HURT
NO!
WE DON'T WANT THE POLICE! I MEAN WE DON'T WANT THEM TROUBLED!
OOOH, GOODNESS GRACIOUS ME. HOW KIND!
THREE HIRED HANDS AND SIR EDGAR...
10164
THAT LEAVES THE GIRL, HER FATHER AND TWO MEN INSIDE, BUT THEY'LL ALL BE WATCHING NOW– YOU SHOULD 'AVE A CLEAR RUN, PRINCESS

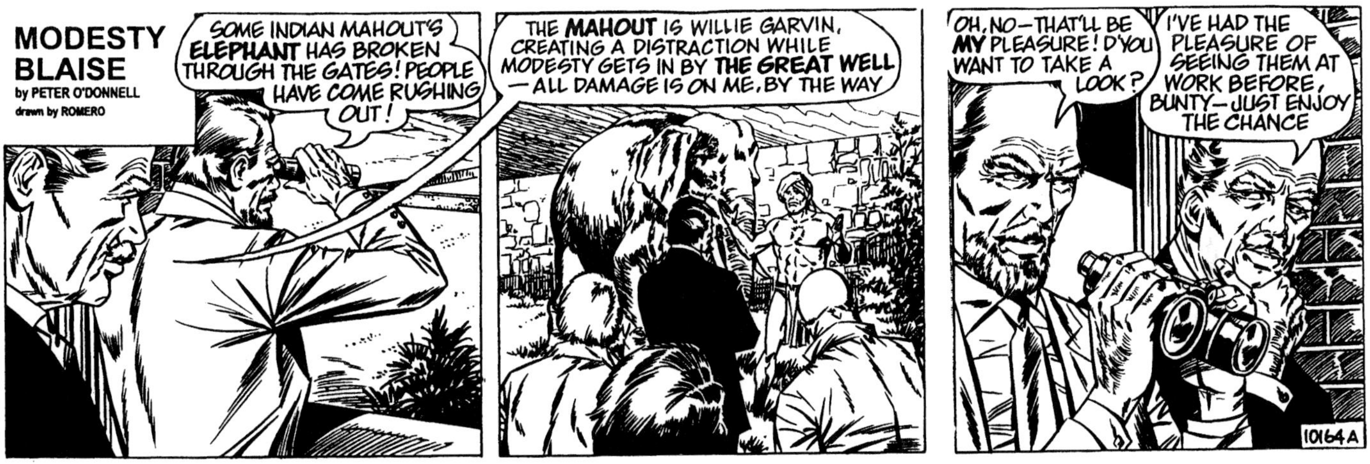
MODESTY BLAISE
by PETER O'DONNELL
drawn by ROMERO
SOME INDIAN MAHOUT'S ELEPHANT HAS BROKEN THROUGH THE GATES! PEOPLE HAVE COME RUSHING OUT!
THE MAHOUT IS WILLIE GARVIN, CREATING A DISTRACTION WHILE MODESTY GETS IN BY THE GREAT WELL —ALL DAMAGE IS ON ME, BY THE WAY
OH, NO–THAT'LL BE MY PLEASURE! D'YOU WANT TO TAKE A LOOK?
I'VE HAD THE PLEASURE OF SEEING THEM AT WORK BEFORE, BUNTY–JUST ENJOY THE CHANCE
10164 A

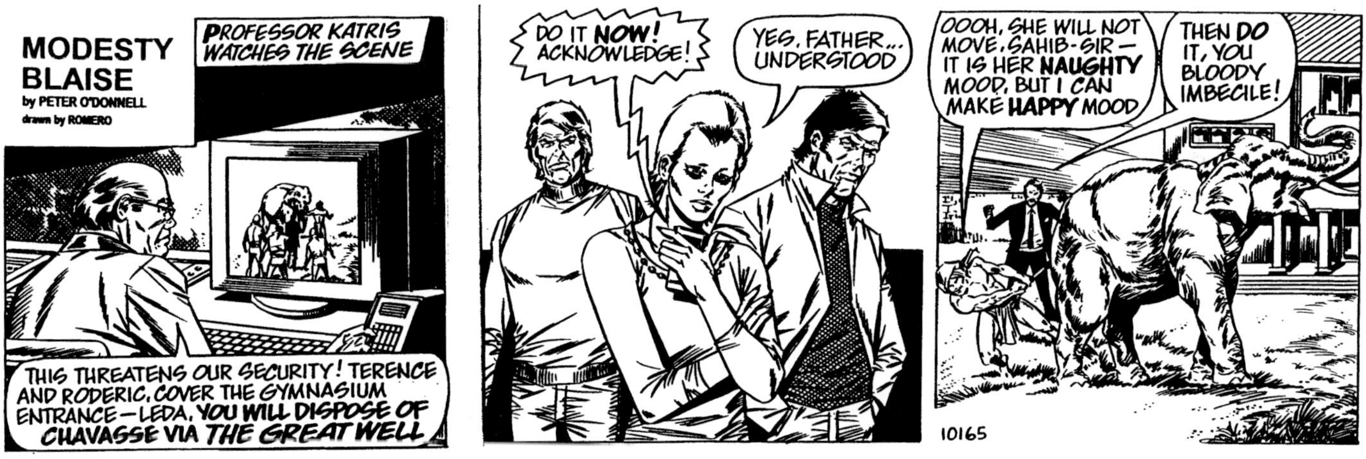
MODESTY BLAISE
by PETER O'DONNELL
drawn by ROMERO
PROFESSOR KATRIS WATCHES THE SCENE
THIS THREATENS OUR SECURITY! TERENCE AND RODERIC, COVER THE GYMNASIUM ENTRANCE–LEDA, YOU WILL DISPOSE OF CHAVASSE VIA THE GREAT WELL
DO IT NOW! ACKNOWLEDGE!
YES, FATHER... UNDERSTOOD
OOOH, SHE WILL NOT MOVE, SAHIB-SIR– IT IS HER NAUGHTY MOOD, BUT I CAN MAKE HAPPY MOOD
THEN DO IT, YOU BLOODY IMBECILE!
10165

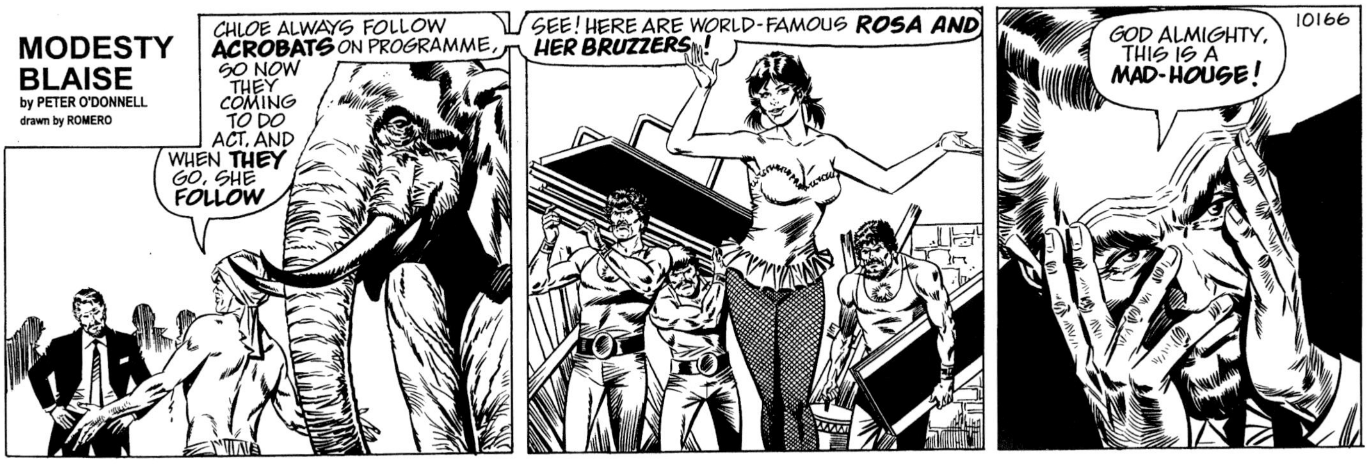
MODESTY BLAISE
by PETER O'DONNELL
drawn by ROMERO
CHLOE ALWAYS FOLLOW ACROBATS ON PROGRAMME, SO NOW THEY COMING TO DO ACT, AND WHEN THEY GO, SHE FOLLOW
SEE! HERE ARE WORLD-FAMOUS ROSA AND HER BRUZZERS!
10166
GOD ALMIGHTY, THIS IS A MAD-HOUSE!

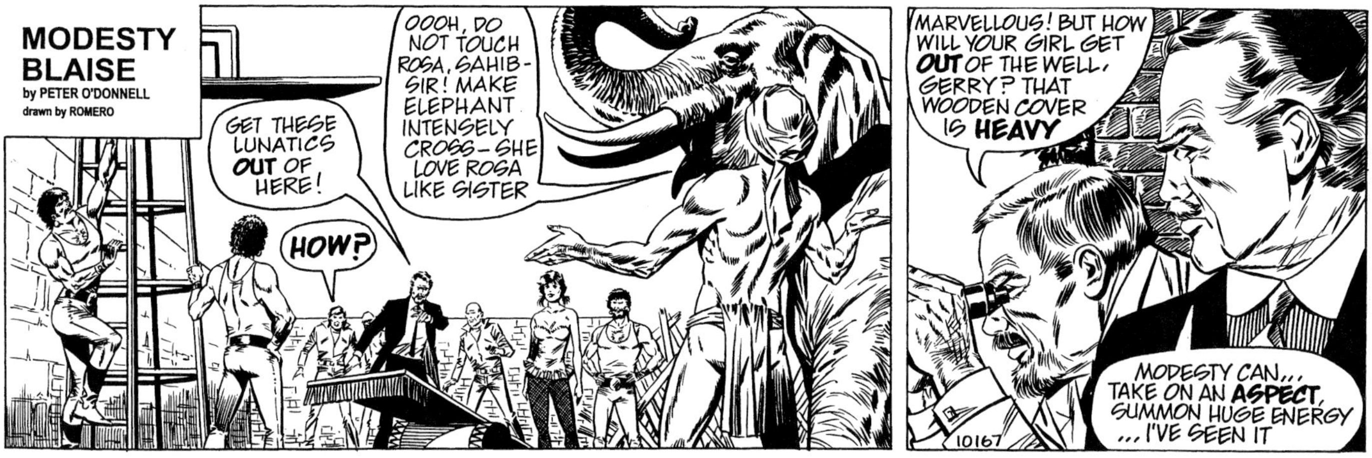
MODESTY BLAISE
by PETER O'DONNELL
drawn by ROMERO
GET THESE LUNATICS **OUT** OF HERE!
HOW?
OOOH, DO NOT TOUCH ROSA, SAHIB-SIR! MAKE ELEPHANT INTENSELY CROSS—SHE LOVE ROSA LIKE SISTER
MARVELLOUS! BUT HOW WILL YOUR GIRL GET **OUT** OF THE WELL, GERRY? THAT WOODEN COVER IS **HEAVY**
MODESTY CAN... TAKE ON AN **ASPECT**, SUMMON HUGE ENERGY ... I'VE SEEN IT
10167

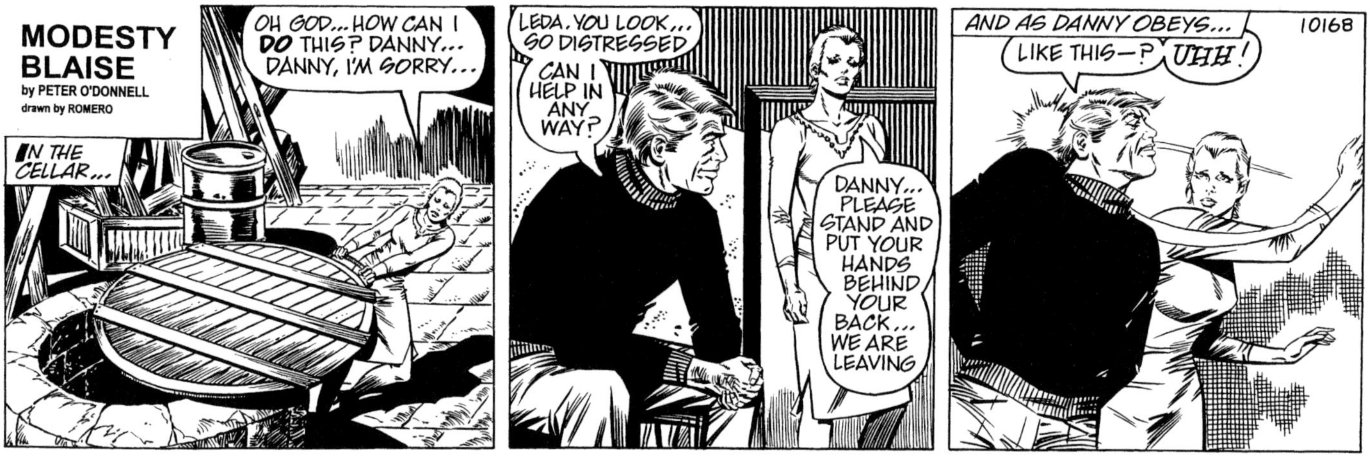
MODESTY BLAISE
by PETER O'DONNELL
drawn by ROMERO
IN THE CELLAR...
OH GOD... HOW CAN I **DO** THIS? DANNY... DANNY, I'M SORRY...
LEDA, YOU LOOK... SO DISTRESSED
CAN I HELP IN ANY WAY?
DANNY... PLEASE STAND AND PUT YOUR HANDS BEHIND YOUR BACK... WE ARE LEAVING
AND AS DANNY OBEYS...
10168
LIKE THIS—?
UHH!

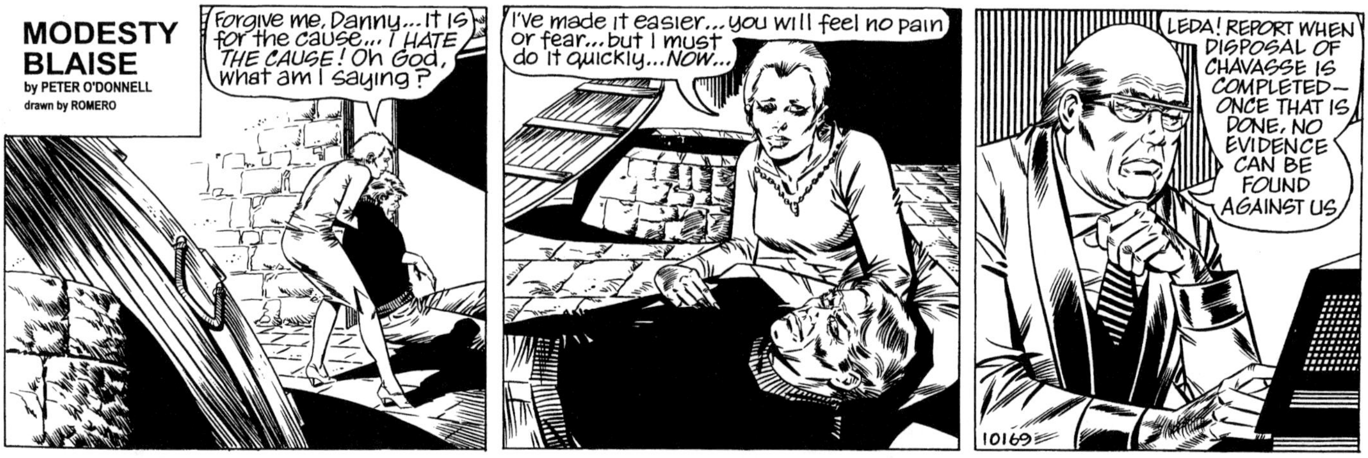
MODESTY BLAISE
by PETER O'DONNELL
drawn by ROMERO
Forgive me, Danny... It is for the cause... I HATE THE CAUSE! Oh God, what am I saying?
I've made it easier... you will feel no pain or fear... but I must do it quickly... NOW...
LEDA! REPORT WHEN DISPOSAL OF CHAVASSE IS COMPLETED—ONCE THAT IS DONE, NO EVIDENCE CAN BE FOUND AGAINST US
10169

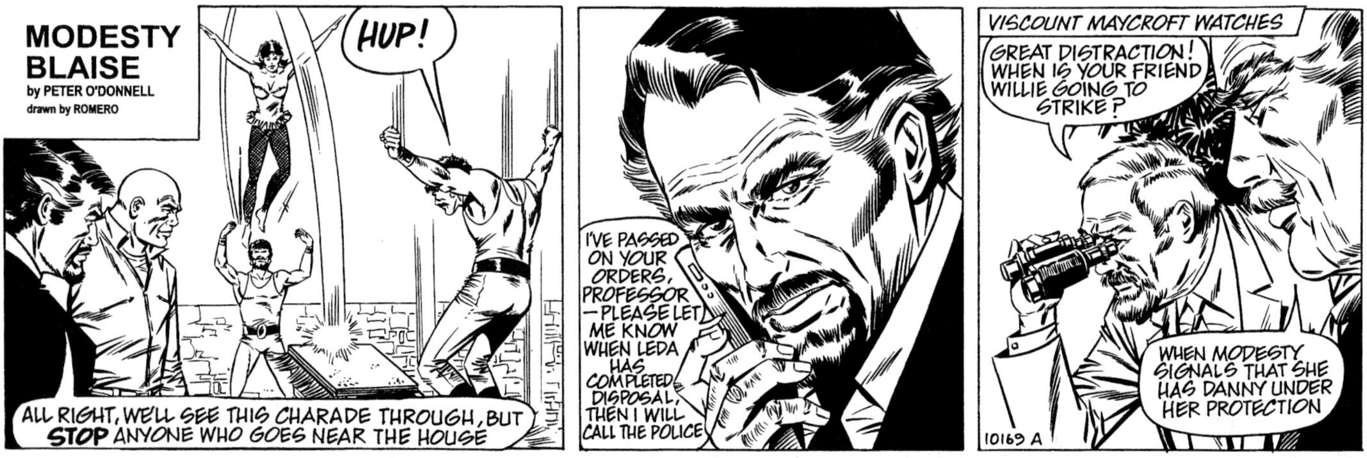
MODESTY BLAISE
by PETER O'DONNELL
drawn by ROMERO
HUP!
ALL RIGHT, WE'LL SEE THIS CHARADE THROUGH, BUT **STOP** ANYONE WHO GOES NEAR THE HOUSE
I'VE PASSED ON YOUR ORDERS, PROFESSOR—PLEASE LET ME KNOW WHEN LEDA HAS COMPLETED DISPOSAL, THEN I WILL CALL THE POLICE
VISCOUNT MAYCROFT WATCHES
GREAT DISTRACTION! WHEN IS YOUR FRIEND WILLIE GOING TO STRIKE?
WHEN MODESTY SIGNALS THAT SHE HAS DANNY UNDER HER PROTECTION
10169 A

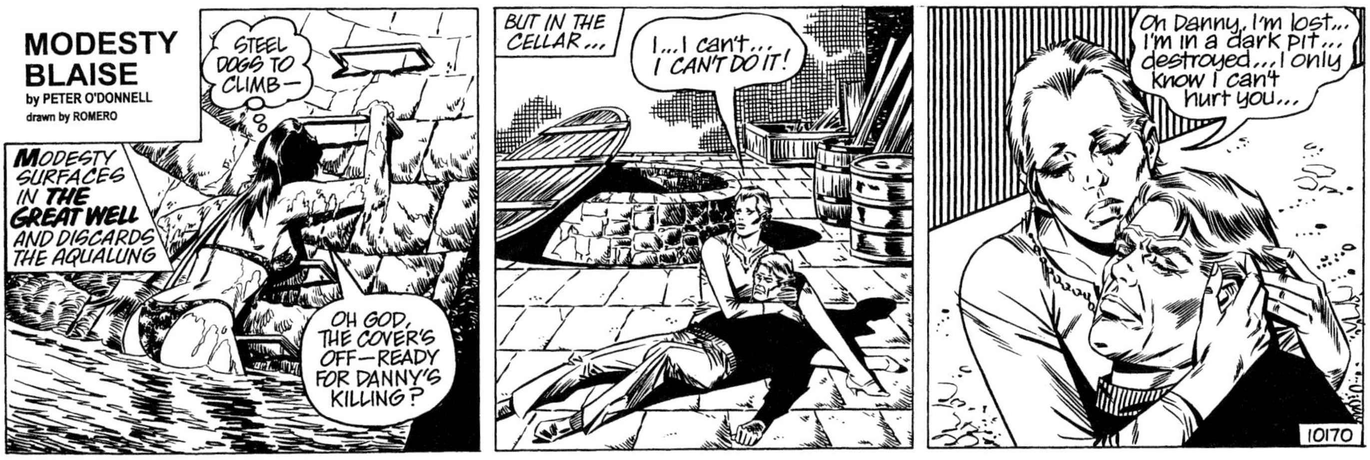
MODESTY BLAISE
by PETER O'DONNELL
drawn by ROMERO
MODESTY SURFACES IN THE GREAT WELL AND DISCARDS THE AQUALUNG
STEEL DOGS TO CLIMB—
OH GOD, THE COVER'S OFF—READY FOR DANNY'S KILLING?
BUT IN THE CELLAR...
I...I can't... I CAN'T DO IT!
Oh Danny, I'm lost... I'm in a dark pit... destroyed... I only know I can't hurt you...
10170

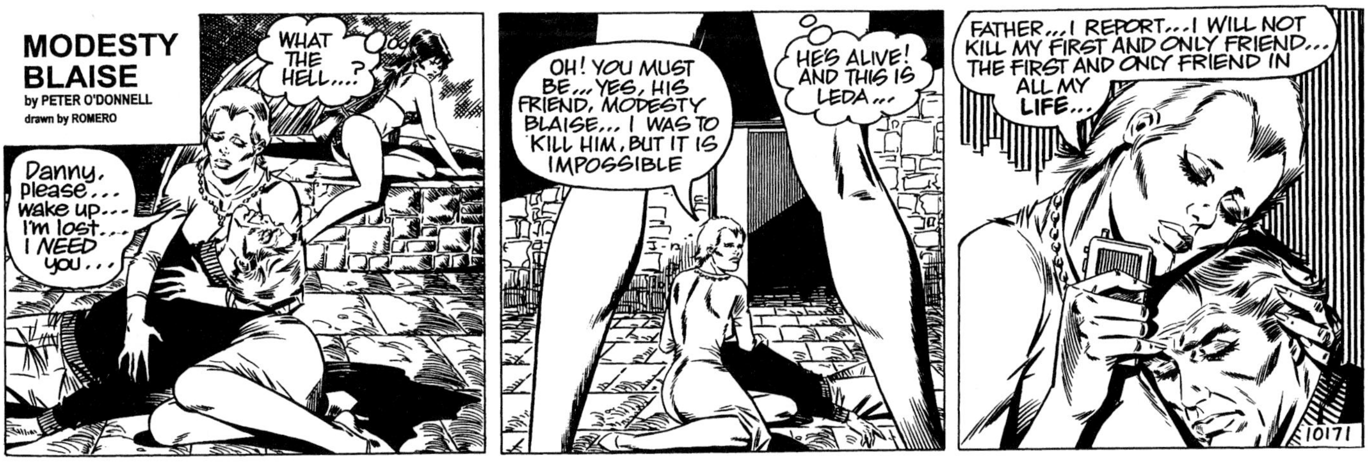
MODESTY BLAISE
by PETER O'DONNELL
drawn by ROMERO
WHAT THE HELL...?
Danny, please... wake up... I'm lost... I NEED you...
OH! YOU MUST BE... YES, HIS FRIEND, MODESTY BLAISE... I WAS TO KILL HIM, BUT IT IS IMPOSSIBLE
HE'S ALIVE! AND THIS IS LEDA...
FATHER... I REPORT... I WILL NOT KILL MY FIRST AND ONLY FRIEND... THE FIRST AND ONLY FRIEND IN ALL MY LIFE...
10171

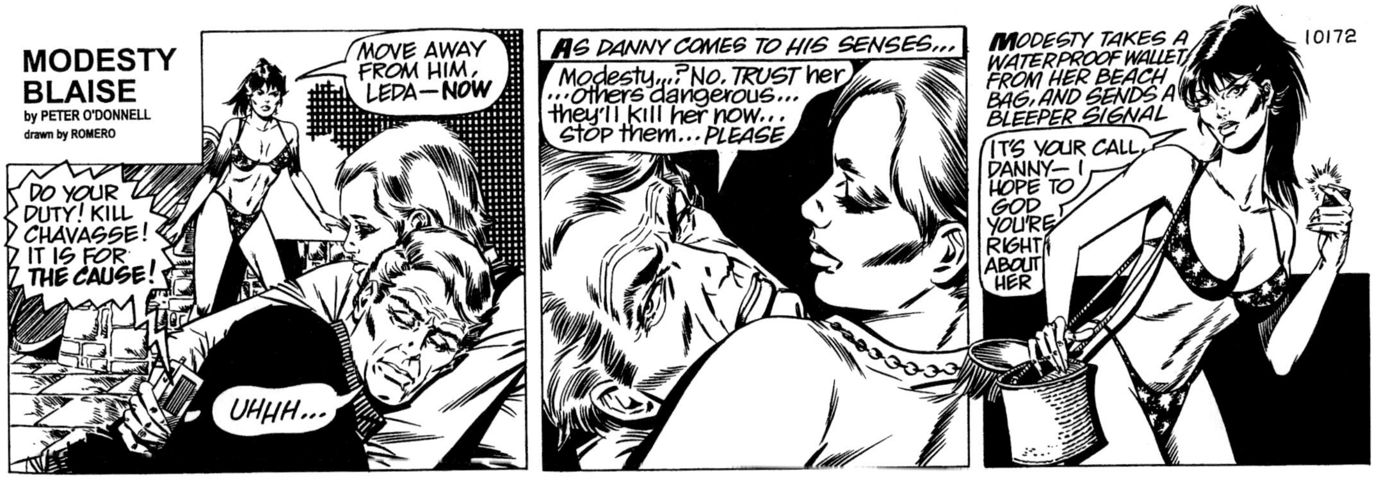
MODESTY BLAISE
by PETER O'DONNELL
drawn by ROMERO
MOVE AWAY FROM HIM, LEDA—NOW
DO YOUR DUTY! KILL CHAVASSE! IT IS FOR THE CAUSE!
UHHH...
AS DANNY COMES TO HIS SENSES...
Modesty...? No. TRUST her ...others dangerous... they'll kill her now... stop them... PLEASE
MODESTY TAKES A WATERPROOF WALLET FROM HER BEACH BAG, AND SENDS A BLEEPER SIGNAL
IT'S YOUR CALL, DANNY—I HOPE TO GOD YOU'RE RIGHT ABOUT HER
10172

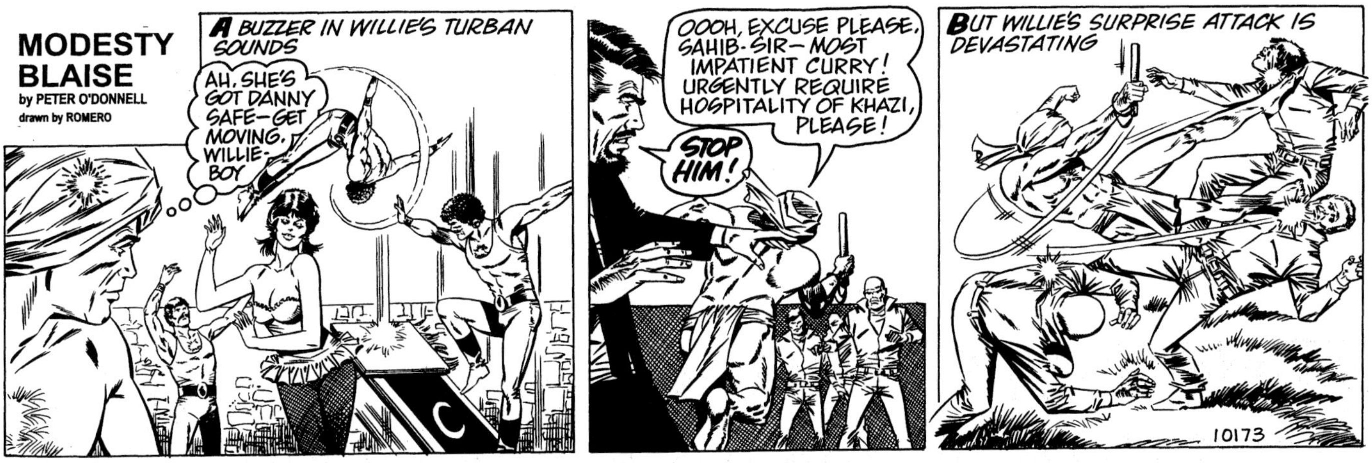
MODESTY BLAISE
by PETER O'DONNELL
drawn by ROMERO
A BUZZER IN WILLIE'S TURBAN SOUNDS
AH, SHE'S GOT DANNY SAFE—GET MOVING, WILLIE-BOY
OOOH, EXCUSE PLEASE, SAHIB-SIR—MOST IMPATIENT CURRY! URGENTLY REQUIRE HOSPITALITY OF KHAZI, PLEASE!
STOP HIM!
BUT WILLIE'S SURPRISE ATTACK IS DEVASTATING
10173

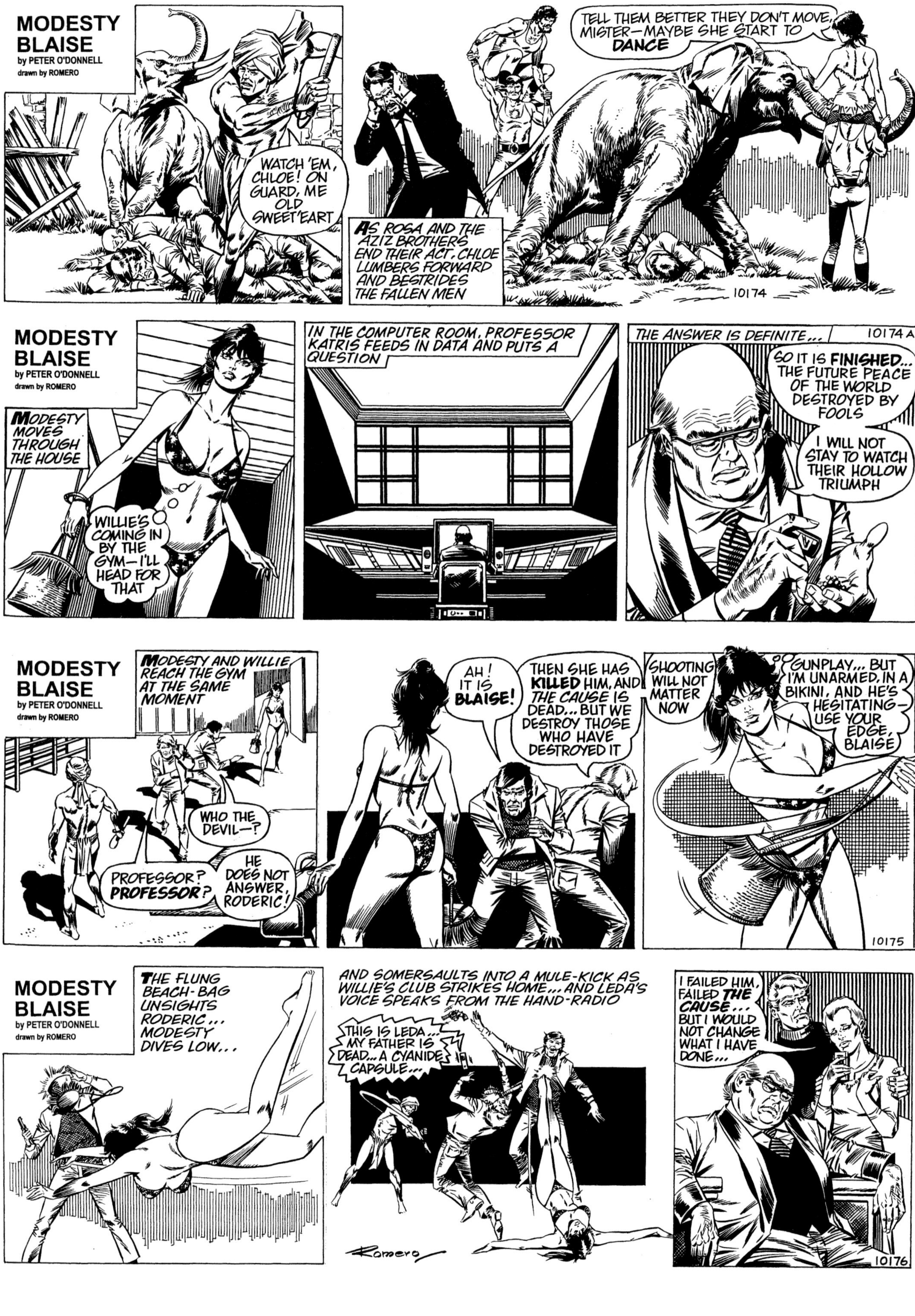
MODESTY BLAISE
by PETER O'DONNELL
drawn by ROMERO
WATCH 'EM, CHLOE! ON GUARD, ME OLD SWEET'EART
AS ROSA AND THE AZIZ BROTHERS END THEIR ACT, CHLOE LUMBERS FORWARD AND BESTRIDES THE FALLEN MEN
TELL THEM BETTER THEY DON'T MOVE, MISTER—MAYBE SHE START TO DANCE
10174
MODESTY BLAISE
by PETER O'DONNELL
drawn by ROMERO
MODESTY MOVES THROUGH THE HOUSE
WILLIE'S COMING IN BY THE GYM—I'LL HEAD FOR THAT
IN THE COMPUTER ROOM, PROFESSOR KATRIS FEEDS IN DATA AND PUTS A QUESTION
THE ANSWER IS DEFINITE...
10174 A
SO IT IS FINISHED... THE FUTURE PEACE OF THE WORLD DESTROYED BY FOOLS
I WILL NOT STAY TO WATCH THEIR HOLLOW TRIUMPH
MODESTY BLAISE
by PETER O'DONNELL
drawn by ROMERO
MODESTY AND WILLIE REACH THE GYM AT THE SAME MOMENT
WHO THE DEVIL—?
PROFESSOR? PROFESSOR?
HE DOES NOT ANSWER, RODERIC!
AH! IT IS BLAISE!
THEN SHE HAS KILLED HIM, AND THE CAUSE IS DEAD... BUT WE DESTROY THOSE WHO HAVE DESTROYED IT
SHOOTING WILL NOT MATTER NOW
GUNPLAY... BUT I'M UNARMED, IN A BIKINI, AND HE'S HESITATING—USE YOUR EDGE, BLAISE
10175
MODESTY BLAISE
by PETER O'DONNELL
drawn by ROMERO
THE FLUNG BEACH-BAG UNSIGHTS RODERIC... MODESTY DIVES LOW...
AND SOMERSAULTS INTO A MULE-KICK AS WILLIE'S CLUB STRIKES HOME... AND LEDA'S VOICE SPEAKS FROM THE HAND-RADIO
THIS IS LEDA... MY FATHER IS DEAD... A CYANIDE CAPSULE...
Romero
I FAILED HIM, FAILED THE CAUSE... BUT I WOULD NOT CHANGE WHAT I HAVE DONE...
10176

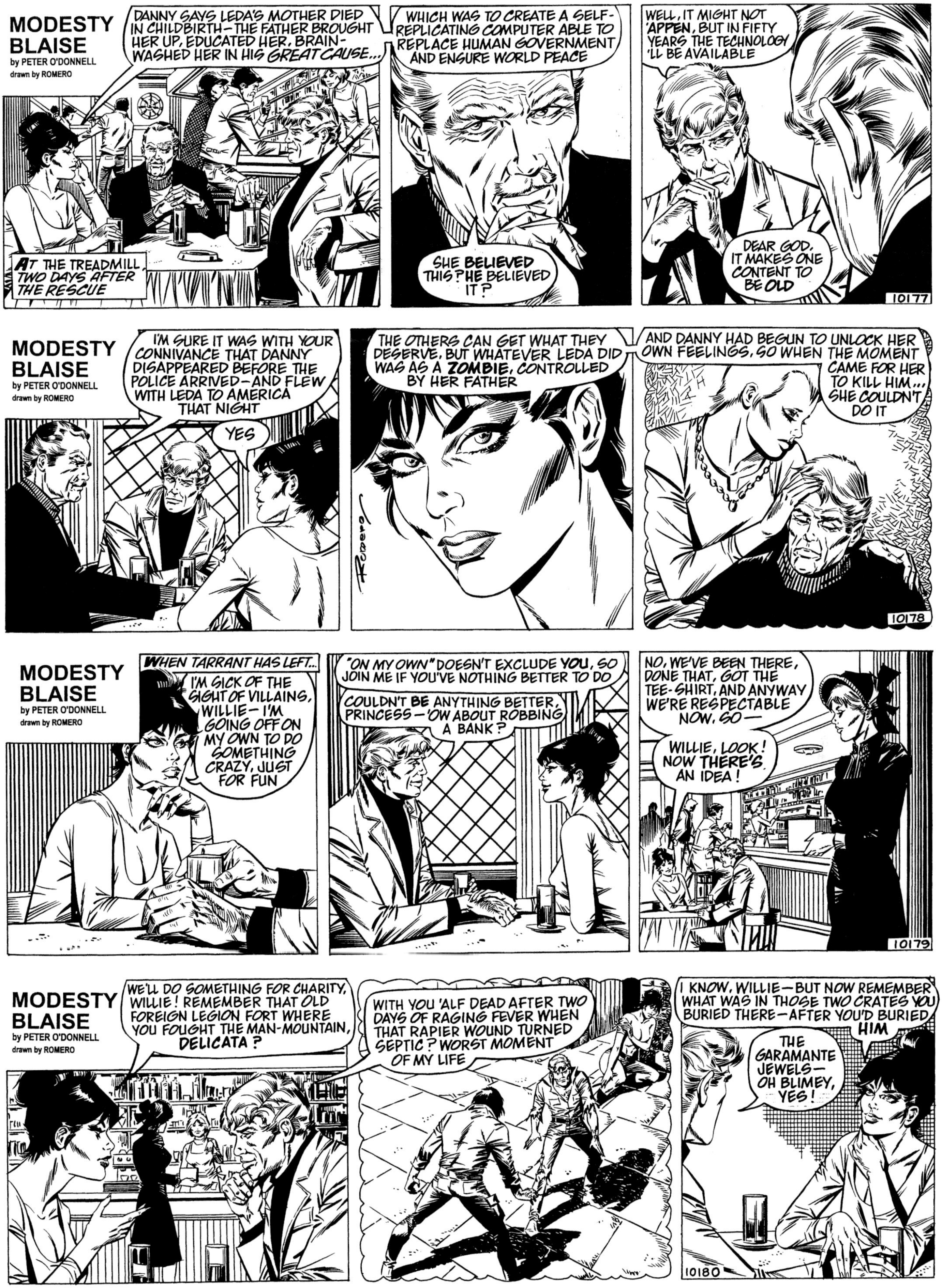
MODESTY BLAISE
by PETER O'DONNELL
drawn by ROMERO
DANNY SAYS LEDA'S MOTHER DIED IN CHILDBIRTH—THE FATHER BROUGHT HER UP, EDUCATED HER, BRAIN-WASHED HER IN HIS GREAT CAUSE...
AT THE TREADMILL, TWO DAYS AFTER THE RESCUE
WHICH WAS TO CREATE A SELF-REPLICATING COMPUTER ABLE TO REPLACE HUMAN GOVERNMENT AND ENSURE WORLD PEACE
SHE BELIEVED THIS? HE BELIEVED IT?
WELL, IT MIGHT NOT 'APPEN, BUT IN FIFTY YEARS THE TECHNOLOGY 'LL BE AVAILABLE
DEAR GOD, IT MAKES ONE CONTENT TO BE OLD
10177
MODESTY BLAISE
by PETER O'DONNELL
drawn by ROMERO
I'M SURE IT WAS WITH YOUR CONNIVANCE THAT DANNY DISAPPEARED BEFORE THE POLICE ARRIVED—AND FLEW WITH LEDA TO AMERICA THAT NIGHT
YES
THE OTHERS CAN GET WHAT THEY DESERVE, BUT WHATEVER LEDA DID WAS AS A ZOMBIE, CONTROLLED BY HER FATHER
ROMERO
AND DANNY HAD BEGUN TO UNLOCK HER OWN FEELINGS, SO WHEN THE MOMENT CAME FOR HER TO KILL HIM... SHE COULDN'T DO IT
10178
MODESTY BLAISE
by PETER O'DONNELL
drawn by ROMERO
WHEN TARRANT HAS LEFT...
I'M SICK OF THE SIGHT OF VILLAINS, WILLIE—I'M GOING OFF ON MY OWN TO DO SOMETHING CRAZY, JUST FOR FUN
"ON MY OWN" DOESN'T EXCLUDE YOU, SO JOIN ME IF YOU'VE NOTHING BETTER TO DO
COULDN'T BE ANYTHING BETTER, PRINCESS—'OW ABOUT ROBBING A BANK?
NO, WE'VE BEEN THERE, DONE THAT, GOT THE TEE-SHIRT, AND ANYWAY WE'RE RESPECTABLE NOW, SO—
WILLIE, LOOK! NOW THERE'S AN IDEA!
10179
MODESTY BLAISE
by PETER O'DONNELL
drawn by ROMERO
WE'LL DO SOMETHING FOR CHARITY, WILLIE! REMEMBER THAT OLD FOREIGN LEGION FORT WHERE YOU FOUGHT THE MAN-MOUNTAIN, DELICATA?
WITH YOU 'ALF DEAD AFTER TWO DAYS OF RAGING FEVER WHEN THAT RAPIER WOUND TURNED SEPTIC? WORST MOMENT OF MY LIFE
I KNOW, WILLIE—BUT NOW REMEMBER WHAT WAS IN THOSE TWO CRATES YOU BURIED THERE—AFTER YOU'D BURIED HIM
THE GARAMANTE JEWELS—OH BLIMEY, YES!
10180

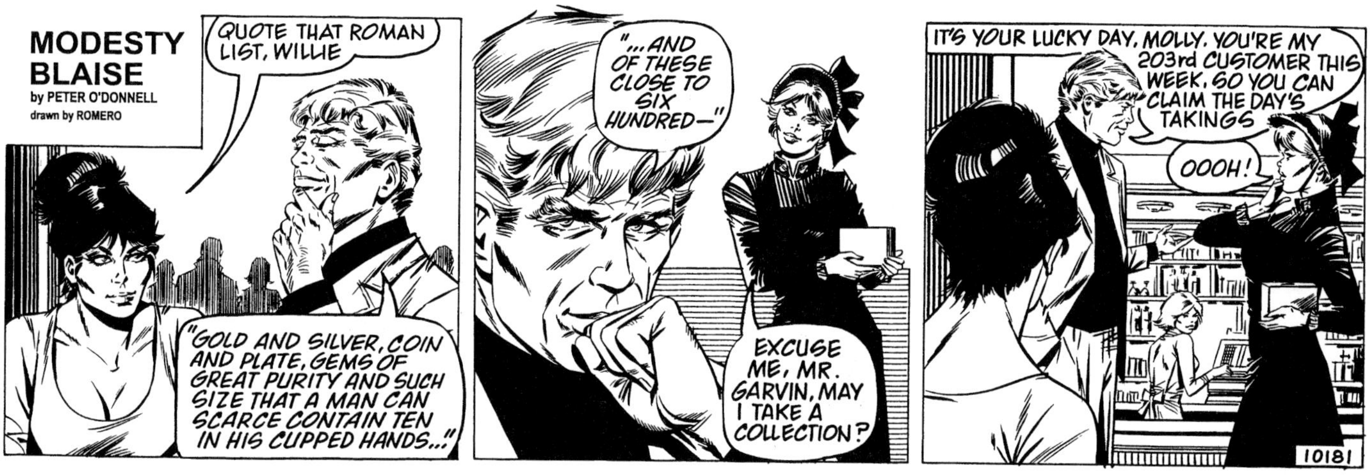
MODESTY BLAISE
by PETER O'DONNELL
drawn by ROMERO
QUOTE THAT ROMAN LIST, WILLIE
"GOLD AND SILVER, COIN AND PLATE, GEMS OF GREAT PURITY AND SUCH SIZE THAT A MAN CAN SCARCE CONTAIN TEN IN HIS CUPPED HANDS..."
"...AND OF THESE CLOSE TO SIX HUNDRED—"
EXCUSE ME, MR. GARVIN, MAY I TAKE A COLLECTION?
IT'S YOUR LUCKY DAY, MOLLY. YOU'RE MY 203rd CUSTOMER THIS WEEK, SO YOU CAN CLAIM THE DAY'S TAKINGS
OOOH!
10181

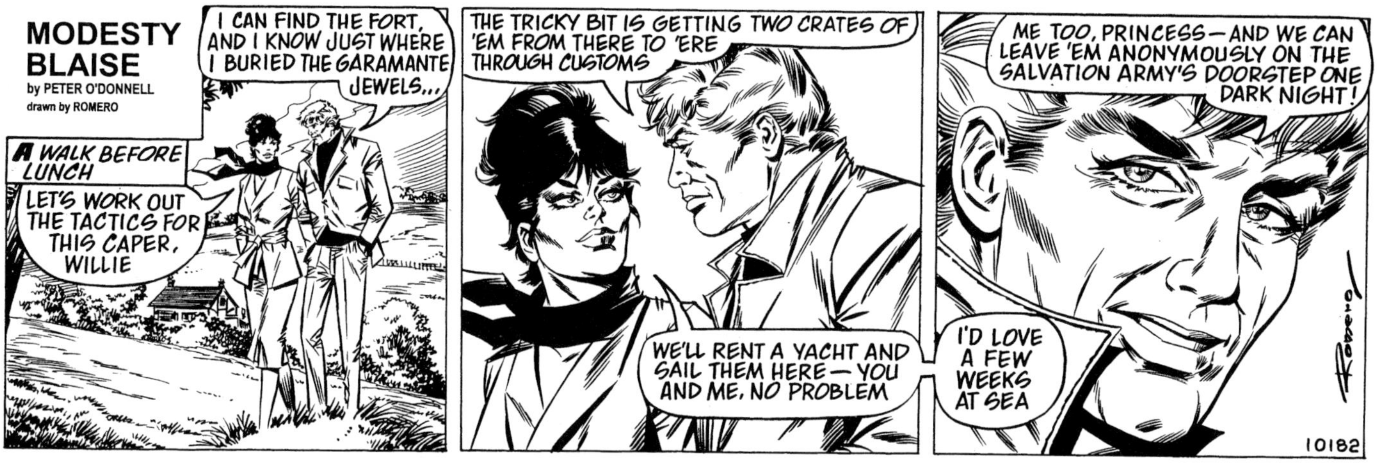
MODESTY BLAISE
by PETER O'DONNELL
drawn by ROMERO
A WALK BEFORE LUNCH
LET'S WORK OUT THE TACTICS FOR THIS CAPER, WILLIE
I CAN FIND THE FORT, AND I KNOW JUST WHERE I BURIED THE GARAMANTE JEWELS...
THE TRICKY BIT IS GETTING TWO CRATES OF 'EM FROM THERE TO 'ERE THROUGH CUSTOMS
WE'LL RENT A YACHT AND SAIL THEM HERE — YOU AND ME, NO PROBLEM
I'D LOVE A FEW WEEKS AT SEA
ME TOO, PRINCESS — AND WE CAN LEAVE 'EM ANONYMOUSLY ON THE SALVATION ARMY'S DOORSTEP ONE DARK NIGHT!
10182

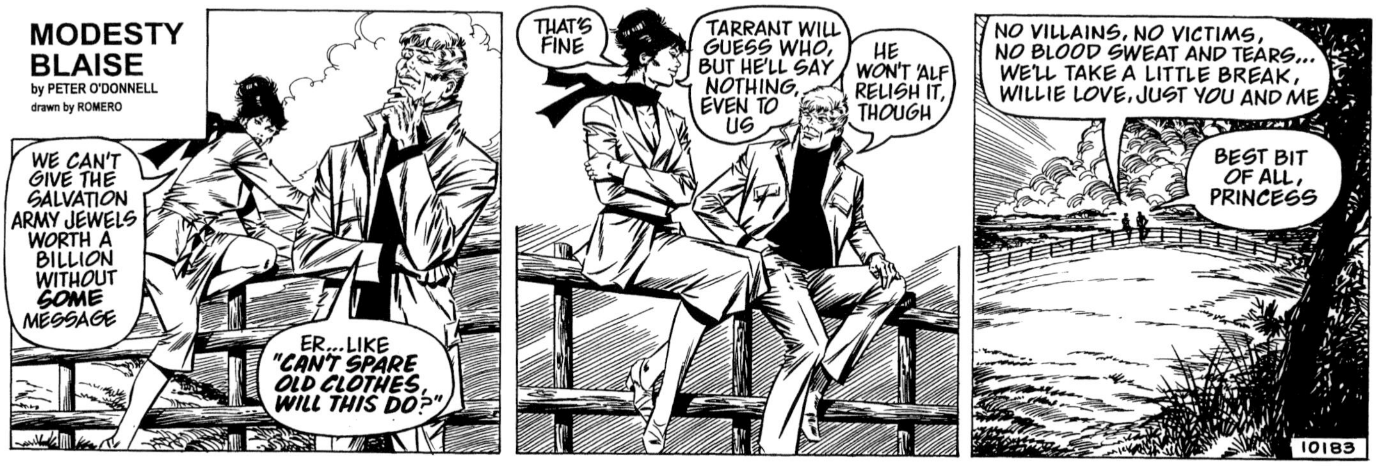
MODESTY BLAISE
by PETER O'DONNELL
drawn by ROMERO
WE CAN'T GIVE THE SALVATION ARMY JEWELS WORTH A BILLION WITHOUT SOME MESSAGE
ER...LIKE "CAN'T SPARE OLD CLOTHES, WILL THIS DO?"
THAT'S FINE
TARRANT WILL GUESS WHO, BUT HE'LL SAY NOTHING, EVEN TO US
HE WON'T 'ALF RELISH IT, THOUGH
NO VILLAINS, NO VICTIMS, NO BLOOD SWEAT AND TEARS... WE'LL TAKE A LITTLE BREAK, WILLIE LOVE, JUST YOU AND ME
BEST BIT OF ALL, PRINCESS
10183

MODESTY IS THE BEST POLICY!

The Gabriel Set-Up
Also features *La Machine, The Long Lever & In The Beginning*
ISBN: 9781840236583

Mister Sun
Also features
The Mind of Mrs Drake & Uncle Happy
ISBN: 9781840237214

Top Traitor
Also features
The Vikings & The Head Girls
ISBN: 9781840236842

The Black Pearl
Also features *The Magnified Man, The Jericho Caper & The Killing Ground*
ISBN: 9781840238426

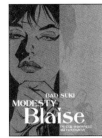

Bad Suki
Also features
The Galley Slaves & The Red Gryphon
ISBN: 9781840238648

The Hell-Makers
Also features
Take-Over & The War-Lords of Phoenix
ISBN: 9781840238655

The Green-Eyed Monster
Also features *Willie the Djinn & Death of a Jester*
ISBN: 9781840238662

The Puppet Master
Also features
The Stone Age Caper & With Love From Rufus
ISBN: 9781840238679

The Gallows Bird
Also features *The Bluebeard Affair, The Wicked Gnomes & The Iron God*
ISBN: 9781840238686

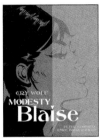

Cry Wolf
Also features
Take Me To Your Leader & Highland Witch
ISBN: 9781840238693

The Inca Trail
Also features *The Reluctant Chaperon, The Greenwood Maid & Those About To Die*
ISBN: 9781845764173

Death Trap
Also features
The Vanishing Dollybirds & The Junk Men
ISBN: 9781845764180

Yellowstone Booty
Also features
Idaho George & The Golden Frog
ISBN: 9781845764197

Green Cobra
Also features
Eve and Adam & Brethren of Blaise
ISBN: 9781845764203

The Lady Killers
Also features
Dossier on Pluto & Garvin's Travels
ISBN: 9781848561069

The Scarlet Maiden
Also features
The Moon Man & A Few Flowers For The Colonel
ISBN: 9781848561076

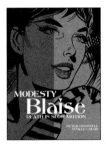

Death In Slow Motion
Also features
The Balloonatic & The Alternative Man
ISBN: 978184856108

Sweet Caroline
Also features *Return of the Mammoth, Plato's Republic & Sword Of The Bruce*
ISBN: 9781848566736

The Double Agent
Also features
The Wild Boar & Kali's Disciples
ISBN: 9781848566743

Million Dollar Game
Also features
Butch Cassidy Rides & The Vampire Of Malvescu
ISBN: 9781848566750

Live Bait
Also features
Samantha and the Cherub & Milord
ISBN: 9780857686688

Lady In The Dark
Also features
The Girl From The Future & The Big Mole
ISBN: 9780857686930

The Girl In The Iron Mask
Also features
Fiona & Walkabout
ISBN: 9780857686947

The Young Mistress
Also features
Ivory Dancer & Our Friend Maude
ISBN: 9781781167090

The Grim Joker
Also features
A Present for the Princess & Black Queen's Pawn
ISBN: 9781781167113

The Killing Distance
Also features
Guido the Jinx & The Aristo
ISBN: 9781781167120

Ripper Jax
Also features
The Maori Contact, Honeygun & Durango
ISBN: 9781783298587

The Murder Frame
Also features
Fraser's Story, Tribute to the Pharoah & The Special Orders
ISBN: 9781783298594

Children of Lucifer
Also features
The Hanging Judge & Death Symbol
ISBN: 9781783298600

The Killing Game
Also features
The Last Aristocrat & The Zombie
ISBN: 9781785653001

VISIT OUR WEBSITE: WWW.TITANBOOKS.COM

MODESTY BLAISE CHECKLIST

The following is a complete checklist of *Modesty Blaise* stories that have appeared in the *Evening Standard*. All stories were written by Peter O'Donnell.

GLOSSARY

KEY TO ARTISTS
JH = Jim Holdaway
ER = Enric Badia Romero
JB = John Burns
PW = Pat Wright
NC = Neville Colvin

DATES
13/5/63 = 13 May 1963

SERIAL NUMBERS
Each serial number represents a day. When the *Evening Standard* stopped publishing on Saturdays the suffix 'A' (e.g. 3638A) was introduced for those papers in syndication that wanted a Saturday *Modesty Blaise*; the *Standard* did not run these strips.

STORY	ARTIST	DATE		SERIAL No.
1. La Machine	JH	13/05/63	- 21/09/63	1-114
2. The Long Lever	JH	23/09/63	- 02/01/64	115-211
3. The Gabriel Set-Up	JH	03/01/64	- 18/06/64	212-354
4. Mister Sun	JH	19/06/64	- 05/12/64	355-500
5. The Mind of Mrs Drake	JH	07/12/64	- 19/04/65	501-612
6. Uncle Happy	JH	20/04/65	- 18/09/65	613-743
7. Top Traitor	JH	20/09/65	- 19/02/66	744-873
8. The Vikings	JH	21/02/66	- 9/07/66	874-992
8A. In The Beginning	JH	1966		(1-12) *
9. The Head Girls	JH	11/07/66	- 10/12/66	993-1124
10. The Black Pearl	JH	12/12/66	- 22/04/67	1125-1235
11. The Magnified Man	JH	24/04/67	- 02/09/67	1236-1349
12. The Jericho Caper	JH	04/09/67	- 13/01/68	1350-1461
13. Bad Suki	JH	15/01/68	- 25/05/68	1462-1574
14. The Galley Slaves (Part 1)	JH	27/05/68	- 06/08/68	1575-1630
14A. The Killing Ground	JH	11/09/68	- 16/11/68	(A1-A36) **
14B. The Galley Slaves (Part 2)	JH	11/09/68	- 16/11/68	1630a-1688
15. The Red Gryphon	JH	18/11/68	- 22/03/69	1689-1794
16. The Hell-Makers	JH	24/03/69	- 16/08/69	1795-1919
17. Take-Over	JH	18/08/69	- 10/01/70	1920-2043
18. The War-Lords of Phoenix	JH/ER	12/01/70	- 30/05/70	2044-2162
19. Willie the Djinn	ER	01/06/70	- 17/10/70	2163-2282
20. The Green-Eyed Monster	ER	19/10/70	- 20/02/71	2283-2388
21. Death of a Jester	ER	22/02/71	- 10/07/71	2389-2507
22. The Stone Age Caper	ER	12/07/71	- 27/11/71	2508-2627
23. The Puppet Master	ER	29/11/71	- 08/04/72	2628-2738
24. With Love From Rufus	ER	10/04/72	- 12/08/72	2739-2846
25. The Bluebeard Affair	ER	14/08/72	- 06/01/73	2847-2970
26. The Gallows Bird	ER	08/01/73	- 12/05/73	2971-3077
27. The Wicked Gnomes	ER	14/05/73	- 29/09/73	3078-3197
28. The Iron God	ER	01/10/73	- 09/02/74	3198-3309
29. "Take Me To Your Leader..."	ER	11/02/74	- 01/07/74	3310-3428
30. Highland Witch	ER	02/07/74	- 16/11/74	3429-3548
31. Cry Wolf	ER	18/11/74	- 25/03/75	3549-3638 a
32. The Reluctant Chaperon	ER	26/03/75	- 14/08/75	3639-3737 a
33. The Greenwood Maid	ER	15/08/75	- 02/01/76	3738-3829 a
34. Those About To Die	ER	05/01/76	- 28/05/76	3830-3931 a
35. The Inca Trail	ER	01/06/76	- 20/10/76	3932-4031 a
36. The Vanishing Dollybirds	ER	21/10/76	- 28/03/77	4032-4141 a
37. The Junk Men	ER	29/03/77	- 19/08/77	4142-4241 a
38. Death Trap	ER	22/08/77	- 20/10/78	4242-4341 a
39. Idaho George	ER	23/01/78	- 16/06/78	4342-4447 a
40. The Golden Frog	ER	19/06/78	- 31/10/78	4448-4542 a
41. Yellowstone Booty	JB	01/11/78	- 30/03/79	4543-4647 a
42. Green Cobra	JB	02/04/79	- 10/08/79	4648-4737 a
43. Eve and Adam	JB/PW	13/08/79	- 04/01/80	4738-4837 a
44. Brethren of Blaise	PW	07/01/80	- 23/05/80	4838-4932 a
45. Dossier on Pluto	NC	27/05/80	- 14/10/80	4933-5032 a
46. The Lady Killers	NC	15/10/80	- 03/03/81	5033-5127 a
47. Garvin's Travels	NC	04/03/81	- 27/07/81	5128-5229 a

STORY	ARTIST	DATE		SERIAL No.
48. The Scarlet Maiden	NC	28/07/81 - 16/12/81		5230-5329 a
49. The Moon Man	NC	17/12/81 - 07/05/82		5330-5424 a
50. A Few Flowers for the Colonel	NC	10/05/82 - 24/09/82		5425-5519 a
51. The Balloonatic	NC	27/09/82 - 18/02/83		5520-5619 a
52. Death in Slow Motion	NC	21/02/83 - 15/07/83		5620-5719 a
53. The Alternative Man	NC	18/07/83 - 28/11/83		5720-5814 a
54. Sweet Caroline	NC	29/11/83 - 19/04/84		5815-5914 a
55. The Return of the Mammoth	NC	24/04/84 - 14/09/84		5915-6014 a
56. Plato's Republic	NC	17/09/84 - 06/02/85		6015-6114 a
57. The Sword of the Bruce	NC	07/02/85 - 02/07/85		6115-6214 a
58. The Wild Boar	NC	03/07/85 - 20/11/85		6215-6314 a
59. Kali's Disciples	NC	21/11/85 - 16/04/86		6315-6414 a
60. The Double Agent	NC	17/04/86 - 15/09/86		6415-6519 a
61. Butch Cassidy Rides Again	ER	16/09/86 - 12/02/87		6520-6624 a
62. Million Dollar Game	ER	13/02/87 - 08/07/87		6625-6724 a
63. The Vampire of Malvescu	ER	09/07/87 - 03/12/87		6725-6829 a
64. Samantha and the Cherub	ER	04/12/87 - 06/05/88		6830-6934 a
65. Milord	ER	09/05/88 - 27/09/88		6935-7034 a
66. Live Bait	ER	28/09/88 - 17/02/89		7035-7134 a
67. The Girl from the Future	ER	20/02/89 - 21/07/89		7135-7239 a
68. The Big Mole	ER	24/07/89 - 11/12/89		7240-7339 a
69. Lady in the Dark	ER	12/12/89 - 08/05/90		7340-7439 a
70. Fiona	ER	09/05/90 - 09/10/90		7440-7544 a
71. Walkabout	ER	10/10/90 - 11/03/91		7545-7649 a
72. The Girl in the Iron Mask	ER	12/03/91 - 02/08/91		7650-7749 a
73. The Young Mistress	ER	05/08/91 - 06/01/92		7750-7854 a
74. Ivory Dancer	ER	07/01/92 - 05/06/92		7855-7959 a
75. Our Friend Maude	ER	08/06/92 - 02/11/92		7960-8064 a
76. A Present for the Princess	ER	03/11/92 - 08/04/93		8065-8174 a
77. Black Queen's Pawn	ER	13/04/93 - 10/09/93		8175-8279 a
78. The Grim Joker	ER	13/09/93 - 09/02/94		8280-8384 a
79. Guido the Jinx	ER	10/02/94 - 05/07/94		8385-8484 a
80. The Killing Distance	ER	06/07/94 - 30/11/94		8485-8589 a
81. The Aristo	ER	01/12/94 - 03/05/95		8590-8694 a
82. Ripper Jax	ER	04/05/95 - 02/10/95		8695-8799 a
83. The Maori Contract	ER	03/10/95 - 01/03/96		8800-8904 a
84. Honeygun	ER	04/03/96 - 02/08/96		8905-9009 a
85. Durango	ER	05/08/96 - 03/01/97		9010-9114 a
86. The Murder Frame	ER	06/01/97 - 06/06/97		9115-9219 a
87. Fraser's Story	ER	09/06/97 - 03/11/97		9220-9324 a
88. Tribute of the Pharaoh	ER	04/11/97 - 03/04/98		9325-9429 a
89. The Special Orders	ER	06/04/98 - 04/09/98		9430-9534 a
90. The Hanging Judge	ER	07/09/98 - 10/02/99		9535-9644 a
91. Children of Lucifer	ER	11/02/99 - 13/07/99		9645-9749 a
92. Death Symbol	ER	14/07/99 - 15/12/99		9750-9859 a
93. The Last Aristocrat	ER	16/12/99 - 19/05/00		9860-9964 a
94. The Killing Game	ER	22/05/00 - 17/10/00		9965-10069 a
95. The Zombie	ER	18/10/00 - 11/04/01		10070-10183

The Dark Angels (with art by Enric Badia Romero): This story first appeared in *Comics Revue* #200 in a longer comic strip form and is not included in this checklist as it is not a true strip story.

this story was written and drawn in for syndication only to introduce the character to its new audience.

**This story was written for the lasgow *Evening Citizen*, an associated ewspaper of the *Evening Standard*, to ver a break in publication of Story 14 the *Evening Standard* due to an industrial dispute in London.

Many thanks to Trevor York and Lawrence Blackmore for their help in compiling this list.

Featuring the iconic comic strips **Goldfinger**, **Risico**, **From A View To A Kill**, **The Man With The Golden Gun** and **The Living Daylights** into a lavishly presented hardback, this is a must have 007 collectible.

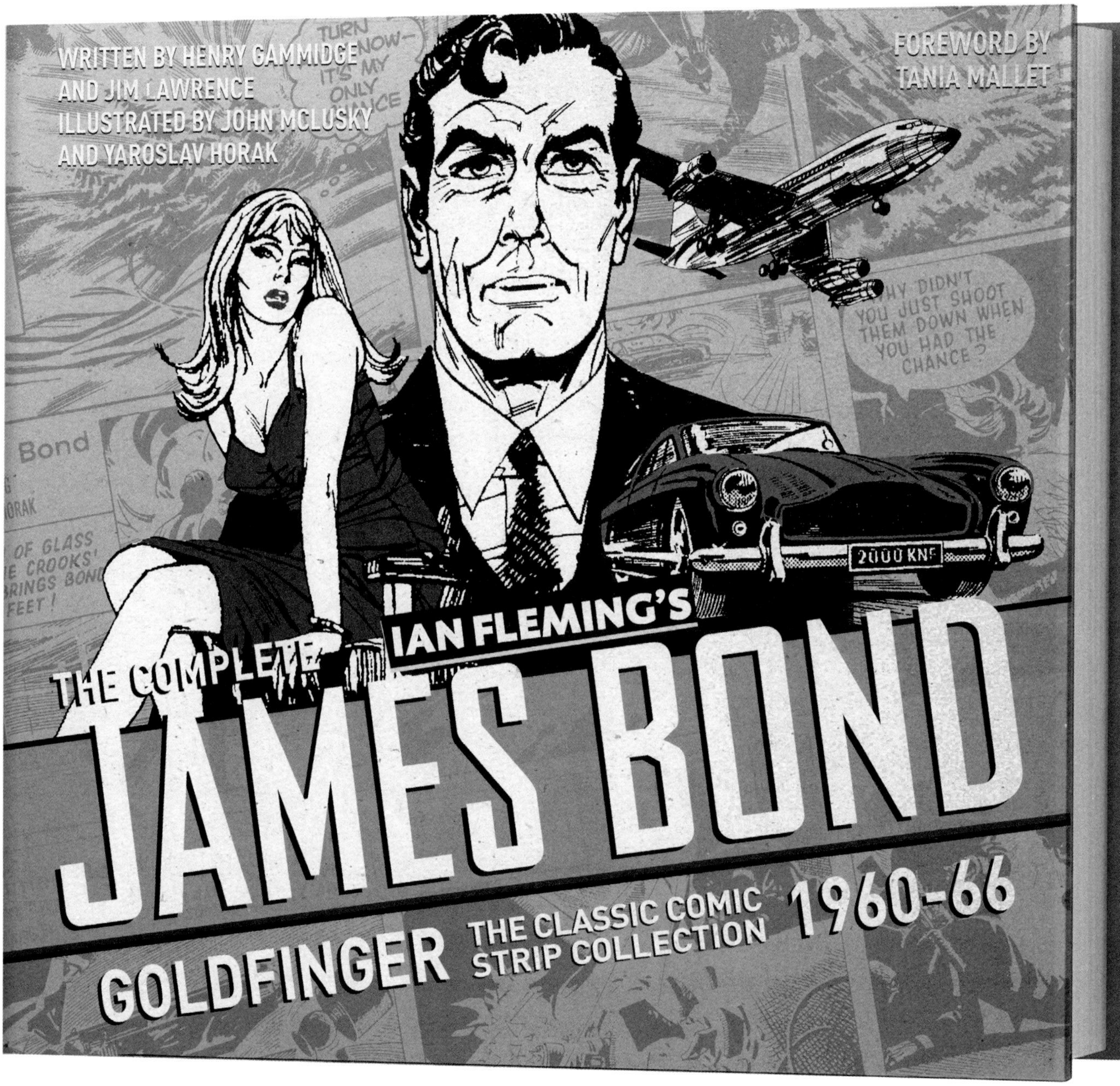

WRITTEN BY HENRY GAMMIDGE
AND JIM LAWRENCE
ILLUSTRATED BY JOHN MCLUSKY
AND YAROSLAV HORAK
FOREWORD BY
TANIA MALLET
YOU JUST SHOOT THEM DOWN WHEN YOU HAD THE CHANCE?
2000 KNF
IAN FLEMING'S
THE COMPLETE
JAMES BOND
GOLDFINGER
THE CLASSIC COMIC STRIP COLLECTION
1960-66

ISBN: 9781785653247

AVAILABLE NOW IN ALL GOOD BOOK STORES